MANCHUKUO

KOREA

JAPAN

PACIFIC OCEAN

P9-ECU-460

FORMOSA

Hong Kong

BATANES IS

PHILIPPINES

YAP

MORON

BORNEO

CELEBES

NEW GUINEA

VA

FIJI ISLANDS

AUSTRALIA

NEW ZEALAND

AN AMERICAN DOCTOR'S
ODYSSEY

Helen L. Read
999. S. Gramercy Drive
Los Angeles Calif
1936.

DOCTOR VICTOR HEISER

An

American Doctor's

Odyssey

Adventures in Forty-five Countries

---

by VICTOR HEISER, M.D.

NEW YORK

W·W·NORTON&COMPANY·Inc

PUBLISHERS

PRINTED IN THE UNITED STATES OF AMERICA
FOR THE PUBLISHERS BY THE VAIL-BALLOU PRESS

ACKNOWLEDGMENT

When I began to write this book I found there were literally huge boxes of memoranda, notes, diaries, and other manuscripts to be sifted and read. Mrs. Rackham Holt, ably assisted by Mr. Walter Hayward, has been of invaluable help in organizing this vast amount of material and in preparing it for publication. I am deeply grateful to them both.

I am also most grateful to Miss Grace Carpenter who as my secretary for twenty years worked so indefatigably over this long period to prepare the daily notes which made this volume possible.

CONTENTS

CONTENTS

AN AMERICAN DOCTOR'S
ODYSSEY

CHAPTER 1.   JUST SHORT OF ETERNITY

ALL during the latter part of May, 1889, a chill rain had been descending in torrents upon the Conemaugh Valley. The small city of Johnstown, walled in by precipitous Pennsylvania hills, was invaded by high water which stood knee deep in front of my father's house on Washington Street.

Nobody seemed particularly concerned at the time over the dam which rich Pittsburghers had maintained high up on the South Fork to provide water for their fishing streams. When the earthen dam had first been constructed, there had been some apprehension. There was a ninety foot head of water behind the embankment, and only a small spillway had been provided. But the dam had never burst and, with the passage of time, the townspeople, like those who live in the shadow of Vesuvius, grew calloused to the possibility of danger. "Some time," they thought, "that dam will give way, but it won't ever happen to us."

During the afternoon of the thirty-first the overflow from the river crept steadily higher, inch by inch, through the streets of the town. Although it had not yet reached the stable, which stood on higher ground than the house, my father became concerned over the safety of his fine pair of horses which were tied in their stalls, and suggested that I make a dash for the stable and unfasten them. The rain was falling so hard that I was almost drenched as I plowed my laborious way through the two feet of water.

I had loosed the horses and was about to leave the shelter of the doorway when my ears were stunned by the most terrifying noise I had ever heard in my sixteen years of life. The dreadful roar was punctuated with a succession of tremendous crashes. I stood for a moment, bewildered and hesitant. I could see my mother and my father standing at an upper window in the house. My father, frantic with anxiety over my safety, was motioning me urgently toward the top of the building. Fortunately, I had made a passageway only a few days before to the red tin roof, so that some necessary repairs could be made. Thus it was only a matter of seconds before I was up on the ridge.

From my perch I could see a huge wall advancing with incredible rapidity down the diagonal street. It was not recognizable as water; it was a dark mass in which seethed houses, freight cars, trees, and animals. As this wall struck Washington Street broadside, my boyhood home was crushed like an eggshell before my eyes, and I saw it disappear.

I wanted to know how long it would take me to get to the other world, and in the split second before the stable was hit, I looked at my watch. It was exactly four-twenty.

But, instead of being shattered, the big barn was ripped from its foundations and began to roll, like a barrel, over and over. Stumbling, crawling, and racing, I somehow managed to keep on top.

In the path of the revolving stable loomed suddenly the house of our neighbor, Mrs. Fenn. To avoid being hurled off by the inevitable collision, I leaped into the air at the precise moment of impact. But just as I miraculously landed on the roof of her house, its wall began to cave in. I plunged downward with the roof, but saved myself by clambering monkey-like up the slope, and before the house gave way completely, another boiled up beside me. I caught hold of the eaves and swung dangling there, while the weight of my body drained the strength from my hands.

For years thereafter I was visited by recurring dreams in which I lived over and over again that fearful experience of hanging with my fingernails dug deep into the water softened shingles, knowing that in the end I must let go.

When my grip finally relaxed, I dropped sickeningly into space. But once again I was saved. With a great thud I hit a piece of the old familiar barn roof, and I clutched with all my remaining power at the half inch tin ridges. Lying on my belly, I bumped along on the surface

4

of the flood, which was crushing, crumbling, and splintering everything before it. The screams of the injured were hardly to be distinguished above the awful clamor; people were being killed all about me.

In that moment of terrible danger I saw the Italian fruit dealer Mussante, with his wife and two children, racing along on what seemed to be their old barn floor. A Saratoga trunk was open beside them, and the whole family was frantically packing a pile of possessions into it. Suddenly the whole mass of wreckage heaved up and crushed them out of existence.

I was borne headlong toward a jam where the wreckage was already piling up between a stone church and a three story brick building. Into this hurly burly I was catapulted. The pressure was terrific. A tree would shoot out of the water; a huge girder would come thundering down. As these trees and girders drove booming into the jam, I jumped them desperately, one after another. Then suddenly a freight car reared up over my head; I could not leap that. But just as it plunged toward me, the brick building gave way, and my raft shot out from beneath the freight car like a bullet from a gun.

In a moment more I was in comparatively open water. Although no landmark was visible, I could identify the space as the park which had been there only a short while before. I was still being swept along, but the danger had lessened. I had opportunity to observe other human beings in equally perilous situations. I saw the stoutish Mrs. Fenn astride an unstable tar barrel which had covered her with its contents. Rolling far over to one side, then swaying back to the other, she was making a desperate but grotesque struggle to keep her head above water.

There was nothing I could do for anybody.

Dr. Lee's negro hostler, all alone and stark naked, was shivering on the roof of his master's house. In the penetrating rain his supplicating hands were raised toward the heavens. As I tore by I heard him shouting, "Lawd ha' mercy on dis pore cold nigger."

I was carried on toward the narrows below the city where the tracks of the Pennsylvania Railroad crossed both valley and river on a high embankment and bridge. When the twisted, interlaced timbers ahead of me struck the stone arches, they plugged them tight, and in the powerful recoil my raft was swept back behind the hill which had saved the lower part of the town from complete destruction and left many buildings standing.

I passed close by a two and a half story brick dwelling which was still remaining on its foundations. Since my speed as I went up this second valley was about that of a subway train slowing for a stop, I was able to hop to the roof and join the small group of people already stranded there. Realizing then that I was, perhaps, not immediately destined for the other world, I pulled out my watch. It was not yet four-thirty; three thousand human beings had been wiped out in less than ten minutes.

For the remaining hours of daylight we derelicts huddled disconsolately on the roof. Now and then we were able to reach out a hand or a pole and haul in somebody drifting by, until finally we numbered nineteen. Though we were in a backwash, many of the houses had been seriously damaged below the water line. Occasionally one would melt like a lump of sugar and vanish. We did not know whether our refuge had been undermined, but there was no way for us to escape to the surrounding hills which rose invitingly above the flood, so near and yet so impossible to reach. The cold rain was still driving down, and it was growing dark. We were so miserable that we decided to open the skylight and climb under cover.

There in the attic we spent the night, starting whenever we heard the whoo-oo-sh which meant that another building had sunk. Ours was straining and groaning. From moment to moment we could not tell whether it were to suffer the same fate as its neighbors. Although exhausted we could not sleep. The waiting, in its way, was almost worse than the previous turmoil, because if our shelter collapsed it would become a trap in which we would drown miserably.

Dawn brought a transcendent sense of relief. The rain had ceased at last, and the water had receded until it reached only part way up the first story. Between us and the safe hills a half mile away was a mat of débris, broken here and there by patches of dirty water. Scrambling over the wreckage, wading through shallows, and rafting the deeper spaces, with an inexpressible feeling of relief I finally set my feet on solid ground again.

I started downstream at once, trying to find my father and mother.

6

Everyone I met was on the same sad errand—looking for parents, children, relatives, or friends. Bodies were already being taken out of the ruins.

As I approached the railway embankment, I saw that it had given way in the night and allowed the water to rush unimpeded toward Pittsburgh and the Mississippi. The consequent subsidence of the flood had left in front of the stone bridge several acres of wreckage in which many people were still imprisoned. This inflammable material had caught fire. I can still hear the maddened shrieks of the men, women and children, as the flames approached. I joined the rescue squads and we struggled for hours trying to release them from this funeral pyre, but our efforts were tragically hampered by the lack of axes and other tools. We could not save them all. It was horrible to watch helplessly while people, many of whom I actually knew, were being devoured in the holocaust.

At last I met one of my friends who lived outside the city and whose house had not been harmed. His family took me in, and gave me food and shelter. The people of the United States were unbelievably generous to the stricken community. The relief trains which soon were pouring in brought me clothes and money.

Day after day I searched among the ruins and viewed with a tense anxiety the hundreds of corpses constantly being carried to the morgues. Two weeks were devoted to this gruesome task, a most agonizing experience for a boy. Eventually the body of my mother was found; my father never was identified with certainty. Most of the victims were buried in the "plot of the unknown dead," but I laid my mother in our own cemetery lot.

I was alone in the world.

CHAPTER 2.   THE LAME AND
                              THE HALT

THE Johnstown flood ended the prescribed course of my life, which until then had been carefully planned for me by my parents. My education had been forced beyond my years. All winter long I used to sit with the other children at my desk in the public school, and, in summer, when all my friends were playing baseball and fishing, I was still sitting at a desk, but this time in a private school. My evenings were spent under a study lamp learning French and German with a tutor by my side. The sole concession to leisure allowed me out of the year was one month on a farm. Although I was particularly fond of sports and hated the steady grind, I rebelled only once. Learning to play the violin was too much.

When the catastrophe came, I was ready for college, but ill-equipped for life.

By a freak of chance, a chest which had stood in the upper hall of our house was found practically intact on one of the piles of wreckage. In it were my father's Civil War uniform with a large old penny in one pocket, a miscellaneous collection of flat silver, and my mother's Bible. The sole value of these slender possessions lay in their associations.

Since everything else belonging to my father had been swept away in the flood, I had to find immediately some way of earning a living. I hired out as a plumber's assistant, and rapidly learned to cut and fit pipe, and even to "wipe" a lead joint, which is generally regarded as one of the most difficult accomplishments in the plumbing trade. But

THE LAME AND THE HALT

I also discovered there was a good deal of truth in the jingle about the plumber who, after the manner of the Assyrian, came down like a wolf on the fold, and

"For nine hours and a half he talked to the cook,
And sixty-five dollars was charged on the book."

My next job was with a carpenter. Framing a house was more difficult than wiping a joint but, to my own satisfaction at least, I soon considered I had mastered carpentry. I aspired also to cabinet making but, fascinating as this was, it too failed to offer sufficient inducement as a life work.

I then decided to become a mechanical engineer. By this time some of my father's real estate had been sold, and with the money thus salvaged I went to an engineering school in Chicago.

Although I did fairly well in my studies, met many people, and gained much worldly experience, I could not be entirely happy. For a youth of seventeen, particularly one who had led so well-ordered a life, to be cast out into the cold world was not an easy experience. Other boys were able to turn to their parents, relatives, or friends, who were genuinely interested in them. I had no experienced person with whom to discuss my perplexities, and had to make my own decisions. For many years I suffered because I could not avail myself of adult counsel and advice. My first lesson in the realities of life was that nobody wanted to be bothered with the problems of others; I had to learn to keep my troubles to myself.

I do not know definitely what turned me toward medicine, but, after my first year at engineering school, I concluded that I wanted to be a doctor. Nevertheless, I have never considered the time wasted which I spent in learning to do things with my hands. The practical knowledge thus acquired has been of incalculable service to me all over the world in the career which I ultimately chose.

I did not have the necessary academic credits for admittance to a medical school of top rating, but I determined to acquire them, and set to work at my books once more. In addition I haunted the public libraries and enrolled in courses offered in such subjects as mechanical drawing and engineering design. To test my progress, I regularly took the examinations of the University of the State of New York, until I had attained enough credits to give me the equivalent of an A.B. degree.

I then entered medical school in Philadelphia, worked hard, and finished a four-year course in three years. Upon graduation from Jefferson Medical College, I was fortunate enough to be accepted for my internship at Lankenau Hospital. There I not only had ward experience, but was given the special opportunity of attending private patients. From both the uncomplaining and the exacting I learned much about human nature and ways of dealing with it.

The spur which drove me was sharp. I was involuntarily following the forcing process of education on which I had been reared. I took on added duties, read books not on any prescribed list, and dashed indefatigably from public ward to private pavilion and to clinics in other hospitals.

The customary routine after finishing at the hospital was to go immediately into private practice. But the more I saw of the latter, the more I came to consider it a retail effort. If I were to make a place for myself in the medical world I must necessarily learn first to be a good doctor, but before I had spent many months as an interne I knew I was not going to be either a general practitioner or a specialist. The prevention of disease on a wholesale basis appealed to me far more.

At the end of my first hospital year, I considered I had earned a vacation, and went to Washington to see the sights, with no plan in mind except diversion. But before I could get well under way with this project, I chanced upon a notice that an examination for entrance into the Marine Hospital Service was about to be held. I had already considered attempting to enter this branch of the Service because of my great admiration for the officer in charge of the Marine Ward at Lankenau. I knew these examinations were extremely difficult, but I thought this was a good opportunity to find out the exact requirements.

In answer to my question, the officer in charge said, "Since you're here, why don't you take the examination?"

"I'm not prepared. I could never pass."

"Well, suppose you didn't, what then? You could come up again next year. If you took it now, you'd have the actual experience, which would be far more helpful than anything I could tell you."

He convinced me there could be no harm in trying. I telegraphed immediately for letters of introduction and credentials to be sent special delivery, and these arrived in time for me to be admitted to the examination at nine the next morning. I was somewhat startled to find I was one of forty-two candidates for only three vacancies, and not encouraged by the remark of one of my classmates who greeted me with, "Why in God's name are you going into this examination? You haven't had any special preparation."

"I'll stay as long as I can," I assured him with an appearance of confidence I did not feel.

The preliminary physical examination was so rigid that twelve aspirants were promptly ruled out. Thirty began the week's ordeal of writing. Each day's paper contained only four questions, and, since eighty was the minimum passing mark, whoever failed in a single one was automatically eliminated. The Board read the papers at night, and just before nine o'clock of the second day the announcement was made, "The following gentlemen will be excused," and five disappointed young men filed out.

I decided there was at least a chance for me to get through. I remembered my classmate's taunt, and my resolve to stick it out stiffened. I wired for my Practice of Medicine, Surgery, Therapeutics, and other text books and, as soon as they arrived, I organized each twenty-four hours. The examinations lasted from nine to twelve and two to five; evenings I devoted to study.

It was July in Washington. I would sit in my room with no clothes on, and, even though the windows and transom were open, the perspiration would run off me in streams. At three o'clock I would tumble into bed and reluctantly out at eight in time for bath and breakfast before the torture began again.

I grew more and more excited as our numbers dwindled. However, I still did not see how I could face the humiliation of walking out. I observed each morning the precaution of placing my hat within easy reaching distance, so that, at the sound of my name, I could make my exit as speedily and inconspicuously as possible.

Happily I was spared, and found myself among the ten who finished the written part of the examination. But the pre-medicals were still to come. We were to be orally examined in history, philosophy, economics, literature, and kindred subjects which I had not studied for four years. I knew I could never get through these on the basis of exact information. I should have to devise some method.

One by one we went up before a Board of three. As soon as a candidate would emerge, damp and perspiring, the rest of us would rush to cross-examine him. We were thus able to get a general idea of the field of inquiry, even though the actual questions might never be duplicated.

My turn finally came. Each examiner interrogated for a half hour; obviously the more delays I could introduce, the fewer would be the questions. If I knew the answer well I would make false starts and hesitate until one of the Board would exclaim in irritation, "Come now, we must get on. Do you know this or don't you?" Just before his patience was exhausted, I would give my answer clearly and briefly.

On the other hand, if I were unable to answer concisely, I would ramble on and on, and try to involve the whole Board in a discussion.

After the pre-medicals, each of the survivors was taken to a hospital and requested to examine and diagnose six patients. Although they had been told to mislead us if possible, the clinical signs were theoretically so obvious that we should be able to make correct diagnoses. The same technique was followed in the laboratory, where we were required to analyze specimens and identify bacteria and parasites under the microscope; many of these slides had been specially prepared to confuse us.

At the end of a grueling two weeks, eight were left from whom the lucky three were to be chosen. I resumed my interrupted vacation, dismissed the examination from my mind, and started off with my bicycle, leaving my cares in the wild Pennsylvania hills. Pedaling vigorously on level stretches, coasting down the long slopes, wandering around the little towns, I soon regained my spirits and was rapidly recovering the twenty pounds I had lost.

The morning of my arrival in Pittsburgh, I saw an announcement in the *Post* that Fricks, White, and Heiser had passed the examination for the Marine Hospital Service. Naturally, I was jubilant over this triumph, but doubtful over the wisdom of accepting the commission, because I was only half through my internship at Lankenau. In the belief that another year's intensive work and study would make me far better equipped I wrote the Surgeon-General a long explanatory

12

letter, hoping he would agree with my conclusions and, furthermore, appreciate the sacrifice I was willing to make in giving up a year's salary for the sake of further training.

The only reply was a peremptory telegram that I should report at once to Boston. I was now in the Service. Since I could not question orders, I necessarily complied.

The reason for official disregard of my proposals was evident. The year was 1898, and many soldiers, desperately ill, were returning from Cuba and Puerto Rico. The facilities of the Boston hospitals were overtaxed by this unprecedented influx, and an appeal had been made to the Marine Hospital Service for help. I was assigned to this task.

Any Federal officer, regardless of his deserts, has much prestige. Therefore, in spite of my inexperience, I was able to advise several hospitals how to deal with the situation.

But when this organizing work was over, hospital routine seemed uninteresting. I explained this to my commanding officer, who said, "Very well, I'll assign you to the medical examination of immigrants. You'll find enough there to keep you busy."

For years the flood of imported cheap labor had poured unchecked through the wide-open gateways of Boston, New York, Philadelphia, San Francisco, and other large ports, bringing with it the lame, halt, and blind. Even lunatics and idiots had not been barred until 1882. Nine more years passed before public sentiment, slowly rising against the foreign labor invasion, forced Congressional action. At that time, not only were the Chinese excluded, but the Marine Hospital Service was charged with the duty of recommending for rejection immigrants afflicted with loathsome or contagious diseases, or those who were likely, for any physical reasons, to become public charges.

The invaders were arriving in such numbers that individual physical examination with our meagre staff was out of the question. A snap diagnosis which stood a reasonable chance of proving correct had to be made in the space of a few seconds. I read everything on the subject that I could find, supplementing my own ideas with the experiences of others, and, after much trial and error, developed a system.

In Boston the medical examinations were always held by daylight on the pier where the ship docked. The stage had to be carefully set so that the immigrants would not be aware that they were being observed. I had it so arranged that they would walk down a lane, in single file, ten feet apart, unencumbered by baggage, and then make a right turn in front of an examining officer. From his apparently casual station at the angle, he could obtain a front, side, and rear view of each passer-by. The path had to be level, so that the immigrant would not have to watch his feet, and also lead away from the water, so that there would be no glare to cause squinting.

Some afflictions were easily picked out. A deaf man in almost every case held his head slightly to one side. Valvular diseases of the heart were often detectable by the ridged nails and peculiar pallor of face and neck, suggesting faulty nutrition. Less simple were cases of favus, a contagious filth disease of the scalp or nails. We would have to be on the alert for the fine, wire-like hair and the betraying bald patches symptomatic of the disease, because a ship's physician would often dissolve off the scales to make the head reasonably clean for our inspection.

I found that a man's walk was often characteristic of his physical and mental state. Hernia, for example, caused a distinctive though indescribable gait, and faulty vision was betrayed by hesitation on reaching the corner. Trachoma, a contagious inflammation of the eyelids, had always to be watched for with special care. It was estimated fifteen percent of the blindness in United States institutions at that time was due to this disease. Clinics in our large cities were overrun with cases which proved stubborn to treat and often impossible to cure. The typical thickening of the lids or roughened condition of the cornea could be caught as the immigrant turned, because the light then struck his eyes at changing angles of incidence.

Though the work was exciting and interesting, it had many distressing aspects. Heartbreaking incidents were constantly occurring when rejections had to be made. A Scandinavian farmer might spend years in Minnesota earning enough money to pay the passage for his wife and their five children. When they would finally arrive, and the long separated family would be reunited, ours would be the painful duty of singling out one of the children, and of saying, "She has trachoma. She cannot enter." The mother and the rest of the children would often have to return to Europe with the diseased one, and, until the boat sailed, the father, wretched and unhappy, would haunt the detention quarters, while his family kept up a constant wailing and crying. But the law was on the statute books and we had to enforce it, regarding the child as a potential focus of infection rather than as a figure of tragedy.

In order to reduce the hardships as much as possible, government hospitals were established in which curable cases might be treated. But inevitably many hard decisions had to be made. Young women with illegitimate pregnancies, whose family or friends frequently had sent them to this country in the hope of covering up their disgrace, were particularly pathetic. The regulations forbade the entrance of these unfortunates, because of the likelihood that they and their children would become public charges.

A detailed examination was impossible, but I had observed that on the left side of any immigrant woman's head was a strand of hair which, under normal conditions, was more or less lustrous. If it hung dull and lifeless over her ear, it marked her at once as possibly pregnant. Other medical men may ridicule the observation, and I cannot explain it myself scientifically, but time and again suspicion turned out to be fact.

The distinguishing differences between a healthy and a diseased person were often subtle, but practice made us reasonably proficient. The system of diagnosis worked so well in Boston that I was promoted to the chief center of immigration at New York, where a new system was to be developed for the inspection of first and second class passengers. Up to this time no examination had been required for these classes, and many immigrants who had been rejected when they had come steerage, were adopting the dodge of traveling cabin. Other defectives, forewarned, were doing likewise. Over the loud protests of the steamship officials, who were fearful of offending their best paying clientele, the regulations had been extended to first and second class passengers.

The government realized it was treading on delicate ground and that such inspections would have to be handled with great finesse. A health officer needed more than technical training to succeed at such a task. In fact, it appeared that diplomacy should constitute a major part of his equipment.

It was vital, first of all, to make sure that no American citizen should be mistakenly included in the examination. Before we had really formulated an efficient working method, one of my subordinates made a serious error. One day he called exultantly, "I've a fine case of acne rosacea."

"Let's have a look at him."

To my horror I recognized the elder Pierpont Morgan. My assistant had been led by his professional enthusiasm to forget the routine question as to citizenship. I have rarely seen such an angry man. At first he would accept no apology, but I explained to him that my assistant was very young, and we really ought to be easy on him because everybody makes mistakes. Perhaps Mr. Morgan, observing my own youth, was amused at these solemn platitudes; he finally began to laugh and said he would forget the incident.

My task was complicated by the intense rivalry which at that time existed between State and Federal authorities over the administration of a quarantine law designed to protect the country against such diseases as plague, cholera, smallpox, leprosy, typhus, and yellow fever. Although Federal laws and regulations applied to quarantine, the local port authorities interpreted them as they saw fit. A ship might dock at Boston under one set of regulations, but, if Baltimore were to be its first port of call, preparations would have to be made for a different set. Because of the resultant confusion, the business interests of the country had added their mite of pressure toward unification, and the Federal government was now trying to arrange for taking over all quarantine services still being administered by State officials. For reasons not always creditable, the latter, pleading their constitutional right to exercise "police powers," resented what they considered Federal interference with their affairs.

The Marine Hospital Service in New York was concerned only with the diseases and physical handicaps of the immigrant, and had nothing to do with the State administration of quarantine laws. The Immigration launch used to go down the Bay at about five-thirty in the morning to meet any incoming vessel, although we were not allowed to board her until she had been released from quarantine by the State officers. We would then employ the hour's passage up the Bay in examining the cabin passengers so that American citizens and foreigners with clean bills of health could be free to leave the moment the ship docked.

One dreary, drizzly March dawn, so thick with fog that visibility was almost zero, our launch approached a French boat which we believed had cleared quarantine. I clambered up the high side and jumped to the deck. To my surprise, Dr. Jenkins, the State quarantine officer, was still there. The sight of my Federal uniform was as a red rag to a bull. He bristled. "Doctor, you're under arrest. This ship's in quarantine for smallpox."

I saw I was in for it. I shouted warningly over the rail to my companions who were already starting up the ladder after me. "Don't come up. Smallpox on board."

The launch pushed off again. As I turned back to Dr. Jenkins, he said with satisfaction, "You'll have to stay in quarantine fourteen days, Doctor."

For a Federal officer to be arrested by a State officer because of assumed ignorance of the law would have made a wonderful newspaper story. In my mind's eye I could already see the headlines. I sat down on one of the damp hatches and, with my head in my hands, gazed up into space, and cerebrated hard.

When Dr. Jenkins had finished his work, he strolled over to me. "We're ready to go. You'll have to spend the next two weeks on Hoffman's Island, Doctor," he rubbed it in.

"I'm not going with you," I said.

"I hope you won't compel me to use force."

"Oh, no, that won't be necessary," I retorted. "But still I'm not going with you."

"Why not?" he demanded.

"Because there's a law in this State that every ship must fly the yellow flag at her masthead while she's in quarantine. If you'll show me any such flag on this boat," I answered, peering up through the fog, "I'll go with you. Otherwise, I'm afraid I must say goodby."

The little man could do no more than stamp his foot helplessly and utter a fervent damn. I hailed a nearby government launch and was taken ashore.

I found the office in a turmoil. When my detention had been dolefully reported, there had been tremendous excitement over the inevitable ridicule. The wires to Washington had been set humming, and only my appearance had forestalled the issue of a writ of habeas corpus.

Shortly after this occurrence I received a summons to Washington, where Surgeon General Walter Wyman congratulated me on my success in having extricated myself from an awkward predicament, and informed me I was to undertake a delicate mission to Europe.

After the International Cholera Convention of 1893, officers of the Marine Hospital Service had been stationed at the main sources of emigration from Europe to attempt to guard against the introduction of cholera into the United States. Later they had extended their activities to making preliminary examinations of emigrants, and to advising the steamship companies which ones were likely to be rejected at American ports of entry on account of physical disqualification under our immigration law. The steamship companies had been glad to cooperate because the rejected emigrants had to be returned to their ports of departure at the expense of the line which had brought them over. But the governments concerned had resented the presence of these inspectors and had insisted on their recall. This action not only had increased the burden on the Service over here, but also had worked hardship and disappointment on those who had to be rejected. Since Naples was the port of departure for the majority of emigrants, it was believed that if Italy could be induced to receive our officials again, other governments would follow suit.

Surgeon General Wyman outlined my job as one of convincing all concerned that cooperation and allowing our officers to be reinstated would be to their interest as well as ours. At the end of the interview he instructed me never to send in any reports in my own handwriting, explaining that its illegibility had cost me first place in the entrance examinations.

"We're presenting you with a new typewriter," he said jocularly. "And we want you to use it."

Since I would have to deal with ambassadors, ministers, consular officers, and other officials, I would have to learn the rudiments of international law and of procedure expected of consular and diplomatic officials, such as matters of precedence and formal calls. Consequently arrangements had been made for me to take a primary course in diplomacy at the State Department.

After a month of learning the things I must do and the things I must not do in ambassadorial halls, and a post-graduate drill in the Immigration Laws, I was ready for Europe.

CHAPTER 3. THE PROMISED LAND

A FIRST ocean crossing holds more glamour than a hundred succeeding ones. This voyage, old to the seasoned traveler, is one of
exploration to the neophyte. I had watched thousands of passengers
stream down the gangplanks of the giant ocean liners. I knew the interior of the one on which I was sailing almost blindfold, but never
before had I felt the throb of the engines on a ship outward bound
beyond Ambrose Light.

To become familiar with the problems I should have to solve in my
new assignment, I journeyed from one capital of Europe to another.
The mellow grime of London, the feverish boulevards of Paris, the
goose-stepping orderliness of Berlin, and the grey ruins of Rome,
each in turn captured my imagination, each was new and strange, no
matter how familiar its external characteristics from books and pictures.

At last I arrived at Naples, melodious with sound and glowing with
color, where I secured reluctant consent from Italian officialdom to
act as temporary medical officer.

Living at a hotel branded me at once as a forestiero, and all foreigners were fair game for cabmen. When I would hand out the proper
fare the cochiero would invariably break out in violent remonstrance,
and my Ellis Island Italian was in no way adequate to cope with
him. To protect myself, I evolved a little strategem, which I used with
great success. After a number of cochiere had insisted they were under-
paid, I tried the experiment of hailing a well-dressed Italian walking
along the street, told him I was a stranger, and showed him the fare

and tip I had offered to pay. "Will you please explain this to the cab driver?" I asked.

The two immediately fell into a violent altercation. I left them on the sidewalk, went into the hotel, took a hot bath, dressed for dinner, and came down to find them in the same place, still indefatigably arguing about the inadequacy of my fare.

The discovery that any stranger to whom I appealed would support my contention I put to good advantage frequently. I once boarded a tram bound for the center of Naples. I gave the conductor my destination, paid him the specified sum, and received in return a pink slip in the true Mark Twain tradition. When we reached the end of the zone, the conductor tapped me on the shoulder and asked, "Are you going further?"

I looked up from my paper in surprise. "Certainly," I said.

"Then you'll have to pay more fare."

"But I told you where I was going," I protested. "It's your fault if you didn't charge me enough." I then turned to the man next me. "Didn't I tell him?" I demanded.

"Yes, yes, of course you did," he chimed in eagerly.

Somebody else stood up and cried loudly, "No, he didn't!"

In no time all the passengers had taken sides and, with shouts and gesticulations, had risen to their feet. The motorman stopped the car and himself joined in. The tumult grew fiercer and fiercer.

Since the matter was now out of my hands, I settled back in my seat and resumed my reading. Time passed. Presently an inspector appeared. "What's going on here?" he called to the conductor. "You're tying up the whole line!"

I looked back; there were literally dozens of trams behind us.

The same psychology could be invoked against the arm of the law. A ship was waiting for its clearance papers one day, and I had only a few moments in which to reach it. I directed the cochiero, therefore, to drive as fast as he could to the pier. The street along the waterfront was fenced off into two parts, one for heavy traffic, and one for carriages. The latter was blocked solid; the former was deserted. I signaled to the cochiero to take the free lane, but no sooner had we started than a policeman waved and shouted, "Get back! You're on the wrong side of the street!"

AN AMERICAN DOCTOR'S ODYSSEY

I expostulated that I was in a hurry, but the policeman did not appear at all impressed. I beckoned to a passer-by, and explained the difficulty. In a second he became my ardent champion, and plunged into the usual argument with the policeman which went on and on. I, also, went on to the ship, signed the papers, and drove leisurely back on the proper side of the enclosure. Through the grating I could see them still engaged in verbal combat over the ethics of my procedure.

I did not long bear the stigma of forestiero. Naturally I was anxious to live as the Neapolitans did, and I welcomed, therefore, the invitation of a young Netherlander, van Berlo, to share with him a beautiful villa on the Corso Vittorio Emmanuele. We used to dine on a veranda, surrounded by roses, geraniums, and oleanders, and look across the deep blue bay to distant Vesuvius. Johnstown, Pennsylvania, was farther away then, perhaps, than ever before or since.

Van Berlo wanted to learn English and I, too, was anxious to improve my languages. We made a bargain that whether it were a question of passing the salt or international politics, we would confine our conversation exclusively to one language a week, using English, French, German, and Italian in turn. At first I sat with a dictionary in my hand nearly all the time, looking up words he used or I wanted to use. We resolutely observed the rules, and by the end of a year were almost unconscious of what language we were using. Each of us, month and month about, ran the house, ordered the meals, and saw that the routine was carried out by the servants, and this gave me much valuable practice in Italian idioms.

But before my tongue was in any way able to keep pace with my thoughts, I was appointed official delegate for the United States to the International Congress on Tuberculosis which was being held in Naples. This added another thrill to the excitement and variety of life. I met the leading specialists from Europe, among them Rudolf Virchow of Berlin, the mightiest lion of them all, the first great pathologist and political opponent of Bismarck. At evening functions I gazed with awe at his coat, which was one blazing mass of decorations and medals; he had been honored by virtually all the royalties of Europe.

King Humbert invited all the delegates to a great reception in the old palace of the Bourbons. According to the rules of precedence, I was at the end of the long line which passed before him as he stood on a dais, speaking a few formal words of greeting to each in turn. In translating my reply, the interpreter hesitated for the correct word and, before I realized what I was doing, I had supplied it in Italian.

I was overcome with confusion, but the King's official attitude at once relaxed. He smiled. "Oh, you know Italian," he said, and, waving the interpreter aside, put his arm through mine, and led me to a window seat.

My knees literally shook. I had been studying Italian only a few weeks, and I knew the King spoke no English.

"I've been wanting to talk directly to an American for a long time, and get some first hand information," Humbert continued.

The King's pronunciation was so clear that I could follow his question about the Spanish-American War. Thinking to myself, "This will end in one second," I replied stumblingly. The situation was saved by the appearance of Queen Margharita, to whose beautiful German I could make answer with a fair degree of fluency. The Crown Prince and Princess also joined us, and they were all so pleasantly friendly that I was soon at my ease.

It was an excessively hot evening. The Crown Princess, fatigued at having stood so long in the reception line, fainted and was carried into an ante-room. Because I happened to be talking with the royal family at that moment, I was asked to attend her. During the hour or so in which she was recovering, I continued my discussion with the Crown Prince, now King Victor Emmanuel III, but somewhat more volubly because of his excellent command of English.

Understanding King Humbert's classic Italian was quite another matter from comprehending the multifarious Italian dialects. But these also I had to learn if I were to dispense with interpreters in dealing with emigrants. The dialects were vastly different. The Genoese would have no idea what the Neapolitans, with their innumerable slang expressions and clipped words, were talking about. The soft Sicilian speech differed from the Calabrese. It was surprising, nevertheless, how quickly the essential words of each could be picked up.

Considerable organization was required to examine expeditiously and properly the three thousand emigrants who would sometimes sail from Naples in one day. Since they were unfamiliar with any folk-customs save their own, they could not understand, for example, why they had to produce their belongings a few days in advance of sailing. Loud complaints usually rose as clothing and bedding disappeared into the disinfecting plant. Not only the procedure but the necessity for it bewildered them.

Practically all the emigrants were inveterate smugglers, with a particular predilection for cheese, on which they thought there was a high duty in the United States. This they would hide in the most impossible places, even sewing it in the lining of their clothes. They would protest violently that they had no cheese, although we explained to them again and again we were not customs officers and had no interest in their cheese beyond preventing damage to their possessions. When the doors of the ten-foot cylinder were locked and the steam was turned on, the effect of the heat was often disastrous. On one occasion when we opened the chamber, a great stream of hot, sizzling, liquid cheese came running out.

Shoes also were favorite objects of concealment. The owner's eyes would start with amazement when a pair which he had tucked away in his mattress roll would emerge from the cylinder shrunk to the size of two watch charms. Only the metal eyelets and the nails would keep their shape, and in the tiny shoes these appeared enormous.

In line with the attitude of cooperation which I was trying to bring about, I had, from the very beginning, asked the Italian doctors to help me in making inspections. But as time went on and nothing untoward happened, they left me to do the work after my own fashion.

My most serious trouble came from an entirely different quarter. I had been in Naples a little more than a month when I encountered the Camorra, at that time a powerful secret organization which, like the modern racket, levied a toll on many civic activities. It was said even the mayor could not act without its sanction.

The power of the Camorra was strikingly illustrated in the disputes which arose between the society and the agent of one of the large German steamship companies. This agent once had the temerity to inquire why the ships of his line should not dock at the government pier, and thus avoid the annoyance and the exorbitant charges of the boatmen who conveyed passengers and baggage from steamship to wharf and vice versa.

A representative of the Camorra informed him, "It will be better for your business if your ships anchor in the harbor. We can't control the boatmen; they are disagreeable people when aroused. If you land passengers on the pier, something unpleasant may happen."

The agent, however, relying on the close relationship between his country and Italy, considered his company was in a peculiarly strong position, and began having the liners brought to the pier.

Nothing happened at first. The society waited until a day when the single pier was already occupied and three ships of this one line were in port. The ubiquitous Camorra had in its ranks people who spoke all languages, and had attired a number of them in Company uniforms. In the confusion attendant upon sailing, nobody noticed the many unfamiliar faces.

As a passenger came down the wharf, he would be asked, "Where are you going?"

"America."

The boatman would reply, "I'll look after your baggage."

The passenger would be put on the right tender and the right ship, but his baggage would be placed on a vessel going to South Africa, and that of a passenger embarking for South Africa would be sent to China.

Almost immediately the offices of the line everywhere were bombarded with the protests of the righteously indignant, and the officials, becoming seriously alarmed over the bad name they were acquiring, threw up their hands and said, "We surrender."

Thus simply did the Camorra deal with such situations.

My own run-in with the society came over the inspection of baggage. One day I was waited upon by a courtly gentleman who remarked that it must be an arduous and difficult task to examine the belongings of so many people. I agreed that it was not easy.

"You might be having a good time out in the country," he suggested. "Not far from Naples are some delightful amusement places, scenic outdoor restaurants, and pleasant feminine companionship. I'd like to relieve you of your burden. I'll give you a thousand lire for each ship, and see that the baggage is properly disinfected. All you have to do is to leave me your official seal, and I'll stamp everything for you."

I assumed the plan of the Camorra was to charge a fee to each emigrant which, in the aggregate, would have brought in a tidy income. "Your suggestion sounds very pleasant," I temporized, "but I'd better think it over before I decide. Suppose you come back in a few days."

Shortly, another gentleman, even more polished than the first, put in an appearance. "I'm sorry," I told him, "but I can't accept your proposition."

He then pointed out other aspects of the matter. "You know yourself a number of people are stabbed here in Naples every night. Few questions are asked. A British engineer was knifed just last week. The British government is a powerful one, but no action was taken. A thousand lire is a fair offer and, if you accept, you'll be protected."

Obviously, the possibility of being killed altered the situation. The only reply I could make at the moment was, "I'll have to think this over again."

"You give it serious thought," he admonished me.

In the absence of the American Ambassador, I consulted Iddings, the Chargé d'Affaires at Rome, who assured me that, if I stood my ground, I should receive the full protection of the American government.

I was not surprised when, in the course of time, still a third gentleman, even more suave than his predecessors, called to see me. Neither he nor they ever admitted any connection with the society, yet he made it apparent that an immediate answer was required.

This time I was able to be definite. "I'm very sorry, but I can't accept your offer. Furthermore, I don't really believe that anything will happen to me."

"What do you mean? There are ways of dealing with this," he warned.

I answered this threat directly. "I'm not afraid. You must surely realize that, if you kill me, another officer will come in my place. You might even kill him. But there are one hundred and fifty officers in my Service, and they would keep coming. By the time you had disposed of several of us, the United States would take action, and the clamor would be world-wide. The American public already has a grievance against your country over the payments we had to make after the New Orleans Mafia riot. The Roman government may be weak in Naples, but my government is strong, and would bring such pressure to bear that the Camorra might be wiped out. You go back to your people and tell them that I'm going to continue running the baggage inspection myself."

This was my first and last difficulty with the Camorra. They held no rancor over the fact they had failed, and eventually many became my friends and more than once rendered me valuable aid.

In the course of the day's work my assistant, Dr. Norman Barnesby, was once obliged to advise against a Neapolitan named Giuseppi. A storm of abuse in which the word "kill" frequently recurred followed the adverse verdict. We paid no attention; such occurrences were common. A few nights later, just after Barnesby had left my house, he was attacked. Because he was a good boxer and extremely agile, he was able to dodge so that the man's knife went through his sleeve, wounding him only slightly.

Barnesby believed his assailant was Giuseppi, although it had been too dark to make absolutely sure. He reported the incident to the police who, with characteristic Latin shrugs, replied, "If we question the man, he will only deny it. You have no witness. We can do nothing."

Barnesby's bride was frantic with anxiety. I, too, was concerned and went for aid to one of the steamship companies. These were my chief supporters. Because it cost so much money to bring back rejected immigrants, my word was invariably accepted as to physical condition; they would refuse to sell tickets to anyone named on my list. After explaining the circumstances to a sympathetic official, I suggested, "If you're willing to take a chance on this fellow, he could sail."

"Suppose we try," he replied.

But when Giuseppi was rejected at New York, he was so anxious to remain in the United States that he escaped from Ellis Island and swam to the mainland before he was recaptured and shipped back to Naples. The morning after his return I found him sitting on the curb across the street from my house. As I walked toward the tram

I could hear his stealthy footfalls behind me. I half turned my head so that he could not come upon me unobserved. On the tram I prudently stood on the rear platform; had I taken a seat a knife might have lodged between my ribs.

All day long Giuseppi sat on a bench in a small park opposite the office, waiting patiently and watching the door like a cat at a mousehole. When I went out to lunch, his pursuing steps followed me. There was no mistaking his intentions; he had transferred his animus to me, convinced I was to blame for his rejection.

Thereafter this dark shadow never left me. Each morning when I arose he was already on guard. The first few days of this I endured with a fair degree of patience. But after a while my nerves were so on edge that I complained to the authorities. They said they could do nothing until Giuseppi committed some overt act; threats and even attacks were not actionable in Naples. I must wait until I was killed, or at least wounded, before steps could be taken.

This espionage went on for so many months that finally I took it for granted. One evening after the opera I forgot my pursuer completely and, without thinking, took a short cut home through a narrow dimly-lighted viculo winding between tall, dark houses. Just as I turned a corner, Giuseppi jumped out at me with a knife in his upraised hand. His shortness of stature gave me the advantage. I knocked him down with an uppercut to the jaw. I did not hurry the rest of the way home; but neither did I dawdle. The next morning Giuseppi was not there but, to my intense disgust, the following day he was back again.

A week later I had lunch on board one of the steamships where I had been making an examination, and told the assemblage about my disagreeable experiences.

It could be assumed that wherever one went in Naples the Camorra would be represented. One of the guests said immediately, "Why didn't you mention this before? The matter could easily have been arranged. But I assure you that there will be no further trouble."

I never saw Giuseppi again.

I had worked almost a year in Naples and was beginning to make progress in winning the confidence of Italian government officials when I received an urgent message from Washington saying one hundred thousand bales of rags had entered the United States unaccounted for. Many of them were readily identifiable as Egyptian robes, some of which might have come from the bodies of bubonic plague victims. I was ordered to Egypt to solve the mystery.

The American public was becoming alarmed over the steady march of plague around the world. Crawling insidiously from Hongkong into the Red Sea ports, it had fastened upon Egypt. Coming slowly West, reaching out to India, it had filtered into Spain and subsequently Italy, England, and France. Its progress could be followed on the map also as it crept around the other way. In 1899 it leaped to Hawaii, and in relatively few months bridged the final gap to our own Pacific Coast.

In 1900 the method by which plague was transmitted, in spite of unremitting research, still remained a riddle. But it was suspected that these dirty, filthy, cotton rags of Egypt, most of which ultimately found their way to the paper mills of the United States, might be sources of infection. I was to determine how these rags were getting into the country, when every port was blocked against them, and also to apply myself to research on the disease.

In Alexandria the plague was endemic; sometimes epidemic. A case would break out in one section of town. It would be isolated at once by the English and German doctors in the employ of the Egyptian government. We would set to work to investigate all the circumstances. Just then another case would be reported from an entirely different section. Since we were certain contact between the two must have taken place, we would follow every clue in the effort to establish some possible connection. Discouragingly seldom were we able to find any. The difficulty of the work was increased because we could not make these Orientals realize the importance of giving straight answers.

The fleas must have been laughing at our ineffectual efforts.

After considerable detective work I traced the Egyptian cotton rags to Liverpool, and found they were thence being reexported to Canada. A final manifest made them appear as Canadian rags, in which guise they could enter the United States freely. I suggested simple legislation requiring shippers to declare the place of origin of the rags. When passed by Congress this bill effectively put an end to the abuse.

The Egyptian rag shippers professed a willingness to comply with our regulations. During the winter I supervised the construction of fumigating sheds and saw that the rags were exposed for three hours to sulphur fumes. After being baled, they were sealed by an American consular officer and shipped directly to the United States.

The cooperation of the rag shippers was forced because they had no true conception of our aims. Although they were actually being saved the trouble and expense of their former surreptitious methods, they thought they were being bothered for nothing. This was my first experience with Oriental guile. I found that nothing irritated the Oriental more than to have to comply with the regulations which sprang from Occidental ideas of sanitation.

One of the favorite subterfuges of the Egyptians was to falsify the time during which the rags had been in the fumigating sheds. Another was to place rags only on the forward part of the trucks, so that when the doors of the shed were opened, the cars would appear to be filled. I would have to prowl about constantly in the alleys between the sheds where women were sorting rags into heaps of colors, whites, and woolens. I would often discover huge piles about to be baled which had never been inside the sheds. The dealers were constantly surprised and disgruntled when I would demand that the untreated rags be fumigated.

I found a sympathetic and responsive listener to the amusing occurrences of the day in Joseph H. Choate, our Ambassador to Great Britain, who was then vacationing in Egypt. My conversations with this profound student of human nature, famous the world over for his wit and his legal pronouncements, proved an inspiration. On many occasions to come, when my duties included drawing up and securing passage of legislation, my recollections of the latter were of great assistance.

As soon as the exportation of rags from Egypt was under control, I went back to finish my work at Naples. The United States immigration officers were gradually being permitted to return, first to Italy, where the government this time welcomed them, and later to the other countries which were sending us their excess population. I had scarcely returned, however, before the Surgeon-General delegated me to stop another leak in the health dam. Back across the water I came.

Immigration laws had been growing more and more effective in our own ports. But their success was largely nullified because the rejected aliens soon learned a method of circumventing them. No matter how incapacitating or contagious the disease might be for which they had been barred, they were finding free entry from Canada.

Canadian steamship agencies in Europe were advertising how easy it was to avoid inspection by traveling to the States through Canada. One circular was printed and distributed which announced:

"For sickly or defective passengers who want to avoid to land in the United States ports, I recommend my new Canadian line to St. John, where passengers are freely landed, without any examination. From St. John passengers can get within a few hours ride by rail to any place in the United States."

It was impracticable to guard three thousand miles of border, but our government had obtained permission to open stations at Quebec in the summer and at Halifax and St. John in the winter, where a Commission could examine every immigrant who applied for entry into the United States. This measure, however, was of only slight assistance, because proportionately few of the defectives announced their intentions beforehand.

In Canada, as in Egypt, I had a dual assignment. Although I was technically medical officer for this Commission, my real function was to persuade reluctant Canada to pass an immigration law similar to ours. Because of their widespread resentment over the high protective tariff of the United States which interfered with their trade, Canadians were not likely to lend a willing ear. They might go as far as to like an individual American here and there, but if the United States wanted any certain thing, they definitely did not want it.

During the year I spent in Canada, I became familiar with the entire border, and knew almost every stream and town along it. Wherever I went, I talked about immigration laws. Ultimately I

31

decided to do the obvious thing and enlist the aid of the railroads, which were then a power in Canadian politics. The Canadian Pacific Railroad had always been on the side of the government, whether Liberal or Conservative, and any government was embarrassed without its support. The road was willing to cooperate with us because it did not want its passengers further inconvenienced by the ever more stringent regulations we found it necessary to impose.

The Premier of Canada, Sir Wilfred Laurier, on whom final action depended, was reluctant to take any steps toward keeping immigrants out of the country, which was large and needed filling. He had first to be persuaded that his policy of settling would be helped and not hindered by barring the same types of aliens we had found undesirable. But, once convinced, he acted immediately. An Order in Council was promulgated which embodied the important provisions of our immigration laws, and later a bill was enacted by the Canadian Parliament which turned the Order in Council into law, and thus largely plugged the immigration leak.

A certain amount of running of aliens across the border still continued. Once when I was staying at Lake Memphremagog, Vermont, some of my friends in the Immigration Service had received word to be at the border the following midnight and, thinking I might be interested, they invited me to go with them. We had not long to wait before a covered undertaker's wagon loomed out of the dark.

"Halt! Everybody out!" called one of the officers.

The driver, in a shocked tone, exclaimed, "You can't interfere with us. I'm taking these sisters of charity to a funeral."

"Let's see 'em," ordered the officer peremptorily.

From the wagon descended first one sister, then another, and another, their white coifs gleaming in the faint light. But when the lantern was lifted to the eight faces, parchment yellow skins and flat eyes were revealed. The officer sardonically requested the pseudo-sisters to disrobe, and underneath the voluminous trailing black garments appeared Chinese cotton trousers and jackets.

The men were all deported under the Chinese Exclusion Act.

Often applicants for entry had to be barred because of some irregularity. Usually these poor people, amid strange surroundings, were almost overwhelmed by their misfortunes. In response to a call to act as interpreter, I arrived late one evening at another Vermont border town, and found in detention an unmarried Swedish couple. Even before I saw the woman, I could hear her loud sobs; the man stood aside resentfully. It seemed hard to send her back just because she was pregnant. I explained to them in my none-too-good Swedish that she would be allowed to enter if they would first get married. They could not comprehend why the American government should concern itself with their private relationship. They were going to get jobs, they said. The man impassively explained that he intended to marry her as soon as he had enough money. I reiterated that, under the law, she could not enter unless they were first married.

After I had talked with them most of the night, the man reluctantly consented. In the early morning I found a minister who was willing to marry them and accept my services as interpreter, though I had many qualms myself as to whether I should be able to translate questions and responses correctly. The service was a sketchy one, but the minister said it was legal, and the bride and groom, not looking particularly happy, departed into the promised land.

After Canada had passed her immigration law, the main reason for my having been sent there was concluded. Four years of study of the immigration problem at Boston, New York, and Naples, as well as Canada, had convinced me that more constructive legislation was needed. During the long winter evenings in Canada I had studied law, which helped me to gather together in legal form the data I considered vital for this purpose. I submitted these to Washington, and they formed the nucleus of the Immigration Act of 1907.

This bill was passed with the active support of labor. During its preparation I frequently met Terence V. Powderly, the former head of the powerful Knights of Labor, who had been appointed to the Bureau of Labor as a concession to those who claimed that the hordes of Europe were being brought in for the use of American capital.

Powderly gave me a valuable piece of advice which has often stood me in good stead. "You probably will have to deal with newspapers a good deal, young man. Here's a little rule for you. If you've anything you don't want published, just give the reporters the whole story and then tell them how much of it is off the record. They'll never go back on you."

I have always followed this precept and have never in any country had a reporter abuse my confidence in a personal interview.

But long before the Immigration Law had been passed, my activities had been completely shifted. I received the appointment of Chief Quarantine Officer for the Philippine Islands on the other side of the world.

At the end of the Spanish-American War the United States was confronted with large responsibilities in the field of tropical sanitation. Suddenly we found on our hands an unsought duty. In the Philippines the Army Board of Health was presented with a medical situation of unparalleled gravity; an entire nation had to be rehabilitated.

The British, the French, and the Dutch had had years of dealing with administration and health in the Orient and the tropics, but, broadly speaking, American medical officers were inexperienced. Almost the only exception—and that a recent one—was the dramatic and successful fight waged in Cuba against yellow fever, which had caused such a high mortality there, and often invaded our own shores. To prevent this danger was one of the principal reasons for our going to war with Spain. Public attention had been focused upon this yellow fever battle conducted by Military Governor Leonard Wood, the Walter Reed Commission, and Major William C. Gorgas of the United States Army Medical Corps.

Discussion and argument over our making another tropical venture had simmered for years and was now coming to a boil. The French effort to build a canal at Panama had broken down because of their failure to conquer yellow fever and malaria, and we were about to make our attempt to cut the Isthmus. Success in this endeavor must rest upon sanitation, and Gorgas was the logical person to supervise it.

The government concluded that, before taking up our posts, both Gorgas and I should be fortified with information as to what was being done in the Orient in the field of tropical medicine, and, therefore, sent us in 1902 to the International Congress on Medicine at Cairo.

Medical officers from most of the tropical countries were present.

THE PROMISED LAND

As is true of all such association gatherings, I learned far more in conversation on the famous veranda of Shepheard's Hotel than I did from hearing papers read at the meetings. I was particularly impressed with the Germans who, at that time, stood at the top of the world in scientific research, and were attacking the problems of tropical medicine with their usual thoroughness.

We spent several weeks in the Egyptian capital, and I found Gorgas a most delightful colleague. We were both reluctant to make public addresses but, since he was my senior, it became his duty to serve as spokesman, and he accepted this obligation manfully. He, who had so reluctantly adopted the mosquito theory of yellow fever, with all the zeal of the convert was anxious to have this Congress formally recognize his yellow fever work in Cuba, and have it on record that the medical profession was convinced the stegomyia mosquito was the sole conveyor of the disease. I argued with him privately as to the desirability of making such an all-inclusive statement, but the Congress, swayed by his magnetic personality, passed the resolution in the form he had written it. A recent expedition into Brazil sent by the Rockefeller Foundation once more raises the question and throws a cloud of doubt over the theory.

After the Congress was concluded, Gorgas returned to await developments on the Isthmus, and I went on my Eastward passage through the hot countries—India, Ceylon, Malaya—alluring names for carefree travelers, but each a tocsin for the health officer from the New World, anxious to redress the balance in the Old.

All along the way I heard the same arguments: the Oriental could not be sanitated; he always had lived in filth and squalor; to persuade him to live in any other way was hopeless; he was happy in his present mode of existence and it would be a shame to disturb him; all efforts, therefore, should be concentrated on making living conditions safe for the European who was obliged to sojourn in his midst.

I listened patiently, but I knew the American people would never sanction such an attitude toward our "little brown brother."

CHAPTER 4.   AND BID THE
SICKNESS CEASE

"WHICH of you, intending to build a tower, sitteth not down first and counteth the cost, whether he have sufficient to finish it."

From the time the slow *Rohilla Maru* left the roadstead at Hongkong there was no peace from the frothing, churning turbulence of the China Sea until, some sixty hours later, she steamed through the Boca Chico, between Mariveles and the Island of Corregidor, into the calm of Manila Bay. There, in panorama, was spread out the teeming water life of the Orient's largest harbor. Little inter-island steamers chugged busily up and down. Praos with lateen sails and crews balanced on outriggers sailed in from remote places. Fishermen's bancas bobbed up and down in the shallows. Scores of bamboo fences jutting from the water enclosed the fish weirs, which looked like fields of rippling grain, marked out in orderly array.

At intervals along the twenty-five miles to Manila the embracing arms were dotted with clusters of little nipa huts, sprouting from the water's edge like four-legged mushrooms. Among them Cavite, the American naval base, gleamed with fresh American paint, and the white ships of the White Fleet rode at anchor.

Toward the end of the day the hot sun, beating on the water, piled up a huge feather bed of fluffy clouds. A faint steam arose, and through the haze glowed sunsets unequaled the world around. I had seen the sun sink behind Capri in gaudy glory, the vivid radiance of the Golden Gate, the torrid blaze of the African desert, and the delicate pastel pinks of New York, but nowhere else, before or afterwards, did I ever see sunsets of such grandeur or so varied in their swift changing colors, ranging over the spectrum even to delicate green.

From far out in the Bay Manila appeared in the distance, with its red roofs gleaming amid the dense green of the cocoanut fronds. Above the royal palms along the Malecon Drive stood out the crosses of the church buildings. Water once lapped about the foundations of these structures, but now the Americans, to make way for new and important commerce, have dredged the harbor, filled in the foreshore, and pushed the tidal flats away from their doors. Great ships, which formerly had anchored perforce in the roadstead, are now escorted to the new piers, and the smoke from their funnels drifts like incense through the naves of the ancient stone churches.

All the long way out to the Philippines I had considered the nature of the task before me. As Chief Quarantine Officer, I was to work with the Health Board so that when the time came to release the Army officers who largely controlled it, I should be ready to add to my duties those of Commissioner of Health. My future was in my own hands.

I had already formulated my answer to the constant reiteration of the British, the French, and the Dutch that it was waste of time and money to sanitate Orientals, who wanted to be left to their ancient unsavory habits. My answer was, "You cannot let people suffer if you have the means to relieve them."

In addition, I had not overlooked the fact, repeatedly impressed upon me in my immigration training, that disease never stays at home in its natural breeding places of filth, but is ever and again breaking into the precincts of its more cleanly neighbors. As long as the Oriental was allowed to remain disease-ridden, he was a constant threat to the Occidental who clung to the idea that he could keep himself healthy in a small disease-ringed circle.

It should also have been evident to employers of colonial labor that human life had a direct monetary value, even though it might be difficult to estimate and might vary greatly with age and race; the Orientals had too long held a position near the bottom of the scale.

I believed that health should be regarded from the economic as

37

well as from the humanitarian viewpoint. To be without it was to be without earning power. A people once relieved of unnecessary burdens caused by sickness and death, could compete on equal terms with races not so handicapped. Cholera, malaria, and smallpox had made any successful commercial development of the Philippines impossible under the Spanish. Again and again they had failed in their efforts to cultivate sugar on a large scale.

In 1903 throughout the Islands death was the one event in a harried life that brought tranquillity and peace to its victims. The population for years had been at a standstill, or even on the decline, as the inevitable result of war and unobstructed devastating disease. Farmers had discarded the plow for the bolo and the gun, and as a consequence the haciendas were idle and the gardens overgrown with weeds. Long years of insurrection, discontent, and discouragement had wrought disaster in every department of government, and in every business interest. The money of the Treasury had to be spent in protecting the loyal people from the bullets of insurrectos rather than from disease.

Whatever the relative importance of the medical man in other parts of the world, he, and the profession he represented, stood first in the Philippines. The health of the people was the vital question. To transform the Filipinos from the weak and feeble race they were into the strong, healthy, and enduring people that they might become was to lay the foundations for the future on a sound basis.

Across the street from my office was smallpox, to the right was plague, and to the left cholera.

We had first to extinguish the conflagration of disease, started long before the American occupation. Plague was creeping through the alleys of Manila. The morgue was piled high with the bodies of cholera dead. Forty thousand unvaccinated were uselessly slaughtered each year by smallpox. Tuberculosis, unconsidered and unfeared, was responsible for fifty thousand deaths annually. The beriberi victims were numbered in the tens of thousands. Every other child died before its first birthday; the Philippines had the unenviable distinction of having the highest infant mortality rate in the world.

More than ten thousand men, women, and children, blighted by the scourge of leprosy, wandered, sad and lonely, among the uncontaminated. Only a few hundred were cared for by the Church. The insane were chained like dogs underneath the houses. Imitation quinine pills were sold at fabulous prices to the wan and shaking sufferers from malaria. Medical relief had never been extended to the three hundred thousand wild peoples of the mountains. Even as simple a thing as a fracture caused severe suffering, lifelong deformity and handicap which could so easily have been avoided by proper setting of the broken bones.

Sections of Manila were so closely crowded that no room for streets or even alleys was left, and the wretched people who lived there had to creep through human excrement under one another's houses to reach their own. Six to eight human beings packed themselves to sleep into a room hardly large enough for one.

With the exception of an antiquated and polluted Spanish water system in the Capital, there was not a reservoir, not a pipe line, and not an artesian well in the Islands. Without let or hindrance the vilest class of food products was shipped into the country. Perishable provisions were sold from the ground, so that dust and dirt were soon intimately mixed with them. No proper inspection of animals was made before slaughter, and diseased cattle were constantly marketed to the public.

In general the people of the Philippines were strongly imbued with superstitions and traditions. They were apparently contented in their ignorance and poverty, and resigned to their many ailments.

I set myself the goal of trying to save fifty thousand lives a year.

CHAPTER 5. LITTLE BROWN BROTHER

MANILA, like all Oriental ports, had a water life separate and apart. The boat people did not mingle with the shore people, except when they went to the markets or to the cockpits to try their luck with their fighting roosters. They lived all their lives in their boat homes on the waters of the Bay, the Pasig River, and the esteros, or canals. They died there and would have had water burial had not a strict and seemingly unkind government forbidden it.

In those days Manila looked as though it might sink into the water. A heavy rain and an inshore wind would invariably flood the low-lying barrios. The storm waters could not be carried off by the time-worn esteros, which served as natural but ineffective drains. The tide was too languid to cope with the accumulated human filth, and a miasma of nauseating odors followed the passage of every boat.

A huge moat stretched around the Intramuros, the old Walled City, holding it python-like in indolent grip. Four sewers emptied into these twenty-five acres of swamp and morass—stagnant, noisome, and crawling with huge snakes. Beyond affording the lazy carabao, the water buffalo, an unequaled opportunity to wallow, and the mosquitoes an unsurpassed breeding place, this slough served no useful purpose. The fussy Americans filled it with good ground, converting the poisonous algae green to the fresh green of grassy parks.

The mighty walls, forty feet thick where the crenelated towers rose above the battlements, had stood siege more than once. It was true they barred entrance to the invader, but they also slowed the plodding traffic stream and excluded light and air. In disregard of the hurt feelings of antiquarians and historians, we admitted Twentieth Century vehicles, and ventilated the quarter by punching holes through the walls. In our holy zeal for sanitation, we might have razed them completely. But fortunately the anguished lamentations of American historical societies were potent enough to stay the execution. Before this happened, however, the river wall was entirely removed, and the quarter made thoroughly accessible.

The old Spanish houses which lined the narrow streets of the Intramuros leaned lovingly toward each other. These heavy masses of stone, weathered and grey, for centuries had withstood the triple threat of fire, earthquake, and invasion. Their cautious owners had locked the doors securely against thieves, but had locked within the damp, insanitary interiors the deadly germs of tuberculosis, dysentery, and cholera, and had invited plague rats to dine with them.

By far the majority of Manila's population of two hundred and fifty thousand lived outside the walled city in more modern houses. The first story often was of sandstone, soft when sawed from the quarries, but hardening when exposed to the air. Above was a projecting wooden superstructure around which was a passage way, forming a double wall and providing air space to keep the interior cool.

The first thing a Filipino did when he rose in the social scale was to build one of these hard material houses with a decorative hardwood floor made of the polished yellow molave, more beautiful than mahogany. If more esthetically-minded, he might alternate the molave with the colorful reddish ipil.

The airy baskets on stilts in which the fishermen and the toilers on land lived were fashioned after the old Malay villages built always on tidal flats or along river banks. Roofs and sides of these huts were of nipa palm, frames and floors of ant-proof bamboo, the whole bound together with withes of vegetable fibres—there was not a nail in the peasant Filipino house. The poles for the floor were split and placed flat side downward, thus making a smooth and resilient surface on which were spread their *petates*, or sleeping mats. Other furniture they had none except, perhaps, the ever-present Singer Sewing Machine. To catch vagrant currents of air, door and window flaps were propped open with sticks. Underneath the houses were the foul puddles formed by refuse dripping through the floors.

The nipa palm, rooted in salt water, grows luxuriantly in the Philippines, but does not occur again until far away Sumatra. The Filipino takes it for granted, but without it his life would be vastly more difficult. It provides him with the roof for his home and with internal warmth. Because it has no insect enemies the crop is unfailing, and until the ocean dries up it can suffer no drought. With little effort, the boats of the harvesters wind their way through narrow water ways, cutting the protecting fans, tapping the slender stalks, and emptying the little cups of their sweet sap. Out of this are distilled alcoholic imitations of beverages ranging from chartreuse to cognac— imitations so closely resembling the originals that only the most delicate palate can distinguish the difference.

The nipa hut, frail as it is, can withstand one enemy to which wood rapidly succumbs. One oppressive November day I went to a Thanksgiving party in Manila, and when, after the home fashion, a huge turkey was brought to the table, instead of bearing the weight cheerfully, the festive board literally groaned and collapsed at our feet. Everybody was startled, but nobody was surprised. Termites had bored up through the legs, leaving only a shell of varnish.

These white ants were the great destroyers in the tropics. At the Mariveles Quarantine Station where, during the first years, I spent much of my time, four carpenters were kept busy as the busy ants themselves, replacing their depredations. If the queen ant could be located and destroyed, the colony would die off, but she was usually hidden so carefully that it was well nigh impossible to find her. Each ant colony was built underground, tier on tier like a huge upside-down skyscraper. Somewhere in the middle of the structure was the boudoir, bed chamber, and lying in room of the fat and bulbous queen, who passed her life there in purdah, because her jealous subjects had designed the exit and entrance tunnels far too small for her passage.

I remember spending almost an entire Sunday afternoon watching these blind workers solve a complex engineering problem, apparently requiring a high degree of reasoning power. Up the side of the bathroom wall they had constructed their tunnel of mud and sand, cemented with a glue-like secretion which, when dry, was hard and fairly waterproof. Opposite the wooden flush tank, their objective, some six inches from the wall, they stopped to consider the question. First they vainly endeavored to bridge the gap with their ordinary tunnel structure by projecting it into the intervening space. When this did not work, they carried out one of the most ingenious operations I have ever witnessed. Against the side of the wall opposite the tank they extended the tunnel horizontally, forming an L, and then waited for it to dry. While a few of them wet it at the joint, the majority took hold of the vertical section and slowly turned it until the horizontal section bridged the gap. Without instruments and without sight they had constructed the connection the exact six inches necessary. Two ants cautiously ran across and fastened it; in a few moments it was ready for use.

Skilled artisans though they were, the habits of these ants were notoriously bad. In the vaults of the Treasury the great silver cartwheel pesos were stored in canvas sacks. The rude and pushing insects entered the cracks of the vault and devoured the sacks. When, for all their nibbling, the silver remained intact, their low and revengeful natures came to the fore. They covered the coins with a thick and horrible deposit which no soap, no water, and no solvents could remove. Small boys earned large sums scrubbing away with stiff wire brushes at the pesos, trying to get them clean.

Many of the hot dusty streets of old Manila presented a grey monotone until the Americans, with tremendous enthusiasm, began planting trees. Growth in the tropics is so rapid that much of the city was soon sheltered. In April and November, when the leaves of the fire tree dropped and the blossoms emerged, the town was aglow with incandescent flame.

Travel on the thoroughfares of Manila was not without its hazards. Ordinary asphalt paving was tried but the continuous heat melted it; similarly, the tar filling around wooden blocks ran away. Until recently there remained only the large cobblestones, heritage of Spanish rule, over which vehicles rattled with careless abandon and deafening noise. In the Escolta and Calle Rosario, ambulances, even when carrying emergency cases, had to proceed at a walk; the violent jolting might easily have caused further injury.

No street scene in Manila would have been complete without the

43

springless, two-wheeled little carts with long shafts and flat platforms. Each was drawn by a carabao, strong as any two horses, moving sedately a mile an hour and hauling behind him a heavy, precariously-balanced load. This stolid animal would not be hurried or pushed aside, and his great wide horns, swinging ponderously, were a constant source of danger to the innocent bystander.

For more select transportation, the quilez, with seats along the side and steps that came down in the back, was preferred by the Filipinos. The driver sat outside in the front and directed a small trotting ox, which clattered merrily along at eight miles an hour.

The common horse-drawn vehicle was the two-wheeled, solid-topped carromata, shaped much like the old-fashioned hansom, except that the driver was perched low between the shafts. As soon as the carromata stopped and the occupant alighted, the driver would leap into the passenger's seat, seize the reins with his toes, and sink into profound slumber. He was able to sleep under all circumstances and for an indeterminate period of time.

The slender, slant-eyed, brown people of the Islands are of many kinds and speak many tongues. Forty-three ethnographic groups have been distinguished and eighty-seven dialects, most of them differing so widely that those who speak one cannot make themselves understood to a neighboring group. The Spanish had never imposed their tongue on the people; only the upper classes acquired it in the course of being educated. With the coming of the Americans, the use of English was gradually extended throughout the length and breadth of the Archipelago, but when I first went there interpreters were frequently necessary. Now the younger men in the Legislature do not even speak Spanish, because they were educated in American schools; English is to be the language of the new Commonwealth.

Though Malay in origin the Filipinos are Christian in their religion and Occidental in their form of government. Largest in numbers and gentlest of the racial groups are the Visayans of Southern Luzon and the central islands—Panay, Cebu, Leyte and the rest. Most civilized when Miguel Lopez de Legaspi established Spanish rule in 1565, they later yielded the leadership to the more aggressive Tagalogs of Manila and Central Luzon, who have been head and front of the independence movement since the old days of the Katipunan, the revolutionary secret society led by José Rizal and Emilio Aguinaldo. To the Northwest are the hard-working Ilocanos, true sons of Martha, who, in their thatched-roof carts, follow the harvests around Luzon.

In the central hills are the five wild tribes, animistic in their religion; and here and there in Luzon, tucked away in the recesses of the Mariveles hills and the East Coast, are the Negritos. Far to the South in the Islands of the Sulu Sea—Mindanao, Jolo, Tawi-tawi—are the fierce Moros, last of the Malay invaders and the only Mohammedans in the Archipelago.

Fortunately, the race question has never proved a stumbling block between whites and Filipinos. Perhaps three hundred years of Christian influence have given the latter an attitude toward Western races not shared by other Orientals. Of *mestizos* there are many, mostly a mixture of Filipino with Spanish or Chinese, and from these are generally drawn the leaders of the people, including Manuel Quezon, a Spanish-Tagalog, and Sergio Osmeña, a Chinese-Visayan, both exceptionally able men.

The Filipinos, with the exception of the wild tribes and the Moros, were devout Catholics. But their grievances against the Church were so bitter that the Revolution had been directed as much against it as against Spain. Many of the Independistas wanted religious as well as political freedom, so that a Filipino might become a priest or a Filipina a sister. In Father Aglipay, who had been Aguinaldo's chaplain and one of the brains of the Revolution, they found a leader.

The schismatics took possession of the Catholic churches in the districts where they were strongest. The question of ownership was taken to the Supreme Court of the United States where the adherents of Aglipay contended that the churches had been built by the people of the community, and therefore belonged to them; the Roman Catholics, on the other hand, claimed that a church once built belonged to the Holy See forever. The Supreme Court decided for the orthodox religion, and the Aglipaists had to give up the churches. They, however, were not to be checked so easily. They erected churches of their own, first of bamboo and wood to serve until, as their numbers swelled to a million and a half and funds increased, they could afford better ones.

The bulk of the population of the Philippine Islands was agricultural. The tao, or peasant farmer, was a friendly creature, simple and uncomplaining. In the old days, half the village might be dead of cholera, but the survivors would be cheerful. Or if his house burned down the tao, with no caviling at fate, would set to work the next day to build it up again.

All the Americans felt sympathy and affection for the tao and wanted to protect him. But this was difficult because of the cacique system, so strongly entrenched that neither Spaniards nor Americans had been able to root it out. The cacique was the rich man of the town, who owned all the property and received a percentage on all the produce. Through his system of usury he kept the tao in a state of serfdom.

In the health service we had to recognize the power of the cacique; usually an intelligent person, his opposition could have nullified our efforts. But as soon as he realized he could get no graft from us, and that, on the contrary, we might bring him added income by making his subject taos more productive, he ranged himself on our side. The tao, who was as unprogressive as he was gentle, often offered passive resistance to Westernizing, but at a threatening word from his cacique he would prove amenable.

It is always easy to condemn a whole people by calling them this or that when, as a matter of fact, the adjective may only be true in part. The Filipinos have been termed lazy, but the tao, the submerged nine-tenths, is anything but lazy. With his carabao he works his plot of ground day in and day out. The class above the tao, on the other hand, is frequently disinclined to physical exercise—carpentering, gardening, or even walking. But even they could not be called mentally lazy.

All Filipinos have the siesta habit, although it was abruptly broken into by bustling American office routine. Americans found it difficult to appreciate the leisureliness of the Filipinos, who, for example, measured distance by the time it took to smoke two cigarettes, or five, or whatever the number might be. The Filipinos, on the other hand, failed utterly to comprehend the importance of time as viewed by Westerners. To an American, an appointment at ten o'clock meant ten o'clock, but to the Filipino it meant the time at which he left his house; he might arrive at the meeting place at eleven.

The net result of centuries of subjection was a tendency to evasion, a characteristic of people who have long lived in a state of dependency. This indirection was carried over into daily conversation. I soon learned that I must never say "no" to an Oriental, because nothing gave greater offense than the direct negative. If a Filipino asked me for the loan of an umbrella, I must not say, "I'm sorry, but I have no umbrella," but rather, "I don't think it's going to rain." He would understand and not be affronted.

Though the Filipino seldom smiled, he was by no means dour. Kindliness was one of his most charming traits. Family life was invariably amicable and friendly. Harsh or scolding voices were seldom heard. Even the little children were polite to each other. No child was rude to strangers or failed to obey. He seldom whined or cried.

Equally endearing was the generosity which welled spontaneously from Filipino hearts. I was once accompanying Jacob M. Dickinson, Secretary of War, on a tour of the provinces when, due to a motor mishap, we had to stop at a village which had not been expecting us. Our party was composed of at least twenty-five, but within an hour an excellent banquet was produced, complete even to such orations as would have made a United States Senator envious. Mr. Dickinson was much impressed with the spirit of hospitality he found everywhere, and at the conclusion of his five weeks' stay among the Filipinos quoted as his valedictory the words of Charles Sumner, "Let us know each other better and we will love each other more."

Former custom had been to "civilize" native populations with the aid of a whiskey bottle, the Bible, and the Krag. The United States was determined that different methods would be employed in the Philippines. Kipling's advice to the American people was noble but unnecessary; in our hearts we had already assumed the white man's burden. President McKinley had sincerely believed, as he said, "There was nothing left for us to do but to take them all, and to educate the Filipinos, and uplift and civilize and Christianize them, and by God's grace to do the very best we could by them."

In harmony with this sentiment he selected men who would also wish to avoid the horrors which usually had accompanied the efforts of a white race to impose its civilization on one of darker color. William Howard Taft was sent to the Islands early in 1900 to head a Commission of Five, two of whom were to become governors after him—Luke E. Wright, Secretary of Commerce and Police, and Henry C. Ide, Secretary of Finance and Justice. One of the others, the dynamic Dean C. Worcester, was to serve ardently, faithfully, and long as Secretary of the Interior.

The views of all these men coincided with those of President McKinley. Their conception of their responsibilities included immediate attention to the material and physical needs of the Filipinos. With that speed and energy which we like to think of as American, one million dollars was appropriated at once for roads and three million for improving Manila harbor, a thousand American school teachers were imported, civil service by merit was installed, a native constabulary formed, a whole new system of government with its manifold ramifications designed and executed.

One of the outstanding acts of Governor Taft's administration was the peaceful settlement of the Friar Lands Controversy. The four orders of friars had obtained most of the desirable land in the Islands, and had rented it out to the Filipinos on terms which they resented. The Revolutionaries had driven the priests helter-skelter, killing or imprisoning any they could catch. Embittered public sentiment was almost unanimously against their return. Governor Taft interested himself wholeheartedly in this important question. To settle the unrest he went in person to Rome and, after consultation with Pope Leo XIII, he arranged for the purchase of these lands for seven million dollars by the Filipino government and their resale to the Filipinos at fair rates.

Economic betterment could not be successful until Filipino confidence had been secured. The Filipino had a difficult time comprehending that anybody should want to do anything for him without expecting something in return; he was always looking for a concealed motive. Service without expectation of reward, in the Anglo-Saxon sense, was outside his cosmogony, and he regarded giving for the sake of giving as absurd.

At the outset, Taft enunciated that the American goal in the Philip-

48

pines was to train the Filipinos to self-government as quickly as possible. To attain this end, as well as to increase goodwill, three Filipino members were added to the Commission. They were participants, and their wishes were carefully considered, but the five Americans retained the deciding vote by reason of their numbers, although it is interesting to note that the vote seldom split along racial lines. Until the advent of the Democratic Administration in 1913, it was a consistent American policy never to delegate authority to Filipinos until they had been trained to responsibility, just as it was the policy to train them to this responsibility as quickly as possible.

Another immediate problem was due to the inevitable friction caused by a military occupation; the soldiers with whom the Filipinos had been at war were naturally still regarded by them as their enemies. Taft had to make himself popular as a necessary incident to initiating a civil government. He was so successful in this endeavor that when there was talk of President Theodore Roosevelt offering him a Supreme Court justiceship, thousands of Filipinos serenaded him with the stirring sentiment, "We want Taft!" His winning smile and his jovial good nature were maintained in the face of every obstacle. The Filipino took life seriously. The Americans were so burdened with the responsibility of their mission that they had little inclination for humor. But Taft, amid the encircling gloom, would tell his stories with such gusto as to command appreciation and delight.

Taft came down shortly with amoebic dysentery, the inevitable result of his constant attendance at banquets. He believed it his duty to partake freely of the soft drinks and the strange food until, as he himself expressed it, his "intestines harbored a first class zoological garden."

In spite of his size, and although the perspiration poured from him, he was a glutton for work. He had a most extraordinary talent for preparing laws. I have seen him dictate ex tempore to a stenographer a legal document running into several pages in which scarcely a word would have to be altered.

Taft created hundreds of laws, but the man who saw to their administration was Luke E. Wright, a former general of the Confederacy, a typical Southern officer with upright bearing and clear, cool eye. His wisdom had much to do with the success of Taft's administration, and when he succeeded as governor, he ably carried out the laws which Taft had drawn up.

Wright was followed by Henry C. Ide who held office only a short time. Then in 1906 came the picturesque James F. Smith, Colonel of California Volunteers, who had served as Customs Collector, Justice of the Supreme Court, and Vice Governor-General. He was likeable, sincere, honest, and, above all, human. It was during his term of office that the railroads of the Islands were built and the government finances stabilized. He could secure Filipino support for his measures, a gift which, as time went on, became increasingly essential.

Each administration reiterated Taft's original promise of independence when the Filipinos were prepared for it. One step toward its fulfilment came in 1907 when the first Philippine Assembly was opened by Taft, then Secretary of War in President Theodore Roosevelt's cabinet, who had made the long journey across the Pacific for this express purpose. The Commission, soon increased by the addition of a fourth Filipino member, then became the upper house of the legislature.

I have known all the governor-generals of the Philippines and, in my opinion, the one most gifted in administrative ability was W. Cameron Forbes. He laid a firm foundation for sound government which might totter in political earthquakes but would not fall. His nine years of service began in 1904 when he became a member of the Commission. As Secretary of Commerce and Police he controlled many of the basic government entities upon which the material prosperity of the Islands depended—Public Works, Coast and Geodetic Survey, Posts and Telegraph, Inter-Island Navigation, and a Constabulary of ten thousand men. He did much to create the forces which would eventually make the Islands fully rounded and self-sustaining economically. Improvement of harbor facilities and reduction or abolition of harbor dues did much to stimulate commerce. His brilliant achievements in all these fields ranked with those of Lord Cromer in Egypt.

This grandson of Ralph Waldo Emerson, the transcendental theorist, used his brains to build up the most efficient government the world has ever known. For a population of ten million he did all the things a government had to do—courts, constabulary, harbors, education, civil service—on thirty million dollars a year. He ran the Philippines as a business; politics were allowed to play no part.

Every item of expense, no matter how minute, was carefully scrutinized by his loyal lieutenant, auditor Lawshee, who would lop off here and whittle there, waging a successful war against the common human failing to pad expense accounts. I remember one occasion when Lawshee's eagle eye was skimming the expense account of one of my subordinates. When it lit upon an item charging two dinners in one day, his inexorable blue pencil ruled it out. My man explained defensively that he had been on shipboard one rough night and had lost his dinner. But shortly the sea had grown calm, and he had been able to return to the dining room and consume a second dinner. His contention was that the first had been lost in the line of duty. But the Rhadamanthine Lawshee brushed this explanation aside, saying one dinner was all that could be allowed.

Philippine revenues were small, and much money was needed to turn into reality the American dream of rehabilitating the Islands. Forbes started in to develop their material resources. But before this could be done, roads had to be constructed. The military caminos which the Spanish had built for conquest had long since fallen into decay and disrepair. Forbes built new ones, also for conquest, but this time intended to seize the treasures of Mother Earth.

According to the Forbes plan, after a road had been built, a caminero was hired to patrol each kilometer on the sound theory that a stitch in time saves nine. He would plod up and down with his little cart, his eyes scanning the surface, and then, with simple tools, a bushel of stone, and a bucket of tar, he would mend immediately each rift or hole.

Though Forbes was doing this work for the good of the Filipinos rather than for their exploitation, he, like every departmental head, had always to battle with the ghosts of past abuses; the Filipinos had vivid memories of the corvee system under which they had been conscripted for road work. Nevertheless, so persistently did Forbes bend his energies in this direction that, half jokingly, half affectionately, he was dubbed Caminero Forbes.

Wealth began to flow along the roads which he had opened. His efforts resulted in raising sugar production from fifty thousand tons to a million and a half a year and in developing the copra industry to an extent hitherto undreamed of. Wherever we went in Southern Luzon we used to see the silvery white hemp fibre hanging out to dry like washing. The staple, ten to fifteen feet long, stronger under water than any other fibre grown, has made Manila virtually synonymous with good rope throughout the world. Forbes encouraged gold mining and the Philippines are rapidly becoming one of the world's leading producers.

Forbes did much to advance the Philippine tobacco industry against the bitter antagonism of American corporations already interested in the Cuban product. As soon as Philippine tobacco, which has a smaller nicotine content than the best Havana and is unsurpassed in quality, began to win popularity on its own merit, reports were circulated that Philippine cigars were made by lepers and syphilitics. Such is the suggestibility of human nature that even the red sentinels at cigar store entries seemed to hold their right hands aloft with, "Thou shalt not enter."

The Bureau of Health, trying to combat this unfounded prejudice, certified that each box exported was manufactured under absolutely sanitary conditions. But a bad name, once given, clings as tenaciously as a lanky hound to the trail. The old stories would keep cropping up. Whenever I would try to purchase a Philippine cigar in the United States, the cigar store clerk would reply, "We don't carry 'em. They'd ruin the rest of our stock." Then he would deliver a lengthy homily on the dangers inherent in even having them in the store. He would show me Philippine cigars with tiny holes in them, and instruct me in the habits of worms, with many details as to how they would infect the good clean Havanas.

My explanation differed from his. Occasionally, as is common to any tobacco, eggs had been laid on a few of the leaves. After they had been rolled into the cigars, the eggs had hatched and the worms bored their way out. But the worms had long since gone their way and therefore could not possibly have "infected" any other cigars.

Forbes' interests were not alone material. He had a strong sociological bent, particularly directed toward penology. The great central prison of Bilibid was becoming much overcrowded. Instead of adding to its great stone walls, or to its wings, radiating from the central tower where the guards unceasingly watched, Forbes established the partially self-governing community of Iwahig, consisting of twelve hundred adult criminals, on the far distant island of Palawan. As in the George Junior Republics in this country, there were no walls at all; Iwahig was designed to reform rather than to punish. Privileges were won by merit. After two years of good behavior a prisoner could send for his family, set up housekeeping, and develop a plot of land independently as though he were at home in his own village. Half of what he produced was his. If he did not care for agriculture, he could learn a trade.

Few escapes were attempted; most of the murderers, highway robbers, and burglars loyally observed the conditions of their parole. After release they were in great demand for servants because of the excellent training they had received, and the reliability they had proved. Paradoxically, released convicts found it easier to get jobs than those who had not served an apprenticeship at Iwahig.

Such was the power of Forbes' personality that it pervaded every department. The esprit de corps was raised to so high a pitch that all labored joyfully and without regard for their own interests; even the office boy was heart and soul a part of the movement and firmly convinced that if he were not there at eight o'clock in the morning the wheels would stop.

Although he worked so hard, Forbes seemed to be able to stretch the twenty-four hours farther than most people. He attended official functions faithfully, and did more than his share in furthering good fellowship between Filipino and American. He was at the height of his success and had attained world renown when in 1913 the administration changed. President Woodrow Wilson subjected him to one of the extreme cruelties so often perpetrated under a democratic form of government. Without warning he received the following curt cable from Washington:

"Washington, August 23, 1913. Harrison confirmed August 21. The President desires him to sail September 10. Will it be convenient to have your resignation accepted September 1. Harrison to accept and take office September 2. The President desires to meet your convenience. Should

AN AMERICAN DOCTOR'S ODYSSEY

Harrison take linen, silver, glass, china, and automobiles? What also would you suggest? Wife and children will accompany him. Please engage for him servants you leave."

Two days later, President Wilson, apparently realizing that something more was due, wrote as follows:

"Washington, August 25, 1913.
My Dear Governor Forbes,

I have appreciated your willingness to remain as Governor General of the Philippines until I might with deliberation select your successor. I realize the amount of excellent work which you have done in the Islands as Secretary of Commerce and Police, and as Governor General, and I desire to thank you for your faithful and careful service. It is my desire that your successor should, if possible, reach the Philippines before October 16, and I therefore accept your resignation to take effect September 1 from the service."

Forbes had performed a great work for the American government in a position which, in administrative importance, ranked next to that of the Presidency itself. Wilson's abrupt action was a poor return for one who had spent his personal fortune freely and had worked so hard, often against the opposition of the Assembly, that his health had given way a number of times.

Under Osmeña and Quezon the movement for independence had been steadily growing, although, in their desire for personal power, the leaders often talked in generalities, either without knowledge of the facts or disregarding them. Forbes had no intention of denying independence to the Filipinos but only of withholding it until he considered these novices in self-government had become experienced enough to manage their own affairs without tariff concessions and military protection from the United States.

The arrival of Francis Burton Harrison, former Congressman and the avowed champion of Filipino independence, was awaited with much speculation and curiosity. Who knew what happy hunting grounds in the various government departments might be opened to the politicos?

As a gesture of courtesy, an envoy was sent to meet Governor Harrison's ship at Nagasaki to answer any questions he might wish to ask about the country he was to administer. When he propounded the rhetorical question, "I suppose I should wear a silk hat and morning coat when I enter Manila?" the envoy, anxious to please, replied politely, "Of course."

But the moment the emissary was out of the presence he sent off warning cables to Manila that the new Governor General intended landing in silk hat and frock coat. The Filipinos were always immaculately and neatly clad but always in white, and even formal occasions called only for mess jackets. There were no more than a half dozen top hats in Manila and no time in which to procure more. They were not to be found lacking in etiquette, however. They organized the official reception in relays. Several hundred people are supposed to have defiled before Governor Harrison, exchanging the six silk hats rapidly behind a screen.

Meanwhile emergency telegrams by the hundred were being despatched to Singapore, Hongkong, and Calcutta calling for hats, but to fill this unprecedented demand the emporiums of the East were able to send hardly two of the same shape or vintage.

Governor Harrison was both amused and embarrassed at the furore he had unwittingly created. After his first appearance he had discontinued toppers, but for many months they were faithfully worn by the Filipinos to the delight of Philistine beholders. When we went on inspection tours it was the custom for the officials of each town to line up in the main street. I used to pull out my binoculars as we approached. Governor Harrison would ask anxiously, "How are they dressed?"

I would take a gleeful look and reply, "They're all out in their silk hats."

Governor Harrison would sigh and say, "I suppose I'll never be able to live that down."

In spite of Governor Harrison's personal charm, he was to create much havoc throughout the Islands. Because he said to the Filipinos, "What you want you may have," his popularity with them was immense. But he had not been in Manila twenty-four hours before he began dismissing American officials of the Philippine government who, as Civil Service incumbents, had considered their tenure permanent. They were informed, often with only a few hours' notice, that their jobs were terminated, and they were left stranded ten thousand miles from home. The blade rose and fell, and one head after another rolled into the basket. Many Filipinos were lifted into positions which they were not qualified to fill.

Two schools of thought about the Philippines existed among Americans. One was to allow the Filipinos to direct the lesser units of government and, as they showed fitness, to turn over to them the higher units. The other, to which Governor Harrison belonged, believed the only way for people to learn how to govern was to let them do the governing as they wished.

Since 1907 there had been two main parties in the Philippine Assembly—the National Independent, which wanted freedom at once, and the Democratic, which was always in the minority and favored going slowly. Additional parties kept cropping up, only to be plowed under again. One of them, the Electric Independence party, wanted independence as fast as electricity could travel.

The two leaders of the National Independent party were Sergio Osmeña and Manuel Quezon. Undoubtedly the latter was even then the chief figure in the Islands. Although our objects were often antithetical, he had such charm that it was impossible to dislike him, and our relations were always friendly. Osmeña, long Speaker of the House, and then President of the Senate, was second only to Quezon in prominence.

After Rizal, Emilio Aguinaldo was the most outstanding figure in Philippine history. He was a full-blooded Tagalog from Cavite, in whose name the Filipino insurrection had been conducted. This school teacher, exiled by Spain for political activity, in spite of his originally peaceful occupation, had shown a certain talent for military tactics. After Funston had captured him by a daring ruse, he gave his parole, and from that moment became a loyal citizen, who did his utmost to help build up the Islands. He retired from active life and concentrated on his farm in Cavite.

In and out of the course of duty I saw Aguinaldo often. He still had a great name. During presidential campaigns, politicians would come all the way from the United States to wring from him his opinion on the progress the Filipinos were making toward independence. Ammunition was always needed for pre-convention speeches.

Senator William J. Stone, a Democrat from Missouri, appeared on one of these missions. Americans in the Islands kept telling him that Aguinaldo had no influence whatsoever politically, but Stone naturally considered that these artful Republicans were trying to lead him astray, and prevent him from tracking down the truth. Stone was a guest of the Governor General at Malacañan, the former residence of the Spanish governors, and Aguinaldo was produced for him. Since no interpreter was present, I was asked to fulfill that function.

"Now, General," Stone began. "Don't you think the Filipinos would have been much better off if we hadn't occupied the Islands?"

"I really don't know," replied Aguinaldo, "but I'm trying to raise some corn in Cavite. Now I understand you come from a great corn-raising state, and I wish you'd tell me something about the essentials of seed selection."

"I haven't ever thought about it. I don't know anything about corn. But you, General, know that the Democratic party in the United States has always stood for release of the Islands. Don't you think you should have independence right away?"

"That's a debatable question, Senator, but now about fertilizers. What fertilizer do you use on your corn?"

"I don't know anything about fertilizer," asserted the Senator firmly and with signs of irritation. "But I'd like to get your opinion on what America should do right now, and whether it wouldn't be the correct policy to turn these Islands over to you. What do you think?"

"Oh, there are many people who know much more about governmental matters than I. But in Missouri—"

"To hell with Missouri," shouted the Senator, and stamped out of the room.

But if Aguinaldo were lukewarm to independence some years ago, he was in the minority, because independence was the burning issue. A school superintendent in Cebu reported that he had received from a small potential voter the following answer to his request for a description of a cow. "A cow is an animal which has a leg at each corner, it has horns and gives milk, but, as for me, give me Independence."

By the passage of the Jones Act in 1916 an elective Senate replaced the Commission, leaving the legislature in financial control. Thereafter Filipino bills were subject only to the veto of the Governor

General. With complacent Harrison failing to assert his prerogative, the Filipinos had affairs in their own hands. Unfortunately, the novitiate had not lasted long enough; the vows of government had been taken too soon. The people had not "had time to absorb and thoroughly master the powers already in their hands."

CHAPTER 6.　　　　　WASHING UP
THE ORIENT

THE Philippine Archipelago stretches along the coast of Southern Asia for more than a thousand miles; a fast ocean liner can pass by in no less than two full days. The only quarantine station in this vast and scattered collection of Islands was at Mariveles. Ships which came into any port of entry with communicable diseases sometimes had to be remanded enormous distances. In order to ease the burdens on commerce one of my first duties was to build a quarantine station at the populous port of Cebu, and later others at Iloilo, Zamboanga, and Jolo.

In Spanish days the quarantine department had been run on a simple system. Whenever a ship sailed into Manila with dangerous communicable disease aboard, its captain would take up a "collection," as it was called. If it were sufficient, the ship would be promptly released without being delayed in quarantine. If not ample, another collection, and perhaps even a third, would have to be tendered. The result was that an outbreak of plague, cholera, or smallpox in China or Japan would usually be followed by an outbreak in the Philippines.

We applied water, soap, and disinfectant rigorously. Whenever ships came in from Hongkong or Amoy, the crews, many of whom had loathsome skin diseases due to filth, were scrubbed, sometimes forcibly. After a few rounds of bathing most of these skin troubles disappeared.

Later we had an arrangement with Hongkong so that the crews of ships about to sail for Manila would be bathed there. The Chinese, who objected strenuously to bathing and who were always highly skilled in evading regulations, promptly formed a guild of professional bathers. A boatload of sailors on its way from ship to quarantine station would change places midway with a boatload of the professionals, and depart to seek pleasure elsewhere. The only certain way to stop this practice was to send inspectors to see that the Chinese performed their ablutions satisfactorily.

A detail, but a bothersome one in the quarantine service, was cleaning up the Spanish-operated inter-island steamers. Everything about them was indescribably filthy. The ice boxes spread abroad a noxious odor which tainted the food. The knives and forks were dirty, and so were the table cloths. Toilets and baths were unspeakable, and drinking water was unsafe. I put every arriving boat in quarantine until it could pass an inspection for cleanliness. The captain would run up a signal when, according to his way of thinking, the ship was immaculate. We then went out and inspected. If it were still dirty, we left the crew again to their housecleaning. They did not understand the meaning of the word dirt until its presence had been actually pointed out to them. But in the end they met our exacting demands and learned how to scrub.

America was literally washing up the Orient.

The Army Board of Health had also inaugurated a general campaign on land of cleaning and sweeping, so characteristic of the American sanitarian. In the four years of its existence this Board, composed of three American surgeons as active members and two prominent Filipino physicians as honorary members, had done what it could in the face of an overwhelming problem. But its work had necessarily been confined largely to protecting the health of the troops and sanitating the city of Manila, although municipal boards of health had been organized to study the requirements of the different towns and suggest remedies.

There was never money enough for all our needs. Hence, anybody was cherished by the Commission who could reduce expenses and at the same time produce results. I bore this constantly in mind. It was astounding to find how the employment of a little ingenuity would accomplish great things economically. I have often thought our work was done more efficiently because things were not too easy. One simple method of creeping into the hearts of my superiors was to save them the annual expenditure of three hundred dollars for a launch awning. The rot in this humid climate was so great that the canvas would quickly mold away. I adopted the simple expedient of having it washed once a week with bichloride of mercury, thereby killing the mold germ and extending the life of the canvas considerably.

The financial stringency under which I worked as quarantine officer permeated all government departments, and was an ever-present and pressing problem in the Bureau of Health. We were at all times handicapped by the shortness of the Treasury purse. Whatever we accomplished had to be done within the revenues of the Islands, and, moreover, appropriations had to be secured from a reluctant and uncomprehending legislature. We had approximately fifteen cents per capita compared with the $3.65 which Gorgas could spend yearly in Panama. Moreover our territory covered a hundred thousand square miles and three hundred inhabited islands instead of the narrow strip of Canal Zone. Contrary to general belief, the Philippines never received any financial assistance except a *million dollars* from the United States to repair the losses of the frightful rinderpest epidemic.

Another handicap with which I struggled for a year was the limited power granted to the head of the health department. For example, under the Health Act as originally drafted, I had to secure the permission of the Governor General and of the Commission before making any important move. When I had to have an assistant the list of eligible appointees limited me to five ex-presidents of provincial boards of health. One had an aortic aneurism which made him a hopeless invalid, one weighed two hundred pounds and could not speak after climbing a flight of stairs, and the others had no technical training.

Governor General Ide, at my request, cabled to the United States for an assistant. When Dr. Burdette arrived, the members of the Commission, angered at what they considered derogation of their authority, refused to confirm the appointment, and offered to pay Dr. Burdette's passage back if he would take the first boat. Within a few hours, however, they had reconsidered and informed me they would confirm Dr. Burdette's appointment, but only because of the expense already incurred in bringing him out.

I earnestly wished to do my duty, but it was impossible to work

61

under these conditions. If anything were to be accomplished it was absolutely essential that the Director of Health have almost military authority, and not be hampered either by politics or personalities. Otherwise the organization would be in such confusion that little could be accomplished. For efficiency and economy the administrative set-up of the department should be changed. I, therefore, submitted a new draft for a Directory of Health which, after much discussion, was accepted, and I was furnished dictatorial powers.

At first I had great difficulty finding medical men who were qualified and at the same time interested enough in the cause of humanity to undergo the innumerable hardships and discomforts to be encountered in the provinces. But ultimately the Bureau of Health had a staff of three thousand employees, two hundred doctors, and many sanitary inspectors. One of our great and continuing problems was to educate such a large force of men, and several million dollars a year were required to operate the complex machinery. Among other things the accounting system had to be elaborate, because we were determined never to have it said that an inspector could be bribed.

We kept ourselves informed in various ways whether the force was carrying out orders. We insisted on detailed reports; daily during epidemics, weekly otherwise. We also made surprise visits, and had inspectors to watch the inspectors. The sanitary squads had to display a big flag to show the section of the town in which they were working so that they could be located immediately if required. Since they might be called at any time, they never strayed.

I cannot now recall one case of breach of trust, although members of the force were often guilty of peccadillos. It was extremely difficult to bring them to book because the Oriental is so adept in extracting himself plausibly from the most compromising situations. I once had an idea that the doctor in charge of a nearby district was in Manila when it was vital he should be attending to his duties in the provinces. I had no definite basis for my suspicions, because his daily reports came in regularly. But, as a test, I suddenly sent an order transferring him to another province. He acknowledged this in the correct manner and telegrams began to arrive from the new headquarters.

Oddly enough, however, telegrams were being received at the same time from his previous station. I summoned him to an interview and waved the telegrams in front of him, demanding, "How could you have been in both Cavite and Laguna at the same time?"

"Oh, that's very simple," he replied disingenuously, "I knew how worried you were about the cholera epidemic, and I told my subordinate to keep on sending reports after I had left. He simply made a mistake and signed my name to them. He shouldn't have done that."

I often used to play the fascinating game of catching an Oriental squarely in a lie. The caretaker of the Manila morgue had the strictest instructions to see that rats were kept out. One day when I made my inspection, it was all too evident that, in spite of my injunctions, rats had been there.

"There are rats here," I said sternly to the caretaker.

"It's impossible," he replied stoutly.

"Oh, yes, there are," I corrected him.

"No, sir, there are no rats," he stubbornly maintained.

"What's that right under the roof?" I asked, pointing to a dark object on top of the wall.

"That's just some old rags I put up there." Rather than take the trouble to remove the cloths with which he had wiped off the tables, he had tossed them up on the rafters. But I knew that cloths could not move of themselves.

"You go get them."

"I haven't any ladder."

I had one brought in and he gingerly climbed up the rungs. The animated bundle of cloths quivered as he approached. The caretaker hesitated.

"Bring them down," I ordered sternly.

He reached over, and the rat, who could retreat no further, bit him savagely. He uttered a bloodcurdling yell.

"Are there any rats in here?" I demanded inexorably.

This was the only time I ever won the game.

My subordinates did not lie with malice but rather as children do. At first they had little comprehension of the essential purposes be-

63

hind the innumerable instructions which they had to carry out. They fulfilled their duties mainly by rote. But they, being under my immediate control, could be trained to see; to move the vast inertia of the populace was far more difficult.

Nevertheless, the sanitary regeneration of the Philippines had to be brought about, not in spite of the Filipino, but with his assistance. It was natural at first that a people should resist measures which, in their inmost hearts, they believed were being enforced by the governing power for the express purpose of making them miserable, unhappy, and uncomfortable.

President McKinley had once promised that the United States would do nothing to interfere with Filipino habits and customs. But the Bureau of Health was constantly doing this very thing, and any measure proposed which the Filipinos did not like was ipso facto not one of their customs. I could sympathize with them; it was doubtless unpleasant to be ordered about by sanitary officers and nurses.

Popular hostility was naturally reflected in the press, and even the doctors joined in the hue and cry when I submitted a sanitary code for Manila. I was invading the privacy of the home. After they had delayed its passage for a year, I called them into conference and asked, "Gentlemen, what corrections would you like to make?" They submitted their proposals. I agreed they were excellent, but needed only a few slight changes here and there of a purely technical nature. I then rewrote the code, essentially as it had been before, and everybody was happy.

I used this same system often in the legislature, where hostility could be converted into active cooperation by the simple expedient of saying to the most violent objector, "Will you draft this bill for me?" His opposition would evaporate instantly, and he would eagerly accept the commission. When he brought it back, I would agree that his version was excellent, and then recast the entire bill. As the bill thereafter bore his name, the theoretical author and I would remain faithful allies forever.

We always had to bear in mind that we had to have public opinion on our side. Public opinion conceives of sanitation in terms of collecting garbage and cleaning dirty streets, removing dead animals, cutting weeds and grass on vacant lots, keeping goats out of back alleys, sweeping sidewalks, penning up pigs, and deodorizing foul smells. We had to do all the things which the public regarded as of most importance, even to seeing that their whiskey was free of impurities.

The citizens were being bitten continually by mosquitoes, and hence mosquitoes became, in their eyes, the paramount health problem. In reality the mosquitoes of Manila, though enormous in numbers, were negligible from a health point of view because they did not transmit any important disease there. Even to free the city of flies was not of vital importance but had to be done. Every householder and stable-keeper in Manila was required to have a garbage and refuse receptacle, which was emptied daily under the eyes of the Bureau of Health employees.

Epidemics of flies, however, sometimes served a good purpose. People never count their blessings until they suffer a little annoyance. If the inspectors became careless, flies would promptly breed. The press would come out with loud denunciations of the Health Bureau. I would dutifully promise, "We'll get rid of them in two weeks." When this miracle was achieved, the people were alive to the fact that they had a sanitary department. I would not have been able to carry them with me in greater things if they had not been able to say, "Manila is the cleanest city in the Orient."

But the public never realized that the real health work went far deeper than this. Water and soil pollution are the root causes of mortality in the tropics. We would have saved more lives in the end if we could have worked on these alone and disregarded the things which were merely irritations and not major health hazards.

A direct correlation is not always traceable between the amount spent for health and the death rate. People talk glibly about the pricelessness of human life, but they really do not believe this. If the cost of saving lives is too great, the money must be spent where it will do the most good. Though we could not install a permanent water system when thousands of people were dying of cholera, plague, and smallpox, I did what I could. According to a consistent governmental policy, anything I could save from my appropriation might, with the approval of the Governor General, be used where necessity demanded. It was my custom to take each peso that became available and use it to free a certain number of individuals of intestinal parasites, or employ it to help drill an artesian well, or vaccinate forty people.

In later years my great satisfaction came from walking along the streets of Manila and seeing that under a certain age nobody was pockmarked. But the public in general was bored by the ceaseless detail which had gone into achieving this result; although after a disease had been reduced, they would be prompt to applaud and cheer to the echo.

It is hard for the white man in the Philippines to work for the joy of it. He is oppressed by the humid heat and has to drive himself constantly. Perspiration begins to roll from him the moment he leaves the shelter of the cool interior, even to walk across the street. Only after sundown is it possible to be comfortable, and then only by establishing sleeping quarters on the windward side. One guest at a hotel will complain at breakfast, "I've had a frightful night," while the canny old-timer will report, "I've rarely had such a pleasant sleep." It all depended where their rooms had been located, whether on the windward or lee side.

The climate of Luzon has its vagaries, though they are well regulated. When the Northeast monsoon comes over the Pacific, it strikes the mountain range which divides the island in the middle, and drops its load of rain on the sparsely inhabited East Coast. In Manila, which is on the West Coast, the seasons are exactly the reverse. The frequent rains begin in June with the advent of the Southwest monsoon, and last until October; for hours each day it may pour in torrents.

The winds at Manila blow five months and change, and five months and change again. November and May are uncomfortable because of the calm that comes when the winds are gradually shifting. Through December until the middle of January is the season to which everybody looks forward, when the nights are cooler than the daytime, and when there is always a refreshing Northeast breeze. Thereafter, however, the country takes on a brown and dead appearance. Vegetation is burned up. Only the beautiful round mango trees, with their tremendous long tap roots seeking water at unbelievable distances in the earth, show spots of green.

In the early summer, the dreaded typhoon season begins. Father José Algue, S.J., in charge of the Manila observatory, first won fame when he made storm warnings public while Dewey's fleet was blockading Manila in the typhoon season, losing his Spanish citizenship thereby. He later invented a baro-cyclometer which invariably indicates the center of the storm. Much of our present knowledge of these disturbances is attributable to his scientific observations.

From the time the typhoons form in the Ladrones until they hit the China coast, or are lost in the China Sea, they are carefully watched and reported, so that every place in the Islands with telegraphic communication is seasonably informed. The typhoons move along certain belts, according to the time of year. The early ones go South and, as the season advances, they gradually move North until they miss the Islands entirely.

Death and destruction are left in the path of a typhoon. I have seen trans-Pacific liners come limping into Manila Bay after passing through such a storm, not only with their boats gone, but with the sturdy iron railings torn away by the force of wind and wave. In one wild blow at Leyte a large steamer was carried half a mile inland, and a huge channel, costing almost as much as the vessel was worth, had to be dug before it could regain the sea.

Since the track of the typhoon is never over fifty miles wide, and its speed is only six to ten miles an hour, any modern boat can run away from it, but most vessels remain prudently in port until the storm is over.

I remember once being caught by a typhoon in the treacherous waters off the East Coast of Luzon, when I was carrying a load of lepers in the government steamer, the *Basilan*. The trembling vessel would climb up and up a huge forty-foot wall of water, and then from the dizzy peak she would toboggan down the other side with terrific speed, and plunge her nose so deep into the trough that she seemed headed for the bottom of the sea. The whole ocean was standing in pinnacles which moment by moment broke, smothering the boat in foam. We had not dared approach the treacherous shore. Toward midnight the captain said the ship could not last more than a few hours; he must take a desperate chance, and make for the narrow, unlighted, rock-bound entrance to the harbor of the little island of Polillo.

It was dark as ink. The boat plunged, pitched, tossed, and rolled, and then suddenly steadied and grew still. The captain let the anchor go, and we waited for what might happen next. In the dim grey light of dawn we saw the rocky shore looming up all around us only a terrifyingly short distance away. This most remarkable seaman had managed to guide his craft, by what could only have been sheer luck or instinct, through the narrow passage and into the very center of the tiny harbor.

On land also the typhoon was a fearful thing. No one who has not been through it can appreciate it. The impressive thing is the way the wind increases, increases, and increases until it seems impossible that it can blow harder—and then it does. One particular typhoon I was able to watch from the reasonably safe doorway of a strong stone house. It was as though I were looking at the stage of a theatre. I alone was motionless. Huge trees would be lifted up, roots and all, and go sailing off into the atmosphere. Small houses dashed after them. In the harbor steamers of ten thousand tons, with noses pointed frantically at the open sea, with the anchors out and steaming full speed ahead, were piled stern foremost on top of the breakwater. Street cars left the tracks; down went the wires. Sheets of corrugated iron roofing soared through the air, sometimes cutting off the arms or legs of desperately hurrying pedestrians seeking shelter.

Then in the midst of the wildest confusion came the ominous dead calm, which marked the so-called center of the typhoon. But the quiet was only momentary. The other edge arrived, the wind reversed, and everything moveable went roaring back again.

Nature in the tropics tends to excesses and forces human beings to set up a wall of apathy to protect the nervous system from constant shocks. The things that happen near the Equator are dramatic and appear with cyclonic suddenness. Earthquakes occur more frequently than typhoons and the inhabitants must become accustomed to these terrifying experiences or each time they would be overwhelmed. During a quake, when I used to look out the window of my office on the narrow Calle Palacio, and observe the houses swaying toward one another, I would have the illusion that they were actually bumping heads.

Before the days of reinforced concrete, sections of Manila would be periodically demolished. I have seen a bottomless crack streak like a flash of lightning across the ground and split a big church in two. Years ago it was observed that these seismic waves came in known directions, and a Catholic priest, wise beyond his generation, instead of building his church on rocks, mounted it underground on rockers, turned in the direction of the waves. It has stood several hundred years, complacently rocking while its contemporaries crumbled to pieces beside it.

On the night of January 30, 1911, the ears of all Manila were shattered by the loudest noise in the world, audible for two hundred and fifty miles. In a few moments the streets were filled with people, gazing with awe and consternation at a titanic Fourth of July celebration. The whole sky was filled with stars, shooting toward infinity. The Taal volcano, thirty-five miles south, standing silent in the middle of a lake since 1754, had presumedly sprung a leak, generated steam, and blown up. It was celebrating its release with a gigantic eruption of lava, mud, fire, smoke, and gas.

Thousands of the inhabitants of Batangas Province lived in the vicinity. Although the full enormity of the catastrophe could not be determined until reports began to come in from the stricken towns and barrios, I set the machinery in motion to organize a relief expedition as quickly as possible. We could not travel by motor car because the old broken-down Spanish roads leading there were impassable. But the next day, with ample hospital supplies, a detachment of the sanitary corps, and a body of constabulary under Colonel William Rivers, we embarked on a government steamer and anchored in Balayan Bay. Thence we made all possible speed the seven miles inland to the scene of the disaster.

The sight was horrible. Not only had all life been wiped out on Volcano Island itself, but also for miles away from the shore of the lake. The dead could wait; our first care was for the wounded and the homeless strays who were without food, drink, and shelter. Temporary hospitals were set up; acres of gauze were used to dress the frightful burns, bruises, and fractures. Many women and animals were found to have aborted, doubtless from the terrific concussion.

The number of wounded was in remarkably small proportion to that of the dead, and the evidence showed that the majority of the fatalities had been caused by the explosion of gases. When nature runs amok, she often becomes pranksome in a ghastly way. The Filipinos are normally so modest that they are never caught with their clothes off. Even in bathing they are well covered. But among the ruins we found Filipinos stark naked, standing upright and embedded in ashes to their knees, still holding protecting umbrellas over their heads. They had apparently been attempting to get away when the ashes rained over them and the vacuum caused by the exploding gases had torn off their clothes.

Only about seven hundred and fifty bodies were recovered out of an estimated two thousand killed. Many had either been buried by the mud or ashes or washed back into the lake by the immense wave which had inundated several barrios and, in receding, carried practically every moveable thing with it.

Our work was interrupted by constantly recurring quakes which continued for several weeks. Colonel Rivers and I slept in the same tent and for the time being adopted the Filipino indifference. Our nervous systems became so adjusted to the shocks that we would sleep soundly at night, but kept a lantern burning in case we should be needed, or should have to make a quick exit. One night came a quake violent enough even to waken me. I returned to consciousness just in time to hear Colonel Rivers utter a startled "Whoo—ooo—ooo" as he sat up in bed and rubbed his eyes. A crack had dug diagonally across the ground covered by the tent, and the earth was sinking fast on his side. He made a leap toward me. I beat a hasty retreat under the side of the tent and he came tumbling after.

In the course of a day or so the quakes settled to their business with clock-like regularity. Every twelve minutes the ground shook, and the earth opened. When we amused ourselves straddling the clefts and riding the quakes we would receive an exaggerated sense of up and down motion. It was much like trying to stand with the right foot in one rowboat and the left foot in another when a light sea was running. These cracks might fall together at the next shock or remain gaping for months before they were filled with débris.

From the dressing stations we hauled the wounded to the coast on high, two-wheeled, canopied, pony carts, using the board seats as stretchers. I was taking a full load on one of these carretelas down a long hill when suddenly a tremendous quake came and a crack appeared in the road directly ahead of us. The cochero could not pull up the pony in time. The animal fell into a crevasse, but the shafts bridged the gap, and the harness held him.

We knew we had twelve minutes in which to work. Saplings were hastily procured, the pony was pried out, and the board seats were laid across the crack. We continued to the coast unharmed. The hardening process we had gone through made this only an incident in the day's work.

Newspaper reporters came from all over the East to cover this catastrophe. Among them were two Frenchmen who arrived after most of the rescue work had been accomplished, and who remarked superciliously that it had hardly been worth their while to come. In the endeavor to make it worth their while, fifty stalwart constabulary were selected, who eagerly entered into the plan. The next night we waited until the Frenchmen were asleep, and then cast a rope over the roof of the nipa shack in which they were housed. The soldiers took hold of either end, and stood poised. When the customary *tremblement de terre* came, they began to sway, pulling back and forth on the rope in accelerating tempo. The bamboo creaked and groaned under the stress as the hut lurched dangerously on its stilts from side to side. The soldiers gathered momentum, and it swung faster and farther, until the terrified Frenchmen catapulted out the window, hit the ground, like Antæus gained new strength, and sped away into the darkness.

We learned later that they had not stopped until they had reached the nearest town, many miles distant, and we read with great interest and amusement their account of the frightful earthquake at the scene of the Taal volcano.

The Filipinos who survived continued phlegmatically with their regular round of duties. I remember watching an old peasant plowing a nearby field with his ancient and resigned carabao. When he reached

71

the lower end, suddenly there came a tremendous quake, and that side of the field sank about three feet. The carabao never stopped, but kept methodically on and around until he came up against the raw embankment which marked the scission. I saw him cock an eye quizzically as though to say, "Where did this come from? I never had to climb anything like this before." And then he wearily hoisted himself over the acclivity and monotonously continued on his way.

Whenever the heat became too great at Manila Americans would make the three day journey to the hills, sometimes by steamer and pony, sometimes by train and four-mule team. The heavy oppressiveness of the capital changed to the sparkling wine-tang of the rarefied mountain air. At night the soughing of the wind in the pines was reminiscent of home. It invited the Americans, exhausted by their labors in a heat strange and difficult for them to cope with; the sick were made well and the tired were refreshed.

The development of picturesque Baguio, a city planned in every detail by D. H. Burnham of Chicago, was, for years, the object of more criticism on the part of the Filipinos than all other American ventures. Nevertheless it created much attention throughout the East, and the French government once sent a delegate to observe and report on the possibility of building a similar paradise for Indo-China. The Governor General asked me to serve as a guide to this representative. The Frenchman showed great interest, asked pertinent questions, and was enthusiastic about what had been accomplished.

We came back on the same train as the Japanese Consul, and I introduced the two. We happened at the moment to be passing a succession of pits along the railroad line, and the Japanese, with the insatiable curiosity typical of his race, asked, "What are those?"

"I can't talk about them," I assured him.

"Why can't you tell me?" he persevered.

"I can't tell you why. I simply cannot say anything about them."

Since it was becoming more and more difficult to avoid his importunities gracefully, I retired to the smoking compartment. When I finished my cigar and was returning down the corridor, I could hear sounds of violent upheaval. On opening the door, I was dumbfounded to find the Japanese Consul on the floor and my French friend on top pounding his head up and down.

With one hand I grabbed the Frenchman by the collar, and with the other pulled the Japanese Consul to his feet. "What in the world is the matter?"

They glared at each other. Then the Frenchman, in lofty dignity, said, "I won't talk about it here."

The Japanese, who was almost inarticulate, managed to stutter, "This is perfectly outrageous!"

With my protégé, who was boiling with indignation, I repaired once more to the smoking compartment.

"Do you know what that Japanese proposed to me?" he sputtered. "He wanted to have me ask you what those holes were along the railroad. Does that scoundrel think a guest of the government would betray a secret? I wouldn't stand for such a thing. It reflected upon the honor of a Frenchman."

For a few moments it seemed probable that an international incident would follow, but with soothing words I managed to calm them down, and finally persuaded them to shake hands.

This required all my diplomacy. What I had intended as a mild joke had got out of hand. Had I explained about the pits it would have been very embarrassing to all concerned and I would have been the object of their joint wrath. The simple explanation was that the Filipinos did not like day labor and hence, when they needed filling material, the railroad engineers had found it much simpler to stake out places for the workers, and say, "When you've dug those out, you'll be paid for so many cubic yards," and the system had left borrow pits along the right of way.

Many of the attacks leveled by the Filipinos against Baguio were not so much on its own account, but because of the unexpected and appalling cost of building the Benguet Road, which was to connect it with the lowlands.

Seventy thousand dollars was appropriated for its construction. It appeared that this was hardly a start. The two hundred thousand which was confidently asserted would be ample also gave out. Half a million more had to be provided and still the road was not completed. There seemed to be a hoodoo upon it. The typhoons hit it, the floods washed it out, cholera scattered the workers, and the engineering difficulties were far greater than had been foreseen. The soil had no cohesion, and landslides covered the road periodically. The building of the road became almost a scandal, but the government was committed to its completion. All the previous investment would be lost by withdrawal. Money, therefore, was poured into it continuously, until finally a million dollars was required to finish it.

But the road would not remain completed. Fresh disasters kept putting it out of commission. The work went on for years, and all this time the Filipinos were vociferating that they were not interested in a cool place, and improvising every variety of criticism which could occur to the exceedingly fertile Oriental imagination.

Although Harrison's arrival caused an upheaval in government, it was apparently pleasing to the forces of nature, because no tornado, no landslide, no flood ever again struck the Benguet Road. The evil spirit was exorcized. The magnificent road wound up and away to this vacation land in the hills.

The Democrats turned their backs upon the project which had just been finished at such great expense, and said to the Filipinos, "This is your road. Since you dislike it so much, you may abandon it if you wish."

The Filipinos, who had assailed it so bitterly, now said, "This is a beautiful road. We love it dearly."

They flocked to Baguio and added the final touches which made it into one of the most beautiful hill stations in the world.

The natives of a tropical climate, generally speaking, are not affected injuriously by the meteorological conditions of their environment any more than are the inhabitants of more temperate climates; their physiological activities are adjusted to their surroundings. But many Island residents are subject to the condition facetiously termed Philippinitis. It has recognized symptoms—mental and physical torpor, forgetfulness, irritability, lack of ambition, aversion to any form of exercise, and want of interest in passing events. It is usually blamed on the climate but, like many other ailments, it often results from direct violation of hygienic laws, especially those governing the production and dissipation of body heat. Many Europeans and Americans eat even more in the Philippines than they do at home. In Manila the daily temperature is usually ninety degrees. Since that of the body is 98.6, fewer heat units are needed than in the temperate zone. I never knew anyone to get Philippinitis who took the proper amount of balanced food, or consumed his excess heat units in regular exercise, and lived a reasonably hygienic life. Like many of the diseases of the Islands, it was self-induced.

The rays of the sun are not a danger in the Philippines. But I never succeeded in convincing the conservative British that tennis may be played the year around at Manila. They always abstained during the hot season, and consequently became so out of practice that the Americans who followed my example could usually excel them.

It was, however, necessary to guard against heat. In the course of experimentation, the army developed a felt campaign hat with a ventilated sweat band so that a current of air could pass over the head. This was much more agreeable to wear than the awkwardly shaped sola topee.

The British were horrified when I appeared in India equipped with one of these innovations. What was good enough for the Britisher's grandfather was good enough for him. My friends said, "If you persist in going out with that on your head, we won't go with you. You'll get sunstroke and we'll have all the bother of bringing you back."

However, I continued to wear this hat to my own satisfaction and comfort.

At one time it was believed all the heat troubles of the white man in the tropics could be ascribed to the ultra-violet ray and that this could be excluded by wearing orange-red underwear. The American Army was interested but skeptical. They decided to equip one thousand men with the orange-red and use another white clad thousand for controls. Five thousand suits were ordered which were intended to last a year. From the beginning the experiment met difficulties. Less than a quarter of the underwear was furnished in the 36 and 38 sizes worn by the majority of the soldiers. Therefore, the unfortunate subjects had to be chosen largely from among the smaller men. When it was discovered five suits a year were not sufficient, the number of victims had to be cut in half.

The experimentees to a man became universally color conscious and protested violently against the indignity. They continued to protest more loudly as the bright garments returned from the laundry a most peculiar and unpleasant shade of muddy yellow. They were taunted by the white controls, and wore them only under strict orders from the officers. It became a disciplinary problem. The soldiers claimed the despised articles retained the heat and the humidity, and asserted they could detect no great improvement in their health; when the year was over the ragged remains of the orange-red underwear quietly disappeared.

In spite of the failure of this great experiment, studies in acclimatization continued. Professor Aron of the Medical School determined that, whereas a Filipino had sweat glands evenly distributed all over his body, those of a person from a temperate zone climate were largely limited to forehead, armpits, back and groin. He observed, however, that after two years' residence, the sweat glands of the soldiers had increased tremendously.

In the effort to decide whether the light rays or the heat rays were responsible for sunstroke, Professor Aron found that monkeys which died when exposed to the sun were unharmed if an electric fan were blown upon them. It seems likely the heat and still air and not the light rays cause the damage.

Health in the tropics is largely a matter of observing simple hygienic rules rather than of climate. The physiological machinery of the body is so adjusted that great variations of atmospheric temperature can be supported without detriment. Indeed, it is very rare that temperature acts directly as a pathogenic factor. The white man's chances of contracting disease are actually less in the Philippines than in the United States.

In the white man and in the brown man alike, everywhere and among all peoples, the spectacular diseases are usually of specific origin, that is, they are almost always due to specific germs.

The germs of many diseases are true parasites, and, to retain their existence, they must pass from host to host. If, during this passage, the temperature of the transmitting medium be too high or too low, the germ dies or ceases to be infective. In this way may be explained the absence from the tropics of a class of infectious diseases represented by scarlet fever, measles, and diphtheria.

The transmission of some other diseases from one human being to another requires the agency of a third or entirely different animal. If this animal is found only in the tropics, the disease will, of course, be confined to the tropics, and may be accurately called a tropical disease.

Most of the more serious diseases in the tropics can be avoided by the observance of a few simple little rules. Anyone who follows these faithfully will be practically sure to remain well. Among these, the first and foremost is never to drink any water that has not been boiled or otherwise sterilized. It may be pure, but the chances are against it. Another, is never to eat raw, any low-growing garden truck, such as lettuce or cabbage, because they may, in spite of laws against it, be fertilized with human excreta. I am certain that at least a third of the people who violate these two laws sooner or later have amoebic dysentery or some other form of intestinal parasite.

The Philippines were a huge laboratory in which my collaborators and I could work out an ideal program. Often in emergencies this would have to be dropped, and months might elapse before we could return to it, but in the end, in my opinion, we had the most complete set of sanitary laws and as good enforcement as any country ever had. In the course of these years we met the chief enemies of man in the tropics, and fought and conquered many of them by simple prophylaxis. The goal of saving fifty thousand lives a year was so soon attained that I realized it should have been set at one hundred thousand.

When I returned to New York the medical profession gave me a dinner. The chairman, Dr. Abraham Jacoby, made many pleasant remarks, most of them dealing with my bravery in facing the pestilential diseases of the tropics, and congratulating me on being safely back in New York. As he portrayed the perils I had faced, I could see on the countenances of those present evidence of sincere sympathy for one who they believed had been exiled by official duty to a service of affliction and danger in a foreign, God-forsaken land.

I thanked Dr. Jacoby for his kindly words. "But in reality," I said, "I come back to the United States in fear and trembling. The diseases of the tropics which sound so terrifying here we know how to prevent. But even among you I see joints gnarled by rheumatism. I read every day of deaths from pneumonia, scarlet fever, and other diseases which practically never cast their shadows over the happy homes of the

Philippines. We know the prophylaxis for cholera and dysentery, the mode of transmitting malaria, the causes of plague and typhus, and the reasons for beriberi. We run practically no danger of contracting them. But there is no prophylaxis against pneumonia or rheumatism. Do not, therefore, condole with me. I assure you I consider you, who live among dangers that you know not how to control, the real heroes."

CHAPTER 7.   THE BLACK DEATH

"The houses were filled with dead bodies and the streets with funerals; neither age nor sex was exempt; slaves and plebeians were suddenly taken off amidst the lamentations of their wives and children, who, while they assisted the sick and mourned the dead, were seized with the disease and, perishing, were burned on the same funeral pyre. To the knights and senators the disease was less mortal though these also suffered in the common calamity."

SUCH is the account of the pestilence which struck Imperial Rome and which, during the ensuing centuries, was repeated again and again. In the Second Century A. D., according to Herodian, the Emperor retired to Laurentium because it was considered the fragrance of the laurels acted as an antidote against the contagion. The people in the city also, by the advice of physicians, filled their noses and ears with sweet ointments and perfumes. Nevertheless, nothing which they could do for themselves saved them from the deadly attack of the bubonic plague.

In the Fourteenth Century the scourge appeared in the East, spread rapidly to Asia Minor, thence to Northern Africa, and followed the trade routes into Europe. By the spring of 1348 it had entered Italy by way of Genoa, and soon had gripped the entire peninsula. Three-quarters of the population of Siena died; seven-tenths that of Pisa. Petrarch, who saw with his own eyes the Black Death at work in Florence, said, "We go out of doors, walk through street after street, and find them full of dead and dying, and when we get home again

79

we find no live thing within the house, all having perished in the brief interval of our absence."

Perhaps best of all contemporary descriptions of the Black Death is that by Petrarch's friend Boccaccio, which forms the introduction to his *Decameron*.

"There appeared certain tumors in the groin, or under the armpits, some as big as a small apple, others as an egg; and afterwards purple spots in most parts of the body; in some cases large and but few in number, in others less and more numerous, both sorts the usual messengers of death. . . . And the disease, by being communicated from the sick to the well, seemed daily to get ahead, and to rage the more, as fire will do by lying on fresh combustibles. Nor was it given by conversing with only, or coming near the sick, but even by touching their clothes, or anything that they had before touched. . . . These accidents . . . occasioned various fears and devices amongst those people that survived, all tending to the same uncharitable and cruel end; which was to avoid the sick, and everything that had been near them; expecting by that means to save themselves. . . . What numbers of both sexes in the prime and vigor of youth, whom in the morning neither Galen, Hippocrates, nor Aesculapius himself, but would have declared in perfect health, after dining heartily with their friends here, have supped with their departed friends in the other world!"

The Black Death took the Channel in its stride and wreaked such havoc in England that the dead were heaped into trenches, Parliament was suspended, and those who could flee the crowded cities did so. The Scots in derision dubbed it the "foul death" of the English, before it leaped their borders and wiped out one-third of them.

During this one year between a quarter and a half of the population of Europe died. An economic and social revolution which proved one of the great turning points in the history of the world followed in the wake of the plague.

The nature of mankind under extreme terror leads him to excesses. The convenient Jews were accused of poisoning the air and the wells. Some individuals considered that, since life was so uncertain, they were entitled to enjoy all license. Others believed that their only hope lay in placating an angry God. The sect of the Flagellants revived. In their despair the people regarded all efforts to stop the progress of the disease as sacrilege. The Duke of Reggio wisely ordered the isolation of the stricken, but "all were more grieved and terrified by this edict than by the fear of the pestilence which, when God permits it, cannot be arrested." During the next three hundred years the plague returned periodically. It reached its climax in England in 1665 when, after carrying off seventy thousand in London alone, approximately sixteen percent of the population, it spread South and East. Pepys faithfully recorded its onset in his diary for June 7th.

"I did in Drury Lane see two or three houses marked with a red cross upon the doors, and 'Lord have Mercy upon Us' writ there, which was a sad sight to me, being the first of the kind that, to my remembrance, I ever saw. It put me into an ill conception of myself and my smell, so that I was forced to buy some roll tobacco to smell and to chaw, which took away the apprehension."

The following year came the Great Fire of London, after which the plague disappeared from England, and shortly from Europe. But it remained endemic in the East.

Toward the end of the Nineteenth Century there was a recrudescence of plague. Hongkong, which had become the second largest port in the world, was the chief exporting point. The British, who were traders first and foremost, had shut their eyes to the need for sanitary control; consequently in the early days, few precautions were observed. From Hongkong the plague girdled the Pacific and, on its way, swept into the Philippines.

The human mind for centuries had been so handicapped by its ignorance of bacteriology that any hope of successful warfare against the plague was vain. But in the eighties some knowledge of microscopic life began to be acquired by the scientific world. The spread of the plague focused attention on Hongkong and there, in 1894, the bacillus pestis was isolated by Alexandre Yersin, the pupil of Pasteur, and Shibasaburo Kitasato, the pupil of Koch, working independently. This discovery marked the first great advance in the history of the conquest of the disease.

The association of rats with plague is so obvious that it was noted long before it could be proved. After the discovery of the bacillus it was a simple matter to identify the epizootic among rats as identical with the epidemic among men, and the close relation of the two was shown to be almost invariable. The problem was how to link them together.

There was a hypothesis, conceived by P. L. Simond of Spain, that plague was conveyed by fleas. He had no supporting proof for his theory; he merely imagined this was the way it happened. His claim was tested by the First Indian Plague Commission which, after investigation, announced that no connection could be found between the flea and the plague.

In the course of my work in Egypt, I had formulated certain theories of my own about plague, and could not reconcile them to the findings of the Commission. The subject had been extensively discussed at the Cairo Medical Congress in 1902. On my way thence to the Philippines I met Captain W. Glen Liston of the Indian Medical Service, and made the trip to India in company with him. He also was dissatisfied with the conclusions of the Plague Commission. As we sweltered in the Red Sea heat, we would lie on deck until late hours, and as we crossed the Indian Ocean pace up and down, discussing the pros and cons of plague theories. When we reached India, Liston enthusiastically took me to inspect the flood of plague cases coming into the hospitals.

One of the most interesting developments in India at the time was the plague vaccine developed by Professor W. M. Haffkine at Bombay. The religious tenet of the Hindus that the cow was sacred had interfered with his use of the beef broth, essential for culturing plague bacilli. He had surmounted this difficulty and had produced a vaccine which aroused the immunity forces of the individual into whom it was injected, though the immunity conveyed was relatively short. It was proving particularly useful for those compelled to work in plague stricken areas.

But while I was there, Professor Haffkine was in the midst of a great battle for his reputation. Part of his process had been to treat his culture with carbolic acid, which killed the bacilli but left the antitoxin. In the effort to fill a quantity demand from the Punjab, the acid was omitted. By an unfortunate accident tetanus germs were somehow included in a particular bottle and all inoculated from it died. However, after prolonged investigation by a special Commission, the Haffkine Laboratory was exonerated of all blame and he was reemployed by the Indian government.

Before Liston and I separated, we agreed to continue plague research, he in Bombay, and I in Manila. I established a laboratory at Mariveles where one of my assistants, Dr. H. S. Stansfield, began research on the flea transmission theory.

Every year came new evidence that fleas and rats were closely connected with the plague in human beings. Liston was surprised to find an outbreak of plague among guinea pigs at Bombay, and an examination showed they were infested with rat fleas. Guinea pigs do not usually harbor fleas, but dead rats were found in the vicinity. By keeping up a constant agitation Liston finally secured the appointment of a second Indian Plague Commission of which he became a member. In 1907 the Commission was able to announce that fleas definitely were the conveyors of plague, and proved its case to an incredulous world with a simple experiment. Cages containing rats were hung at different heights with plague fleas hopping about below. The rats which dangled enticingly above the fleas' four inch high jump record did not catch plague; the unfortunate ones which hung lower sickened and died.

In all my study of the rat I never was able to solve the enigma of his life's ending. It would seem he transported himself bodily to his heavenly granary. The statistics are incontrovertible. It is conservatively estimated that in every city of the world there is one rat for each two persons. I once made a determined effort to locate the tomb of the rat in Manila, which, at the time, had a population of three hundred thousand. Estimating the average life of a rat even at five years, there should have been a mortality from natural causes of twenty-five hundred rats a month.

The rat catcher gangs of over three hundred men seldom found a dead rat that had not died of poison placed for it, or from some other readily explainable cause. My curiosity was aroused; I stationed inspectors at the public crematories in which was incinerated the daily collection of all garbage, refuse, and street sweepings. They personally examined the contents of each container. Only one dead rat was discovered in the course of a month.

If dead rats had been found by householders they would automatically have been placed in the refuse cans or left lying on the streets. They would not have been burned, because stoves were unknown, and the small primitive fires of bamboo sticks would not have been likely to have consumed the carcasses entirely.

It was possible, of course, that a certain percentage of the rats had died in inaccessible places. But owing to the rapid decomposition in a tropical climate, the odors which would have arisen would soon have attracted attention; comparatively few nuisances of this kind were reported.

The rats were barred by fine gratings from access to the sewers. The generally swampy nature of the ground prevented burrowing, and the few spots where holes could not be flooded, we had sealed with concrete.

It was suggested that the dead rats were eaten by their brethren, but carcasses or even skeletons of partly eaten rats were not encountered. The riddle of the rat's last resting place still awaits its Oedipus.

With the links of plague transmission joined, research made rapid progress. Any rat may harbor the plague flea, but the chief danger comes from the long-tailed, blackish mus rattus, who, an unbidden guest, makes man's home and food his own. The reddish-gray short-tailed mus norwegicus is a fiercer fighter and seeks his shelter away from man.

The plague-stricken rat, like the human, has fever and septicemia. He moves very slowly. He shows no fear of human beings, but looks up at them without shying or running away. He may sometimes recover, and, after long years of exposure to plague, may even develop a certain immunity. In India this is greatest in places which in the past have suffered most severely. At Bombay, for example, local rats cannot be used for experimentation, but must be obtained from Madras, where the disease has never struck.

Out of the multitudinous varieties of fleas the principal culprit was proved to be the Pulex cheopis. Later research showed that on rare occasions others, such as the astia, might convey plague. But unless the rat acts as host to more than four fleas, there is little danger.

The flea has a hollow tube, called the epipharynx. With this it pierces the skin, and then with its jaws enlarges and lacerates the hole. It pumps saliva down its epipharynx into the wound, which rapidly becomes congested. The blood that collects is sucked up through the hypopharynx, or prolongation of the lip.

The oesophagus of many types of flea has a valve which retains the blood once it is swallowed, but in the cheopis and astia the apparatus is lacking, and an overdose frequently causes regurgitation. If the flea is infected, the fluid will contain plague bacilli. As many as five thousand may be lodged in the body of one flea.

When the rat sickens and dies his boarders leave him and hide in a crack or a pinch of dust. They may survive for two months, growing ever more hungry, and, if no rat appears, rather than starve, they will content themselves with a meal from a human or any other animal. The laboring class in tropical countries customarily goes barefooted and barelegged to the knee. This gives the flea the advantage.

When man is bitten, he scratches, inflames the wound, and makes a way for the plague bacilli to enter more easily. These multiply with appalling rapidity. Although the incubation period may last as long as seven days, plague normally appears within forty-eight hours. The toxin affects first the lymphatic system. One of the functions of the lymph glands is to repel invading poisons, but because they are unable to cope with the plague bacilli, the buboes, or glandular swellings, the sight of which had aroused such terror in the ancients, are formed, usually in the groin, more rarely in the armpit. After this system of defense has broken down, the whole body is invaded. Delirium shortly sets in, vital organs are poisoned, and the patient ordinarily dies between the third and fifth day.

In the septicemic type of plague, so much and so powerful a toxin is liberated that the body defenses are overwhelmed before nature's normal protections can become effective. These are brushed aside, and therefore no bubo appears. In most epidemics the mortality is over ninety percent, and no treatment has been found of much avail.

Only in pneumonic plague is the disease transmitted directly from man to man. The bacilli reach the lungs, and the fine spray from the coughing is charged with the deadly microbes so that those who breathe them are infected. The serum exudate in the lungs is so great that the victim is literally drowned. Death comes with shocking suddenness. None survives.

The Philippines were always threatened with plague. Once when the steamer *Zafiro* arrived in Manila from Hongkong the routine medical inspection was made, and no illness detected. But twenty-four hours later a Chinese member of the crew who had apparently been in excellent health the night before was found dead in his bunk of pneumonic plague.

Two days later the *Loonsang* arrived in the harbor, also from Hongkong, with a dead Chinese on board. While hauling spiritedly on a rope, he had toppled over in an apparent faint, and had died in the course of a few hours. He also had had pneumonic plague.

Chinese reports claim that ptarmigans and marmots, as well as rats, are subject to plague in septicemic form. But when their fleas bite man, he contracts pneumonic plague. Every year Chinese laborers migrate to Manchuria in vast numbers. There they live huddled in dirty sheds. If only one laborer is infected with the pneumonic type, he may, by coughing, transmit the disease to a crowded trainload returning at the end of the harvest, and, as the coolies scatter to their homes, plague will spread like wildfire, sometimes wiping out whole districts. The coolies stop overnight, sleeping in crowded little shanties along the way, where they become infected, and travel on the next day, starting new foci of infection all along the route. Whenever they are segregated, or even made to wear gauze masks, the disease declines rapidly.

The plague had made its appearance in Manila in December, 1899. The measures adopted against it then were very strict and in full accord with the status of current medical knowledge. The sick were sent to the hospital, and the dead taken in charge by the Army Board of Health. The houses and their contents were completely renovated and disinfected. Partitions and cubicles were torn down, court yards opened up, and obstructions to sunlight removed. Circular letters were issued, giving the salient points of plague diagnosis, theories of transmission, and the course to be pursued when a suspected or genuine case had occurred in a locality. All vessels arriving during the epidemic were disinfected. Although it was not known at that time that the rat flea was the communicating agent for the plague, many of the measures taken had resulted in the destruction of the rats which carried the fleas.

Later, anti-rat measures were invoked and the Board of Health had spent $350,000 in the effort to wipe out all the rats of the city. But rats are difficult to exterminate because they breed so rapidly. Three to five times a year, after a gestation period of only twenty-one days, the female brings forth from six to sixteen young, and these in turn produce offspring when they are less than three months old. Thus a single pair in one year might be responsible for hundreds of descendants. At the end of five years when I took charge the rat population of Manila was apparently as plentiful as ever, and plague was still present.

At one time a bounty of five centavos was paid for each rodent whose tail was offered in evidence of death. But difficulties soon arose. Certain enterprising inhabitants of Manila began breeding rats. The outlay was negligible and the profits high; a tail was a tail, whether from a baby or a grandfather. The bounty system had to be stopped.

Experimentation showed that spring traps were seven times as efficacious as the cage type. We also spent much time and thought on the subject of poisons. Our greatest success came from mixing cheap and tasteless white arsenic with rice, which was the natural diet of rats in the Philippines. Every rice grain was impregnated with enough poison to kill one rat. But the rat was apparently able, in some mysterious fashion, to warn his brethren of danger. After only a short time the rats would refuse the poisoned tidbits, although their savor was unaffected by any detectible taint. We had to provide meals varied with such foodstuffs as fish and tomatoes.

To catch the rats was easy enough, but other factors complicated the campaign. It was always possible that a child might unsuspectingly swallow a portion of the poisoned bait. For the greater good we had to take this risk, but we used to provide for the contingency. When an epidemic broke out and intensive methods had to be used, antidote stations were located every few blocks so that, in case of a casualty, sesquioxide of iron could be administered immediately. As we had feared, a few children did succumb to the temptation of the rice, but due to our precautions no fatalities resulted.

87

Constant guard had to be kept to see that plague did not slip through our defenses. Manila was within a few days' steaming distance of badly-infected foreign ports. Passengers, crews, rodents, and vermin all might arrive well within the incubation period of the disease. Plague was detected from time to time upon incoming vessels, but such infections were invariably intercepted at quarantine. As a preventive routine measure, all ships which had not touched at plague ports were fumigated with sulphur at not greater than six month intervals.

We had big sulphur furnaces at the quarantine station, and Dutch ovens to take on board where we could not run the hose. The sulphur killed everything it reached, but, as a rule, it did not dispose of more than eighty percent of a ship's rat population.

Sometimes unwittingly we helped to smoke out other travelers, mostly Chinese who were always trying to smuggle into the Philippines. On one occasion, after the customs officers had examined a boat from stem to stern, my men started fumigation. Hardly had they battened down the hatches and turned the sulphur pots loose when suddenly there came a rap-rap. As soon as we could locate the sound, the hatch was opened, and three Chinese stumbled into the fresh air, spitting, "pfft, pfft, pfft," as they came. By signs we asked them, "Any more?" They shook their heads.

Again the hatches were battened down; a few moments later came another knocking. In front of our astonished eyes, forty coughing coolies, one after another, emerged with streaming eyes through a thick veil of billowing yellow smoke.

For the third time the hold was sealed. But in no more than a few moments the knocking began again. The remaining hardy souls in the coal bunkers who had thought they could stick it out tumbled gasping and nearly suffocated on to the deck.

The ship had carried one hundred and two stowaways.

Hydrocyanic gas, which is now employed instead of sulphur, is far more effective, but also more dangerous to handle. When the technique of applying it is not followed, an occasional fatality results, although we were fortunate enough in the Philippines never to have this happen. The customary routine was to fumigate a ship for several hours, and then expose everything to fresh air. But some drunken sailor would disregard instructions, find his bunk, and turn in; enough gas would still remain in the mattress to kill him. To avoid such casualties, ships are now completely ventilated with air jets before anyone is allowed on board.

Our primary concern in the Philippines was to keep rats from landing. Under exceptional circumstances rats will swim. I have seen them scuttle down the anchor chain of one ship and paddle furiously over to that of another. Vessels were made to remain at least six feet from the pier, special iron ratguards were placed on all lines leading to shore, and the gangplanks lifted at night.

As a final precaution, we built in Manila the first ratproof wharves. They were of concrete throughout so that no rat could gnaw his way through, and so flashed with steel sheathing underneath that the rat could not find a foothold. Clever as he is, he has never yet contrived a method of walking upside down on smooth metal.

Rats are noted travelers though their names never appear on the passenger list. For centuries their presence on ships was taken for granted. No one even inquired into the reasons therefor. When it finally became apparent that these rats were a menace to every port where cheopis fleas existed, all efforts were directed at clearing them out of ships and preventing others from entering. Over thirty countries joined in an international agreement to this end.

As I learned in my Philippines experience, the most effective way to deal with any pest is to interfere with its natural breeding places. A rat has to have a protected home and an adequate food supply. If he is not afforded harborage near man, his fleas are less likely to reach man. Thus the danger from plague can best be reduced by building him out.

The rat is expensive to get rid of, but even more expensive to maintain. The rats of New York cost the residents more than ten million dollars annually for meals. Crop destruction is also enormous, so that both urban and rural dwellers suffer loss. The world rat bill amounts to staggering sums. At least a cent a day must be expended to feed a rat on shore, and twice that on ships where the garbage is dumped overboard and where he must live on clean food. On shipboard also, there is the additional expense of fumigating twice a year. Almost fifty thousand dollars used to be spent on the *Mauretania* to keep her free of rats for twelve months.

In 1924 the United States Public Health Service placed a technical assistant on the *Leviathan*, and during a year's study of the rat problem he found fifty-three structural defects which were responsible for rat harborage. The ship was then ratproofed; thereafter no rats haunted the store rooms or lurked around the pipes. The British, the Germans, and the Dutch followed the American lead. Only the French, reluctant to spend money on new schemes, held out. But even they were convinced when the *Lafayette* had to be fumigated after her maiden voyage because of the many rats which had boarded her while she was on the ways.

The *Normandie* was ratproofed.

Building the rat out of Manila was a far more difficult undertaking, requiring the reconstruction of the city, and obviously was a matter of years. We began by having a municipal ordinance passed that all new houses or major repairs had to be constructed according to plans which would make it impossible for rats to find shelter. No hollow walls, partitions, floors, or structural parts were allowed. The foundation had to be of concrete, brick, stone, or mortar, extending three feet above the ground and several below it.

The house plan of the wild mountain tribe of the Ifugaos served in part as models for civilized Manila. The Ifugaos use their homes as granaries, and an economic rather than a sanitary motive had produced an efficient method of protection. Their thatched houses stood on posts, each of which was fashioned with a shoulder large enough to prevent the rat from creeping around it. It cost only a small sum to protect the nipa huts of Manila similarly by placing flashing along the sides of the building.

Rats are very fond of burrowing into the hollow ends of bamboo poles, out of which the floors of nipa huts are almost universally made. They did not gnaw through the smooth, hard, resistant surface, but could and did enter the open ends, biting their way through the joints until they found safe shelter. Such floors we ratproofed by cementing the ends of the bamboo poles. If the rat happened to be inside at the time, it was so much the worse for him. The bamboo fences were treated in the same way.

Most of the objections to ratproofing in Manila came from the Chinese, who controlled the mercantile trade and owned most of the rat-infested bodegas. The adobe walls of these warehouses were often several feet thick and contained rat burrows. Under the board floors the earth was honeycombed with runs. However, opposition began to lessen as soon as the caretakers of premises began to report unwonted freedom from rats and it became apparent that absence of rats not only meant immunity from plague but was also of great economic value.

Our problems in the Philippines were simple compared with the situation in India, where over a million persons were dying annually of plague. The Hindus would take no life. No rat could be killed in India; any live thing might contain the soul of an ancestor. Consequently, they stubbornly opposed the killing of rats. One method of driving out rats and at the same time compromising with religious sentiment was to lift off the roofs of the houses and let the sun in, so that the rats, who abhor light and crave privacy, would retire to some darker refuge. In other cases, a self-curing method was used. When plague appeared in a native village, the inhabitants were all moved out into the fields under temporary canvas shelters. At the end of six months the rats had moved out, and the townspeople moved in again.

Ratproofing was a preventive measure. An epidemic called for instant and concerted action. Plague slipped by the defenses in Manila, in 1905, and again in 1912. On the latter occasion we were prepared. One morning reports came in that plague had broken out in several widely separated districts of the city. But the flying squads of rat catchers, clad in flea-proof clothing, and with powdered naphthalene or kerosene on neck, wrists, and ankles, at once started as though to a fire.

Any block in which the disease occurred was regarded as infected. Radiating lines, usually five in number, were prolonged like the spokes of a wheel to the outskirts of the city. Plague rats were seldom found more than a few blocks away, but rats all along the lines were caught and examined. The furthermost points at which infected animals were detected were then connected with lines running from spoke to spoke, and the space enclosed was regarded as the area of infection. Instead of throwing a force of rat catchers into the house where the case of plague had occurred, which would have scattered the scurrying menace in all directions, the entire force of a hundred and fifty men was concentrated along the border of the infected section.

As the rat catchers closed in, the blocks were thrown out of commission. Every house was gone through in systematic fashion, starting at the top and moving down. Every box, barrel, or receptacle which might harbor a rat was opened. All dirt, filth, and straw in the yard was moved and burned. Woodpiles, which were favorite harboring places for rats, were invariably taken down and re-piled well above the ground and away from any wall, so that dogs and cats might keep the rodents out of them in the future. Rat nests, when found, were sprayed with insecticide.

When live rats were encountered, these were killed at once. Some of the rat catching gang had fox terriers, imported especially from Australia for their lightning-like swiftness. Others had trained ferrets which would come to their masters' call like dogs, and were even more effective. The rat stood no show. You could hear the crack as the ferret's sharp teeth severed the spinal column. He never shook the rat as the terriers did, and never attempted to eat him. He was a killer, pure and simple.

The Filipinos also grew unbelievably skilled in catching rats with their hands. As the animal would start to run from its hiding place, a man would grab it, and, before it could bite, would stun it against the wall and finish it off with a club.

Always as the rat catchers closed in, the ratproofers followed in their tracks, making it certain that the area would not be reinfected. One section after another was treated in this way. Once weekly thereafter, rats were caught in previously infested sections, and at other places which were known to be insanitary.

By the practical application of this system plague was twice wiped out of Manila, the only large city until recent years where an imported infection has been thus completely eradicated.

THE BLACK DEATH

In the Philippines, as elsewhere in the East, Europeans and Americans who lived in more cleanly surroundings were rarely attacked by plague. But there was one outstanding exception. One day William Crozier, editor of the *Manila Daily Bulletin*, was taken violently ill, and forty-eight hours later died at the San Lazaro Hospital. While the sanitary squad was carrying out the insecticidal and other anti-plague measures in his office, an inspector pulled the upper drawer of his desk out to the end. Live fleas were seen hopping around, and in the very back lay the body of a mummified rat. A hole in the rear of the drawer showed the manner of its entrance. After the rat had died its fleas had deserted it. Crozier, who was presumably working in his shirt sleeves because of the heat, must have reached into the drawer and been bitten by one of these fleas. We found a wound on his arm later. Plague bacilli were recovered from the fleas and the rat in the drawer.

Plague remained of vital interest to me long after I had left the Philippines. The Rockefeller Foundation, generously recognizing this, was always glad to make my services available to any government which requested aid in dealing with the disease.

One of my visits to Ceylon happened to coincide with a bad outbreak at Kandy. People in Ceylon were generally accustomed to having natives die horribly of plague, but when members of the nice clean English club also began to die horribly, consternation reigned. Some had already died, many more would die, and the instant the news became public, the tourists, on whom the material prosperity of Kandy largely depended, would seek a safer playground.

Immediately upon my arrival at Colombo, I was called in as a consultant. I repaired to Kandy and went over the ground with the plague expert of the Health Department. We spent hours poking about in native houses and dirty narrow alleys. I could point to nothing which had not been done. Sometimes, however, the obvious is overlooked. A large English store on the main street backed upon the plague area. At the end of a long day, I asked, "Have you investigated that?"

"No," my colleague explained. "That is a European store which is kept perfectly clean. If there had been any sick rats around, they would have been noticed."

"I'd like to go over it just the same," I said.

Accordingly, he introduced me to the manager. I examined the first and second stories without finding any suspicious indications. Then I asked, "What else do you sell?"

"We have a feed department in the basement," he answered.

No further information was needed. As soon as he had taken me downstairs, I singled out the piles of baled hay and straw. "We ought to take those down," I suggested.

Inside were dead and dying rats by the dozen. Some traveler rat or flea, plague-stricken, had entered with a grain shipment and infected the local rodents. The English club had been well within the radius of the infection.

Stamping out the focus stopped the plague in Kandy.

I really enjoyed the detective work often involved in completing the deadly triangle of the rat, the flea, the man. It was extraordinary but true that incredulity as to the relationship still persisted. Only a few years ago, Sir Herbert Samuel, governor of the Palestine Mandate, sent word to me that plague had broken out and that he desired advice. On my arrival, he presented his particular problem. "Our health service says it will take a half million dollars to get the plague under control. That's an enormous sum for a small government to spend. Before embarking on this program, we'd like an outside opinion, although, of course, we'll spend the money if it's necessary."

"I'll talk it over with your Health Officer," I said.

This official showed no resentment at what might have been regarded as interference with his duties on my part; instead, he gave me a hearty welcome. However, he said he did not agree with my published report that dead rats were always associated with plague. No rats had been found during the present outbreak, and, therefore, he was forced to conclude that my deductions must be wrong.

"Where is the plague center?" I asked.

"Jaffa."

"Could we go there?"

"Certainly," he agreed.

Accordingly, he conducted my young North Carolinian assistant, Dr. W. P. Jacocks, and myself to one house in Jaffa where seventeen people had just died of plague, but where nobody had seen a dead rat.

"Where did the first person die?" I asked.

I was shown a bed against a wall in a downstairs room.

"I'd like to have a hammer," I said.

I began to tap the walls, listening carefully to the sound. As I was working my way towards the large crack which I had noted above the bed, the Health Officer interrupted me.

"You're evidently not familiar with house construction methods here. There are no hollow walls."

"I'm probably a damn fool," I replied, "but, if you don't mind, I'd like to satisfy my own curiosity."

He made no further objection, and I continued tapping until I reached the crack, where the wall gave forth an unmistakably hollow sound.

"Will you have a man dig into the wall just here?" I asked.

In a few moments the workmen had uncovered an open shaft, and in the shaft was a small shelf on which lay a dead rat. "The flea came through the crack," I explained.

"You seem to be right," the Health Officer admitted, "but how would you account for this one?" and he led me upstairs to a bed set squarely in the middle of a room.

I glanced at the ceiling and located another crack. "If you'll send a man to the attic, you'll find a dead rat just about there," I said, pointing to a particular spot above the bed.

The corpus delicti was there.

I glanced at Dr. Jacocks, but instead of the expression of satisfaction I expected, I saw that his face was as white as his linen suit. I was startled. "What's the matter with you? Are you ill?"

"Look at me!" he shouted.

"What is the matter?"

"Look!"

To my utter horror he was literally covered with fleas. They were crawling all over him, black spots against his white clothes. Everybody rushed to pluck them off, and we soon had them in bottles which were hurried to the hospital laboratory. After an hour of great anxiety, we received word that they had been identified as merely dog fleas.

When we had recovered from our fright, we returned to the search for the focus of plague infection. Two dead rats did not explain the origin of the epidemic.

The house we had just examined was one removed from the corner, around which was a blacksmith shop. We repaired thither. I engaged the owner in conversation and casually inquired, "Do you ever see any rats around here?"

"Oh, yes," he replied. "Lot's of 'em. But they're the funniest rats I ever saw. They come out of that hole over there and just stand. They don't seem to be afraid or run away, and all we have to do is hit 'em with a hammer and throw 'em in the fire."

"That's very interesting," I commented. "Where does that door lead?".

"Into a vacant lot."

I promptly followed it through and behind the high wall enclosure found from three to four feet of débris remaining from the wreckage of a house. I procured some Arab laborers at once. Underneath the rubbish they came upon a wooden floor, ripped it up, and uncovered hundreds of dead rats.

But my work was not yet done; these mute bodies offered no explanation of the tragedy which had overtaken them.

I scouted further, and came upon a grain store across the street. Such an establishment is always suspect, because the mus rattus is an epicure, and loves best the food which humans eat. I learned that this store had been importing rice from Rangoon, one of the plague centers of the world. Since vessels there were loaded from lighters coming direct from the heavily rat-infested godowns, or warehouses, it was safe to assume that plague rats, or fleas, had been unwittingly imported, and had brought the infection to Jaffa.

The final step was to have specimen rats collected from towns and villages in Palestine. The orders were sent out for this to be done.

I was suddenly awakened two nights later by the jangling of the telephone bell. "Dr. Jacocks is very ill," I was told. While I was hurriedly pulling on my clothes, I kept thinking, "There must have been some cheopis fleas that were missed." In the full realization that it was I who had been responsible for taking him to the plague house, I spent some harassed moments before arriving at his bedside.

To my intense relief, the dread triangle was incomplete, and he was in no mortal danger. His illness was malaria with chills and fever contracted in his own Southland.

Meanwhile the fleas of Palestine were coming to the laboratory. Out of them all only the rats of Jaffa and Haifa proved to be infested with the cheopis variety, and the plague was cleared out of Palestine for a few thousand dollars.

A far greater amount has been expended in the effort to eradicate the plague menace in this country, gradually spreading eastward from California, where it had landed in 1900. It is reasonable to believe that, if proper measures had been taken, the disease could have been wiped out at that time. The Federal government, which had been steadily assuming more and more responsibility for the entrance of dangerous communicable diseases into this country, sent Dr. J. J. Kinyoun there to take charge. But the people of California so bitterly resented the suggestion that bubonic plague might be present in their midst that he was publicly assaulted and even spat upon in the theatre.

At first the disease was confined to Chinatown, where Dr. Kinyoun asserted plague-infected persons were actually found. When the California authorities denied this, a plague commission was appointed to go to California, headed by Dr. Simon Flexner, then Professor of Pathology at the University of Pennsylvania. The Commission found unmistakable evidence of the bacillus pestis among the Chinese, but California was still unconvinced, and the press was almost unanimous in denying it.

Then the Federal government delivered an ultimatum to California: "You are a sovereign state. You may do as you please within your borders, but if you do not take steps to control this vital danger, we will establish a quarantine entirely around you, and every person and every piece of goods crossing your state line will have to go through this quarantine."

Only under this duress did California finally surrender.

But the capitulation came too late. The rats had infected the ground squirrels. In spite of the expenditure of millions of dollars, these infected ground squirrels have not been eradicated. They do not live near human habitations as do rats. Carbon bisulphide, poisoned fruit and grain, and sharpshooters have not sufficed for their extinction. Always some get away to infect others. In the fall of 1919 fourteen cases of pneumonic plague occurred in Oakland, and all but one of these died. In the epidemic at Los Angeles of October, 1924, thirty died out of thirty-two cases.

Even now there is an occasional case of plague in California. The ground squirrel infection has extended over the Coast Range, which barred the way for a long time, and has recently crossed the Rockies. In 1935, plague-infected squirrels were found in Nebraska. Plague will probably never flourish in this country, but its prevention may become exceedingly costly. The great hazard lies in the possibility of the squirrel, which avoids the presence of man, transmitting his fleas to the rat, which lives with man. This danger might have been avoided had the people of California been reasonable in 1900.

It is now beginning to appear that if plague has been endemic for thirty years in a community, it tends to vanish by itself. I noted this first in Basra, and later in Canton, Hongkong, and Bombay. In Canton the disappearance was certainly not due to direct prophylactic measures, because none was taken. At Hongkong, on the other hand, by 1910 a housewifely sanitary force had cleaned and dusted the whole town twice a year; every piece of furniture had been set on the street while the fumigation, cleansing, and airing was proceeding. But the plague mortality in slovenly Canton was no higher than in tidy Hongkong.

Bubonic plague, a name synonymous with disaster to the Ancient and Mediaeval World, need not exist in the Modern. This is a great human achievement. The scourge had seemed to attack blindly and without reason; neither rich nor poor, high nor low, old nor young, knew who might be the next victim.

People no longer need wring their hands in futile terror and despair at the appearance of plague. The mystery of its cause has now been solved by the laboratory worker; the link in the chain of transmission has now been broken by the prophylaxis of the watchful and resolute sanitarian. If plague does creep by the outer defenses, it can still be dealt with swiftly and with certainty. Finally, the health officer, who stands sentry at the port, knows when it is safe from any attack. Flea surveys are now made to show what species are present among the denizens of the rat underworld. A port may be considered non-infectible when the flea population of the average rat contains no more than one cheopis.

New York is a safe port. The New Yorker may seek his Sabine Farm as a pleasant refuge; he need never be driven there by the blind panic which possessed the citizens of Florence when the Black Death had stormed their walls and taken their city in "a sad and wonderful manner." But the citizens of San Francisco, Mobile, and New Orleans must still exercise vigilance if they wish to sleep in peace.

CHAPTER 8.   EAT, DRINK, AND BE MERRY

I HAVE been walking along a street in Manila, and ahead of me have seen a man, as though jerked by some inexorable force, leap into the air, and then fall back sprawling on the ground. He would be dead before I could reach him.

But although the toxin of cholera, like strychnine, sometimes stops the heartbeat with the swiftness of lightning, it is not always so merciful. More often into the few days of its fearful course is compressed an infinity of suffering. The victim of cholera is a terrible object. A cold, clammy sweat is upon him, his skin shrinks and grows dark grey from the terrific purging. Cramps of unbelievable intensity occur in the calves of the legs and in the arms. His thirst is unquenchable. His circulation finally grows so sluggish that even cutting the veins fails to produce a flow of blood.

Little can be done for the sufferer beyond alleviating his agony. The injection of salt solution in the veins replaces some of the lost fluids and relieves the cramps. The cholera patient never loses consciousness. His face is puckered into an expression of anxiety, due as much to the draining of the fluids from his body as to terror.

I well remember one afternoon at the cholera hospital when, in the course of my rounds, I entered the ward in which eight American Negroes had been placed. Each bed had a number and, by one of those strange coincidences which become more striking because of the macabre nature of the occasion, the Negro in bed No. 1 had died first, to be followed rapidly by the inmates of beds Nos. 2, 3, 4, and

5. Beds Nos. 6, 7, and 8 were still occupied when I entered the room. Fully expecting that he would be the next to go, the Negro in No. 6 had pulled the sheet over his head to shield himself from the sight of the gruesome succession of corpses being taken from the room. I drew it aside. His eyes were at first tight shut. As he gradually opened them, I could see the whites shining in the semi-darkness of the room.

"Boss, is I daid?" he inquired anxiously.

He was fairly close to it. Death, however, had paused by his bedside. He and his two companions left the hospital on their own feet, none the worse for their harrowing experience, but with no assurance that they might not find themselves in beds Nos. 1, 2, and 3 the next time.

In all my experience in the Philippines not one medicine ever proved of any great value in the treatment of cholera. Many so-called specifics were recommended. An old doctor in far away Ohio dogmatically proclaimed that it was unnecessary for anyone to die of cholera; that our wanton disregard of his quinine cure was unjustifiable.

Because we had ourselves been vainly searching for a remedy, we had already given his treatment a trial, hoping that by some miracle it would prove beneficial. Convinced it was worthless, we had discontinued its use. When the old doctor received no satisfaction from us, he wrote President Theodore Roosevelt to the effect that the bureaucratic physicians in the Philippines were prejudiced against him. He knew his remedy would cure and we were sacrificing thousands of lives by failing to use it.

President Roosevelt, in his forthright manner, cabled us suggesting that the treatment be given a trial at once. The epidemic of 1905 was in its most virulent stage, and patients were dying in large numbers. In any event, quinine could do no harm, and the suggestion had come from the President of the United States.

The medicine was given in strict compliance with the inventor's prescription. But it failed to save the life of the first man upon whom it was tried. The second man died also. A few days later we cabled the President saying we had tried the quinine remedy on six patients, and that all of them had died. "Do you wish it continued?"

"No!" came the quick reply.

Iron bars and thick stone walls had served for centuries to protect the cloistered nuns of Santa Clara from the prying eyes of the outside world, but could not guard against the entrance of the penetrant cholera. One nun after another was stricken, until the bodies of half a dozen had been placed outside the great wooden doors. Then terror became so great that the Mother Superior appealed for help to Archbishop Harty. He advised that the rules be abrogated and that I be asked to attend. On my way to and from the Ayuntamiento I had often passed these lofty walls, but it was with a sense of dread that I stooped to enter the little door set within the larger one, and placed my feet upon the stones over which no man had walked for a hundred years or more.

The Mother Superior, of commanding presence, conducted me down the long hall, grim in its austerity, where through years of poverty the once white walls had grown darkly stained. The corridors seemed alive with restless, swishing, grey-robed figures; eyes which had long forgotten how a man appeared stared curiously from white faces. I passed the chapel, gleaming with many flickering candles, where nuns knelt silent in perpetual adoration. At last I entered the dormitory and there, with what meagre facilities science had to offer, ministered to the desperately sick nuns.

But something could be done for those as yet untouched. I turned to the overshadowing problem of seeking the way by which the disease had crept into these forbidden precincts. In the long bare inner court I found the nunnery well from which all had drunk. As so often before, in so many countries, cholera had sprung from this unguarded source.

I sterilized this death-dealing menace, explained the simple rules for avoiding cholera, and took my departure, leaving the nuns once more to their cloistered seclusion. There were no more cases.

The first suggestion of the connection of cholera with contaminated water had come in 1855 from Dr. John Snow of London. The previous year he had traced an epidemic to a pump on Broad Street. He found that only those who had drunk of this water were attacked by the disease. He ascertained that a cesspool drained into this well, and that there had been a case of cholera in the house served by the cesspool. He proved that the intestinal discharges of the sick had polluted the water supply. His classic reply to the query, "How can we stop this cholera epidemic?" was, "Remove the pump handle." Dr. Snow wrote an account of his discovery that seemed of such little interest to the publishers of his day that he was forced to print it at his own expense. Nevertheless, though recognition was late, the English people, goaded by fear, began to install uncontaminated water supplies.

In 1884 Robert Koch, often referred to as the founder of bacteriology, after having already isolated the bacillus of anthrax and of tuberculosis, discovered the cholera vibrio. Although it creates such great damage, it is subject to many inimical forces; like the rare orchid it must be nurtured in exactly the right environment. In one hour the sun can destroy it, acid kills it, drying sterilizes it, almost any other bacteria can choke it out. If it is to flourish, it must somehow or other get from one human intestine to another. In spite of these serious handicaps, the vibrio manages to find transportation, and has circumnavigated the world more than once, and always without a ticket.

Cholera has been one of the great scourges of modern times. At four different periods in the Nineteenth Century it was pandemic. In the sixties it was taking toll through large parts of the United States. Terrified England was twice swept by the disease.

Seven great epidemics since 1820 ravaged the population of the Philippines. When the deaths in Manila reached a thousand a day, not enough people could be found to bury the dead. Nightly the streets to the cemeteries were blocked. The priests, leading the religious processions of atonement, could with difficulty find a path through the calesins, carromatas, and slow carabao-drawn carts, all bearing the dead for burial.

Mediaeval theologians had taught that all illness and deformity were manifestations of divine wrath; plague, pestilence, and famine were visited upon the people for their transgressions. Where this doctrine had become powerful enough to regulate the life of the Christian world, the progress of medicine had come to an almost complete standstill. The Filipinos were still living in this mediaeval atmosphere; they were resigned to their angry God, were used to his punishments, and preferred their own ways to those of strangers.

Beyond establishing free medicine stations, the Spanish authorities had been powerless. Instead of taking those simple measures of health and sanitation which would have prevented these destroying epidemics they had bowed their heads and prayed while the death rate mounted to its inevitable peak.

When the Americans came, they were not disposed to tolerate such resignation. Because they had to protect their troops, they decided that something must be done about cholera. March 3, 1902, the attention of the Chief Quarantine Officer at Manila was called to the existence of Asiatic cholera in Canton. Five days later came news of it at Hongkong, from which large quantities of fresh vegetables were constantly being shipped to Manila. In the effort to ward off infection, the port authorities at Manila immediately placed an embargo on low-growing vegetables. This step was necessary because the Chinese were accustomed to sprinkle human excreta in liquid form on growing cabbages, not only for fertilizer, but also for protection against insect pests. If cholera were present in the vicinity, it was always possible that each fresh, crisp, tender leaf would enfold a myriad cholera germs.

Under the terms of the embargo, a large shipment of cabbages from Canton was refused, and the angry shipmaster thereupon dumped the cargo into Manila Bay and sailed off, leaving the surface of the water literally covered with the bobbing heads. From the nipa huts of Farola, Tondo, and Meisic, the Filipinos swarmed to the water front, launched their praos and bancas, and went fishing for cabbages. They welcomed the succulent vegetables as manna.

In the light of subsequent knowledge it is doubtful whether cholera entered the Philippines in this way. There is no doubt, however, that one of the most terrible epidemics of modern times had begun. A few days later two cases of cholera were admitted early in the afternoon to San Juan de Dios Hospital, through whose ancient portals so many thousands had preceded them. Before the day was over, two more arrived. Within forty-eight hours doctors and nurses were rushing about distractedly trying to find beds in which to put the sufferers.

Responsibility devolved upon Secretary of the Interior Worcester.

He was a man of magnificent physique, respected by the Filipinos for his size and courage, but feared and disliked for his personality. He was brusque, and did not ask for cooperation; he demanded compliance with his orders. He always insisted that the established sanitary fact of the morning must be the rule to be observed for the evening. In following out what he considered right, he paid no heed to Filipino public opinion.

Worcester was taking vigorous steps, and cholera was not claiming so many victims as in Spanish days. The more ignorant of the populace, therefore, said this disease could not be cholera because not enough people were dying. Many Spanish and Filipino physicians, who, under the old régime, had been the most influential class politically and socially, jealous of the authority of the Board of Health, criticized its measures and fanned the antagonism of the people.

A land quarantine was established around Manila in the effort to keep the disease from the provinces. In the state of resentment over what seemed the dictation and ruthlessness of a military occupation, the Filipinos could not comprehend the theory of paternalism which said, "We are doing this for your own good." Eluding the futile cordon at night, or slipping across the fields by day, people already sickening of the disease escaped to start new foci of infection.

Within a few weeks seven thousand temporary employees of the Board of Health were in the field. But the force was new and untrained, and undoubtedly in exercising its duties it was guilty of discourtesy and even abuse of power.

The Farola district, a narrow neck of land along the Pasig River running out into the Bay, covered with warehouses, coal piles, and a crowded mass of small filthy nipa huts, was the apparent focus of the disease. Worcester ordered it evacuated and burned. Under a blazing sky the terrified and resentful owners watched the shooting sparks as shack after shack crackled and collapsed. The report spread about that the homes of the poor were being burned to make room for future dwellings and warehouses of rich Americans. Further rumors that the foreign doctors had poisoned the wells were also widely credited; it was even said the American aim was to annihilate the Filipino race.

It was true that, in the effort to stop the spread of infection, the Americans sometimes may have overridden the private rights of individuals. Uniformed men clattered up with ambulances and without ceremony lifted the sick from their mats and carted them away from their wailing families. The husbands, wives, and children could not understand why they were forbidden to follow. Four times out of five this was the last they ever saw of their loved ones until shortly they received a curt notice to come to the hospital and claim their dead.

The severity of this treatment gave rise to even more extravagant rumors. It was said that in the detention camps where contacts were segregated all sorts of horrible abuses were being perpetrated, and at the emergency hospitals the sick were being deliberately murdered.

The state of popular apprehension amounted to hysteria. Whenever possible, the sick were concealed by their families and the dead thrown into the esteros or the Pasig River or the Bay, thus adding further poison to the already poisonous waters.

Measures were taken to control sea traffic. All vessels leaving Manila were quarantined five days at Mariveles, and for a longer period if cholera broke out. A water patrol was established on the Bay, but here also many small boats evaded the watch. At the time of my arrival the emergency was so great that the quarantine service was extended to cover the Manila waterways.

The people were often, in their pitiful ignorance, hastening their own destruction. One morning I came down to my office. My first glance, as always, was towards the big map on the wall. I was startled to see that, according to the arrangement of the colored flags which marked the location of every case, cholera had suddenly burst forth in little isolated groups all over Manila.

An investigation was begun at once. This soon revealed that two days earlier a fisherman had come in from the Bay with a marvelous story of how he had seen bubbles rising in the salt water which, as they rose, formed the vague outline of a great cross. He had tasted the water and found it sweet. Crossing himself, with wonder in his heart that he had been chosen to discover this portent, he paddled furiously to land. Others, at first incredulous, tasted and then believed. The fisherman escorted to the spot a priest, who blessed the water and declared it a miracle. The Filipinos were such ardent seekers after wonderworking that they would cry out "I believe" when any prophet proclaimed, "Lo! A Miracle!" Dwellers along the shore poured themselves out on the Bay in anything that would float and eagerly scooped up the holy water in bottles, jugs, pans, and pails.

Together with the Manila health officials I was soon on a launch, which nosed its way through the conglomeration of native craft. A glance was enough to show us that this was no miracle but a dire calamity. The sewer line, which emptied far out in the Bay, had broken. If access to the miracle were shut off immediately, we knew that, in the prevailing state of incipient rebellion against health measures, the believers would feel deeply outraged and would be ready for any violence; the health service would be attacked for interfering with divine providence itself. On the other hand, action was imperative if cholera were not to run riot in the town.

We went to the Governor General and asked for constabulary to patrol the area and keep the people from committing mass suicide. Instead of acceding immediately to our request, he hesitated. "It's quite possible there'll be a minor insurrection if I do this," he argued.

"It's quite certain there'll be a major catastrophe if you don't," I retorted.

"Well, I don't know," he drawled. I was well enough acquainted with the Governor's legal turn of mind to realize that he was weighing all contingencies before making a decision. To me there could be no question as to the necessity, and, moreover, speed was of the essence.

"We are advising you in the strongest terms that the constabulary be called out. The situation is serious, and if you want to assume the responsibility, we can't do anything further about it. But we want to have it plainly in writing that it is you who are responsible."

We could state our position no more plainly.

The Governor did realize the danger, the police and the constabulary prevented the collection of the water until the sewer was repaired, and, on this occasion at least, the disturbances which ensued were of only a minor character.

When I took charge of the Bureau of Health in 1905, cholera had broken out again. If a fire is to be kept under control, it is imperative

107

to prevent a state of panic. My experience in the previous epidemic had taught me that quiet, effective measures and persevering kindness were far more potent than martial law and armed forces.

Beyond placing guards on the Benguet Road and trails leading to the Mountain Province from badly infected towns, no attempt was made at a land quarantine. An efficient blockade would have required an army of fifty thousand and the expenditure of vast sums of money. If we could keep the populace from becoming alarmed, they would perhaps stay in Manila.

Simultaneously with our efforts to keep the infection localized, we were isolating the sick in hospitals as quickly as possible. Most of them were taken to the newly completed San Lazaro buildings which, I believe, harbored more pests than were ever before concentrated at any one spot in the world. But instead of barring the friends and relatives, we built glass partitions so that they could see and realize the patients were being properly cared for. However, memories of old wrongs die hard. In spite of our efforts to calm the panic, the vernacular press accused us of exercising the same ruthless measures as had been enforced in the previous epidemic, and of being lacking in pity and humanity. One article described how the naked bodies of the dead, tagged and with feet tied together, lay about the entrance. Widespread terror among the lower classes was prevented only by Worcester's prompt action in compelling the paper to print a public retraction.

Isolation was the most important weapon against cholera, but our inability always to locate cases in their early stages prolonged the epidemic. Even with house to house inspection by police and constabulary, from two to twenty-four hours often would elapse before the Bureau of Health was informed. A quarantine guard was at once placed upon an infected house and its inmates, and from that moment the particular focus was adequately cared for; yet in the hours before these measures could be taken, other individuals almost inevitably had been infected.

In order to reduce the risk as much as possible, we mapped out the city of Manila in districts, and disinfecting carts were maintained like fire apparatus. At the sound of an alarm, the disinfectors would set out on a mad gallop, and in most cases would be at work in a few moments. Nothing but prepared food was destroyed or damaged. Clothes, blankets, mats, crockery, all went into a tub filled with carbolic acid solution. There was rarely a second case in a house which had been thus treated.

The spread of infection was often due to the kindly Filipino habit of visiting any neighbor who fell ill. Friends and relatives literally crowded to commiserate with him. But upon discovery of the nature of the disease, or upon notice from the doctor that he had to report the case, they promptly scattered and went to their meals without washing their infected hands. Many times they carried from the house mats, clothing, food, and drink, to save them from the disinfectors. We tried to trace the homes to which these articles had been carried, but it was always difficult and often impossible to locate them all.

In giving foremen their instructions, we laid great stress upon the necessity for displaying courtesy at all times. They were told to take part in no argument with householders or anybody else, and to do their work with consideration, but none the less thoroughly.

In one epidemic we had six hundred men working. The daily consumption of disinfectants was enormous. About seven hundred gallons of carbolic acid and seventy-five tons of lime were used. The entire stock of the former was consumed in one month and emergency shipments had to be secured from Hongkong and Japan. In this crisis Dr. Paul Freer, the Director of the Bureau of Science and a brilliant chemist, suggested that sea water could be electrolyzed, forming a disinfecting fluid which, according to laboratory tests, would kill cholera vibrios promptly. This provided us with a cheap and inexhaustible supply of disinfectant.

To sanitate people with fixed abodes was comparatively simple when compared to the problem presented by the harvesters of rice, sugar, and tobacco. These semi-nomads moved rapidly from place to place seeking employment. They stubbornly persisted in stating that the disease was not cholera, but poison introduced by *los Americanos* under the guise of disinfectants.

In addition to active opposition, we had passive obstruction to deal with. At times when the immediate isolation of a case of cholera would have saved a town, factional disputes might either prevent the Municipal Council's convening for lack of a quorum, or, if it did meet, it might decide that guava water was a more desirable disinfectant than carbolic acid. If the town health officer happened to be persona non grata through religious, political, or personal differences, his salary might be reduced to the lowest possible limit.

Doctors were still reluctant to settle in the provinces, so that there were many sections without skilled medical aid. Even where they were stationed, I had occasional difficulties with them. The following exchange of telegrams is self-explanatory:

"Dr. ——, San Fernando, Union: Governor, Zambales, reports cholera San Narciso. Proceed immediately take charge situation. Answer."

HEISER.

The reply came, "Health, Manila, am sick. Impossible for me to travel."

"When will you be ready?"

"Have itch: am making house my office. Shall advise when cured."

The telegrams were sometimes even more laconic. A young Filipino graduate of Rush Medical School in Chicago had returned sartorially garbed in the height of American fashion with the latest thing in neckties and toothpick shoes. His first assignment was to a cholera outbreak in an isolated town ten miles beyond the end of a railroad line. He found not even a carromata taxi at the terminus.

"No conveyance. What shall I do?" he telegraphed me at once.

"Walk!" I wired.

But I am reminded of an earlier occasion on which the zeal of a subordinate had created unexpected difficulties. The first indication that I had of anything wrong came in the form of a summons to an interview with Governor Taft. Trying to compose his jovial features into an expression of severity, he began the conversation. "Look here, Doctor, I want to help you all I can, but your department is going much too far."

"What's the matter?" I asked.

"They've been stopping the ringing of church bells in Batangas. Why?"

"I'm sure I don't know," I answered, "but I'll find out at once."

I summoned the inspector and asked for an explanation. He admitted readily that he had stopped the bells. "But that's not a sanitary measure," I pointed out.

"Oh, yes, it is," he insisted. "When the church bell rings, it lets everybody know another person has died of cholera. This news casts a gloom over the whole community. You know, yourself, Doctor, that any depressing news interferes with the secretion of the gastric juices, and that one of the best protections anybody can have against cholera is strong gastric juice. Now, when the church bell rings, the gastric juice of all those who hear it is reduced in strength, and they are much more likely to get cholera."

Still inexperienced with Oriental sophistry, I was taken aback by his reasoning. It is true that a deranged digestive system and a weakened hydrochloric acid offers a happy hunting ground for cholera germs. But even so, I was well aware that the inspector was moved by anti-Church feeling rather than true scientific spirit. I accepted his explanation, however, merely admonishing him that he was not in the future to interfere with religious observances.

I relayed his explanation to Taft who roared with laughter, and admitted the logic was incontrovertible.

The basis on which I worked in attempting to control cholera was that it could only be contracted by the introduction into the mouth of contaminated food or drink. "You can eat cholera, and you can drink cholera, but you cannot catch it." Almost absolute safety against infection could be secured by the simple precaution of using safe, potable water and cooked food. My greatest task was to convince the Filipinos that this assumption was correct.

Large portions of the population were ignorant and inaccessible. Much superstition existed, one of the most popular beliefs being the supposedly injurious character of boiled water. The time-honored custom had been to keep water in large earthen jars into which anyone who was thirsty dipped his half cocoanut shell and, incidentally, his fingers. The eating habits were equally simple and primitive. Food was conveyed to the mouth with the fingers from a general bowl used by all the household. The sterilization of water and the preparation of hot food was difficult and expensive, because all heating and cooking had to be done over infinitesimal fires of bamboo sticks.

The question of the perishable food supply of the inhabitants of Manila was almost as important as water. It had to be inspected so that nothing diseased, unsound, or unfit would be sold or consumed. We erected large airy buildings of concrete, which were to serve as central markets. This system of distribution proved to be one of our few innovations which pleased everybody. The city liked it because of the income, the dealers because of the cheap rents, the housewives because of the wide choice of foods and the convenience of being able to buy all their supplies in one place. Finally, it served the purposes of the Bureau of Health because it gave us an opportunity to control the sale of foodstuffs. Manila has the distinction of being the only city in the world where perishable food may be sold only in a public market. We also took advantage of these gathering places to teach the Filipinos habits of sanitation by instructing them in the use of public latrines.

The low-growing vegetables, as usual, were barred, but the sale of fruits that grew high on trees, such as bananas, cocoanuts, and mangos, was not dangerous and not interfered with. Forks were provided in the meat stalls, but much education and patience was necessary before the old custom of handling one piece of meat after another could be stopped.

Every market had a large number of stands which catered solely to the chewers of betel. The kernel of this nut, fruit of the Areca palm, is taken from its thick husk, much like that of a walnut or butternut, and is then cut into disks. The pieces are covered with lime, wrapped in moist green buya leaves about the size of those of a morning glory, and placed in an earthen pot. They are thoroughly sprinkled every few hours, but the old water at the bottom of the vessel is seldom replaced.

The Filipino purchaser is very particular as to the tenderness of the leaves. He puts his hand into the jar and feels them all carefully before making his selection. Naturally, if his fingers are infected, he spreads the contagion throughout the pot.

The habit of betel nut chewing was so ingrained among the Islanders that any attempt to forbid it would have been useless. Its mildly stimulating effect was apparently no detriment to health, although it was incidentally injurious. The Filipino would push the cud between his teeth and cheek, and the pungent essence of the nut would irritate the mucous membrane, often causing buccal cancer. Since we could not stop this habit, which was more common than gum chewing in the United States, we prohibited the sale of the nut outside the markets.

In an epidemic we used to rope off the market so as to leave only one possible entrance. There we stationed a uniformed guard, and placed by his side a barrel filled with a weak solution of bichloride of mercury, mild enough to be harmless to human beings. The guard saw to it that each person entering the market rinsed his fingers in the barrel. Since no towel was provided, the disinfectant perforce dried on his hands.

The Filipinos regarded this procedure as a rather childish American practice which hurt nobody. They dipped in their hands and then, with shouts of laughter, splashed one another with the disinfecting solution. Nothing could have served our purposes better.

Even more important than bullfighting to the Spaniard is cock-fighting to the Filipino, because every man, no matter how poor, can participate in the sport. In many homes the cock is the most valued possession. In case of fire the Filipino is popularly said to rescue first his cock, then his wife, and lastly his children. A cock costs money, a wife nothing, and children are easily come by. One of the commonest tableaux in the Islands is that of two men holding their cocks by the tails and letting them scratch and pull towards each other to strengthen their muscles.

Around the cockpits, which are in every village, amphitheatres are built of bamboo and nipa, and each Sunday the seats are filled from dawn to dark. Usually a white cock is matched with a colored one, so that each may be readily distinguished. Before a contest begins, the owner brings in his cock and, holding it firmly by the tail, allows it to struggle and strain in order to display its fierceness and strength. The audience of inveterate gamblers makes its appraisal promptly and the betting begins. Cries of, "Five on the red," or, "Ten on the white," alternate with the clink of money thrown into the pit. The attendant shouts, "Any more bets?" and when none is forthcoming, he sweeps up the silver and paper with a broom.

Each cock has fastened on one leg a steel gaff of razor-like sharpness, and one of the combatants is disemboweled quickly or runs away. The slain heroes, although tough, eventually find their way into the family soup pot. The pay-off, which takes place without any apparent system of accounting, is a most amazing performance. A man comes up to a little window and merely says, "I bet five on the red," and receives his money. I never saw a single dispute about the amount of the wager.

In times of epidemics any gathering of people was dangerous. We could not ride roughshod over the customs and the religion of the people; often we had to compromise. The fiesta is a time-honored institution in the Philippines, and the principal event in the yearly history of each town. Save for its religious aspect, it resembles one of our county fairs, bringing together thousands of people of all ages and conditions, who, for the time being, lose themselves in festivity.

The greatest single hazard to health during the year came from the annual celebration of the feast of *Nuestra Senora de Paz y Buen Viaje* at Antipolo. For several weeks ten thousand persons or even more would congregate in the small town containing the shrine. Feasting was one of the essential features. Food was brought from cholera-infected districts and even from invaded homes, and, with that sincere hospitality so characteristic of the Filipinos, was distributed to all who would partake. There was a natural tendency to excess in eating, and the indigestion thus induced might have afforded just the opportunity for the development of a case of cholera or typhoid or dysentery.

Patients in the incubation state of cholera often mingled freely with the well, and, since the means for the disposal of the excreta of so many people were usually inadequate, it was quite obvious how the disease might spread. After visiting the Virgin, the pilgrims used to bathe in the Mariquina River, which was nearby, and the drinking water was scooped up farther down the stream.

Almost immediately after Antipolo, cholera would crop up simultaneously here and there about Luzon. The villagers could find no other explanation than that some mysterious fermentation was working in the soil. But to the members of the Bureau of Health who were studying the route maps of the returning pilgrims, it was apparent that the lines of infection radiated in all directions like the spokes from a hub. The devout travelers might have escaped contagion at Antipolo itself, but too often it was obvious they had stopped at Pasig, where they must have purchased low-growing vegetables fertilized with human excreta alive with cholera organisms.

Quarantine as an emergency measure and, as more permanent preventives, the disposal of excreta and the provision for pure water, were our only prophylaxis against cholera in the early epidemics. But it was obvious that other factors, as yet unknown, entered the equation.

Cholera had always broken out at crowded Bilibid Prison in every epidemic. When I was first called upon to cope with this disease, the prison medical service was under the complete control of an official called the Director of Prisons. As the death rate was mounting to over two hundred per thousand, Governor Wright asked whether I would find out wherein lay the trouble.

"I'll try," I said, "but I can do this only if I have the necessary authority. Will you instruct the Director of Prisons to carry out any reasonable requests I may make?"

"But that would be infringing on his domain. I don't see how I can do that," said the Governor.

Realizing that my work would be useless without complete control, I said I was sorry, but that I should have to decline. Governor Wright considered for a moment, and then decided that the emergency required the cutting of red tape. "This outbreak must be stopped. I'll do as you say."

I went to the prison and, after searching all morning, had discovered nothing. The sick had been promptly isolated, the food was cooked, and the water was pure; there seemed to be no reason for the constant recurrence of cases.

Then the dinner gong rang. The prisoners trouped into the dining room, and I noticed the flies from the toilets went with them. In those days little was known about the possibilities of carriers and insect transmission. Flies, however, were a danger in any epidemic, because they might carry on their feet any intestinal disease. They frequented disease breeding spots and purposely hunted for filth. If there were no filth, there would be no flies. I ordered the toilets to be screened and the entrance to be provided with a vestibule and spring doors. Within forty-eight hours the cholera epidemic in Bilibid Prison stopped with dramatic suddenness.

The prison medical service was shortly thereafter placed under the Bureau of Health, and Bilibid became a laboratory where we could study disease under controlled conditions. The death rate there dropped to the level of the most famous health resorts.

Flies might explain an outbreak in an institution, but could not make clear why, in spite of all our sanitary measures, cholera kept cropping up in widely scattered districts of Luzon. An epidemic would start in Hagenoy, and a few days later break out in Pampanga. By rigorous methods we would be able to declare Hagenoy clean, but while we were concentrating on Pampanga, Hagenoy would somehow be reinfected. And no sooner would Pampanga be cleared up and we would proceed to another district than it would be reinfected from Bulacan. Often cases were few and dissociated, but the endless chain went on. An infection dispersed so broadly, so elusive, and so slight as to be scarcely noticeable, could with great difficulty be combated. Nevertheless we knew that any relaxation in vigilance would surely be followed by a major outbreak.

In studying the causes of the tragic Hamburg disaster of 1892, when eight thousand people had died in three months, the doctors of the period had offered as a theory the possibility of cholera carriers —people who, though themselves not ill, were yet able to distribute millions of germs and infect many others. The explanation had not been proved and was lost sight of until Dr. Allan J. McLaughlin, one of the outstanding members of my department, working on the German hypothesis, determined the existence of carriers in the Philippines. Thereafter, in our measures for controlling cholera, we took cognizance of the potential danger from this source.

If the bacteria carrier washed his hands often enough and at the proper times, he would not transfer infection from his dirty fingers to the food or drink of others. Otherwise, he was a great menace to the public. We kept very close track of all carriers and isolated them whenever they gave positive results. Even when they were negative, it was possible that they might become positive at any time.

Consequently, before the season for cholera came around, we used to have them examined.

Once in possession of the fact that cholera carriers existed we were able to guard the Philippines against the entrance of cholera from other countries. We required bacteriological examination of all passengers at quarantine, a system which has now become an essential part of safeguarding any port from cholera carriers or those slightly ill with the disease.

In 1911 I happened to be in New York on my vacation when cholera broke out at Brooklyn. Three thousand immigrants were coming in almost daily, and it was assumed cholera carriers among them must have brought in this infection. Wholesale bacteriological examinations were obviously necessary, and, because of my previous experience with cholera, I was asked to help. An emergency appropriation was secured, a laboratory was set up at Rosebank, New Jersey, and thirty women technicians were employed to find the carriers. Instead of sweeping the country as had so often happened, cholera was stopped in its tracks.

The system we installed at Rosebank has now become the recognized one throughout the world. Although it is most useful in preventing cholera, it does not give absolute assurance. All threatened towns or sections must always be prepared to fight the disease.

Combating epidemics was temporarily stopping the leak in the dam, and cleaning and renovating were essential, but all would be of no lasting value unless the coming generation were educated in the necessity for and knowledge of prophylaxis through inculcating cleanly habits in eating and the disposal of feces.

The children made the handiest tools to work with. The little Filipinos were exceedingly studious; such a thing as a child not preparing its lessons was unknown. There were never enough schools to go round, and it was pathetic to see them standing outside the schoolhouse looking longingly in, hoping that some boy or girl would not appear and one of them might enter in his or her place. Teaching by precept and example and literature did a great deal. We organized Knife and Fork Societies among them. In some cases they carried this lesson in table manners home, but the older people were seldom affected; their eating habits were fixed, and the danger quite beyond their comprehension. Nevertheless, we continued to encourage the children to repeat what they learned to their parents who, although they themselves could neither read nor write, were also eager for learning.

Simple rules of hygiene were placed in the newspapers and on handbills in English, Spanish, Tagalog, Ilocano, Visayan, and various other native dialects. With the cooperation of the Bureau of Education, these circulars were sent to every school teacher in the Islands. They were to be taught to the children so that they could repeat them verbatim to their parents. We also had the rules printed on large flaring red posters which were placarded on municipal and other public buildings.

We spent much time in the preparation of a primer of sanitation, destined for the bending of these young twigs whose homes possessed no running water, no stoves, and no bathrooms. When it was put in words of one syllable, it became the standard for schools throughout the tropics.

To get the best results in our campaign of education we concentrated on one subject at a time—beriberi, cholera, tuberculosis, or whatever was most important at the moment. Talks, pamphlets, newspaper articles, and demonstrations were all used. We would gather the people together wherever we could and illustrate our points with lantern slides. We secured a car from the railway, and made it into a traveling exhibit with a Filipino lecturer to accompany it. Later a Healthmobile and good roads enabled us to reach many more. To those who were still inaccessible we sent miniature exhibits on porters' backs, and a lecturer went from house to house expounding.

A prime requisite in the campaign was the cooperation of the churches, because of the great respect which the Filipinos generally paid to the words of their religious instructors. I first went to Archbishop Harty, a very intelligent man without whose help I could have accomplished little. I explained to him the highly infectious nature of cholera, and pointed out that it did not make any difference whether a Catholic or a Protestant swallowed the germs—they both died. Our aims were identical. His priests were intelligent men, but as long as they taught their flocks that cholera was a punishment for transgression and merely commiserated with them, they helped rather than hindered the spread of the disease. Every death was furthering destruction by bringing together large groups of people, and during an epidemic it was vital to stop these wakes.

"I do not want to ban them arbitrarily," I explained to the Archbishop, "because I should gain nothing in that way. The people would probably hold their wakes in secret. But you can instruct your priests and they will faithfully obey."

He agreed to help me.

I then broached an even more important subject. I wanted him to distribute simple rules for cholera prevention. He promised that they would be preached from every Catholic church in the Islands.

Armed with Archbishop Harty's assurance, I approached Monsignor Aglipay, the head of the Independent Catholic faction. "Your Grace," I began, "the Roman Catholics are sending out cholera circulars. Don't you want to save the lives of your people also? If you do, here are the handbills which will teach your parishioners how to avoid this disease."

In his eagerness, Father Aglipay almost snatched the circulars from my hands.

I then made the rounds of the Protestant denominations and said to Episcopalian, Methodist, and Presbyterian in turn that the Catholics were sending out circulars, and suggested they might wish to do the same. They also promptly agreed.

In this manner I brought into my camp the best educational and religious forces of the country.

Month after month and year after year we labored by every possible means to persuade the Filipinos to boil their water, but with no great success. One of my American doctors, valuable because of his knowledge of the Tagalog tongue, was especially good at coping with cholera outbreaks. I knew that wherever he went he would stress the necessity for sterilized water. When the cholera rate remained high in his province of Pampanga, I went in person to investigate. I began making the rounds of the houses and in each one I asked, "Do you use boiled water?" and in each received an affirmative reply. By the time I had reached the fifth house, I decided I had better go into the question somewhat more thoroughly. "How do you use this boiled water?" I inquired.

"We take a teaspoonful three times a day."

The wise Chinese are the only Oriental people who apparently do not suffer from cholera. They know the use of boiled water and cooked food. They drink tea and eat hot rice. Perhaps far back in the Shang, or the Chou, or the Tsin, or the Han dynasties, certain Chinese preferred fragrant tea to insipid water when they were thirsty. Cholera passed them by. But those who did not practice the delicate art of brewing and drinking tea, in the course of time perished, leaving a nation of tea drinkers.

In the Philippines it was found that the Chinese who were stricken had betrayed their ancestors by adopting the Filipino mode of living. In Manila there was one case of cholera out of a thousand Chinese, one out of seven hundred Americans, and one out of two hundred and fifty Filipinos.

The Chinese always drink boiled water, the Americans generally drink boiled water, and the Filipinos seldom drink boiled water.

CHAPTER 9.   WATER, WATER,
                              EVERYWHERE

FOR many years the indifference of the Filipinos toward the
question of better water seemed almost impossible to overcome. If a bridge fell down and ten people were killed, the public
would be wrought up to fever pitch, and an investigating committee
would at once be appointed to fix the responsibility, but the deaths
of hundreds of people who died of poor water went totally unre-
garded.

Whether water was safe and potable seldom seemed to have been
inquired into from a scientific standpoint, nor was the enormous
amount of labor to be saved and the convenience which would result
by having it delivered through pipes seriously considered.

The Spaniards had put in a pumping station for Manila which
elevated water from the Mariquina River to a reservoir and then
distributed it by pipes. But this system did not reach all the people
in Manila. As a result, the poorer classes, among whom the danger
from cholera was greatest, were accustomed to take water from
shallow wells, ponds, esteros, or other questionable sources, not only
for washing clothes and kitchen utensils, but in many instances for
drinking purposes. We tried to forbid this practice, but more often
than not our orders were ignored because some barrios were located
so far from the nearest hydrants that the people had to carry water
a long distance in bamboo tubes or the emptied Standard Oil tins
which litter the East.

One of the first steps in a cholera epidemic was to guard the water supply from pollution. We closed all the wells, except a few in the more distant barrios. These we treated with permanganate of potash; nobody would then drink the blood red water. Wherever possible, all stagnant places were drained by digging ditches, and certain small infected esteros were patrolled by the constabulary. Until simple disinfection with chlorine became available, the United States Army was also called upon in emergency to guard the banks of the Mariquina and prevent soil pollution. Communities aggregating ten thousand were located along the banks of the river, and from time immemorial had been accustomed to bathe and to wash there.

In the 1905 epidemic, a few days after the first cases of cholera appeared in Manila, reports of an outbreak came in from San Mateo, one of the towns in the Mariquina Valley. A certain young Filipina, living nearby and called by her admirers the Queen of Taytay, was performing miracles. She was bathing in a galvanized iron garbage disposal tank which had been abandoned by the Army. Villagers from near and far were standing in line all day long waiting to drink the water after her ablutions. They believed that she was endowed with such miraculous curative powers that the hundreds of those who drank would be healed.

No doubt some who came to drink had cholera germs upon their hands and, as they dipped in their containers, the water had become infected. Cholera organisms remained in the residue, which was not removed, so that each fresh tankful was reinfected.

Faith healing has always had a tremendous hold over all people of all times. This is particularly true of a country which has been disease-ridden for centuries. To tamper with the Queen's miracle when Rizal Province was in such a state of emotional excitement would, as in the case of the broken sewer in Manila Bay, have been a hazardous undertaking. But it was even more dangerous to let her continue.

Although the Queen of Taytay was invading my precincts, I could think of no legal way in which she could be stopped. The Bureau of Health always tried to proceed along the lines of law and order, but every avenue in this case seemed to be blocked. The Attorney General went through the Philippine statute books, and he also was unable to offer any solution.

WATER, WATER, EVERYWHERE

I had to resort to guile. I repaired to Taytay and went into conference with the father and mother of the Queen. I conceded that she might be doing good, but I pointed out that in the capital she would have wider scope for her activities. Where hundreds could drink in Taytay, thousands could drink in Manila. I promised here and cajoled there, and in the end I persuaded them. Even the Queen, after a day of earnest argument, consented to come to Manila. In addition, I made solemn affidavit to the whole village that she would be given ample opportunity to bathe as much as she pleased, and that we would take good care of her.

A procession was formed. The Queen and I led the van during the twelve mile walk to Manila, and many of the inhabitants of Rizal accompanied us to make sure no harm should befall her. Before she disappeared within the hospital, I addressed the multitude, which, after the manner of crowds, had increased enormously in numbers.

"Your Queen," I said, "must go inside to do her bathing and perform her miracle, but once an hour she will come out on the balcony, so that you may see that she is safe."

Though the assemblage did not seem to be altogether convinced, no open protest was made.

Curiously enough, we had no difficulty with the Queen herself. At first she took her baths regularly, and regularly we let the water run away after she left and drew a new one for her. She seemed to have no concern over the disposition of the water. As time went on, she bathed less often. Since she was being fed well and having a pleasant time, her interest in miracles rapidly waned.

For the first few days the Queen's balcony appearances had been dutifully made. At night we had even turned a flood light on her so that her faithful watchers would have hourly reassurance. But gradually they grew tired of their long vigil and went home. She walked on less and less frequently as the numbers of her followers diminished. By the end of a week she had played her final performance. After two weeks we told her she might go home, but that she should bathe in the tank no more. If she were overpowered by the need for performing miracles, she should come back to us and perform them at the hospital.

The Bureau of Health did not subscribe to miracles. We put our faith in a new water system. We went thirty miles farther up the Mariquina to a sparsely inhabited watershed, and across the pure white marble gorge of Montalban we built a dam. Necessarily, the few inhabitants had to be moved elsewhere; not all wanted to go. I can still see Worcester in his customarily forceful language talking to one recalcitrant whose stables and sty stood beside a small stream which emptied into the Mariquina above the dam. He said this little river belonged to him, and refused absolutely to budge.

"All right," said Worcester. "We can't put you out of your home. But we can forbid you to let one drop of your polluted water flow over on our area." The farmer could not very well keep his river at home, and surrendered.

After the new water supply was turned into the pipes, eight hundred fewer deaths annually occurred in the city of Manila than ever before. We were to be given even further proof of the vitally important role played by water in the tropics. The Filipinos were always dynamiting the streams to get fish, and by chance they once set off a charge directly above the water main where it crossed the river bed. We had to send all the way to Glasgow for new lengths of pipe. This accident, combined with a severe drought, compelled us to go back to the old Spanish system. Although we tried by every means to induce the people to boil their water before drinking, yet three hundred and ten more died than in any similar period since the new system had been completed. As soon as the pure water was in use again, the death rate came down, not only from water-borne, but from all other diseases.

This was directly in line with Hazen's statement that when drinking water was made safe, each death avoided from typhoid fever caused the avoidance of two or even three other deaths from diseases not regarded as intestinal-borne.

It would never have been possible to guard all the streams and shallow wells of the Philippines against pollution. Furthermore, if pure water could be provided, we should be spared the never-ending task of inculcating the boiled water habit. We asked the Legislature for twenty-five hundred dollars with which to bore a few experimental artesian wells. With the greatest reluctance this money was appropriated. The members, almost to a man, regarded this as a new-fangled notion of the Americans which could not possibly be of any utility to their constituents.

The first well was drilled in 1906 in the province of Pampanga. It came in successfully and began flowing large quantities of pure, potable water. But the people would not come near it. They said, "If God had intended us to drink water out of a hole drilled in the crust of the earth he would have put it there." According to their ancient custom, they continued drinking out of the streams in which carabao wallowed, and the wells into which filth drained.

We sent a Filipino doctor to explain to the Pampangans in their own dialect the virtues of this new water. In the effort to give them a practical example of its benefits, he almost water-logged himself, but to no good. The people remained indifferent. Other doctors were despatched; hostility grew. One of them had to flee for his life, pursued by bolos. Rumors began to circulate. "If you drink this water," the villagers said, "your hair will fall out. If you don't believe it, look at the Director of Health at Manila. He drinks this water. Look at him!"

I could make no valid defense to this conclusion. It posed a neat problem, because the Filipinos are so proud of their hair that they will go to almost any lengths to conserve it.

For several months the well bubbled invitingly, but none partook. We had led the Filipinos to the water but they would not drink. Then we were ourselves vouchsafed a lay miracle which brought to pass instantaneously and simply the results we had so long struggled for. This well was located a short distance from a town. A weary and sick stranger was passing along the road, and in his great thirst drank of the water. Almost from the first sip he began to feel his sickness leave him. He sat down beside the well and drank more. The more he drank the better he felt, until finally he was entirely recovered.

The traveler hastened to tell the villagers what had happened to him, and of the great medicinal value possessed by this water. Nothing could have been better adapted to Filipino psychology. The villagers streamed to the well. The parish priest blessed it. The news spread to the surrounding districts by grapevine telegraph. Inside of a week people were coming from points as distant as one hundred and fifty miles to get some of this marvelous water, taking away as much as they could carry.

We went again to the Legislature for money, and this time encountered no difficulty. In a few years "artesian wells" became one of the leading public questions of the day. Assemblymen who wanted to be elected would always come out in their platforms for artesian well appropriations. The demand became far too great for the supply of money, although three hundred thousand dollars was appropriated in 1915 gladly and willingly.

We watched very carefully to see the effect upon the mortality in villages where wells had been drilled. It was gratifying to observe that a death rate of forty to fifty per thousand would drop in one year to twenty or twenty-five. Nevertheless, the villagers still did not understand the true purpose of the wells, although they liked them and used them. We would sometimes find upon investigation that the pumps had been primed with water from the nearest ditch.

There were many deaths in the Philippines traceable to intestinal causes which did not find their way into the statistics under this head, and in addition perhaps even a greater number which were indirectly due to lowered resistance or other factors not clearly understood. For each death directly ascribable to intestinal disease, there are at least ten cases of illness which incapacitate an individual for ten days. Practically every Filipino had some form of intestinal parasite; often several varieties in combination. This condition was directly due to soil pollution, which for centuries was responsible for more deaths and illness among soldiers than have ever been slain on the field of battle. In recent years vaccination against typhoid and cholera has greatly reduced the military danger.

As far back as there is any historical record, the disposal of human wastes has been a sanitary problem. Nomadic peoples, such as the Indians of North America, would move on to a new place as soon as their camp grounds became filthy. Those who lived on the seashore depended upon the tides to keep their abodes in a cleanly condition.

Moses, the leader of a wandering people, was among the first, as far as history shows, to make written sanitary regulations for the proper disposal of human wastes. For many years his laws were in operation throughout the world, and even today are practised by those who live a camp life. The pit system used in the armies of the world is but a slight deviation from that enforced among the Ancient Jews. Moses had no knowledge of disease germs, but he had learned from experience that if he did not keep his camp grounds clean, his people became sick.

Cholera, typhoid fever, and dysentery are due to soil pollution. No one would think of throwing a substance known to be poisonous into the yard, or leaving it uncovered in the house; yet human wastes are more dangerous than arsenic or strychnine, and a thousand times more likely to be carried to the supply of drinking water, or to be brought in contact with the food, than are vegetable and mineral poisons.

The public generally is not interested in the subject of soil pollution. The excreta of a great city can be safely disposed of with a modern sewer system, but in the Philippines there were no sewers. In the nipa hut districts of Manila, houses had been built promiscuously all over an interior plot of ground without regard to street or alley lines. Access to many was only by means of a narrow path, not even wide enough for a cart. Others had to be reached by going under the neighboring houses.

In these closed barrios, made up of collections of miserable shacks, without proper kitchen facilities or even surface drainage, and with overcrowding worse than the old "lung" blocks of New York or Chicago, the difficulty of finding and combating epidemic disease was very great. Kitchen refuse, and even human excreta, were dropped through the interstices in the bamboo floors; the waiting pigs were the only sanitarians.

Pigs are omnipresent and offensive in the Philippines, but as scavengers they are invaluable. These starvelings ran loose in Manila until the olfactorily-sensitive Americans passed a law whereby they had to be locked up. Thereafter most Filipino homes had bamboo runways under the houses. The gastric juices of a pig are so powerful that they destroy practically any bacteria he eats. Cholera vibrios which would have killed a human being in a few hours, were as nothing to the pig. We concluded he was a help rather than a hindrance.

127

In a way the cholera epidemic helped us in our efforts to reclaim the nipa hut interiors. The attention of the better class of Filipinos was thus called to sections of their city into which few of them had previously penetrated. Many had honestly considered that the Bureau of Health was only persecuting an inoffensive class of poverty-stricken unfortunates.

As soon as cholera had disappeared from Manila we set about a determined effort to do away with these districts. But it was only after years of effort that we succeeded in securing sanitary barrios, on easily drained land and subdivided into streets, alleys, and lots according to a definite plan. It was interesting to note that the criminal rate, which had been highest in the insanitary sections, went down as soon as health was improved.

The installation of a new sewerage system in Manila also did a great deal to reduce health hazards. But many people would not obey the local ordinances, and we had to go to the Supreme Court of the United States to enforce sewer connections. The opposition came chiefly from the owners of large tenement houses, but, once the legal decision was made, we had no further major difficulties.

In contrast to the dread inspired by cholera everywhere, there is the greatest indifference to typhoid. Yet the presence or absence of typhoid is often regarded by many as the chief index of the sanitation of a given locality. Typhoid is usually thought of as a disease of civilization, and when the Americans first came to the Islands, Filipinos apparently suffered very little. But as communications improved, it began to spread, and with thousands of miles of good roads the infection was scattered broadcast. It circulated rapidly, was extremely virulent, and caused a high rate of mortality.

Since typhoid is conveyed in much the same way as cholera, the same measures of prophylaxis are applicable, although the typhoid bacillus is not so easily destroyed as the cholera vibrio. The administration of typhoid vaccine is a preventive, but it is expensive, and immunity grows less after two years. The principal way to combat the disease is through a pure water supply.

The study of health records in the tropics shows that the great enemies of man are diarrhea and dysentery, and not the spectacular cholera and plague. Dysentery caused more deaths, more disability, and more time lost from gainful occupations than all other tropical diseases combined. Annually dysentery assumed an epidemic form in a number of localities, shortly after the beginning of the rainy season. Curiously enough, it usually did not spread by extension as did cholera, but kept within certain bounds. Sometimes it appeared simultaneously over a widespread territory. It might break out on an island which had had no communication for weeks with the mainland at the same time as in the thickly inhabited Dagupan Valley.

Dysentery is of two kinds. It may be caused either by a bacillus or an amoeba, although the symptoms are much the same. The amoeba is a slightly greenish, microscopic, unicellular parasite, which is able to move around with considerable freedom. In the early days we thought all amoebae could convey dysentery, and, since all water in the Philippines contained amoebae, we would have to sterilize it all. This would have been so costly as to be practically prohibitive. The problem was turned over to the Bureau of Science, and its experts proved that amoebae were of pathogenic and non-pathogenic types. Since the ordinary amoebae did not hurt anybody, this made it possible to exclude from treatment a great many water installations.

It was long known that the drug ipecacuanha was useful in treating dysentery. In 1658 it had been brought to Europe from Brazil and sold as a secret remedy to the French government. But the use of this drug caused disagreeable and exhausting nausea as well as actual vomiting, because of the large doses essential to obtain full curative effects. Many vain efforts were made to coat the pills with salol or keratin, so that they would pass through the stomach undigested, or to check the vomiting with opium, chloral hydrate, or tannic acid.

Ultimately, Captain Edward Vedder of the United States Army Medical Corps, in the Philippines, discovered that emetine, the principal alkaloid of ipecacuanha, had the power, even in high dilutions, of destroying amoebae in test tubes. He did not, however, experiment with this drug on human beings.

Leonard Rogers of the Indian Medical Service, later knighted for this distinguished contribution to science, happened to read on shipboard the pamphlet in which Vedder described his experiments. He could hardly wait to reach India and try emetine on dysentery patients. By administering it hypodermically, he obtained results that seemed scarcely short of miraculous. He hastened to make the discovery known before the impending rainy season brought the inevitable increase in cases. The new treatment was immediately adopted and proved of inestimable benefit.

It was generally assumed by powers which colonized in the tropics that the native populations were immune to dysentery, but we made one thousand consecutive autopsies on Filipinos who had died of other causes, and found that three hundred of them had ulcers in their intestines from this disease. We knew then that dysentery was a problem among the Filipinos as much as among Europeans and Americans. There was a certain difference in its course, however. Among Filipinos and Chinese the tendency was toward recovery, and the abscesses of the liver which so often occurred among white victims were not so frequent.

Curing disease has never seemed to me of equal importance with its prevention. But I could not agree with the British, who always insisted that woolen belly bands protected them against intestinal diseases and guarded them against chills. I ridiculed the practice, saying it was much better to harden yourself against chill, and what would happen to you if you went out some time without your belly band? In any case, it was hot and uncomfortable, and it took more than a belly band to kill an amoeba.

There were certain omniscient ones among Americans, also, who said it was all foolishness to drink sterilized water; they never did. I always replied mildly that their luck would hold only so long, but the chances were that sooner or later they would have their bouts with dysentery. There was scarcely ever a transport or liner leaving Manila that did not carry back invalids who had caught dysentery as the result of not drinking boiled water.

On the month-long inspection trips through the Mountain Province I always had servants bring my canteen to me as soon as it had been filled. If it were not piping hot, I would know the water had not been boiled. I also saw to it that each member of the party took half-gallon canteens. He was thereafter supposed to make sure only water properly boiled was placed in it.

We could carry no ice, of course, on such trips, and the contents of the canteens were often warm and unpleasant. But those who disobeyed the instruction to partake only of boiled water invariably became sick. One by one the foolhardy ones would succumb to temptation. We would arrive at a mountain stream which rippled invitingly across the trail. They would be so hot, and the water would look so clean and cool, that they would lie down and put their dry thirsty mouths into it and drink. For the moment they would be refreshed, but they would soon find to their cost that they had been imbibing contamination from the villages above. I remember one particular expedition when out of twenty men Forbes, Worcester, and myself were the only ones who did not have to be carried in litters to the coast and shipped back to the Manila hospital.

Among the wild tribes, who had the best opportunity to disseminate infection, there existed dense ignorance in regard to the nature of bacteriological cleanliness. To them a germ was a bug, something that could be seen and dealt with by means of a bolo. The difficulty of explaining to a primitive race the nature of microbes and their wicked doings was excellently illustrated by the endeavor of Winfred T. Dennison, Secretary of the Interior under Harrison, to teach the Igorots about the amoeba.

Mr. Dennison was a little man, and therefore not so much admired in the Mountain Province as his predecessor, the gigantic Worcester. He was convinced that he could turn the Igorots' belief in evil spirits to good account, and asked that a motile amoeba be mounted for him on a microscopic slide. A lusty specimen was accordingly provided.

We went on the annual tour of the Mountain Province, and, at one of the chief towns of the Igorots, Mr. Dennison decided to give his demonstration. He had one of the chiefs brought over and said to him, "I want to show you an evil spirit that causes diseases. The white man can control him. If you look through this you will see him."

The *Apo* looked as directed, and grunted.

"What do you see?"

No reply could be elicited.

Mr. Dennison then handed the *Apo* a pencil and paper, and said, "Draw what you see."

The *Apo* produced a very good likeness of an amoeba jumping about.

Mr. Dennison then triumphantly exclaimed, "That's what causes diseases that kill you, but we can kill it."

"You say that little thing can kill a man?" queried the *Apo* incredulously.

"Yes," came Mr. Dennison's confident reply.

"Well, it might kill a little white man like you, but it wouldn't hurt a great big *Apo* like me."

I have followed my own rules of exercise, cooked food, and boiled water faithfully for years in the tropics, and only once have I had any so-called tropical disease. This was in the nature of an experiment. I was attempting to test my thesis further. I began to drink water casually on ships and in hotels without making precise inquiries into its source. After two months of this nonchalance, I came down with amoebic dysentery at Calcutta.

CHAPTER 10.　　NOT WITH BEAT
OF DRUM

I HAVE always found that, no matter what the color of a person's skin, if you can relieve him of pain, he becomes your friend. This is especially true among primitive races, who are more lavish in their gratitude than many civilized people I know.

In the mountainous interior of Northern Luzon lived three hundred thousand wild tribesmen, untamed wards of the government who, for lack of a better name, were commonly called non-Christians. But they were not savages and, because they had so recently abandoned the practice, they were sensitive to the opprobrium conveyed by the term head-hunter. The principal reason for their long isolation was geographical. The narrow passes which led into the mountains could be easily defended against a considerable military force. Furthermore, the land was poor and the people fierce and warlike. It had never been worth the Spaniards' time or money to conquer them. For centuries also a feud had smoldered between Christian lowlander and animistic mountain dweller, and for a long time it was questionable whether friendly relations between the two could be established.

In general, the mountain people were exceptionally healthy and sturdy, and the normal death rate from disease was not so high as in the lowlands, although many children died of malnutrition or improper feeding. The mothers used to chew up rice, camotes, and meat, and feed infants of a few days directly from their own mouths, as a squab is fed.

All five tribes suffered appallingly from a disease called yaws, which is communicated under conditions of filth and poverty, and

by actual contact. Although not venereal, it had many of the pathological characteristics of syphilis, among them a positive reaction
to the Wassermann test. It usually began with a large cauliflower-like
excrescence known as the mother yaw, and thereafter the lesions
spread over the entire body. In later life it often caused paralysis
and deformities. Children were particularly susceptible to this disease,
which frequently and tragically robbed them of their childhood.

Our first step in peaceful penetration was to provide medical service for these mountain dwellers whom civilization had overlooked.
In the Igorot country, which lay just beyond our doors, we began
the attempt to relieve some of the suffering caused by yaws. We were
making slow progress with the old potassium iodide treatment for
syphilis, when luck unexpectedly came our way. Dr. Paul Ehrlich
sent some of his newly developed salvarsan (606) to Dr. Richard
P. Strong, who experimented with it, and found it marvelously
effective in yaws, working miraculous cures. Armed anew with this
discovery, we opened a small dispensary on the edge of the Igorot
territory.

The healthy Igorot wore nothing but a breech clout, but when he
fell ill he immediately took his blanket and wrapped himself into
his misery. There was no clock, no sun-dial, no hourglass in the
Mountain Province, but the sun rose every day. Every medicine man,
brown, black, yellow, or white, often practises hocus-pocus. To an
Igorot whose sufferings had overcome his suspicions, we handed a
stick with fifteen loops of string tied around it.

"Be up at dawn each morning," he was admonished solemnly.
"Have your bolo ready. Watch carefully. Just as you see the first
yellow tip of the sun, cut off one loop. Do not take off your blanket.
Do not look at your skin. At every sunrise cut one more loop. When
the last one is gone, throw aside your blanket. You will be well."

Having pronounced these words, we injected the 606, and sent
the Igorot on his way.

One of our doctors was most anxious to describe the magic treatment for a medical journal. He had selected six particularly interesting cases, and sent for a photographer from the Bureau of Science,
asking the six Igorots to be present on a certain morning. The morning
came, and so did the photographer, but no Igorots.

"That's just the way with these ungrateful people," the doctor irritably exclaimed. "You cure them with great trouble and cost, but when you ask some little favor, that's the last you see of them."

Two weeks later the doctor heard a great hullabaloo. He went to the door of the dispensary, and there were his six "ungrateful" patients, triumphantly leading several hundred of their afflicted brethren, all coming for their sticks with the fifteen loops.

By healing the people we gradually extended our dispensaries, until we had penetrated into the heart of the non-Christian country. The tribesmen began flocking to them, carrying their sick in litters and welcoming physicians and nurses into their homes.

Eventually at Bontoc, the capital of the Mountain Province, we built a modern hospital, made of brick baked in the hills. It took much time to teach the people our new and strange ways. Just after the hospital was opened I remember making an inspection visit one night and finding all the beds empty. I had seen the ward full only a few hours before. As I was looking around for some explanation of the phenomenon, I noticed a pair of bare brown feet sticking out from under a bed, and stooping down, I found all the patients in similar positions. We had to permit them to sleep on the floor until we could convince them a bed really had its advantages.

The non-Christians were much averse in the beginning to staying in an enclosed space for any length of time, ignored the advantages of quiet in producing a cure, and abhorred all treatment which limited the usual quantity of their daily food. They much preferred to remain in their homes and enjoy the *canao*, or feasting, which, according to them, was the best cure for their infirmities.

But in the end they turned out to be excellent publicity agents. A man who had been operated on for a large benign tumor would say to a friend in the same sad case, "You go down to those American doctors. You go to sleep in a room. When you wake up, it is gone."

When we first went into the mountain country, tribe warred against tribe, all hunting each others' heads. The mutual ferocity and hatred was unbelievable. The people were compelled to huddle into villages for protection from their head-hunting neighbors, and spent hours traveling from their distant fields to their homes. Men from Village A would not even carry our baggage as far as Village B. They would go half way, lay down their loads and retire, whereupon those from Village B would come forward and pick them up.

Almost every house had its head rack, and the number of skulls, which might range from two to several dozen, indicated the social standing and prestige of the owner. Head-hunting was a sort of game; if one village took three heads, the enemy village had to prove its manhood by securing four in return. There were great ceremonies, with speeches and songs, when the heads were carried home in triumph. Any warrior decapitated in one of these encounters was considered to have cast such discredit on his community that he was buried under a trail where his resting place would be trampled upon. The Igorots had a fundamental sporting instinct; they would send timely warning to the village to be attacked, and sometimes met by mutual appointment.

In later years the warriors would stage sham head-hunting battles for us with spear, head axe, and shield of stout wood lashed with rattan. It was a beautiful sight to see with what accuracy they could hurl the wickedly barbed, long steel-tipped spear, but gruesome to watch them manipulate, even in play acting, the terrible head axe, pointed at one end to puncture the enemy's skull, and fashioned and sharpened at the other to cut off his head.

Head-hunting was forbidden by law, but the enforcement of such laws is not easy. In most backward countries, the white man's usual method is to shoot the offenders; we did it chiefly by changing the nature of the rivalry. We substituted athletics, reduced to their simplest terms. Instead of allowing the villagers to cut each others' heads off, we would say to those of Village A, "Choose eight of your strongest men. Village B is going to do the same. Then you will meet in a tug of war and whichever team can pull the other over the line has proved that he belongs to the better village." These contests became life and death matters; in this way the tribesmen sublimated the violent emotions which formerly had found outlet in bloodshed.

I made many solitary trips into the Igorot country, usually forewarned by anxious friends that I would certainly be killed, because I could not tell when the savages would turn upon me. I was going along one day in a remote part of the country when my ears were

136

startled by the most stupendous uproar of yelling and shouting. It sounded ominous, but there was no help for it. I had to go on. These agile runners could have outdistanced me and cut off any possible escape had they been so minded. The only thing to do was to keep quietly on as unconcernedly as possible.

The din increased as I proceeded. Suddenly I emerged into a clearing, but, instead of spears and bolos, my eyes were startled with the sight of bats and balls, and the fantastic picture of a savage, naked save for a string around his middle and a great wire catcher's mask before his face. An inter-village baseball game was in progress. Nobody paid any attention to me; nobody knew or cared whether I had arrived. The teams were fairly matched, and I was soon raised to almost the same pitch of excitement. With one man on first base, a young Igorot came to bat and, with a resounding crack, hit the ball into left field. The man on first started for second, but it seemed almost certain he would be put out. With one accord the cry arose from the throats of the wild men, "Slide, you son of a bitch, slide!"

The Igorots had watched the games of the American soldiers at the hill station, and were letter perfect in their lines.

The mountain tribes had some characteristics and habits sharply distinguishing them from one another. The Igorots, largest in numbers and highest in the scale of development, were still not far removed from barbarism. Their bodies were strong and lithe, but around their tattooed limbs they often wore coiled brass rings or bands, which in time became so tight that they impeded the circulation and made the veins stand out in snakelike ridges. Their teeth were filed to sharp points as a mark of beauty. Their hair was banged on the forehead and long behind, confined in a little basket-woven cap of scarlet, yellow, and brown. When matches were introduced, they were kept with the tobacco in this tiny hat on the back of the head. On their chests hung necklaces of dogs' teeth, saved from their feasts.

On the Benguet Road I often used to see Filipinos, bound for the Saturday dog market at Baguio, each dragging along on a leash six to ten yellowish-brown curs. It was hard to imagine why these lean and hungry beasts, which had never been fed anything beyond the scraps of garbage and refuse they had picked up, were so prized as

137

articles of diet. But the meat hunger in this country which had little game or fish, had given the Igorots a keen appetite for proteins. The favorite method of preparation was to feed the starving animal with rice till his belly bulged full and round. When he could swallow not one grain more, he was promptly killed and, thus neatly self-stuffed, was roasted and eaten. The undigested rice was esteemed the greatest delicacy of all. General Wood remonstrated with the Igorots, and, partly due to their fondness for him, and partly to the tinned salmon with which they were then being supplied, they agreed to give up the practice.

Since meat could not be preserved, whenever a family had an animal to kill, it was the occasion for a *canao*, to which all friends were invited. There was no wastage; viscera and head disappeared with the flesh as everybody gorged. When the head of a family died, according to the Igorot "Share-the-wealth" plan, all his property was given away or consumed. If he were rich, if he had plenty of carabao, pigs, and camotes, the native tubers, there would be a splendid festival which would continue until the fortune was entirely eaten up. The feasting mourners would squat in the house of the deceased, and custom demanded that the corpse be there with them, propped up in a rude chair with a smoke fire going under him to keep him. I have known these affairs to last six months, and in that warm climate the corpse, even in its smoked condition, was likely to become rather high.

The neighboring Ifugaos had an unattractive practice of eating their carabao alive. The beast was turned loose and hamstrung with the first blow so that he could not escape, and then everybody attacked him with bolos, cutting the raw flesh from the living animal. In a few moments, the carabao was chopped to pieces. I have often seen the crowd so frantic with meat lust that the flailing bolos inflicted serious wounds, even cutting off fingers. It was a job for several doctors to sew up the injuries after one of these affairs. Later the practice was forbidden and, instead, the meat was properly slaughtered.

Igorot and Ifugao were obliged to depend for their daily food on camotes and, more particularly, on rice. Both were hard-working agriculturists and cultivated the land to the limit of maximum productivity. Each year during the dry season thousands of acres of rice paddies were planted in the dry river beds, the stones were cleared out. dikes were erected, and earth was carried in by hand, and each year during the rainy season they were destroyed by the floods and all had to be done over again the following year.

The land in the river beds was only a fraction of that required for sustenance. There was little level ground elsewhere, only hill after hill, the soil of which had no adhesion or cohesion, and slipped incessantly. With marvelous engineering ability the tribesmen had terraced the sides of the high, steep slopes, and had led water to them for irrigation, building stone and clay walls from four to ten feet high to keep the rice paddies from being washed away. From the very top of the mountains they stretched, "Down, down, and away over the mighty hills like stairways of the hosts of heaven."

The Ifugaos displayed the greater skill in all building operations. The Igorot house was merely a depression in the ground with logs and stones heaped around and covered with a high grass roof. But the Ifugao dwelling, built on stilts with board floor, wooden sides, and thatched roof, was a remarkable structure. The door posts had interesting designs carved upon them, and invariably the supports had the projecting shoulders to keep the rats and vermin from getting into the granary and store room. Chickens were hung at night in cages, like parrots, from the beams underneath the hut. Below these prowled the scavenging pigs, the dirtiest, leanest, and hungriest specimens I have met with on my travels.

In the Igorot country the girls and unmarried women lived in one large house, where young men of the village sought companions for the *oolug*, or trial marriage. Most of these were successful from the beginning; the partners in the experiment really wanted to see whether they could live happily together, and childlessness was usually the only cause of dissolution of unions made in this way.

As far as I could observe, the Igorots possessed a natural sense of morality. If pregnancy occurred, the mother and father married. Abortion was not popular; those who were compelled to practise it regarded themselves as prostitutes. The Igorots claimed knowledge of a certain vegetable extract which would help to cause abortion during the first two months of pregnancy. But under controlled conditions this drug was tested and proved ineffective.

139

The animistic religion of these tribes was as uncomplicated as their sexual customs. The spirit of life and death was the beneficent Luma-wig who, they believed, appeared to them in ghostlike form. But they had always to propitiate the *anitos*, or spirits, which were embodied in everything alive and inanimate—bird, beast, snake, grass, wood, or stone.

The folklore of the mountains was extremely limited. The most common story was that of an old woman who had two boys. She was never satisfied with anything they did. They brought in all kinds of wood, but she always said it was either too green or too old, and for punishment began depriving them of food. The boys grew thinner and thinner until one day one of them climbed a tree and called to his companion. "I'll get some wood to satisfy the old woman." First he threw down one leg, then another leg, then one arm, then the other arm, then his trunk, and lastly his head. "Take those to the old woman," he said. He had given up his whole body and was now an *anito*. In the form of a bird he directed the other boy by the shortest path back to the house.

To the Western mind this story, in its incompleteness, adorns no tale and points no moral. But it is typical of the simplicity of the primitive mind which demands no explanations.

Far more backward and more difficult to make contact with than Igorot or Ifugao were the Ilongots, who suffered agonies from their superstitions, and propitiated the evil *anitos* with shrines. They were forest dwellers, small in size and numbers, who lived by hunting game with their large bows and arrows, and waged constant war against the more civilized peoples. Lying concealed along traveled trails, hiding behind their light wooden shields of dull brick red, they attacked from ambush, rushing upon the enemy and decapitating them. Worcester called them "a good deal more than half devil, with the balance half child, but peculiarly treacherous, vicious, and savage man."

Penetrating north, further and further from the settled territory, was like pushing back the curtains of time. Each successive tribe was one step backward in progress, and ferocity increased with each onward step.

The small tribe of the Kalingas, Mongolian in appearance, lived on the open spaces and the bare hillsides. Their houses were, however, often nested in trees, and even when on stilts were cleaner and more orderly than those of Igorot or Ifugao, so often grimed with soot and ashes. Their costume was especially colorful; they ornamented their hair with tufts of scarlet feathers, tipped with yellow. Their fighting regalia was as gay as their dress. They had black shields, quite different in shape from those of their neighbors, and brilliantly ornamented with scarlet and yellow, or black and white.

In making the first overtures among them, one of the white Constabulary officers formed a bundle of the lances thrown at him, and sent them back to the Kalingas, suggesting this was not the proper way to treat a would-be friend. Ultimately these tattooed devils, whose name means "enemy," were turned into effective agents for the maintenance of law and order.

Once the Kalingas had accepted the proffered amity, they showed a childlike curiosity in the devices of modernity. One of the officers displayed a phonograph to a Kalinga chief who could not believe that the sound which delighted him came from the machine, but ascribed it to some supernatural origin. When the phonograph was taken away, he dug deep into the ground with his bolo, attempting to locate the pipe which had conducted forth the sub-terrestrial harmonies.

Fiercest of all the mountain tribes, and the last to be persuaded of our peaceful intentions, were the Apayaos. They were supposed to be the remnant of a band of Moro raiders whose wild natures had been attracted by the wildness of the country, and who found as good hunting there as in Mindanao, a thousand miles away. The result had been a strange people, warlike, but fond of fiestas and gaudy clothing.

Forbes took a paternal interest in the welfare and happiness of the five tribes, and each year went on a tour of inspection, accompanied by his aide, Secretary Worcester, in whose department lay the care of the non-Christians, Governor Pack of the Province, the five subgovernors of Benguet, Ifugao, Bontoc, Kalinga, and Apayao, and a few favored visitors. I went along to keep everybody healthy, as well as to inspect medical progress.

The trip, which had to be made on horseback, required about a month. The baggage train would consist of carriers from the local province. Igorots, for example, would meet us at the edge of their territory. They would all pick up their fifty-pound loads and dash off over the hills, rarely following the regular trails, but taking a short route of their own. We never gave a thought to our unlocked baggage thereafter. It was invariably safe when we arrived in camp for the night; in my experience I have found that primitive peoples seldom lie or steal. Not merely was everything in its place, but the carriers with huge banana leaf umbrellas had kept everything dry in a country where rain fell almost daily.

Before Governor Forbes was to make his first inspection trip, he suggested that we ride his thoroughbred polo ponies. I had been over the rough, precipitous trails on other occasions, and was practically certain that I would have difficulty in handling the high-bred nervous animal assigned to me. Two weeks before we started, therefore, following a presentiment, I began to practise mounting and dismounting on the wrong side. By the time we set out I was quite adept at getting on or off either side of the horse.

On such trips I was frequently stopped by urgent requests to visit the sick. Medical attention was still rare; we had not yet had time to establish enough dispensaries in these almost inaccessible mountains. I happened to be delayed one day by one of these professional calls, and the main party went on ahead. While I was hurrying to catch up with them my skittish horse shied at a fluttering leaf, slipped, and left the trail. I leaped from the off side to safety. As he fell, he rolled over and over down the mountainside, loose rock clattering and banging after him. I peered over the edge, never expecting to see him, but by some miracle his forefoot had caught on a vine just at the edge of a sheer drop of hundreds of feet.

I was standing helplessly pitying the dumb animal, when the baggage train came trotting around the bend. Here was a possible solution. The sure-footed Igorots clambered down goatlike to the edge of the precipice and, while five or six held the poor beast, one cut the vine with his bolo, and others hauled the pony by the bridle. He came scrambling up the steep hillside, badly scratched but with no bones broken.

The most forlorn mountain village at news of our approach would be transformed into a bower of bamboo and greenery. The reception parties would come to meet us and escort us in under the triumphal arch with a grand hurrah. Always a *canao* would be held and native dances to the rhythm of an Umpah, Umpah, Umpah, beaten on an instrument that looked like a copper skillet, sometimes assisted by a nose flute or a stringed instrument of bamboo. Although the warriors would seem mirthful and gay at such a reception, we always had them stack their spears, over which two of our party were told off to keep a close eye, because in case of trouble their first movement was toward their weapons.

One of the essentials in the welcoming ceremonies in any Ifugao village was the passing of the *bubud*. To the foreigner this fermented rice drink was a vile tasting mixture, but to refuse the proffered loving cup as it made the rounds was an unforgivable offense. It had to circulate until it was emptied. Furthermore, if anyone entered the company before the ceremony was completed, he had himself to down an entire bumper. I had observed that Dr. Strong always happened to be absent while we were undergoing the ordeal by *bubud*. This made it necessary for everyone else to imbibe just that much more of the fearful stuff. I called Forbes' attention to Strong's defection; he nodded meaningly.

We reached Banaue, the next village, in a driving rain storm, and were received in a fragile lean-to. Dirty muddy water was rushing through a ditch past our feet. Just as the inevitable *bubud* made its appearance the prudent Strong, as was his custom, melted away. Manfully the rest of us kept at the container until finally we saw the bottom. At this point Strong returned unobtrusively and sat down debonair and smiling. The moment Forbes caught sight of him, he turned to the Apo and said, "Dr. Strong has not yet had his *bubud*."

With his dirty toes, the chief immediately retrieved the cannikin from the ditch, poured *bubud* into it, and offered it to Strong with a fine gesture of courtesy.

Strong was now in for it. He would take a swallow of the nauseating stuff, but it would not stay down. It would have been a bitter insult to have spit it out. We gloated fiendishly over his predicament. Large tears appeared in his eyes, and he had many chances to taste it both going down and coming up before it finally stayed down.

Strong was never again late for his *bubud*.

143

Presents had always to be given at a *canao*. Since there were thousands who had to receive them during a trip, this might have seemed a difficult job for anyone but Santa Claus, but these grown-up children were perfectly satisfied with strips of white paper, which they tied gleefully around their black hair. A big strong man might obtain two, or perhaps three, in the grab. Such shouts of joy were never heard even on Christmas morning.

Needles and skeins of colored yarn spread equal delight among the women. At one time Worcester who, because of his regal manner, was regarded with special deference, took along suitcases of such yarn for the women. To handle the expected rush, he used a large cabin into which they were admitted one by one, and passed out by another door. But after half a dozen had secured their yarn, the women, unable to restrain their excitement, stormed the guard, threw themselves into the room and buried the worsted, and Worcester as well, in a tremendous scrimmage.

A number of us rushed to the rescue. Only waving arms and legs could be seen; it seemed quite likely that the Secretary of the Interior would be suffocated. We seized the Igorot ladies bodily and tossed them through the window until we had dug down to where Worcester lay helplessly tangled in the skeins.

By such means as the giving of simple presents and entering into their festivities, we worked toward winning the friendship of the non-Christians, and bringing them law and order. But only little by little could tribal hatreds be broken down. Once when we arrived at Ifugao we found that an Igorot, in an attempt to escape from the jail, had been caught by the Ifugao guard, who had reverted to their ancient tribal hatred and cut him up badly, even breaking some of his bones. Taking no chances, they had then put irons on him.

Dr. Strong, after working over the prisoner for some time, was of the opinion he would probably die within eight hours, and could almost certainly live no more than ten. Since there was no possibility of his escape, Dr. Strong asked to have the irons removed, and laid him on the veranda of the guard house to die in peace. But because the feeling against Igorots was so strong, Captain Galman gave strict orders to the Ifugao sentry that the prisoner was not to be harmed in any way. If an Ifugao were given a direct order by his commanding officer, he would never disobey.

For a time all was quiet. The sentry paced up and down outside the guard house and Governor Pack sat inside doing his accounts. Then suddenly warned by a slight sound, Pack looked up to see the delirious prisoner, given up for dead, coming at him with leveled bayonet. With a convulsive and almost instinctive leap, he was through the window, calling to the sentry, "Shoot! Shoot!"

The sentry paid no attention, but continued placidly walking his beat. Governor Pack dodged in through the door, the "sick man" after him, and in a second leaped through the window again, closely followed by the small dark figure. The foot race continued. Round and round they went—from the garden into the guard house and out again through the window. Governor Pack was a big man and easily winded, so that he could never gain a safe lead over the prisoner who, wounded though he was, kept at his heels. The Governor was staggering when Captain Galman arrived on the run to see what all the noise was about.

"For God's sake, tell the sentry to shoot!" panted Governor Pack.

Captain Galman gave the order. The sentry came to attention, raised his rifle deliberately, and shot the prisoner through the head. Then he put the gun back on his shoulder, and resumed his beat as though nothing at all had happened.

The behavior of these Ifugaos was an exception. In general, the men of that tribe formed the best Constabulary companies, and practically always won the annual rifle competition. When the Americans came, the undress uniform was "back and side go bare, go bare." The government had to consider this prejudice in forming the constabulary. The Ifugaos liked the nice blouses with shiny buttons, but drew the line absolutely at trousers and shoes. As they strode along, it seemed like the march of civilization—strong splay toes gripping the ground firmly, brown legs twinkling in the sun, buttons on their blouses shined according to regulations, uniformed hats jauntily perched on their heads, and Springfields over their shoulders instead of bolos in their hands.

As soon as the health service was well entrenched in the hearts of the people, the educators followed through this opening wedge. The young Igorots learned English rapidly, the school idea spread quickly, and the mountain people often erected their own buildings with free labor. The most promising pupils were sent to Normal School, and are now teaching their own people.

After the schools were established the Church brought up the rear, both Catholic and Protestant, and began to capture pagan souls.

I once met a most disconsolate looking old Igorot sitting by the roadside. He looked so absolutely wretched that I stopped and asked, "What's the matter?"

"I feel so bad," he answered.

"Why? Tell me about it."

"Oh, Bishop Brent is coming here tomorrow."

"He's a nice man," I said reassuringly. "He won't hurt you."

"Oh, yes, I like him too," agreed the Igorot.

"Then what's wrong?"

"When he was here last he gave me a hat and I became an Episcopalian."

"That's fine. It's a good religion."

"Well, a little later a Catholic priest came along and gave me a pair of pants, and I became a Catholic."

"Catholicism is also a very good religion," I assured him.

"But what is Bishop Brent going to say? I don't want to make him unhappy."

The Igorot meditated until finally I asked, "Well, which are you going to choose?"

"I think I'll give the bishop back his hat and the priest his pants, and just be an Igorot again."

Far more primitive than any of the wild tribes were the Negritos. Only in August, during the dry season, was it possible to cross the East Coast barrier reef of Luzon to the country where most of them lived. They had once spread through the Archipelago, but they were a vanishing race, only scattered remnants of them remaining. They were dwarfish, with thick lips, knock knees, and black kinky hair. Many of them had curly beards. Their arms, like those of the African pygmies, were disproportionately long. That they were true Negroes was shown by the one piece cartilage in their spreading noses; all

146

other races have a split cartilage. Even the octoroons show this negroid characteristic, which is regarded as a reliable test for Negro blood.

As far as health work was concerned we could do nothing for the shy, mild, little people any more than we could for the deer in the forest. They spoke neither Spanish nor English—only a gabble of their own. They had no houses; for shelter they ripped the bark off a tree and stood it against another tree. They used bows and arrows smeared with deadly poison, the merest scratch from which was supposed to be fatal. Like the natives of Yap, they made scar patterns by cutting their skins with sharpened pieces of bamboo and rubbing dirt into the open wounds. They were wonderful woodsmen but good for little else. The Filipinos had tried to use them as house servants, but they were hard to domesticate. Though they did not slave-raid themselves, these improvident people, when they suffered from hunger, used to sell their children into slavery. Sometimes they came into the cultivated country during the harvest season and worked in return for rice; otherwise they lived on game, fruit, and roots.

A small colony of them had settled back of the quarantine station on the slopes of Mount Mariveles, where on Sunday afternoons I used often to go for a stroll in the hills. On one occasion I had proceeded but a mile or two along a trail when I met a little naked Negrito girl about ten years old.

"Hello," I said without thinking.

"Hello," she responded with an American accent.

I did not believe I could have heard aright. To test my ears I said, "What would you like to have?"

"A chocolate ice cream soda," she answered without the slightest hesitation.

I would have granted this simple wish had it been possible. Instead, I inquired further and found she had been one of the exhibits in the St. Louis Exposition of 1903, and there had learned English so that she could speak it as well as any American child.

One amusing old fellow in her tribe used to call himself a chief, but his sole distinguishing claim to such rank was an ancient silk hat, his only article of clothing, given to him by a Spanish official. It always remained a mystery how he kept it dry and prevented it from molding in a country where dampness and heat were so incessant. But in the course of years it became tattered and torn. Worcester was so delighted by the chief's unusual costume and afraid that it would not last indefinitely, that he brought a new silk hat from the States and presented it to the Negrito.

The hat must long since have passed to the old chief's descendants, but to this day I have no doubt that its lucky owner is accorded a position of honor and dignity among the shy Negrito survivors of the Mariveles Hills.

During my first years in the Philippines I had little to do with the Southern Islands of Mindanao and Jolo and the other Mohammedan lands. They were administered by the Army, and their health service was also under military control. It was always the endeavor of the civil régime to extend its sway to these Islands as soon as they could be pacified. This was difficult, because the Spaniards had been shooting them for several hundred years, and our Army and Navy was similarly engaged for over ten. Pershing had "subdued" them, and Wood had led a great attack to the center of Mindanao. Each time the Yakan Moros, more savage, more cruel and more aggressive than the Ilongots, had retaliated in kind.

The chief potentate to whom all the *dattos* were subject was the Sultan of Sulu, who lived on the island of Jolo, but was also Sultan of Borneo under British jurisdiction. The remnants of his former power could only be exercised over petty offenses and religion. In spite of being subsidized both from Philippine and British sources, he was always notoriously hard up.

On one of my visits I was accompanied by Professor John Mulholland of Columbia University who, in his lighter moments, practised magic and was expert at this art beyond most professionals, always maintaining that it consisted solely of trickery. Together we paid a call on the potentate and, in order to entertain him, I asked the Professor to work some of his magic. He agreed and went through the usual rigmarole of making things disappear and reappear, and then turned to the Sultan with the remark, "I can't possibly understand why money should be so scarce in Jolo when even the air is full of it."

He thereupon took off his coat, rolled up his sleeves, and pulled silver dollars out of the air until the floor was littered with them. The Sultan's eyes popped so far out of his head that they could have been knocked off with a stick. To think that the air was so full of money and he who needed it so much had not been able to discover it! He was inarticulate with amazement, and I do not know to this day what he really thought of the performance.

It was not until we changed our policy to one of peace that any real progress was made among the Moros. In 1914 the change from military to civil government was finally brought about, and Frank W. Carpenter was put in charge. As Governor he showed the same sagacity as he had displayed when councillor to the successive Governor Generals of the Philippines. Tremendous progress was made toward pacifying this race of warriors under his administration; the bolo and the rifle were replaced by the hoe and the plow. Much time was also spent trying to organize schools to which the Moro women could go, but the men always retorted, "We don't want our women educated."

The Moro health service was brought under the central office in Manila and reorganized by Colonel E. L. Munson, who had done so much to help formulate the sanitary laws of Manila. Hospitals and dispensaries were established, and produced the same calming and civilizing effect as among the wild tribes. Colonel Munson was succeeded by Dr. Jacobo Fajardo, who carried the work yet further and accomplished it so well that he eventually became Director of Health of the Philippines.

With three hundred islands to inspect, scattered in a huge thousand mile crescent from the tip of Luzon in the North to the Celebes Sea in the South, much of my time was inevitably spent upon the water. Some of the Islands—Cebu, Mindoro, Negros, Samar, Leyte, and Panay—were large and easily accessible. Others seemed lost in the immensity of endless sea and sky. Once a year only the mail boat went to the rocky Batanes, tiny Christian outposts anchored firmly in the windswept Bashi Channel. The tidal maelstrom which separated them from Formosa rushed by with such fury that no swimmer and no boat propelled by oars could make headway against it.

One of this isolated group, only ten miles in diameter, was the curious and remote coral islet of Ibayat. It formed almost a perfect circle, cupped around a lake in the center which furnished the few thousand inhabitants with water. Ibayat rose sheer from the sea; an ocean liner could steam close to its edge and still find no anchorage.

Fierce as was the tide below, the wind on top was even fiercer. The houses had to be tucked half into the ground, and the roofs fastened on securely. In some areas, each stalk of sugar cane had to be pegged to the ground.

There was no break in the circular rim; not even a goat could clamber up. The island provided unexcelled grazing land, and the herdsmen had devised a method of exporting cattle which, although it seemed cruel to Western eyes, served its purpose. The animals were driven to the edge of the precipitous cliff and then ruthlessly prodded into space. I have watched them drop with helpless legs asprawl, all the while bawling in mortal terror. There would be a splash and a thud, and a splash and a thud; then bobbing heads would emerge and the poor frightened creatures would swim madly in all directions. Rowboats from the steamer would close in to pick up the short ropes previously tied around their horns, and when five or six had been towed within reach of the steamer's winch, one by one they would be hauled aboard by the horns. As many as three or four hundred would be taken away on a trip.

At rare intervals I paid a visit to inspect the work of the resident medical officer. To admit the visitor, the Ibayat hermits, like the monks of Athos, let down a basket dangling at the end of a long vine. We maneuvered underneath and, what with the rocking of the boat and the swaying of the basket, almost simian agility was required to scramble in. I clutched its sides firmly as it swung perilously back and forth; the vine stem seemed a fragile hold to life. I watched the top of the cliff slowly approach and could not prevent a sigh of relief when the basket bumped on solid ground.

CHAPTER 11.   FOR THEIR OWN
GOOD

THE Bureau of Health was like the tree of life, Yggdrasill. Worcester, Forbes, and I were the three Norns who assiduously watered its roots, which pushed their way around stones and through clay into the not too clean earth of Filipino existence, so that it might reach from the Hell that was to the Heaven that might be.

Necessarily we had to invade the rights of homes, commerce, and parliaments. We had to guard against the entrance of dangerous communicable diseases by strict measures, even when they conflicted with convenience or personal necessity, and segregate the cases of leprosy which might endanger the health of the greater numbers. Hospitals for the sick had to be built, and doctors and nurses trained. The physical welfare of the morally ill had to be cared for. The helpless insane and orphans had to be provided with homes. Births had to be recorded and resting places found for the dead. What the people ate, what they drank, where they went, and how they traveled had to be safeguarded. Finally, the great majority had to be taught how to arm themselves against disease and death.

But always we tried to tangle the threads of Filipino lives as little as possible.

When we arrived the hospitals were of the most primitive type. There was not a good operating room in the Islands and no laboratory facilities. Modern medicine had not penetrated far. To remedy this condition Worcester, in 1900, had formulated a plan on a noble scale to build a hospital, a medical school, and a laboratory of science all in one integral group—the medical center idea adopted in the United States so much later.

After the Bureau of Science was started in 1901, the next step was to train doctors. The ancient Santo Tomas University already had a medical school attached to it, but it was inadequate. In 1905 we secured an appropriation for a government institution with American curricular requirements, which later was to become part of the government-owned University of the Philippines. When the Church school saw the more modern one in operation, it raised its standards so that, in addition to turning out our own graduates, we were, by our example, assuring a further supply of well-trained young men. The Filipinos made excellent physicians, once their dislike of dirtying their hands was overcome.

But the project was not yet completed. Session after session and year after year Worcester presented to the legislative body a request for money with which to build a modern hospital in Manila. As often as he came away disappointed, he returned to the charge. After eight years of steady pounding he was rewarded with success. The Philippine General Hospital was authorized in 1908 and completed in 1910.

Hospitals are too often bare and bleak. We tried to make ours, built on the pavilion system, open on all sides, cool, pleasant, and cheerful as well as practical. By polished molave and media aguas we endeavored to soften its white austerity. For the first time hospital beds were equipped with wheels; they could be rolled on to the spacious verandas so that the eyes of convalescents could be made glad by the sight of royal palms and the gorgeous acacias, which twice yearly made the grounds a sheet of flame. What the patients ate at home was not good for them, and we had no wish to make them adopt our food, which they did not like; we handed over the problem of modifying their diet to imported dieticians.

But a fine hospital was not enough. The imported American nurses would soon go home and it was essential to have Filipinas to take their places. In the effort to train them, we came up at once against the strongly rooted social custom which decreed that women should do no manual work. My constant endeavor was to interest the Filipinas in health work; through them we could reach the men also. Rarely did a Filipino take any action without first consulting his wife. She held the keys to whatever there was of value in the house. She was the business manager and, as a rule, she was the more intelligent. The man cooked, washed the dishes, made beds, and also labored in the fields. Hospital nursing was foreign to the Filipina of the upper social strata. This prejudice had to be overcome.

I first persuaded five girls at the Normal School to include a course of nursing which in the beginning was to be entirely theoretical. They seemed to enjoy learning out of a book how much of this or that drug should be given for this or that ailment, but luring them into practising their knowledge was another matter. Only after much cajolery on my part did they consent to wander around the wards of the hospital for a few hours each day. But then they struck. It took candy and flowers to bring them back, and no sooner had I shepherded them into the hospital than they walked out again. After this had happened three times, I effected a compromise by installing a small sick bay in the Normal School, where a few students would pretend to be the patients. Half-heartedly for a few days the girls practised bed making, giving baths, and dishwashing, and then declared, "This is servants' work. We'll have no more to do with it."

At this turn of affairs, I threw up my hands. Not even Miss Mary Coleman, who was in charge, could, by any form of persuasion, get the young ladies back. Finally, in a moment of inspiration, she announced, "We'll have to write a play."

"But I don't know anything about playwrighting."

In the end, however, we composed a remarkable drama. I supplied the technical details and Miss Coleman the plot. We engaged professional actresses to play the roles of the nurses, who were all co-starred.

The performance was attended solely by invitation and sparkled with social tone. The wives of the highest ranking officials were all patronesses, and the tickets were distributed to a specially selected group, including our former pupils. The play, which was produced before a capacity audience, proved an unbelievable success. Crisis followed crisis. Almost every instant a situation arose where a nurse saved the day. Whenever one of the numerous heroines would rush in and snatch half a dozen lives from the jaws of death, loud and enthusiastic applause would shake the hall.

The next morning the five girls were back again, this time to finish their preliminary course.

As soon as it seemed safe, I ventured to send them to the hospital, with the intention of having them practise two hours a day in the wards. The morning after their first experience, I was sitting at my office desk when the attendant brought in a sheaf of cards. The briefest glance informed me that I was in for a mass attack from the parents of the girls.

As they stormed through the door, the leader said, "Our daughters have been humiliated and disgraced. We are taking them home at once."

"Why?" I inquired innocently.

"My Rosita was asked to go into a room where a man was in bed. She never can hold up her head in society again."

I tried reasoning, but with no success. Nothing I could say would cause these offended parents to change their minds. I then played my last card.

"I've been very patient with you," I said. "Now I'm tired of all this nonsense. Our American women are just as fine as yours, and they take up nursing careers without loss of dignity or self-respect. If you're so far behind in the scale of civilization that you can't realize this, take your daughters out of the school at once. I don't want them there any longer. I've given them the opportunity to learn an honorable profession. But you're just exactly what your critics—"

"Wait a moment," they interrupted in concert, "let's consider this further."

"No! Not for a second," I asserted firmly. "Take the girls away."

They began to plead with me. Their arguments turned to entreaty.

"No!" I said haughtily. "There's nothing more you need say."

But they said much more. Only after an hour's ardent effort were they able to persuade me not to dismiss their daughters.

The next year the class increased to thirty. Finally we had to make provision for two hundred. We distributed application blanks among the schools, which were to select the most desirable girls. Not only the chosen ones put in an appearance, but an additional one hundred accompanied them. I was pleased with their enthusiasm, and told them I genuinely regretted we had no room for the extra ones.

FOR THEIR OWN GOOD

All Filipinos, men, women, and children, petition the Legislature when anything displeases them. The hundred rejected girls appealed to the Philippine Congress. They said I was refusing them an education, and demanded entrance to the school.

The Legislature subpoenaed me, read charges against me, and intimated that my resignation was in order.

When this ceremony was over, I asked, "Will you hand me that digest of laws over there?"

In the course of my professional duties I had been obliged to familiarize myself thoroughly with the volume in question, because such contingencies were apt to occur at any moment. I flipped the pages to the paragraph I wanted and read it aloud. It was to the effect that any public officer who incurred an expenditure not specifically authorized by the Legislature would be subject to fine and imprisonment.

I closed the book with a bang, laid it down, and struck an attitude. "I am acting in accordance with your own law," I told them. "If I admit these girls, I shall have to feed and house them. You have given me no money for this purpose, and I refuse to disobey the law!"

"We see that, we see that," they chorused eagerly. And immediately a law was passed appropriating the money necessary to include the extra hundred students.

In a way the question raised by the Legislature was most gratifying. It showed that nurses were making a place for themselves in the life of the community and that there was a desire on the part of the law-making body to give them protection. The long struggle to establish nursing in the Philippines on a sound basis with standards that would compare with the world's best now began to look as though it could be won. In this I was not only thinking of the Philippines but other countries in the Orient. There was hope that the sick of China, Japan, Siam, Java, and other Eastern nations could have much more adequate care. A career was in prospect for the women of the Orient through which they might have an important part in alleviating unnecessary suffering. If nursing on a proper basis could be established in the Philippines there was much reason to believe that it could be done in other Asiatic countries.

155

Once the nurses had accommodated themselves to Western ideas, they worked faithfully and fulfilled our highest expectations. They were invaluable because they knew the local language, customs, and prejudices far better than we, and, therefore, could teach the people how to apply the sanitary regulations. During a major outbreak of bacillary dysentery at Cebu they went from house to house, showed the inhabitants how to dispose safely of bodily excreta, sterilize water, prepare food, and demonstrated the importance of clean hands; dysentery disappeared almost in their wake.

In the midst of our worst cholera epidemic four young Filipina nurses not yet graduated volunteered for duty at the San Lazaro cholera hospital. With the dead and dying all around them they performed coolly and capably some of the most disgusting services that could be demanded of any human being, and with full knowledge that any slip in disinfecting themselves would change them in a few hours from cholera nurses to cholera victims.

Many of the graduates ultimately came to this country to study higher nursing. Some passed the United States Civil Service examinations with high marks and occupied nursing positions in America with great credit, and some returned home to teach in newly established nursing schools. Many of the nurses became adept public speakers, and were powerful politically. Whenever I wanted to have a particular health measure enacted into law expeditiously and inexpensively, I would request a committee of these women to talk to the legislators.

Until Filipino doctors also could be trained I necessarily had to depend to a tremendous extent on my American staff. These were of many types and gradations, but one and all supported me loyally. Efficient in a medical way, but one of the shyest and most retiring men I have ever known, was one of my quarantine officers, Dr. Turnipseed. It was the custom when going on board an incoming vessel to call on the captain first to have him sign the quarantine papers. One morning Dr. Turnipseed boarded a big ship from the Pacific Coast, went to the bridge, and knocked timidly on the captain's door.

"Come in," commanded a big gruff voice.

Turnipseed edged through the door and said apologetically, "I am Dr. Turnipseed."

"Well, you haven't anything on me. I'm Captain Garlic."

FOR THEIR OWN GOOD

Many of my doctors later attained eminence in the medical world, but one of the greatest geniuses among them achieved no such reputation. Dr. Gilbert I. Cullen could do more things well than anyone I have ever known. Whenever any place was mentioned, he had been there; whenever anybody was in a tight spot, Cullen was able to extricate him. His feats of legerdemain sounded so improbable that many people considered his experiences fabricated. But I saw him often in action, and I am sure the things I did not see must also have been true.

Cullen had come out in 1899 with the Philippine Volunteers, and had served in Hell Roaring Jake Smith's contingent at Samar, where the insurrection was raging most violently. All the signal men had been killed in the initial fight, and there was no way of communicating with Manila. Somebody familiar with Cullen's versatility suggested he might be able to use a telegraph key.

"Oh, yes, I can telegraph," Cullen admitted readily. For a month he alternated clicking out messages in Morse with dressing wounds and tending the sick. The Army was so grateful that a line was diverted to his tent from the main cable, through which all the news of the world came to him. It was always possible that Cullen, in the course of satisfying his curiosity, might stumble upon information of value.

Cullen served the Army well not only by his varied knowledge but also by his physical courage. When it was almost certain death for any American to set foot in the Pulajan country of Samar, the Constabulary asked him, because he had already familiarized himself with the native dialects, to undertake a mission into the interior. He went alone, and by methods of his own arranged for the surrender of the rebels.

When Cullen came under my jurisdiction I appointed him Health Officer of Samar, where his really thorough knowledge of medicine coupled with his unrivaled knowledge of the Island made him invaluable. His intimate acquaintance with Army affairs often stood us in good stead. One day he walked unannounced into my office at Manila. "What are you doing here?" I asked. "I didn't give you any orders to leave Samar. You're supposed to be there attending to your job."

Government appropriations were meagre, as Cullen was well aware. "I know how important bargains are to you," he replied. "There's going to be a big clearing out sale of Army medical supplies. I wanted to tell you ahead of time."

"How do you know?" I asked.

All Cullen would vouchsafe was, "I've ways of finding out."

That same noon I met the Quartermaster in charge of Army supplies and remarked, "I hear you're having a big sale of medical articles."

"Oh, no, we're not having any sale," he assured me.

I sent for Cullen. "I've just seen the Quartermaster and he says there isn't going to be any sale. I assume you had some private reason for coming up here. The best thing you can do is to get back as fast as possible."

"You'll get notice pretty soon," Cullen replied confidently.

Two days later the Quartermaster approached me. "Do you remember you asked me about a medical supplies sale? Well, I don't know how you found out, but we've just had a cable this morning telling us to clear them out."

Thereafter I believed in the accuracy of Cullen's information, though I never did find out how he obtained it.

Cullen had also had training as a lawyer. He was able to plead eloquently in court, and often defended the poor without thought of a fee, usually winning his case. But whatever his extra-medical activities might be, he never allowed them to interfere with his work. He was one of those rare individuals who require only a few hours of sleep; he did his reading and experimenting at night. Furthermore, he was so proficient mechanically that he was able to start a stubborn fire engine when Iloilo was burning up, and even build himself a radio set out of odds and ends when he was confined to a hospital bed.

After Cullen had served at Samar for some time, I had him transferred to the laboratory of the Bureau of Science with the idea of having him acquaint himself with the more recent developments in science. He had been there no more than a week when the head of the department asked me, "Why did you send Cullen here? He knows more laboratory procedure than we do."

FOR THEIR OWN GOOD

At another time a plan for the Coast and Geodetic Survey of the Islands was being developed by George Rockwell Putnam, who wanted to determine the exact spot in the Philippines on which to base his survey. This problem in triangulation was extremely difficult, and an expert in geodesy was brought from the United States.

Dr. Cullen happened to drift into the Survey office at Manila and asked inquisitively, "What are you fellows doing?"

"We're trying to plot a base position," he was told.

"Let me see what I can do," said Cullen.

With some merriment the data were handed over to him, but he surprised the experts by rolling up his shirt sleeves and setting efficiently to work. Their amazement grew as he completed step after step and arrived at the correct solution.

Cullen was past master of practically all branches of higher mathematics. A coast guard cutter was once about to leave Samar when the officers decided they needed a purgative. Somehow they confused a bottle of bichloride of mercury with Epsom salts; several died and the others were completely incapacitated. Nobody was left on the bridge. When Cullen volunteered the information that he had officer's papers, he was thankfully told to take command, and he navigated the ship safely back to Manila.

Cullen was always immaculately dressed. When everybody else was hot and untidy, he was clean and cool. Dr. George Shattuck of Boston went with me on one of my leper collecting trips. When we were off the East Coast of Samar, he said, "I'm terribly embarrassed, but I've left my toothbrush behind. I don't suppose there's any possible way of getting one here."

The place was remote and the nearest shop many miles away. But I automatically said, "Cullen will be able to take care of you."

Cullen did not let me down. To my question he replied, "Certainly, I have a new prophylactic brush right here," and reached into his dufflebag.

"How about some chocolates? Got some of those too?" I asked jocularly.

"Would you like a box?" he asked, and, like a magician producing rabbits from a hat, he handed out a pound carton.

One of the inevitable duties of any department of health is the compilation of vital statistics, which are an indispensable measuring rod of sanitary progress. Before we took charge in Manila not over forty percent of the births there were recorded, and the percentage was far lower in the provinces. By persistent efforts we gradually collected the necessary data. Sanitary inspectors on their rounds would make inquiries as to whether there had been any new births, and baptismal information was obtained from churches.

The cemeteries proved to be one of the most vexatious of all our administrative problems. In Spanish times the practice had been to deposit bodies in rented graves or in leased niches, the lease period being usually five years. When the time expired, the well-to-do would renew their leases or remove the bodies to their final resting places in the crypt. But unless another cash payment were made the bones were thrown out.

When the Americans came to the Islands their first messages to the homeland told of the ossuaries, or human bone piles, back of every church, and many a femur and tibia found its way to the United States as a relic from this far away and very odd country. In less than two years all the bones in the ossuary of Paco cemetery disappeared. Sometimes a section of a skeleton would turn up under queer circumstances, and we were never quite sure whether a murder had taken place.

No records seem to have been kept as to the exact location of bodies in the majority of cemeteries, which were scattered helter skelter over Manila, and mourners not infrequently had to witness the uncovering of remains in the same graves in which their own dead were about to be laid. Five or more bodies had sometimes been interred in one grave.

Governor Taft was amazed and distressed at the condition of the cemeteries, and had a law passed which compelled each one to secure a license. Being able to think of no other agency, he put the enforcement of the ordinance into the hands of the Health Department, even though the problem was one of esthetics and not of disease.

We had to examine each cemetery and listen to complaints which, in some cases, led us into legal complexities, and many times into conflict with the people, a situation we were most anxious to avoid.

As the schism in the Church proceeded, the followers of Father

Aglipay were not allowed to bury their dead in the Roman Catholic cemeteries. Constant fights and reprisals took place. An Aglipay health officer would declare a Catholic cemetery insanitary and close it. A Catholic of the old faith would complain to me there was grease on the top of his well, which must have come from some grave in the Aglipay cemetery near his house.

Whenever we had to close a filled cemetery, the Church had to find new ground. Formerly the government had supported the Church; now fees had to be collected directly, so much each for baptism, marriage, and burial. The Filipinos were not used to paying fees, and paid them seldom if ever; the priests had very little to get along on.

An Aglipay cleric one morning came to my office, and begged for a permit to bury a rich parishioner whose family ardently desired to have him placed in a cemetery I had ordered closed.

"I'm sorry I can't open this cemetery for you," I said. "It's far too crowded already."

"Oh, I should so like to eat some meat," he moaned. "I've had nothing but rice and dried fish for so long a time. You could make it possible for me to get some meat. All I need is a temporary permit for this one burial, and I could get some meat again."

I could not make an exception for him, but compromised by buying him a meal with meat included.

I not only had to watch over the cemeteries, but also concern myself with allied activities. There was an undertaker in Manila named Dell who had erected a new and first-class establishment for which he had to get a license from the Municipal Board. But all was not plain sailing, and he sought aid.

"You've helped me with the plans for my mortuary, and you know I've fulfilled all the health requirements. But the Board is going to vote me down. I don't know what I'm going to do. All my money is invested in this, and I'll lose it all."

"How do you know you're going to be turned down?" I asked.

"They've got a petition signed by a thousand people saying my establishment would be inimical to business and bad for trade."

"How much time have you before the hearing?"

"Only three days."

"That's time enough. Write yourself a flowery petition. Tell how your establishment would enhance values and be an asset to the city. Show how desirable it would be. Make it elegant."

"But all the people in the neighborhood have signed the other petition."

"Get their signatures first of all and then go further afield."

Here was an opportunity to test the truth of the current belief that anybody in the Philippines could get any petition signed for anything pro or con. There was a story of how, far back in Spanish times, charges had once been filed with the Governor General against a Provincial Governor. When shown the scroll with thousands of signatures affixed, the latter had asked, "May I have a week to answer?"

At the time specified he had returned with a long petition signed by twice as many people, which read, "To our personal knowledge the Governor General is a son of a jackass."

Dell accepted my advice and had his lawyer draw up a beautiful petition which he circulated. Every shopkeeper and householder whose signature was on the other paper was equally complacent when asked to affix his name to the new one.

At the hearing Dell's opponents read a petition signed by a thousand citizens against granting him a license. His lawyer thereupon rose and read a petition in favor of granting him a license, signed not only by the thousand who had endorsed the other, but by many others as well.

Dell obtained his license.

As a person wielding much authority over many activities, I was constantly being importuned for favors of one type or another. A gravestone manufacturer once came to find out whether I would let him print his advertisements on the back of the official death certificates; in return he promised to cut and erect me the finest tombstone in the cemetery.

I also had the usual difficulties in warding off ambitious salesmen from the States. A shrewd Irish American named Kelly, realizing it was a problem for our small staff to be in all necessary places at once, was constantly after me to buy some of the new-fangled motor bicycles for our sanitary inspectors. His argument was that they would be able to cover more ground with these contraptions. He had the proverbial pertinacity of his kind, and it was not easy to avoid him.

On my way to lunch at the Army and Navy Club I used to pass by the old Luneta, which during the late afternoon and early evening was filled with carriages and promenaders. One noon as I came across the park, practically deserted during the siesta hour, Kelly hailed me from his motorcycle.

"Please give me a minute. I want to show you how well it runs."

I had done some amateur bicycle racing, and was naturally interested. He inveigled me on to the seat. I was admiring the gadgets and fiddling with them when, without meaning to, I pressed something, and the thing started off like a shot. I had never been on one before, knew nothing about it, and had not the faintest idea how to stop it. All I could do was to guide it around and around the Luneta.

Kelly shouted directions at me, but the machine was making such a racket that I could hear nothing as I tore past. He rushed across the oval to intersect me, cupped his hands and yelled at the top of his lungs, but still to no avail. I sped along wondering how much gas there was in the tank and praying that nothing would get in my way before it was gone. I lapped the Luneta at least ten times, while Kelly shuttled back and forth, his face getting redder and redder, still screaming futile directions.

Suddenly a carromata loomed ahead. I swung sharply to one side to avoid it, and in so doing I happened to twist the handlegrip. To my amazement the machine increased its dizzy speed. This astounded me. In my bicycling days it had been essential to have the grips firmly cemented, and it would never have occurred to me that a grip could serve as a control on a motorcycle. But such was obviously the case.

Feeling safe in the knowledge that I had mastered the infernal machine, I thought I would have a little fun. I turned the rubber grip until I was going sixty or seventy miles an hour. Kelly was nearly crazy. There was no use now in his racing back and forth; he merely jumped frantically up and down.

After three or four turns, I took pity and pulled up to a neat stop right beside him.

"These things are very nice," I said as I dismounted nonchalantly and strolled on toward my lunch.

The Bureau of Health depended to a great extent on the Bureau of Science for aid of all sorts. Worcester's greatest achievement had been to assemble under one administration, as far as practicable, all the scientific work of the government, building up in one unit the most modern organization in the laboratory field that any country had ever evolved. Under the able direction of Dr. Paul Freer, discoveries were made which are even now just beginning to be utilized elsewhere in the world.

The Bureau of Science Biological Laboratory performed all the microscopy for the general hospitals, and diagnosed specimens of all kinds. Four hundred thousand rats were examined for plague bacilli. A routine examination was made for all cholera carriers. When a cure for any disease was announced the laboratory would test its value. Quack native remedies were often advertised as being cure-alls, and the people were apt to have more faith in them than in foreign importations. For any type of experimentation prisoners from Bilibid would always volunteer, because they would receive perquisites and even have their sentences commuted if they were to incur serious risks.

All vaccines or serums developed in any part of the world against disease were manufactured at the laboratory. Diphtheria antitoxin and the Pasteur treatment for hydrophobia were kept in readiness. Over two million units of vaccine against smallpox were made annually.

In addition to the routine at least half the laboratory was working on independent research. Extensive studies were made for eradicating the locusts which caused hundreds of thousands of dollars damage to agriculture annually, and years were spent in developing a rinderpest serum. Dr. Marshall Barber investigated the role played by cockroaches and other insects as carriers of cholera, bacillary dysentery, and typhoid. Dr. E. L. Walker worked more than a year on amoebic dysentery, and succeeded in differentiating pathogenic from nonpathogenic types. Over three thousand examinations were made of Philippine water supplies to determine their biological content.

The botanists combed the Islands, and for the first time classified the flowers and plants and studied the insect pests and the fungi, the forest products, fibres, seeds, dyes, and tans. The entomologists studied methods of exterminating mosquitoes, flies, and termites. They also conducted extensive research on the possibility of introducing silk culture, though the industry never gained a foothold because of too keen competition from China and Japan. The ornithologists collected the common forest birds, and showed which ones were injurious and which helpful. Worcester himself discovered the nesting place of the frigate bird, an enormous creature like the albatross. The Island of Bancanan was thickly covered with these strange birds, which refused to give the human trespasser the right of way, biting when any attempt at force was made.

The *Philippine Journal of Science* became rapidly one of the leading publications of the world in its field. The central scientific library, the largest East of Suez, was accessible to anybody. In the museum were assembled the tools, weapons, agricultural implements, costumes, and basketry of the various peoples. One of the most valuable collections of pictures in the world was gathered by the photographic department. A proof of each was filed so that the negative could be procured for use at a moment's notice. The wild peoples were photographed at regular intervals, showing the stage of civilization to which they had arrived year by year.

The chemical laboratory also had a vital function to perform. Ten thousand samples of cement were tested to see which would best stand the tropical quakes and downpours. Paints were tried out against Philippine sun and rain. The first steps were taken in developing industries. Soils were analyzed, copra production improved, gums, perfumes, and essential oils tested and experiments made in the extraction of sugar from the nipa palm.

The Food and Drugs Act in the Philippines could not be enforced until definite knowledge became available; first, of the effects of certain substances upon the human organism, and, second, until laboratory methods for examining foods had been still further perfected. But it was obvious that lime juice adulterated with five percent sulphuric acid, jellies with formaldehyde, peas with copper, cheap flavoring extracts with wood alcohol, and coloring matter with arsenic or mercury were highly deleterious to health. Moreover, the people were not being fairly treated when they bought butter with rennet added to increase the weight, or baking powder with starch added up to fifty percent, or lard with water added up to twenty-four percent, and mixed perhaps with starch, lime, alum, and salt. Sausage often contained nitric acid. Many shipments of milks contained formalin and other preservatives which might readily have been responsible for much of the indigestion among children.

Ice cream made in Manila had almost everything in it except what the name indicated. When brought to book the dealers claimed it was impossible to make proper ice cream in a tropical climate. Such claims were promptly disproved by the chemists, who demonstrated beyond question that good ice cream could be made as well in Manila as anywhere else in the world.

The chemists of the Bureau of Science were exhaustive in their search for these adulterated foods. One of them determined, for example, that certain imported lard contained cocoanut oil. Although Armour & Company denied categorically that it had been adulterated by them, our chemist stuck to his guns. It finally developed that the lard in question had been rendered from Oregon hogs fed on copra, and that the cocoanut oil globules had been deposited by nature in the tissues of live hogs.

When another of the chemists stated he had discovered salicylic acid in Hires root beer, that company almost burst with indignation. They said their chemists were as competent as any in America, and they could certify on their honor that their extract contained no salicylic acid. However, it turned out oil of wintergreen had been included among the flavorings, and when the extract had been shipped through the hot tropics the wintergreen had been chemically transformed into salicylic acid.

Then formaldehyde was found in Swiss strawberry jam. The Swiss said this was impossible, but it eventuated that certain sugars in the strawberries of Switzerland had the peculiar quality of turning into formaldehyde under the influence of heat.

The Chinese were naturally the great food importers, and controlled ninety percent of the business in Manila. They knew that a hundred centavos made a peso and paid more attention to the one which they did not have than to the ninety and nine which they had safely hidden. When we found adulterated articles on their shelves, we had to seize and destroy them. They meant to be law abiding, but they could not understand what we were trying to get at. In his bewilderment, one of them approached me and exclaimed plaintively, "The green the peas, the green the peas, the green the peas," over and over again. It was hopeless to try to explain to him that the peas contained copper.

We made life fairly miserable for the poor Chinese. On one occasion I stopped a shopkeeper on the street. Divining from my uniform that I was an official of some sort, without a word he brought out from under his shirt the leather bag in which he carried his valuables. First he presented me with his certificate of residence. I shook my head. Then out came his immigration certificate. I assured him I did not want to see it. He kept hauling out more papers—the cedula which proved he had paid his head tax. I shook my head again. He produced his merchants' tax receipt, looking up hopefully at me. Again he was wrong. I had given up trying to stop him by this time. His plague inoculation certificate did not satisfy me, nor did the license which showed he owned a stall in the market. Finally, he pulled out his vaccination card, which happened to be what interested me at the moment. I had never realized before what a bale of papers the poor Chinese had to carry about with him in the Philippines to prove his right to exist.

At the time the civil régime was instituted in Manila, there were two hundred or more places where the Chinese could buy a pipe and table space for twenty cents. Their contention was that opium, as they used it, was no more detrimental to their health than whiskey and soda to a foreigner. But while they were satisfied with the drowsiness and visions they obtained from their tiny pipes, the Americans and Europeans, when they took up the drug, wanted the full effect. In the fear that the Filipinos might become addicts to the opium habit unless some means could be found of preventing its spread, a commission was appointed. After studying the opium question throughout the East, it recommended that the drug be excluded entirely from the Islands two years from that date.

The first day of March, 1908, was "Black Sunday" for opium habitués. The truth and seriousness of the situation finally dawned on those who had sinned away their two years of grace between the passage of the law and its going into effect. The behavior of the victims in the face of the government's determination to save them by legal force would truly characterize them as fiends. The term fiend is used liberally by the laity, but becomes appropriate when a victim is deprived of the drug.

In sheer desperation the sufferers sought the hospital treatment provided by the government. The rush was so great and the task so hard that the San Juan de Dios Hospital, which had previously cared for drug addicts, asked to be released on the ground that it lacked proper facilities for the accommodation and restraint of so large a number of frenzied patients. Accordingly, to meet the emergency, the government made ready several wards of the new insane department of the San Lazaro Hospital. There the addicts fought, screamed, threatened, and sulked until they realized that the government meant business, when they quietly submitted.

Experience demonstrated that the opium habit was not particularly difficult to treat, especially among the smokers. Those who took the drug by mouth experienced more inconvenience, and those who were in the habit of taking it hypodermically suffered considerably. We used the Towne treatment as recommended by Dr. Alexander Lambert. Severe as it was, it was justified by the results. As soon as the craving for opium was gone, we proceeded to build up the patients. How many relapsed after being discharged from the hospital was, of course, unknown, but many habitués professed profound relief at being cured. Alcoholism could also be similarly treated. It gave me great satisfaction to pick up beachcombers and by the same method turn them once more into self-respecting citizens.

Upon the exclusion of opium and the closure of the public resorts, the price of opium promptly went up, which made it prohibitive for Filipino purses. Moreover, the Chinese were not particularly anxious to force the habit on the Filipinos, once they had to depend on illegal sources for their own supplies.

The Chinese are, without doubt, the world's most adept smugglers, and they soon devised ways and means of satisfying their simple needs. We were always finding opium in the most unheard-of places. One day, in my routine examination of imported foods, I made an unannounced inspection at the Customs House. A huge shipment of jam had just arrived. I had no reason for being suspicious, but as my eye traveled over the stacked cases I said to one of the inspectors without knowing exactly why, "I'd like to see one of those tins."

I took it in my hands, looked it over, and saw it was correctly labeled strawberry jam. Nothing apparently was wrong. Nevertheless, "Bring me a plate, please," I asked the inspector. When I emptied out the contents of the tin, it seemed an unusually small amount compared to the size of the container. Examining it more carefully, I found it had a false bottom. Every one of the forty-eight tins in the crate was then opened, but only four contained opium. An examination of the several thousand crates in the shipment showed that the Chinese, mathematically computing the probabilities of detection, had filled just four cans out of each forty-eight in every case.

Other smuggling devices were even harder to cope with. Although the Filipino backyards were overrun with chickens and roosters, eggs were comparatively scarce. Consequently, huge quantities were shipped from China. A favorite ruse of the opium smugglers was to insert a hypodermic needle into an egg, withdraw carefully all the albumen and then refill the cavity with opium. When the hole was expertly sealed, the illicit contents could only be discovered by breaking the eggs. Thousands of dozens were shipped by each Tuesday's steamer from Hongkong, and for a time the customs inspectors broke every single egg that came in.

But it was obviously impossible to open every tin of food or break every egg that passed through the various customs houses, and undoubtedly a great deal of opium must have slipped through, no matter how alert the inspectors were. In fact, the Chinese succeeded in getting large shipments of bulky and perishable lettuce and cabbages passed in right under our noses. They could always be bought in the Chinese quarter. Once we found a case labeled shoes which, under the first layer of slippers and boots, was made up of forbidden vegetables.

In 1908, just before sailing for the United States on leave of absence, I went to say goodby to Governor General Smith.

"I'm sorry you're not going to be here for our monster opium bonfire," he said. "It's going to impress the Chinese tremendously, don't you think so?"

I explained to him that in my opinion the Chinese, instead of being impressed with our high moral purpose in burning the seized opium, would think we were merely playing a colossal trick upon them. It would be inconceivable to them that we would destroy anything so valuable. I illustrated my point with an experience I had once had. At the request of the State Department, I had gone to China to carry out a diplomatic mission. I had no sooner arrived than I was offered fifty thousand dollars by one group of litigants. Although I paid no attention ultimately I had, in fairness, to decide in favor of the disputants who had offered me the bribe.

Hardly had I returned to Manila when I began to be besieged by Chinese wanting my advice. They would be sitting in my office every hour of the day and would ask my opinion on every conceivable subject—whether they should get married, whether a certain investment were good, whether they should buy more land. I could not understand it.

Then one day a Chinese came in who had been born in America and could both speak and understand English better than his compatriots. I asked him, "Why do all your countrymen keep coming to see me? They never used to."

"They think you are a very wise man."

"That's nonsense. What really is behind all this?"

He hemmed and hawed but finally told me the truth. "We all know you were offered fifty thousand dollars in China to decide that case the way you did. We also know you did not take that offer so that you must have received a better one. We had your bank accounts and all possible hiding places searched, and we have not been able to find a trace of it. Anybody who could successfully conceal so much money must be a wise man."

"That," I said to the Governor General, "is typical of the Chinese attitude. They'll never think you're burning opium, but will be sure you're pocketing the profits and substituting molasses."

"Then what would you suggest?"

"I'd have the opium shipped to the United States and made into pharmaceutical products which we could use for the poor in our dispensaries."

He accepted this suggestion, and for years thereafter the Bureau of Health had an ample supply of the drug.

FOR THEIR OWN GOOD

The Filipinos, in spite of our best efforts to persuade them of the value of the Bureau of Science in the development of the Islands, had never appreciated it fully, regarding it mainly as a place for the white collar class to earn an easy living at the expense of the populace. Governor General Harrison encouraged them in this misapprehension and his Cabinet naturally reflected his own attitude.

I remember the indignation of the new Secretary of the Interior Dennison, upon receiving an estimate of some sixty odd dollars for the photographing of certain molluscs. He even made a speech on this subject, which aroused great antagonism and a storm of articles in the press. His theme was that since the Filipinos were not interested in the Department of Ichthyology of the Bureau of Science, why should they pay money to provide a few scientists with pictures to gloat over?

"I could pay the whole share of the insular government in one teacher for the Mountain Province for the cost of these photographs. I am not unaware that the world outside of the Philippines may possibly prefer the photographs of the molluscs to teachers in the Mountain Province, but can there be any doubt in the mind of anyone that my duty is to spend that money for the interest of the Philippines rather than to further what may be considered the interests of the scientific world at large?"

Mr. Dennison, however, had not taken the trouble to inquire into the purpose of the appropriation. In the Philippines there was no window glass; in its place the window frames were filled with three-inch panes of the translucent mollusc shell. The Department of Ichthyology had learned how to propagate the mollusc and was trying to extend the market for this purely Filipino industry to the United States where other uses could be developed. To this end the disputed photographs were to be sent to the Smithsonian Institution. Mr. Dennison assumed that it was his function to determine whether the money should be spent on what the Americans thought was good for the Filipinos or for what the Filipinos themselves wanted.

During the years of Governor Harrison's administration the Bureau of Science almost entirely lost its reputation, and so many unscientific reports were published in the *Philippine Journal of Science* that its professional standing also was undermined. If the Bureau of Science were to be of utility, it was necessary to have on its staff men who loved research for its own sake. Such men could not do good work in the midst of the political atmosphere which existed from 1913 to 1921 in the Philippines, where almost every newspaper issue brought rumors of reduction in their salaries or even abolition of positions, and where scientific work was subject to constant hostile discussion by members of the Legislature. In a few years the Bureau was dismembered, its staff dispersed, and its appropriations for research restricted almost to the vanishing point.

The Bureau of Health suffered almost equally from the change in administration, but it was strangely due to Governor Harrison himself that one of the most advanced pieces of legislation in health was put through. My personal relations with him were always extremely pleasant. He probably found me useful as a consultant, because I had been through all the preceding administrations. I was accustomed to have breakfast with him often at Malacañan, and afterwards we would ride downtown together.

One particular morning Governor Harrison's attention happened to be attracted to a peculiarly lurid example of patent medicine advertising on a billboard. He pointed it out to me. "Isn't that a bad idea?" he asked.

"Frightful," I agreed. "Poor people waste their small savings on things which are useless, expensive, and often habit-forming. Here in the Islands the credulous population will accept as truth the wildest claims to a panacea, and the patent medicine evil flourishes like the green bay tree."

"Why don't we stop it then?"

"I'm surprised you ask that question. There's the red clause in newspaper contracts."

"What of it?"

"Your experience in the American Congress must have taught you nothing effective can be done in legislating against the proprietary medicine interests because they are too powerful."

"Anyhow, you draft a bill and bring it to me tomorrow."

"That's only twenty-four hours. I can't do a good job on it in that time."

FOR THEIR OWN GOOD

"I want it quickly. Tomorrow."

I sat up all that night pounding out a draft on my typewriter, and then marking out here and inserting there with a pencil until I myself could hardly make sense of it. I worded it far more stringently than was really necessary, but wanted to have enough extras in it so as to be prepared for the inevitable and necessary compromises. At daylight I had a rough draft ready which I took to the Governor General's office as soon as it was open.

Governor Harrison glanced through it hastily and said, "That's fine. Just what we want."

"Then I'll take it to the Attorney General and get his advice."

"Oh, no, no, no. The bill is all right as it is."

"But it may not be in the proper legal phraseology. I'd much rather have him go over it."

"You've written lots of laws, Doctor, and I'm a lawyer myself. This looks all right to me."

"Well, at least let me make you a clean draft."

"No, I want it just as it is."

He was Governor General. He kept the document.

At six the next morning a boy knocked timorously on the door of my room at the Army and Navy Club, and said some gentlemen had called to see me on business.

"Tell them I'm in my office every morning at eight," I replied crossly. "I'll transact business with them then."

The door was shut. I was preparing to resume my slumbers when the knock came again. "They won't go away, Doctor," the boy explained, looking a trifle scared. "They say it's important and they must see you immediately."

With resignation I put on my dressing gown and started down the long stairway to the lobby. Even before I had reached the bottom, the waiting group spied me. All had papers which they began waving excitably in my face. "You're the fellow who committed this outrage," one of them shouted.

"What are you talking about?" I asked in amazement, and then suddenly recognized two or three representatives of the patent medicine interests.

"You had this outrageous law passed," another shouted.

173

"I don't know anything about any law. When the proposed patent medicine bill goes to committee you'll have an opportunity to present your views."

"How can we? It's a law already. It's been enacted." He shoved a paper into my hand and there was my bill, word for word as I had drawn it up, the strictest of its kind ever passed.

It was undoubtedly a law, but the history of its mysterious passage still required explanation. Subsequently I learned that, as soon as I had departed from the Governor General's office, he had had it copied and sent by special messenger to the Upper House. The President of the Senate had said, "Here's a bill which our very good friend Governor General Harrison has sent down. He's apparently much interested in it. It doesn't affect any of us, and I propose that, if he wants it, we suspend the rules, read it by title, and pass it."

The motion had been made and seconded, and the bill had been passed by acclamation.

When the House had met at four that afternoon, the Speaker had risen and announced, "Here's a bill which our very dear friend Governor General Harrison wants. The Senate has just passed it. Let's show our respect for the Governor General and pass it also."

By six o'clock the bill had been back on Harrison's desk. He had signed it immediately, and it had become a law. I was given the job of enforcing it.

The law was so stringent that magazines containing patent medicine advertising could not be shipped into the Philippines unless the formulae were published. Patent medicine concerns from all over the earth raised a howl. Our only counter to this was that we had not attempted to prohibit the sale of nostrums, but merely required publication of formulae. If this were done, however, anybody could see that the ingredients of pink pills at one dollar a box were probably nothing but Blaud's carbonate of iron which could be bought in any drugstore for fifteen cents.

Because the measures of the Health Bureau had been so criticized, when Governor Harrison had arrived and had begun dismissing Americans on every hand, it was assumed that I should be among the first to go. When the weeks passed and I still remained, a newspaper war began to wage around the rumors. The United States press, of all shades of political opinion, and even the trade journals took part. Telegrams, letters, and newspaper clippings made a pile waist-high, all protesting against my being interfered with and stating that my dismissal would be an outrage. Finally President Wilson stilled the troubled journalistic waters by issuing a statement that I was not to be removed. Governor Harrison then broached the subject for the first time by echoing the President's words and saying such an idea had never entered his head.

Paying no attention to the clamor, I proceeded with my duties.

CHAPTER 12. THE HEAVENLY FLOWER

SMALLPOX is as loathsome as leprosy and claims many more victims. Millions of people, who could so easily have been saved, have died of this disease. Hundreds of thousands have been doomed by smallpox to lifelong blindness. Every bazaar in India is filled with these helpless and pitiful martyrs, groping their way through eternal darkness, or led stumblingly about by those who are already overburdened with poverty and sickness.

This heartbreaking condition is due to the stubborn refusal to accept the simple and effective remedy that science has to offer. The world, if it so willed, could be free of this most horrible disease.

One of the most satisfying successes of the Bureau of Health in the Philippines was the almost complete obliteration of smallpox. It was the more satisfying because it need never be feared again. Forty thousand people, most of them children, were alive at the end of each year who, in times past, would have been dead, and thousands upon thousands were saved from blindness and disfigurement.

The microbe which causes smallpox has never been discovered. But the disease is one of the most contagious of all human afflictions. The eruption on the skin, the breath, and the clothing of the patient can apparently convey the disease to others. There is even a strong possibility that the infection may be carried through the air. Smallpox patients used to be kept on board hulks anchored in the Thames, and it was noted that people who lived on the lee side of the smallpox ships suffered badly from the disease, while among those to windward there were few cases.

Smallpox has existed as far back as we have any records. It was in India and China in 300 B. C. In the sixth century A. D. it was epidemic in Southern France and Northern Italy. Among the Crusaders it wrought fearful havoc. The first settlers brought it to this country where it killed more Indians than the bullets of the Puritans. In virgin territory it reaped a frightful harvest. With the increase in travel during the Eighteenth Century it was spread far and wide.

Long before vaccination was discovered, attempts had been made to lessen the ravages of smallpox. It had already been observed that anyone who had once had the disease would never sicken of it again. The Hindus, Chinese, and Persians practised inoculation; that is, they transferred pus from the pock of a sick person to one who was well. This "sowing the smallpox," as it was called, caused a true case in the person so inoculated. One most unpleasant Chinese method was to soak a shirt in smallpox pus and put it on the victim; another was to blow the dried pus into his nostrils. The hope, often futile, was that smallpox thus contracted would be milder in form, but too often the procedure ended in fatalities.

In India, where inoculation was directed by Brahmins, it was somewhat better managed. The prospective patient, to get him in the best possible physical condition, was placed on a special diet and rest routine before the ordeal. The Brahmins would then soak a pad in pus mixed with holy water from the Ganges and apply it to the upper arm.

As time went on and attempts to reduce mortality spread westward, methods of inoculation began to approach the modern idea of vaccination. In Turkey a wound was made in the upper arm, the pus inserted, and a walnut shell tied over it. Lady Mary Wortley Montagu, wife of the British Ambassador, indefatigable observer and chronicler of everything and nothing, described the inoculation parties at Constantinople in 1716. Groups of people would gather and arrange to have an old woman come "with a nutshell full of matter of the best sort." Lady Montagu's correspondence with friends at home was responsible for introducing inoculation into England.

Macaulay wrote a particularly graphic description of smallpox

177

during the Seventeenth Century in England, where it had been estimated that only five out of every thousand escaped, and one out of four died.

"The smallpox was always present, filling the church yards with corpses, tormenting with constant fears all whom it had not yet stricken, leaving on those whose lives it spared the hideous traces of its power, turning the babe into a changeling at which the mother shuddered, and making the eyes and cheeks of a betrothed maiden objects of horror to the lover."

More than half those living had borne pockmarks. To be without them had been conspicuous; an unmarked face had been useful in describing a fugitive. Two-thirds of the inmates of the early blind asylums of London were there because of smallpox. The disease could not be shunned and each new generation had brought new victims.

The English fashion of inoculation was to take smallpox virus from a fully developed pock and insert it under the skin of a well person. It was found the disease when induced in this fashion was much milder, and gave a mortality of only one percent, but since it was as contagious as smallpox normally contracted, this method involved isolation for a number of weeks. Friends used to be inoculated at the same time and pass the period of seclusion in each other's company.

Apparently the Sanskrit texts made mention of the protective qualities of cowpox. But although this vital fact may once have been known, it had long been buried in an oblivion from which it did not emerge until the end of the Eighteenth Century when Edward Jenner investigated the dairy maid's chance statement that persons infected from sores on the udders of cows with cowpox escaped the more fatal malady. In 1796 he vaccinated eight-year-old James Phipps with virus taken from the sore on the hands of a milkmaid who had been infected while milking a cow. Six weeks later he inoculated this same boy with smallpox, and the disease did not take.

Jenner's paper, announcing his discovery, was rejected by the Royal Society, and he, like Dr. John Snow, had to publish at his own expense. However, unlike many of his confreres, he attained high honors during his lifetime from universities, learned societies, sovereigns, and even from the American Indians. The enlightened ones of a world who had so long suffered from this blight recognized that his contribution, differing from so many which had been mere steps in the conquest of a disease, heralded the possible annihilation of smallpox.

Immediately after Jenner's announcement a storm of controversy, for and against vaccination, arose. It was possible that, having seen the too often fatal effects of inoculation, the great mass of the people accepted this heritage of fear and classed vaccination with previous experiments towards immunization. Professor Benjamin Waterhouse of Harvard University took up the cudgels for vaccination, as Cotton Mather had done almost a century before for inoculation. He vaccinated his own family, only to find that the newly born but already lusty anti-vaccinationists were at once up in arms. He had to take his children to the smallpox hospital and actually expose them to the disease before people would believe they were immune. When he was asked to argue the merits of vaccination, he always rejoined that one fact in such cases was worth a thousand arguments, and he was ready to demonstrate the fact. Waterhouse sent some of the virus to President Thomas Jefferson in 1801, and himself vaccinated some of Jefferson's family.

Spain, often considered an unprogressive country, has been a leader in introducing vaccination into her colonial empire. In 1803 a ship sailed down the Guadalquivir with twenty-two children on board. During the voyage they were vaccinated by passing the contents of the vesicles from arm to arm so that it could be preserved until they reached Manila. Three years later that city had a Bureau of Vaccination, and in 1850 an institute for the manufacture of virus. Systematic vaccination was inaugurated in many of the provinces, but at best the work was sporadic and often interrupted by lack of funds.

Smallpox existed throughout the Philippines. Under a Spanish law vaccination had been compulsory, but lack of efficient organization preceding the American occupation had made it largely ineffective. Each year during the dry season a huge temporary hospital had to be erected at Manila to take care of the hundreds of victims, the great majority of whom died. The Filipinos were not against vaccination per se, but they had become accustomed to see the law not observed. The strong fatalistic philosophy which ruled their conduct permitted them to take chances that their better judgment condemned as unnecessary and hazardous.

When the Division of Vaccination was reorganized in 1905, my aim was to vaccinate all the seven million inhabitants of the Archipelago, including every new-born baby by the time it was a month old, and, furthermore, to see that everybody was kept vaccinated. For the safety of all each newcomer had to be included also.

The authority under which I acted required that every person in the Islands who could not furnish satisfactory evidence, either by certificate of recent date from a president of a municipal board of health, public vaccinator, duly qualified physician, or such other person as I might designate, to the effect that he was immune against smallpox, should have to submit to vaccination as often as might be required by the above-mentioned authorities. The greatest error with which any person can delude himself is that because he has been in the presence of the disease and has not taken it, he is immune. Many lull themselves also with the idea that one successful vaccination, perhaps in infancy, is protective for all time to come.

The first plan was to have the local Filipino health authorities take charge of vaccinating everybody who lived in their districts; but it did not work. In most instances, the health officer did not appreciate the necessity and importance of vaccinating every individual, without exception. He often would permit his friends, or perhaps influential caciques, to go unvaccinated.

As soon as it was demonstrated that Filipinos were often negligent and were apt, under pressure, to break rules, a new system was organized. An American physician, with some twenty or thirty vaccinators, began at one border of a province and literally marched across it, only going forward when all behind could display the evidence on their arms.

Reliable vaccinators were hard to get in sufficient numbers. Not until they were taught antisepsis were they allowed to go to the provinces and use the vaccine. Fortunately for our expense account, a Filipino who was learning any trade was willing to work for very little money, and we were able to accomplish a great deal at small cost by taking on *aspirante* vaccinators.

In 1905, the first year of the campaign, the stupendous number of

1,687,767 people were vaccinated. It was not all smooth sailing. In some districts the vaccinators were regarded as busybodies interfering with the routine of life. In Iloilo much patient effort was required to overcome the false rumor openly circulated by the mal-disposed that vaccine had been purposely infected with leprosy and that all those whom the lancet touched were doomed to the living death. In another outlying district, it was necessary for the mayor, the head of the police force, and myself, to be publicly vaccinated before the timid were reassured.

In provinces where violent objections were encountered, the vaccinators were as a rule withdrawn at once. We bided our time. In six months an unvaccinated pueblo would turn its eyes enviously from its own sick to the fortunate neighboring pueblo where tiny arm scars had taken the place of horribly disfiguring pocks, blindness, or death. The chief men in the unvaccinated pueblos would themselves request that the vaccinators return. For example, in the province of Albay, bitter opposition was encountered in Tabaco and Malinao. Many of the inhabitants fled before the vaccinators. But in the following year there were forty deaths in those two localities alone, and not another one among the 234,000 population of Albay.

Similarly, great opposition was encountered at first in Antique Province from intransigents who even threatened the lives of the vaccinators. However, by the use of tactful persuasion, a number submitted. Shortly afterwards smallpox broke out, and the death rate mounted. Here was visible proof that those who had been vaccinated, even when they were nursing the sick, did not contract the disease. The people of Antique cried for help and welcomed the same vaccinators whom a short time before they had driven away.

Patience worked wonders in Albay and Antique, but the outlying districts presented an entirely different type of problem. Bagac was an isolated barrio of two thousand inhabitants in the province of Bataan, situated in the path of the monsoon, accessible by sea only during short seasons, and by land requiring strenuous travel over a wretched trail. From 1896 to 1901 the district had been in the throes of war and rebellion and therefore neglected. But in the 1905 epidemic of smallpox, there was an outbreak at Bagac, and it would have been criminal negligence had we not attempted to protect it. As soon as one of the villagers had brought the news that every house in the barrio had one or more cases, I immediately loaded a launch, sturdy as a tugboat, with vaccinators and supplies. We plowed down the Bay, through the Boca Chico, and up the coast until we arrived off the village. Twenty-four hours a day, while the Northeast Monsoon blew, the great rollers piled up on the sandy beach where great boulders protruded here and there. The shore shelved so steeply that anchorage was out of the question. We had to lower a boat in the open sea, and thought ourselves lucky to surge through on top of a huge comber and land on the beach without upsetting.

The results proved worth the effort. Two weeks later there were no new cases of smallpox in Bagac, and soon the disease had disappeared completely.

Many regions in the Islands were so remote that to reach them required from two to three weeks of toiling over rocky trails and through morasses. Since the ordinary glycerinized lymph would not remain potent off the ice for more than ten days at the longest, no vaccination seemed possible. We tried to get ordinary lymph to these communities, but it had lost its potency and our time was wasted. Vaccine in powdered form was tried, and also the so-called dry points, but the percentage of success was so small and the danger of infection so great that their use was abandoned.

Unless everybody could be vaccinated, the danger of infection always lurked in the background. It was important to reach to the uttermost parts of the Islands. Since I could not improve the transportation, the length of time for preserving the potency of the lymph had to be extended. I devised a small portable ice box which nearly doubled the period during which the vaccine could be kept potent after it had left the laboratory.

A tight box, filled with ice, was placed inside a larger box, so that the airspace between the two would serve as insulation. The virus was put in small opaque receptacles and laid upon the ice. The whole was then locked and sent to the district medical inspector who had a duplicate key. Sometimes the boxes went by government launch or by bancas, sometimes by carretelas or carabao carts. Where there were no roads into the wilderness, the carts were mounted on skids so they would slide over the mud, and the carabao would follow the streams, sometimes half swimming. Whenever the animals grew hot and tired, they would lie down and wallow, but somehow or other they would manage to get through. Even occasionally the little ice boxes reached their destinations on the backs of runners.

The empty boxes were returned by the same devious routes to the Bureau of Health; there was a continuous stream of them going in and out of the central office.

With all our efforts it was impossible to reach some of those who, through no fault of their own, were maintaining the seedbed of the disease. When I was home on vacation in 1908 I spent an evening at Menlo Park and submitted the question to Edison. He already had wealth to spare and was planning to devote the rest of his life to inventions which would be valuable to the world though they might produce no money. In a small black book were entered just such problems. He had already experimented with a box which would give out carbon dioxide, but the little escape faucet kept freezing and defeating its own purposes. He was so interested in what I told him that he said he would set to work again to try to overcome this difficulty.

But Edison never solved the problem. An even better solution was discovered in Java by the Dutch, who are a very resourceful people. They utilized the knowledge that the strength of a virus may often be stepped up by inoculating from one type of animal to another. They introduced human seed vaccine into a rabbit, rabbit vaccine into a calf, and calf vaccine into a carabao. The resulting serum was emulsified with two parts glycerin, and then sent out in glass tubes enclosed for safety in bamboo containers. This vaccine, which will last more than a month in tropical heat, is now saving thousands of lives in the East. In 1915 the Indian government was about to erect vaccine plants at great cost in the mountains, because vaccine could not be manufactured during the hot season in the lowlands. I had just learned of the Dutch discovery, and suggested that use be made of it. By adopting the Dutch method India was saved the expenditure of thousands of rupees.

We had developed a system of making our vaccine which was efficient and cheap. We would buy carabao calves, shave a place two feet square on each one, and with a knife dipped in cowpox vaccine make stripes an inch apart, crossing them with other stripes until the bare space looked like a gridiron. On this surface vesicles would appear in great numbers. Out of one calf we would secure about three hundred cubic centimeters, or enough to vaccinate a thousand people. As soon as the calves had recovered from cowpox we would sell them back for what we had paid for them.

A complete vaccination of the Philippines could not be accomplished in one year or even two. We worked as fast as we could, taking first those districts where the scourge was worst. I remember in December, 1910, the *Basilan* was returning to Culion with a full complement of lepers. It was obvious that we should arrive too late in the evening to land. I knew I was somewhere in the vicinity of Caluya, a small isolated island I had never visited. Since I did not wish to waste six hours riding at anchor in Culion Harbor, I suggested to the captain, "Let's put in at Caluya. I'd like to have a look at it."

Accordingly, the *Basilan* lay to off the beach and a boat was lowered. The first thing I noticed as we approached the shore was that the usual welcoming throng had not come pouring down to meet us. In fact, the beach was deserted. I walked into the town. It, too, was silent and lifeless; not a human being was in sight. I peered into the dim interior of the nearest nipa hut. The air was fetid with the poisonous discharges of smallpox pustules. Eight fevered bodies were tossing restlessly. I went to the next hut, and there were seven more. Some were in the early stages of pains and fever, their faces covered with hard red pimples not yet broken; some were already approaching death.

From the third hut I extracted a Filipino youth who, although terror-stricken, showed no signs of the disease. In the ten houses I inspected I found only one other Caluyan untouched. Each had a perfect vaccination scar. "How did it happen that you two were vaccinated and not the others?" I asked.

"Last year we were visiting in Calapan when the vaccinators came and we were vaccinated, too."

Out of the thousand inhabitants of Caluya, five hundred had died. The epidemic had started with the arrival of an infected person from Antique. An old woman, in the attempt to prevent the spread of the disease, had harked back to the Eighteenth Century, taken the contents of a pustule from the smallpox case shortly before death, and inoculated a number of the inhabitants. In a little over two weeks the epidemic had followed. The population of the islands in the group totaled two thousand. One thousand already had the disease before my vaccinators, for whom I sent immediately, could arrive. Of the remaining thousand, eight hundred were vaccinated, and of these not one contracted smallpox with a successful vaccination two weeks old. Two hundred had fled in terror of the disease and we could not find them.

The Filipinos in the outlying islands, in their ignorance, were apt to be afraid of vaccination until they became accustomed to it. There were always evaders; even on shipboard where we rigorously enforced vaccination we had to watch carefully. I happened to be out on business in the harbor one day and passed by a ship on which the crew was being vaccinated. One Chinese after another was swarming down a line into a lighter tied to the stern. After my vaccinators were satisfied that everyone on the ship had been accounted for, I ordered one of the crew to cast off the lighter. When we boarded it, I never saw a more astonished lot of coolies. They chattered and gibbered in dismay at having been caught as we lined them up and ordered them to bare their arms.

Legally I had the right to have anybody vaccinated; if necessary I could call on the police for assistance. But I preferred to use other means if possible. The Filipinos seldom made any protest after the first few years. Most of the objectors were unvaccinated Americans, among whom the mortality was twice as high as among Filipinos. When any of my vaccinators encountered one of these conscientious objectors, he had instructions to send him straight to me.

One noon hour I was sitting all alone in my office, and a great enormous American blacksmith entered. "You're the guy who's goin' to vaccinate me, are you?" he began truculently.

"No, I'm not," I answered. "I don't want to vaccinate you if you don't want me to. My duty is to tell you what risks you are running. This contagion is so widespread that I don't know any unvaccinated person who hasn't caught the disease. A health officer's joys are few. It gives me pleasure to attend the funeral of someone who has died of smallpox because he was not vaccinated. Only last week I went to one of those funerals. All I'm going to do is tell you that you're running a terrific risk, but if you don't want to be vaccinated, it suits me perfectly. I'll announce in the afternoon papers that you are an anti-vaccinationist. When you come down with smallpox, I'll have that item printed also, and I'll do the same with your death notice. You know, of course, that you have less than a fifty-fifty chance to pull through. But I'm delighted that you are offering yourself as a human experiment."

"Aw, come on, vaccinate me," was his only retort to this harangue. Like a well-disciplined dog he followed me to the special little vaccination office maintained to accommodate any who came to be vaccinated.

No force, no persuasion, no wiles, were necessary on the German Island of Yap. I observed when I went there in 1911 that vaccination day was a holiday. Native runners were sent out in advance to advise the communities that at a certain time the doctor would arrive prepared to vaccinate all who might desire it. The entire village would appear en masse to avail themselves of this wonderful opportunity to be ornamented with the scars of which they were so proud. Vaccination was a rare treat because the Yaps were accustomed to inflict wounds upon themselves and to keep them open by frequent scratching, or by rubbing with sand, bamboo, or shells. As soon as a scab formed from the vaccination they would scratch it off, so as to make the resulting scar as large and round and white and beautiful as possible. The doctor in charge told me that natives frequently asked to borrow vaccine and a lancet with the idea of vaccinating themselves and adjusting the size of the scarification to their own fancy.

In Mindanao, which was under military rule, and where the influence of the Bureau of Health was nebulous, the Army doctors as a matter of routine vaccinated the troops, and for protection also vaccinated the Moros in the vicinity of the military posts. In the course of time it became evident to the Moros of the back country that their brethren who had been vaccinated did not get smallpox.

One day about three hundred Moros, all armed with krisses, appeared with a flag of truce outside one of the Army camps. "We have come to be vaccinated," their *datto* announced.

THE HEAVENLY FLOWER

The post surgeon met the *datto* in a field nearby and said, "I'm very sorry, but I can't vaccinate you. I haven't any vaccine."

The *datto* replied in a matter-of-fact way, "We came to be vaccinated, not to listen to any foolishness."

The surgeon caught the glint and heard the whisper of drawn krisses. He thought quickly. "Without doubt you're in urgent need of vaccination," he agreed. "I'll see that you are accommodated at once."

He retired, therefore, to his office, and returned shortly with a bottle of distilled water. With a scarifier he carefully scratched each arm and applied the sterile water.

When he had finished the last brown arm, he said to the *datto*, "One time is not enough. There will be no scar from this. You must come back again on the tenth day."

The satisfied savages returned to the jungle and the doctor hurried to the telegraph operator. His message to me requested a large supply of vaccine, which I despatched to him at once. It arrived in time, and at the end of the ten days the Moros all reappeared. This time they were effectively vaccinated.

Our vaccination record in the Philippines was unique both in its wholesale nature and in the total lack of injurious after-effects from infection. In the course of a few years we performed twelve million vaccinations; practically no cases of smallpox occurred among the properly vaccinated, no one died as a result of vaccination, and not one arm or leg was lost. This was absolutely unprecedented; even in Germany, where the most modern sanitary practices prevailed, out of every million vaccinations several people died or lost arms or legs because of infection in the wound. I had conceived the notion that, if the scarification were not dressed but allowed to dry, tetanus germs would be less likely to gain a foothold. Much to our gratification it turned out that, in trying to avoid tetanus, we avoided nearly all infection. Of the hundreds of nurses who served in our hospitals, only one contracted smallpox. She had been vaccinated, but, since she did not believe in the practice, she had rubbed the virus off with alcohol.

In time our system worked with a high degree of efficiency. The death rate was reduced from forty thousand annually to seven hundred, and the fatalities occurred in districts too remote for us to reach or among unvaccinated children. Childhood furnished the smallpox reservoir. The Filipinos who reached the adult stage had either had it or were immunized. There always remained a few who took to the hills, climbed trees, or hid in cellars to evade the vaccinators, and those kept small foci of infection perpetuated. If everybody in the Islands had been vaccinated there would have been no smallpox. In Manila, where we had complete control, there was not one death from the disease in the seven years prior to 1914, where before there had been thousands.

One of the greatest catastrophes in modern times began in the Philippines in 1918 when fifty thousand people, most of them children, lost their lives from smallpox, and the total eventually reached almost a hundred thousand.

I had been away from the Islands for three years, traveling from one out of the way place to another, and had just arrived in the United States. I was on the train from New York to Boston and from the window saw signs which in effect asked, "People of Massachusetts, how much longer will you stand for this frightful practice of vaccination? The Philippine Islands, which have been cited and vaunted so much as having been freed from smallpox, now have one hundred thousand deaths. What better evidence do you want of the valuelessness of vaccination?"

Soon afterward I was recalled to the Philippines as one of General Wood's advisers under a return of the old régime. He, as an administrator, was appalled and worried by the smallpox situation; as a physician he was intensely interested in the causes of this recrudescence of an infection once stamped out. He joined me in my search. We started with the children. We looked up their health records, which certified they had all been vaccinated. We then inspected the Health Service at Manila and found the vaccine had been manufactured and sent out regularly. To make a final check we went to the schools. In classroom after classroom we found to our indignation that, in spite of the records, the children had not been vaccinated. Naturally we wanted to fix responsibility. We discovered that local health officers had consistently falsified their reports. In some instances many more vaccinations had been reported by them than would have been possible with the quantity of vaccine sent to the vaccinators. In other cases, rather than do their jobs they had thrown the vaccine into the waste paper baskets where we found it.

Thus a huge unvaccinated population had come into being, and it had only been necessary to blow upon the ever present spark to start the conflagration. The bellows had been used; the spark had kindled into flame. Century-long exposure to the disease had bred no immunity. The Filipinos had died like flies, and the heat of the conflagration was so intense as to affect those who were only semi-fireproofed by vaccinations of too long standing.

Between 1918 and 1920 the Islands had lost twice as many lives from smallpox as the United States had lost from casualties in the World War. The death toll could have been avoided. The figures showed conclusively that ninety-three percent of the deaths had occurred among the unvaccinated. I described to Wood my previous methods which had proved so successful. He put the same regulations into effect and the Islands were once more freed of the disease.

The problem of eradicating smallpox from the Philippines was no different from that anywhere else; it merely involved the thorough and repeated vaccination of everybody, without exception. Unless local sanitary officials in every country can be made to realize that infants must be vaccinated shortly after birth, that unprotected transients must submit to the operation, and that everybody must be periodically revaccinated, smallpox will continue to prevail.

If the so-called special visitations of Providence for the purpose of convincing people of their errors, could be logically considered in the category of sanitary measures, then the awakening of a sanitary sense of the people caused by a virulent epidemic is productive of good. If the tenets of the believers in New Thought and Christian Science were true, this class of people would never have smallpox. For surely no bigotry could be more pronounced than that manifested by the anti-vaccinationists of the Philippines. Fortunately these fanatics, although vociferous, were small in numbers and not influential in the Legislature, and the unvaccinated among them contracted smallpox so regularly that they were no problem.

It seems almost incredible that, in spite of the absolute proof that effective vaccination makes smallpox impossible, there should still be dissenters. Daniel Webster, in one of his less inspired moments,

189

said, "Compulsory vaccination is an outrage and a gross interference with the liberty of the people in a land of freedom." He failed to realize that freedom must not be granted to those who have proved themselves unworthy of it by endangering others. The construction of fire hazards is not permitted; why should anti-vaccinationists be allowed to generate sparks which threaten the lives of the public? Even now, in these supposedly enlightened days, the ill-founded claims that vaccination produces harmful effects during menstruation, pregnancy, lactation, and early infancy are too frequently respected, even by the advocates of vaccination.

In the United States and England societies have been founded of those whose one idea seems to be that all the ills of the world are due to vaccination. Strange to say, occasionally the prime movers in these anti-vaccination societies are physicians, although it is difficult to understand how any observing medical man could question experience and the evidence of science so far as to doubt the thoroughly established fact that vaccination prevents smallpox.

Simon Louis Katzoff, to quote only one out of many, asks in *Physical Culture:*

"How long are the poisoned pus peddlers to be allowed to run wild and fatten their purses and the insane asylums, hospitals, and graveyards? Priestly despotism is bad, but medical despotism is intolerable.

"Smallpox is a filth illness which follows closely upon flagrant violations of the laws of hygiene and health. No person is susceptible to smallpox or any other filth disease so long as he is in a state of health. . . . Compulsory vaccination ranks with human slavery and religious persecution, and is one of the most flagrant infringements upon the rights of the human race. The more vaccination is practiced to the neglect of sanitation, the more smallpox flourishes, but when sanitation is practiced and vaccination neglected smallpox disappears. Vaccination will be neglected and smallpox will disappear when medical superstitions and medical intolerance have disappeared."

In Denver, Colorado, chiropractors loudly proclaimed the uselessness of vaccination as a protection against smallpox, and for a time succeeded in winning a large section of the public to their point of view. But just as surely as a dry shaving will burn when a match is applied, just so will the unprotected contract smallpox when exposed to the contagion. As time went on, it became increasingly apparent that the unprotected were furnishing all the victims while the properly vaccinated were escaping. Finally the unvaccinated chiropractors began to contract the disease. One of them who fled not only himself died, but started smallpox in faraway Arkansas which had previously been free.

I have always felt strongly on the question of vaccination, because smallpox is a disease we ought not to have. On almost every one of my world trips I used to meet anti-vaccinationists. I remember in particular one man who was traveling with his beautiful daughter. He was rabidly against vaccination. When she contracted smallpox and died in Singapore, I never saw a man burdened with greater remorse. His lesson was a bitter one. He said to me, "I alone am to blame. I pitted my puny opinion against the judgment of the medical world, and this is what has happened."

Anti-vaccinationists should be attacked everywhere as a menace to the welfare of mankind. The disfigurement, blindness, and death for which they are responsible should be brought home to them. Their false doctrines are too costly and should not be allowed to spread.

There are very few anti-vaccinationists now in the Philippines. Most of them have died of smallpox.

CHAPTER 13. ALAS AND A LACK

IN 1908 I was delegated to attend an international convention on tuberculosis at Washington, and it was decided that Dr. Francisco Calderon, a prominent Filipino physician, should accompany me. Since he was being groomed for an important administrative position, it was judged desirable for him to see how affairs were conducted in the United States and, incidentally, what was being done for Filipinos in American universities. After leaving Washington we were to circle the globe, inspecting progress in the treatment of tuberculosis in Europe on our way. I started for Hawaii a month ahead so that I could visit the leper colony at Molokai. Calderon joined me at Honolulu and together we set sail for San Francisco.

I had not been in the United States for five years, and when we reached San Francisco I was so busy talking with friends who had come to the boat to greet me that, for the moment, I forgot all about Calderon and his inability to speak English. When I looked for him he was not to be found. Finally I located him in a Customs enclosure.

"Que pasa?" I asked.

He shrugged his shoulders and professed entire ignorance. A Customs inspector interrupted, "He's been trying to smuggle cigarettes. He had ten thousand which he didn't declare. That's smuggling on a large scale."

I pointed out to the inspector that ten thousand cigarettes were not so many under the circumstances. Dr. Calderon was a Filipino, and everybody in his country smoked all day and half the night. He would be uncomfortable without his own brand, and was merely taking a supply with him to last during our world trip. Moreover, he was an official representative to an international meeting to which he had been invited by the United States and, as such, entitled to diplomatic immunity.

"He can't do anything like that," insisted the obdurate inspector.

"Well, if you won't let him off, I'll have to go down and interview the Collector of the Port, who's an old friend of mine," I replied. When I reached his office, he had gone to lunch, and I had to wait until two o'clock before he returned. I told him the story and, although he demurred at first, finally, on my statement that Calderon was a prominent Filipino on a diplomatic mission, he gave me an order for release. I returned to the pier, exhibited the document, and saw Calderon restored to freedom.

Since my own baggage had not yet been inspected, I went off to attend to it. But when I returned I found no Calderon. I discovered him again under guard.

"What's the matter now?" I demanded.

"I don't know," he lamented. "This is a terrible country."

I sought the inspector and asked, "What's my friend done now?"

The inspector, who had been somewhat annoyed over Calderon's release, exclaimed triumphantly, "He is a smuggler. You got him out of the cigarettes, but let's see you get him out of this. You said he was a Filipino. Then what's he doing with this big sealskin robe? How could a fellow from a hot place like the Philippines have any use for such a thing? You can't tell me he isn't trying to smuggle it into the country."

I knew better than to argue; I hailed a taxi and returned once more to the office of the Collector of the Port. After I had explained the nature of the new contretemps he said, "I'm afraid I can't help you this time. The inspector is perfectly right. We can't overlook such a serious offense."

"You'll cause a lot of trouble," I interposed. "This man is a guest of the nation. I assure you he has merely borrowed the robe from a friend in Shanghai because he's afraid it's going to be cold in Siberia."

After much persuasion and the assurance that the robe was not to remain in the United States, the Collector of the Port reluctantly agreed to sign a second order for Calderon's release. This time I took no chances, but watched over him as though I were his keeper.

The train for the East left at seven o'clock, and once we were well under way I went forward to the club car, leaving my colleague to amuse himself in the Pullman. I had not been there long when the porter came rushing in after me. "You'll have to come back to your friend right away."

"What's the matter?" I queried.

"He's undressing in the aisle. We can't allow it."

I returned and admonished Calderon. "Look here, this sort of thing isn't done in America. You'll have to undress in your berth."

"How could anybody undress in that little hole?" he protested.

I admitted the art of Pullman travel was a difficult one to master, but I explained its technique as best I could.

"But how do you get your trousers off? There's no place to sit down except in the aisle."

"You get in that berth," I commanded. "I'll see you in the morning."

I went back once more to the club car, but I had not finished my cigar before the porter sought me out again. "What's the matter this time?"

"That man is sitting in the observation car in his pajamas."

"Well, they all do that in his country," I explained. "It's September, and it's hot, and he probably wants to cool off."

"But he can't do it. You'll have to get him back in his bunk. He doesn't understand me."

I went to the observation car and found Calderon contentedly smoking away on his smuggled cigarettes.

"You can't sit here in your pajamas," I began firmly.

"What kind of country is this?" he demanded indignantly. "I've been lying in that infernal bunk where it's hotter than at home, and it's very pleasant here."

I eventually persuaded him to conform to American notions of propriety and return to his bunk.

Until we reached New York everything went smoothly. There we registered at one of the large hotels and started for the elevator, Calderon following behind me—an Oriental always walks two paces in the rear. The door slid shut and, before I realized he was not with me, the elevator was on its way to the twelfth floor. I waited there for some time, but he did not appear. With visions of his being lost in a city where things moved far too rapidly for him, I returned to the ground floor.

Calderon was nowhere in sight. I asked the starter whether he had seen anybody answering Calderon's description.

"Oh, yes," he assured me. "He's just gone up."

"Then I'll go up again, but if he comes down while I'm gone you keep him here until I get back."

I returned to the twelfth floor, but he was not there.

When I once more emerged into the lobby, I burst upon a tremendous scuffle. Calderon was loudly shouting as he struggled with the starter, "He's trying to arrest me!" He had mistaken the uniform for that of the police. I placated the starter, explained to Calderon, and, taking him by the arm, conducted him to his room.

This was by no means the end of my troubles. October came, and the days grew fairly cool. When Calderon donned his bright yellow overcoat he attracted attention wherever we went. A group of small boys would often follow us, shouting derisively, "Look at de guy in de yella coat!"

I spent half my time plucking Calderon bodily from in front of automobiles and street cars, interpreting for him, and trying to find the kind of food which he found palatable. I was almost a nervous wreck before I located a Filipino to look after his wants. Thereafter I could leave Calderon happy and contented in good hands while I went about more important business.

Calderon had received an invitation to go to the Lake Mohonk Conference, which was concerned with helping the Indians and other dependent peoples of the United States. He thought this might afford an opportunity to obtain additional funds for his Gota de Leche Society in the Philippines which had for its object the distribution of milk to poor children. Calderon, who was an extremely well educated and intelligent man, wrote an excellent address in Spanish, which his Filipino guide then translated into English. It was still effective, because the Spanish idiom is beautiful even in translation. He practised his speech daily and, although he scarcely knew the meaning of the words, he could repeat them perfectly in English. He made such an impression that a considerable sum was voluntarily contributed to the Gota de Leche, even though, as a rule, money was not solicited at these conferences.

Calderon's success had been so great that I suggested we interview Nathan Straus, who had done so much for the cause of pasteurized milk in America and Europe, and see whether we could interest him in donating a pasteurization plant for Manila. We were received by both Mr. and Mrs. Straus. The former was not impressed with our story, but his wife showed great interest. When he objected that he had put in all the milk plants that he cared to, she reminded him that this was an American responsibility, and he ultimately agreed to have one which happened not to be in use shipped to the Islands.

Calderon had become so amusing in his idiosyncrasies that I wanted to continue the fun. Accordingly, when we embarked for Hamburg in December, I placed over the door of his stateroom a little sign which read, "Professor of Music." Thereafter he was constantly being invited to play and sing, particularly by the ladies, who took a tremendous fancy to him. He was totally unable to understand his popularity. He refused each frequent request to perform, and I invariably explained he was too shy to make a public appearance.

As we drew nearer and nearer to Hamburg, I noticed that he was becoming miraculously stouter and stouter. I finally grew alarmed and said, "How is this? Your trousers are so tight I'm afraid they'll burst."

The explanation was simple. He had bought a dozen suits of long underwear, and as the days grew colder had added the suits one by one until he was wearing four, and looked exactly like a stuffed porpoise.

In spite of his underwear and the robe, he was shivering when we reached the Customs Office on the Russian frontier. It was bitter cold. Just as the train was about to leave, two American ladies appeared, much distressed because they had no reservations.

"We'll offer them our compartment," I said.

There was no place for us except third class, and we had had no breakfast. Russian was not included in my linguistic equipment, but I had a French time-table, and I believed that by comparing this with the time of arrival at stations, I could pick out a dining place. But the train did not keep its schedule, so that I soon lost track of where we were. At every stop I rushed out to try my languages, one after another, but the big, whiskered Russians shook their heads in bewilderment. By the time I had finished asking in six languages how long the train was going to stop, it was usually pulling out again.

The thermometer was far below zero, and still we had had nothing to eat. Poor Calderon was nearly congealed; I have never seen anybody so cold in my life. I took his pulse and found it so weak I was afraid he would literally freeze to death. When we reached Warsaw I was trying to figure out whether he could be buried there, and what my duties were to a friend under such circumstances.

About seven in the evening an ancient Jew entered the compartment, and I immediately addressed him joyfully in Yiddish. He was the first person during that long, miserable day who had been able to understand a word of what I had said. He informed me the train would stop about ten at an eating place, and I promised him anything he wanted for supper if he would lead us to food. Three hours later he produced steaming borsch, black bread, and tea. Calderon's face began to resume its natural color, and he was soon able once more to articulate.

The next morning we were at St. Petersburg. The great cold of Russia was naturally uppermost in Calderon's mind, and when he discovered a French-speaking staff at the hotel, he had listened morbidly to their harrowing tales of unfortunates who had lost limbs or had been frozen to death. I asked him whether he cared to walk along with me to call on the American Ambassador, and explained that the exercise would keep us warmer than if we hired a sleigh.

According to his usual habit, Calderon kept trailing behind. It grew colder and colder; his hands were practically ankylosed. I had to do something to make him move faster and stir up his circulation. "If you don't hurry up, you'll lose an ear," I warned him. He kept in step with me for a few moments, and then began to dawdle again at his usual gait.

Finally I turned around. An expression of simulated horror came over my face. "It's too late! You've lost an ear!"

He clapped his hand to his head, but it was so cold he could feel nothing. "What am I going to do without an ear?" he wailed.

"If you don't hurry, you'll lose the other one," I admonished him pitilessly.

From that time on it was I who had difficulty in keeping up with Calderon. As we drew near the Embassy he became worried about his appearance. "If you keep your head away from the Ambassador, he won't notice it," I comforted him. "And we'll only be there a short time—it won't warm up enough to bleed."

All through the interview he kept his head carefully averted, and on leaving pulled his coat collar up over his head. As soon as we returned to the hotel he rushed to the mirror. He was so relieved to find his ear intact, that he forgave me on the spot for the trick I had played upon him.

Soon afterwards, homeward bound on the Trans-Siberian, we arrived at the end of the line at Mukden. In order to buy a ticket on the Chinese railway to Peiping I had to have Chinese money, but it was then three o'clock in the morning. I found a nook slightly sheltered from the wind where I deposited our many pieces of baggage with Calderon to watch over them. Because trunks had to pay first class postage rates, we had lightened ours by putting everything possible in bags which could be kept in our compartment.

I started out to find a place to change my twenty-dollar gold pieces, and hurried along the dark streets until I saw a light over the entrance to a gambling place. Much time was taken up in haggling over a satisfactory rate of exchange, but I was ultimately content and started to retrace my steps toward the station. As I drew near I could see Calderon fast asleep, and a big Chinese in the very act of picking up one of the trunks and hoisting it on his shoulder. I yelled and sprinted after him over the frozen rice paddies. Before I could overtake him he dropped the trunk but kept on running. Without its weight he gathered speed, and his pigtail stood out behind him. I had no intention of carrying the trunk back. I caught hold of his pigtail, slowed him down, turned him around, marched him back to the trunk, made him pick it up, and we returned together.

This was the last of my adventures with Dr. Calderon. In spite of not feeling at home in a strange environment, throughout our trip he had acquired an amazing amount of scientific information, which he had assimilated thoroughly. He became Dean of the Government Medical School in Manila and later President of the University of the Philippines.

ALAS AND A LACK

The problem of tuberculosis had its peculiar and complicating features in the Philippines. The dietary was unsuitable for its cure; but, in addition, the people had the insanitary habit of eating with the fingers, a lack of proper exercise, superstitions concerning the contraction of the disease, and an almost unshakable fear of night air as a poisonous thing. They usually slept closely together in groups on the floor. Betel nut chewing made the custom of expectorating in public and private universal and practically incurable. Legislate as we might, the filthy habit of spitting still continued, even among the more intelligent. Added to this was their utter resignation to the disease as a thing inevitable.

Not only did we have the ordinary preventive and curative measures against tuberculosis to organize and enforce, but we had to devise ways of cooking and preparing native products so that they would be both nourishing and acceptable to the masses. But it is often easier to be bad than good, and, similarly, easier to be insanitary than sanitary, and the East likes best the easiest way. We began an active educational campaign for the prophylaxis and treatment of the disease. But curing the people of their superstitions was as great a task as converting them to a new religion; tuberculosis had long been regarded by the public as necessarily fatal, and it was difficult to convince the afflicted that it often yielded to the simplest hygienic measures; they wanted a sign before they would believe.

In the Philippines more people died of tuberculosis than of any other disease, and there was hardly a family that had not lost at least one member. One-sixth of the deaths were directly attributable to it; only Calcutta approached Manila in its mortality rate from this cause.

The tubercle bacillus, which was discovered by Koch in 1882, is exceptionally hardy. If not exposed to sunlight, which kills it in a few hours, it may live for six months. The defensive forces make every effort to kill the tubercle when it gets into the body, but can only succeed when the blood is rich and healthy. The frail physiques of Filipinos make them particularly susceptible.

For thousands of years doctors have tried to find a remedy that would cure tuberculosis, but so far have had to fall back on nature. Sunshine and fresh air are the enemies of disease the world over. Formerly it was the practice to recommend a change in climate, but experience has amply demonstrated that treatment is more dependent on proper nutrition and rest than on meteorological conditions. The benefits of favorable climatic environment are oftentimes more than offset by the inconveniences of travel, loneliness, and homesickness, and the necessary status of patients among strangers.

However, proper hygiene and diet, the attention to the little things peculiar to each individual case, together with appropriate medication for special conditions as they arise, can best be supervised in a sanitarium. One of the principal objects of such an institution is to teach the patients to help themselves and not be a danger to others. The influence exerted by those who have recovered is the greatest power in the educational crusade against this disease. One enthusiastic patient returned cured is worth more than all the circulars and literature that could be produced on the subject.

No disease makes such a drain on the resources of families, for its long, insidious course prevents its unfortunate victims from earning their living, thus oftentimes enforcing a condition of debt and actual want. I considered that the government should take up the burden of providing a tuberculosis dispensary and a hospital for chronic cases at Manila and a sanitarium at Baguio. Even if the great misery, suffering, and despair of stricken victims, of relatives and friends and those dependent upon them, were to be ignored altogether, and the question considered from its financial aspect alone, it would be, I thought, a matter of wise, public policy to relieve, in part at least, this drain on the productive capacity of the country, which was measured in millions every year.

Dr. Calderon and I returned from our trip with a good knowledge of what the rest of the world was doing. But I realized that the hope of freeing the Philippines was in large measure dependent upon raising the economic standards. Until the Filipinos could obtain better food and make more general use of milk they were tremendously handicapped.

This was excellently illustrated by the situation in Europe where before the War the tuberculosis rate in Austria and Germany compared favorably with that of Great Britain and America. As the War progressed, tuberculosis began to increase. In some sections it ran as high as in the past. But after the War, even though overcrowding was universal, even though there was no money, the tuberculosis rate at once climbed down because the Austrians and Germans were again getting the fats and other food essentials of which they had so long been deprived.

Nature evidently intends that every child born should take part in the great drama of life and live until all the purposes which have called it into existence have been satisfied. So determined is she that her plans be successful that she has apparently established a law fixing a direct ratio between the birth rate and the infant mortality rate.

A high death rate among infants, unless brought about by epidemic diseases or other special causes, is normally offset by a higher birth rate. Nevertheless, it is the duty and desire of the health officer to save as many of them as he can. No one wants the children to live more than the health officer, because the bearing of healthy children is a blessing to womankind and to the world at large, while the bearing of sickly children soon to die is a misfortune to humanity. The tiny graves in the cemetery are seen by many, but few hear of the efforts made by self-sacrificing physicians and faithful workers in the children's cause to prevent these graves.

The death rate among young Filipino children was appallingly high. In Manila every other baby died before its first birthday. General debility was a common condition among children. The bodies that these babies inherited from weak parents could not withstand the germs of disease. Another cause was the obstetrical practices which prevailed. If a woman had too small a pelvis to give birth easily, not infrequently a rope was wound around her waist with a man pulling at each end to force the birth. Many children also had died of tetanus neonatorum, because the midwives, according to an ancient and common Oriental custom, had dressed the cord with manure.

The midwives were an organized but untrained and unlicensed group. By the exercise of much diplomacy we took the leaders among these old women into camp, teaching them more scientific and humane methods. In a great campaign of education we issued free packets by the hundreds of thousands for dressing cords, and finally they were used. When the midwives had been converted, midwifery schools were started over the Islands, and the decree went out that before any woman should practice obstetrics she must procure a license.

But improper nutrition was the major cause of the high infant mortality. The struggle for more adequate food has been long and still continues. The use of milk on a large scale was practically unknown in the Philippines, as well as in many other tropical countries. The poverty of the people made properly marketed cows' milk, either fresh or canned, impossible to obtain except by charity. Ordinary cows' milk was extremely expensive, because cows did not do well in the Islands. The native grasses had little spines which, when eaten, caused tiny wounds in the intestinal tract. When these healed over they left scar tissue which ultimately caused such contraction that the natural glands were destroyed and the cow could not absorb what she ate. She literally starved to death. In my early enthusiasm, I tried to start a herd of a hundred and fifty, but all died.

Goats were common and flourished, but the Philippine variety gave very little milk. It occurred to me that if we could cross an Island goat, which could stand the climate, with a Maltese goat, which lactated generously, we might get a satisfactory hybrid. The agricultural department took this up and a breed of goats was produced which seemed to fill the requirements. I believed we could use the slogan, "a goat in every family," and have another cheap method of securing milk, but the Filipinos did not take to the idea.

Whatever milk the poorer classes used came almost exclusively from the caraballa, or female water buffalo, which is, by nature, a dirty animal and doubtless contributed its full share to the sum of impurities that vitiated the infants' milk.

The Filipinos have a degree of understanding with the carabao which the white people have never seemed able to attain. When Manila was first occupied by American troops, a Major, in his delight at getting ashore, went for a long walk on the outskirts of the city. While crossing a field he was observed by a carabao, which promptly charged him. There happened to be a tree in the middle of the field, which he reached with three leaps and a bound. It was then about five in the afternoon. He lifted his voice in plaintive appeal but nobody answered. He would remain quiet for a few moments and then cautiously begin to descend, but each time a warning, "pff-shshsh-oo-oooo" would send him hurriedly back to his perch. Hour after hour the Major sat in a crotch of the tree, and hour after hour the carabao waited untiringly below.

The long night passed. Finally, at about six in the morning, a four-year-old child toddled over the field and led the carabao unprotest-ingly away by its nose rope. The brave Major then made good his escape.

The Major had probably been wise in his policy of watchful waiting, because many people have been gored and killed by infuriated carabao. The animal has no sweat glands except in his nose, and if he does not have an opportunity to soak himself once a day in water, or at least in mud, he will go *loco*. Though ordinarily slow and deliberate, under such conditions he will attack anything on sight, preferably a white person. At all times he loves mud and filth, and if, while dragging his cart or sledge, he comes to a mud puddle, he will promptly lie down, and only under the most urgent suasion will he move on.

The scarcity of milk was accentuated by the rinderpest epizootic which, in its slow girdling of the world, had finally reached the Philippines. It carried away from seventy-five to eighty percent of the carabaos—hundreds of thousands of animals that were indispensable in cultivating, reaping, hauling, and disposing of the agricultural prod-ucts upon which the prosperity of the Islands was totally dependent.

Rinderpest is a dysentery in cattle which has a ninety percent mor-tality rate. I have gone through fields where hundreds and hundreds of these dead animals were lying. At that time we could do nothing for them except keep a strict guard at the quarantine stations and try to prevent the infected animals from rubbing noses with those as yet untouched. So many cattle perished that for years meat had to be imported from Australia, and milk became almost an unknown quan-tity. Finally, an army veterinarian named Kelser developed a vaccine which made cattle immune to rinderpest, but the Filipino owners were suspicious of it, and the veterinary corps were not always considerate of their sentiments and prejudices. It was extremely pathetic when the only animal upon which a family depended for the necessary work of the rice field succumbed to the disease. No money with which to in-demnify the owners was available until the United States Congress appropriated a million dollars, *the only money ever contributed to the Philippines.*

Even when the caraballa had recovered in numbers, difficulties arose about the nature of the milk, which contained twice as much butter fat as ordinary cows' milk. It could be diluted in half and still have the proper amount of fat, but such dilution made the carbohydrate content entirely out of proportion. To remedy this, the dealers in caraballa milk tried all sorts of experiments, hoping to make the product correspond to cows' milk—rice, starch, and other substances, many of which produced weird looking mixtures and bacterial counts that would have staggered a statistician.

Regulating the trade in caraballa milk was complicated because there were no big producers, and keeping watch over every caraballa owner was an obvious impossibility. We tried at one time posting inspectors on the roads, but there were so many tracks and trails by which milk could enter Manila that the attempt proved a failure. As always, our recourse was education. Nurses went from home to home to talk to the housewives.

Ultimately, several substitutes for fresh cows' milk were discovered. The Swiss developed a method of preparing natural milk with no preservative and not heated enough to coagulate the casein. It kept well, would not transmit disease, and could not be infected so long as the tin was unopened. It could be bought for eleven cents a quart at the grocery store, and in time it came to be generally used throughout the East.

Another discovery, made at the Peiping Hospital, was that a substitute for milk itself could be manufactured from the soya bean. With the addition of cod-liver oil and calcium it closely resembled natural milk. A number of children were fed only on this food from the time they were three weeks old, were examined regularly, and proved to be healthy and normal in every way. I was convinced that the "eat only what you crave" idea was nonsense when I saw how children who had never had any other food loved this soya bean milk, because to an adult it was one of the worst-tasting decoctions that could be imagined.

A Filipina college graduate in chemistry from Columbia University then made her contribution. She found that extract of banana added to the soya bean mixture made it taste like fresh milk. The Filipina housewife can now make this milk in her own kitchen, using a little handpress for the bean and adding the other ingredients according to the prescribed directions.

The soya bean has proved of inestimable value to the East and promises to enlarge the dietary. I once attended a delicious full course lunch in the Bureau of Science Laboratory in Manila where everything from soup through steak to cake was made from this bean.

Another food deficiency was responsible for one of the most debilitating and crippling diseases of the Orient. Beriberi is as needless as smallpox and a disease about which I feel as strongly. Each year it takes a toll of over a hundred thousand lives. In the War of 1895 between Japan and China nearly half the Japanese troops had it; in the Russo-Japanese War of 1904–05 eighty-five thousand cases were reported. It was estimated that in the Philippines at least five thousand died and twenty-five thousand were made ill from it annually.

Among the poorer classes beriberi was particularly prevalent; people for whom the government was directly responsible suffered badly. Bilibid Prison was filled with it. On more than one of my leper collecting trips the captain of the *Basilan* pointed out a lighthouse where there was no light, and on investigation we would discover keeper and assistants dead of beriberi. Or more often the American flag would be flying upside down as a signal of distress. In almost every instance we would find the crew, although still able perhaps to tend the lamps, seriously ill.

Beriberi caused a multiple neuritis affecting both the motor and the sensory nerves. The extremely painful inflammation brought about a partial and even complete loss of the use of the muscles supplied by these nerves, and particularly affected the heart. One of the most apparent manifestations was the dropsical appearance. The patient ultimately became bedridden, and large numbers died from heart failure. I remember the impression made upon me by the huge hospital for beriberi incurables at Singapore, where these poor people were crawling around on their hands, dragging their paralyzed legs behind them. The disease was too far advanced for a cure; it might easily have been prevented.

Many causes were assigned for beriberi, such as overcrowding and poor ventilation. The French clung to the theory that it was infectious long after it had been proved otherwise. Many claimed it was due to bacteria on rice which produced a toxic condition. The discovery of the true source came with the opening up of huge rubber plantations in the Straits Settlements and Malay States. Chinese and Indian laborers were imported, and promptly developed beriberi. The British government employed two scientists, Henry W. Fraser and A. T. Stanton, to work on this problem. They arrived at the startling conclusion that this horrible affliction was due to a food deficiency; that beriberi was a disease brought about by the absence of certain chemical constituents essential to the nourishment of the human body. They gradually found out that Vitamin B was missing from rice which had been polished; the outer surface of the rice grain containing substances essential to nourish the body had been ground away. Those who ate unpolished rice did not get beriberi. Europeans and Americans did not have it because they received Vitamin B from other foods which Orientals ordinarily did not eat.

After trying out their theory on chickens, Fraser and Stanton tested it on inmates of the insane asylum at Kuala Lumpur. The results were the same. Those who ate polished rice came down with beriberi; those fed only unpolished rice remained healthy. They then tried a further experiment. The government was building a railway in Malaya, and three hundred of the workers joined in the test. Half were put on a diet of unpolished rice; half on polished. The latter group came down with beriberi. Then the diets were reversed. The sick group recovered and the well group came down with the disease. It warranted the deduction that a diet which included Vitamin B was a preventive for beriberi.

After the British had made the discovery, it developed that Professor C. Eijkman in Java had caused beriberi in chickens but had never applied the same test to humans as the British had done.

Fraser and Stanton determined further how to tell whether rice was polished to the danger point. If when stained with methylene blue or iodine the grains took a deep color, then the rice was deficient in Vitamin B, and, therefore, beriberi might result. If the grains stained slightly, the rice was safe to use. This test was extremely valuable, because it was so difficult to judge with the naked eye how much of the coating had been removed from the kernel. A more exact index was to determine the amount of phosphorus pentoxide. If it contained four-tenths of one percent or more it was safe; if less, it might cause beriberi.

At the first meeting of the Far Eastern Association of Tropical Medicine at Manila, in 1908, the two British scientists read the story of their epoch-making discovery. I decided to try it out at once among those for whom I was directly responsible. Before the Fraser and Stanton report, we had striven in vain to wipe out beriberi entirely at Culion. By adding to the rice more meat and mongos (beans resembling lentils), the number of cases could be reduced, but many of the inmates preferred to deny themselves food rather than eat mongos, so that we had starvation as well as improper diet to deal with. At the beginning of 1910 the use of unpolished rice was made compulsory, and beriberi stopped immediately.

With this evidence Forbes issued an order that only unpolished rice should be used in all government institutions. But soon commissary officers, prison wardens, and others directly charged with carrying out the order began to be besieged with complaints, and it was but natural that they should take a course of least resistance and recommend that the use of unpolished rice be discontinued. It was asserted that a penurious government was attempting to cheapen the diet at the expense of inmates and employees, who, consequently, often refused to eat it. However, we insisted upon strict obedience, and when its use finally became general, the results were startling. The thousand deaths from beriberi in government institutions that formerly occurred annually ceased altogether.

During the autumn of 1911 a great shortage of rice occurred throughout the Orient, and certain grain interests attempted to corner the world market. The price soared one hundred percent. In some instances to protect its people from extortionate prices, the Philippine government also plunged, and bought and bought until it had broken the corner as far as the Islands were concerned. In a short time it had the cost to more normal figures, but in so doing had been forced to buy great quantities of polished rice. So much was on hand that large issues were made to Culion in November, 1911, and continued until February, 1912. I was away at the time or I should have protested.

During January cases of beriberi broke out among the inmates, and the general mortality rate rose rapidly. As many as fifty deaths a month were occurring. Immediately upon my return in February, I ordered rice polishings, which contained the essential Vitamin B, fed with the rice, and soon beriberi disappeared again.

We could control inmates of government institutions; one year after Forbes' decree beriberi had disappeared from the prisons, the lights burned steady and true along the coast, and the United States Army Scouts marched with firm step. We then turned our attention to teaching the general public to eat the more healthful rice. But the Filipino, like all other Orientals, is very fond of his polished rice. Any time the Filipina housewives decided to wipe out beriberi from the Islands they could do so. But even to this day they have not been convinced.

The solution of the beriberi etiology unexpectedly shed much light on one of the important causes of infant mortality. In Manila the death rate curiously was much higher among breast-fed children than among those fed from a bottle. The exact reverse is true in America and Europe. Since the staple article of diet among the masses was polished rice and fish, neither of which contained the requisite nutriment for mothers' milk, the breast-fed child was not properly nourished and became irritable and fretful, cried, failed to sleep, and did not gain weight. Ultimately it became paralyzed. This condition was called *taon*, and was thought to be due to a toxin in the mother's milk.

Major Weston P. Chamberlain and Captain Edward B. Vedder of the United States Army Board began a series of experiments with *tiqui-tiqui*, or rice polishings, and made an extract from these. Vedder had noticed that the Filipino cocks grew strong and sturdy if given *tiqui-tiqui*. He knew that polyneuritis among chickens and beriberi among humans were due to the same causes. If, then, *tiqui-tiqui* were good for roosters, it might also be good for babies. The two Army doctors sought out babies on which to try their extract. This was not easy, because parents whose children had *taon* were usually poor and ignorant, and their ignorance made them distrustful.

No one who did not see the effects of administering *tiqui-tiqui* extract to these children could believe the quick results which followed. A child who for days had slept no more than a few hours, who had been whining and crying constantly, would fall into a quiet sleep. In a day or two its weight would begin to increase, and the paralysis to leave its limbs. It was just like a miracle.

Nevertheless, we were dealing with a symptom and not getting at the cause of the disease. Another paper outlining progress on beriberi was read in 1911 at the Hongkong meeting of the Far Eastern Association of Tropical Medicine. Among the most convincing proofs were that the Hongkong jails, formerly riddled with beriberi, had been freed of the disease, and the entire native army in Java had been cured. The Association adopted a resolution that all governments with Eastern possessions should be petitioned to have white rice barred and only unpolished rice used.

The next day the French delegates moved to reconsider, asserting they would like to present certain facts. At Saigon, in Indo-China, there was a monastery and a nunnery. Both monks and nuns ate the same diet of polished rice. If we could explain to their satisfaction why the women always had beriberi and the men never, they would be glad to join us in signing the petition. We had no answer at the time. It remained for a Netherlander, Kuenen, years later, to discover that if rice were thoroughly washed, the protective substance was removed as effectively as though it had been polished. In Saigon the dirty men had not washed their rice, while the cleanly women had rinsed theirs thoroughly. The campaign against beriberi was held up for years because of French dubiety.

I realized that solution of the beriberi problem would be of tremendous humanitarian and economic advantage and be one of the great forward steps of modern times. A simple method of protecting the poor against themselves would be to tax white rice. This would work no hardship on them, because the price of unpolished rice would not be raised. But harmful polished rice, even at a few cents' higher price, would be put out of their reach. On the other hand, those able to afford the polished rice would not be hurt by it because their living scale would allow them to include a more varied diet.

In spite of much opposition, I managed to get a bill to tax white rice passed by one House of the Philippine Legislature, but adjournment took place before the other House could consider it. Later, owing to the unsettled condition of the rice market, the Legislature was not disposed to take any action.

For years I have peddled my tax idea around the world. Over and over again I have pointed out that its action would be automatic, because people would buy the cheaper unpolished rice and beriberi would disappear. The War interfered with my plans. Afterwards I interested Sir William Osler, then Professor of Medicine at Oxford, and Viscount Bryce, who agreed to use their influence with the British government to impose such a tax. But before they could take any action, both of them died. Though progress has been slow, I continue to peddle the idea.

It is perfectly amazing that, in face of the miraculous results from so simple a dietary reform, incredulity, with its attendant sacrifice of life and health, should still persist. But I am convinced that if somebody could prove today that cancer was caused by the eating of white bread, twenty-five years from now most people would still be eating white bread.

CHAPTER 14. THE HOUSE OF PAIN

HUNDREDS of thousands of lepers still exist throughout the world as social pariahs, thrust out of society because they have, through no fault of their own, contracted a repulsive disease. Far beyond their physical suffering is their terrible mental anguish. No criminal condemned to solitary confinement is confronted with such torture and loneliness. Shunned by friends and acquaintances, who are in terror of even coming within speaking distance, the unfortunate victims soon find themselves alone in a world in which they have no part. The few who come in contact with lepers instinctively draw back from them, so that normal social relationship dies at birth. Patients, when avoided by everybody, sit idle and brood; a human being devoid of hope is the most terrible object in the world.

The treatment of cases of leprosy today is sometimes as inhuman as in former times. In India a leper is often cast out by his own relatives, and has to go to the government for relief. The Karo-Bataks of the East Coast of Sumatra expel a leper from their villages, and at night surround and set fire to his hut, burning him alive. The Yakuts of Siberia, in their great terror of leprosy, force the leper to leave the community, and he must henceforth live alone unless he finds some other leper to keep him company.

Even in the United States lepers have not always been treated kindly. The people of a West Virginia town, when they once found a leper, placed him in a box car and nailed the door shut. The train departed. It was the middle of winter, and before the door was finally opened, the man had starved and frozen to death.

Leprosy is the most ancient and exclusively human of diseases. It has followed man in all his migrations. The ancient records are not precise, and it is impossible to say with certainty that Egyptian papyrus, or Sanskrit *Rig-Veda*, or Chinese parchment, or Jewish *Old Testament* referred definitely to what we know as leprosy. Syphilis and yaws and various skin ailments have clinical symptoms often readily confused with it. One of the oldest works in Chinese medicine, called *Su-yen*, 400 B. C., described a disease which certainly had the characteristics of leprosy. Tradition ascribes an existence of more than two thousand years to leprosy in China. It is claimed that Buddhist priests used to frighten people into conversion by threatening them with the disease should they close their ears to the holy teachings. For centuries overpopulation and misery have sent the Chinese out into all parts of the world, and they have carried leprosy with them.

Leprosy among the Jews is undoubtedly very old, although from the description in *Leviticus* (14, 4–8), many different forms of disease appear to have been included with leprosy. Moses, one of the first great sanitarians, laid down a system of regulations for those having leprosy, threatening the Jews with the wrath of Yahweh if they disobeyed. At intervals of seven days the isolated ones were examined by the priests, who attempted to cleanse them by the following ritual:

4. Then shall the priest command to take for him that is to be cleansed two birds alive and clean, and cedar wood, and scarlet, and hyssop.

5. And the priest shall command that one of the birds be killed in an earthen vessel over running water.

6. As for the living bird, he shall take it, and the cedar wood, and the scarlet, and the hyssop, and shall dip them and the living bird in the blood of the bird that was killed over the running water.

7. And he shall sprinkle upon him that is to be cleansed from the leprosy seven times, and shall pronounce him clean, and shall let the living bird loose into the open field.

8. And he that is to be cleansed shall wash his clothes, and shave off all his hair, and wash himself in water, that he may be clean; and after that he shall come into the camp, and shall tarry abroad out of his tent seven days.

If after the alternate periods of examination and isolation the lesions persisted, the accused was declared leprous. He had to go out with clothes torn and dirtied, bareheaded, with his face covered, and hair uncut, crying to all he should meet *"Tame! Tame!"* "Unclean! Unclean!"

The origins of leprosy are hidden in the mists of antiquity. But the routes of travel, for trade or for conquest, have been the paths of disease as well. The Phoenicians may have bartered leprosy for sandalwood and spices; the Achaians crossed the wine-dark sea for Helen, but their slaves may have brought leprosy back to the shores of Greece; leprosy is supposed to have followed the armies, and was brought by Pompey's legions from the conquest of the East; and the Soldiers of the Cross who set forth to rescue the Holy Sepulchre, staggered back bearing the cross of leprosy to the Christian world.

By the middle of the Twelfth Century leprosy was in Scotland, Norway, the Shetland Islands, Holland, Denmark, Sweden, and parts of Russia. There were many leprosaria in England—seven in London alone, among them St. Giles, founded in 1101. In Scotland the leper houses were called spetels, and the disease to the Scots was the mickle ail.

There is great controversy and doubt as to how many leprosaria existed in Europe in the Middle Ages. One reading of Mathew Paris gives nineteen thousand in 1244, but this is vehemently disputed. Certainly there were many thousands. Mézeray, the French historian, says that in the time of Philip Augustus, 1223, there was no city or town which was not obliged to build a hospital for lepers, solid and durable. Louis VIII in 1226 left legacies to two thousand leper houses. In Spain the first leprosarium was founded by Ruy Bivar, the Cid. In 1284 sequestration was required by Sancho IV of Castile. The Castilian monarchs had a special interest in the disease, because more than once a leper had sat on the royal throne.

Some contend that in the Fourteenth Century the religious orders began to found hospitals for the lepers, known as Hospitals of the Holy God, but more popularly as lazarettos, in honor of St. Lazarus, the Bible beggar, while others say the name derives from the island of St. Lazarus in Venice, which was the site of one of the first leprosaria.

The leprosaria in the Middle Ages were directed by the ecclesiastics of some nearby monastery. They were endowed in different ways. Many of the rich lepers had to take at least a part of their patrimony with them. The service of the houses was done by Brothers or Sisters, clothed in the leper livery, and wearing on their sleeves a piece of red cloth, so that they might be recognized when they walked abroad.

In general the leprosaria were for the rich. The poor, if there were no hospice nearby especially dedicated to them, were treated in quite another manner. A complaint was lodged against anyone suspected of leprosy, and a hearing held before the ecclesiastical judge. If he were accused and convicted of having the disease, he was cast out of the world. In nearly all countries the ceremony, called the *separatio leprosarum,* was similar and differed little from the offices for the dead. According to the ritual of Paris, the leper knelt before the altar, his face covered with a black veil, and listened devoutly to mass. The officiating priest three times took a spadeful of earth from the cemetery and let it fall on the head of the leper while saying, "My friend, this is a sign that thou art dead to the world, *'Sis mortuus mundo.'* " And in consolation he added, *"Vivus iterum deo."* Thou shalt live again with God.

Then the priest read the following rules which the leper was to observe:

"I forbid you ever again to enter in this church, or the market place, or the mill, or the public fair, or in any company or assemblage of people whatsoever.

Item, I forbid you ever to wash your hands and all necessary things in fountain or in brook or in any water whatsoever. And if you wish to drink, take water with your jug or some other vessel.

Item, I forbid you henceforth to go without the habit of lepers, so that you may be known to others, nor shall you go barefooted except within your own house.

Item, I forbid you to touch anything that you wish to buy in any place whatsoever, but point to it with rod or staff, so that what you wish may be known.

Item, I forbid you, while going through the fields, to reply to anyone who may question you, except first, for fear you might infect someone, you step off the road to leeward. And also henceforth you shall not go by the highway for fear that you meet someone.

Item, I forbid you, if necessity requires that you take a path through the field, to touch the hedges or bushes on either side, except before this you have put on your gloves.

Item, I forbid you to touch little children, or any young people whatsoever.

Item, I forbid you henceforth to eat or drink with companions, save they be lepers."

The leper then put on the leper garb of black with a veil over his mouth, and received from the priest the cliquettes with which he must warn of his approach. The priest finally took leave of him in these words, "Thou shalt not be disconsolate for being sequestered from all others, for thou shalt have thy part and portion of all the prayers of Holy Mother Church, as if in person thou wert daily attending divine service with the others. Only take care, and have patience. May God be with thee."

In some districts the leper at the close of the ceremony was made to descend into an open grave in the cemetery and undergo a pretended inhumation, but more often was merely led outside the church and in procession conducted to his cabin in the fields. Before his door was planted a cross on which the priest hung a box for alms.

The leper houses of wood, surrounded by palisades, were invariably located outside the villages in the country, but usually in close proximity to a traveled highway, so that begging might be fruitful. At a leper's death, his household utensils were broken if of earthenware, burned if of wood, and passed through fire if of metal. The corpse was buried under the cottage and, in certain regions, a cartload of lime was thrown into the grave.

At a later period lepers were very rarely kept strictly to their houses, in accordance with the prohibitions given by the priest. Privileges were often accorded them which would seem to fit in poorly with the theory that the Middle Ages were cognizant of the extremely contagious nature of the malady. They had the right to circulate in the environs of the town, provided they did not pass a certain road, square, bridge, or river. On certain days and hours of the day they might enter the city, although they could not eat there nor frequent taverns. But they had to beg, and a begging space was usually carefully specified. Often a well person would be there to receive alms for them. They also had to buy provisions, and attended church, where a special place was assigned them, since they were not admitted to the common confessional.

Usually at Easter the lepers would go "out of their tombs like Christ himself" and enter for several days in the cities or villages to participate in this universal Christian festival.

On the other hand, lepers might be subjected to extreme severity. At Vicenza anyone who found a leper wandering in the city or its environs had a right to hunt him out with a whip, even though he were ringing his "leprous bell."

The treatment of lepers was a curious compound of horror and compassion, in which, as the years went by, the latter gradually gained the ascendency. The diseased ones became something sacred; in France they were called *les malades de Dieu, les chers pauvres de Dieu,* or *les bonnes gens.* Anyone who helped them reached the heights of sacrifice, and thereby attained the greatest honor. Hans Holbein painted a picture in 1516 of Elizabeth of Hungary, patron saint of queens, succoring a group of lepers. Albrecht Dürer also treated the subject by painting the limbs of the lepers as crippled or amputated, and the skin covered with blotches like those of a leopard. It is obvious that the horror rather than the accurate portrayal of the disease was the artists' aim; they desired to express the heroism of those who helped lepers. Matilda, wife of Henry I of England, Countess Sybil of Flanders, Rochilde of Hainaullt, and St. Catherine of Siena were among the great personages who believed they were honoring themselves by caring for lepers.

And Ambroise Paré, physician to Henry II of France, and often regarded as the father of modern surgery, at the end of his discourse on leprosy gives the advice that, when the lepers are separated from the world:

> "one face them as kindly and gently as possible, having in mind they are like to ourselves, and, should it please God, we might be touched with the same malady . . . And it is necessary to admonish them that although they are separated from the world, yet at all times they are loved by God while bearing patiently their cross."

At the time throughout Europe it was a consistent policy to stamp out the disease by isolation in colonies or hospitals. Even a healthy person who had been known to have been touched by a leper might be banished from society. Probably such measures had a most important influence in preventing the spread of the malady. The leper house period in England lasted roughly from the Eleventh through the Fourteenth Century. The disease died down in Europe much in the order in which the countries had been attacked. One of its most remarkable features was its rapid decline in the Fourteenth and Fifteenth Centuries.

Nobody knows why leprosy occurs in one place and not in another. As Frank Oldrieve, Secretary of the British Empire Leprosy Relief Association, expressed it, "There is a caprice of distribution which it is difficult to explain, and it does not seem to depend directly on climate, geological formation, or such-like physical conditions; for leprosy is found in mountainous districts, on the plains, on the coast, in the interior, in all varieties of climate, and on all kinds of geological strata."

Leprosy never breaks fresh ground unless it has been introduced from without by a leper; and a sure and safe way of stamping it out is by isolation. For example, lepers were unknown in Hawaii until 1859, but thirty-two years later one out of thirty of the population was leprous. A Chinese introduced the disease into New Caledonia in 1865, and four thousand cases grew up in twenty-three years. The first instance in the Loyalty Islands was in 1882, and on one tiny islet six years later there were seventy cases.

It is generally assumed that a sufficient concentration of cases in any small area will soon result in the appearance of other cases among persons who frequently come in contact with them. This is strikingly illustrated in the Island of Nauru in the central Pacific Ocean, south of the Equator. Although only about twelve miles in circumference it supports a population of about twenty-five hundred. In 1920 there were four cases of leprosy on the island, in 1921 sixty, and in 1927 three hundred and thirty-seven, or about one in seventy of the population.

More than three million lepers are supposed to exist in the world, the great strongholds being India, China, and Japan. India has a million or more cases, and China is in much the same position. There are forty thousand in Burma alone. South America has had large invasions; Colombia is said to have over one hundred thousand lepers.

Also the islands of Ceylon, Java, Hawaii, and many islands in the West Indies have suffered terribly. In Korea, curiously, the disease is confined to the southern half of the peninsula.

Leprosy occurs now in Europe only in sporadic form; a few centers remain in Italy, Finland, Russia, Norway, and Sweden, but they are diminishing rapidly. About sixty years ago the disease in Norway was declining, but then it began to spread once more. It also reappeared in Holland after a long absence. Although there are many persons in England today afflicted, there have been no indigenous cases for the past fifty years.

The weight of authority would seem to indicate that leprosy did not exist on the Western Hemisphere before the coming of the Spaniards, but afterwards it spread throughout South America, and was augmented by the traffic in slaves, among whom were lepers. Cortez erected the first hospital of San Lazaro in Mexico. In 1573 the first white man of prominence was declared a leper in Cartagena, Colombia, then the center of the slave trade, and still a focus of leprosy.

Leprosy was brought to the United States with the slave traffic, the French settlers of Louisiana, and worldwide immigration. The disease now spreads in but four of the states—Florida, Louisiana, Texas, and California, although at one time it could be contracted in Minnesota. If the same incidence prevailed in this country as in the Netherlands East Indies, where the rate sometimes runs as high as ten cases per thousand, we would have over a million lepers instead of a few hundred.

New York State proceeds on the theory that cases of leprosy introduced within its borders are no danger to others, and is loath to segregate, especially if there is any objection on the part of the patient or his friends. In New York City there are dozens of lepers, but no one contracts the disease from them. Massachusetts had a leper settlement on Penikese Island near Buzzards Bay, of which the normal capacity was nineteen. All but one of these were of foreign birth or parentage.

A very interesting story is told in connection with the entrance of leprosy into the Philippines. One of my predecessors, Major E. C. Carter, had put in print a story to the effect that the Japanese, annoyed

THE HOUSE OF PAIN

by the efforts of the Spanish Catholic Church to implant Christianity in Japan, had, in retaliation, loaded one hundred and thirty-four lepers on a ship and despatched them to Manila, saying, "If it is converts you want, begin with these."

Japan resented Major Carter's statement so deeply that the United States was requested to make a public withdrawal and an apology for this alleged outlandish charge. It devolved upon me to make a defense. Accordingly, I had the royal documents at Seville searched. In Section V, drawer II, bundle XXIII, it was recorded that Philip IV, King of Spain, acknowledged the receipt of a communication from the Captain General of the Philippine Islands, on June 8, 1632, in which His Majesty had been informed that one hundred and thirty-four "converted Christians" who had been sent over by the Emperor of Japan, had arrived in Manila Bay. The Most Christian King had directed that the "converted Christians" be welcomed with a parade, and that, in addition to the five hundred reales already set aside for their reception, two hundred more be expended for their maintenance. In that same year one hundred and thirty of them were admitted to San Lazaro Hospital.

These facts were submitted to the Japanese government, which then reported they had already confirmed the story from their own records and withdrew the demand for retraction. They were, however, of the opinion that these lepers had been deported from Japan for sanitary reasons, but admitted cautiously that there might have been some lepers among the Japanese Christians who were banished when the feudal system had become dominant in the Empire.

By royal decree promulgated in 1830, leper settlements were established at Manila, Cebu, and Nueva Caceres, in which some four hundred lepers lived. Only those were gathered up who were in such advanced stages of the disease as to be loathsome to the public or objects of charity. Even though not allowed to live in the same houses as the healthy, frequently they were permitted to mingle freely with the people in the markets and other places. Friday under Spanish rule was lepers' day, when the afflicted walked the streets seeking charity. If alms were not forthcoming, they would squat patiently in groups in front of a residence or alongside a ship. No effective guard was maintained at Cebu, where at one time whole parties of lepers left the

219

hospital and settled down in nearby towns. San Nicolas and Opon, which are now foci of leprosy, were in all probability two of the points to which they fled. Supposedly due to this early laxness, two-thirds of the Philippine lepers now come from Cebu, which has only a seventh of the population.

When the United States Army arrived in the Philippines thousands of lepers were at large. Some were eking out a miserable existence on isolated sandspits, others begging in the market place, and still others trying to earn a pitiful living. Their labors, which of necessity had to be those requiring little strength, sometimes, most unfortunately, had included making cheese or handling foodstuffs in grocery stores. The spread of the disease had been practically unchecked. The attitude of the Filipino public had fluctuated between a great horror of it, amounting almost to panic, and the greatest callousness.

The San Lazaro Hospital for lepers at Manila is an old stone building constructed by the Franciscans in 1784. It was maintained by the income from the district of San Lazaro outside the walls, granted the Fathers for this purpose. At the time I took control, the Hospital contained two hundred and forty-three lepers.

Here, as in so many other instances in the Philippines, success in dealing with the leprosy problem could be obtained only through a program of educating the public. The people had to be taught not to shun the leper, but leprosy, and that the leper who concealed his disease was a constant deadly menace to the community in which he lived.

Leprosy is one of the most repulsive ailments that afflicts man. Of the two main types, one, the neural or anesthetic, exhibits little outward evidence, and the other, the cutaneous or hypertrophic, is marked by lesions which form on the surface tissues. The two types often occur together. In neither are the lesions confined to a single tissue.

The first signs of leprosy are often indicated by an enlargement of the lobe of the ear, or an infiltration or ulcer of the septum of the nose. Then erythematous, or red spots commonly appear, on which all sorts of ointment are apt to be tried, none of which is efficacious. When I have described these symptoms at lectures, I have often noticed how here and there a member of the audience would feel his ear. Occasionally after one of these addresses I have had someone come knocking at my hotel door late at night, saying "Doctor, I seem to have a nodule in my ear. I want to have an examination to see whether I have leprosy."

Leprosy begins insidiously, progresses slowly, and may last for twenty or thirty years. Aretaeus, a Greek physician of Cappadocia who came to Rome in the First Century A. D., wrote an account of the disease which holds true today:

"Shining tubercles of different size, dusky red or livid in color, on face, ears and extremities, together with a thickened and rugous state of the skin, a diminution or total loss of its sensibility, and a falling off of all the hair except that of the scalp. The alae of the nose become swollen, the nostrils dilate, the lips are tumid; the external ears, especially the lobes, are enlarged and thickened and beset with tubercles; the skin of the cheek and of the forehead grows thick and tumid and forms large and prominent rugae, especially over the eyes; the hair of the eyebrows, beard, pubes, and axillae falls off; the voice becomes hoarse and obscure, and the sensibility of the parts affected is obtuse or totally abolished, so that pinching or puncturing gives no uneasiness. This disfiguration of the countenance suggests the idea of the features of a satyr, or wild beast, hence the disease is, by some, called satyriasis, or by others leontiasis. As the malady proceeds, the tubercles crack and ultimately ulcerate. Ulcerations also appear in the throat and nose, which sometimes destroy the palate and septum, the nose falls, and the breath is intolerably offensive; the fingers and toes gangrene, and separate joint after joint."

The ancient world often mistook other diseases for leprosy. There is an innocent skin disease, characterized by white spots which changes the epidermis and turns the individual affected into the Biblical whited sepulchre. The lesions of yaws and syphilis may resemble leprosy; lupus vulgaris, or tuberculosis of the skin, may be as disfiguring as leprosy, but can usually be cured by proper treatment. Once at Oris in Samar I found awaiting me in a leper compound at the edge of town a hundred of the most mutilated, repulsive individuals I had ever seen. For years these tragic figures had endured the stigma and mental anguish inseparable from leprosy, but not one of them was a leper. A temporary hospital was opened, the cases were successfully treated, and the patients were released.

The manifestations of leprosy differ widely throughout the world. The incidence in the Philippines is relatively high but the type is mild compared with certain other countries. India has the more serious nerve type, and the tuberculoid form is predominant in South Africa. In the Philippines about one-quarter of the cases are purely cutaneous, without much nerve involvement. In such instances, the disease first appears with a small round patch on the skin, white or red, or whitish and scaly in the center with a red margin. No pain and no itch are experienced, the principal symptom being the lessened sensitivity to feeling. After the disease has lasted a few years the nerves usually become involved, and, ultimately, in those who live long enough for the skin manifestations to disappear, only neural manifestations remain.

Americans are not immune to leprosy in the Philippines; as far as can be determined the incidence among those who live in the lower social strata is as high as among Filipinos.

Anesthesia among lepers is extremely common. One of the earliest authentic accounts of the anesthetic features of leprosy occurs in the chronicles of William of Tyre. He tells how it was discovered that Baldwin, son of Amory, the King of Jerusalem, was a leper:

"One day the future king was playing with his comrades and in the course of the game the hands and arms of all were scratched. The other children uttered cries, but Baldwin made no complaint. His tutor remarked upon it. At first he believed that the child, through valiance and bravery, was hiding his pain, but Baldwin, questioned, affirmed that he felt none whatsoever in the region of the scratches. His arm and hand had gone to sleep, and even when his tutor bit him, he did not feel the bite."

I have often seen a lighted cigarette burning into the fingers of a leper without his being at all aware of it. Even the odor of burning flesh did not attract his attention, because the sense of smell was also gone.

Anesthetic leprosy attacks the trophic nerves, which carry impulses throughout the body, causing the blood to bring essential elements to damaged tissue. Ordinarily, if the fingers of a well person are merely drawn across a piece of paper, a few surface cells of the skin are rubbed off. But nature telegraphs by means of these trophic nerves to headquarters that tissue has been removed, and at once the blood supply opens, the repair is made, and the hand heals. But this telegraph system in lepers is completely out of order. Nature is not aware that any cells have been removed, and the result is they are not replaced, but are gone forever. Lepers frequently have worn their hands down until they are no more than bats.

Wounds in anesthetic cases heal with great difficulty. A slight injury, such as caused by running a thorn in the foot, often starts an unhealable ulcer that produces a deep hole and discharges foul pus. We keep such wounds dressed and try to make them bleed, but the ulcers often become so bad that the bone is exposed and the feet often have to be amputated. A characteristic lesion is interosseous atrophy, where the tissue between the bones at the back of the hand is absorbed.

The anesthesia is not accompanied by paralysis, because the motor nerves are not affected and still retain their functions. The nerves of the eye are sometimes attacked, often resulting in frightful suffering from iritis. The larynx may be affected and the voice becomes hoarse.

Leprosy is horrible to live with and difficult to die with. Death seldom comes unless from some other cause. The average life of a leper is probably about ten years after the disease first becomes apparent. At Culion a pathological survey of the causes of death showed that twenty-four percent died of tuberculosis and sixteen percent of nephritis. The mortality at the colony was high, but it was believed to be materially lower than it would have been among these people in their homes. Many of them had been beggars and wholly dependent upon public charity for their living. The great majority of cases during the early years were so far advanced when admitted that they were practically beyond human aid.

There are usually two male for one female leper. Why this is so no one has been able to tell. When I visited any leper colony for the first time I used to ask, "How many men have you?"

"We have two hundred."

"Then you have one hundred women."

The invariable reply was, "Yes."

Gerhard Armauer Hansen, a Norwegian doctor of Bergen, in the early 1870's first proved leprosy due to a bacillus. This microbe, which usually grows in bundles of rectilinear sticks resembling the Chinese puzzle, is too small to be seen with the naked eye. Whenever this bacillus can be demonstrated in the tissues, it may be stated beyond question that leprosy is present. Scientists have tried to advance the study of leprosy by attempting to transmit it to guinea pigs, Japanese dancing mice, rats, and monkeys, but without success because no animal contracts it. They have also attempted to isolate and cultivate the lepra bacillus in the test tube. Many have claimed to have succeeded, but their claims so far are open to question because the experiment could not be satisfactorily repeated by others.

In acute leprosy, accompanied by fever, bacilli abound in the rash which covers the body, and it is quite easy to recover them from the scales constantly being shed and from the serum that oozes from abraded surfaces of the epithelium. Such cases are assumed to be extremely dangerous. From the mucous membrane of the nose thousands of bacilli are discharged from lepers who at the time show no cosmetic or anesthetic evidence of the disease.

The nose still continues to be the site where mycobacteria of leprosy can be detected with the greatest frequency and certainty. A scraping from the septum mixed with the serum drawn from the scarification remains a standard test.

Falsehood is a hare and truth is a tortoise which travels slow to its destination. I have been severely criticized for allegedly having stated that the lepra bacilli were found in secretions of the nose. I have denied this again and again and again. But the statement, "Heiser is entirely mistaken in his nasal secretion theory," continues to crop up. I had never made mention of any nasal discharges; I had said only that a scraping from the septum of the nose would show the existence of leprosy more frequently than other tests.

To recover the bacilli in the neural form would necessitate cutting into the nerve trunk to scrape off the sheathe, but this painful process is unnecessary because the clinical signs of anesthesia are unmistakable.

We have learned how leprosy affects the body but not why. As in tuberculosis, we still lack the knowledge to attack the disease by breaking a link in the chain of transmission. Nobody knows how leprosy is contracted, except that it apparently requires prolonged intimate contact. Because the incubation period is unknown also, one of the disquieting features of handling lepers is the long period which may elapse before the disease manifests itself. The shortest known time is about two years, and in some cases it has been over twenty. This makes it extremely difficult to obtain any positive proof as to the exact time at which the disease was acquired.

Some people have believed that mosquitoes were responsible for the transmission of leprosy. But lepra bacilli are found only in the intestinal contents and do not reach the proboscis of the mosquito, which is inserted directly into a blood vessel of its human victim. The evidence against flies is greater; their feet could easily carry bacilli from the sick to the well and it has been proved that flies retain the bacilli in their intestinal tracts for several days after feeding upon leprous material.

Something more than ordinary contact is apparently necessary before transmission can take place. What this is we do not know. But it is also true that leprosy does not occur in areas in which there is no leper. This fundamental fact was the foundation stone on which I built my policy.

The segregation of lepers has been subjected to much criticism in the past. Many have held that attempts at rigid isolation have generally defeated their own ends because victims of the disease were driven into hiding, whereas if treatment were offered and assurance given that there would be no forcible detention, lepers would voluntarily apply for medical attention and thus open cases could be rendered much less communicable. However widely eminent medical men may differ upon this question, the incontrovertible fact remains that every leper who is capable of giving off lepra bacilli is at least one center of infection if the bacilli can find suitable soil in which to lodge.

The real gains against leprosy are due to the disinterested co-operation of physicians, research workers, and sanitarians who have shared their knowledge and experience and helped governments and institutions to organize systematic measures of isolation and treatment. Their aim has not merely been to relieve the afflicted but to protect whole populations. These modern crusaders will not be content until leprosy has been banished from the world. The recent trend has been for more and more countries to recognize their responsibilities and earnestly to try to control the disease and give the lepers adequate care.

The United States has a creditable record in taking care of leprosy at home and in its dependencies. When I made my first trip around the world in 1908 I spent a month at Molokai, where Father Damien had labored so long. At that time this place was foremost in the treatment of leprosy. The colony occupied only half the island, but the three hundred and fifty inhabitants were cut off by a precipitous mountain from all communication with the other section.

Leprosy was called *mai pake,* or the Chinese Evil, by the Hawaiians. It had probably been brought out by the coolies imported for work on the sugar plantations. It had spread rapidly in the Islands, due partly to the fact that the Hawaiians do not shrink from those afflicted with the disease. They had tried various remedies of their own, scarifying themselves with pieces of glass, eating the flesh of cats, drinking Pain Killer, and consulting the *Kahuna,* or medicine man.

A place of isolation had first been set aside by Kamehameha, and the United States government had carried on the work. Not only was everything done for the lepers' comfort and for advancing our knowledge of the disease, but many luxuries had been introduced.

The lepers also profited by exercising their franchise. The political parties of Hawaii were about evenly divided, so that the votes of the lepers could almost swing the election. Hence they were cherished solicitously by the leaders of both parties. Native orators harangued the inmates of the colony, but took care to have the platforms erected near the shore and with palm leaf screens to protect themselves from possible contagion. But more substantial bait was required. The fermented taro dish called *poi* was particularly delectable to the Hawaiians. One political aspirant would guarantee, in case he were elected, to provide each leper with one pound of *poi* a day. The other aspirant would then promise two pounds of *poi.* At the time of my visit the bid had been raised, and each leper was entitled by law to seven pounds of *poi* a day, far more than he could possibly eat. The lepers were taking advantage of their strategic position and favoring a law which would give them the right to sell the *poi* which had been thrust upon them and retain the proceeds.

A study of the history of leprosy in Hawaii shows that until isolation was carried out, the number of lepers was constantly on the increase. It may be argued, however, that the Hawaiians are unusually

226

susceptible to leprosy, while the Japanese, who are now numerically predominant, are not. Thus, although the total number of lepers in Hawaii has been reduced, it is not certain whether this reduction may not be due to the lesser susceptibility of the Japanese and other introduced races.

When I became Director of Health of the Philippines I realized that one of my most important duties would be to isolate the lepers whose numbers were estimated anywhere from ten to thirty thousand, although officially a little less than four thousand were recorded. There were twelve hundred new cases developing every year and practically nothing was being done about them.

Segregation is always cruel. We did not want to separate husband and wife or children and parents. But segregation is cruel to relatively few whereas non-segregation threatens an entire people. I believed that isolation not only protected others from contracting leprosy but, furthermore, was the most humane solution for the leper himself. Instead of being shunned and rebuffed by the world, he could have an opportunity to associate with others of his kind in pleasant relationship. In the Philippines the lepers were sensitive and proud and quick to notice any infringement upon their human rights.

Among the Filipinos family ties are unbelievably strong. Every step would have to be taken most tactfully; otherwise the Filipinos would conceal their lepers, or even actively oppose segregation. First, the colony would have to be prepared, and, then, the Islanders would have to be educated to the benefits of the plan.

Almost at the very inception of the civil government, negotiations had been carried on by Worcester which led to the setting aside of Culion Island for a leper colony. Culion is one of the Calamianes group between the Sulu and China Seas, two hundred miles southwest of Manila. It is twenty miles long and twelve miles at its widest point. The population was then about eight hundred; more than half were harmless, wild Tagbuanas, without fixed abode or title to land beyond that of possession. Outside the town of Culion there were only eight small houses.

The Bay of Culion is almost landlocked, and is surrounded with marvelous green hills. Through the water, calm and blue and crystal clear, are plainly visible coral and marine plants of almost every conceivable hue. Across the Bay is the Island of Coron, over which hangs in the early morning a diaphanous blue haze. The rising sun gradually clears the air, only to have the mists gather again as the sun sinks. Coron has long been a lodestone for those who specialize in coral. Beautiful to look at, it is almost impossible to investigate. There are some tiny coves with a little sand in them where a boat can be landed. Otherwise the whole shore is a sheer cliff, usually undercut three to four feet; at low tide a rowboat can glide beneath comfortably.

The greenish-blue surface of Coron is built up of thousands of razor-sharp plates, like meat cleavers, set perpendicularly and so sharp and so close together that the toughest leather is sliced to ribbons after a few steps. Only one man has been able to penetrate any distance. When his shoes were completely shredded, he bound twigs upon his feet, proceeding cautiously for a few paces, and then repairing the damage with more twigs.

Culion was valuable for its forest products and had good fishing grounds. Thus it was a constant temptation for poachers. In addition, the many wild carabao were a lure to sportsmen. We were glad to have these dangerous animals shot, and we would grant special permits to those who wished to try their skill. But so many mighty hunters had come to grief at the horns of the carabao, that it was customary for a small relief expedition to be kept in readiness.

Once the brother of Governor General Harrison, an internationally renowned Nimrod, scorned our warnings, and set forth boldly. When dawn of the next day broke without his having returned, the relief party started out and discovered him, gunless and hatless, in the topmost part of the tallest tree in the vicinity.

At first the plan had been to locate the leper colony outside the old town of Culion at a place called Halsey Harbor. In January, 1903, fifty-nine laborers and two foremen had arrived, constructed a weir to supply fresh fish for the camp, and tried to get the natives to saw planks for a wharf, but this had proved to be beyond their skill. Moreover, siesta hour for the Filipinos had seemed to come the moment the foreman turned his back. Lonesome for their women, and discontented at the working conditions, as soon as they were paid, they had said, "We want to go home." Finally beriberi and malaria had set in, and the site had had to be abandoned for another.

A little over a year later steps had been taken to purchase the village of Culion and transfer its inhabitants to the Island of Busuanga, near Coron. There were a number of good houses, and also an old fort, dating from the time of the Moro raids, where the Filipinos, although outnumbering their assailants twenty to one, had judged it more prudent to hide than to fight.

The problem of Culion was one of the most arduous which faced me when I took office. I became wholly responsible for the undertaking, which proved more difficult than I could ever have anticipated, even in my wildest dreams. The actual building began in 1905. Every imaginable type of social question presented itself. Not only houses and a hospital had to be constructed and separate quarters for the non-lepers built, but streets had to be laid out, wharves constructed, buoys planted, a sewer system installed, amusement halls and a postoffice planned. Arrangements had to be made for public order, for municipal ordinances, for banking, and for disinfecting letters.

We never could be sure of holding labor any length of time. Good mechanics had no desire to undergo the isolation. Some left after a few days' work, and the class that could be induced to go often lacked skill and made blunders which sometimes took months to correct. At one time three hundred workmen laid down their tools and retired to a safe distance at the first report that a shipload of lepers was soon to arrive at the Island.

Delays were constant and inevitable. There was no telegraph, and mail steamers arrived only once every three weeks. Moreover, captains of vessels carrying building materials who were unfamiliar with the port often would anchor far off, and the supplies had to be laboriously landed in small boats. Sometimes a part of a machine would be lost in transit. This island in the China Sea was ten thousand miles from a market; all supplies had to come from the United States. It took four to five months to procure even an odd screw which might be missing.

In May, 1906, we prepared to transfer the three hundred and sixty-five inmates of the San Lazaro Hospital at Cebu to Culion. Often, before and afterwards, we had to contend with fear. A government boat had been set aside for the purpose, but as we were about to sail the entire crew deserted. Only the chief engineer and the skipper, a Maine Yankee named Tom Hillgrove, stuck to the ship. Even after a new crew had, with great pains, been assembled, I had qualms about setting forth over the treacherous waters of the China Sea, because the skipper had fortified himself with such huge quantities of alcohol. But he was so good a navigator that he was equal to all emergencies, and we arrived safely at Culion, where Father Valles, a Jesuit priest, and four Sisters of the order of St. Paul de Chartres were on hand to receive the lepers.

I wanted to popularize Culion so that the lepers who were at large would come there willingly. I had photographs taken of the colony, and even moving picture reels made, a great achievement in those days, showing how attractive it was. I invited leaders of public thought to come to the Island, trusting they would write home about it to their friends. Agents were sent to the various towns to explain the purpose of Culion, and tell the lepers what they would find there, the type of house they would live in, the food they would eat, and the facilities for treatment. The Filipino is cautious, and not many came at first. But those who were persuaded found they were much better off than at home. The first two years we received enough volunteers to tax all our resources.

My plan was to remove lepers first from well isolated islands which had comparatively few victims, so that the spread of the disease could be prevented where it was not firmly entrenched. For the leper collecting trips we chartered the *Basilan* which could accommodate one hundred and fifty. Orders were telegraphed a few days ahead to the local health officials to have the lepers assembled at central points in preparation for my arrival, giving them the date.

In collecting lepers, as in every other activity, expenses had to be watched carefully. The Bureau of Health was prepared to bear all reasonable charges, but it was found necessary to inform the municipal authorities in advance that only a limited amount of money was available. If not so notified they would usually erect expensive quarters instead of the temporary shelters which would adequately serve the purpose.

Many municipalities used to try to evade their responsibilities by presenting for transfer to Culion their insane, blind, cripples, and other incurables who had become public charges, and some were surprised and pained when we rejected them. In the first collections only about half those reported as lepers were authentic cases.

In the early days the very word leprosy struck unreasoning terror into the hearts of those suspected, and a number went into hiding. There was a young leper girl in Cebu whom the local authorities were never able to produce when we arrived. Finally her brother was stricken and taken to Culion. On our next visit she gave herself up voluntarily. When I asked her how she had eluded us so long, she explained that the telegraph operator was her friend, and had informed her in advance when we were due. She would then speed away to a cave back in the hills where she had always had enough food cached to last her until we had gone.

I have never seen remorse that equaled hers. Her heart was broken. I used to talk with her each time I visited Culion, and each time she would say to me, "I thought I was fooling you and all the time the only person I fooled was myself. I infected my brother, and if only I had given myself up it would never have happened."

One of our most prolific sources of information as to evaders was the anonymous communication. If a Filipino wants to secure revenge on an enemy, he spies upon him until he discovers some evidence to report to the authorities. Curiously enough such delations as we received were, in the main, correct. On one occasion we were told that if we were to go to a certain house in the center of Manila, and knock three times, and then again once, a trap door in the ceiling would open, and there we would find a leper. We followed these instructions, and found the leper. Somebody had a grudge against his family, and was trying to get even.

The anonymous letter writer was not always accurate, however. We once received information that the son of a mayor in a small provincial town was ill with leprosy. When we went to the house we found him in bed with all his clothes on. There was nothing wrong with him but malaria and a skin rash. We furnished him quinine and a cake of soap, with the stern advice to use both. He recovered shortly.

The Filipino is also likely to be unscrupulous when he is attempt-

231

ing to secure a political advantage. When I arrived one day at a small town, the mayor reported he had all the local lepers ready in waiting. On the way to the detention building one of the prominent citizens approached me and asked me to help him, saying his daughter, who was perfectly healthy, had been shut up with the lepers. Since this was a very common story, I was not particularly impressed, but told him I would look into it.

I was somewhat surprised to find that he was right. His daughter, a beautiful girl, had been herded into camp with real lepers, although she had not the slightest sign of the disease. I ordered her released and then demanded of the local health officer, "Why did you lock her up?"

"The mayor told me to, and I have to obey his orders."

"But what reason did he have?"

"Her father is a candidate. The present mayor thought he could win the election if he could brand his rival's daughter with the stigma of leprosy."

At the very inception of gathering up the lepers it became our fixed policy not to confine anyone at Culion from whom leprosy bacilli could not be recovered and demonstrated by microscopical examination. Filipinos had so many skin diseases that an occasional mistake might easily have been made in diagnosing non-lepers as lepers. We never placed anyone on the ship until from three to five leprosy experts, acting as a Board, were unanimously satisfied that the man or woman had leprosy. If we erred it was on the side of safety, but, as far as I know, no mistake was ever made. The reason more cases are now being found is that since those days many refinements in diagnosis have been made. The more recent complete knowledge is of great value because the early stages of the disease are the most infective.

For the clinical examination of the anesthetic form the suspect was blindfolded. Then his skin was touched with a cotton swab, a feather, a camel's hair brush, or a paper spill, and he was asked to indicate where he had been touched. The head and the point of a pin were pressed alternately against suspected spots, and the patient was asked which caused the more pain. Test tubes, one filled with hot water and the other with cold, were held against his skin, and he was asked to tell which was warm and which was cold. Finally, a scraping was taken from the septum of the nose with a blunt, narrow-bladed scalpel, and put under the microscope.

The actual work of collecting the lepers and caring for them after they were gathered together presented obstacles, many of which at times seemed insurmountable. Most people have a spontaneous impulse toward charity and a social conscience which impels them to do good, but these emotions are often dissipated in the face of actuality, particularly where the task is loathsome and repellent. When it came to transporting lepers to a seaport, providing their subsistence, aiding them aboard the steamer, making the necessary medical examinations, and attending to their needs, experience again and again demonstrated that only those of my doctors who were possessed of superior courage and capable of supreme self-sacrifice could be induced to continue at the work.

Often lepers had been confined in a barbarous manner by the local officials at the outskirts of towns. Once when we arrived in a province we found them in an abandoned warehouse, where they had been shut up for weeks pending our arrival. Some were literally rotting away. I had several doctors with me, most of them long experienced in work of this kind, but they became so nauseated by the foul stench from the gangrenous, putrescent ulcers that they could hardly bring themselves to handle the patients. One old woman in particular was no more than a mass of decaying flesh, rotten as a corpse long exposed; she looked as though she were going to fall to pieces. It was with the utmost difficulty that I finally summoned the courage to gather her up and carry her on board in a basket.

There was always, of course, the danger of infection. On one occasion cholera broke out on the *Basilan* in the midst of a collection trip in the Southern Islands. I ordered the boat to make for Culion as quickly as possible, but at best it would take several days, and the quarters on board were too small for effective isolation. After we arrived at Culion, I immediately segregated the lepers in groups of ten, so that if one group should become infected, it alone would have to be quarantined. One leprous woman was not only violently insane, but also came down with cholera. She would keep no clothing on and, since she was completely uncontrollable, she was a deadly menace to everyone. It required a physical struggle, but I finally succeeded in pinioning and imprisoning her. In the process she scratched me so deeply in the arm that I still bear the scar. It is extremely unpleasant to be scratched by an insane leper with cholera, and I lost no time in drenching the wound with disinfectant, though I could not be certain that it would prove effective. There is no way to tell who have and who have not immunity to leprosy, but my mind is now at rest, because the twenty years of possible incubation have passed, and I have not yet evidenced any signs of leprosy.

In the light of our present knowledge I believe that isolation is the best course in a country such as the Philippines, but it will take a long time to prove that it can wipe out the disease, because many cases in the incubation period cannot be detected.

By 1908 at least one collection of lepers had been made all over the Archipelago, and a number in many provinces. Four years later every recognized leper was in confinement. Certain elements in many communities were not open to persuasion, and there force was necessary. The obstreperous cases often belonged to the criminal classes, so that sometimes we had to resort to legal compulsion. But most of the patients who were to become the inhabitants of Culion were persuaded rather than compelled to go. Gradually the terror it caused was lost through our educational propaganda, and lepers were lured there by hope of cure.

It must be said to the credit of the Filipinos that the effort to segregate lepers was never seriously opposed. In the majority of cases they cooperated, even though this often involved the lifelong separation of wife from husband, sister from brother, child from parents, and friend from friend. Only in comprehending this can it be realized what forbearance was exercised by the Filipinos.

I can still hear ringing in my ears the cries of anguish of the relatives and friends who used to follow us down to the boat drawn up on the open beach. As we rowed out to the *Basilan,* and the *Basilan* steamed out to the open sea, I could see them standing there, and hear faint echoes of their grief. It was an experience to which I never became hardened. I knew that even as the *Basilan* was hull down on the horizon they would still be there, straining for a last glance at those whom they never expected to see again.

CHAPTER 15. PRISONERS OF HOPE

THE *Basilan* had no sooner landed its first grim cargo at Culion than I realized that my responsibilities toward the lepers whom I had uprooted from their homes had only begun. Transporting them there and providing them with food and lodging was merely a prelude to the real work.

After the novelty of their surroundings had ceased to attract and divert the lepers, they often became homesick, and yearned for their old associations. In every way we tried to make their life as nearly as possible like that of their own villages, always remembering Culion was a town of invalids. We put Tagalog with Tagalog, Ilocano with Ilocano, Visayan with Visayan, Moro with Moro; they would mix during the day but at night liked to be with their own kind.

Little by little we beautified the place with trees, palms, and shrubbery. I designed a semi-open air theatre, with Chinese spirals and other roof decorations, but the workmen were unable to follow my intention so that when finished it resembled no known style of architecture. It served its purpose, however. It was so constructed that those who needed protection could sit under the roof, and the rest in chairs around the outside.

Filipinos are born actors and the lepers took eagerly to dramatics. Besides putting on plays of their own, they enjoyed greatly the films with which generous motion picture companies kept me supplied.

Filipinos are natural musicians also. I have always believed it would be possible to hand fifty band instruments at random to fifty

Filipinos and hear sweet music at once. The Filipinos have made music for the entire East. I have heard the rhythm of their Spanish melodies echoing from dance floors and theatres at Calcutta, Bombay, Singapore, and everywhere else in the Orient.

The lepers were no exception. Culion took great pride in its band and practised faithfully. This we encouraged, because the music cheered them enormously. The lepers at San Lazaro at Manila had a particularly good stringed orchestra which used to greet me on every visit. Once after a long absence I was welcomed as warmly as ever but observed with surprise that no music was on hand. "Why don't you play?" I asked.

"We can't."

"Why not?"

In dumb reply they held up their hands; they had literally played their fingers off.

Our first collections of lepers were composed of those who were so ill as to be nearly helpless. The disease had produced such contractions of limbs, destruction of tissues, losses of fingers and toes, impairment of muscular power, and general debility, that only a few could perform the heavy work connected with agriculture, which we hoped would divert them as well as contribute toward their support. Also, many had fever several days during the month, and more were entirely bedfast.

It was not easy to keep the semi-well occupied and distracted. Because of the public's great fear of infection, they could not weave hats of palm or dresses of jusi cloth, carve knickknacks or hammer brass ash trays for general sale. We did not even advocate the manufacture of these handicrafts because the innate Filipino disposition to take life easy, while deplorable for the healthy, is not at all a bad thing for lepers. They did little work other than that entailed by their own domestic requirements.

At first we tried serving cooked food in a cafeteria, but when our Occidental methods of preparation obviously did not please our patrons, we gave them the raw food and let them prepare it to suit their own tastes. Some years later Miss Hartley Embrey, an able food chemist, went to Culion as a volunteer to devise ways of combining proper dietary with Filipino gustatory preferences. The most

advanced cases had been collected earlier; the later comers were in
the initial stages of the disease, and consequently not so badly incapacitated. Basing his action on Miss Embrey's advice, General Wood
arranged for the employment of competent gardeners. Ubi tubers
were introduced from the Batanes and leafy vegetables were grown
with great success. They started tiny sugar plantations, the output of
which was purchased by the government and reissued as food to the
lepers.

Cattle raising was started. We also encouraged them to fish, and
they paddled little balsas of lashed bamboo to the huge fenced fish
traps and to other waters. They did well at fishing, and daily we
purchased large quantities. In addition to buying their produce we
gave them a gratuity of twenty cents a week, and established a store
at which small comforts were sold. In order to avoid all risk of
infection outside, special money was used, which circulated only in the
colony.

We helped the townspeople to set up an organization with a
presidente, or mayor, and ten councillors, all of whom they elected
themselves. They were allowed to make their own regulations, and
punish offenders. The first woman suffrage in the East was established at Culion in 1908. The women were influential in elections,
and invariably picked out the best looking man for *presidente,* no
matter what his qualifications.

A former sergeant of Constabulary who had developed leprosy was
chosen to captain a leper police force of twelve, which grew in size
with the expanding colony. We did not attempt to restrict the liberty
of the inmates; as far as we were concerned they could escape whenever they were so minded. The idea was that they were to prevent
themselves from running away.

Very little went on in the colony that the police and secret service
men did not know. Nevertheless, being lepers themselves, it sometimes happened that they were at one with those who grew too
lonely. The refugees would make rough rafts of bamboo with sails
woven of palms, and hide them away in some safe place. Then, when
the occasion was propitious, off they would sail into the China Sea.

Often the lepers came from distant islands, hard to reach with
improvised craft, and in the endeavor to gain home an occasional one

was shipwrecked and drowned. A few of the deserters leaving Culion escaped, because the Islands are dotted so closely that the voyage from one to another is not far and could be negotiated even with their frail balsas; under favorable weather conditions the crossing to Luzon could be made without excessive risk. The lepers would be missed when they did not show up for their gratuities, and occasionally we could rescue them in a launch. Escapes were comparatively rare and never were a source of great trouble. Even those who reached their homes usually gave themselves up after they had satisfied their nostalgia.

The comparative contentment of the lepers was in great measure due to the Sisters of St. Paul de Chartres, who had dedicated their lives to the care of these unfortunates. Outwardly calm and happy, the Sisters spread an atmosphere of cheer around them that was truly magnificent. Whenever the *Basilan* came into port, they would have to dress the nauseating, disgusting wounds of the newcomers, and each day thereafter throughout every year, this routine had to be repeated with never a break. In emergencies they had to perform amateur surgical operations.

I had always had a notion that cleanliness was an important factor in the prevention of leprosy. If those even in the closest contact kept free of vermin and washed their hands and bodies frequently and thoroughly, I believed they would incur little danger. Although I could not confirm this theory scientifically, I had noted that nurses and attendants who worked at leper colonies and did not keep themselves clean often did contract the disease.

I asked the Sisters to promise me solemnly that when they entered the hospital from their quarters in the clean part of the colony, they would remove their clothes in a room provided for that purpose before walking into the next room, where disinfected clothing would be waiting. When they left, they were to reverse the process, bathing themselves with disinfecting soap, stepping into the clean room, and there putting on their own clothes. Some of these nurses have been at Culion almost thirty years and not one has contracted leprosy. I have always ascribed this to the faithful manner in which they have carried out my initial instructions.

Among the loyal band of nurses Sister Calixte Christen was outstanding. As a young woman she had left Chartres and her family and friends to devote her life to lepers, the most friendless of human beings. With her own gaiety she lightened the burden of the hopeless. She had an extraordinary facility for languages, which she cultivated so that she might bring to each of the patients under her care added cheer. In June, 1926, General Wood and his staff attended the ceremony of presenting her a gold medal, cast especially for the occasion and given in recognition of her remarkable services over this long period of time.

Graduates from Philippine nursing schools are now sharing the burden. Their zeal, both from a scientific and humanitarian point of view, spurs them on to great heights of self-sacrifice.

Individuals who are willing to abandon the pleasures of the world for lepers are rare, but, when found, usually exhibit complete abnegation of self. The American lay brother Dutton, who insisted on remaining at Molokai, was a case in point. No one knew whether he were truly a leper, since he would never allow himself to be examined, merely implying that he was leprous. To the lepers around him he was a friend, reading to them and advising them. He worked toward their interests indefatigably, writing letter after letter to cabinet ministers, politicians, millionaires, and presidents. By his solitary efforts he succeeded in raising moderate sums, which he turned into the common fund for lepers.

The doctors who went to Culion, although again they lacked the religious inspiration of the Sisters, possessed in full measure professional zeal and enough human charity to enable them to stand the loneliness of the life and the particularly trying and disgusting duties. The treatment of the foul-smelling gangrenous ulcers on a single patient often required more time than a major surgical operation.

I remember one occasion and only one when a physician deserted. I had promised him a relief in ten days, but several Filipino doctors had found excuses at the last moment for not sailing, and I was unavoidably detained in the endeavor to find one courageous enough. Nevertheless, I regarded my tardiness as no excuse for abandoning a post of confidence and trust, especially as he had left the hospital full of sick.

Life for the staff at Culion was exceedingly monotonous. Few diversions and little humor broke the monotony of the daily round. The coming of visitors was heralded as a great event. One of the doctors, who was something of a wag, was asked to be prepared to entertain a gentleman who was coming to inspect the work, and whose reputation for prohibitionist sentiments was well known. Prohibitionists have always been a temptation to jokesters. The doctor had a boy climb a cocoanut tree, puncture a nut with a hypodermic needle, draw out some of the milk, and replace it with whiskey.

The prohibitionist in due course arrived, and after half a day's inspection in the hot sun, his tongue was hanging out with thirst and his mouth was cotton wool.

"Wouldn't you like to have a drink of cocoanut milk?" asked the doctor. "There is nothing quite so delicious when you are hot and tired."

The visitor welcomed the proposal and the boy was sent up to fetch down the doctored cocoanut. The top was slashed off and the juice poured out before his eyes. After draining the bumper, he smacked his lips and said, "I've never tasted anything so pleasant in my life."

The inspection was finished in a spirit of hilarity.

Each time I paid a visit to Culion there was usually a public reception, complete with banners, a band, and an impressive parade. The duty of presenting petitions weighs heavily upon all Filipinos, no matter how unimportant the subject matter may be. My coming offered an unexampled opportunity to fulfill this obligation. Such petitions I was usually able to handle with a fair degree of diplomacy, but once I found myself obliged to retreat ingloriously from a mass attack of the women of Culion on the question of segregation of the sexes.

We had provided separate sleeping quarters for men and women but did not forbid them to mingle by day. Certain well-meaning persons who had interested themselves in the lepers were horrified. They brought pressure to bear on the government, and the Governor General issued orders. One part of the Island was to be set aside for the women and surrounded with a very high barbed wire fence. It was all finished and prepared for occupation when I arrived on my next trip. But I found that the sequestration had not been carried out in accordance with the decree. "Why hasn't this been done?" I asked the doctor in charge.

"The women simply won't go," he replied. "Short of a couple of regiments of constabulary we can't do anything with them. If you think you can persuade them, you go ahead and try."

"Let's call a meeting," I suggested. I had often addressed them before and anticipated no trouble. When the women were assembled, I climbed up on a soap box and stood under the blazing hot noonday sun, looking down on the bobbing mass of black umbrellas, tipped back to frame the furious faces. I explained to them that separation was believed to be for their own good, and that in any event the instructions of the Governor General must be carried out.

The Filipino women are even better orators than the men. One of them rose and delivered a fervent harangue to the effect that the rest of the world, after having segregated them, had not before seemed to concern itself with their welfare, and why should it take this unpleasant interest in them now? The women of Culion had asked for no protection from the men and did not want any.

Another rebel followed with an even more impassioned address. She worked upon the audience, already aroused, until they began to shout, "Kill him! Kill him!"

The umbrellas shut with a loud concerted swish, and with steel points sparkling, they converged towards my midriff. As the rush began, there flashed through my mind a picture of the ignominious fate which awaited me—punctured to death by umbrellas.

I held up my hand and shouted at the top of my lungs. "Wait a minute! Wait a minute!"

Fortunately one of the leaders heard me, and with a stentorian voice repeated, "Wait a minute! Let him talk! Let's hear what he has to say."

The umbrellas were poised in mid-air, steel points still aimed at me.

"If you feel so strongly about this, I promise you will not be

241

isolated until I have had a talk with the Governor General! I give you my word that no further attempts will be made to carry out the order until after we have had this conference!"

Slowly the points were lowered, and the women disbanded. I was saved. I went to the Governor General as I had promised. "It's no longer the responsibility of the Director of Health to carry out such orders. I've made every reasonable effort, and I'm not going to risk my life again."

He agreed that other means should be found to meet objections. The women continued to live as they had done formerly, but ultimately homes were established for the young girls. The Sisters took charge of them, and saw that the doors were securely locked at night, although a rumor was current that a Sabine raid had once been planned and executed.

We had discouraged marriage because we did not want the lepers to contract lasting relationships which might entail suffering later if one partner should be cured and dismissed from Culion. But when they produced offspring without benefit of clergy, moral necessities obtruded upon medical ones, and our religious advisers insisted they must marry. Our concern before had been to prevent propagation, but now the birth rate began to increase.

Leprosy is most easily contracted in childhood; the earliest age at which it can be detected is about two, although generally it evinces its presence at from three to four years. Possibly the contraction of the disease in infancy is due to the close contact of leprous parents and children. Statistics show that if babies are not removed from their mothers before they are six months old, approximately half of them will become leprous.

That heredity plays little part in the transmission of leprosy has been shown at Molokai, where the children of lepers are removed a few days after birth to beautifully appointed homes in Honolulu, one for boys and another for girls. There they are cared for until they reach the age of twenty-one. During the thirty years this system has been in effect, not one child, according to the report, has ever developed leprosy.

The problem of what should be done with the children born at Culion offered great difficulties. No law existed, as in Hawaii, whereby we could take them from their parents. The duty seemed to devolve upon me of persuading the mothers of Culion to surrender their babies. I used to get them together and harangue them for hours, appealing to their mother love, and explaining how their children would almost certainly contract leprosy unless they were put in a safe home outside the colony. After having my pleas fall on deaf ears time after time, on one occasion my persuasive powers must have become transcendental, because twenty-six mothers, inspired with the spirit of self-denial, offered me their children.

> "He that will not when he may,
> When he will he shall have nay."

"All right," I said. "The boat sails tomorrow morning at eight. Have the children ready."

I ordered the *Basilan* prepared at once. Canvas was stretched around the railings, so that the babies could not fall overboard. I arranged to take six Sisters with me to watch over them and give them proper care on the twenty-four hour trip.

Long before eight o'clock the children arrived at the beach. Everybody was crying; the children were crying, the fathers were crying, the mothers were crying, and the friends were crying in sympathy. Lamentation was loud in the land. I could stand it only so long and then rushed to the bridge and told the Captain to be ready to leave the moment the last child was on board. The hawsers were cast off, the engine room bell jingled, and we slowly pulled out, leaving a weeping band behind us on the shore, and reducing the audible criers to twenty-six.

The *Basilan* puffed placidly over the beautiful calm waters of Culion. The Sisters could be seen moving about efficiently in their starched caps, quieting the children, and feeding them. I viewed the peaceful scene complacently, proud of the way I had managed the whole affair.

But just as we left Coron Passage I felt the first faint suggestion of roughness. The *Basilan* shifted uneasily, rocking gently from side to side and up and down. Then things began to happen that I had not anticipated. The English Channel is a mill pond compared to

243

the China Sea. First one Sister became sick and silently retired, then another followed, and another, until finally I, a bachelor, was left alone on the after deck with twenty-six babies.

The ship began to pitch and the seas grew heavier. Easily identifiable noises came from the cabins, and buckets were in demand. Now and then a wave curled over the deck. The rolls grew more prolonged. The *Basilan* would lurch to one side and babies and water and I would be awash in the scuppers. Each moment I expected to see one of my charges go overboard. Clutch and grab as I might it was impossible for me to contain all twenty-six in one embrace. Back we would go in the scuppers on the other side. During a lull I would get the babies all collected on a high spot, but although I held on to a leg here and an arm there, each roll sent some tumbling.

The loud, incessant, and nerve-wracking wails kept up from nine in the morning until three in the afternoon. Everybody gave me a wide berth. I was all alone with the sea-urchins in this dreary game of pitch and toss.

At last a sailor hove in sight. Filipino men were as good nursery maids as any women. I hailed him.

"I've had no lunch, and I must have a rest. You'll have to take care of these babies for a while."

When my sense of honor drove me back to the nautical nursery, a most amusing sight greeted my eyes. The sailor was seated flat on the deck, a baby on his right arm, a baby on his left arm, a baby under his right knee, a baby under his left knee, a baby hanging on his right ear, a baby hanging on his left ear. He had filled a beer bottle with milk. Whichever child howled loudest would find the neck thrust into its mouth. Until the baby subsided he would keep it there; then he would pull it out and stick it into the mouth of the next yowler.

The weather was so rough on this trip that the usual twenty-four hours lengthened into forty-eight. Since the time of which I am telling was before the days of wireless, I had to wait until we approached Corregidor to announce our arrival. But the instant we were within reach of the signal station, a message was sent summoning doctors, nurses, and ambulances to meet the ship at Manila. As we drew alongside the government pier, I made one of the longest broad jumps in history. Doctors, nurses, and ambulances were there ready to take over, and I streaked for my office. I figured that I had done my share in delivering the babies from the devouring sea.

I was just relaxing before the huge pile of mail which had accumulated in my absence when the telephone rang.

"Hello," I said unsuspectingly.

"This is the hospital. You'll have to come up here right away."

"Why? What's the matter?"

"We can't register those babies of yours until they've been identified. We don't even know their names."

"That's simple," I assured the head nurse. "Each child has a tag around its neck, giving its name, age, and parents' history."

"They may have had tags when they started, but they're ravenously hungry and must have eaten them. They're not here now."

I sighed resignedly and set off for the hospital. Sure enough, the tags were missing.

I picked up a baby, turned her over a few times, and then said, "This is Pepina de la Cruz." I laid her down and picked up the next. "This is Juan Cabonegro," and so I went down the line. After the first five or six identifications, the watching nurses accused me of hocus pocus.

"Come on now, Doctor, you're making up those names."

I assured them I was not, and fortunately was able to prove it. During the voyage I had had plenty of time to become acquainted with the babies and, since I had a numbered list, I scratched the number of each baby on its finger nail—merely as a precaution. Number 1 was Pepina, and Number 2 was Juan, and so on. Long before we reached Manila the names and corresponding numbers were engraved in my memory.

My original intention had been to put the children in an orphanage, but meanwhile they were kept in the hospital, theoretically to recover from the effects of the voyage. A week went by, plaintive appeals from the hospital coming in daily. "Please take these babies away. They're perfectly healthy. They don't belong here, and they're taking up space that we need for the sick and eating us out of house and home."

I was conscience-stricken, but was also in a quandary. If I put my twenty-six charges in the orphanage, I might be exposing four hundred other children to leprosy. The babies were possibly in the incubation stage of the disease, even though they bore no evidence whatsoever of illness. I temporized and left them where they were. I simply did not know what to do with them.

One afternoon a reporter from the *Bulletin* appeared in my office to get a story. "I'm terribly sorry," I said, "but I haven't anything for you today, and besides I'm very busy. You'll have to excuse me."

The reporter settled himself more firmly in his chair. "The editor says you're always good for a story, and I'm supposed to stay here until you tell me one."

I was suddenly inspired. Filipinos were very fond of children. It occurred to me that, if properly approached, they might be induced to adopt my babies. I had no qualms because the risk was slight if they were taken into private homes. "I'll tell you a story," I said to the reporter. "But I'll do it only if you'll promise to put it on the front page and give it a four-column head."

It was a slack day for news and the reporter agreed. I then told him about my homeless babies, whom I could not put in the orphan asylum because I might thereby be endangering many others. I urged him to pull the *vox humana* stop as much as he liked but, in order that nobody might be misled, he must make it perfectly clear in every paragraph that these were the children of leprous parents. "Put in your article that we'll have them at the office at eight in the morning day after tomorrow. There will be lawyers on hand to draw up the documents for legal adoption, and the babies can be taken away at once."

The reporter did a beautiful job. Martin Egan's *Manila Times* and the other afternoon papers seized his story and elaborated upon it. When I arrived at the office the following morning, I could not imagine at first what the shouting, milling crowd was there for. It turned out that these hundreds of people were clamoring for babies. I pushed my way into the office and found that the infants were being disposed of with great celerity. Guarantees were being given, signed, and sealed before a notary public, and everything was in perfect form. I left the details to the office force, and turned to my daily routine.

At ten o'clock the chief clerk sought me. "You'll have to go out there," he said.

"Why, what's wrong?" I asked.

"The babies are all gone."

"That's fine. What more is there for me to do then?"

"But the people are still there. They want babies. They won't go away without babies. And there aren't any more babies."

"Well, tell them there aren't any more."

"I have told them, but still they won't go away."

There was nothing to do but tend to the matter myself. Barely had I opened the door when I heard the cry, "We want babies! We want babies!"

"My good people," I expostulated. "With the best intentions in the world, we cannot produce babies on such short notice—"

"We demand babies! You promised us babies!"

At this moment a second inspiration struck me. Among my other responsibilities was the orphanage. Without any great success I had tried for years to arrange for the adoption of these orphans, who were without home care and love.

I held up my hand to still the clamor. "All right, you'll have babies," I promised. "We'll have more babies in here tomorrow morning—a choice collection and plenty to go around."

Fifty orphans were brought to the office and by noon they too were all gone. As quickly as possible I installed a regular baby department with shelves put up where the babies could be placed.

Rarely were the foster parents particular as to type. Usually they took the babies as unquestioningly as those bestowed by nature. But one morning a woman returned, carrying a baby on her hip. "I don't want this one," she complained.

"Why, it seems like a nice baby. What's the matter with it?"

"I think it has some Japanese blood. I don't like the Japanese."

"That's all right, we'll take it back." I tossed it up on the shelf, pulled down another, and handed it to her. "How is this one?"

"Oh, this one is fine," she said, and departed.

But in no time she was back again. I was slightly annoyed. "We can't keep exchanging babies every few minutes. What's wrong with this one?"

"I bought the Japanese baby a whole outfit of clothes. This baby is much bigger. Nothing's going to fit him."

I turned to the shelves, looked here and there for a moment, and then pulled down a third baby. "Will this one fit the clothes?" I asked.

"Yes," she agreed, and went away with it.

On the whole my device had been a great success, but it was only an expedient and could not be repeated.

Children born thereafter at Culion, during the Harrison régime, were left in the colony, and many of them contracted leprosy. When General Wood took control some permanent compromise had to be found. The plan ultimately adopted was to allow the babies to remain with their mothers for six months, and then place them for two years in a nursery situated outside the leper limits. Those who became afflicted with the disease during that period were returned to their parents; those who remained free of it could be sent, with their parents' approval, to Welfareville near Manila. Only a small percentage of the children treated in this manner became leprous.

When I went to the Philippines little was known, except in a general way, about the treatment of leprosy. The prospects of cure were most discouraging. Hundreds of remedies had been tried, but only failure had followed. From time to time an isolated cure had been reported. This could be ascribed to a number of reasons: the diagnosis might not have been satisfactorily confirmed, the recovery might have been spontaneous, or the reliability of the reports might have been in doubt. Experience with thousands of lepers in the Islands taught me that occasionally individuals alternately recovered and relapsed, and during the period of temporary recovery it was impossible to prove leprosy, even by microscopical methods.

Many treatments for leprosy, like those for tuberculosis, seemed to cause some improvement. Furthermore, under better hygienic conditions and hospital care, or for other reasons not understood, the disease is often arrested; in a few instances improvement results, so that occasionally apparent cures may take place without any treatment.

The people of the Islands had employed various native remedies.

The Filipinos used to tie on the leprous lesions certain leaves which had a caustic effect. The Moros, who called the disease *Epul*, practised charms upon it. The patient was taken to some unfrequented spot in woods or mountains, put naked into a disemboweled bullock, and left there twenty-four hours, during which the tomtom beat incessantly to accompany the incantations of the medicine men. This was supposed to transfer to the carcass all the impurities of the human body. Whether the charms had any effect is doubtful, but throughout the treatment of leprosy it has been observed that heat may have a beneficial reaction. In Japan the value of thermal springs has been known for hundreds of years.

Hot baths to elevate the temperature are a desirable part of all modern treatments. The protein reaction and fever caused by vaccination was also decidedly helpful. For a time we had high hopes from the use of X-rays, applied as near the burning point as possible without actually inflicting permanent injury. In two cases slightly burning the skin produced an apparent cure, but the method was so severe that it could not be generally used.

The Bureau of Health continued a policy of trying any suggested remedy which seemed to give hope of affording relief. Other apparent cures occurred, but unfortunately all of the cases relapsed or died from some other disease after a period of one year. In the case of relapse the infection had simply existed quiescent, unperceived, only to break out again under propitious circumstances.

It sometimes seemed as though the mere intuition of the less progressive people grasped more than the scientific wisdom of the Western World. The common people of the East can often, by a mere glance, detect a leper when the American or European physician, after a clinical examination, fails to find evidence of the disease. In such cases, bacteriological examinations will often show that the ignorant native is right. Dr. Strong was once riding through the streets of Manila in his carromata when a Filipino sanitary inspector stopped him and informed him the driver was a leper. Dr. Strong was outraged, but the inspector's diagnosis turned out to be true.

It has long been known to the natives of India that chewing the leaves and the twigs of the chaulmoogra tree has a beneficial effect on leprosy. There was a pre-Buddhist legend, centuries old, that a leprous king of Burma had entered the forest and cured himself by eating the raw seeds. Eventually the Indians deduced that it was the oil of the chaulmoogra tree, and this is found most abundantly in the nut, which contains the curative substance.

In 1907 Dr. Isadore Dyer, Professor of Dermatology at Tulane University, brought the properties of chaulmoogra oil arrestingly to the attention of the scientific world by reporting its successful use at the Louisiana colony for leprosy in Iberville Parish. I visited there the following year and gained a most favorable impression of the treatment.

As soon as I had returned to the Islands Dr. Dyer's treatment was given a thorough trial. The drug had to be taken by mouth, and most patients became so nauseated that only one out of three hundred could retain the oil over a period long enough to be effective. The poor lepers would say, "Doctor, I'd rather have leprosy than take another dose!"

Then began an extended series of experiments to develop some method of administering the remedy without the resulting nausea. Chaulmoogra capsules were coated with salol or other substances so that they would pass through the stomach without digesting. Enemas were tried. Most of all we wanted to inject chaulmoogra hypodermically, but the oil would not absorb.

At this point a letter was written to Merck & Company, in Germany, in which we asked whether they could suggest any substance to add to the chaulmoogra oil which might cause it to absorb when injected hypodermically. They replied that they had no practical knowledge, but theoretically it was possible that the addition of camphor or ether might give the desired result. The testing of this possibility was done by Elidoro Mercado, the house physician at San Lazaro. He added camphor to Unna's old oral prescription of resorcin and chaulmoogra oil. To our great joy we found that this combination was readily absorbed.

Many came forward to volunteer for the new treatment. In fact, had I announced to the lepers of Culion, "If your right arm is cut off, you will be cured," dozens would have stepped forward.

The camphor-resorcin solution proved a great advance. After the first year we were able to announce to the world that a number of cases had become negative. We promised that if any patient remained so for two years we would release him. When this actually happened, for the first time in history hope was aroused that a permanent cure might be found for this most hopeless disease.

Few can imagine with what a thrill we watched the first case to which chaulmoogra was administered in hypodermic form, how we watched for the first faint suspicion of eyebrows beginning to grow in again and sensation returning to paralyzed areas. We took photographs at frequent and regular intervals to compare progress and to check on our observations, fearing our imagination might be playing tricks upon us, because in hundreds of years no remedy had been found which had more than slight influence on this disease.

But I was not satisfied. The treatment was still so slow in bringing about improvement or recovery that, after the first flush of excitement, the interest of doctors, nurses, and patients all began to wane. To remedy this and to discover more effective preparations of the oil, we brought over chemists from America. They failed. As we went deeper into the subject it became more and more clear that the world's knowledge of leprosy was still very primitive. If further progress were to be made, the resources of science should be coordinated.

In 1915 I visited Calcutta and there met Sir Leonard Rogers, who had just succeeded in curing amoebic dysentery with the emetine treatment. I endeavored to interest him in our research work, telling him we were on the first rung of the ladder but, strive as we would to reach the next one, we could not secure a footing.

Although Sir Leonard was interested he said, "I've been in India many years now, and I feel I'm entitled to a rest. I'm just about to retire and return to England." But he had made a mistake in having me as his guest. I kept after him hammer and tongs until he agreed to postpone his retirement and work on my problem. In only a few months, with the assistance of an Indian chemist, he was able to make a chaulmoogra oil preparation which halved the time of treatment.

I continued my efforts to enlist the services of as many scientists as possible. When I next passed through Hawaii, I called the attention of the Molokai authorities to the progress in India, and suggested that they take up the work in their laboratory from a new angle. The use of ethyl esters allowed us to ascend at one bound several rungs of the ladder of progress. Many cases so treated recovered and only eight percent relapsed after a year or so.

By this time the United States Department of Agriculture considered chaulmoogra of such vital importance that J. F. Rock was sent around the world to make a survey of the potential supply. The true chaulmoogra is the Taraktogenos kurzii. It has a fruit about the size of an orange, covered with a tawny-colored, fibrous rind and containing numerous oval, bean-like seeds. The oil in warm weather is a brownish-yellow liquid; when cool it is a soft solid with a characteristic odor and acrid taste.

The collection of the seeds, which were offered in the native bazaars of Burma, Siam, and even in China, was in the hands of the jungle people of Burma, who allowed at least fifty percent of the crop to be eaten by wild pigs and other animals, when they were not themselves frightened away by tigers and elephants. The dealers in the oil had never seen the tree in its native state.

When the crop of Taraktogenos failed in 1912, the oil of a related species, the Hydnocarpus wightiana or anthelmintica was used. This led to years of experimentation to see whether the oils of allied trees had the same effect as Taraktogenos.

As experience accumulated it gradually became apparent that the oils of any of the trees of the family to which the chaulmoogra belonged were equally efficacious. Many contradictory reports, however, had to be sifted and tested.

Mr. Rock had found forests of Hydnocarpus in Burma, some of the trees fifty to sixty feet tall, covering the steep hillsides in the back country. In Siam the trees were, in some places, so common that soap was made from the oil. Plantations have since been started in many countries, so that the supply of chaulmoogra will be assured.

The Hydnocarpus group is now most commonly used in the form of ethyl esters, which cause less local irritation than the other chaulmoogra oils. However, the choice of which to use is determined by the ease of procuring, cost of delivery, purity and freshness, and keeping qualities.

Success in treating leprosy has become as important a factor in preventing its spread as segregation. It is obvious that if a child with an infective lesion is promptly discovered and successfully treated a most important focus of infection is eliminated. The course of leprosy is of such great chronicity that final conclusions about the therapeutic value of a drug or method cannot be arrived at until after it has been used for several years. Both clinical estimates and microscopic examinations are subject to many errors.

I sometimes compare the treatment of leprosy with an automobile which has been going down hill with no brakes. Present day treatment has provided brakes. These do not always stop the car, but they do slow it down; sometimes they stop it completely, and occasionally it is possible to reverse the machine and put it back on the road to health.

Although of no case is it possible to state definitely that it can be cured with the present chaulmoogra oil treatment as standardized at Culion, ten percent of the patients recover, and fifty percent have a cosmetic cure, that is, the outward lesions disappear and the disease makes no further progress. In the case of thirty percent the disease is arrested, and ten percent are entirely uninfluenced and keep on getting worse. Among lepers who have not had the disease more than four or five years and are not beyond the period of young adult life, in certain groups varying with the country, sometimes twenty-five percent can be paroled. Such lepers are ordinarily examined at stated intervals for a reasonably safe period.

The earlier a case of leprosy can be detected, the greater the likelihood of recovery. In Zamboanga live two girls who were paroled in 1911 when they were ten and twelve years old. I have been watching them since their childhood. They are grown up and married, and have children of their own. They bear a few scars which will never disappear, but they are well, and show no signs of leprosy.

Several thousand lepers have now been freed from Culion after having the treatment, but one of the great unsolved problems is what to do with those who have recovered but who are badly disfigured. Many were deeply conscious of the stigma attached to them when they returned to their old homes. Often they begged to be allowed to stay at Culion, and a clean section of the Island was set apart for them where they could earn their living.

Although chaulmoogra oil produces a certain measure of success, the search continues constantly for more effective remedies. Mercurochrome, bismuth, neo-salvarsan, X-ray, diathermy, anything that offers even the remotest hope is tested out. Dr. Gordon Ryrie, an expert in dye therapeutics, became interested in leprosy and went to the Sungei Buloh Leper Settlement, near Kuala Lumpur, in Malaya. He argued that since coal tar dyes, which are used to stain bacilli, promptly kill them in the laboratory, why should not the same result be produced in the human body?

After some experimentation Dr. Ryrie found that the blue dyes had a definite therapeutic effect. First he tried methylene blue, and then trypan blue. It was a most startling sight to see him work. Within a minute and a half after the intravenous injection, the surface lesions of leprosy became clearly outlined, just as though they had been painted upon the skin. Even lesions not ordinarily visible to the eye became blue, and gradually the whole body turned indigo. At the end of a week the leprous nodules began to soften and to be absorbed. The blue color vanished about six weeks after the last injection. Sometimes in three months all the external symptoms disappeared and the case became negative. For a time it looked as though a real remedy had been found, but unfortunately many of these cases shortly relapsed.

Fluorescin is being given intravenously, and acts as well as trypan blue. Recently a California pharmacologist named C. D. Leake produced a synthetic preparation which he called chaul-phosphate. This is now being tried out at the Brazil leprosarium at Rio de Janeiro, and the lepers of Panama are being injected with it.

Too many disappointments in the past prevent us from becoming excited about a supposed new remedy until it has been completely tested. So far none has proved more efficacious than chaulmoogra ethyl esters. But meanwhile the quest goes on.

Dr. Ernest Muir of Calcutta, one of the foremost leprologists of the world, has made many contributions to the theory of the disease. I have never seen any man whose whole soul is more in his work. He is always ready to talk of leprosy, works with it all day long and probably dreams of it all night.

PRISONERS OF HOPE

The British Empire has more known lepers than any other political entity. After Sir Leonard Rogers returned to England he was instrumental in organizing the British Empire Leprosy Relief Association which, in turn, organized branch societies in India and many of the colonies, and made a survey of leprosy in Africa, Ceylon and the West Indies, and through its sister society a survey of India was made. Recently, with adequate isolation, much has been done in Jamaica, British Guiana, Cyprus, and other places.

Christian religious societies have always interested themselves in caring for lepers, and have been virtually the only ones. All other religions have, as a rule, held aloof. But sympathy for the afflicted, a Christian tenet, has done much to alleviate the sufferings of these unfortunate people. The American Mission to Lepers, fostered by the American Churches, works in many foreign countries, particularly in India.

Leprosy in the United States, although not commensurate in importance with many other diseases, has received a great deal of attention. Estimates of the number of lepers here vary from twelve hundred to two thousand. Most of the sufferers are aliens in whom the disease had not been sufficiently advanced to be detectible at the time of their admission. But, since they were here, their care automatically became a national obligation. As early as 1913 Surgeon General Rupert Blue was advocating a National Leprosarium. The American Mission to Lepers took a leading part in demanding such legislation. In 1917 Congress appropriated two hundred and fifty thousand dollars for the construction of a hospital in which all lepers in the United States should be cared for free of cost.

The government then had the problem of selecting a site. Almost insurmountable obstacles were encountered. Senators, representatives, chambers of commerce, business men, one delegation after another, raised a tremendous uproar at the slightest rumor that a leprosarium might be established in their particular vicinity. A well-known publicist began writing articles criticizing the government for its delay in choosing a site. A year had passed and no hospital had been started. The government could make no adequate defense.

I happened to be in Washington at this time. The Assistant

Surgeon General, who had been on my staff in the Philippines, said, "I'm worried over all this criticism. Nobody wants to have a leper hospital anywhere near. Haven't you any suggestions?"

"It sounds easy enough to me," I replied.

"What would you do?" he asked eagerly.

"I'd appoint a committee of three to locate this disputed site, and since this man has been your chief critic, I'd make him the chairman. Cut out the red tape. Let them have a liberal traveling allowance. They think it's so easy. Let them struggle with the problem."

The members of the committee set out on their travels. Like Yellow-Dog Dingo, they ran until their tongues hung out, and wherever they picked out a likely place, no one would let them stop.

Their hunt went on and on and on; I had forgotten all about them. One drizzling November night I arrived at Gulfport, Mississippi, with no idea in my head except how comfortable it would be to get to the hotel and into bed. But no sooner had I stepped off the train than I was surrounded by an exceedingly determined-looking crowd of men.

"This is the guy," one of them shouted.

"Come along with us," growled another threateningly.

I could smell pungent hot tar, and caught sight of a bag of feathers not very well concealed in the offing. "What have I done?" I demanded.

"You've done enough," came the menacing reply. "We're going to make an example of you."

Things were going very badly until one of the ruffians, peering more closely, said, "Say, we got the wrong fellow. This guy hasn't any whiskers."

Then, rather belatedly as I thought, they asked who I was, and when I was able to prove my identity, they let me go with rather surly apologies, but with no explanation as to what it was all about.

As soon as I reached the hotel I asked the clerk at the desk if by chance any member of the leprosy committee were staying there.

"Shshshshshshsh," he whispered. "Keep quiet!"

"Why, what is it?" I whispered back.

The sibilants continued. "There's a vigilance committee that wants to tar and feather one of them. It's suspected he's going to recommend locating a leper colony on Ship Island just off the coast. He's hiding up in his room and we're going to smuggle him out of town on the first train in the morning."

The next time I saw the Assistant Surgeon General he was again despondent. "The whole committee wants to throw up the job," he complained. "What shall I do?"

"Don't accept their resignations. They undertook to do the work. Let them finish it."

Eventually the committee recommended the purchase of the Louisiana State Leprosarium at Iberville. The avarice of man intervened between this charitable purpose and its accomplishment and Louisiana put a prohibitive price on her institution, plainly trying to hold up the federal government. But finally the purchase went through in 1921.

Leprosy had been endemic in Louisiana more than two hundred years, and had been sustained by contact with tropical America. Not until 1894 had any attempt been made to segregate the lepers. Before that they had begged on the streets, eaten at public restaurants, and traveled in public conveyances. Even after a home had been found for them on Indian Camp Plantation, Iberville Parish, seventy miles from New Orleans, they had had to be transported there by night on a coal barge, towed by a tug, and the feeling in the parish for a long time had been so strong that the existence of the home had been threatened.

On the site of the old leprosarium the government has now erected at Carville the best equipped leper colony in the world, until recently in charge of Dr. Oswald Denney. Its laboratories contribute much to the study of the disease. Most of the four hundred inmates are Asiatics or West Indian Negroes.

Saddest of the inmates are the leprous representatives of the creole families of New Orleans. Because of the assumed disgrace attached to their state, they rarely report their cases until they are in so advanced a stage of the disease that it is impossible to help them. A large percentage of the creoles develop leprous iritis, one of the most agonizing afflictions in the world. Leprosy itself is not normally painful, but it frequently takes this particular form in Louisiana. Its victims suffer so frightfully that morphine can hardly be given in large enough quantities. Most of the time they sit begging pitifully to be killed. There was one woman of the highest social class there, once handsome, now horribly disfigured, who day after day suffered this torture. I, a doctor, felt sad and humble that I could not prevent such suffering.

Everything imaginable is done at Carville to make the lot of the lepers easier. Specialists of all sorts come weekly for consultation. I particularly admired the resident dentist. Leprosy affects the jaw bones frequently, and artificial reproductions have to be made. When leprosy gets into the respiratory passages the breath becomes unbearably foul. A special machine has been devised to pump gas into the affected areas to make them less offensive. But what makes the work heroic is that this dentist is constantly running the danger of breaking the skin of his hands and allowing the infection to enter. Not long ago a surgeon in Paris cut himself while operating upon a patient and later developed leprosy.

Golf and tennis instructors are available, and a moving picture machine affords entertainment in the evening. In the magnificent new hospital building every inmate has a private room, beautifully furnished and equipped with a radio.

This seemed to me a very paradise, and I said to one of the lepers, "You must be very happy in your new quarters."

"Ahhhhhh, the government should a done it long ago."

The inmates of any public institution usually feel that they are entitled to whatever they can get from the government. At Carville the independent spirit is enhanced by the fact that the patients are allowed to decide for themselves what treatment they want to take and how long they want to take it.

No other leprosarium in the world approaches Carville in comfort or lavishness of equipment. At Culion I had always had to struggle with pitifully inadequate funds. Even so, it took approximately a third of all the appropriations of the health service and a twentieth of the entire revenue of the Islands to care for leprosy. When Governor Harrison handed over the reins to the Filipinos, I sadly watched the calesin of government hurtle toward destruction. It is true the Philippines were poor, but they were wasting what money was available in non-essentials, or misusing it like children.

I had many detractors among the Filipinos, who for years had conducted a campaign against me. The Oriental is adept at making charges. If I had permitted it, all my time would have been taken up in answering the accusations leveled against me. But when the Legislature decided to cut in half the appropriations for the Health Department, thus threatening our provisions for lepers and insane, I knew the time for action had come.

I appeared before a Committee of the House, all hostile, all with their minds previously made up. For a whole day I talked to them, pointing out the inestimable services the Health Bureau had performed for Manila and for the Philippines. I made no impression. They merely listened imperturbably. After I had argued for half the next day, I realized that I was losing rather than gaining ground. I had only one recourse left.

Before the Americans had come, the insane had often been chained like dogs under the houses. Fires were common in the dry nipa palm huts, and, in the frantic rush to escape, the insane had usually been forgotten and abandoned to horrible deaths. We had gradually built hospitals for the insane and taken in as many as we could of the worst cases.

Grimly I played my last card before the impassive Committee. "Gentlemen," I said, "you know that the only lunatics in your asylums are of the most dangerous kind. Among them are murderers, incendiaries, and the like. I can barely maintain them with my present funds. If you cut the appropriation according to your proposed bill, I shall have to release half of these maniacs. But to make it clear that the responsibility is not mine, I shall have a sign fastened around the neck of each: 'Dangerous Lunatic. Likely to Kill. At Large Because the Philippine Legislature Refuses to Provide for My Care.' This will make a great newspaper story. It will go over the whole world, and bring you a reputation."

"You wouldn't really do such a thing, would you?" one of the Committee asked in obvious alarm.

"Certainly I would, and, what is more, the same holds true for Culion. Half the lepers there will have to be turned loose. They are in an advanced stage of the disease, and not pleasant to view. They are capable of spreading leprosy wherever they go. I have just enough money left to bring them to Manila. But I want everybody to know that when the lepers are freed in the streets, I am not responsible for this act, either, and around the neck of each will be a sign: 'Released and at Large, Because the Legislature Refuses to Appropriate Funds for My Care.'

"That will make an even better newspaper story. It will be news everywhere, and particularly in America. You are demanding your independence and say you are capable of self-government. What impression do you think this will make in the United States?"

They capitulated and the appropriation was restored.

I had won my victory, but it was short-lived, because, with my departure to join the Rockefeller Foundation, the Legislature had its way.

Governor General Leonard Wood took particular interest in the leprosy problem. He was horrified to find that, because of lack of funds, only one out of six of the patients at Culion was receiving the ethyl ester treatment. To secure further appropriations, he used all his influence with the Legislature, which in the early days was great. A more scientific staff was installed, a first-class chemist employed, and an expert on nutrition set to work. Dr. H. Windsor Wade was transferred from the chair of pathology at the University of the Philippines and made pathologist at Culion. Most important of all, the manufacture of chaulmoogra oil ethyl esters was undertaken at the colony itself, thereby reducing the cost of the treatment and permitting many more to receive it. The effects were almost instantaneous; two thousand cases became negative in a few years.

But the lack of funds was still a severe handicap. Every morning General Wood used to meet with his advisers and conduct informal discussions on every conceivable project which might be of utility to the Islands. Leprosy was often on the table. General Wood was of the opinion that it would be a comparatively simple matter to raise one million dollars from the generous American public to establish a laboratory at Culion and build a hospital for lepers at Cebu.

It seemed to me that it would be essential for General Wood to lend his name to the undertaking. But he could not be made to see that this would have any drawing power. I talked to him off and on for days, saying that what he had done for Cuba would soon be forgotten, but the world would always remember him for his efforts on behalf of lepers. His other advisers were unanimously with me in this opinion. Finally he agreed.

Mrs. Dorothy Paul Wade, the wife of Dr. Wade, offered to help in any way she could. General Wood said he would write out an appeal, and, if she could get this published in the press of America, he was sure the response would be ample. Those who had had experience in raising funds were not so certain that this method would get us what we all wanted, but, since Wood enjoyed such popularity, they admitted they might be wrong. It must be said to the credit of American journalism that, although Wood had incurred much opposition during his candidacy for the Presidential nomination on the Republican ticket, the entire press of America, Republican and Democratic alike, published his appeal in the form of an editorial. The results, however, were disappointingly small; only a few hundred dollars were raised.

It was then suggested to the General that the only way to make the campaign successful would be to place it in the hands of experts in the money raising field. This was abhorrent to his New England conscience. Believing that the entire amount should be devoted to the purpose for which it was intended, he could not bring himself to allow a percentage of any money raised to be diverted toward the cost of the campaign.

Mrs. Wade worked with amazing celerity and by the end of a month had arranged for a series of magazine articles on this great human need. The magazines, like the newspapers, were liberal with their space, but again the results were terribly meagre. After trying faithfully to do the job as General Wood wanted it done, Mrs. Wade begged him by cable to allow the campaign to be put in the hands of professionals. Among those who seconded her appeal was Peter B. Kyne who wrote the General in part as follows:

"The needs of a lot of poor Filipino devils of lepers on the other side of the world will appeal to our public with just about as much force as the starving Armenians appealed to them. The Filipino isn't a romantic figure and nobody cares a hoot about him. . . . I have no faith in the average human being having born within him a hunch that he ought to do something for another average human being; I think there are about five percent of the human race who have anything like a noble aspiration . . . About ninety percent of man's inhumanity to man is quite unconscious and unmeant. However, we cannot escape acknowledging the fact that all human beings appear to have a little peacock blood in them. They like to do the popular thing and they like to get credit for it. The humble worker in the vineyard who sits quietly down at his desk and mails his check to the Bureau of Insular Affairs for the spiritual satisfaction it gives him will be found to be as rare as the dodo. Somebody has to set a public example, somebody has to take them by the nose and lead them forward while somebody else prods them from the rear. Then and then only will you achieve results."

Time was slipping by and nothing was being accomplished. It fell again to my lot to appeal to the General, and, after "much argument, about it and about," although not altogether convinced, he bowed to the wisdom of his more practical-minded advisers. The campaign was then handed over to professional money raisers, two million dollars were secured, and the Leonard Wood Memorial for the Eradication of Leprosy came into existence. It has on its Board such men as Henry L. Stimson, General James G. Harbord, General Samuel McRoberts, and Owen D. Young. The purposes and plans of the Wood Memorial, quite different from those of charitable organizations, are "to the extent of its financial ability to leave no scientific step untaken that holds any promise of finding the ultimate solution to this age-old curse of the human race."

Half of the initial two million dollars went to erect a new hospital for lepers at Cebu and to improve the Culion laboratory, both in equipment and personnel. The Cebu hospital was helped by a large donation from Eversley Childs, and was transferred to the Philippine government, which now maintains it.

The Memorial considered that the physical care of lepers was the merest start in solving the leper problem. The income from the second million was used with business efficiency in the research field. One of the first actions of the Board was to call the Leonard Wood Memorial Conference on Leprosy at Manila in January, 1931. Only scientists who had done distinctive work in leprosy were invited, and they laid down a set of principles for the guidance of leprosy research throughout the world.

The next international activity undertaken by the Memorial was to subsidize the International Leprosy Association so that it could publish a quarterly *International Journal of Leprosy*, under the editorship of Dr. Wade. In the past a discovery made in India might not be known in Brazil. Now the Association attempts to coordinate the fields of research carefully, so that there may be no duplication of effort. It serves as a clearing house for information, and focuses the newer methods of research upon leprosy. The Memorial also financed a world-wide survey of tropical diseases undertaken by the National Research Council. A Medical Board was formed to supervise the research activities in pathology, bacteriology, and epidemiology of leprosy.

Great acumen has been shown in husbanding the resources of the Memorial. The trustees desired to use the brains of the best possible scientists, but salaries for such men would have been a tremendous drain. Therefore, they arranged to work through various American universities; each year, for example, a professor of one of the sciences goes to Culion on his Sabbatical leave, his traveling expenses being defrayed by the Memorial. He approaches the problem with a fresh point of view, and usually tours the tropics, observing progress elsewhere, before returning home. He becomes so interested in the subject that, upon reaching his university, he utilizes the resources of his own department on leprosy, thereby tremendously enlarging the scope of research.

The Memorial aids as well in discovering young scientists with talent who need more training, and gives them fellowships to go to Culion or other places to study. It also works in close conjunction with the League of Nations, which several years ago appointed a Commission on Leprosy with a full time Secretary. The efforts of this Commission have resulted in steps to organize international research centers at Tokyo and Rio de Janeiro.

For thousands of years any man, woman, or child on whom the blight of leprosy had fallen, knew himself condemned to a living death. Even thirty years ago no hope could be held out to these unfortunates, who were not even permitted by an unkind Providence to die of their disease, but must linger on for years of untold suffering and degradation. Wherever I have gone over the face of the earth I have visited colonies of lepers, and the change that has taken place is no less than miraculous. Nothing in my life has given me so much joy as to see the light of hope slowly kindled in faces once set in lines of despair. The lepers now feel themselves on the threshold of deliverance. They are patient because of the chance, however slight, that they may be once again restored to the world of men and life.

"In his nipa hut, high on the hill of the Leper City, old Lazaro de Paerusza sits in the little bamboo doorway staring seaward with eyes that leprosy has long since blinded. He turns over and over in gnarled patient fingers a battered pair of binoculars. One of the padres gave them to him when his sight first began to fail to help his dimming eyes grope seaward towards the ships—the little trudging coastwise ships that, once in three weeks, in four, in six, come tacking through the reefs with help for Culion. Each day he waits, listening, for the new ship that is to bring America's mercy to those who live beyond the grave. 'No ship today, *matanda?*' they ask him at the end of an empty day. He listens. He hears the night. The reefs chant under the moon. The wild dogs howl in the hills as they rummage among the shallow graves. He shakes his old head and smiles, wisely and believingly as children smile. '*Darating. Darating din Bukas,*' he says in the vernacular—says it for all the patient, buried thousands at Culion—'tomorrow. Tomorrow it will come.' "

CHAPTER 16.　　　DIVIDENDS FROM
PHILANTHROPY

BY 1914 I believed that my work in the Philippine Islands had
been accomplished. The great pestilences had been brought
under control, and the Archipelago had become a healthful place for
the white man to live in. The Filipinos, who had been a nation of
invalids, were well advanced in convalescence. A permanent health
organization had been established. In the course of creating this,
it had become increasingly apparent that the logical method of
eradicating disease was to attack it at its source and to create conditions under which it could not flourish. It was this larger field of
preventive medicine which drew me, but I was not certain as to the
precise form my participation should take.

I was still a member of the United States Public Health Service,
which had expanded from the Marine Hospital Service, and I had
remained in close touch with the Surgeon Generals. The Service was
constantly spreading out, and at the moment was undertaking a campaign for pure water, a matter which would affect millions of people
and in which I was vitally interested. Furthermore, many opportunities for usefulness outside the Service had presented themselves
during my later years in the Islands. The Canadian Pacific Railroad
had asked me to install a combined railway and steamship medical
system which would be more economical and efficient than their
existing one. I had been consulted frequently on sanitary measures,
and had often drawn up plans for civic health organizations. I had
contributed various suggestions to a new state health law for Massa-

chusetts which Governor David I. Walsh had asked me to administer as soon at it was passed.

This was the opportunity which appealed to me the most, and I was negotiating with Governor Walsh when Wickliffe Rose, the able, resourceful, and constructive leader of the newly-created Rockefeller Foundation, came to Manila to discuss proposals for the development of health work throughout the Eastern Hemisphere.

We considered plans for the prevention of disease, which subsequently came to have tremendous influence upon the destiny of the inhabitants of the Orient. This opened for me an opportunity for world-wide service. I told Mr. Rose that I was coming to the United States in a few months and then would go further into the matter of joining the Rockefeller Foundation.

On July 13, 1914, I left Manila with mixed emotions. I was in many ways glad to get away but, on the other hand, I was leaving the place which had become home to me. As I sailed down the Bay, almost every building on the skyline called up memories. I had hard work overcoming the sad reflection that, after all, the masses of the people had no conception of what had been done.

On my arrival in the United States I went to see Governor Walsh. I told him how much I appreciated his courage in placing training and experience above political clamor in favor of a native son and seeking a health officer from far away Manila. Having heard that he had obligated himself to appoint me State Health Officer to organize the service under the new law, I realized the embarrassing position in which I was placing him, yet I had to ask him to release me. The potentialities for world service under the aegis of the Rockefeller Foundation seemed to fit in better with my aspirations.

I joined the Rockefeller Foundation forthwith. Nobody had any clear idea exactly where any of us were to fit in, but we already had our motto. We were to become heartily sick in the ensuing years of its incessant repetition; nevertheless it expressed the concept on which we were to conduct our operations—"The Well Being of Mankind."

Before Mr. John D. Rockefeller, Sr., began to dispose of his wealth on a large scale he sought a plan for distributing it commensurate with the superhuman efficiency with which it had been accumulated. He allowed it to become known that he was open to suggestion. Naturally, innumerable ideas were eagerly presented. He looked into them carefully; none appealed to him.

In 1901 the Reverend Frederick Taylor Gates, who had begun his association with Mr. Rockefeller by securing from him six hundred thousand dollars for the University of Chicago, read Sir William Osler's *Practice of Medicine*. With unbounded admiration and enthusiasm he rushed to Mr. Rockefeller and said, "I have the idea! The world isn't getting its full share of benefit from scientific discoveries. This knowledge must be distributed in a practical way to relieve the ills of the world."

Mr. Rockefeller was already convinced that education and health, two words almost synonymous in his mind, rather than indiscriminate charity, would make philanthropy produce dividends. The Gates suggestion coincided with his own sentiments, and the attempt began to find a definite application. In 1901 the Rockefeller Institute for Medical Research was chartered with a pledge of two hundred thousand dollars from Mr. Rockefeller for grants-in-aid to investigators in institutions. Later, millions were available. Dr. Simon Flexner, Professor of Pathology at the University of Pennsylvania, became its leader and the Rockefeller Institute developed into the outstanding research laboratory of the country.

Intensive investigation was begun on a special group of temperate-zone diseases about which comparatively little was known. The resources of the Institute were brought to bear upon the medical sciences for science' sake, but practical application was also kept in mind. Studies were made and improved treatments were developed for such diseases as rheumatism, infantile paralysis, diabetes, and heart affections. The knowledge of pneumonia was greatly extended and mortality tremendously lowered by various sera.

With Dr. Flexner was associated Dr. Alexis Carrel, whose manual dexterity in special phases of surgical technique is unsurpassed. He became famous particularly for his successful transplanting of living organs, and growing tissue in a test tube.

In accordance with the changing theories of the importance of preventive medicine, however, Mr. Rockefeller did not wish to spend his money primarily in curing disease, but also desired to educate man in avoiding it. This process would extend over many years and require millions of dollars. It must inevitably prove futile unless a way could be found to reach uneducated minds.

Mr. Rockefeller invited a small group of leaders of the medical profession to meet him. "I want to ask you gentlemen a question," he said. "Is there a disease affecting large numbers of people of which you can say, 'I know all about this and I can cure it, not in fifty or even eighty percent of the cases, but in one hundred percent'? Furthermore, it should be possible to prevent by simple means. It should be a disease of which the cause can be clearly seen—nothing so vague as microscopic bacteria, but something visible to the naked eye. If you could name me such a disease you would not have to discourse in vague generalities about public health, but would have something concrete which the masses could understand, and concerning which they could be convinced by large-scale demonstrations."

Nobody had ever before presented such a problem to these eminent physicians. They shook their heads and said, "We must have time to think this over."

Fortunately for the answer, Dr. Charles W. Stiles of the United States Public Health Service was writing and propounding the tremendous importance of hookworm, or uncinariasis, in the South, and Dr. Bailey K. Ashford had pointed out the destruction it had wrought in Puerto Rico.

Fortified by this information, the little group of scientists returned to Mr. Rockefeller. "We have your disease," they said. "It is hookworm. It affects millions. We know all about it. It can be definitely cured, it is preventable, and the worm can be seen."

The hookworm first came into prominence in connection with the building of the St. Gothard Tunnel in 1880, although it had been identified by the Italian Dubini in 1838, who named it ancylostoma, hook-mouth. The Italians, who are the tunnel builders of the world, supplied most of the laborers for the St. Gothard. They fell sick in such numbers that the work came to a standstill. The calamitous illnesses were ascribed to the evil eye or to the mountain's anger at being bored full of holes.

But science offered another explanation. The tunnel had been polluted by the workers. Through ova in the feces the disease was diagnosed as ancylostoma infection. The heat had compelled the men to work naked, so that the worms had been allowed free entrance through the skin, and the disease had spread rapidly. Not until sanitary measures had been taken was it brought under control. Somewhat later the common affliction among miners, known in Cornwall as Miners' Anemia, was found to be due to the same cause.

But the flurry in hookworm was soon over, and for many years the disease became merely a matter of record in medical textbooks.

Hookworm next became a subject of importance just after the United States had occupied Puerto Rico. When a frightful hurricane had wrought tremendous damage, Dr. Ashford, of the Army Medical Service, observed that the people were not recovering from their privations as speedily as, with good food and proper care, they normally should. Their skins were white and colorless, their gums pale, their hair dry and brittle. Their blood was of such poor quality that it was incapable of nourishing their bodies properly. Their appetites were unnatural and they were constantly fatigued. Children were stunted; their bodies so emaciated that they had angel-wing shoulder blades. Obviously they all were suffering from anemia.

Dr. Ashford wanted to find out why the inhabitants of an entire district should be anemic. In examining them thoroughly he found, first, ova and then the worms themselves. Although the latter did not correspond to the description in his textbooks, he had no doubt they were hookworms and responsible for the unparalleled anemia. He brought specimens to America which were later examined by Dr. Stiles, his former Professor of Helminthology.

Dr. Stiles had already suspected that the people of the South had hookworm. The cotton-mill workers, like the Puerto Ricans, suffered frightfully from anemia. They would rest all day Sunday, work well Monday, get along fairly Tuesday, be all tired out Wednesday, and thereafter do little work the rest of the week. In North Carolina the sufferers were eating clay. Nobody knew exactly why. Nature may have been appeasing a hunger in this strange diet, since the native clay contained iron, one of the best remedies for anemia.

Dr. Stiles identified Dr. Ashford's find as a new variety of hookworm, which he named the necator americanus, or New World hook-worm. It was slightly smaller in size than the ancylostoma, which was about half an inch long, the thickness of a coarse thread, and had fewer hooks. The difference between them was slight and their effect identical.

As time went on it was discovered that the necator was not at all a New World hookworm, but had been brought over from Africa with the slave traffic. Folk migrations have been traced by studying the occurrence of the worm. Dr. Samuel T. Darling has made a good case for such a movement of peoples from South to North in India. The necator has proved itself to be one of the world's greatest travelers, and wherever it has established itself, it has remained.

Hundreds of thousands of dollars have been spent in the study of the life cycle of the hookworm. These parasites live in the small intestine. They usually occur in great numbers; one person may harbor as many as ten thousand, although it takes only five hundred to produce serious symptoms. They attach themselves by their little hooks to the inner coat of the intestine and suck blood. Ten thousand worms can drink a great deal, and the wounds they cause in securing their horrid meals continue to ooze more blood. These tiny punctures leave openings for infection, and when they heal leave scar tissue. It has been asserted by some investigators that the worms cause further damage by throwing off toxins of their own.

Hookworms live a long, long time in the small intestine, creating havoc all the while, but they cannot multiply there. In the course of six or seven years they die, and the human host would be free of hookworm if reinfection did not usually occur. The worms lay eggs in tremendous quantities, sometimes ten million at a time. If these eggs, when expelled with the feces, happen to fall on warm, moist soil in dark places, in one or two days they hatch out into microscopic embryos. These little creatures rapidly acquire organs of digestion, and eat any available animal or vegetable matter. After casting their skins for the second time, they begin to stir about, and can explore the terrain for four inches around. If they are not destroyed by sun or cold they can climb up any vertical surface, and if this should happen to be a blade of grass, as is likely, they stand there on their tails, waving coaxingly back and forth in the breeze. They are capable of remaining in one spot for many weeks in patient anticipation of a foot or ankle.

It was once believed that the young parasites entered the human alimentary canal by being swallowed in water or food or carried on earth-soiled hands or utensils to the mouth and thence to the stomach. This is possible in theory, but, actually, never seemed to occur.

Later investigations have shown the worms have elected to travel by a much more complicated route. Looss, the German Professor of Parasitology at the Cairo Medical School, put a patch of infected mud on his hand and discovered from the small punctiform places that the worms had penetrated the skin. He mistakenly supposed entrance had been made through the hair follicles, but it has now been determined that the worms can squirm directly through the epidermis with astonishing rapidity, sometimes even overcoming the obstacle of socks or stockings. The resultant irritation, known as ground itch, produces ulcers when scratched. Those who go barefoot are more likely to contract hookworm, because their feet are apt to come in direct contact with ground which has been soiled by human discharges.

Once inside the human body, the young worms wriggle their way into the lymphatics or veins, are carried along to the right heart, and are then pumped to the lungs, where they abandon swimming and take to the air. Nature tries to expel these foreign substances; they are coughed up through the windpipe and then swallowed. Down the oesophagus and through the stomach they go, finding their journey's end in the small intestine, where they set up housekeeping and in less than a week begin in their peculiarly roundabout way the business of raising a family.

Any people who have to feed a collection of intestinal worms as well as themselves are bound to lose the race against those not so handicapped. By dwarfing their bodies, inhibiting the development of their minds, and rendering them more susceptible to other diseases, directly and indirectly, hookworm has caused incalculable damage. It has slaughtered members of the human family by the thousands, and rendered them ill by the millions.

Mr. Rockefeller made available a million dollars to develop methods for the control of hookworm. Having set the machinery in motion he characteristically retired from all further connection with it. Wickliffe Rose was lifted from the chair of philosophy at the University of Tennessee to head the Rockefeller Sanitary Commission, as it was called. This new organization was to operate in the South, where the Rockefeller General Education Board, favored with a Federal charter and endowed with more than thirty million dollars, had already broken ground with its agricultural improvement program.

Mr. Rose, himself a Southerner, was well aware that merely setting up dispensaries in rural communities for treating hookworm under the Sanitary Commission's auspices would not prove feasible. Local jealousy of this Northern philanthropic invasion would immediately be aroused, and the project would be stopped before it was well started. The longer way, but the only promising one by which the desired ends could be obtained, was to secure the goodwill of the already existing state health agencies and work through them. This plan had the added advantage of supplying a permanent organization which would be prepared to continue when the Rockefeller Sanitary Commission should withdraw. This theory of having the government carry on the work, and other principles which Rose laid down, made him one of the soundest administrators I have ever known. They were the signposts which later guided the International Health Board in a far larger sphere of activity; success was assured as long as they were adhered to.

The beginning was not auspicious. The name Rockefeller reeked of oil and all its unpleasant connotations. The view of Judge Kenesaw Mountain Landis that Mr. Rockefeller, for his Standard Oil misdeeds, should be "thrown into jail like a common felon" was widespread. The people were suspicious and the press inclined to be hostile. The abuse of the Rockefellers was worse than anything Ida Tarbell ever penned in her muckraking exposés. Even in Congress resolutions were constantly being introduced to stop the work in the Southern states for fear we should corrupt them.

As Rose had foreseen, indignation was also loudly expressed in the South itself. "We do not have hookworm," the papers stated. "Such an accusation is a reflection on the fair name of the South. But even if we do have it, our own doctors are good enough to look after it. We do not need any Yankee help." They chose the surest way to kill any campaign, showering hookworm with ridicule by dubbing it the "lazy worm disease."

Dr. John A. Ferrell had been chosen to lead the attacking forces in North Carolina. Under his direction survey after survey was made, with the utmost caution and care, to determine the extent of hookworm incidence in the South before any further step should be taken.

Dr. Ferrell happened one day to meet Josephus Daniels on the street in Raleigh. Mr. Daniels, then editor of the *Raleigh News and Observer*, had obligingly been running a great deal of publicity in his columns showing the widespread hookworm infection as proved by the surveys. Latterly his attitude had changed.

Dr. Ferrell seized his opportunity. "What's the matter, Mr. Daniels? You don't seem to like our hookworm campaign any more. You've been pretty critical lately. Why?"

"You've told us how bad we are in the South. But you don't do anything about it. When are you going to start?"

"Right now, Mr. Daniels," Dr. Ferrell said. "You are a fair minded man. I want to make you a fair proposition. You know what a ne'er-do-well John Doe is. We believe he's a ne'er-do-well because he's too tired to work, and he's too tired to work because he has anemia, and he has anemia because he's filled with hookworms. Will you do me a favor and watch what happens to him in the next two months?"

"That's fair enough," replied Mr. Daniels. "Certainly I will."

Inside the allotted period, by the use of thymol, which was then the accepted hookworm vermifuge, John Doe gained weight, was proud of his muscles, got a job, and started in earnest to support his family. Mr. Daniels was as good as his word; he observed the cure and faithfully reported it.

When dispensaries were opened in rural communities and each and all were invited to come for examination and free treatment, they were at first, even though under semi-public supervision, eyed askance. But other wonders continued to be worked. The same children who before hookworm treatment had shown low mentality according to the Binet test, when given the same test after treatment showed a vastly increased intelligence quotient. Among the adults a grateful population was eventually restored to gainful occupations. Those who were cured were the best allies. Even the physicians, who had been so hostile, claiming that the Commission was taking away their business, came to realize that the gradually increasing earning power of the breadwinners after treatment enabled them and their families to seek medical aid much more frequently for minor ailments, and business was actually growing. Ultimately the doctors also lent active support.

Slowly the tide began to turn. The first demonstration had been made; the disease could be cured by eliminating the worms from the body. The next step, a far more difficult one, was to show how it could be prevented. Over half the rural people of the South polluted the ground as nonchalantly as the animals of the field. Every conceivable method of instruction was used to convince them that, if they would build proper latrines and use them, they would do away not only with hookworm but with typhoid, dysentery, and other intestinal-borne diseases. The process was slow but the idea was finally implanted.

When the converts saw the results, they asked in their simple way, "Can't you rid us of other diseases?"

"You yourselves have got to do something first," the Commission doctors replied.

"What?"

"Support your local health department."

"Is that all?"

"Yes, because in that way you will be aided in controlling other diseases that are preventable."

Hitherto a Southern health service had been mainly a statistical bureau where men untrained in preventive medicine might find a political haven. In all twelve states of the South only two hundred and fifty thousand dollars annually had been appropriated for health purposes, and even this had been given with reluctance. But now the most illiterate farmer who paid taxes on his small holding could see that his few pennies were bringing tremendous returns in well-being. For the first time in the history of Southern sanitation, money was freely offered. Health services began to spring up in the wake of the Sanitary Commission. The outcome resulted in ideas which, at comparatively low cost, affected the human race fundamentally. Eventually the expenditures of the states themselves increased to two and one half million dollars, or tenfold over what they had been.

Mr. Rockefeller himself was pleased. "This thing seems to have worked out very well," he commented. "I know now what I want to do with my money. I made it all over the world and will spend it there. Get the people interested in their diseases. Hookworm seems the best way, although something else may come up later. But get knowledge into the minds of the people." Accordingly he capitalized the Rockefeller Foundation at a hundred million dollars.

As the field of activities broadened, many changes were to take place, but the Rockefeller Foundation as first organized, had four subsidiaries. An investigation of Industrial Relations was to be undertaken under the directorship of Mr. W. L. Mackenzie King, but since he was unable to participate because of the War and his rapid political advancement, this portion of the program was dropped.

In the War emergency a temporary War Relief Commission was established which dispensed vast sums to the stricken nations of Europe.

The function of the China Medical Board was to establish higher standards of medical education in China. The already existing missionary schools, owing to the paucity of their financial resources, were badly staffed. The China Medical Board undertook the job of substituting schools which would function more efficiently. Eventually it bought out the Medical College at Peiping, and built in its place one of the finest groups of medical school buildings in the world, sending members of the existing staff to America for further education.

The Rockefeller Sanitary Commission, which had operated only in the South, was superseded by the International Health Board, which disregarded boundaries, working among any peoples and in any climes. The eventual aim of this organization was to build up the health departments of countries needing assistance in dealing with their own diseases. We would help them set up a machine with the hope that in time it might be able to function efficiently by itself. In order to do this, an opening wedge had to be driven by teaching

275

control and preventive measures against hookworm, malaria, and yellow fever.

Wickliffe Rose, the Director General of the International Health Board, was assisted by Jerome D. Greene, Secretary of the Rockefeller Foundation. Among the members of the International Health Board were Starr J. Murphy, Mr. Rockefeller's confidential lawyer and personal friend, President Charles W. Eliot of Harvard, my old confrere General William C. Gorgas, and Walter Hines Page, publisher and Ambassador to the Court of St. James. All these men were specialists in fields in which Mr. Rockefeller considered himself a novice.

One of my first duties with the Rockefeller organization was to attend a conference of some of the leaders in medicine called to discuss the question of a school to train men for public health service. Among them were Harry Pratt Judson, President of the University of Chicago, Dr. Milton J. Rosenau of Harvard, whose volume on Preventive Medicine was a classic on the subject, and Dr. William H. Welch of Johns Hopkins, honored as the dean of American medicine.

Unexpectedly the demand from the South for men trained in public health had surpassed the number of those available to fill the jobs. The ordinary physician lacked the special education to fit him for a position of this type. Unless the demand were met quickly, much damage might be done by improperly trained doctors. Experience had proved it unwise to place an M. D. without additional qualifications at the head of a health service. He might concern himself too greatly with direct questions of medical relief, rather than the larger problems of preventive medicine.

It was decided to establish master schools to train leaders and teachers. After a thorough survey Johns Hopkins was endowed with a million dollars and Dr. Welch became Director of the first modern school of hygiene in the United States. A few years later Harvard was similarly endowed.

I had been introduced to the great Dr. Welch for the first time when I had been a medical student. At this second meeting we became great friends and remained so during his lifetime. He was probably the most brilliant and able medical man produced in the

United States. After studying extensively in Germany, he had returned to found the first pathological laboratory in this country at Bellevue Hospital, New York City. Later, in the nineties, he was mainly responsible for the organization of the Johns Hopkins Medical School on a system which ultimately had a profound influence in shaping American medical education and giving it world leadership. Many of the most eminent members of his profession, such as Dr. Simon Flexner, Dr. William G. MacCallum, and the Nobel Prize winner, Dr. George Whipple, had been his pupils.

When Presidents and other high officials wanted medical advice, Dr. Welch was sent for. He was acclaimed not only in his own country but throughout the civilized world. Nobody knew how he managed to keep up with all his appointments; he faithfully attended the meetings of the Rockefeller boards, and also those of the Carnegie, the Milbank, and other benefactions. He engaged in countless additional activities, and never missed one of his classes.

Now, at the age of sixty-five, Dr. Welch was undertaking to organize this new School of Hygiene and Public Health at Johns Hopkins. He traveled over the world and in the end evolved a postgraduate public health institution, different from the others, which has become the model for all later schools.

Nobody ever saw this fat little man, perfectly bald, with pointed Van Dyke, take any exercise. But he had most amazing physical stamina. He was over seventy-five when he attended the opening of the Peiping Union Medical College. Some of us had laboriously climbed the Mountain of the Ancients at the Summer Palace, from which one of the finest views around the Chinese capital could be obtained. As we reached the summit and the beauty of the vista spread before us, one of our party panted, "Too bad poor Dr. Welch can't see this," just as we caught sight of the old gentleman himself, calm and unwinded, smoking away on his big cigar.

One of the outstanding characteristics of Dr. Welch was his intellectual curiosity. One day as we were walking in Manila and I was detained for a moment, he wandered off and returned beaming. "What's the history of the monument in that little square around the corner?" he asked.

"What monument?"

277

"The one to the Spaniard who introduced smallpox vaccination into the Philippines."

During all my years at Manila, and in spite of my intense interest in the subject, I had never known that such a statue existed.

Dr. Welch was never too busy to talk to those who sought his advice, and was kindly and gracious to all. But he would seldom answer letters. The Filipino doctors were naturally most anxious to meet him. He was extremely affable and would say, "Now you must write me what you are doing. I'm always interested to hear." But I knew that in his room in Baltimore were piled stacks of letters which he had never opened. In fact, the only way to get a reply from him was to send a telegram. He could not be reached by telephone except at the school or at the Maryland Club which, in his day, used to revolve around him.

The personality of this human dynamo was so vivid that all present were electrified when he entered a room. Conversation ceased; everyone waited for what he might have to say. To any medical subject he could bring color, and could hold the uninitiated enthralled. He could discourse brilliantly on politics, or, if the conversation should turn to New England cemeteries, he could quote quaint epitaphs by the dozen.

The stories told about Dr. Welch were innumerable, particularly in regard to his uncanny memory. Once he was traveling across the Pacific with Dr. Flexner on the Committee that resulted in the organization of the China Medical Board. At one of the inevitable ship's entertainments Dr. Flexner recited a poem of sixty verses. Dr. Welch, who had listened attentively, murmured apologetically afterwards: "Dr. Flexner, didn't you make a mistake in the second line of the eighteenth verse?"

Dr. Flexner, who took great pride in his own memory, was annoyed. "I couldn't have done such a thing. I'll show you the text," and sought the correct version in the ship's library. But Dr. Welch was, as always, right.

Dr. Welch was as familiar with other medical subjects as with his own. On one occasion at Peiping Dr. Robert T. Leiper, of bilharzia fame, in the midst of an address on helminthology, was taken ill and fainted. The situation was awkward. Dr. Welch was asked whether he would speak to the audience. He obligingly took up Dr. Leiper's speech and to our amazement continued it.

Nobody ever saw a note on the innumerable speeches made by Dr. Welch during his many years of public life. When honored by President Hoover on his eightieth birthday, he considered it would be discourteous not to have something prepared. He ascended the platform, put his manuscript down on the desk, and, as he went along, regularly turned page after page. Afterwards a reporter asked him for a copy. "Certainly," replied Dr. Welch, with a twinkle in his eye, and handed over the sheaf of perfectly blank pages.

But after Dr. Welch died, bundles of musty papers and memoranda were discovered under an old stairway in his home. Many and many of the postprandial talks he had given had been previously outlined on scraps of paper. Apparently anticipating that he would be called upon, he had prepared himself, and at need had probably directed the conversation along lines to which his talk would be apropos.

My first month with the Rockefeller Foundation I spent at its offices in Washington, going over the various phases of future operations with Welch and Rose. It was agreed I should make a thorough survey of the East and thereafter propose a plan based on the same effective methods already in use in the United States. First of all, I had to return to the Philippines to close out my work there, and then continue to Borneo, Java, Malaya, Siam, Ceylon, India, and Egypt.

In addition to making surveys of health conditions and the possibilities of working in the various countries, I was to report on the status of medical education. Rose believed that one of the important means of extending medical knowledge was to provide fellowships so that earnest young men from Tokyo, Sydney, or Bangkok could learn from Paris, Berlin, or London, Boston, Baltimore, or New York.

According to the system we developed, our fellows were not necessarily recruited among those who had graduated at the heads of their classes. By the more usual method of selection, a fifty percent success had been high. We chose instead those who had in practical work demonstrated ability and capacity for leadership. It was sometimes difficult to make this plan understood in the countries for which fellowships were being considered. The Indian government, for example, kept presenting me with lists of those who had passed their examinations with the highest marks. By our method we rarely had a failure, and a large number of our fellows now occupy leading positions throughout the world.

In the course of many years I interviewed thousands of these enthusiastic seekers after knowledge. I always tried to give personal attention to those whose choice had fallen upon American schools, and arranged to have them invited into homes, so that when they returned to their far countries, they would have a broader picture of what we were like.

It was equally necessary to present the habits of the East to our own young staff members, not only to show them how inexorably the Orientals were yoked to their ancient and onerous customs, but that patience must be cultivated before the yoke could be removed. These promising young men were being trained variously as specialists, directors, advisers, and teachers. Many did fine work in the field. I have always been proud of them and profoundly grateful, for they were constantly dealing with people who did not understand what they wanted, who were often suspicious, sometimes antagonistic, and almost always apathetic. At extreme personal sacrifice they isolated themselves from home ties and friends and, year after year—three hundred and sixty-five days on end—faithfully carried out our projects.

One of the hardest abnegations was entailed by our stipulation that the local health organization should receive credit for whatever success might be accomplished. As a rule our men were never heard of in the outside world. Scientists usually want the fruits of their labor in the shape of public recognition, but we could not allow this. I sympathized deeply, but could do nothing save encourage them in their work.

Some of our men received flattering offers outside the Foundation at much higher salaries than our organization paid. We were not sorry to see them go elsewhere, because in so doing they were carrying out the larger purpose of extending health knowledge; in many cases we even helped them to go. We ourselves always made a special point not to employ persons who were already doing good work under other auspices.

When I joined the Rockefeller Foundation, Mr. John D. Rockefeller, Jr., had already given up his business directorships and was devoting himself to social service under the able tutelage of the men his father had chosen. But before many years had elapsed he had taken his place at the head of the table, not by right of inheritance, but by right of ability. Sober and serious, with a stern sense of moral obligation springing from his religious background, home environment, and the strict school of piety in which his father reared him, he regards himself as a trustee for the millions placed in his keeping.

On the other hand, Mr. Rockefeller, Jr., has a lighter side not often realized by the public. He has a fine sense of humor, loves good stories, and likes to tell them himself. He has found time to make himself a connoisseur of porcelains, one of the most esoteric of collectors' hobbies. At Hongkong we went through Sir Paul Chater's collection, which was supposed at the time to be one of the best in the world. As his discerning eye wandered over the cases, again and again he would point to a piece and say, "That is not genuine." When Chater died and the collection went to the British Museum, many of the items were discarded as counterfeit.

Traveling with Mr. Rockefeller was an amazing experience. He was hyper-conscientious about his customs declarations, sometimes including more than the law demanded. He was equally sensitive to the requirements of the swarms of newspaper reporters and photographers who awaited him at every station. While the rest of us would employ our brief stops in stretching our legs and pacing up and down the platform, he would devote himself to the unpleasant duty of being interviewed.

The incredibly bad-mannered curiosity about the whole Rockefeller family was a revelation to me. On shipboard Mr. Rockefeller could never escape impertinent inquisitiveness. Everybody would gather around to watch him play deck tennis. As we would sit after dinner in the Rockefeller suite, a window would be raised cautiously, and several pairs of eyes could be detected avidly peering in.

Not a day passed that Mr. Rockefeller did not receive several dozen letters from passengers on board, all asking for aid. When we visited the Philippines, airplanes circled overhead dropping requests on the ship. He took all letters seriously, insisting on knowing the contents of each, so that nothing might be overlooked for which he felt responsibility. He spent his time indefatigably on such matters. I always felt sorry for him, because he seemed to have so little time for recreation. Almost everybody who came near him had an ulterior motive. As we left the hall after one of the big banquets during the dedication ceremonies of the Peiping Union Medical College I sought to get a few words with him concerning our program for the next day, but during the short walk from the table to the door, at this purely social function in his honor, he was accosted by three different individuals begging for money. Dozens of times I have been asked for letters of introduction by people who sought to use me as an approach.

The magic of the Rockefeller name extends to the Foundation. Innumerable requests are received which are not included within the general scope of its divisions; these range from the reasonable to the ludicrous. "I'm a widow. I have a mortgage coming due next week. I need two thousand dollars. Please send a check by return mail"; or, "Would like all literature on the harmfulness of cigarette smoking. My boy is twenty-one and smokes a cigarette a day." A mother asks help for her baby suffering from eczema, a man wants aid to improve his eyesight, a woman desires medical advice about her sister's sinus, a father would appreciate a monthly pension of forty dollars to educate his five daughters, a doctor wishes a subsidy to permit him to reduce his fees, amateur societies suggest infallible schemes for world peace if provided with funds, an inventor seeks investigation and promotion of his hair root resuscitator, a note from an immigrant at Ellis Island says, "Here I am, Mr. Rockefeller, please send my check for a million dollars here."

All such mail is carefully perused. The same courtesy is shown in the offices of the Foundation as Mr. Rockefeller himself displays in his personal correspondence.

The scope of the Rockefeller Foundation was not sufficiently broad to include all the philanthropies of Mr. Rockefeller, Sr. His wife had had many charities which he wished to have continued, including the Constantinople College for Women. But one of the peculiarities of the existing Rockefeller organizations was that each one, almost immediately after birth, had developed a policy. In referring requests for aid to his various philanthropies, Mr. Rockefeller, Sr., would often be met by the reply, "This does not fall within our policy." Finally he established the Laura Spelman Rockefeller Memorial, which among other things was to carry on Mrs. Rockefeller's benefactions and serve as a catch-all. Following the policy of all the other philanthropies, however, the Memorial promptly developed a policy of its own.

Mr. Rockefeller, Jr., experienced the same type of difficulty as his father in his benefactions. When insulin was first discovered the appeals were almost beyond belief in number and poignancy. Although the wording was practically identical at times with the fantastic examples just given, the genuine need behind them was obvious. "My only son has diabetes. I'm a poor woman and a widow. I cannot afford to buy insulin. Can you, Mr. Rockefeller, with all your millions, sit still and see my son die?"

Mr. Rockefeller showed these pathetic letters to the Institute, and asked whether something could not be done about them. "This matter does not fall within our policy," he was told. "It would interfere with our other work."

He then appealed to the Foundation. "Oh, no," was the reply. "We're only interested in preventing people from getting sick. We're very sorry indeed, but we can do nothing."

He finally took his problem to the Spelman. "Oh, no. We cannot go into this, it does not fall within our program."

In one of our conversations, Mr. Rockefeller told me of his deep concern. "This is a real need and must be met somehow," he said.

"Then you'll have to set up some organization to take care of it," I warned him. "It's humanly impossible for one person to investigate all those claims, some of which are certain to be fictitious. You would also have to have some method of distributing the insulin to the authentic cases."

"Can you suggest how this could be worked out?"

"I can think of one way. The administration of insulin requires a great deal of skill and knowledge. The medical profession now has no opportunity to learn the necessary technique. Why not give money to several big hospitals, strategically located throughout the country. Fifty thousand dollars to each would suffice. They could then give free instruction in administering insulin, and supply the drug free to those who applied. Each appeal could be directed to the nearest center, which could handle the whole matter."

The plan was adopted and proved successful.

Mr. Rockefeller continued his benefactions and by 1926 the following separate entities had come into existence: The Rockefeller Institute for Medical Research, which occupies several blocks in New York at Sixty-sixth Street between York Avenue and the East River; at 61 Broadway there were first, the General Education Board; second, the Rockefeller Foundation, under which the International Health Board operated, the Division of Medical Education and the Division of Studies; third, the China Medical Board, which was under the joint direction of the General Education Board and the Rockefeller Foundation; fourth, the Laura Spelman Rockefeller Memorial; and fifth, the International Education Board. All of these organizations worked independently, and subsequently they were partially consolidated. By 1936 the Rockefeller Foundation had added divisions for the Social Sciences, the Natural Sciences, and the Humanities.

It was under the Presidency of Mr. George E. Vincent that the Rockefeller Foundation so largely expanded its activities. Mr. Vincent, a past master in the art of public speaking, could say things that from anyone else would sound outrageous, but he phrased them so amusingly, and was so lacking in malice, that he never gave offense or was even criticized for his remarks. Once one of the vice presidents of the Foundation was delegated to substitute at an address during one of Mr. Vincent's absences. Much worried that he might make some strategic error, he procured an outline of one of Mr. Vincent's most successful speeches. He committed this carefully to memory and delivered it, secure in the conviction he was doing the safe thing. The next day the newspapers assailed him for expressing such views.

I have traveled with Mr. Vincent for a week at a time and heard him give virtually the same address each night in a different town. But always it was as new to me as though I had never heard it before. The framework was identical but new trim had been substituted. Speaking on one occasion at the same banquet with Winston Churchill, Great Britain's acknowledged best, in English in which the most critical could find no trace of abhorred Yankeeism, he aroused vociferous praise from audience and press alike.

Mr. Vincent's memory was comparable to that of Dr. Welch. Like the best public speakers he was able to incorporate into his repertoire any anecdote or bit of description. We would often ride uptown together on the crowded, rumbling, rattling, rolling subway. His attention would apparently be divided between his newspaper and the amusing incidents I was telling him. A week or two later my stories would appear refurbished in his own inimitable manner.

Whenever anybody wanted to know anything that might have a remote connection with the health field, he came to the International Health Board. At the home office, the most important achievements were frequently off the record. Countries unable to obtain laboratory and hospital supplies asked for assistance in filling their orders. Cities large and small, near and far, solicited advice—how to plan and staff their health organizations, where to obtain competent instructors for their medical schools, how to purify their water, how to build their sewers, and how to construct their hospitals. We welcomed the opportunity to extend aid of this character.

The International Health Board's achievements in proving the importance of hookworm eradication had aroused interest in the medical laboratories of the world, and many were anxious to do research for their own countries. The laboratories at Amsterdam were exceedingly desirous of studying dog hookworm, which was analogous to the human type, but, because the canines of the Netherlands never had been attacked by uncinariasis, we were requested to send them a thoroughly infected animal.

Rose asked me whether I could supply one. I wrote to a dozen friends in the South, trusting that among so many I could procure a specimen. But not a single reply was forthcoming. When the time came for a follow-up, I resorted to speedier methods and sent twelve telegrams. A few days later, to my amazement, not one but twelve dogs arrived, all in the same afternoon. The offices were filled with sounds of yelping, whining, and barking.

Sailings to the Netherlands were infrequent. Each of twelve girls of the office staff agreed to take a dog home for a few days. But when the next sailing was delayed, it was too much to ask them to keep the dogs longer. I secured quarters at the Rockefeller Institute.

On the morning the ship was to leave I took a sad-looking little yellow cur, the commonest of its kind, to the American Express Company. No sooner had it been delivered on board, however, than rumors began to spread that it had a strange disease. An hour later the dog was put off and returned to me. I hurried down to the pier and argued the captain into accepting it. But further complaints that the dog was a menace to the passengers caused it to be put ashore just before sailing time.

I taxied the forlorn little object back to the Institute to join its fellows, all of whom were being cherished in case something might happen to the yellow dog. I was getting desperate. With good food and care the dog appeared to be losing his hookworms rapidly. From time to time I used to look anxiously to see whether there were any left. I sought other means of transportation, ultimately finding the captain of an Antwerp freighter who agreed to take the dog if I would secure him a certificate from the Dutch Consul that it would be admitted to the Netherlands and would not remain on his hands.

Another snag arose. The Belgian Consul refused altogether to give the diseased dog a permit to travel across Belgium. I made a return visit a few days later, this time appealing to his emotions rather than his problematic love of science, reminding him of the services of the United States in feeding the Belgians during the War, and pointing out that they owed us a debt of gratitude. He was still doubtful. I then said, "If you can't do anything about it, I'll have to send a cable to the King himself," and I sat down at the desk and determinedly took up a pen.

"I'll do it! I'll do it!" the Consul hastily interjected, and cabled his home office, shortly receiving permission for the dog to land, provided he did not stop anywhere in Belgium.

It was with a sigh of relief that I saw the little dog, who had appeared sadder with each frustrated trip to the pier, sail down the Bay on his designated mission.

In spite of their varying policies, all the Rockefeller organizations had the same end in view of serving people everywhere. When they were needed, the International Health Board borrowed the brighter lights of the Rockefeller Institute. For example, Hideyo Noguchi helped us in our yellow fever research.

When Dr. Flexner had first been in the East, Noguchi had wanted to return with him to the University of Pennsylvania, but Dr. Flexner had refused on the ground that there was not room in his laboratory, and had forgotten the incident. A year later Noguchi had walked in, saying, "Here I am. I'm your assistant." He had proved such an apt pupil in Philadelphia that Dr. Flexner had found him indispensable and had brought him to the Rockefeller Institute. Sometimes he would work night and day for forty-eight hours steadily, without eating or even telephoning his family. He was full of temperament and scarcely anybody but Dr. Flexner could get along with him.

This curious little fellow had been so long from home that his own countrymen could not understand him, and his English was equally incomprehensible to us. But in a siege of typhoid he unexpectedly learned Spanish, which apparently came easier to him, and thereafter he and I compromised on that language.

Though Noguchi was valuable to the world, the members of the accounting department could have dispensed with him gladly. He drove them almost frantic. They would give him a thousand dollars for expenses and a little book in which to note down his daily disbursements. But when Noguchi returned, his little book would invariably be blank. It went without saying that the money had been legitimately used, but it was only possible to guess in a general way the manner of its spending.

Publicity came to Noguchi unsought; he was a man who attracted attention. But he was unfortunate in that his undertakings which seemed to promise the most brilliant results did not always eventuate. When he was sent to Guayaquil, Ecuador, to study yellow fever, which he had never seen before, cases were produced for him which both the local physicians and a clinician sent down from Chicago certified as authentic.

Noguchi took blood from these patients and found organisms new to science. He cultured these and injected them into guinea pigs and rabbits, thereby producing a disease which was apparently yellow fever. Assuming that the diagnosis of the physicians had been correct, he believed he had discovered the yellow fever organism; unfortunately for his reputation, it turned out to be one which caused a form of the infectious jaundice known as icterohemorrhagica, or Weil's disease. He had already worked on this disease, but the type of organism he found in Ecuador differed from that with which he was familiar.

Since icterohemorrhagica had first been discovered in Japan, Noguchi was extremely anxious to obtain some of the original strain for comparison with American jaundice, and two unsuccessful attempts were made to transmit the culture. Once when I was at the Kitasato Institute in Tokyo, Dr. K. Shiga, head of the bacteriological laboratory, asked, "Will you help us get a strain of icterohemorrhagica to the Rockefeller Institute?"

"What do I have to do?"

"Oh, very little," I was assured. "You just have to take a few guinea pigs with you on the steamer, and every eight days you inoculate a healthy one from one that is dying or has just died. We'll supply you with everything necessary, and put the guinea pigs on the ship."

"All right," I agreed, and promptly forgot about the whole matter. The Canadian Pacific liner, *Empress of Russia*, was crowded; every cabin was taken. In mine I found waiting for me six guinea pigs, two of which had been inoculated the day before, and four healthy ones to carry on the strain, together with bales of leaves and cabbages. My room companion at once objected violently to the idea of traveling with sick pigs. I sympathized with his repugnance, because the odor in the hot confined space was undoubtedly disagreeable. I had only been in the room a few moments when the steward informed me the guinea pigs must go back on shore. My only hope was to interpose delays. The steward was still objecting and I was upholding my end of the argument with undiminished vigor when the ship got under way.

"If you'll let this go overnight, I'll fix it in the morning," I promised, and he finally departed.

But before I could do any fixing, the captain and the purser and the doctor all paid me an official visit. The captain delivered the ultimatum. "You'll have to get rid of the whole lot. We can't run the risk of infecting our passengers from sick pigs."

"But it is most important for me to get them to the United States."

"I won't have them on my ship. The whole business has got to go—all your old fodder and everything else."

"Could I discuss this first with the doctor?" I asked.

With the captain's consent I appealed to the doctor's professional instincts, explaining my objective. "You tell the captain it's perfectly safe to have these pigs on board. You know they can't infect the passengers. I can understand the objections to having them in the room, but if you ask him to let me keep them in the ship's morgue, I'm sure he'll agree."

The doctor added his entreaties to mine, and cages and food were transferred to the morgue. For a few days the gentle guinea pigs, which suffer so uncomplainingly from so many of man's diseases, scampered around merrily and nibbled their cabbages, unaware of how nearly they had come to an ignoble end under the butcher's cleaver.

From the time we left Tokyo it was raining and blowing, and almost all the passengers on board were seasick. But the pigs remained in good health. On the eighth day I inoculated a nice little white-eared pig. The next morning the pigs found a new roommate lying on the rubber slab above them. A Chinese passenger had died. According to the custom of his race he had paid a deposit in return for a guarantee from the steamship company that he would not be buried at sea, but would be returned to the tomb of his ancestors, in order that he might receive proper homage from his own descendants.

That morning the storm reached gale proportions. I found that my guinea pigs were apparently very sick from the effects of the formalin with which the corpse had been embalmed. The second Tokyo-inoculated pig had died during the night, and it was necessary that one of the well ones be inoculated immediately. I sat flat on the floor with my feet well braced and picked up the healthy black pig. According to instructions, I prepared him by shaving the hair from his belly, and put him aside temporarily. Selecting a shiny scalpel, with the greatest of care I began to cut out the liver from the dead pig.

Just as I was at the most delicate stage of the operation, the ship gave a tremendous lurch. The dead Chinese above me slid off the table, and sat on my shoulders, with his legs around my neck. I did not dare move. The slightest slip might mean a cut and consequent infection from a disease with a particularly high mortality. With the pig before me and both hands occupied with scalpel and tweezers, I had to continue. The ship would roll one way and a cold naked leg would swing in front of me, then back it would roll in the opposite direction and the other leg would jolt my arm. I had to leave the icy, stiff body straddling my shoulders until I had finished extracting the liver and rubbing it on the denuded belly of the black pig. The moment I had finished I heaved the body back on the table and, with the aid of the morgue attendant, lashed it down so that such an accident might not recur.

When we reached Vancouver, only three pigs were left. They had already endured much and the condition of two of them was dubious. It was midwinter and they had to be kept warm. I took them into the sleeping-car with me, concealed under my raincoat. But that evening they were discovered; the conductor peremptorily told me to remove them to the baggage car.

"But it's so cold the guinea pigs will die."

The conductor pulled out a book of regulations, and I had no recourse but obedience. By this time we were well up in the Canadian Rockies and it was eighteen below zero. The first thing in the morning I hurried forward the long length of the swaying train to look at my guinea pigs; they were all frozen stiff. I sent a telegram to the Institute at once, informing them of the mishap, and received a return wire to bring them along, but be sure to keep them frozen.

Tremendous excitement attended their arrival at the Grand Central Station. A Rockefeller Institute ambulance, uniformed attendants, and even Noguchi himself were there. The train had barely slid noiselessly to a stop when the guinea pigs were snatched from the baggage car and rushed to the laboratory, where Noguchi, in spite of the many misadventures, succeeded in reviving the icterohemorrhagica organisms.

The pigs had fulfilled their destiny.

CHAPTER 17.   A DRUMMER OF
IDEAS

IN undertaking the position of Director for the East of the International Health Board I was obligated to spend most of my time away from the United States and practically ostracize myself from any permanent ties of family or home. For twenty years I traveled furiously on my mission, peddling my line of ideas. Research workers in the United States would be brimming with experiments they wanted tried out in the tropics, and tropical health officers were eager to have projects tested in the big laboratories of the outer world. I carried in my head health ideas gleaned up and down the whole creation.

Until a few years earlier the various medical services of the East had been united only in their laissez-faire policy toward the native populations, looking with suspicion upon one another and jealously guarding their own secrets. Each health service had revolved smugly in its little sphere, and much labor had been wasted in solving problems which had already been successfully met in other lands.

Governor General Forbes had given concrete form to the idea of international medical cooperation. He had issued invitations to all countries East of Suez to send delegates to the first meeting of the medical men of the Far East to be held at Manila, March, 1910. Japan, China, Tsingtao, Ceylon, Hongkong, Straits Settlements, the Federated Malay States, India, Siam, Netherlands East Indies, and Australia had responded, and the Far Eastern Association of Tropical Medicine had come into being.

More important than the papers read or even the ideas exchanged had been the personal relationships established among the medical representatives of widely divergent races and countries. Yellow, brown, and white had met in a common cause, and each had learned that the essentials of his problems were common to all. Thereafter our brethren throughout the East, in full fraternity, had met with us every other year at some Eastern capital. The results of these meetings were so gratifying and so valuable that on my trips for the Rockefeller Foundation I varied my itinerary whenever necessary to attend them.

Usually I followed the sun on my journeys, and Vancouver was my first stop. British Columbia already had a health service, but sometimes officials were unsure of themselves and felt the need of being confirmed in their procedure. They would present me with many problems, and we would pore over them, trying to pick out the sound kernels which might bear fruit.

Generally I traveled from the Pacific coast to Honolulu. Although we had neither personnel nor money invested in Hawaii, not only the government but also private organizations of business men were spending liberally in promoting health. The Americans in Hawaii had established such high standards of plantation sanitation as to make Hawaii a paragon throughout the East. Here I could learn much. The give and take in ideas exceeded that in any other place. I could study the methods of leprosy treatment at Kalihi, and in return help with plans for the eradication of plague, which was endemic in the back country of Maui, and which was looked upon as a stigma.

Each country I visited had a different set of questions to be answered. The Japanese would accumulate a huge quantity of statistical data without being themselves sure of what to do with it. Their interest in science as practised in the laboratory was tremendous, but not sufficiently vital to induce them to sink their professional rivalries for the good of the country. The aim of the Foundation was to bring about concerted action in health work and I, as its representative, tried to make myself persona grata to rival factions. Out of respect for the Rockefeller Foundation they would come together, and this was a big step toward conciliation.

A DRUMMER OF IDEAS

From Tokyo I went to Peiping, where the China Medical Board was already at work. Its activities did not fall within my province, but I was frequently consulted.

I already had had experience in China. In 1911 I had been asked to organize a health service in South China. Many of the questions put up to me, however, had been far afield from sanitation. The first thing the authorities had wanted to know was what to do with the army which had just conquered Kwantung Province and refused to go home. "How can you disband an army?" they asked me.

After prolonged cogitation I suggested that the wall along the water front of Canton should, in the interests of sanitation, be demolished. "Why not set your idle army to tearing it down?" I suggested.

The soldiers were put to work, and the wall had practically vanished before, one by one, the disgruntled laborers had abandoned their unexpected task and had slipped away to their homes. At one and the same time the ends of health had been attained and the army difficulty settled.

The problem in China was controlled by the value placed on human excreta. China has no sewers. Each night in urban centers the excrement is collected by coolies, who carry it in wooden buckets to barges along the river. These are pushed up the streams and canals into the interior, and almost everywhere farmers and gardeners may be seen purchasing their supply, which they convey to their fields of rice and mulberry. There they dig it into the ground for their crops, or moisten it with water and sprinkle it over growing vegetation. Thus a relatively light infection in Chinese cities may become a serious factor in spreading the disease to agricultural districts and, through the infected vegetables, back to the cities. All gardeners and rural coolies work barefooted or bare-legged. Under the mulberry trees, where it is dark and shady, the hookworms wait for the unwary.

At Shanghai, as a private individual, I used to meet the authorities of the International Settlement at dinners and luncheons, and talk over a dozen different things. I used to impress upon newspaper editors the need for better water, so that they would begin intensive campaigns; ultimately both water purification plants and sewers were built in Shanghai. In the normal course of events, this would have taken place of itself, but perhaps I helped to speed it up. I could do such things without having them appear in any reports, and the results in health were infinitely greater than could have been accomplished in fighting any particular epidemic.

After a quick swing through the interior of China, I usually ended at Hongkong, which in my opinion vies with Sydney as being one of the most beautiful harbors in the world. From the water front at night when the mountain side is lighted, the scene defies description. Along the zigzag road which curves back and forth up the Peak, the traveler can be carried in chairs or take the inclined railroad, all the way passing homes built into the hillside, each with its beautifully terraced garden radiant with bloom.

In Hongkong diplomacy was essential. The British prided themselves on having created an island oasis of health, despite the fact that it happened to be inexplicably ridden with malaria. I would cultivate the chief medical officer, reporting progress in malarial countries here, there, and everywhere, but never mentioning Hongkong. Finally he would say, "We have some malaria here. What do you think we should do about it?" Since this was the opportunity for which I had been waiting, I would promptly make my suggestions.

The University of Hongkong and the Health Service had long been furiously jealous of each other. The latter controlled the hospitals. Hence the medical school, which the British had started, could not secure clinical material. Due to this feud, as well as lack of funds, the school was not doing the good work it should. The Foundation judged it exceedingly important that the school should graduate well-trained doctors who spoke Cantonese and would have influence on the governmental affairs of South China. My job was to effect a rapprochement between the University and the Health Service, which eventually took place.

Sometimes I used to take ship from Hongkong to Saigon where the French have reared a little Paris from the swamps of Cochin-China, and with typical insularity have transported there the boulevards, shops, sidewalk cafés, and hotels of their *patrie*. On arrival I paid my respects to the health officials of Indo-China. The service was primitive; it protected the French population, but little was done for the natives. Cholera had been raging in Indo-China for years and had never been brought under control although, as always where French influence predominates, a Pasteur Institute had been erected. One thing that impressed me was the intense French jealousy of other nations. I was told, for instance, that it was a criminal offense for any native of Indo-China to come to the United States for an education; he would forfeit his citizenship thereby.

The ruins of Angkor Wat in Cambodia rank with the seven wonders of the world. A complete city, with a magnificent style of architecture to be seen nowhere else, had been built by the Khmers. Where this race had come from nobody knows, and where it has gone is equally shrouded in mystery. This amazing city, supposed by the natives to have been built not by men but by mighty demons, was only discovered in 1860, and no start to clear away the jungle was made before 1908. Since then the French have worked long and hard to make it accessible to travelers. They also desired to bring home to their own people some impression of its grandeur, and when I was there they were taking impressions of some buildings for the French Colonial Exposition in Paris of 1932. To test out their carefulness, I made scratches on a block of stone; when I examined the replica later in Paris I saw even these scratches exactly reproduced.

Since I could bring little to the French in Indo-China and take little from them, I went there seldom. More often on leaving Hongkong, I sailed to the Philippine Islands, where I was coming home. I was still regarded as Director of Health, and was deeply touched by the many kindly attentions of the Filipinos, who had come to realize what I had been trying to do. At Malacañan with each Governor General I would go over the problems which, though familiar, were always changing. I would greet old friends, revisit old haunts, never failing to pay a friendly call at the Culion leper colony.

After about six weeks I would start South, invariably stopping at Zamboanga. Here Dr. Fajardo, head of the Mindanao health service, displayed the affection of an old boy greeting his former master. He was trying out all sorts of advanced preventive methods, among them cholera vaccine, which up to that time even Manila had hesitated to use.

From Zamboanga across the Sulu Sea to Sandakan was not a long jump. British North Borneo was run by a chartered company for dividends, and was, naturally, not particularly interested in health expenditures. The task there was to arrange for hookworm surveys and to show the planters how better sanitation would not only improve the health of their laborers but, what was of more immediate interest to them, decrease their operating costs. The planters were not at first able to see the self-evident connection between profits and health.

In 1915 a heavy outbreak of beriberi had been serious enough to handicap the production of rubber, for every pound of which a world at war was clamoring. The impotent health service was well aware beriberi was caused by eating polished rice, but was powerless to induce the planters to accept the idea. Upon my suggestion Governor Pearson, who had autocratic powers, issued a mandatory order that only unpolished rice should be used on plantations. Not until this order had gone into effect and beriberi had automatically disappeared in its wake were the planters convinced.

I received every consideration at Government House, and being the Governor's guest had certain great advantages. He would ask me whom I wished to see. "I don't know," I would answer, "but I'll tell you what I have in mind."

The Governor would then invite the particular group of people who were in a position to tell me what I desired to know. Because everybody who came to Government House was supposed to talk, I was able to secure a mass of information which would never have come my way in the course of ordinary interviewing.

Governor Pearson told me about an interesting criminal case which had arisen in connection with a Malay woman who was subject to the nervous affliction called latah. The characteristic of this disorder is that the afflicted person will involuntarily imitate every motion made by another. In this instance the woman was traveling on a steamer with a baby in her arms. A man near her made a motion to throw something into the sea, and she imitated him by throwing the child into the ocean, where it drowned. The court held that since the man knew she suffered from latah, he was guilty of the crime.

I spent a great deal of time visiting the various plantations, often starting in the early morning and enjoying the gorgeous sunrises, the infinite variety of birds, the cool air, and the winding trails. One nine hundred acre plantation was run by a canny Scot who had made the steps to his house double the ordinary height to save lumber, and was tapping his trees in two places, although it was an accepted fact that a rubber tree could stand no more than one.

Another rubber estate was located on rich soil, said to be ten feet thick, which had been the bottom of a lake within the memory of the older residents. Between the trees had been sown the creeping passiflora fetida, which shut out all other growth and could, at intervals, be rolled up like a carpet, leaving the ground bare and free of weeds.

The poles of the recently completed telegraph line between Sandakan and Jesselton, the other capital of Borneo, were kapok trees, which have only straight, right-angled branches upon which the wires were strung. These telegraph poles had the advantage of not deteriorating and also of raising a valuable crop of cotton. In other places where ordinary poles were used, for some unknown reason, wild elephants took exception and pulled out the posts and threw them away almost as soon as they were replaced.

The Rockefeller Foundation representatives in Borneo sometimes had a hard time socially because the feeling against Americans was very strong, and few amenities were extended. The planters blamed the Americans for the bursting of their rubber boom; from the height of opulence in 1925 they had been plunged into depression a few years later. It is not a simple task to gain the cooperation of people who believe they have been robbed.

I would go along the coast of Borneo, occasionally stopping at the Island of Labuan and the Protectorate of Brunei on the way to Kuching, the capital of Sarawak. There I was the guest of Sir Charles Vyner Brooke, the White Rajah, who governed the country under British protection.

To my surprise the British in Sarawak seemed to have lost the art of polite living in the British sense. My experiences gave me the distinct impression that visitors were not particularly desired. The Brooke family took little interest in health work, and the authorities in charge seconded this attitude. I was amazed to see that everyone seemed so afraid of the Rajah that he was not discussed even in whispers. Because I had credentials from the Colonial Office in London, I was admitted to conference with His Highness and explained to him how two courses were open in a backward country such as his. A little might be done in many fields, and such action, though it would have only a slight effect on sickness and death rates, would be commended by the lay critic; or, something essential, although less spectacular, might be done which, at comparatively small outlay, would produce larger results.

We kept a man there under salary for over a year and a health plan was worked out, but the government never put it into effect.

From Kuching I sailed to Singapore, in Malay, the "City of the Lion," which had been transformed by Sir Stamford Raffles from a fishing village into the Emporium of the Orient. It was now a great world trade center and Great Britain's monster naval base in the East. Chugging to Johnson's Pier through the diversified shipping was a fitting introduction to the conglomerate life of this extraordinary cosmopolis. The Raffles Hotel, one of the famed hostelries of the world, was almost always crowded. World tourists were arriving on every steamer and people were dropping in from China, Japan, the Philippines, Siam, Burma, India, Ceylon, and Europe. On the huge verandas overlooking the Bay, amid beautiful palm trees, the punkahs swayed noiselessly back and forth, ice tinkled in glasses, and constant calls were heard for stinga whiskey and soda.

Before Rose had started his 1914 tour of the East, he had realized that knowledge of hookworm control was not yet perfected. A fundamental question had to be answered, "Was anemia from hookworm distinguishable from that caused by malaria or other diseases?" Malaya seemed to offer the best opportunity for a survey. With the cooperation of the government a commission was appointed by the Rockefeller Foundation, composed of the American doctors, S. T. Darling and M. A. Barber, assisted by the British doctor, H. P. Hacker.

Dr. Darling, the head of the Commission, had been in Panama with General Gorgas, where he had made important contributions toward the success of the health service. Dr. Barber had been Professor of Bacteriology at the Kansas Medical College. One of his most brilliant laboratory achievements had been the discovery of a way of isolating a single bacillus. The great Koch was told about his method at the Tuberculosis Congress of 1908, but Koch had pooh-poohed it. Dr. Barber had then successfully demonstrated it to him. Because he had so well proved himself, we brought him over to the Bureau of Science in the Philippines, where he made many practical discoveries, brilliant in their simplicity and revolutionary in their effect on the control of disease-bearing mosquitoes and other aspects of tropical medicine. After he joined the International Health Board, he developed a method of segregating hookworm eggs by which examinations were immensely facilitated and speeded up.

One of my first jobs in the Federated Malay States was to prepare the way for the Darling Commission, find a place for its members to stay, arrange interviews, and, since they had no licenses to practise there, to secure the necessary permission. In addition, I drew up a list of points on which further hookworm knowledge was desired, such as whether thymol or chenopodium was more efficient, the after effects of the treatment, what kind of purge to use, the diet, the relation between the age of the patient and the severity of the infection, and whether necators were less resistant than ancylostomes. The final point was to determine to what degree uncinariasis infection was a menace to the health and working efficiency of the peoples of the Orient. The Commission planned to make the same type of survey in Java and Sumatra, and to check their findings in Fiji, where no malaria existed to complicate the study.

Much hookworm work was eventually done throughout the Straits Settlements. Dr. Paul Russell gave many lectures at Malacca, where large numbers of Chinese and Tamil laborers had been imported to build a new dam. His audience took to heart the letter if not the spirit of his exhortations. A group of Chinese coolies, after hearing one of his talks on hookworm infection, almost killed two Tamils who had violated some of the regulations he had laid down. Another Malay convert was inspired by his teachings to build a latrine of which he was so proud that he fastened the door with a padlock lest anybody defile it.

In Java as well as the Federated Malay States I secured permission for the Darling Commission's survey, but accomplished little else for many years. It was difficult to make headway against the hard-headed

Dutch who, because of their brilliant achievements, considered themselves self-sufficient. In the beginning, I was under suspicion on the theory that I was there for the chief purpose of winning approval for a Standard Oil concession. I could have answered any direct charge, but nebulous implications are not so easily combated. The Dutch authorities, however, were always hospitable and courteous in listening to suggestions. It required a long time for an idea to penetrate the heads of this stubborn people, but, once it was in, they could be counted upon never to let it go. And so I persevered.

From Batavia I retraced my steps to Singapore, and thence continued to Siam, where in the uplands of Chiengmai we turned old Buddhist temples to our uses, transforming them into theaters where we could display the life cycle of the hookworm. Thence I took the train back to Malaya, stopping for a few hours at the beautiful island of Penang. The congestion of small watercraft at this port of entry into Siam and the northern coast was terrific. No adequate docking facilities were available, and people and merchandise had to be landed in small boats.

It is an overnight journey by train from Penang to Kuala Lumpur, known locally as K-L, the capital of the Federated Malay States. It was one of the first cities in the world to adopt town planning, brought about by a woman's organization. Every house plan had to be submitted and accepted as harmonious to the whole. At Kuala Lumpur, during and after the War, I saw flourishing one of the most affluent governments in the world. The shipments of rubber and tin were so large that only a slight export duty on them sufficed to provide for all government needs. It was a taxpayers' Utopia. Commodities of all sorts could be had for little or nothing; good Havanas were ten cents apiece. I thought travel in the United States was comfortable, but it did not compare with that of Malaya. For fifty cents I could acquire a compartment with a bed, screened windows, shower bath, fans, and running water.

Owing to its tremendous wealth, the government of the Federated Malay States did not feel in need of our financial assistance; all it desired was ideas.

In Sumatra, by suggesting methods of hookworm and beriberi control, I was able to prove the commercial value of sanitation to foreign firms with huge plantations just coming into production. The Dutch treatment of the malarial mangrove swamps taught me in turn much which could be used elsewhere.

From Belawan Deli, the chief port of Sumatra, I went to Rangoon, capital of Burma, rich with oil, rice, teak, and rubber, and boasting the great golden Shwe Dagon. The Burmese were a docile, easily led race, inclined to be lazy. The health service sought the help of the Hpungis, the priests, who would assist, for example, in rounding up the people for vaccination. The upper classes assimilated knowledge readily, but gambling and the pursuit of pleasure often made them unreliable in medical work. Students had to be paid to attend the medical branch of the University, and the government had to let them bring along their valets. The Burmese were so ashamed of their medical school that they would not even permit me to see it.

Personal habits were not a problem among the Burmese. They were cleanly and used latrines. But the heavily populated part of the country was low-lying, and when the subsoil water rose in flood time, the people became infected with hookworm from the overflow.

Next I landed at Colombo and spent approximately three weeks looking over operations and studying, in the field, the development of the hookworm campaign. Ceylon was one of the most important stops on my route. In the early days the Foundation was using this island to demonstrate the results of hookworm research. We concentrated much effort there, because we believed that what was accomplished in Ceylon would be applied in other British colonies. Even though the obstacles were great and the discouragements many, in Ceylon we learned more about the practical application of hookworm knowledge than anywhere else in the world, and in the end the results were gratifying.

Then I crossed by Adams Bridge into Southern India, first stopping at Madras, and afterwards going north to Calcutta in Bengal. I would spend days and evenings getting acquainted with the men of the Indian Medical Service, the most effectively organized body of medical men in the world, who had contributed the great bulk of our knowledge of tropical medicine. The British who composed it, able, efficient, and unassuming, proceeded steadily toward their goal in spite of the magnitude of their problems.

Sometimes it would seem desirable for me to go to Simla. Two nights and a day were consumed in a journey which might have borne a superficial appearance to a vacation, but it was made for a purpose; I met the important people there at a time when they had leisure for discussion.

Many of the research problems of India were being worked out at the Bombay Bacteriological Laboratory. I used to stay with the commanding officer on the grounds, and, consequently, valuable time was not taken up in establishing my status. The Indian Medical Service was trying to start a school of hygiene, a project dear to my heart and one in which I was delighted to be of assistance. Bombay, one of the scientific medical centers of India, was disputing with Calcutta for its location, although ultimately Calcutta won.

On the long voyage from Bombay through the Red Sea and the Suez Canal I had time to collect my thoughts, and most of my material had been organized when I reached Egypt. The World War had stopped our hookworm labors there, and for years my visits were of an advisory nature only.

Egypt was one of the most tempting countries in which the Rockefeller Foundation could be of service. Its resources were tremendous but the knowledge of how to apply them effectively was meagre. Egypt also offered unequaled opportunities for research, being one of the few places in the world where the ancylostoma exists alone without the necator. Furthermore, it is afflicted with the outstanding problem of bilharzia.

Thousands of tourists, the cultured of all countries, well-informed, intelligent, and thinking people visit Egypt each year, and have been doing so for a century or more; scarcely one among them has even heard of bilharzia. Yet out of the twelve million Egyptians who are crowded into the narrow, desert-bordered belt of fertile green that fringes the sinuous course of Father Nile from Alexandria in the Delta to Assuan by the cataracts, six million have this disease, three million are seriously handicapped by it, and one million are bedfast. A tiny trematode worm, called a fluke from its fish-like shape, holds the descendants of the Pharaohs in a self-imposed but none the less vise-like grip.

Here, as everywhere else in the tropical world, the chief responsibility for disease rests upon the lack of cleanly habits. Bilharzia could be eradicated if these could be inculcated. With other research workers the Rockefeller Foundation is now engaged in attempting to solve this problem. Until Egypt has been freed of this devastating disease, she will always be under a serious disadvantage in taking her place among the nations of the world.

From Alexandria I embarked, sometimes for Athens, because we were conducting malaria investigations in Greece, sometimes for Naples, and sometimes for Constantinople. Wherever I landed, after a short stay I would take the train for a brief tour of the capitals of Europe. I would spend a few hours at Budapest to inspect the Institute of Hygiene, and then go on to Vienna which, long before the social conventions had permitted it in other countries, had made clinical material available for students.

Czecho-Slovakia held special interest because it had a newly-organized government with young ideas and an enthusiasm unhampered by an already existing bureaucratic administration and weighed down with precedent.

In Germany the great problem after the War was to know how to apply sanitary measures with the consent and help of the people. In the imperial days an order had no sooner been given than it was carried out, and usually carried out well. But the Republic had to instruct and persuade.

I never omitted Paris, where the Foundation maintained an office for the Commission on Tuberculosis, which was making extensive surveys—a work later taken over by the French. I learned a great many things that could be successfully applied in such places as the South Seas, where the tuberculosis incidence was high.

The French, although they may well claim to be among the world's most intelligent people, had steadfastly refused to be convinced of the soundness of our conception of medical education. Because we wished to disseminate this special type of knowledge through French-speaking people, the Foundation tried to accomplish this purpose by helping the Belgians at Brussels to develop a modern medical school.

At Amsterdam and The Hague I would interview people from cabinet ministers down, and discuss particularly the problems of Java. My chief point of contact was Dr. W. Schüffner, famous authority

303

on tropical diseases, whom I had first met in Sumatra. It was through these Netherlands visits that I eventually broke down the barriers to our entrance into Java.

London, although last, was the scene of my most important diplomatic labors. The health officials of the colonies looked to my visits there to help them get through measures they desired. The Colonial Office in turn was anxious to have impressions of its agents abroad. The authorities made my path infinitely smoother by seeing to it that I was officially received wherever I went in British territory, and secured for me the necessary invitations to make surveys.

From a health standpoint, Russia was, without doubt, one of the most interesting countries of Europe. Although I traveled there in 1929 as a private individual, naturally my chief interest lay in finding out what was being done in my own field. Because I wanted to guard against receiving purposeful misinformation, I was careful to confirm what I heard from the Soviets by checking at such unprejudiced sources as the Jewish Relief, financed from the United States, and the well-informed Americans at the Near East Relief headquarters. In no case did I find I had been deceived.

Under the Czar medicine had been encouraged as an art, but had not been widely disseminated among the general populace. But under Soviet rule Russia had evolved a modern health organization which was laying particular stress on popular education, using all the resources of propaganda, at which the Soviets have proved themselves so expert. The government acted on the theory that the public must be intelligently prepared for health measures. The radio, which could be heard in farthest Siberia, was of inestimable value in reaching the illiterate portions of the population. Foreign pamphlets and posters from all over the world had been collected and such parts as were applicable to Russian conditions were being used.

At Moscow I had a most interesting interview, conducted in German, with Dr. Vera Assatkine, one of the chiefs of the Bureau of Health. She described the Soviet health achievements—general mortality in Moscow had been reduced one-third, infant mortality one-half; attendance of mothers at post-natal clinics had been increased over ninety percent, health protection was being extended rapidly to rural districts. When populations were transferred from unprofitable lands to virgin fertile regions, the train that carried the people had a hospital car with doctor, nurses, medicines, and complete hospital equipment.

A special plague section had been formed in the Health Department. In various cities larger and more scientific laboratories had been erected which made smallpox and cholera vaccine. Before it had been possible to organize health work, a great smallpox epidemic had broken out and many deaths had resulted. But now every infant over four months old had to be vaccinated. Russia also had had frightful malaria after the War, but within a few years had installed the most approved system of combating it. Anti-malaria stations were opened and distribution of quinine arranged. Russian delegates made a practice of attending foreign meetings on malaria, and working industriously they steeped themselves in the world's knowledge of the disease.

I was particularly struck with the manner in which the Health Department handled venereal disease, which was being treated solely from the infectious standpoint. This is in great contrast to our attitude; ostrich-like, we stick our heads into the sand and refuse to recognize that syphilis causes greater havoc than any other disease in the Christian world, and that efforts to deal with it should not be handicapped by regarding it as punishment for sin. Venereal disease, like cholera or plague, is primarily infectious and should be handled accordingly. The situation will remain hopeless as long as a prominent health officer of the leading state in the Union can be refused the use of one of the great radio broadcasting systems because he mentioned the word syphilis.

After the Revolution of 1917, when the experiment in Communism was just beginning, the Soviets made one serious error in the health field. They had assumed that no special preliminary education was needed before a student could enter medical school. Four or five years were lost before they learned that good doctors could not be made in this way. Their excuse was that the Marxian doctrine is not complete; here were beams too short for Marxian houses. Nevertheless *Das Kapital* remained their Bible, albeit in modified form.

The friend with whom I was traveling was accustomed to paying well for what he desired. But at the hotel in Moscow, in spite of his lavish tips, we received practically no service. We could seldom finish a meal in less than two hours. A party of Germans seated near us would come in, be expeditiously waited upon, and depart while we were still impatiently awaiting our first course. Finally I went over to their table to ask them their secret.

"You don't do it right," was the answer. "You can't buy these people with money or treat them as servants. If we want a fork we say, 'Kamerad, would you mind, when you are coming on another trip from the kitchen, to bring us a fork? We would be so glad if you would.'"

We changed our tactics and stopped tipping, and thereafter received every consideration.

The aim of the Soviet is, as I understand it, in simple language, to work out better sociological conditions, and if they succeed other nations will, no doubt, wish to adopt them. As long as they confine these activities to Russia, we have little cause to object if they choose to turn themselves into a social laboratory.

I often altered my itinerary at other points than Russia. Occasionally my trips were varied by a tour of Central America, which was recognized as a health menace to the United States. Lack of public order made stable health services there impossible. The men in charge of the Foundation work had to be encouraged and heartened over and over, because only a Disraeli could have survived the ups and downs, the fusillade of bullets, the constant repetition of "the President has been shot, long live the President."

Sometimes I went to the South Seas or Australia. In the latter country at first I encountered such opposition that it was difficult to tell whether the bitterness was due to the Rockefeller name or directed against Americans in general. Certainly capitalists were not popular. But in the end the country united to laud the efforts of the Rockefeller Foundation in promoting health.

Whatever my route, once a year I returned to the United States where one of my busiest times began. Progress in medicine and health would have been so rapid that after my long absence I would find myself far behind. I would go to Canada, Boston, Philadelphia, Baltimore, Washington, Chicago, San Francisco, delivering lectures and attending meetings, renewing old associations, making new contacts and investigations, and picking up new ideas which would be helpful during my next world tour.

CHAPTER 18.   MUCH HAVE I
                                    TRAVELED

M OVEMENT, change, flux have governed the pattern of my
life for many years. The throb of engines, the mournful
warning of foghorns, white-jacketed stewards, tourists vocal with er-
roneous information; gentle seas, rough seas, calms, and typhoons,
landfalls once strange but later familiar, golden sand and green
jungle, heat and dripping humidity; alien customs and alien faces,
white skins, yellow skins, brown skins, black skins, the patter of many
tongues; trains swaying along uneven roadbeds and hurtling over
level ones, shrill whistles in the night, hotels with sleepy porters; cots,
feather beds, wooden pallets; low-humming Rolls Royces and rattling
Fords, flat roads meeting the horizon, white roads curling up mountains; cities large and small with prideful citizens anxious to display
civic wares; hospitals everywhere, "This is the ward for such and
such, and this is our operating theater, and this is the laboratory, and
so on"—I can still repeat the whole story backward and forward—
it makes me weary now to think of the hundreds of miles of hospital
corridors traversed in contemplating medical education in lands near
and remote; interviews with those friendly and hostile, tongue dry
with hours of talk, pointing sprightly stories with hidden morals, explaining the same thing over and over, mustering the old arguments
of merit against politics.

Almost always I took with me one of the younger doctors, either
from New York or his post in the East, to show him what was being
done in countries other than his own. Often I had pleasant companion-

ship which was not directly in the line of duty. In 1916 I was accompanied by one of my old friends, Dr. William George MacCallum, who had become one of the world's leading pathologists, and was author of one of the best textbooks on this subject. Dr. MacCallum, who was then enjoying his Sabbatical leave from Columbia University, said he was tired of performing autopsies on victims of the same old diseases and the same old races; he wanted to see what he could learn from the victims of tropical maladies. But in the beginning of our journey the opportunities for autopsies were so few that he was reduced to dissecting sharks.

MacCallum was still harping on autopsies when we arrived at the Fiji Islands and loudly expressed his annoyance because nobody had died recently in Suva. At the Governor's dinner I sat next to the Chief Justice and endeavored to amuse him by describing MacCallum's macabre enthusiasms.

"Well, I think I could arrange something for him," the judge remarked.

"How?"

"Two criminals are going to be executed here next Monday. I could easily arrange to have their bodies turned over to him."

I explained that unfortunately MacCallum could not wait until Monday, because we were sailing Sunday.

"Oh, that's easily enough arranged. I'll have the execution advanced to Saturday. That'll be a simple matter."

Confronted with this proposition, I had to beg off on the ground that I could not feel responsible for hurrying two wretches into eternity before their time.

I preceded MacCallum to Manila where I arranged to have him temporarily appointed a city pathologist. I told him the glad news when I met his boat at six in the morning, but, omitting all mention of the current cholera epidemic, warned him that, if he once accepted, he must perform autopsies on all bodies brought to the morgue. MacCallum was so delighted at this opportunity to increase his knowledge that he hurried through his breakfast and rushed me off to the morgue. Five bodies were already awaiting him. I left him bubbling with enthusiastic anticipation. He did not appear at lunch, nor at dinner. At eleven in the evening he dragged himself wearily into the

309

hotel, having seen a great deal more of cholera than he had bargained for. Ten more cases had come in before he had finished the first five. After the second day he was ready to resign, but I told him he would have to remain at least two weeks to establish his good faith. The result was that the cholera chapter in the revised edition of his book was one of the best.

MacCallum had done special research on malaria and had made one of the great contributions to the knowledge of the disease by his discovery of the sex life of the malaria parasite. At Singapore he was overjoyed to find many victims of malaria on whom he could perform autopsies. These were so profitable in adding to his store of information that some years afterwards he returned to make further studies. But in the meantime the British had performed the Herculean task of reducing the disease to a negligible figure. Practically nobody in Singapore was now dying of malaria. He railed at me for months thereafter. "You sanitarians have ruined the business of the poor pathologist."

Unfamiliar with the vagaries of tropical climates, MacCallum had great difficulty in adjusting his clothing to the differing temperatures. On reaching Vancouver he had stocked up with winter clothing and discarded his light weight suits. At Fiji he had reversed the process, throwing away his newly-acquired winter outfit, and buying a summer one. At Sydney he had purchased new winter clothes and left behind his summer ones once more. I lost track of the number of times he went through this jettisoning process, but when he arrived in Java he was in his winter clothes and dripping in the insufferable heat, always protesting to me that he was, "Very comfortable, thank you." Not until his resistance had been overcome to the point where he would admit he was genuinely suffering did I produce his latest edition of tropical clothing, which I had surreptitiously retrieved. His pride by this time had completely melted, and his gratitude was unalloyed.

Through so much traveling I had had to learn all sorts of expedients and prepare for all sorts of emergencies. My wardrobe had to provide for a wide range in temperature, and social, business, and sport requirements. I found there was only one way of being sure I did not leave anything essential behind. I made an all-inclusive list, a copy of which was kept in each bag. By this means nothing was ever lacking, even when I had to pack and set forth at short notice.

I carried an office desk with me in the shape of a specially designed wardrobe trunk. When it was opened, a leaf in the middle could be pulled down, thus converting it into a desk. There were plenty of pigeon holes. One drawer held a traveling library, another served as a catch-all for papers, and below was a suitcase ready packed with everything I needed for brief trips, including a typewriter and complete desk equipment. In the other half of the trunk my clothes were concealed behind a folding door.

It was a painful experience to see the massive trunk being moved inch by inch up the ship's gangway; one slip and it would have gone to the bottom of the sea. Only in Egypt where the stevedores are reputed the strongest in the world did I ever feel confident; but there one of them would pick up the three hundred pound load, walk up the gangplank with it on his shoulder and deposit it on the deck. A turn of the key and I would be ready to work; through the tropics it was pleasanter on deck. I always suffered considerable anxiety until I had the trunk in my possession. Once when I had to search for it in the hold, I found it labeled, "Dr. Heiser, deceased," and had great difficulty in proving that I was alive.

Seasickness is a malady of moment only to the sufferer, but it is nevertheless very serious to the constant traveler. I am not one of those fortunate ones who are naturally immune, but I did learn how to prevent its occurrence. Until I had become more or less immune, my simple but effective remedy was to lie in bed with my feet higher than my head, even eating with my head at this lower level. A still better cure is to have some absorbing interest to divert the mind. Once in weather so rough I could hardly stay in my bunk, where I was coddling myself, a sick call came from the steerage. I somehow staggered to my feet and answered it. Shortly I became so occupied that I forgot all about my unpleasant nausea.

In 1915, when the War was well under way, some of the steamers delegated for neutral passenger traffic were unspeakable. I always chose an upper berth, because of its advantages; I could look out the porthole and, if my cabin mate were seasick, I preferred to be located aloft. One night, while traveling on the Union Steamship Line, I was awakened by the most terrific pain in my big toe. Wriggling it only made it worse. I thrust my foot over the edge and my anguish increased. When I hurriedly switched on the light, there was a huge rat hanging on with a bulldog grip. The more I shook, the harder the frightened rodent held on, and the further his teeth sank into my toe. But as soon as I pulled my foot back on the bed, he let go and scampered off, leaving me to dress my wounds.

In addition to rats, the ship carried a full complement of roaches. They would run over the tables, even in the daytime. But they had some compensatory attributes. No chiropodist could have made his living on this line. Passengers who were afflicted by corns would find them neatly removed by morning. The roaches would gnaw down until they reached a sensitive spot, the foot would then automatically be moved, and, thus disturbed, they would scamper off.

Even more annoying than the Union Steamship Company was that far famed line, dear to all British hearts—the Peninsular & Oriental. I have experienced all the vexations and humiliations which Kipling has described so well, and, in addition, many of my own. My introduction to the P. & O. came when I boarded one of their ships at Suez, en route for the first time to the Philippine Islands. I had left my heavy baggage at Port Said while I went to Egypt, and had arranged for the ship to pick it up there because I planned to meet it at the other end of the Canal.

The officials of the line would not vouchsafe the time of the vessel's arrival at Suez. But, fortunately, I had one eye open when it finally came at three in the morning. With a natural anxiety to find out before we left whether my baggage had come on board, I repaired to the purser and made inquiries. He was as offended as though never in his life had he heard such a question. He grew redder and redder, and swelled and swelled like a turkey gobbler. Finally he managed to sputter, "The luggage is the business of the Fourth Officer."

"Where is the Fourth?"

"I don't know."

After searching here and there on the darkened ship, I finally crawled down the hatch ladder and located the Fourth in the hold with the cargo. Again I inquired politely for my trunks. He looked at me in a stern and lofty fashion. "Do you really expect me to keep in mind all the luggage that comes on board?"

"I thought you might be able to refer to your list."

"We have regular hours for attending to luggage. Tomorrow at four."

I could not see how that information would avail me if my trunks were not on the ship. But his decision was final, and I went to bed.

I was still tired when I awoke at nine and decided to have breakfast in my room. I rang for the steward. He came. I ordered breakfast.

"Are you ill, sir?" he inquired.

"No."

"Breakfast is only served in the cabin when the passenger has a certificate from the doctor that he is too sick to come to the table," he parroted.

I tried to induce the steward to change his mind, but he persisted it was against the rules of the company. Since I was more tired than hungry I stayed in my bunk until noon. Then I repaired to the dining room for lunch, expectantly anticipating my soup. When I indicated to my waiter that I was ready, he corrected me with the information that I might be ready but the captain was not. Fortunately for my appetite, the captain, a proud individual in a grand uniform, soon entered and was majestically seated. Then, and not until then, a special steward by his side banged on a big gong, and the soup course appeared.

I soon learned the rigid etiquette of dining on the P. & O. A hardy individual who said, "I won't have any soup, steward, I'll have the fish," was met by a stolidly reproving glance. "The soup is being served, sir."

The hungry man would have to possess his soul in patience until another sonorous bang announced the captain had finished his last spoonful of soup and the fish was being borne ceremoniously through the swinging doors. Whoever came late had to start with the course which the captain was then engaged in consuming.

I remember one dinner at Aden where we had arrived late in the afternoon. The customary rule on most lines was dinner jackets in the evening, although if a passenger had been ashore until too late to dress, it was automatically waived. But not so on the P. & O. Sitting next to me at table were a young Hungarian count and his bride, neither of whom spoke English. He came on board just as the soup gong had struck, rushed into the dining room, and sat down.

The steward said, "I'm very sorry, sir, but we can't serve you."

The Count obviously did not understand and pointed again to what he wanted on the bill of fare.

"You'll have to leave the dining room, sir. We do not serve anyone who is not in evening dress."

Still the Count did not understand. The waiter then stepped behind him, lifted him out of his chair, and escorted him from the room.

In later years a great concession was made to the tropic heat going through the Red Sea. I saw a sign which read, "Gentlemen will be permitted to dance in flannel trousers, but this will not excuse them from formal dress at dinner."

Conversations on shipboard are always the same, people get tired of deck tennis, organizing ships' concerts, betting on the daily run, and avoiding bores. By way of divertissement, I sometimes submitted my list of ten words, which nobody yet has spelled successfully. I usually prefaced it by remarking that President Eliot of Harvard had missed three, and that newspaper editors had been known to miss five or six.

The spelling test worked with equal efficacy on land. On one occasion the copper king, John Ryan, was present, took the test, and missed four. A few weeks later I met him walking along Broadway. He came up to me with his big beaming smile. "I haven't seen you since I boasted I was the champion speller of Michigan."

"Are you sure you can spell those words now?" I asked.

"Of course I can."

"I doubt it."

"I'll show you. I'll do it right here."

There in the middle of crowded Broadway, jostled by passers-by, he scribbled out the words as I gave them to him. Again, to his great chagrin and surprise, he missed four. His experience was by no means unique.

I learned to count upon certain responses which were almost in-

314

variable. Though numerous and diversified, the explanations offered for mistakes followed a set pattern. The British always used to claim I was using the American way of spelling. I would refer them politely to the Oxford Dictionary. With eager look one of them would rush to the ship's library. Sure that he was right, he would skim over the pages until he came to the word. Momentarily dashed, he would then rush with equal confidence to the next word he had missed, only to have his hopes once more blasted.

On one trip I had been asked by Mr. Rockefeller to make a report on the Constantinople College for Women, which was anxious to secure additional funds. I went through the various divisions until finally I reached the English Department. I was introduced to the head, a spinster, forbidding in demeanor. To alter the monotony of the inspection I began as follows: "You're the head of the department?"

"Yes."

"You teach English?"

"What else would I teach?"

"I suppose you give instruction in spelling?"

"We pride ourselves on our spelling."

"Would you mind if I tested you?"

"What do you want to test me for? I know how to spell."

"Of course," I said, "if you don't want to give me information—"

The President of the college, who was standing by trembling in her boots, conveyed to the English teacher in whispered asides that it was important to treat me with civility. An abrupt change in attitude followed. "Certainly you may test me," the English teacher said.

"Have you a pencil and paper?"

"I usually spell out loud."

"We'll use pencil and paper if you don't mind."

I gave her the list. Confidently she wrote down the words and handed the slip to me. Seven were wrong. Further whispers followed, which evidently convinced her of the enormity of her guilt; I never saw a balloon collapse more quickly than she.

I had already determined that the time was not propitious to recommend more money for the institution, but to this day those women probably believe they did not receive a further grant because the head of the English Department had fallen down on the spelling test.

These are the words—inoculate, embarrass, harass, supersede, innuendo, rarefy, vilify, plaguy, desiccate, picnicking.

The Australians, on whom I also experimented, countered with "Can you name for us five adjectives ending in 'dous'?" I was delighted to add this to my list of parlor games. When I tried it on General Wood, he was so exasperated with his inability to name them that he had his secretary go through the dictionary until ten had been painstakingly culled.

Pleasant memories stretch behind me of kindly hospitality in government mansions and native huts, friendly clubs and charming homes. Everywhere people went to great pains to entertain me. In addition to the round of dinners and banquets, my hosts produced for my delectation the local forms of diversion, among which dancing was naturally prominent.

In all Eastern countries dancing is a highly formalized art to which the performers are usually trained from childhood. It has attained a degree of perfection remarkable to behold, though often unintelligible to Western minds.

One of my trips stands out for the quantity and variety of dancing exhibitions to which I was invited. The Japanese government, always lavish in welcome, wished to show me the beauty of the graceful geisha dances, and staged an elaborate display. I found it delightful and said so. My next stop was Peiping. The Chinese, who had heard how impressed I had been with Japanese dancing, were not to be outdone, and produced the best their sing-song girls could offer. I then went to Canton, and the Cantonese did their utmost to prove that dancing in South China was the finest in the land. When I reached the Philippines the girls at the Normal School had been learning old Filipino folk-dances, and proudly reproduced them for me. At Bali I saw the world-famed symbolic interpretations of Hindu legends, acted by masked dancers whose every tiny gesture was significant. But at Djokjakarta the Dutch said the genuine Javanese dances performed to the haunting melodies of the gamelan orchestras were incomparable, and proved it. I even saw the temple dance at

Angkor Wat, which is supposed to be the acme of Oriental perfection.

Unaware that their efforts were being wasted upon me, country continued to vie with country. But by this time I knew that I did not care to see more dancing. When not a word of it was breathed at Singapore I sighed with relief. I thought I was finally done with spending evening after evening at this business.

But at Siam the word that I was a connoisseur of dances had again preceded me. The Crown Prince had arranged a special exhibition, beginning at nine and ending at three in the morning. Beautiful as they were my appreciation was dimmed by the fact that I had to be up and about my duties at eight.

I was now sure I must have seen the end of dancing, but hardly had I stepped ashore at Rangoon than the wife of the Governor said to me, "We've held up our annual dancing fête until your arrival. We thought you, as an authority on Eastern dancing, would be particularly interested to see it." That afternoon she gave a tea party to which all social Rangoon tore its hair to be invited, and I was regaled with the native dances of Burma.

I went to India. In Madras, Travancore, and Bombay the nautch dancers swayed to the shrill piping flutes. I continued to Egypt—the dancing girls of Cairo swung wildly to the monotonous minor of Arabic music. Not until I had left the East did the competition for my unofficial approval finally end.

In the diverse forms of entertainment offered me I could more readily adapt myself to the dinners and the luncheons, though they were often composed of strange foods consumed according to strange customs. I remember my first formal Chinese dinner. Graciousness is inherent in Chinese hospitality. When plans were being perfected for a National Health Service in China, I was tendered a banquet at the Winter Palace of the former Empress Dowager. We were rowed in the moonlight to one of the lake pavilions on a barge, beautifully decorated with palms and wistaria and varicolored paper, which might have belonged to the glamorous Tsu Hsi herself.

Apologies were many and profuse that the sixty-course dinner was not enough for my honor; it should have consisted of one hundred and twenty. At seven o'clock we were seated at a round table, each with a little bowl before him. In the center of the table was a large bowl from which the guest of honor first served himself with chopsticks; after that a general scramble took place. Each diner retained his own bowl, but the center one changed as course followed course in amazing succession—sharks' fins, birds' nest soup, unrecognizable foods which, nevertheless, had a delicious flavor. The ordering of such a formal Chinese dinner was a fine art; two days might be devoted to planning the appropriate dishes and their fitting sequence.

After two hours, even though my portions had been small, I began to feel that I had had enough, but by ten o'clock I had digested the first courses and had gained my second wind; it seemed to make no difference thereafter how much more I ate. The meal reached a high point when we were served eggs, black with age, buried for three hundred years. They were not so unpleasant as might be assumed, but tasted rather like poor quality cold storage eggs. The Chinese esteemed them as one of their greatest delicacies, and cherished them for their antiquity. I considered this merely part of their ancestor worship.

The Westerner at a Chinese table cannot identify much of what he is eating, but the initiate knows the dinner is nearing an end when the rice and tea appear. The fruit course is never served at the main table; the necessity for shifting to a side one where it is displayed provides an opportunity to change partners.

Watermelon seeds, which are eaten before, during, and after the dinner, are much prized. My hosts would skillfully extract the kernels with their teeth, but I found it took practice. Chinese wines of varying flavors are freely served; I found Suchow most to my taste. Glasses are constantly replenished and tongues are loosened at these bright and charming Chinese functions. The Japanese affairs often compare with them in length but not in sprightliness of conversation.

Most Chinese foods are pleasant. But occasional exceptions are found. At a dinner given me in Hangchow the *pièce de résistance* was many-legged, live bugs several inches long and resembling roaches in color. These were served in a bowl covered with a glass bell. It is bad form not to accept a helping, no matter how small, of everything offered. I was supposed to lift the cover quickly, grab the wriggling animal with my chopsticks, pop it into my mouth, and crush it before it could start to crawl. I found that I needed considerable courage to bite this unfortunate insect, and, since I was a novice at the practice, it would invariably begin to squirm around my mouth before I could administer the quietus.

I have eaten all sorts of food in all sorts of places. It has always astonished me that Americans and Europeans in the tropics spend much money importing fruits when they are surrounded by all varieties of delicious native species; on a short trip through Central America I once encountered fourteen fruits different from those in the United States.

For some reason or other when I first went to the Philippines I had never heard of the mango. The *Rohilla Maru* had landed me in Manila about six in the morning, and I reached the hotel in time for eight o'clock breakfast. My table was located near that of an American woman who had ordered a strange-looking fruit of a rich yellow color. I was avid for new experiences and wished to make myself at home in this new country. "I'd like to have one of those," I said to the waiter.

Not wishing to appear ignorant, I watched how the lady handled hers. She tilted it on end, with a dexterous stroke cut down the two sides, and then ate each of these with a spoon. It looked very simple. I tilted back my mango similarly, and started to cut. But when it did not slice with the ease of hers, I exerted force. The juice exuded and spurted over my arms and on to the tablecloth. When I had hacked it open, I set to work with my spoon, but again the juice would not stay in the fruit; a geyser spouted up to my chin. I wondered uneasily how many people were watching my exhibition.

Stealing another look at the lady, I observed her take the four-inch kidney-shaped seed, insert her fork into it, and eat it delicately with absolute unconcern. I adopted the same nonchalance. I pressed my fork against the seed as I had seen her do; it would not go in. I pressed harder, but to no avail. The breakfasters began to nudge one another, and I was conscious of eyes focused upon me. In desperation I tried again. The more pressure I exerted, the less successful I seemed. The veins of my neck became turgid and my face cyanotic. By now the whole dining room was watching me. I was determined to succeed. With a final terrific thrust the fork slipped and the large

319

flat stone shot the length of the long dining room, hit the opposite wall with a crash, and fell to the floor with a loud thud. A roar of laughter went up from my delighted audience.

I was shortly set right as to what I should have done. My first mistake had been that I had not cut from the stem end, and consequently had been working against the grain. I had made the same error in eating the fruit, also spooning it against the grain. Finally, when I had essayed the seed, I had not known that I should have inserted the fork, one prong at a time, into the soft places between the ridges.

Even with the best of care mango eating is apt to be messy. The juice makes an irremovable stain which in a moment turns black; in mango season hardly a white napkin can be found in the Islands. It was always popularly said that the proper way to enjoy the fruit was to relax in the bathtub.

After my not too brilliant first performance I set to work to master the fine art of mango eating and this eventuated in securing me many dinner invitations at Malacañan. Whenever any Governor General had distinguished visitors who had never eaten mangos, I received a summons. Since it would have been indelicate for him to give directions on how to handle the fruit, he would introduce me as the Director of Health, who would expound the proper method of eating mangos hygienically.

I became Philippines instructor in the technique of mango eating.

A very strange fruit is the durian, which grows on a large tree and is larger than the largest orange. It is protected by spines and filled with seeds which turn black as it ripens. I once tried to eat one. I held my nose and found it not so bad as I had feared. A traveler, who more than half a century ago wrote a book on the Malay Archipelago, described the savor of the durian as a "rich butter-like custard, highly flavored with almonds . . . but intermingled with it come wafts of flavor that call to mind cream cheese, onion sauce, brown sherry, and other incongruities." It possesses one of the most penetrating and disagreeable of all odors in the world. A polecat or limburger of the ripest vintage are mild in comparison.

On one occasion I was traveling with my chief assistant, Dr. Wilbur A. Sawyer, now Director of the International Health Division, on the train from Bangkok to Penang. The train had no diner, and we had, therefore, taken our luncheons in a hamper. About the middle of the day a Chinese, the only other occupant of the compartment, bought a ripe durian at a station and began his lunch by slicing it carefully in half. Bad as a durian is while yet unopened, it is infinitely worse when the rind is cut. We called a guard, told him we were absolutely overpowered, and asked him to persuade our traveling companion to eat his durian on the platform. The Chinese gathered it up and obligingly departed.

We unwrapped our ham sandwiches and began to eat them shortly after our fellow-passenger had come back. We had scarcely bitten into them when he started to make gestures of repulsion, shook his head, and ejaculated, "Whew! Whew! Whew!" as though he were overcome with disgust. Then he, too, called the guard to whom he spoke in Malay. The guard turned to us and asked whether we would mind stepping outside to eat our lunch. Since the Chinese had been so polite in acceding to our request, we felt we could do no less than return the favor. To a final "Whew!" we also left. When we had finished our innocent sandwiches and returned, the jocular Chinese looked up at us with a big, broad grin on his face.

I cannot imagine why, but nothing would satisfy Dr. Sawyer after this until he also could secure a durian. Not finding any ripe enough for immediate consumption, he compromised on a green one. At Penang he packed it away in a wicker hamper which, with the rest of our baggage, was left in a storeroom of the hotel at Colombo while we made an inspection trip of the provinces of Ceylon. As we approached the hotel on our return, even a block away we were aware of a terrible odor. It grew stronger and stronger as we drew nearer. We were astonished to see the whole courtyard in an uproar. The hotel staff was opening doors, poking at the ground, searching vainly to find the source. It was as though a hundred rats had been dead for some weeks. When Dr. Sawyer called for his baggage and the door of the storeroom was opened, the smell almost knocked us down. The durian, a fruit unknown in Ceylon, had been ripening successfully in the hamper.

The dauntless Dr. Sawyer was still determined to eat it. I said, "You certainly won't be allowed to open it around here, but if you go out along the breakwater, you'll be a half mile away and perhaps nobody will mind."

With his durian Dr. Sawyer retired to the very end of the mole. Even so, occasional whiffs of the evil odor came drifting in on the sea breeze.

Amusing and sometimes dramatic experiences often befell me on my voyages. Inevitably I missed boats, sometimes because the sailing date had been changed, sometimes because ships had been condemned or had sunk. At least four times to my knowledge I have been saved from almost certain death by pure coincidence.

In 1901 I had come down from Canada and was stopping at the Murray Hill Hotel in New York City, awaiting orders from Washington. When several days had passed without reply to my report, I sent a telegram, "Still awaiting orders."

The answer came almost instantly, "Return to Canada." I took the train at once. That same night an explosion occurred in the old Interborough tube, then under construction. The Murray Hill Hotel was badly damaged, and the man who was sleeping in the bed I had occupied was killed.

The second event occurred in Mexico during the Revolution. I had had great difficulty getting into Mexico City by the San Antonio-Nueva Laredo route for a conference with Carranza. I decided to return by way of the longer but less uncomfortable road to El Paso. I had already bought my ticket, made arrangements, and notified the Foundation of what I proposed to do. But just before train time I received a wire, "Services urgently needed in Brazil. Take most direct route to New York." I canceled my ticket at once. The train on which I had planned to travel was held up by bandits the next afternoon, and all the white passengers were taken out and shot.

The scene of the third coincidence was on the other side of the world. I had always wanted to travel the road to Mandalay, but had never seemed to have time. Once when at Rangoon I had concluded my essential duties and still had a few days before my ship was due to sail. This seemed an ideal opportunity. At the railroad office I started the process, interminable in the East, of procuring a ticket. Before the extended arrangements had been half concluded my conscience began to trouble me; my time could be better employed in attending to unfinished details in Rangoon. "I'm awfully sorry," I said to the agent, "but I don't think I'll take that ticket after all."

The train departed, but had proceeded only a hundred miles when it was wrecked; over fifty persons were killed and several hundred wounded. My three days were employed in helping to set bones and sew up wounds.

The fourth escape occurred at Bagdad. Mr. Charles R. Crane, the former Minister to China, with whom I was traveling, urged me to accompany him in his motor car the next morning, but the exigencies of my itinerary called for my arrival at Damascus at a certain time. We were both dinner guests of King Feisal, and as we parted at eleven o'clock I announced my decision that I had to go by the more direct route. Mr. Crane left at six in the morning; at nine his automobile was ambushed by Arab tribesmen. The man sitting next to him on the back seat of the automobile was killed. I would almost surely have been that man.

My first trip for the Rockefeller Foundation in 1915 was in many respects the most interesting of them all. The War, so recently under way, complicated almost all of our undertakings. But having set ourselves to the task, we could not turn back, even though we had to mark time in some places and surmount unexpected obstacles in others. Echoes of the battle could be heard in many countries of the East.

At this time the British had their hands full not only with their avowed enemies the Germans, but also with native unrest. When I arrived at Singapore, the recent mutiny of the Fifth Light Infantry, an Indian regiment some seven hundred strong, was still the all-absorbing topic of conversation. Nobody knew the exact cause of the outbreak, but the mutineers had killed Britishers wherever they could find them, thirty-seven in all. They had then gone to a camp where three hundred Germans were interned and, after driving off or killing the guards, had invited the Germans to come out and lead them. This offer had been refused.

Singapore had been entirely unprepared for the outbreak, and pandemonium resulted. The small British gunboat *Cadmus* landed seventy-five men, and these, with a few hundred Singapore volunteers, met the largest groups of mutineers and dispersed them. Four hundred gave themselves up within forty-eight hours, and said they had been forced to join the mutiny by their comrades, but had never fired a shot. Two thousand territorials shortly arrived, a Japanese gunboat landed some marines, and the man hunt was on. At first, the mutineers were shot on sight, but many escaped and hid in nearby swamps, where they were not found for several weeks. As soon as they were caught they were tried by military court martial and many, as examples, were condemned to be shot.

I attended the impressive function, March 25, when twenty-two of them were executed before a crowd of ten thousand, mostly Malay and Chinese. Outside the grey, moss-grown walls of the prison the white volunteers formed an open square. To the beating of drums and the blowing of trumpets, the prison doors were flung open, and a section of turbaned Sikhs emerged with the prisoners. Each of the twenty-two marched steadfastly, without a sign of fear, to a post of wood, quite new, which had been driven into the turf. Each came to attention while being tied, and, with eyes unbandaged, stoically faced the square. The officer in charge read in clear tones the findings of the court martial. The khaki-clad territorials faced the condemned men. "Present"—a pause, "Fire!"—and a sharp crash. The territorials were willing but their marksmanship was not perfect. All the mutineers were not dead, and the officers of the firing squad had to despatch those still living with final bullets.

I watched for an expression of hatred, or pity, or horror, on the faces of the multitude. No emotion whatsoever was displayed—nothing but stolid indifference.

Borne by human, animal, and machine power, on sea, on land, and in the air, I have traveled over the globe. Almost everywhere in the East human muscle is the most important factor in transportation. Rickshaws are omnipresent, pulled by one man on level ground with amazing speed and endurance. But in the mountains of India, where the grades are steep, rickshaws are manned by two, four, and even six runners. At the base of each hill in the uplands of Japan pushers wait and, at the rickshaw's approach, dash out to assist their fellow coolies up the hill, and then, with their coppers, return to resume their patient waiting.

MUCH HAVE I TRAVELED

Often where trails forbade wheeled vehicles, I have reclined in litters carried by four bearers. In China I have been lifted in sedan chairs, and also bumped in wheelbarrows with huge wheels which have benches along each side where four or more passengers sit back to back and have little places for their feet. One coolie trundles this enormous load, the wooden axle groaning and howling with each revolution of the wheel. The excellence of a wheelbarrow is judged by the character and volume of its squeak; no luck will attend the journey on a squeakless one.

In some places I have been carried ashore from boats, my legs dangling around the neck of a porter half my size who somehow staggered through the shallow water under what must have been an almost overwhelming weight, invariably landing me dryshod.

I have embarked on every imaginable type of water craft—hand propelled houseboats, lighters, barges; canoes on Canadian rapids, punts on the Thames, gondolas in Venice, sampans on the Yangtze-kiang; in the Philippines unstable bancas and enormous cascos holding fifty tons; on the Nile, dahabeahs, aided by soft winds against their towering sails; in the vale of Kashmir, luxurious, awninged boats, made comfortable with cushions of gay colors, drifting down the Jhelum toward the Indus, past the towering peaks of the Himalayan wonderland; sailing vessels of every description—schooners, junks, praos, and swift, two-masted lorchas, which used to speed from Iloilo to Negros with such celerity that only a good steamer could keep up with them; greyhound liners, battleships, private yachts, coastwise steamers, tug boats, and wheezy launches in which I would sit by the hour waiting for the engine to be started.

On land I have driven behind six-mule teams and the horses of Egypt, of purest Arab stock, racing the twelve miles from Cairo to the Pyramids in an hour. I have ridden in the gharry of India, and the four-wheeled carriage of Singapore; calesins, carromatas, calesas, carretelas, and carts of the Philippines; buckboards, droshkies, sleighs, and sledges. Perhaps the most amusing animal-drawn vehicle was the two-wheeled sadu of Java, sometimes pulled by a horse so small that, reversing the role of passenger and burden bearer, I have stuck my head between his front legs and carried him. On one occasion, when the horse apparently saw the house in which he had been born and started toward it, my companion and I simply leaned backward in the sadu and lifted him off the ground between the shafts, holding him pawing ineffectually in the air until he had recovered his mental balance. The only smaller animal that I have known was the diminutive trotting ox of Ceylon, clatter-clattering along on his tiny, shod hooves, a joke edition of the more common and stolid specimen.

I have jogged hundreds of miles on horseback—ranging from polo ponies to percherons. I have bestridden minute donkeys, hunching up my legs and gripping them with my knees to prevent their walking out from under me. I have clambered into the howdahs of ponderous elephants and clutched the cumbrous, wooden saddles of the nasty-tempered, rocking camels.

I have journeyed thousands of miles on luxurious Pullmans with seats of comfortable plush—corridor and compartment—combination freight and passenger, and even construction trains; funiculars, and baskets swung perilously from crag to crag in the Dolomites; camions, trucks, and buses; and airplanes and hydroplanes, swiftly winging over mountain, desert, and river, even the Great Wall of China winding snake-like below.

I did not roam from wanderlust or curiosity as to other lands, not to criticize ways alien to my own, not to bring back adventurers' tales to those who must travel in armchairs. My mission was to open "the golden window of the East" to the gospel of health, to let in knowledge, so that the teeming millions who had no voice in demanding what we consider inalienable rights should also benefit by the discoveries of science, that in the end they, too, could have health.

CHAPTER 19.　　SNAKES IN EDEN

WHEN the British in 1795 added Ceylon to their Empire, they became overlords of a country with a storied past but no apparent future. The massive ruins of Anuradhapura, once a city covering two hundred and fifty square miles, was no more than a shrine for pilgrims, who came to gaze with reverence upon the sacred Bo tree, grown from a slip of that under which Buddha himself had sat at Benares. It had survived two millennia, and bade fair to continue for several more. The island, which had known the yoke of Hindustan, Portugal, and the Netherlands, retained only vestiges of its ancient riches—few divers descended to the famous pearl fisheries, the gold mines were abandoned, the people had grown weary, and grubbed but listlessly for topaz, sapphire, and ruby, the palaces were tumbled down, and the jungle had crowded into the groves of cinnamon and cardamom; it was said the British had conquered no more than an empty shell.

But, once again, after many vicissitudes, the Fragrant Isle has bloomed. Although not many decades ago the coffee trees on the great plantations were destroyed by blight, and the cinchona industry was lost to Java, in place of these, pungent tea shrubs now flourish luxuriantly on every mountain side, and latex flows from the rubber trees and have brought new prosperity. In the lowlands the fronds of the useful cocoanut shade broad roads, and add to the country's riches.

Because of its economic prosperity, Ceylon was looked upon in the East as a prize colony, although many serpents flourished in this Garden of Eden; the hookworm infestation was heavy and widespread. If we could prove the importance and the practicability of a hookworm campaign, funds would be available to carry on the work, and the already existing Health Service would provide the machinery. A second reason for concentrating on Ceylon was that other British colonies tried to emulate it, and hence a successful campaign there would serve as an entering wedge elsewhere in the Orient.

But the internal situation in Ceylon was exceedingly complex. Economic, political, and social conditions made it desirable for us to work first on the large estates, which, in turn, required securing the cooperation of the powerful planting interests. This was necessary but dangerous, because a hostile-minded press might have attacked us on the ground that we were one group of rich men working for another group of rich men rather than for the poor down-trodden masses.

Living is easy in Ceylon, and the Sinhalese, the native born, choose not to work for the planters. Therefore, laborers had to be imported for the year-round task of gathering the leaves in the tea estates. Fortunately, an inexhaustible supply of Tamils exists in the great Presidency of Madras, which sprawls down the eastern and up the western coasts of South India. When the Rockefeller Foundation decided upon Ceylon as a demonstration center, about one hundred thousand coolies, including their families, were going annually to the Ceylon tea and rubber plantations.

These primitive Dravidians of Madras, coal black with Caucasian features, ignorant, superstitious, and servile, unresponsive, uninterested, only five percent literate, entirely lacking in ambition, were also docile. They were willing workers, but depressing to look at because of their blank countenances; there was hardly a smile in the entire race. They still spoke in their ancient dialect, and had brought with them to Ceylon their own habits and preferences. They ate their strictly vegetarian meals from banana leaves, and objected at first to the substitution of tin plates.

A detention camp had been built at Mandapam, at the tip of India, through which half of these coolies passed on their way to the estates. According to contract, the planters provided their living and hospital care, but otherwise did little more than cater to their insurmountable

328

caste demands. Hindus, for example, lose caste whenever they leave their country and travel over water. This could be restored by religious ceremonies at the temples of Dhanushkodi or Rameswaram when they returned from Ceylon.

Because the Tamils had a superstitious fear of light, no windows were built into the barrack-like "lines" in which they lived on the plantations. Each family had two rooms; in one they slept, and in the other cooked on the floor. Smoke and dirt were everywhere. More insanitary than all else was the indiscriminate soil pollution. This was a greater health hazard to the Tamil than to many other peoples because his skin was as thin as that of the white man, and hookworms could penetrate it easily.

The planters had long before made up their minds they would allow no interference from the local health authorities. They would neither give nor receive aid in dealing with the hookworm situation, because they were convinced the intrusion of sanitarians would hurt business. I was well aware that Lord Crewe, when at the India Office, had threatened to stop their labor supply unless they took active steps to deal with the hookworm situation; they had then made evasive but plausible answers, and things had gone on as before.

The resistance of the planters had to be overcome, but our policy demanded also that we conduct our work under the official auspices of the Health Service. Consequently, my first step on landing at Colombo was to call upon the incoming head of the department, Dr. G. J. Rutherford. After the amenities had been complied with, we began discussing the new venture in health launched by the Rockefeller Foundation and what it purposed to do. "What's the present hookworm situation in Ceylon?" I asked.

"It's frightful," he promptly admitted.

"Why should that be? You have laws enough to cover any action you might take, haven't you?"

"Yes, we have, but the tea planting interests are all-powerful, and they are opposed to taking adequate measures against hookworm. We issue a regulation—they get it suspended. We're helpless."

"Would you have any objection to a survey made under the auspices of the Rockefeller Foundation—supposing it could be arranged with the planters?"

329

"Not at all, provided your men operated under our Health Service."

Since this had been my objective from the beginning, I assented readily to his condition.

That evening at the Colombo Club I was fortunate enough to meet the Chairman of the Estates Agents Association, which represented the absentee landlords of England and was the dominant force in local politics. In the pleasant club atmosphere I was able to establish friendly relations. "They tell me you've lots of hookworm in Ceylon," I said, seizing the opportunity, "but they also say you planters won't allow anything to be done about it."

"You're jolly well right we won't."

"Why not?"

"We're not going to have a lot of health fellows crashing into our affairs. Look at what happened last year. There was a plague scare just when our best harvest was due. It amounted to nothing, but those health inspectors came along threatening to inoculate our laborers, and almost before we could turn around thousands of them were on their way back to India. It nearly ruined us. If we ever let the Health Service get started on hookworm, all our laborers would run away, and we couldn't harvest our tea and rubber. No! No health business for us."

"Well," I replied, "I'm not a reporter or a writer for muckraking magazines. But if I wanted to, I could make your actions look like the Belgian Congo atrocities. Here you are—rich Englishmen—sacrificing thousands of lives just to get your tea harvested."

"But we have no such intentions," he indignantly protested.

"It's actually happening. Why don't you do something about it?"

"Nothing can be done with Tamils," he asserted with an air of finality.

"That's all I've heard in the East for fifteen years. When I first began working with a peasant population, I was informed everywhere 'Nothing can be done.' But it was done in the Philippines."

"Perhaps American millions did accomplish a little there. But nothing can be done with our coolies."

"We won't get very far by my insisting it can, and you that it can-

330

not. Let's talk about this as a business proposition. How much does it cost you to bring a laborer here from Madras?"

"That's a commercial secret."

"I don't care about your exact figure. I'm not in business. But does it cost you a hundred rupees?"

"All of that."

"How many laborers do you have to import?"

"About a hundred thousand a year."

"That runs into quite a sum of money, doesn't it? Now, on every estate you have a hospital. It may be large or small, but it is constantly occupied. Doctors and nurses alone must cost you a lot. And am I correct in assuming that you have to pay your laborers whether or not they are working?"

"Yes."

"Suppose we could reduce the hospital expense by half."

"That would certainly save us a great deal."

"Here's another important point to be considered. The Tamil women tend to be sterile because of anemia from hookworm. If they could produce children, you wouldn't have to bring over fresh labor all the time. You could raise your own. Wouldn't that be advantageous in the long run?"

"It would increase our profits tremendously—that goes without saying."

"So health and the planting business have something in common after all? Now, there's a way to test out these arguments I've been giving you. Suppose you were to pick out some estates employing several thousand laborers and allow the Rockefeller Foundation to bring in experts to demonstrate whether we could cure them without having them run away. You'd be the judge of our success."

"I don't see how that could do us any harm. But we wouldn't want our own Health Department concerned in any way. They're all tangled up in red tape, and would only make a lot of trouble. You'd have to leave them out of it."

"I'm afraid we couldn't do that. If you don't like your present Health Department, it's your privilege to recommend a change. But we cannot go anywhere at the request of a commercial organization

331

alone; we must have an official invitation from your Governor."

"Well, I'll talk this over with my Board of Directors, and let you know in a few days."

In the interval I made calls assiduously on everybody who might be concerned, hearing everywhere that all hookworm conversation ended merely in talk. I was, therefore, much gratified when the representative of the Estates Agents reported that the planters were willing to let the Foundation go ahead with the demonstration. I had some difficulty, however, in making clear to him that the Foundation must supervise its own expenditures. Finally, he accepted my condition that the planters pay their share.

The Governor of Ceylon, Sir Thomas Chalmers, K.C.B., had previously indicated that he did not want any Yankee men or Yankee methods introduced; Ceylon was capable of running its own affairs and paying for its own health work. The Estates Agents Association, however, brought its influence to bear, and in the course of a week the Governor capitulated. Letters were exchanged, and we prepared to begin operations, but, because the submarine campaign was in progress, and the Germans were constantly torpedoing boats with our supplies on them, we were delayed some months in assembling a staff.

But when finally we did get under way, as was almost inevitable, we incurred immediately the enmity of the native herb doctors, who considered we were interfering with their practice. They said we were in league with the British and were administering capsules to the coolies which would explode inside them at the end of five years; thus the Germans would find no labor when they possessed themselves of Ceylon. This rumor, which seemed so plausible to the coolies, was not easy for us to combat, especially as the War was going badly for the Allies at the moment. Our demonstrators might swallow capsules by the dozen to combat the accusation, but this constituted no proof that at the end of five years their stomachs would not explode.

For many years thymol had been used as the standard vermifuge, but owing to the War this drug became expensive and difficult to obtain. The Dutch had already discovered the virtues inherent in oil of chenopodium and had called my attention to it. Chenopodium had the advantage of expelling all worms, even the long-lived and tenacious tapeworm, and had a ninety-one percent efficiency against hook-worm as compared with thymol's eighty-three. Carbon tetrachloride, tetrachlorethelene, and hexylresorcinol are being used now.

Our first action in the Ceylon campaign was to treat thoroughly a small number of estates for hookworm. The results were amazing. Hospital attendance and charges dropped immediately, and the general death rate was soon greatly reduced. Whereas before the campaign large numbers of coolies failed to report for work, afterwards the labor turnover was reduced. The treatment was rapidly extended to other estates, and in 1921 two hundred thousand coolies were being freed of worms.

After demonstrating what we could do in the way of cure, it was time to start education in preventive measures against hookworm. The coolie lines in 1915 were not equipped with latrines. Every planter believed it futile to build any because he was convinced the Tamils could never be induced to use them. But by this time we had proved the economic value of our methods so completely that we could lay down conditions. We notified the plantation owners that we would do no more work on the estates until they had installed them.

Accordingly, the planters erected latrines and we helped to instruct the coolies in their use. An effective method of enforcing compliance was to fine a coolie a few cents for each dereliction. We had not been installing latrines for many years before a Tamil who was preparing to sign on again would ask whether the particular plantation to which it was proposed to send him was equipped with them. Districts now vary from thirty to ninety percent in installation, and their use has become an accepted part of the customs of the people.

In time the number of Tamils imported from India was reduced, because the working force on the plantations was not so depleted by sickness and death, and the women, having recovered from their anemia, began to bear children. In the end the planting interests co-operated whole-heartedly and themselves went through many a struggle on behalf of sanitation.

After we had demonstrated under controlled conditions on the estates that hookworm could be both cured and prevented, the campaign was extended to the villages, a far more difficult undertaking.

We were now dealing with the intractable Sinhalese rather than the stupid but amenable Tamils, but, even so, we kept the idea in the forefront that it was their responsibility.

Ceylon, like India, was split along religious and racial lines. The Sinhalese, who made up half the population, were followers of Gautama; the largest minority were the Hindu Tamils, and next to them the more energetic Mohammedans. An important factor in the population were the Christian Eurasians, known locally as the Burghers. Under supervision by the whites they ran a great deal of the administrative machinery of the island and the plantations.

Politics in every Eastern country is inextricably mixed with religion. This always complicates the health problem to a degree inconceivable to Western minds. Our work in future years was to be delayed by the rising tide of Sinhalese nationalism. The first day I was in Colombo I heard the slogan, "Ceylon for the Sinhalese," on all sides, and was offered also a glimpse of native religious unrest.

May 25 was Wesak, a Buddhist festival, customarily celebrated by making pilgrimages to shrines, feeding the poor, and feasting. But in 1915 the religious tension seemed extraordinarily acute, particularly at Kandy, a very holy place because of its temple where one of the teeth of Buddha reposes on a golden lotus leaf within its seven jeweled caskets. Riots flared up when the Buddhists held their procession in defiance of an injunction secured by the Mohammedans. The worshippers of Allah had irritated the erstwhile peaceful Buddhists to the point of violence by disrespectfully tweaking the noses and twisting off the ears of the calm and contemplative images of the Enlightened One.

The unrest spread along the railway toward Colombo. Volunteer white guards mobilized, cannon were dragged through the streets, armored automobiles filled with soldiers dashed about. The concentration point seemed to be at my hotel.

A week later trouble began in earnest. The street cars stopped running, soda water bottles filled with sand were hurtling about, and the broken glass interfered seriously with motor traffic. Groups of people were collecting everywhere, ships in the harbor were unable to coal, the government commandeered all motor cars. The Mohammedans were the shopkeepers; hence they were the creditors and the

Buddhists the debtors. I would see a crowd gathered in the street; one man would point to a shop and all, with a concerted rush, would dive into it. Three minutes and the place would be gutted, and not a trace of "accounts due" would be left. Dr. Rutherford told me one hundred and fifty injured were brought into the hospital during one night.

This was by no means the end of the disturbance, although a Colombo paper soothingly stated that everything was "practically quiet in Kandy except a few assaults and murders." Finally British territorial troops restored peace.

The Mohammedans, in retaliation, started many lawsuits for damages, which were upheld by the courts. Bitter resentment was felt against the government by the Sinhalese, some of whom are still paying costs.

Our work was going on in Ceylon when the Donoughmore Commission's recommendation for self-government went into effect. This movement was synchronous with the rising tide of Indian national feeling. An attempt had been made in Ceylon to safeguard the rights of minorities, but the Sinhalese, who were in the majority, tended to disregard the claims of Tamils and Burghers to hold office, even though they had been born in the country. Under British control many Burghers had been taken into the Civil Service, but now their advancement was threatened by the Sinhalese.

The political situation in Ceylon was typical of that encountered elsewhere in the East. Petty politics, unwarranted attacks launched by ambitious office seekers, vague promises never fulfilled, evasions and procrastinations, public announcements conveniently forgotten, were everyday happenings. Politics had to be considered at every turn. There often seemed to be no chance whatsoever of getting action on our many plans and projects. Our representatives sometimes became so down-hearted that they recommended withdrawing until things should settle down.

But in spite of individual discouragement, the Rockefeller Foundation persevered in its attempt to make Ceylon a modern health community. Experience proved that the best way to popularize a movement so foreign to the customs of the people as hookworm prevention was to prosecute it as though it were the only thing in the universe left undone. The history of the devious life and habits of this wily worm had to be brought home to every resident of Ceylon.

To prepare the way, lantern slide lectures were given and public exhibitions arranged, showing the parasite and its eggs under the microscope. To make the demonstrations more convincing the villagers were allowed to take part. They were first asked to scoop up moist earth, and put it in a glass funnel. Water was poured through this and they could watch with their own eyes the larvae being washed out of dirt they had walked over daily.

People universally seemed to show more interest in the biological problem involved than in the ravages caused by the disease. The aim was to make even the most backward members of the community thoroughly familiar with the biology of hookworm, thus creating better understanding of the methods for its control.

A small dispensary was often opened in the house of the Headman of the town, who was instructed to persuade the villagers to apply for treatment. When they showed reluctance, the simple device was adopted of treating everyone for hookworm who applied at the hospital or dispensary, even though his complaint might be as far afield as a broken leg or a toothache. The number treated in this way rose to over a million a year.

Hookworm relief was supplemented by the establishment of Health Units throughout Ceylon, which assumed responsibility for all work in a particular district. They were staffed by a doctor, a number of public health nurses, midwives, and sanitary inspectors. When no epidemic loomed in the offing, these nurses always directed their attention toward maternity and baby welfare work, because the problems of both are constant and serve as the best avenues of approach to general education in health measures.

These Health Units did not blossom forth overnight. They met opposition from all classes and religions. A doctor would approach the Mohammedan chief of a village with a list of questions. "What's your death rate?" he would begin.

"It is the will of Allah that all die; some die young, some old."

"What's your number of births?"

"Allah alone can say."

"Is your water safe and potable?"

336

SNAKES IN EDEN

"History records no death from thirst."

"What is the hygienic condition of your village?"

"Allah sent Mahomet who proved the truth with fire and sword. Now, Lamb of the West, cease your questioning. It can do you or others no good."

To train doctors to cope with these and all other possible situations which might arise, better instruction had to be provided in the Medical School. This presented a major problem. The Sinhalese believed their school to be one of the best in existence, and support for any radical change was almost impossible to obtain. Practically all the instruction was by lecturers of the old didactic type. Criticism of the general lack of interest and the inefficiency shown by the doctors in the hospitals always brought the triumphant rejoinder that they had qualified before the British General Medical Council with flying colors. Though I might be convinced that both diagnosis and treatment were often incorrect, I could make no answer.

When the Sinhalese gained political control, they insisted on having the teaching of the ancient Hindu system of Ayurvedic medicine supported by the government. As the protagonists of modern science, we had to discourage a method by which a practitioner, en route to a patient's bedside, would determine the treatment he was going to prescribe by the number of buttons on the coat of the first man he met.

In the renaissance of Indian nationalism, Ayurvedic medicine had naturally been stressed, and many schools had been started all over India. One of the largest of these was at Benares. When I was taken on the usual tour of inspection, the President, a Hindu, solemnly displayed the most ridiculous things. After he had finished I said, "I trust you won't consider me rude, but how can you believe in what you have been showing me this afternoon?"

"You never get very far or go very fast by attacking an established institution direct," the Brahmin replied. "You have noticed that by the side of courses in Ayurvedic we have installed others in anatomy, histology, and chemistry. Wherever possible, we encourage our students to take these courses. Those who do so are intelligent enough to see the absurdities in Ayurvedic, and will discard them of their own volition. But if I were to challenge the Ayurvedic system

337

itself, I would not get the money I need for the school, and the little we have gained would be lost."

This answer impressed me as being sound in its psychology, and seemed to offer hope that the time would come when we would not have to contend with this particular obstacle.

Because the claims of this extraordinary materia medica were put forward by such leaders as Gandhi, who dogmatically asserted modern medicine was sorcery, the government of India, under Colonel Chopra of the Indian Medical Service, has spent thousands of dollars in the endeavor to determine whether it possessed anything of value. So far the results have been meagre. It is true that certain Ayurvedic drugs were found to have properties with which we were not familiar. But we had developed drugs for the same purpose which were far more efficacious. For example, Ayurvedic boasted about its kurchi as a cure for dysentery, but carbasone is so far superior as to be beyond comparison.

The march of medical progress in the East for a time was retarded by the poet-philosopher, Rabindranath Tagore. He had arrived at Peiping on his way through the Orient, addressing huge audiences everywhere and advocating a return to Eastern idealism instead of following Western materialism. This was virtually an attack on modern science. Because he was being hailed by all the dark-skinned races as an example of an Eastern intellect acknowledged by the West as of equal calibre, his words carried great weight and were extremely detrimental to the objectives of scientific medicine. I might very likely fail, but I thought I could do no less than try to divert the trend of his lectures.

Such vast numbers of admirers were besieging Tagore's quarters that I had great difficulty in securing an interview, but finally was ushered into his presence. He looked like a patriarch, with his beautiful, long, white hair and flowing beard, and he charmed me with his soft, persuasive voice and delightful manner. We talked for a long, long while of this and of that. He elaborated his theory that nothing permanent or worth while in health could be accomplished unless the spiritual and human interest of the masses were first won. He apparently was impressed by my observation that disease had made it largely impossible for Indians to smile, and agreed thoroughly with my stand that no government or private organization could give health; people had to achieve it by their own efforts.

Tagore was of the opinion that the Indian Medical Service had failed because it had not established itself in the hearts of the people, and intimated that if the Rockefeller Foundation were to work directly through him its results might be very much better. I answered that, though we required the formality of government cooperation, we used our own judgment and our own methods in establishing ourselves in the hearts of the people, very much as he advocated. Tagore's suspicions of us as allies of the government he so mistrusted were allayed, and he was persuaded that we had the same end in view as himself. But he was convinced that the only right way to go about attaining it was through the system of ancient India which he was so stoutly recommending.

This remark gave me the opportunity for which I had been looking. "You've had a Western education," I said, "but you're decrying everything Western science has contributed to the world. Yet the mere fact you are here is a testimonial to its accomplishments. The steamship which carried you could never have been produced by the old culture which you uphold."

"I could have come overland."

"Not in your condition of health," I replied. "You couldn't have come at all. But I'm most interested in what you have to say about Hindu materia medica. You claim it has much value. But you don't know, and the only way of testing its merit is in the modern research laboratory, the greatest institution for truth that man has ever evolved. It is absolutely impartial, its findings are not colored, it is simply seeking the truth. A lot of the remedies which you suggest as effective have been scientifically proved of no value. I think you yourself would be satisfied if you followed the steps in the laboratory that have been taken to arrive at this conclusion. Before you say anything more, would you go and see in this city of Peiping one of the finest laboratories in existence?"

The philosopher agreed to go, and I made arrangements for his reception at the Medical College. This was our only conversation on the subject, and I had no opportunity to find out when I saw him later whether his visit had converted him to my way of thinking.

339

But I followed his addresses carefully, and never again to my knowledge did he speak against Western medicine.

Obstacles and discouragements were of almost daily occurrence in Ceylon, but in spite of them our efforts were eventually successful. With the assistance of the Rockefeller Foundation, Ceylon now has one of the most modern health services of any country of similar population in the world. Our function was to hasten this accomplishment by several decades.

Ceylon was the best illustration that could be found of what Mr. Rockefeller had meant when he said, "Philanthropy must pay dividends." Both from the economic and the humanitarian standpoint, benefits accrued far beyond our expectations. Not only was the health of the population improved and its happiness increased thereby, but this very improvement in health produced wealth in increasing proportions. The fifty thousand dollars we spent to widen the circle still further, over the years brought about governmental appropriations for health of at least five millions.

Important as it was to complete the hookworm demonstration in Ceylon, the eventual goal was to make such demonstrations unnecessary by tracking hookworm to its place of origin and eradicating it. It would be useless to wipe out the disease in Ceylon if reinfection were constantly to recur from the source of labor supply. To persuade the authorities of India of the shockingly high Tamil hookworm infection was the first step in the long march toward stamping hookworm out of Madras, which was a radiating center of infection, sending Tamils thousands of miles westward across the world to Trinidad and British Guiana, southward into Malaya and the lower tip of Africa, and eastward to Burma and the South Seas.

As soon as preparations for the survey in Ceylon had been made, I had set off for India. Whatever elation I may have felt over the successful outcome was dampened by having to start the same laborious round over again. The provincial Health Service of Madras disclaimed all authority. In a country which had an average of one hundred and ninety-five persons living on each square mile, the idea that hookworm was controllable was denigrated. It was the old cry of the impossible job; it could not be done. After interviewing men here and there—at Calcutta, Delhi, and Simla—trading health ideas as I went along, I found, surprisingly enough, that the source of authority was the man at the top, Sir Charles Pardey Lukis, Director General of the Indian Medical Service.

I called immediately upon Sir Pardey at Simla. He was an intelligent and pleasant gentleman, but skeptical of the hookworm figures with which I presented him. He could not believe that our estimates of over seventy percent infestation could be correct, but assured me he was open-minded and willing to be convinced. He intimated, however, that it was out of the question for anything to be started in war time. I retorted with a description of British colonies in which health work was going on in spite of the War, and described enthusiastically the impression I had received that the British government was very proud of those officials who could keep things moving in a normal manner, and even undertake new things during war time.

The next day I went into the matter with Major F. Norman White, the Assistant Director General, sounding him cautiously on the prospects. He also was affable, but less easy to convince. He said he feared the government would decide to postpone any such undertaking as a hookworm survey until after the War because the Indians might take advantage of war conditions to start an uprising. Any innovation might have an unlooked-for effect, however innocent or philanthropic its real objects might be.

Major White attempted to discourage me further by saying it was inconceivable that an American doctor, new to the infinite complexities of Indian psychology, could make any headway when the Indian Medical Service doctors, with years of experience behind them, had such great difficulty. I suggested that many of the things which appeared theoretically hard often proved simple in actual practice, and we believed the best plan was to proceed cautiously with test demonstrations, working out the procedure as we went along. Any man we sent could be relied upon for tact, and with Major White as guide might achieve success.

I returned later to the attack on Sir Pardey, and we spent several evenings talking until midnight. At the end of these conferences he asked me to submit a letter with our proposals. I did as he asked, but, because the chiefs of the Indian Medical Service did not believe the hookworm situation could be as serious as I had represented it, they decided to have their own men verify my estimates. Since almost all their regular members had been absorbed in the War, Sir Pardey selected to make the investigation a native doctor, Mhaskar, and a Catholic priest, Father Caius, the latter a competent chemist who had already been working in his laboratory on various remedies for hookworm. The two investigators reported a ninety-seven percent infection, a figure far higher than ours. The Indian Medical Service was horrified over the enormity of the problem, but the War took so much of its attention that several years elapsed before we were called upon for any further part in Indian health affairs.

Meanwhile, research work on hookworm was proceeding in many quarters of the world. Dr. Norman Stoll, with Dr. John Grant, who had been studying the disease in China, evolved a method for determining the severity of infection. By counting the number of eggs in one gram of feces, he could estimate the number of worms in the individual. Dr. Wilson G. Smillie, working in Alabama and Tennessee, found that the presence of fifty hookworms or under did not constitute a serious menace to health and could be disregarded; many more were required to produce anemia.

As soon as the government of India was free of its war obligations, and had asked the Rockefeller Foundation to cooperate, we turned this newly discovered knowledge about hookworm to practical use in Madras. It had been estimated that the cost of a hookworm campaign averaged about one dollar per person. Therefore, it would cost fifty million dollars a year in Madras alone. We did not have this money; neither did the Indian government. Even had we had it and treated the population, it would all have had to be done over again the following year. Obviously such an enormous problem would remain unsolved until some new method of handling it could be evolved.

To begin with, we stationed men at each emigration camp, and ploddingly examined every outward-bound Tamil for his degree of infestation, including plotting his birthplace on an enormous chart. At the end of three years' painstaking examination, it was apparent that the emigrants with heavy infestation came from a few well-delineated districts. If these foci could be cleaned up, it was probable that less heavily infected centers would eventually become free, because hookworm tended to disappear of itself. We checked our information by looking up meteorological records of certain swampy areas and found they were distinctly correlated with the major hookworm infestations. We then knew exactly where to direct our attack at a cost within the grounds of possibility. Since this section of India was disseminating uncinariasis throughout the tropical world, a tremendous step toward its conquest will have been taken when it is stamped out of Madras.

CHAPTER 20. THE WHITE MAN'S LAST REFUGE

CEYLON was a large scale demonstration for the entire East where the Rockefeller Foundation helped to spread modern health concepts. There we were dealing with a native population to whom sanitation and health had meant practically nothing; in the Australian democracy, with white labor already health conscious, almost one hundred percent literate, and fully vocal, little was needed except encouragement.

In 1916 I had to approach British countries armed with credentials from the Colonial Office at London. With this meagre equipment I launched my attack against the important, self-sufficient citadel of Australia. Not until some years later was Rockefeller Foundation aid eagerly sought everywhere and were we able to lay down more and more stringent conditions.

With pleasant anticipation, I entered beautiful Sydney Harbor, dotted with Goat, Shark, Cockatoo, and innumerable other islets. I saw again the sloping green hillsides from which emerged the picturesque red and pink tiled roofs of the houses. The sun was full upon the city and the sight gorgeous beyond description.

My reception at the pier was decidedly in contrast to this inviting prospect. That I was an American was proclaimed by my passport. The customs officer, glancing at it, asked peremptorily for my luggage. Forthwith, suits, shirts, handkerchiefs, collars, socks, papers, books, toilet kit, all my possessions were soon scattered over the dirty floor.

THE WHITE MAN'S LAST REFUGE

When not a single object remained in the gaping bags, he turned away. "You can go," he said gruffly.

"Who's going to put my things back in the bags?" I mildly inquired.

"You are!"

Before I could think of an effective rejoinder, there was a loud honking from the street, and a brilliantly appareled officer brightened the doorway. "Is this Dr. Heiser?" he inquired. "I'm the Governor's aide. His Excellency has asked me to look after you. Is your luggage ready?"

I waved my hand toward the wreckage. "The customs officer has been making an inspection."

The aide turned to him sharply. "Dr. Heiser is a guest of the government. Repack his bags immediately and if one thing is missing or dirty, you'll hear from His Excellency."

We left a subdued inspector, meekly dusting, folding, and packing.

On this visit I found Australia generally inclined to be inimical. In the first place the friendliness she had formerly evidenced to the United States had been metamorphosed into hostility, and the resentment against Americans as such was strong because they alleged we were avoiding the risks of war while reaping the financial benefits of neutrality. They took delight in annoying us whenever and wherever possible.

I, personally, suffered under the further handicap of being an emissary of the Rockefeller Foundation. Even the august tutelage of the Governor General could not help me in that quarter. The odium and curiosity attached to the Rockefeller name was inevitably reflected upon anyone associated with it. My life would have been a burden had I even had the Foundation address printed on my baggage.

In those days offers of help from the Foundation were looked upon with suspicion, particularly by the anti-capitalist Australians. The Standard Oil Company was in such bad repute that the health officials, although we had been friends since the days when they had visited the Philippines, shied at the sight of me. Instead of receiving me in their offices, they would conduct interviews walking

345

up and down in the park, where our conversations could not be overheard or our association be so obvious.

Any representative of the Rockefellers was bound to be looked at askance in a country which had been pro-labor and anti-capital from its very beginnings. Most Australian legislation had been drawn up to the end of fettering capital. In the eyes of Australians I was the agent of the arch capitalist. The deep-seated hatred of large corporations was enhanced by a lurking suspicion that our work was in the nature of a scheme to superimpose American economic control upon ingenuous foreign countries.

The influence exercised by labor in Australia was enormous. Even when I had first gone there in 1911 anybody could be arrested for working more than eight hours a day, and many papers had listed violators. New South Wales carefully defined the minimum wage as one which provided food and adequate shelter for a man, his wife, and two children, and, in addition:

"fuel, clothes, boots, furniture, utensils, rates, life insurance, savings, accident or benefit societies, loss of employment, union pay, books and newspapers, train and tram fares, sewing-machine, mangle, school requisites, amusements and holidays, intoxicating liquors, tobacco, sickness and death, domestic help, unusual contingencies, religion, or charity."

I was constantly running into other examples. One of the most extravagant was in the Northern Territory. Originally part of South Australia, which saw it go with little reluctance, this vast expanse of desert, interspersed here and there with grazing land, has turned out to be a white elephant to the Federal government.

Port Darwin, the chief city, seemed like one of our own Western towns with its right-angled streets and one story buildings, its lack of trees, and the red soil which rose in clouds of dust under the great heat. Even in this latitude of only twelve degrees south the air at night felt almost crisp. The prosperity of the town had depended on a huge, million-dollar plant which the Vestry Meat Works of London had erected there, drawing its cattle from the big ranges to the south.

But labor, in the so-called slow strike, had forged a deadly weapon to satisfy its demands. The normal daily load carried by sixty-five stevedores was three hundred tons. But when a ship chartered by the Vestry Corporation would come in to take on cargo, this would be reduced to fifty tons, thereby increasing the loading time sixfold. Since all vessels have demurrage clauses in their charters, if they are delayed in port too long, the profits are entirely consumed. The meat plant had to close.

The laborers, who had thus done themselves out of the only existing jobs, were soon in a starving condition, and the Australian government had to support them. I was once on the *S.S. Montoro* which was taking free supplies to Port Darwin. When we arrived Sunday morning the foreman of the stevedores came on board. He told the captain, "If you want us to unload your ship today, you know you'll have to pay double." Dock laborers in Australia were paid a base rate of eighteen shillings, with nine extra for tropical service, and double rates for Sundays and night work. The captain might fume but, to avoid demurrage, he had to agree, even though the ship was bringing food to be distributed to these very men as a dole.

At eleven the foreman came truculently on board again and demanded drinking water. One of the ship's officers lost his temper and shouted, "To hell with you! Get your own water!"

In this labor democracy stop work orders might be issued on all occasions. The foreman, judging the water situation warranted drastic action, issued a stop work order. Immediately all the stevedores adjourned to the town, which was some distance from the harbor, for a drink. By noon they had returned, but, since union regulations did not permit them to start work until one, another hour was lost. At five o'clock their supplies were not yet unloaded and the foreman dictated, "We'll have to get double wages for night work." Again there was nothing to do but submit and pay the quadrupled rate. The captain estimated that each laborer had received twenty-five dollars for carrying his own groceries.

On another occasion the *S.S. Victoria* had cargo to transfer to another ship and pulled alongside the vessel in order to make the shift directly. The union issued an ultimatum which compelled her to dock on the other side of the wharf and pay regular unloading rates for having the cargo placed on the pier. Each piece had to be weighed and then transferred on trucks the few feet to the other side. Regular rates had to be paid for the reloading operation also.

Had the *Victoria's* captain not submitted, he would have been in the same sorry predicament as the captain of another vessel on which I was once a passenger. Fifty mules were awaiting shipment at Townsville, Queensland. But because it was a holiday, though only a minor one, the stevedores refused to load them. Rather than delay sailing until the next day, the captain commandeered his crew and, with the volunteer aid of most of the passengers, the refractory animals were brought on board. But the captain paid dearly for his expedient because he found himself on the black list and could not return again to Townsville.

Australia is a country full of curious phenomena. The aborigines, termed blackfellows by the Australians who, even though they have lived in the land only since 1788, called themselves the natives, are more primitive than the Negritos of the Philippines. These survivors from the neolithic age build no houses, wear no clothes, cultivate no crops, but live on wild fruits and game, killed by boomerangs and clubs. Their only social grouping is in clans, each bearing the name of its totem, usually a bird, and their only taboo is that no man and woman of the same bird name shall marry. Though only an estimated fifty thousand are left, their wild nomadic life has kept them comparatively free of the diseases of civilized man.

The bird life is equally strange. The emu, the national bird, cannot fly, but kicks sidewise as well as backward; the mallee hen makes its own incubator out of decomposing vegetable matter; the bower bird builds playhouses and gardens, and adorns them with shells and bright seeds; the kookooburra, or laughing jackass, is a friendly fellow, with an uproarious laugh.

Australia is geologically the oldest land surface, and the rivers rise near the coast and flow inland. It was cut off from the rest of the earth before the development of mammals beyond the most primitive marsupial stage.

The kangaroo, which should have ceased living thousands of years ago, is of many species and ranges in size from that of a mouse to that of a man: the wallaby bounds along with gigantic leaps at fifteen miles an hour; the beaver-tailed, duck-billed platypus, web-footed yet clawed, lays eggs and suckles its young, has no external ear and yet can hear; the striped anteater also lays eggs, but hatches them in her pouch; the bear-like wombat and the rat-like bandicoot are other denizens of this strange land.

Lower still and more anachronistic in the scale of evolution are the iguanas which corkscrew up trees after birds' eggs, and the legless lizards, known as slow worms, two feet long, so brittle they break in several pieces when grasped, and the abundant skinks, in which legs have disappeared, leaving only a solitary toe.

My own eyes were witnesses that these things were so, but I had to take on faith the yahoo, whose feet point backward, so that when running from you it seems to run toward you, and the bunyip, the great Beast in the Bush, which none has seen and survived to record its horrendous properties.

However mythological these latter beasts may be, undoubtedly a tremendous wild buffalo with a space of ten feet between the tips of his horns roams the backcountry, and the Great Barrier Reef is haunted by shellfish which can bite an oar in two. The little brown rifle fish swims along until it sees an appetizing bug poised on a limb, takes aim, and brings it down with a well-directed squirt. At the museum in Dunedin, New Zealand, I saw the extinct moon bird, and heard the well-confirmed story of the kea bird, the harmless mountain parrot which, after tasting the fat of dead sheep, developed a voracious appetite for this delicacy, attacking the live animals and killing so many that a price was put on its head.

When some sport-loving Briton introduced the rabbit into Australia, an animal familiar to us but a novelty in this outdated land, the result was startling. Only an adding machine could cope with the rapid increase. Poisons, bounties, and packs of half-tamed dingos failed to diminish them. Finally, to keep them from digging the very grass roots out of the grazing lands, a hundred thousand miles of fences were erected. The fences had to be extended further and further until eventually they overlapped and enclosed the rabbits instead. The Australians have at last turned the tables and have converted these "vermin," which, as white men, they themselves will not eat, into a profitable crop; one ship sometimes carries a million rabbit carcasses to London.

The Australians had even more trouble coping with the cactus, which had escaped from a decorative garden bed and now covers virtually thousands of acres. The plants often grew higher than a man's head, and were so hazardous that cattle often became imprisoned among them. Scientists sought the world over for a cactus pest, and have only recently secured some promising insect enemies.

In a country where the principal tree, the eucalyptus, held its leaves sidewise to conserve moisture, and where cherries had their pits on the outside, which had to be crushed to reach the fruit, the inhabitants also naturally had peculiarities. For instance, any man or woman who resisted the opportunity for self-expression to be found at the polls, under the compulsory voting act, had to pay a fine.

Because of the laudable determination that everyone should be allowed ample time for recreation, Sunday was observed with the utmost rigidity; double fares were charged on the trams and not even a bottle of soda water could be bought. Picnicking in parks or in the outskirts of the cities was a universal pastime, and horse racing was a passion among all classes. So great was the enthusiasm for games that a cricketer who showed extraordinary prowess had a purse made up for him which sometimes amounted to thousands of pounds.

Australians were so determined that their country should belong to the white man that they put into effect the most stringent immigration regulations, even rigidly controlling British subjects. Their simple device was to present the prospective immigrant with an educational test. The Indian, for example, who was constantly appearing on the doorstep, might be asked questions on trigonometry or ancient history. Since he could not possibly answer them satisfactorily, he was automatically returned to his port of origin.

Cultists of all kinds were also unwelcome, although there was no legal barrier to their entrance. When Christian Scientists began their propaganda, the doctors of Melbourne sent them a public challenge, saying the superiority of mind over matter would be freely admitted if they could refrain from vomiting after being given a certain injection. Since sports overshadowed all else in Australia, the populace was agog to see the ordeal by apomorphine, but the Christian Scientists refused to submit, and when their answer was heralded by the press they were discredited.

Intruders might be kept out by various means, but Australian internal difficulties had by no means been settled. Warfare of one sort or another was always being waged against a neighboring city, state, or even the Federal government. Because each state considered itself autonomous, interstate jealousy, political and economic, was intense. Railroad gauges changed at each boundary, New South Wales being the only one to possess standard width. This was discouraging to a traveler, who had to clamber off and on trains five times in making the journey from Brisbane to Perth.

Great Britain itself was not exempted from jealousy. I soon learned that I would have to omit Colonial Office, governor general, and imperial completely from my vocabulary. But it was rather odd, in this democratic country, to see how knighthoods were prized, and the kingly palace in which the Governor General was maintained.

No state would consent to have the capital of the new Federation, which was created after fifty years of bickering, permanently located in the city of another state. This rivalry finally culminated in abandoning a perfectly good capital at well-to-do and slumless Melbourne, beautifully set beside the river among hills and trees and already equipped with public buildings and innumerable metropolitan facilities, for the desolate district now known as Canberra, halfway between Sydney and Melbourne and many miles inland.

A hundred years from now Canberra will probably be one of the world's finest cities. The streets are beautifully laid out in accordance with modern town planning schemes, ornamented with statues and fountains and planted extensively with trees. But at present it is a little trying for the visitor. Building has been started on opposite sides of the immense rim, and it is often miles from one government edifice to another.

I could do little at Sydney in 1916. The Federal authorities were not sufficiently powerful to compose state differences and embark on a national health program. Only Queeensland was eager to have the Rockefeller Foundation make a hookworm study, and invited me for a consultation. Most of the land route to Brisbane lies through valleys and over mountains much resembling those of the Berkshires. Scenery of great beauty lies beyond Toowoomba, as the railroad winds down the jeopardous slopes through tunnels and over fantastic bridges which the Australians build three times as strong as ours, with a triple factor of safety.

South Australia was in the temperate zone; Queensland was tropical, and at Townsville was located a flourishing and interesting Institute of Tropical Medicine which was trying to prove that the white man could work and thrive in the tropics. In the sugar plantation country of Queensland I first encountered this all-absorbing problem. There I saw white men working in the fields, something unheard of elsewhere in the tropics. I observed that, although the temperature was rather low at times, a mango which I had sent as a mere shoot from Manila several years before had become a tree and was bearing fruit. Nevertheless, the country lacked the intense verdure to which I had become accustomed in hot countries. It was curious to see the banana and apple—tropical and temperate zone fruits—growing side by side. Areas of poor soil were indicated by the stupendous magnetic anthills, so called because they pointed north. These mammoth oblongs were sometimes higher than a man on horseback. A tropical region where white labor wore shoes presented unusual conditions, and may have accounted for the fact that Australia came nearer eradicating hookworm than any other country.

Dr. J. S. C. Elkington, Quarantine Officer in Brisbane, an old friend, discussed with me the hopes he and his associates entertained for a Federal Ministry of Health. I stated frankly that, in my judgment, the prospect seemed poor unless public opinion, which must be enlisted to back the project, could be assured and that local governments would cease their childish wrangling and follow a national policy.

In the five years which elapsed before I next saw Australia in 1921, the idea of a Ministry of Health became a popular issue. The troops coming home from the War had threatened the introduction of malaria, typhoid, dysentery, and venereal disease. Cerebrospinal meningitis paid no heed to the jealously guarded state borders.

THE WHITE MAN'S LAST REFUGE

The influenza epidemic, which spared no corner of the continent, brought to light the inefficiency and confusion of the states in dealing with a disease of such vital concern to all. A plan was formulated to centralize health operations under Federal control, with each state remaining responsible for most of its former functions; hence it would cooperate rather than criticize. The Quarantine Service, which was already Federal, was to be the nucleus of a National Health Service.

The great obstacle to the establishment of the proposed Ministry of Health was the alleged opposition of Prime Minister W. M. Hughes. This Australian leader, who had conducted his country brilliantly through the War, was a person of importance. The frequent requests for his presence in London had added to his prestige.

By 1921 a Rockefeller representative was no longer held in anathema. In fact, he was welcomed in an advisory capacity. As a neutral, without an axe to grind, I was asked to approach the dreaded little man with arguments for the Health Ministry. Dr. J. H. L. Cumpston, Director of the Quarantine Service, arranged the interview with Mr. Hughes.

I had no premonition of the unexpected turn the conversation was to take. In the first place, it was disconcerting to find the Premier so deaf that my arguments, well practised for intonation and phrasing, had to be shouted.

Deaf people usually fall into two categories: either they whisper so low that no one can hear their words, or they are under the impression that everyone else is also deaf. Premier Hughes belonged to the latter persuasion. He could hardly curb his impatience while I was setting forth the arguments for the new ministry. As soon as I had finished, "I don't believe in your ministry," he roared up at me. "It's ridiculous!! It's wrong!! I'm not going to have any more ministries!"

"How do you think it ought to be done?" I bellowed down.

"No more ministries!! Have enough of them already! Doctors don't know how to run a ministry! Make it a division! Start on tuberculosis!"

"That's absurd!" I practically screamed. "It's an illogical plan! There's nothing sound about it!"

He looked at me in amazement. "Yes," he agreed, "it's bad."

His amazement hardly equaled mine. The great man whom everybody had approached on hands and knees was actually being meek. Before he could retract his admission, I followed up my advantage with further screams, "You're only a lawyer trying to tell me about something at which I've spent my life!"

I had out-shouted him completely. He was in a virtual state of collapse. "How do you think it ought to be done?" he asked.

"You've heard the plan! That's what you ought to do! You've a great opportunity before you! If you don't accept it, you'll deserve to be called backward."

"Well, why can't we do this ourselves? We've plenty of men."

"You haven't a man with modern training," said I, still yelling at the top of my lungs.

"How should we go about it then?"

"We'll lend you our men, and we'll have yours trained for you in Europe and America to replace them as soon as possible. The whole thing is for the benefit of Australia. Great Britain has a Ministry of Health, and so should you!"

"Perhaps we should," he agreed.

I was not going to give him a moment's pause in which to rally his scattered forces. "Certainly you should," I yelled. "You ought to have done it long ago!"

"Will you help us?" He was almost timid.

"Of course we'll help you. I don't hold anything against you just because you are not familiar with health administration."

"All right, I'll do it."

I could hardly believe that I had heard aright. The tumult and the shouting died. I told him I would submit the plan for a Ministry of Health at once to the Rockefeller Foundation, and bring him the reply as soon as received.

"I'm very glad you talked this way to me," he said with a humble and a contrite heart, as I took my departure.

Dr. Cumpston was so encouraged that he said even though nothing should come of this promise, meanwhile he was living on great dreams.

THE WHITE MAN'S LAST REFUGE

In two days I had the agreement of the Foundation to its part in the plan, and returned to Mr. Hughes' office. I read him the cabled offer to assist in the formation of a Ministry of Health, and presented him the plan. With some return of his former pugnacity, he began, merely from habit, to pick out insignificant paragraphs here and there to criticize, saying it appeared we thought hookworm was as important as the Ministry of Health. "The public can only grasp one idea at a time. Any proposition which expects to win popular approval must contain sections which will apply to each individual."

This was sound statesmanship, but I could not afford to let him get the upper hand. My voice rose immediately. "Of course, hookworm is important. That's the way you're going to get people interested—focus their attention on public health. Then you'll get the thing that Australia needs the most—support for a central health service."

Having made this last stand, he whole-heartedly approved the entire proposal.

By means of an Order in Council, a Ministry of Health was established the next week. Labor gave it unanimous support. When we finally withdrew from Australia, which had been so antagonistic in the beginning, the Federal Parliament passed a vote of thanks commending the Rockefeller Foundation for its work there.

New Zealand bore the standard of the white man's last refuge even higher than Australia. The cost of democracy was equally high, and the same labor troubles were in evidence. Once my steamer stopped at Auckland during a big strike in which practically all shipping was tied up and more than a thousand people were stranded. No cargo could be unloaded. The strikers, however, respected the sacrosanct character of the mails, and were willing to undertake their delivery to the pier, but when they found that a little cement dust had sifted on to the mail sacks, they immediately demanded double rates for landing "dusty cargo"; ship and passengers were detained two days pending the settlement of their claim.

The eight-hour law was observed most punctiliously along the water front. I remember once at Wellington watching horses being

355

loaded onto the ship. One by one slings were fastened about them and they were swung from the wharf to the deck. When the twelve o'clock whistle blew the winches stopped, and a horse was left dangling in midair for an hour, until activity was again permitted.

Even more than Australia, New Zealand was preeminently a land of strange laws and social experiments. Every farmer was obliged to feed and give a night's lodging to any swagger, or tramp, who applied. Regardless of income tax, every employed person had to contribute five percent of his salary toward the unemployment fund. The New Zealanders were cultists; the vegetarian idea had taken firm root. Nevertheless, they had their little snobberies. The bars were run with three separate counters—one for well-dressed people, another for laborers, and a third for soldiers.

Railroads, trams, telephones and telegraphs, water power, insurance, mines, totalizers for betting, workmen's dwellings, hospitals, old age pensions, banks, and arbitration and conciliation committees between capital and labor were under government control and, in actuality as well as in intent, seemed to be operated for the public benefit. I was struck not only by the number of branch libraries everywhere, but that they were so arranged that the public might draw books with the least amount of inconvenience.

New Zealand had been largely settled by missionaries and retired army and navy officers. The average intelligence was high and the illiteracy rate the lowest in the world. No smallpox, no plague, and little malaria attacked its homes. No snakes, no white ants, no ferocious animals disturbed its peace. Nearly all plant parasites were absent; few bugs or pests ravaged its gardens. The country for years has had the lowest general mortality and infant death rates. Its system of child hygiene has been regarded as a model for all to follow.

A very nice question presented itself in such a seeming health paradise. In the War New Zealand soldiers had suffered a higher morbidity rate than the English, and the same held true of New Zealanders traveling in foreign countries. Was it better to correct the environment of the New Zealanders still further, thus making them relatively susceptible to introduced infections, or to build up their immunity so they could both withstand these invasions and go abroad with greater safety? None of the members of the medical profession with whom I discussed this paradox had a solution to offer.

The New Zealand government was taking seriously its responsibilities to the original inhabitants, the Maoris, and was trying to give them the benefits of modern civilization. Over seventy-two thousand of this most advanced group of the highly intelligent Polynesians still existed and warranted every effort made in their behalf. They were found in all walks of life; the Minister for the Cook Islands and the Maoris was himself a full-blooded Polynesian.

But the conscience of the government spread beyond its own confines. Far away to the northeast it had a dependency in the shape of a small group of islands named after the explorer Cook, and supposed to be the original home of the Maoris. The Cook Islanders had by no means progressed so far as the Maoris, although they were not wild people in the sense of the Igorots or Moros of the Philippine Islands.

New Zealand also accepted the League of Nations mandate for Western Samoa, and has spent huge sums, infinitely greater than any return it has ever had, in elevating the living standards of the Samoans. These kindly, hospitable, and docile Polynesians, like the rest of the inhabitants of the South Sea Islands, were decreasing yearly in numbers. New Zealand was much chagrined over the slow progress of her health work, and welcomed our assistance. Our campaigns against hookworm and yaws among the Cook Islanders and Samoans were only two out of many such labors which we undertook in this island-studded section of the broad Pacific.

CHAPTER 21.   PARASITES LOST

AND

PARASITES REGAINED

SOME years after the World War had ended, I was sitting one day in the office of the Australian Minister of the Interior at Melbourne, engaged in a lengthy discussion of health affairs. When it was evident that our conversation would continue for some time, the Minister asked, "Would you mind if I interrupt? There's a man outside who has been waiting to see me for some time. I know what he wants and it will only take a few minutes."

In the shabby individual who entered I recognized the man whom once I had looked upon as among the most enviable of mortals. His appearance recalled to my mind the long-ago morning when my steamer was approaching an island north of New Guinea. Slowly and peacefully it rose from the sea until it appeared like the green and gold lid of a sugar bowl resting alone on a bright blue tablecloth and crowned with a white knob which, as we drew nearer, resolved itself into a spacious house. From the white coral sands of the sea's edge thousands of cocoanut palms flowed like a green tide up the gentle slope toward the summit.

Two German brothers were the sole possessors of this enchanting island of Moron. I later stood with one of them on the crest of the rise, with the sea rim curling below us, as he described his idyllic existence. All the land that he could see was his. No work, no worry troubled him; nothing disturbed the solitude of his existence save the slow procession of ships bound for Singapore, Tokyo, Sydney.

PARASITES LOST AND PARASITES REGAINED

When the fancy took him, he might fish or cruise in his magnificent schooner yacht, or he might bide at home, reading a book from his well-stocked library, illumined by light from his own electric plant, while sipping drinks cooled by his own ice machine—a luxury then unheard of in the South Seas.

This calm and this sumptuousness were the fruits of the hundred thousand cocoanut palms, each of which produced an annual revenue of one dollar. Turn and turn about one brother would take the hundred thousand dollars and scatter them lavishly over Europe, while the other sat idly on the veranda and watched the workmen gather the cocoanuts.

But the War came and Australia and New Zealand eagerly snapped up the rich German spoils of the South Seas. Now here was my host of that halcyon day, who had lost his earthly paradise, tramping from ministry to ministry in the vain hope of its return.

From the first time the eyes of white men feasted upon the beauties of the South Seas, these islands have symbolized escape from a world that is too much with us. According to tales brought back by travelers, nature on sea and land offered a freedom from trouble and from labor, the air was soft and balmy, and the women beautiful and kind. The sea was full of fish, wild hogs ran everywhere. As soon as a child was weaned, it was put on a diet of taro root, and taro grew so freely that an effortless kick brought it from the bountiful earth. The United Fruit Company, with all its research and cultivation, produced no finer bananas than those which nature, unaided, here provided, and everywhere cocoanuts and oranges supplied both food and drink. For the Islanders life consisted almost entirely of diversion, and they questioned the greater satisfaction to be derived from work as compared with leisure. Even Europeans, after a short sojourn among them, tended to accept this view.

The South Sea Islands, generally speaking, are those east of Australia and south of the Equator. With the exception of American Samoa, they are all under the sovereignty of the British Empire or the French Republic. The origin of the Islanders is largely a matter of conjecture, but by drawing a line north and south through the Fiji Islands they may be divided racially into Polynesian and Melanesian, although the Gilbert and Ellice Islands are inhabited by so-

359

called Micronesians, light in complexion, but with the slant eyes which betray a Malay strain.

To the east are the Polynesians, the pure race of tall, brown, straight-haired men. To the west the Polynesian strain fades out until it vanishes in the negroid interior of dark Papua. In the middle islands the admixture is called Melanesian. The course of the Polynesian migration eastward may be traced by isolated islands still remaining predominantly Polynesian.

The long, straight hair found in the Cook, Samoan, and Tonga, or Friendly, groups gradually coils to become a frizzy mass on the head of the Fijian, and kinks tighter and tighter until in Papua it is a mere wool. The Fijian dandy takes such great pride in his black, or sometimes reddish, poll that he spends hours in trimming it, so that not one hair shall be out of place. He will, however, have no hair on his face. Should any have the hardihood to appear, he, with equal hardihood, usually plucks it forth with two clam shells. Sometimes he shaves, using sharks' teeth, broken bottles, or perhaps a knife of split bamboo.

The Fijians, with their beautiful shoulders, narrow waists, great thighs, and handsome calves are more perfect physical specimens than the Polynesians who, although large and well-formed, are apt to be soft from too little exercise. The beauty of the Fijian body was well displayed by the picturesque *lava lava*, much like the Malay sarong, six feet long and a yard wide, varying in fashion and color with the tribe. For women the modest Mother Hubbard, the missionary's contribution to morality in the South Seas, was universal. Only now, with the decline of missionary influence, is some small trace of waist line beginning to creep in.

Throughout the South Seas the missionaries were, in the Nineteenth Century, the dominating force. On their arrival they found the Islanders enjoying a system of communal ownership. If a new house were needed, all joined in and built it. Nothing was spent on maintaining law and order; there was nothing to steal because the goods of one belonged to all. For any little infractions of their customs, the elders of the village held court of a kind; but there were no prisons nor jails.

The missionaries were horrified at these conditions. In the Cook

Islands they insisted that property must be secured from aggression by posting it with cocoanut branches nailed to the house. If a man should take a pig for his own use, he must not only return the one feloniously removed but an additional one as well. In their efforts to reform native morals, they had enacted some highly amusing legislation. No gentleman, for example, could go walking with a young lady after dark unless he carried a lighted torch in one hand.

The Islanders amiably but stubbornly clung to some of their ancient practices. In spite even of recent government pressure, the Fijians will not be persuaded to give up *kere kere*, a custom which requires that anyone must surrender any possession another of equal rank may demand. The Governor told me the unhappy experience of a Fijian Oxford graduate who imported silk shirts which so caught the fancy of his friends that he lost them as fast as they arrived.

Some connection might be traced between the universal aversion to work and the popularity of religion which, until the advent of the movies threatened to displace it, furnished diversion but required no expenditure of effort. The Tonga Islands seemed to me to consist almost exclusively of churches and yet more churches. Methodism was the state religion and long wielded enormous power. Even as recently as twenty years ago, when a restrictive sanitary and medical act was drafted and about to be voted upon by the native Parliament, the Church quashed it in its entirety because it contained a provision that only qualified doctors could practise medicine, and the proponents of the bill refused to excise it. As a means to an end the missionaries had been dispensing a tract with each pill, hoping that both would reach the proper destination. They would lose prestige if, merely because they did not know how to practise medicine, they were debarred from doing so.

Anthropologists believe that Rennell Island, one of the Solomons, although it lies far to the west of the dividing line, is Polynesian, or possibly even pre-Polynesian. The Rennell Islanders have had practically no contact with white people, and their religion is undiluted by Christian doctrines. Here is to be found a primitive religion in a practically pure form. Two main gods, a grandfather and grandson, are tremblingly worshipped. The sinner entreats his ancestors to intercede with the grandfather god, who may thus be induced to intercede with the greater and more fearful grandson god. The priest, however, standing before his people with his talking stick in his hand, communicates directly with the grandson god in a strange hobble gobble, and interprets the holy answers to a cowed and submissive populace.

The taboo is all-powerful; the Rennell Islanders are governed by fear of everything—their environment, their enemies, and even their friends. Ritual directs every act of their lives, and all sickness is, ipso facto, punishment for some infraction of the taboo; they recognize that somehow they must have offended against the orders of the grandson.

Not far from tiny Rennell lies the huge mysterious island of New Guinea, peopled by a myriad wild tribes. Only the fringe of Papua has been explored thoroughly; no one knows what riddles of race or sorcery lie hidden in the jungly interior. The cannibals and killers who dwell there are also ruled by terror of unknown forces. As throughout the South Seas, sickness and health are dependent upon *puri puri*—witchcraft. *Puri puri* is not picked up casually; the finer points are expounded in a school which accredits its graduates in sorcery.

The death of an enemy may be secured in Papua with great simplicity by employing the village sorcerer. This medicine man, who always has some distinguishing mark upon his house, serving the purpose of the doctor's shingle, assumes full charge of the affair, and the person seeking revenge may retire from active participation. In the Mekeo district, the sorcerer studies the habits of the prospective victim, particularly the paths along which he is accustomed to go and the hours at which he frequents them. Next the witch doctor secures something which has been close to him, such as a loin cloth, although it is claimed even a hair will do.

The sorcerer unstops the end of the bamboo rod in which he keeps a venomous snake always on hand for just such emergencies, releasing it into a pot. Then he builds a fire under the pot, in which the piece of cloth has already been placed. The unsuspecting victim walks along the usual path at the accustomed hour and the snake, released from the pot, associates the odor of the man with that of the maddening heat, and makes straight and unerringly for him.

PARASITES LOST AND PARASITES REGAINED

Another Papuan method of carrying out vengeance is for the witch doctor merely to point a sharpened human bone in the exact direction of the man to be killed, the theory being that the bone will speed straight through the air, pierce the body, and return to the sorcerer's hand so quickly that its flight may not be seen. Strange as it may seem, cases of death from such fantastic conjurations have been reported on evidence that cannot be lightly dismissed. In such instances, however, the man who is to die has been informed a curse had been put upon him. Bad aim is impossible; if death does not follow, the failure is ascribed to the employment of a more powerful opposing sorcerer.

Opportunity to observe *puri puri* at first hand was afforded on the sugar plantations of Queensland, which had been obliged to import hundreds of Kanakas, as the South Sea Islanders are popularly called, to serve as temporary labor. A Kanaka worker from one of these plantations once came into the little hospital at Mossman, and said the finger had been put upon him—he was going to die Thursday at eleven. "Sun he come up," he pointed to the horizon. "He come along here," his hand rose almost to the meridian. "Now he stop along place," his outstretched arm was motionless. "Close up me die."

Dr. Philip Clark, the physician in charge, examined the Kanaka thoroughly—blood, urine, heart, liver, lungs—nothing was wrong. Nevertheless, the man persisted he was going to die, lay down upon a cot, and refused to rise again. Dr. Clark had had previous experience with the effects of mental suggestion upon Kanakas. When he could not jolly the victim of the spell out of his *idée fixe,* he sent for his foreman to persuade the Kanaka nothing whatever was the matter with him; that he was not going to die. The foreman came, leaned over the bed, peered into the black man's eyes, shook his head, and turned away. "Oh, yes, Doctor, close up he die."

At precisely eleven o'clock on Thursday morning the man's heart, which Dr. Clark testified to be normal, suddenly ceased to beat.

Dr. S. M. Lambert, then in charge of the Rockefeller Foundation's work in Queensland, several times came into direct contact with this form of *puri puri.* On one of these occasions he happened to stop at a Seventh Day Adventist Mission Station, around which was a

363

collection of Kanaka villages, largely dependent for food and to-bacco on the missionaries. The latter were puzzled by the strange condition of a Kanaka named Rob who had come to them in terror announcing that Nebo, most influential of the neighborhood witch doctors, had placed a spell upon him. Rob, without physical appear-ance of illness, was at the point of death. Dr. Lambert found he had no temperature but an alarmingly weak pulse; since he could dis-cover no trace of disease, there was little he could suggest as a rem-edy.

As a last resort, one of the missionaries went directly to Nebo and spoke severely. "If you do not remove the spell upon Rob, you and your tribe will get no more food or tobacco. You come back with me and tell Rob that he will get well."

Dr. Lambert watched carefully what happened. Rob was lying helpless on the bed. In spite of all that had been done for him, his vitality was steadily ebbing. Nebo leaned over the sick man and as-sured him no spell had been cast upon him; it was all a mistake and there was no need for him to die. Rob's face slowly broke into a broad smile. Before the day was over, his grey, dull skin, that in-fallible index of illness in the black man, was shining healthily and he was about his work as usual.

In Fiji the witch doctor's curse is known as *ndraunikau*. The sor-cerer makes a little fire and then, according to ritual, circles around and around, reciting his incantations and throwing strange and horrid objects upon it. "When I do that, the man dies," the witch doctor says, and each Fijian believes implicitly that he himself can be so willed to death.

Ndraunikau is a problem in the English colony of Fiji, where witchcraft has to be denied officially, and where a man cannot be jailed for a crime that does not exist on the statute books. But in Australian Papua witchcraft is a criminal offense. Once when a work-man on a Papuan plantation announced he had had a spell put upon him and was about to die, the skeptical owner, who would stand no such nonsense, said, "Well, maybe so, but you'll die from this first," and he took a whip to him, and when the man ran, he chased him. The man did not die; the white man's magic was stronger.

The Australian Commonwealth had an economic interest in the

diseases of those living along the coast, because of the rapid development of rubber and cocoanut plantations there. When it appeared
evident that the natives were heavily infected with hookworm, the
Rockefeller Foundation was invited to make a survey.

The Melanesian aversion to labor was not so strong as the Polynesian, but in order to keep a force of eight thousand steadily at work
the year round, three times that number had to be held in readiness;
on the average the Papuans would not stay on a plantation more than
a year at a time. This disturbing habit of theirs caused considerable
hardship to the planters, but was an advantage from our point of
view, because the larger the number employed, the larger would be
the number receiving instruction in anti-hookworm propaganda.

Dr. Lambert carried out a remarkable demonstration of what could
be done with savages who had no communication with neighboring
tribes. Papuan dialects could be numbered by the hundreds; in some
regions he found as many as three language groups in five miles.
Along the coast, however, pidgin English offered a common speech.
This idiom had been introduced in the early Nineteenth Century by
the sandal-wood traders, in order to facilitate their commercial dealings.

Dr. Lambert learned pidgin English.

Wherever a superstition would serve his purpose, he was prompt
to utilize this also. The snake, which played so large a part in Papuan
life, was, among other things, believed to cause disease by taking up
its abode inside the bodies of the sick. The sorcerer who, to give him
his due, worked harder at curing than at killing, with incantations
pretended to suck the ghost of the snake from the mouth, ear, or
umbilicus of the patient. Afterwards he gave ocular demonstration
of his power by spitting a small snake from his mouth. If the sick
man happened to be suffering from a fear malady, naturally he
would often get better.

This snake theory gave Dr. Lambert his opportunity. Holding in
his hand a little bottle of hookworms, which his audience accepted as
snakes, he would begin the story of the hookworm cycle:

"You altogedda boy. You listen good 'long dis story. One big fella sick
he stop 'long bell' b'long altogedda boy. Name b'long dis sick him he

365

hookworm. You look 'long dis bottle. Gottem plenty small fella snake he stop. Dis fella he stop 'long in bell' b'long boy. Tooth he gottem. Him he kai kai bell' b'long boy. Blood he come. Him he kai kai blood b'long boy. S'pose boy he kai kai. Kai kai he no b'long boy. Snake he catchem fust time. Now dis fella snake he allee same pidgin. He gottem hegg. S'pose boy he go 'long bush. Now hegg he come out 'long ground. Now rain he come down. Sun he cook him dis fella hegg. Bimeby one small fella pickaninny snake. Him he come up inside 'long hegg. Now hegg he broke him. Now him he walk about ground quick fella too much. Boy he come 'long. He put him foot 'long dis small fella pickaninny. Quick fella he come up inside foot b'long boy. Now he go, he go, he go. Bimeby he come up 'long heart b'long boy. Now he come 'long wind. Now he come 'long t'roat b'long boy. Now he scratch him t'roat. Boy he swallow him. He go down 'long bell' b'long boy. Now dis long time dis fella pickaninny he stop inside bell' b'long boy. He come in fust time he small fella too much. You no sabe look him 'long eye b'long you. He small fella too much. You sabe look him 'long big fella glass. Now he stop 'long time in bell' b'long boy. He more big. Now he come 'long bell' b'long boy. He gottem tooth. He sabe kai kai bell' b'long boy. He sabe kai kai blood. Boy him he lose him blood. He weak fella too much. Him he sick too much. Close up he die."

Although the Papuan had accepted the explanation of snakes as perfectly natural, he had to be constantly reassured that he was not putting himself in jeopardy by allowing examination of stools. His unquestioning acceptance of the superstition that the body excreta, as well as the paring of his fingernail or a dropped hair, might expose him to his enemy's vengeance made it doubly difficult to win his confidence.

The work was, as usual, started on the plantations. But prisoners in the Central Jail at Port Moresby, none of whom could very well protest, also made excellent subjects. The prisoners were not merely under complete supervision, but, due to the peculiar system of promotion effective in prison circles, they also offered an excellent means of spreading health education in the districts we could not reach.

The Australians have tempered their own severe ideas of justice to the mores of their subject people. Murder has to be treated in the light of the Papuan conception that taking human life was no crime, because a man was not a man, native style, until he had killed. The police query, "Did you kill this man?" directed to the culprit, always elicited a boastful, "Oh, yes." Only at rare intervals was a gallows set up for a public hanging, and then almost always to serve as a warning to leave white men alone. In the ordinary course of affairs the guilty ones were let off with a short jail term, and, after having learned the rudiments of civilization, they graduated and were sent back to their own villages as constables. Badges were hung on their naked chests to distinguish them from their fellow tribesmen, and they became the sole representatives of law and order in their own neighborhoods, where they usually performed their duties with vigor and determination.

In Papua as well as other places in the South Seas the Rockefeller Foundation made a demonstration in hookworm control, but it concentrated its efforts in Fiji, a British crown colony which to all intents and purposes represented the center of the South Sea Islands. Of the more than two hundred islands in the Fiji group, only Viti Levu and Vanua Levu are of any size; many of them are mere atolls almost awash at high tide.

In spite of the inviting verdure, the cooling breezes, and the pleasant prospects, Captain Cook had sailed straight through the middle of the group, not risking a landing because of the fierce aspect of the natives. The sandal-wood traders began timorously frequenting Fijian shores at the beginning of the Nineteenth Century, but not until 1826 did the missionaries first arrive. During our Civil War British commercial interests had seen an opportunity for profit, and the fields in harvest time were white with bursting cotton bolls. This industry died a natural death in the seventies when the United States again captured the markets. Then in the eighties the Colonial Sugar Refining Company brought renewed prosperity. Sugar and bananas were exported by the energetic planters.

Travelers sailing eastward from the coast of Asia have often noted that the variety of vegetable and animal life steadily diminished with each successive landfall. Apparently the Archipelagos of the South Seas, like Australia, had been cut off from the mainland before the development of mammals; the ubiquitous pig was introduced by Captain Cook. Fiji does not even possess bedbugs, white ants, leeches, snakes, or crocodiles. But it has a few native marsupials, among them a species of rat which gnawed down so many canes in the plantations of the Colonial Sugar Refining Company that the mongoose was imported from India to get rid of it. This little animal, which at home put up so brave a fight against snakes and rodents, when transplanted to its new environment promptly began to multiply beyond all reason and, far from warring with the rats, made friends with them and hunted zealously for birds. Similarly, the myna bird, cousin of the starling, was introduced to pick off the cane borers, and now its incessant and clamorous conversation is heard throughout the land.

Fiji has had a number of economic setbacks in recent years. The cocoanut palm was destroyed so completely on Viti Levu that many grown Fijians today have never seen a cocoanut, elsewhere the staple product of the South Seas. Another blow was the barring of Fijian bananas by Australia, which wished to develop the industry in her own state of Queensland. But the government of Fiji, in spite of the depression, continued to spend about twelve percent of its entire revenue on the care, cure, and prevention of disease. I was constantly astonished that so few people could maintain a government that could accomplish so much, even under these conditions of storm and stress.

The cultivation of sugar requires monotonous sustained labor. The Fijians possessed a physical endurance consonant with their great stature, partly due at least to freedom from malaria, but they refused steady jobs. They were willing to labor temporarily at loading ships or being boatmen, draymen, or house builders, or would toil spasmodically in the gold mines, because miners were fed well and housed well. But even when working in company with others for short periods it was important to employ a jester to amuse them. Fijians cared nothing for money; a full belly and simple recreation were their sole essentials. Their personal needs were simple and easily come by. The Fijians' economic nonchalance was assured, because the British government managed and rented out their public lands at good prices to the plantation owners, returning the income to them.

The planters, in despair over the amiable obstinacy of the Fijians, decided that if production were to be put on a profitable basis Tamils would have to be imported, even though their working capacity was only half that of the Fijians. The first influx of Tamils brought the question of health to the fore. The planting interests could not protest against health measures, because the government was the more powerful and they were afraid of losing their indentured labor.

The Darling Commission in 1915 determined that hookworm had not been started by the Indian coolies as at first assumed, but was endemic among the native population. The survey was simplified because no mixture of blood had taken place between Tamil and Fijian; hence the two could be examined separately. It was found that, although the Tamil coolie was almost one hundred percent infected, his was the ancylostoma whereas the Fijian harbored the necator. Curiously enough, half-caste and European children were almost free of worms, although they ran barefooted throughout the year.

Nobody knows how the Fijians would get along if a paternalistic government should force them to compete on equal terms with the Tamils, who have a monopoly on industriousness. Few of the Tamils imported to work on the plantations now return to India. They like the Fiji Islands, and it is a long way home. After they work out their indenture the Colonial Sugar Refining Company sets them up on small plots of land, where they can have their own fields of sugar cane. Now half the population of Fiji is Tamil.

When I first saw these Indians in Fiji in 1916 they lived in miserable houses and filthy villages and seemed to have no desire for anything better. I was much interested in 1934 to see the changes one generation had wrought. Everything was in vast contrast to the conditions which still exist in India. The Tamil had dropped many of the handicaps of his religion, and much of the caste system had been abolished. Lately a movement among the older Indians and their holy men to induce the new generation to return to the ways of their fathers met with little success. They were happy where and as they were.

They had been miraculously transformed from a dejected, downcast, docile, uninterested people, who could not even play, into one which was healthy, alert, sport loving, and mentally so progressive that they were agitating for schools and the vote. They owned fine fat cattle and rich lands, and had, on their own initiative, built a superior type of house, each with its neat latrine. They had well earned their reputation for industry and thrift.

This regeneration had been accomplished by mass treatment for

369

hookworm. Nothing like it has ever happened in history. At last the Tamil smiles.

Carnegie with his libraries had been before us in the Fiji Islands, and his donations had been well publicized. The local newspapers, confusing the two philanthropies, announced that I had come to Fiji to study the habits of the bookworm, assuming perhaps that the Carnegie volumes had somehow become infested. The school children, anxious to show respect to the newly-arrived bookworm investigator, entered a competition, and one inspired Fijian young lady turned in an essay entitled "Parasites Lost and Parasites Regained." I have always believed that no more fitting title could, by any fortuitous circumstance, have been chosen.

Hookworm prevention was the primer used in teaching the peoples of the South Seas that it was possible for them all to have sound bodies. But because of the prevalence of yaws, which all the Islanders had heretofore taken for granted, neo-salvarsan injections provided an open sesame to their hearts, although they were at first timorous of treatment for fear of "driving them in." Many of the children were being entirely deprived of the physical exuberance which is the inalienable right of childhood. Some, with the aid of canes, had to hop on their heels because of the ulcers on their toes, or walk on their toes because of the ulcers on their heels. Others could not walk at all, but would hitch themselves along in a sitting position. One of the times when I have been proudest of being a member of the medical profession was when I saw the cures wrought among the children of the South Seas by the practitioners, who gave them back their childhood, so that they were able to laugh and run and play once more.

The second great curse of the South Seas was filariasis, or elephantiasis. Patrick Manson, a Scotch physician in Amoy, made the brilliant discovery in 1879 that the filaria bloodworm was conveyed from one human being to another through the agency of the mosquito.

When I was traveling about with Dr. Lambert through Fijian and Samoan villages I often slept in native grass huts and, though we both carried nets, I was frequently bitten by the vicious mosquitoes which swarmed everywhere. The knowledge that almost half the people around me had filariasis made me feel distinctly uncomfortable, because any one of these mosquitoes which were biting me might already have dined on one of the nearby sufferers. Dr. Lambert, whose skin had apparently become immune, could sit around in his pajamas and apparently not be bitten, while I would be complaining and scratching incessantly at the huge welts.

After Manson's original observation it was later discovered that the filaria is a white thread-like worm which, after being deposited by the mosquito on the skin, bores its way into the lymphatics and blocks them. Due to this blockage, a tremendous enlargement of the tissues may take place. A leg, for instance, may attain the size of that of an elephant, hence the name.

Filariasis, which is fortunately not painful, takes years to develop. Although the presence of embryos can be detected at an early stage by blood examination, no cure has yet been found. Unless the victim can be removed to a temperate climate soon after infection, the progress of the disease cannot be arrested. Surgical operations give only mechanical relief, but any surgeon who could cut out one hundred and twenty-five pounds of excess tissue naturally found favor in the eyes of the Islanders, and many such operations were performed. If the adult filaria could be tracked to its hiding place, a patient could be cured, but it is often so securely concealed that even the most thorough autopsy, sometimes lasting for days, in which every organ is dissected, fails to reveal its presence.

Not until something was learned about the breeding habits of the filaria-bearing mosquitoes was any effective measure possible against this disease. Only a few years ago it was determined that discarded cocoanut shells which were filled with water by every tropical shower furnished ideal breeding places. With this information in its hands, the Samoan government passed a law compelling cocoanut shells to be broken up, burned, or piled upside down. The incidence of filariasis in Samoa has been declining since then.

Unlike the French, whose interest in their colonies did not seem to include much humanitarianism, the British were greatly concerned over the progressive depopulation of the South Sea Islands. Scientists generally believe that the main cause of the diminishing numbers is the lack of immunity to introduced diseases. It has been generally held that British nationals had been largely responsible for the high death rate from this cause, although the Chinese trader must also bear a portion of the blame. Much evidence, however, has been accumulated to prove that infant mortality is largely due to diet deficiency, as well as the difficulties in inducing Polynesian mothers adequately to care for their young.

The fostering of communications caused these newly introduced diseases to run through the populations like wildfire. Tuberculosis, measles, and pneumonia took a terrible toll. Waves of bacillary dysentery swept over the Archipelagos. The measles epidemic in Fiji was the major catastrophe of its history; over a third of the population died. More recently, influenza was imported, causing an estimated loss of ten to twenty percent in the districts affected.

It is interesting to speculate upon the physical changes which must take place in a people during the process of acquiring immunity. Those who have not been exposed to such diseases as measles and tuberculosis will probably have certain characteristics which are lost to the world by their death, and the survivors will have certain physical qualities which will make for a different line of evolution in later generations.

Recently an airplane bound for the goldfields of New Guinea discovered in the interior a strange people as yet unknown, lighter in skin, who lived in villages, had streets and neat fields, carefully fenced. A doctor could experience no more exciting adventure than to explore some such community, hitherto completely isolated from all contact with civilization, to tabulate the indigenous diseases, and also to experiment with methods of providing against the ravages of disease when the communication barriers are broken down.

Nothing definite was known in 1915 about the relative importance of the causes of depopulation in the South Seas, except that the process was going on at a rapid rate and something should be done about it. The Polynesians were very desirable residents for British colonies. They were such delightful, charming people, and their culture so perfectly conformed to many amenities of life that practically everyone became immediately friendly to them. They got on well with white people. Their high degree of intelligence qualified them to rank equally with the British in education and in privileges, and, as they disappeared, the unassimilable Japanese and Chinese were taking their places.

It had always been difficult to get doctors from home for service in the South Seas because of the extremely isolated life. This isolation caused many who did make the journey to become addicted to alcohol or drugs. Furthermore, such efforts as had already been made to give medical instruction to South Sea Islanders had been inadequate. I have visited hospitals where I found untrained natives handling dangerous medicines of which they scarcely knew the dosage, and making diagnoses such as "feverish," "bad food," and "bad blood."

Australia, New Zealand, and Great Britain were all endeavoring to find some solution. The Australians proposed to balance the birth and the death rates by a system of hospital ships traveling from port to port. The utilization of the waterways for this purpose sounded as reasonable to them as it had to me when we had first tried it out among the Moros in the Philippines. However, I had learned then that hospital ships were not feasible. The expense was heavy, and only relatively few people could be benefited; the sick could not be brought easily to the ports.

The British had first sought the cooperation of the League of Nations and then had approached the Rockefeller Foundation. We, as interested spectators of the varied efforts, were delighted at the chance to offer suggestions. Teaching the people to take an interest in their own health problems was one of our fundamental tenets. In this case we were encouraged by the sanguine expectation that a school for training Polynesians and Melanesians in medical practice had a better chance for success than those erected in many Oriental or Latin countries where the experiment had been tested out previously.

"Why don't you provide a suitable medical education for these people?" we asked. "British doctors—white men on high salaries requiring long vacations—cannot be depended upon for any certain tenure. Furthermore, you should have medical representatives who already know the customs, languages, and superstitions of their own people, who can live among them permanently, who have the interest of the country at heart, and who could do the job at a cost the government could sustain. You have a unique opportunity here, because

373

you have a people intelligent enough to absorb the necessary knowledge."

A small, primitive school was already operating at Suva, the centrally located capital of the Fiji Islands. With a population of about five thousand, more than a quarter white, it was already a thriving port of call for many steamship lines. Several three-story concrete buildings gave an air of commercial prosperity to the main street, and a trio of moving picture houses, an Otis elevator, and other fleshpots of civilization catered to the universal desire to be amused.

The hospital ship idea was abandoned and, without any great enthusiasm, a plan was agreed to whereby the Rockefeller Foundation would assist in reorganizing the Suva school and turning it into an institution to serve the whole South Seas. Ultimately seven Island administrations—American Samoa, New Zealand Samoa, Tonga, Fiji, the Solomons, Cook Islands, and one of the French islands—sent students and helped to support the school.

Dr. Lambert, Deputy Central Medical Authority of the Western Pacific High Commission, with amazing good nature and tact, has been able to conciliate the various Island administrations and settle their differences. His most notable achievement has been to induce them all to join in the support of a central leper colony at Mokogai, Fiji. His latest proposed development is a Western Pacific Health Service for the entire South Seas, in which a system of promotion by merit will spur white health officers to ambition through the knowledge that they will have an opportunity to advance from remote posts to more active ones.

When the Central Medical School was first started no more than a three-year course for training medical practitioners was contemplated. Although I already had great faith in the mental capacity of the Polynesians, even I was astounded at the facility with which the students forged ahead. Nor was it mere rote learning which would enable them to pass examinations; it became obvious they were entitled to further education, and the three-year course was lengthened to four, in preparation for turning out regularly qualified physicians.

The most striking aspect of the school was the spirit of vitality which infused it, and the eagerness for learning evident in every classroom. In the course of one of my routine inspections, the Professor of Anatomy suggested, "Would you like to ask any question?"

I feared that, according to the time-honored custom, some prize pupil had been groomed to impress the visiting examiner. "May I ask anyone I wish?"

"Oh, yes, anyone."

I looked around and selected a student who I was sure could not have been a brilliant Samoan strategically placed for my attention, and requested him to describe the brachial plexus. To his query, "Would you mind if I demonstrated on the blackboard because I can do it better in that way?" I said of course not. He thereupon took up some red, blue, and white crayons, and made a drawing superior to any such extemporaneous art I had ever seen, all the while commenting fluently on the complicated nerve network. Fortunately, I had been handed a textbook, or I should have been completely lost in trying to follow him.

The practitioners from the School went back to their native villages dressed in the tribal style except for the formal addition of a coat, so indivisible from the idea of British caste. But they were thinking along new lines, and bearing neo-salvarsan and hookworm demonstration paraphernalia. Their health propaganda, so enthusiastically supported by the people, brought about a larger percentage of latrine installations and use than any other country has achieved in a similar space of time. Depopulation stopped where health work was well established, and the numbers of Polynesians and Melanesians in the South Seas, with the introduction of modern preventive medicine, are apparently increasing year by year.

Our task was not finished when we graduated medical practitioners; we had to make sure no slip-up should occur after they had been back in their own environment for some time. It was inconceivable that young men, straight from their grass-roofed huts, bred to the terrors of spells and charms, and with only a relatively slight amount of training, would not occasionally sink back to the level of the community.

Even in the classroom the face of every Fijian student became like a carven image when *ndraunikau* was mentioned. Not one of them

375

could be induced even to discuss it. No Westerner can comprehend the degree of courage displayed by Malakai, the best medical practitioner turned out by the School, who once dared to challenge the power of the chief of the witch doctors, although he well knew many had died at the time appointed for them by the curse. "Why don't you kill me? You say you can *ndraunikau* me. Go ahead! I defy you! It's all nonsense! If your system of medicine will work, show me what you can do!"

Malakai proved his faith in what he had been taught, and his bold defiance brought him no harm.

Part of our plan was to have traveling officers—men who would go in a friendly, helpful spirit and not one of criticism—inspect these medical practitioners after they had been at work for some time on their islands. I also wanted to see how they were applying their knowledge. Samoa, the home of the most intelligent of the Polynesian strain, was naturally expected to show the best results. In company with Dr. Lambert I made several interesting trips there, the more pleasant because of his popularity; his avoirdupois coincided with Samoan ideas of beauty and this, added to his talent for speechmaking, made him irresistible to them.

Almost at the outset of the War New Zealand had seized German Samoa, but found that these reputedly most gentle of the pure Polynesians did not greet the change in masters with the expected rejoicings. Insurrection has been in progress ever since. The Samoans resent bitterly being a colony of a dependency; they would not have minded so much being directly subject to Great Britain. Moreover, color intolerance, so conspicuously absent in the case of the Maori, is said to have had much to do with their sense of grievance.

The Samoans have been rebelling over something or other for a hundred years or more, usually as to which was the ranking house, that of Mataafa or Malietoa, and by this time have had so much practice that they have attained a high degree of efficiency. The rebellion against New Zealand, or Mau movement, has taken the form of non-cooperation; for example, the Samoans blandly refuse to pay their taxes. At one time New Zealand tried to exact compliance by troops, but it was out of the question to shoot a man simply because he would not pay. Samoans were adept at thinking up schemes to annoy. Before the rebellion they had, to a great extent, used latrines but, because the New Zealand Health Department approved this practice, they promptly abandoned it, and, in derision, even polluted the doorsteps of the officials.

On the whole New Zealand was lavish with money and attention, and used force only to assert her sovereignty. But finally, her patience near exhaustion, she withdrew the medical practitioners, and in remote districts closed hospitals and dispensaries. At the time of my visit with Dr. Lambert, the people in some rural areas had had only herbalists on whom to depend, and many sick were brought to us for our ministrations.

I interviewed many of the chiefs. The most powerful among them was Fau Mui Na, weighing three hundred and nine pounds, fisherman and philosopher. It was said that but for his intervention, the Europeans in Apia would have been wiped out at the beginning of the Mau movement. I also met Mataafa, a descendant of the former King of that name, who had been educated for the priesthood and spoke beautiful English, German, and French. His daughters entertained us with sitting, knee, and standing dances.

Near Foa (pronounced, "Fona," because the early missionaries' printing outfits had been deficient in certain letters) we had an important public meeting with thirty-four chiefs and orators. At times it looked as though we might become involved in Island politics, but finally we made them understand that in all civilized countries neutrality exists in medical affairs; even between people who are at war.

The Samoans were afflicted with much illness. Filariasis was common there as elsewhere in the South Seas. Blindness, due to ophthalmia and also trachoma, was frequent. But out of the population of fifty thousand only twelve insane were in confinement, and no others were known that required restraint. This may have been due to the absence of syphilis, which in turn was due to the high incidence of yaws; we conducted three successive campaigns in Samoa for the treatment of yaws. Yaws is a horrible disease, but it has this virtue that to its presence may be due the absence of syphilis, which commonly makes its appearance with the white man's advent.

Samoa impressed me primarily as being a land of unfinished churches. Every one of seven villages had one or more, usually con-

AN AMERICAN DOCTOR'S ODYSSEY

crete, with a capacity far in excess of any conceivable use. In some villages of four or five hundred a Catholic, a Seventh Day Adventist, a Methodist, and a Mormon Church would vie for favor. It often happened that while one was under construction, another village would erect a larger one, and the first village then had to cease building, tear down what it had already constructed, and start over again on an even larger scale. It was said that each year when the time for raising funds for new churches drew near, prostitution and burglary increased commensurately.

Certain formalities had to be observed on visiting a Samoan village. Dr. Lambert, because of his long sojourn in the South Seas, was able to guide my steps so that I would not offend our kindly hosts. They appreciated being informed in advance of our arrival because they had certain preparations to make for the welcome of foreign guests. A delegation of villagers would don their best clothes of tapa, a cloth of hammered bark, soft as silk and artistically decorated. Thus attired they would meet us at the outskirts of the town or, if we came by sea, would paddle out to greet us.

We were usually welcomed in the great oval *fale,* the community house, held up by big round posts, beautifully carved timbers, and marvelous trussing in the interior which I have never seen outdone by European or American engineers. The *fale* was open to every breeze; if a sudden squall swept down, a mere pull of a cord released the protecting fibre curtains on the windward side, which shut out the lashing rain while the ceremony proceeded without interruption.

The ceremonial surrounding even the lives of the humble in Samoa compared with that of a royal family in Europe. The head of the table had always to sit with the long axis of the house and the ranking guest sat on the sea side with his back to it. All guests were announced, in order of precedence, by a special official in a loud voice. When a roast pig was served, the head had to go to the chief, the part under the belly to the *taupo.*

No woman was permitted entrance into the *fale* save the *taupo,* the village virgin and its most guarded treasure. She was usually the handsomest daughter of the chief; if he had none, he would adopt a young girl worthy of carrying on the tradition. The entire village saw to it that she remained a virgin until the chief decided the time had come for a political union with a neighboring tribe and a new *taupo* took her place. When she slept, four women surrounded her, one at either side, one at her head and one at her feet. She was the center of all life in the community—entertained visitors and officiated at the mixing of the *kava*.

Kava, the universal South Sea drink, might be considered semisacred; two people never met for conversation without the bowl between them, and no welcome was complete without it. The degree of ceremonial varied with the importance of the occasion. Any visitor who could not play his part in the highly formalized and set ritual was branded as a barbarian. The government encouraged *kava* because its elaborate preparation fulfilled all convivial needs without the inebriating effects of alcohol. In my experience every Oriental country had indulged in a native alcohol made from cocoanut, sugar, or rice. The absence of such a beverage among the South Sea Islanders must have had a profound influence upon their history, and especially their sex life.

At the first *kava* ceremony I attended, the *taupo* placed a small quantity of the pounded, shredded, and dried root of the piper methysticum into a huge iron sugar kettle, added a little water, then swooshed the spongy mass up and down time after time, wringing it out as though it were laundry and tossing it aside for her helpers to shake. With this and new root constantly added, the process was repeated again and again until the *kava* reached the proper strength.

The serving of the *kava* was tremendously important. The *taupo* filled a half cocoanut shell and handed it to the cupbearer who, gorgeously arrayed, taking so many steps this way and so many steps that, finally, with a deep bow and a genuflection, presented it to the guest of honor. Before I put it to my lips, I spilled a few propitiatory drops on the ground. This libation stamped me as someone who was familiar with local customs, and won approval. As I drank the *kava*, which had a flavor reminiscent of root beer, everybody sang and clapped. In some villages etiquette demanded that each gulp should be attuned to the rhythmic beat of hand on hand and I was conscious that my Adam's apple was the focus of attention. When I had drained the cup, I sent it spinning with a twist of the wrist into the center of the *fale*. Not until it stopped its gyrations did the cup-bearer pick it up and present it to the *taupo* for refilling.

Simultaneously with the *kava* preparation, speaking was going forward. Samoans look upon oratory as an art for which there should be special training, and, unlike ourselves, they endeavor to discourage amateurs from engaging in after dinner speeches. The position of tribal orator is hereditary, and he is next in rank to the chief. In some places he is prime minister; in others he is more powerful than the chief himself. I never heard the Rockefeller Foundation acclaimed in such glowing terms as a great humanitarian force which exercised its beneficence in the furthermost recesses of the globe, even extending to this poor little island. I must admit I was flattered to hear extolled so eloquently virtues I had never before known I possessed. Where the orator had obtained the romantic story of my past I do not know, but even more amazing was his discriminatory use of the English language.

I was no such master of my native tongue. I was contemplating with dismay the prospect of having to reply in kind, or at least try to explain gracefully away my elocutionary shortcomings, when my apprehensions were allayed by being informed that another orator would take my place.

My mouthpiece replied to the praise of the Rockefeller Foundation with praise of the virtues of the tribal chief and his queen in well-rounded, beautiful phrases such as I could never have uttered. The words of the virtuoso sparkled so entertainingly that the chief's speaker was spurred to emulation. Fortunately, the competition did not become so keen as at some *kava* ceremonies where these verbal tourneys sometimes took hours.

After the *kava* cup had proceeded down the line in strict order of rank, and after the last oration had been made, the dances began, endless in their variety. Both men and women engaged in these, although they rarely touched each other, usually sitting cross-legged, twisting their bodies and arms, swaying to the accompaniment of strings and drums, sometimes moving silently, sometimes singing melodies of surpassing beauty based on hymns learned from the missionaries, and more poignant even than those of our own South. At evening entertainments the dances often continued from nine until four in the morning. The spectators at this late hour were exhausted, but the performers would have kept on with unabated zest as long as any audience remained.

The missionaries have discouraged many native dances. The hula is seen no more either in Samoa or Fiji, although it is beginning to reappear in the Cook Islands, where the government has not discouraged it.

In Fiji, as in Samoa, I was able to visit many of the remote islands. The Governor kindly lent us his yacht, the *Adi Beti*. The friendly Fijian people also expressed by ritual and symbolism the courtesy which was part of their daily lives. As soon as the native canoes drew within hailing distance of the yacht, a great shout of *"Sabua!"* (sambula) would greet us. We would call back the correct reply of *"Moli!"* which meant literally "orange juice," or, "your words are sweeter than oranges." Then would follow the impressive ceremony of presenting the whale tooth *tabua* (tambua), a compliment bestowed upon those whom the Fijians esteem their friends. The original *tabuas* were of wood, and probably had some phallic significance. Their exchange was an affair among chiefs, and acceptance obligated the recipient to grant any request the donor might choose to make. The whalers had left in their wake the teeth of the great cetaceans, and the bulk of the *tabuas* in use today still date from the days of Moby Dick. Any additions to the floating supply have to be gleaned from dead whales washed up on the beach.

The Fijians also had their *kava* ceremony which they called *yaqona* (yanggona). This was held in the *mbure*, or assemblage place, but in Fiji each person had to make his own speeches, with the aid of an interpreter if necessary. Here, too, we were entertained afterwards. I remember in particular one occasion at Masi, where Nitavua, chief of the Curomoce tribe of firewalkers, set before us an elaborate repast of five kinds of root vegetables, excellent crabs, shrimp, duck, chicken, roast pig, and oysters. But even the *yaqona* and the feast did not satisfy Nitavua's sense of hospitality. He arranged a firewalking ceremony for our benefit.

The secret of firewalking, supposedly the exclusive property of this tribe, had been handed down for many generations. It seems that once, many years ago, a *ratu*, or chief, caught a devil devil in the form of an eel. The devil devil began to tempt the *ratu* in exchange for his freedom.

"I'll make you the richest man in the Island," it promised.

"I'm already the richest man."

"I'll make you the biggest chief."

"I'm already the biggest chief."

"I'll get you the most beautiful women."

"I have them already."

Finally the devil devil said, "I'll confer upon you the ability to walk through fire without being hurt." The extreme form of punishment among the Fijians was to drive an unfortunate victim through hot pits so that he died, and the promise of immunity from this torture was powerful enough to win the *ratu*. The devil devil whispered the secret to him, receiving freedom in return, and thereafter the initiates could walk unharmed through fire.

In preparation for our arrival at Masi a fire had been kept burning for days in a pit some four feet deep and fifteen feet in diameter; the layer of limestone boulders above and below had become red hot. Even after all the embers were raked out and the stones had paled to grey, they still radiated such intense heat as to set fire to the clothes of anyone who stood too near the edge of the pit. Just before the firewalking was to take place, I tied a folded handkerchief over the end of a long pole and touched about a dozen stones, one after the other, with the weight and speed which I estimated would approximate that of a man walking quickly and lightly over them.

At a given signal about a dozen barefoot Curomoce rushed into the pit and stepped rapidly across its diameter. I was amazed to find when they emerged from the pit that their feet gave no evidence of burning or reddening.

My handkerchief also, after being washed clean of soot, showed no evidence of having been burned or even scorched. One explanation, though it does not quite satisfy me, was that each performer curled his feet to form an insulating air cup. Before this could be heated to an intolerable temperature, he had stepped to another stone.

382

PARASITES LOST AND PARASITES REGAINED

As soon as the last man was out of the pit, *massawe*, a sugary vine, and earth, were thrown in to make a bed on which taro and yams were left to bake for several hours. While one of the firewalkers was arranging the tubers, the heat was still so intense as to set his grass skirt on fire, and rapid action had to be taken to save him from burning.

I sometimes found it difficult to reconcile the friendly hospitality and good fellowship of the Fijians whom I encountered with the tales of their former cruel practices. Heavy war canoes, sometimes a hundred feet long, were for good luck launched over the live bodies of men used as rollers. It was also the custom to put a live slave in each posthole of a chief's house before setting in the post. Far from objecting to this sacrifice, the slaves esteemed it a great honor; they would ask to be so buried and grasped the post with both hands as it was put on top of them, thus assuring their future happiness.

The Fijian habit of which everyone has heard was cannibalism; a prisoner was thrown into an oven similar to but larger than that used for firewalking. Cannibalism, shocking as it is, served two purposes for the Islanders. It prevented the spread of disease, because the inhabitants of one village never dared stray far beyond their own boundaries, and it also satisfied a meat hunger. In the back countries there was no game, and sea food was carried up with much effort. This does not explain cannibalism on the seacoast, where fish were abundant. Long before we were acquainted with vitamins, the Islanders knew the value of fish livers.

In the old days the *ratu* used to have his prisoners brought out early in the morning for an inspection, to see on which he and his warriors would dine that day. Eating human flesh was a ceremony —the heart for courage, the liver for wisdom, the genitals for virility. A prisoner's only chance to escape being roasted was to sneeze, because thereby he showed himself lacking in fortitude, and no self-respecting cannibal would eat any but a brave man. "I will give you life," the chief would scornfully say, and the prisoner would humbly reply, "*Moli.*" But after this craven action he could never for the rest of his days associate with his fellows.

Cannibalism is supposed to be extinct in the South Seas, but occasionally in Papua, and doubtless other places, "boys" still disappear from the plantations, and little doubt remains in the minds of those familiar with native ways that they have been eaten.

The last official record of a cannibal feast was in 1867. Missionary Baker had been afflicted with more than the usual martyr's zeal. Against the advice of those experienced in Fijian conduct, he went with a companion into the dark interior, protected only with high leathern boots against the jungle dangers. A certain *ratu* on the coast disliked the missionary intensely and wanted to get rid of him. Since the *ratu's* village was under the strict eye of Great Britain, he was afraid to resort to the simple expedient of his forefathers. He fell back, therefore, upon the ancient rite of the *tabua* whereby the recipient must grant any request he might make. Along with Baker the wily *ratu* sent a runner who, at each village where the party stopped, was to offer the *tabua* to the head man. But in each case, as soon as the messenger attempted to present his gift, the sight of Baker was sufficient warning to bring about a courteous but firm refusal to accept it. The *ratu* could readily divine the nature of the request, and he had a wholesome dread of British retribution.

Finally, the clever runner darted ahead of his party and proffered the *tabua* to an unsuspecting *ratu*, who graciously received it. But gratification rapidly evaporated when Baker put in his belated appearance. "Now I know what you want me to do," he said sadly to the runner. "I would never have taken the *tabua* if I had been warned."

But his tribal sense of what was due and fitting compelled him to accede to the expected request, and Missionary Baker went into the pit, boots and all. According to custom, the choicest bits were sent around to neighboring villages, and the story, which has become apocryphal in the telling, relates that one *ratu*, who received a delicacy in the form of a roasted foot and leg, encased in well-seasoned leather, commented, "Don't these missionaries have tough hides?"

I remember once on a remote island meeting an ancient chieftain whose son was then in the Central Medical School at Suva. He was reputed to have been a cannibal in the good old days, but seemed to resent the term extremely. He informed me ingenuously that when he was young and his warriors had beaten a tribe thoroughly, and that tribe again made war on them, they would capture a man and eat him—not for food, but as an extreme form of punishment.

Then the missionaries came along. The chief had not invited them and had not been at all interested in what they had to offer. But the missionaries would not go away, even though he kept asking them to depart. Finally, the tribe had to eat a few to make them understand they were not wanted. The old gentleman assured me earnestly and with conviction in his eye it was no pleasure to eat the missionaries; he found them extremely tough.

CHAPTER 22.   FISH STORIES

THE beauties of tropic nights on moon-bright waters have been sung by poets for centuries. But even a poet can convey no more than an impression. A scientist finds the reason behind this magic effect equally full of wonder. He knows that when the oars of his boat drip silver and gold, and the wake is like molten metal, this enchantment is caused by certain minute organisms at breeding time.

I have often been traveling at night in a launch, and from the bow watched the startled fish, like luminous arrows, flash right and left. If we were speeding fast enough, the phosphorescence set up by our passage, red and green or white and blue, would send so bright a glow into the air that a newspaper, held near the water, could be easily read. A Japanese discovered that, after being dried, these tiny bodies still retained their radiancy. I once saw a professor of chemistry rub some over his face which, when the light was extinguished, shone pale and eerie as a ghost.

This was not the only natural reading lamp which I chanced upon. One black night I was coming down the Butuan River in Mindanao, and saw ahead a reflection so brilliant that I wondered what traveler might have built his campfire there. As the boat swung round the bend, I saw it was a tree all illuminated with the flickering lights of a myriad giant fireflies, brightening and dimming in unison.

The flying fish of the Philippines, which seemed bigger than those in other waters, were never ending sources of interest. We used to spend hours hanging over the rail of the *Basilan,* watching the gossamer winged fish leap, skim, and dive. My cabin was close to the water, and the electric light by which I read shone out over the waves. Many times these cold and clammy visitors from the deep would come shooting on to my bed. I would revenge myself for the shock by sending them to the galley, and the next morning would enjoy a tasty fish breakfast.

In the early days in the Philippines Governor General Forbes was an enthusiastic fisherman, and I learned about fishing from him. There were no bright trolling spoons then, and, although we fished industriously, we caught comparatively little. Governor Forbes later brought out the first modern trolling outfit, and most of us soon had similar ones. Immediately we began pulling in the most beautiful fish—tremendous fighting pompano which grew in Island waters to eighty pounds, Spanish mackerel, bonito, barracuda, and the lapu lapu, a species of grouper blue with red dots, or bright red with blue dots. Governor Forbes, who displayed the same vim and energy in his play as in his work, had a neat trim boat built with a square stern in order to have free play with the rods.

I remember once in clear, deep water, when Governor Forbes had a good strike, I looked over the side and said, "You've hooked a sea bass."

He also leaned over, and replied, "You're wrong, that's a red snapper."

I peered more intently, "It's a sea bass or I never saw one."

Meanwhile he was slowly reeling in his tackle, and when it came to the surface, we looked triumphantly at one another. One hook had a sea bass and the other a red snapper.

In the course of my inter-island voyages I had discovered many good fishing waters, and was able to introduce General Wood to them. One morning in 1924 we were cruising off Apo Reef on the West Coast of Mindoro. After a fairly good morning, a lull came. Finally the General's line began to run out slowly. I sank back on the cushions, saying, "General, it's hardly worth drawing in. That can't be much of a fish. There isn't enough pull to it."

"Oh, I don't know. It may be a long thin one swimming toward us," he replied defensively, "and that's why it doesn't offer much resistance."

But just as he had reeled the fish almost alongside and I had my gaff ready, the line started off furiously and quite a length was out before the tension slackened.

"I've a bigger fish than you think," exclaimed the General triumphantly.

"Oh, it's not so much," I retorted.

He began taking up the slack, winding and winding until the spool was almost filled and we were expecting the fish to break the surface any second. Suddenly the reel started zing-g-g-g, and the line cut through the water like the bow of a ship. It curled up spray a foot or more as it boiled out.

"Now you'll have to admit I have a big fish," boasted General Wood as he applied the brake ineffectually. The line ran out to within a few feet of its four-hundred-yard length. The General, with a jubilant glance in my direction, began his labors once more. The reel spun and whirred as he lost all that he had gained. He battled with his catch for an hour before it was exhausted enough to bring within gaffing distance.

Looking down into the transparent water I saw an eight-foot shark still lashing around. I gaffed it and we hauled it in. "General, that was never the fish that was on your line when you had the first strike," I said firmly.

"It may have been," he insisted.

"No, never," I repeated, and turning to a sailor I said, "Hand me a knife."

I ripped open the shark and inside found a three-foot Spanish mackerel. The General showed some surprise, but the smirk of satisfaction did not leave his face.

"What's more, you never had that Spanish mackerel on the first time," I asserted.

"Go as far as you like."

I cut open the mackerel and found inside a little ten-inch, polka-dotted lapu lapu, Jonah's dinner, with the hook through its lip.

Baron Munchausen would have had difficulty in improving on this story. I took the precaution of having General Wood sign an official affidavit testifying to its truth, and seal it with the Great Seal of the Philippine Islands.

FISH STORIES

The South Sea Islanders had perfected methods of catching fish which surpassed anything developed by Westerners. "You think you Americans are sportsmen," they would say to me. "You don't even know what sort of fish you're going to catch. We're choice in our tastes. We like only certain kinds."

The young men proved their contention unmistakably by showing me how they did it. In the late afternoon several of us would paddle toward the reef. When fish were seen swimming below, one of the youths would put on water goggles, which fitted tightly into the eye sockets and fastened with a strong cord around his head. With clear underwater vision thus assured, he would dive over the side and glide so quietly down among the fish that they did not seem to become alarmed. The water was translucent, and I could readily watch from the side of the canoe what was going on. The Islander would select a likely fish and, stroking it gently on the belly, gradually work his hand toward its head. Then, with a quick movement, he would slip a finger into its gills and bring his prize to the surface. If it met approval, it would be hauled in; if not, he would descend again for another. The less skilled fishermen used a pole with a barbed end on which the fish was hooked.

Going fishing for bonito in Samoa with Chief Fau Mui Na was a pleasant experience. We paddled out in his special bonito canoe, built sturdily to hold his enormous weight. He was very proud of it; the woodwork was all lashed, and the joints were sealed with lead and tar. Fore and aft it was decked over, and raised pegs indicated his rank as chief. The paddles were heirlooms from his grandfather. He trolled for bonito from a flexible bamboo pole set upright in the canoe, and used a barbless hook of tortoise shell tied to a piece of mother of pearl.

While at Beqa (Bengga) I saw an entire Fijian community join in their remarkable fish dive. At low tide, when about a foot of water covered the selected mile-long reef, a party of fifteen was stationed at each end. All were spaced equally across the reef along a vine rope, tied together, which must have been a half mile in length. Gradually the two parties approached one another, each man holding the vine with one hand and beating the bottom with a pole as he moved forward. Curiously enough, the fish, which were swarming in with the rising tide, never attempted to escape under the slack vine. By the end of about two hours of this slow motion, the gap between the two parties had become no more than a few hundred yards across. About a hundred more villagers now rushed in and grabbing the vine with shouts and laughter, helped to herd the fish toward the V-shaped aperture which was being formed and where others were holding a huge net in readiness.

By this time the water had come up almost to the shoulders of the participants, who whooped and danced and beat the surface with their paddles until the leaping, churning fish were driven into the net. Then still others sailed a boat to the outer edge of the reef, and the net was heaved on board, laden with a ton of finny prizes.

Each island group in the South Seas has its own fishing customs. In Papua nets of tremendous strength are made from the webs of giant spiders, which indefatigably spin their geometrical patterns from tree to tree. The Santa Crucians use spider webs in an even stranger manner. Out of cocoanut fronds they construct an octagonal kite, the tail of which serves as a fish line. The lure is merely a mass of cobweb, trailing along the water. When the garfish leaps for it, he entangles his recurved teeth inextricably in the sticky substance and is easily retrieved.

In Australia the fishermen of the Great Barrier Reef use dynamite in a special way. Ordinarily the detonation bursts the bladder of the fish so that they sink and must be gathered up by diving. But the bright Antipodeans have discovered that if the dynamite is placed near tree coral, this phenomenon apparently does not take place, and the stunned fish float on the surface.

The Cook Islands are great lumps of coral into which the ebbing and flowing tides have eaten caverns, and there the sharks, replete with food, love to lie. But the semi-amphibian natives are equally familiar with these lagoons and know also the favorite resting places of the somnolent sharks. A Cook Islander, according to report, will dive until he finds one that pleases him, and then "talk to it." His right hand strokes its throat while his left, with forgivable duplicity, slips a noose around the body of the great fish, which is then hauled, ignominiously, tail first to the surface. It is also said that an old woman in Samoa was on even greater terms of familiarity with sharks.

She would stand on the foreshore and call until the vicious brutes came silently to her.

Fishing for sharks is great sport as long as the fisherman himself is not the bait. In 1923 I was inspecting health progress in Central America where there were no roads from one country to another and, as yet, no airplane service. Because the capitals of these countries are all far inland, I had to make the long journey around by sea. The hot, humid, and dusty journey from Guatemala City to San José was especially tedious and trying. I left at six in the morning, and it was not until late afternoon that I arrived at San José.

From my hotel window I could see the gentle swell of the broad, empty Pacific purling on a fine sandy beach. The cool-looking water was so alluring that I changed quickly into my bathing suit and hurried down to the deserted pier.

As I gathered speed for a running jump off the end, I was faintly conscious of shouts and yells behind me, but the water called me irresistibly, and I dived in. I swam slowly and steadily until I began to tire, and then rolled lazily over. My gaze was idly wandering when it was suddenly arrested by the pierhead, which had miraculously become black with people. Faint cries of *"Tiburon! Tiburon!"* came to my ears.

Almost at the same moment huge, dim shapes loomed through the crystal-clear sea. The water seemed suddenly icy. I was entirely surrounded by enormous sharks, their yellow-green eyes all fixed unwinkingly upon me.

My first startled impulse was to frighten them away by splashing and making a noise; but my reason checked this rash action. I had swum out leisurely with long, steady strokes, never moving fast. The sharks had not yet attacked me, and perhaps would not so long as I made no violent move. I resumed, therefore, my studied, rhythmic motion, turning quietly toward shore. Playfully the sharks swung around with me. Occasionally one would come so close that I could almost feel the clammy brush of his tail, and imagined I could see the ominous white of his belly. Nobody who has not looked into the cold, glassy eye of a shark swimming beside him in the water can ever realize what a horrible experience it was.

I began the long swim back, the longest swim, I believed, that anybody ever had, and, stroke for stroke, the sharks kept pace with me. I steeled my muscles to their deliberate mechanical task. Using a side stroke I swam like a slow-motion picture, with hardly a ripple or splash.

After what seemed hours, I was off the end of the pier, and could see the agonized expressions of the people, who were momentarily expecting to see me devoured. But when I reached the little iron ladder I did not obey my impulse to leap for it. I grasped one rung cautiously. Nothing happened. Then I lifted the other hand with equal deliberation. I put one foot on the ladder. Still nothing happened. Another foot. Nothing.

Once free of the water I swarmed up the ladder without pausing to wave farewell to my late companions. Not until then had I dared to take a full-sized breath.

The next day the steamer I was to take came into the harbor and anchored just where I had met the sharks. The sailors began fishing for them with salt pork. As soon as one was hooked, they let down over the line a rope with a noose on its end, and eased it along until it reached the shark's tail. Then they tightened it suddenly, so that the shark was firmly caught, and the ship's winch could lift him. One of the sharks weighed more than a ton, and could have swallowed me easily, with room to spare.

I was thankful over my escape, but puzzled as to why I had not been attacked.

Later when I became acquainted with Fau Mui Na I told him that I had heard of his expertness in lassoing sharks, and I asked him whether he would show me how he did it.

"We'll go out this very afternoon," he promised.

Accordingly, we embarked from his private fishing island in a precariously balanced outrigger canoe, accompanied by a mother ship.

"We don't catch our sharks with salt pork bait," the chief said. "We really fish for the fun of it. Catching sharks with a hook isn't considered sporting here. We use our hands as bait."

"Don't people ever lose their hands?"

"Practically never."

"How do you do it?"

FISH STORIES

"I'll show you."

We paddled just outside a barrier reef. The chief put his hand in the water, and trailed it slowly. Soon a shark drifted up and moved as gradually after his hand. As the fish drew alongside the canoe, a noose was gently dropped between it and the hand; the shark, unheeding, followed through. When the rope had passed back of the first fin, it was cautiously pulled tight. If it were to slip over the tail, the shark would struggle and the boat might be upset.

The moment the noose was taut, Fau Mui Na withdrew his fingers. "It's all in knowing how," he said. "If you move your hand slowly, the shark will also move slowly. If you move it quickly, off will come your hand."

The shark was allowed to swim off lazily for about fifty yards, and then was eased around and pulled near the boat. A member of the crew was standing ready with a long-handled mallet, and, as it came within reach, stunned it. The line was then passed to the mother ship, and the great fish was hauled aboard. In two and a half hours we caught more than a dozen specimens, each from six to ten feet long.

This exhibition may afford an explanation as to why I had escaped unscathed at San José. My instinct had been right, and slow-motion was probably the secret.

The report has often been spread about that a South Sea Islander with no other weapon than a knife will engage a shark in submarine combat. Dr. Lambert made the offer of twenty-five dollars in many islands to anyone who would perform this feat. Even though such a sum of money represented a fair-sized fortune in those latitudes, no one volunteered.

There has been much controversy as to whether sharks bite human beings. But Manley Beach at Sydney, Australia, has to be surrounded with iron fences behind which swimmers are supposed to stay. Airplanes patrol the air above and, when a shark is sighted, an alarm is sounded and the bathers flee to safety. Even so the papers almost weekly carry stories of reckless people who have disregarded the warnings and been mangled by sharks.

In my hospital experience I have treated patients whose legs had been bitten off by sharks. A crocodile may also bite off a man's leg,

393

but its canine teeth tear and crush; a shark's curved razor-like teeth shear cleanly through the bone, leaving an unmistakable mark.

I was anxious to do my part in quashing the fallacy that sharks do not bite human beings. A cocksure English magazine had long offered a reward to anybody who would send in an authentic account of a shark bite. I watched as the years went by, and no case apparently was submitted; the reward was continued. Finally, I carefully photographed a femur showing the easily identifiable toothmarks, and claimed the money. My letter was unacknowledged. I wrote again, and, after a third communication, I received a notice that the reward had been withdrawn.

CHAPTER 23.   A GREAT LITTLE
PEOPLE

"WE ARE spending seventy-five million yen a year on health," said the Japanese when, in 1924, they requested that a general survey be made. "We are not accomplishing as good results as other countries in our class. Either it is useless to spend money on health, or we are not doing it in the right way. Every ministry has been instructed to receive you and give you all the information you want. We have provided you with an interpreter. Use him or not as you wish. Everything is wide open to you. We want to know what is wrong."

By boat, by train, by motor, and by rickshaw I traveled up and down Japan in search of the difficulties. To ride in an automobile in Japan was a harrowing experience. The chauffeurs drove like mad through streets so narrow that pedestrians had to flatten themselves against the walls to avoid our headlong rush. From one end of the Archipelago to the other all roads were a moving mass of humanity, where no one seemed to give precedence, and bicycles and rickshaws and handcarts darted here and there, all in the greatest confusion. Every street was filled with color, sound, and motion. Smiling butterfly girls in gay kimonos clop-clopped on wooden *getas* over uneven pavements. From little handcarts or dangerously swinging poles men sold their wares.

The appearance of the landscape of the Island Empire was as fragile and delicate as a print by Sesshu. This country where every tillable acre was in cultivation, and where tillable acres were so few, presented an endless panorama of mountain and valley, of cherished views of sacred Fujiyama, of the torii of the Inland Sea, of red lacquer bridges connecting islet with islet, of dancing paper lanterns and glittering fireflies on beautiful winding streams, of giant lacy cryptomerias, twisted dwarf pines, and gorgeous chrysanthemums, of flowering cherry and plum in the spring and blazing maples in the fall.

I found the perfection of this formal fairyland, designed with such variety of charm, had been sadly marred since I had last seen it. The road to the incomparable summer resort of Miyanoshita, so beautiful with its gardens and pools, had been almost completely destroyed in the great earthquake of the year before, and, after the rains, was little more than paste upon the sides of the precipitous slopes. Huge slides had stripped the steep mountain of its loose volcanic material. The journey up along the road, which was scarcely wide enough for the car, reminded me of my hazardous days with the Italian army in the Dolomites.

In Japan, vehicles follow the English fashion of driving on the left hand side of the road. Because we were circling up the mountain on the left, we had to take the outside whenever we met vehicles coming toward us. Usually we had to back down the curving dangerous road to a place which we hoped would be wide enough for passage. Below us was a gorge thousands of feet deep, and on the inner side of the road a big, heavy oxcart that at any moment might topple us over the brink as it ground ponderously past.

In the towns the completeness of the demolition by earthquake and fire was much greater than anything I had anticipated. In one open square at Yokohama the fleeing inhabitants had sought refuge, dragging their household goods with them. But sparks had fallen on the bedding and, in the resultant conflagration, fifteen hundred people had died. I sadly viewed the ruins, where I could find no vestige of the homes in which I had been so many times lavishly entertained, and for all my searching could not trace my former hosts. My friends had disappeared and nobody knew what had become of them.

Nine months after the shock, Yokohama was still as depressing as the waste lands of the Johnstown flood, or the vicinity of Arras after the German bombardment. Twisted iron, brick, and non-inflammable débris were piled high. Only a few of the streets had been shoveled clean.

At Tokyo, only seventeen miles away, the damage had also been considerable. Only properly erected, reinforced concrete buildings had withstood the shocks and the fire. The escape of the Imperial Hotel, that fantastic structure designed by Frank Lloyd Wright of Chicago, whose contract was said to have called for making it earthquake proof, was most astonishing. Its enormous size and its immense, unsupported ceilings had marked it for destruction. That it stood intact in the midst of falling ruins was a great triumph for American design and construction.

Rebuilding was going forward rapidly, but well-informed foreign residents told me that the Japanese did not fully realize the far-reaching financial effect of the tremendous disaster, and that, had they done so, they would not have continued to create a bad impression by attempting to maneuver the foreign insurance companies, especially the British, into paying fire losses. Common opinion seemed to be that the Japanese, officially and privately, were trying to exploit foreigners. In the effort to prevent them from owning land, the government was prohibiting permanent reconstruction in the city or port areas, claiming time was needed to permit the earth to settle before making a survey for a new town plan.

Any Japanese in a foreign country was apt to be a spy, usually self-appointed. I was told that the government had received literally thousands of unsolicited notebooks and photographs made by its nationals in other countries. Examples of amateur spying had frequently occurred in my Philippine experiences. Japanese fishermen, who had virtually controlled the industry around Manila, had surreptitiously but meticulously sounded the entire Bay, although the information could do their country no possible good; for twenty-five cents a Geodetic Survey chart of those waters, scientifically accurate in every detail, might have been purchased by anybody. Apparently the Japanese could not believe the charts were accurate.

This was no isolated instance. At another time a Filipino with a broken leg had been carried to the nearest doctor, who happened to be a Japanese. But the "doctor," to everybody's consternation, after fumbling for some time, had finally confessed he did not have the faintest idea how to set the bone. His admission had naturally been reported to the Constabulary who, in searching his office, had found, instead of pills and instruments, plans of the United States Naval Station at Olongapo.

Because of their counter fear that foreigners might discover their military secrets and thereby gain some foothold in their country, the Japanese had enacted all sorts of protective rules, including a provision that no foreign warship might enter Tokyo. A week after the earthquake, however, an American Naval vessel, in defiance of regulations, is said to have steamed straight to the city and made fast to a government pier. The Japanese folded their hands; in a few hours they expected to see the American flag flying over Parliament House. But, to their bewilderment, instead of manning the guns, the middies were panting and sweating over unloading rice, medicines, bandages, splints, even building materials hastily despatched from Manila.

The Japanese lacked a sporting instinct in the Anglo-Saxon sense, and could not understand it in others. We were among the first upon the scene with assistance, and they looked upon our action with amazement; it was not only compassionate but startlingly efficient. "How could we have been so mistaken?" they asked. "We have sent all our young men to Germany to be educated. What a blunder! If we had trusted to American ideas, what progress we should have made!"

For a short time thereafter no country stood higher in Japanese estimation than the United States; we were regarded as true friends, and could have had anything we wanted. Japan, always avid for learning, showed her admiration by deflecting hundreds of her students to this country.

We rebuffed this gesture with scant courtesy. By our Japanese immigration legislation, California inspired, we immediately and loudly proclaimed that no Japanese should enter the United States. Although this prohibition did not include students, visitors, merchants, or those who were classed as temporary residents, the bill was regarded as a national affront. The goodwill which had come as a result of our generous action was lost almost overnight.

Resentment against America was extremely bitter in all quarters.

A GREAT LITTLE PEOPLE

The subject was on the lips of everyone in government circles with whom I talked. The American Ambassador, Cyrus Wood, in a conversation with me, stated that his previous relations with the government had been so pleasant that the merest suggestion on his part of a course of action had been followed. This had been particularly helpful whenever Japan's actions to close the Open Door in China, in accordance with her Twenty-One Demands, had seemed inimical to the United States.

An American adviser to the Ministry of Foreign Affairs, with whom I talked, was well qualified to interpret the Japanese point of view because he spent half his time in Tokyo and the other half in the Japanese Embassy at Washington. He told me that after the first unofficial intimation that an Exclusion Bill was under consideration, Prime Minister Hanihara had despatched a "grave consequences" note which Secretary of State Hughes had seen and with which he had apparently sympathized. Japan had been awaiting the negotiations customary to abrogating treaties, even one so nebulous as President Roosevelt's Gentlemen's Agreement by which, if we passed no Exclusion Act, Japan would prevent all emigration. The Japanese had kept the pact in spirit and in letter, but our passage of the Exclusion Act, though within our legal rights, had broken it in spirit.

We lost by our rash action. Had we put them on a quota, something like one hundred and fifty could have entered the country legally, and we should have had the aid of their government in its enforcement. But the moment the Gentlemen's Agreement was abrogated, they were under no obligation to keep their nationals from coming to the United States. It is more than likely that California is receiving more Japanese, via Mexico, since the Exclusion Act was passed than before.

One morning when I was calling on Foreign Minister Shidehara, an intelligent gentleman who had been educated in the United States, he lamented, "It's too bad this should have happened. I'm afraid public resentment is going to last for years. If Washington had only let us know before taking this step we might have prepared our people, and it would have been so much better."

"I don't see how that could have helped."

399

"It would have been simple. If your government had informed us in advance that it intended to pass a bill excluding all Japanese labor, we would then have had an opportunity to announce it to our people in the form of an agreement that no American labor could come to Japan. Since you don't send any labor here anyhow, this would have accomplished your object and at the same time have saved our face."

I myself could verify the state of animosity in the attitude of the daily press. When I came to breakfast one morning at Kobe, I was greeted with flaring headlines stating that rioters, in protest against America's action, had broken up the Saturday night dance at the Tokyo Imperial Hotel. The article claimed it was part of a larger movement to evict all Americans. Some papers expressed it one way, some another, but all featured the story, because it showed how high feeling was running. *Mainichi* of Osaka said it was nothing but a five-year-old boy dancing around with a paper stage sword and the Americans had become frightened and run away. The *Japan Chronicle* of Kobe gave a conservative statement of what appeared to be the facts; the dance had been broken up by members of Japanese patriotic clubs who had distributed handbills requesting that Americans be expelled and their goods boycotted.

The press was only reflecting popular sentiment. Signs in the Kobe stores read, "No goods sold to Americans." At a huge mass meeting a demand was made for the expulsion of American missionaries, the boycott of American goods, and a law to prevent Americans coming to Japan until Congress should modify the Exclusion Bill. Ships' officers complained that the hatred was shared by stevedores, who were delaying the unloading of American vessels by wrecking the winches. On returning to Tokyo, the center of anti-American agitation, I found the entire city under the spell. The Imperial Hotel, instead of being gay with the weekly dance, was shrouded in darkness.

I always suspected that I was guarded by government secret service agents. Whenever I would start to light a cigarette, a match would be all too hastily proffered me by a stranger. Even the omnipresent politeness of the race would not seem to account for the fact that I suffered unpleasantness only once. On this occasion I had boarded a tram already well filled with Japanese and had hardly seated myself when the gentleman beside me rose, bowed, and with a sweep of his hand indicating the other passengers, asked coldly in English, "Shall we leave the car at the next corner, or will you?"

Since it was their country I replied, "If my presence is objectionable to you, I'll leave," and accordingly I alighted at the next corner.

The intensity of feeling thus expressed eventually died down, but the hurt and the slight remained in the backs of the Japanese minds. John D. Rockefeller, Jr., always sympathized with the Japanese sensitiveness, and, to show that all America did not feel hostile, he gave a million dollars personally to rebuild their once fine library. They accepted this gift, even though, I fear, they privately looked upon it with suspicion, lest some string might be attached to it. We might, for instance, try to impose an American style of architecture. Nevertheless, the gift helped to create, in academic circles at least, a more favorable attitude toward the United States.

The Rockefeller Foundation had no cause for personal complaint in making the survey; cooperation was complete and full. Every office was open, every request was granted, every record was available, even to the accounting systems. It was hard to determine whether these apparently open facilities were being offered frankly or only as a means to an end. I sometimes gained the impression the Japanese were merely tolerating the presence of our men in order to have their own trained.

On all my Japanese trips I took with me Dr. John B. Grant, Professor of Hygiene at the Peiping Union Medical College, an extremely able young man whose popularity in China and Japan was unparalleled. He was one of the best administrators developed by the Rockefeller Foundation and was of inestimable aid on this survey. When Dr. Grant discovered what he took to be a discrepancy in the Japanese accounts, the greatest distress was aroused. As I was going out of the hotel one day I noticed a truck unloading huge volumes borne by a staggering line of porters. The sight was, to say the least, unusual, and in curiosity I followed them, to find the tomes being deposited in Dr. Grant's room. Although the Finance Department had merely changed its fiscal year, it was going to prove that nothing had been falsified.

The Japanese are the most hospitable people in the world, and entertained me as I have rarely been entertained elsewhere. I shall never forget my first dinner at the Maple Club, given by the Japanese Cabinet, at which Dr. Grant and I were the only Americans. Because I had been a bachelor for many years, a hole in my sock below the water line made little impression upon me. But, since shoes are not worn in Japanese houses, such nonchalance would not do; I had, as a precaution, provided myself with a supply of new black silk socks so that I would have a new pair available for each function. For this particular dinner I garbed myself in morning clothes, the accepted attire for evening wear in Japan, and one of my new pairs of socks.

Thus confidently fortified I entered the limousine which had been sent for me. The Japanese realize that the difficulties a stranger experiences in any foreign country are increased in theirs because he cannot even read the signs. Therefore they always thoughtfully provide means of transportation.

We arrived a little before six. My shoes were whisked away but, instead of being conducted directly to the reception room, I was regaled with the beauties of the Maple Club's rock garden, reputedly the finest in the country. It was a perfect late afternoon in June, the height of the iris season, as the summer months are characterized in Japan. My guide conducted me down winding paths and over little bridges, and past fern grottos where goldfish twinkled, rippling little waterfalls, shrubs, and flowering plants. Everywhere bloomed gorgeous iris, the most lovely I have ever seen, shading from purest white to deepest purple. Posed here and there among the rocks were geisha girls in brilliantly embroidered kimonos of the latest summer style. Feasting my eyes upon the attractions of the scene, animate and inanimate, I did not notice that the many steps I had taken along this maze of gravel paths, tortuous as the dwarf tree trunks, had had their effect upon my frail silk socks. Not until I reached the reception room did I suddenly realize that one of my toes was peeping shyly forth.

Instead of bending over as was my wont in Japan, I drew myself up to my full height, so that the short Japanese with whom I was conversing would have to tilt their heads up at me. By the use of this subterfuge, I trusted the disgraceful condition of my toe might

402

escape unnoticed. I carefully covered the exposure with my other foot, and congratulated myself that nobody had apparently remarked it.

After a round of courteous conversational exchanges, the paper doors were slipped aside, and we entered the dining room. I was unable to hide my foot discreetly under the table, because there was none. The seating was on the floor in the shape of a horseshoe, and I, as guest of honor, sat in the depth of the curve. I tried unsuccessfully to fold my legs under me in the approved fashion. I imagined I could see dotted lines from the guests' eyes focused upon me, and then I noted with unbounded horror that there had been a hernia of the big toe and it had popped through the sock. Tightly constricted as it was, it had become as fiery red as the tail light of an automobile. I hastily concealed it under my leg, but try as I might it would slip out and the burning gazes were renewed.

Japanese dinners last a long time. A geisha sits before each guest, entertaining him with song and sprightly talk; if he is English she speaks to him in his own language. Sometimes she drinks *sake* with him. As the waitresses patter in with each course, she prepares his food, and, realizing that taking a bird apart with chopsticks is no easy feat, she assists him. Between courses all the geishas join in a ballet. But even the delightful witticisms of my charming geisha failed to make me oblivious of my toe, and the *sake* in this instance proved no Lethe.

For at least two hours I struggled with the recalcitrant digit, but when at last the dinner was over and the signal was given to rise, another embarrassment was in store for me. At Japanese banquets hot *sake* is always served in tiny porcelain cups, and courtesy demands that each diner approach the guests of the evening and with a profound bow drink a cup of *sake* with them. Although this is not a particularly strong drink, if there are forty diners the odds are heavily against the guests and considerable alcohol is consumed. Dr. Grant, who was sitting some distance down the horseshoe, failed to rise with the rest of us. A horrible thought struck me. Mr. Rockefeller was the premier prohibitionist of the world, and one of his officers was so drunk at a Japanese banquet that he could not rise to his feet!

I approached Dr. Grant with a firm tread and whispered severely, "You've got to get up!"

He looked up at me appealingly but made no effort to rise. I took him by the arms and lifted him; he sank limply back again to the floor. In even sterner tones I said, "You've simply got to stand up!"

I lifted him again; again he sank back. "Are you drunk?" I demanded.

"No!" he replied indignantly, "certainly not!"

"Then why don't you stand up?"

By this time our whispers had risen to audible tones and our Japanese hosts were hovering solicitously about. "I can't. My legs are paralyzed."

Immediately the Japanese bent over him concernedly, massaged his legs vigorously, and Grant was soon on his feet.

Probably my contortionary efforts to hide my toe had alone been responsible for saving me from the same cramps. I realized also that in my efforts to conform to the customs of the country I had erred on the side of elegance. Thereafter, at all functions, instead of silk socks I wore stout cotton ones similar to those with which the Japanese protected themselves from such predicaments.

Because of the universal politeness and courtesy of the Japanese, many situations that might otherwise have proved awkward were smoothed over. Courtesy is extended even to that stronghold of rudeness, the customs service. If a customs officer discovered tobacco in my baggage, he would say with a bow, "You probably won't need this in Japan. We'll keep it for you and return it to you when you leave." Any attempt to bribe them would probably be followed by a jail sentence. The honesty of the Japanese public services contrasts strikingly with conditions elsewhere in the East.

One of the national handicaps was the Japanese inability to learn foreign languages well. I sometimes found it extremely difficult to discourse with men who supposedly were educated in English. German helped me enormously, but, even so, conversation was disconnected. It seemed very difficult for them to grasp the spirit of a question, and their abbreviated vocabularies were distressing. When

I came to know them better, they would often confess their humiliation. A great part of their bowing and scraping was due to embarrassment; it also gave them time to formulate their answers.

Another obstacle to mutual comprehension was the lack of a sense of humor as Americans understand it. Our oral fun-making was readily intelligible to the Chinese—which may in part account for the greater ease with which we get along together. But the Japanese found cause for laughter chiefly in the vulgar joke.

The people are, nevertheless, at heart merry, and sometimes, to my own amusement also, played pranks upon me. In this country of small people, nothing is built for tall men. The berths on the sleepers, some of which are compartment trains, are only five foot ten, and are so narrow that when I lay on my side my doubled-up knees protruded. One hot night I had been twisting and bumping this way and that in acute discomfort when a brilliant idea struck me. I adopted the simple expedient of stretching out full length and letting my feet stick through the window. With a sigh of relief I sank into deep slumber.

I do not know how long I had been thus happily occupied when I returned to consciousness with a convulsive start which jerked my feet back into my compartment. The train was no longer moving. To see who or what had so disrespectfully tickled my toes, I peered out, and found my window surrounded by a group of adult Japanese, convulsed with laughter, to whom my large, bare, white feet had proved an irresistible lure.

Only a tall person knows what another tall person suffers. Heads are always being bumped under low doorways, feet or shoulders protrude from blankets. But in New York hotels, at least, his feet will not stick out. The Constitution of the State, due to the efforts of the Six Foot Association to alleviate his agonies, provides that no hotel bed shall have a sheet shorter than eight feet. In my Eastern travels I was happiest in Java, where appurtenances are built to fit the tall Dutch; I was apt to become stoop-shouldered in Japan.

The Japanese were very sensitive about their size. Newspaper reporters used to come daily to my hotel for a story. I had early developed a method of sidetracking them. "Gentlemen," I would say,

"I'm a guest of the government. Whatever you wish to know must be obtained from official sources."

This shunting device worked beautifully; medical officials, always inclined to be jealous of outside interference, were disarmed because they realized I was not trying to steal their thunder.

After I had made my excuses to the reporters for some time, one of them said, "Look here, we've been around day after day and you always put us off. Come on now, give us at least one story."

"All right," I said. "I can't give you one, but, if you'll keep my name out of it, I'll tell you where you can get one. You've a scientist here in Tokyo who has made a certain fish extract which possesses the property of stimulating growth tremendously. The children to whom he is giving it are growing larger and larger. If you see Dr. ——, he'll give you the details of his experiments."

The next morning the story of the magic growth powder appeared in all Tokyo newspapers. Because this was such important news to the Japanese, the Associated Press and Reuter correspondents picked it up, and, to give it more than local interest, sent it out over their wires under my name. When I reached the United States I found awaiting me bundles of newspaper clippings and letters by the hundreds from little short people all over the world. The tenor of the latter was, "I saw in —— paper that you said a Japanese had invented a growth powder. I am five feet tall. I want to be six. How much of the powder would I have to take to grow this extra foot? How much would it cost?"

The volume of letters was so great that it taxed the office force considerably to answer them and express my regrets at being unable to help. I never saw a story persist as long as that of the magic growth powder. Finally, it was put into plate and syndicated throughout the world. My name was inextricably linked with it, and hardly a voyage passed that somebody did not ask for further information about it.

The members of the Japanese press are as pertinacious and resourceful as their brothers of the fourth estate elsewhere. One warm June morning, worn out after the long night's train ride and the many courtesies tendered me, I stepped off the train at Tokyo to face a camera squad ready for action.

A GREAT LITTLE PEOPLE

"Have you seen Dr. Heiser?" one of the photographers asked me.

"Oh, yes," I replied mendaciously. "He's just behind me on the train. He'll be off in a minute."

I had no desire to answer questions, and certainly not to pose for photographs, an ordeal which I have never faced with composure. I was hot and tired, and aspired solely to a refreshing bath. I betook myself quietly to the Hotel Imperial, and soon was merrily sloshing around in the sunken tub provided for captious foreigners.

No locks safeguard doors in Japan; the Japanese have never felt the need of them because, unlike Christians, they do not indulge in petty pilfering and have no sense of personal privacy. Having finished my bath, I walked unconcernedly toward the outer room, but just as I was framed in the doorway my startled glance fell upon several cameras in position. With one bound I knocked aside a hand, poised to set off the flash. "Even in Japan," I protested, "you wouldn't run a photograph like that—of a man without any clothes on."

"Oh, no," one of them replied. "We'd cut off the bottom and nobody would know the difference."

The picture of a bald-headed man in this décolleté pleased me little more than the idea of the full-length nude. I had prevented a major catastrophe by my prompt action, but I was still unclothed, and there is something about such a state that produces a distinct feeling of helplessness. In the ensuing argument I found myself at a great disadvantage. The photographers had been sent on an assignment, and were determined not to return to their papers without pictures. Nevertheless, while keeping up my end of the controversy, I was slipping on a garment here and there, and, as my self-confidence returned, my arguments increased relatively in potency. Once safe inside my clothes, I was a match for them, and was able to persuade them to retire.

Everything had to be done strictly according to rule in Japan; no deviation was allowed. At the smaller hotels in the interior the ritual of bathing was an experience to remember. Although the people were unbelievably clean, the result was accomplished by means of a little two-quart receptacle of water, not much bigger than a wash-basin. But, because they suspected that the Anglo-Saxon might be up to his well-known trick of plunging, before he had washed himself, into the big tub which had to serve for everybody, diligent maids constantly pattered in and out to see that bathing customs were not violated. Only after I was supposedly cleansed was I given an opportunity to sit in the extremely hot water of the tub and rest, relax, and contemplate. When the time came to emerge, I was as red as the proverbial boiled lobster.

The hotel maids were equally determined that I should get no fresh air at night. I wanted the panels between my room and the out-of-doors left open, but this was contrary to Japanese custom. After retiring I soon heard light footsteps, and the panels were noiselessly slid shut. When all was quiet, I would steal catlike to open them again, but would soon awaken to find them once more closed. Such battles often continued through the night.

In the morning the constant entrance of the same smiling maids, regardless of the state of my attire, was embarrassing to me but apparently not to them. Shaving seemed to afford particular amusement. At one hotel the entire staff gathered eagerly to watch the operation. The departure from this same hostelry was rather touching. From manager to porter all seemed to be as sincere in their farewells as in their greetings. They did, however, expect the traveler's tip to equal the hotel bill; if he were a real gentleman he would double it.

The clean and sociable Japanese made pleasant fellow travelers, although their hospitality on occasion was carried to excess. Whenever a new passenger entered a compartment on a train, he passed around a box of laxative pills. Courtesy demanded that one be accepted and swallowed. I did not mind taking one, but the Japanese were constantly getting off and on, and each newcomer would inevitably produce his little box. On long journeys I had to resort to sleight of hand.

But in spite of their embarrassingly frank customs and their strict observance of tradition, the Japanese were enamored of Western ideas. It seemed to me they copied everything American, even to the numbering of their sleeping cars, and the rubber-tired electric baggage motors were reproduced to the last screw.

I became much impressed with the efficiency of this people. The trains were run on time. I could set my watch to the minute by comparing their scheduled arrival with the time-table. All waste motion was eliminated in loading ships or freight cars, and the muscular coordination of the coolies, notwithstanding their handicap in size, was admirable.

The Japanese showed the same efficiency in all their operations outside the country. When I first went to Manchuria in 1916, in the days when it still belonged to China, the Japanese-owned South Manchurian Railroad was the acme of perfection, with beautiful roadbed and American-type Pullman cars. The railroad had a fine hospital and maintained a medical school.

It is extraordinary to observe that the Japanese are the only Orientals who have been able to rise above their own self-satisfaction and have, furthermore, disturbed the mass inertia of other Orientals with whom they have come in contact.

In Korea also, which Japan was endeavoring to pull up to Western standards, a good job had been done from a machine standpoint, and much more money was being spent than was collected in revenues. Enormous public works had been undertaken, agriculture developed, schools introduced, and hospitals built. The Japanese did not seem favorably disposed to the efforts of the missionaries, and hence taxed their property heavily. Apparently in an effort to ease them out entirely, the Japanese would build bigger and better hospitals of their own near missionary dispensaries, and thus greatly aided in elevating the standards of medical practice.

In 1916 I saw the border Japanese town of Antung, planned along the best lines, with wide streets and proper drainage, in the making, but it seemed to cause no emulation in the Chinese town across the Yalu River. Korea was hilly and full of huge loose surface rocks. Even so, the valleys were intensively cultivated, mostly with rice. Oxen were apparent in large numbers, carrying great loads on their backs. The countryside was brown and sere and heavy in frost. Everyone was dressed in white cotton cloth and this, in the prevailing freezing weather, gave me a chilly sensation. The stiff, silly, black horsehair headgear worn by the Koreans to protect their topknots looked like silk hats several sizes too small, and contrasted grotesquely and startlingly with the whiteness of their other clothing.

In spite of the Japanese improvements over Korean ancient customs, the Koreans were extremely hostile to their overlords, and often assassinated them. Supervision was so rigid in Korea that tyrannicide was practised mostly outside the country. I once happened to be at Government House in Singapore when the present Mikado, then Crown Prince, was touring the East. He was naturally invited to an official dinner, and a guard of honor was sent to the pier to escort him. Fifteen minutes before the appointed dinner hour the telephone rang, and the request was made that identical arrangements for receiving the Prince be made at another pier, but to leave the first guard of honor where it was. Government aides scurried around in mad haste, and a second guard of honor was made up and despatched. The hour came and went without a Prince. Twenty minutes later he put in an appearance with no guard at all. After his official guardians had been satisfied with their complex preparations to throw off any possible assassins, they had sent him ashore in a sampan, and he arrived at Government House in a rickshaw.

I had an extremely interesting interview with Viscount Goto, former Home Minister and generally regarded as one of Japan's ablest statesmen. He was a fine looking old gentleman, with a goatee, and had charming, courtly manners. He was at first exceedingly cautious, but in the end my frank treatment of the situation called forth an equal frankness from him. He greatly deplored the Japanese tendency to analysis rather than to synthesis and admitted this tendency stood in the way of their progress. He said the Japanese regarded Burbank as being unscientific and only successful accidentally. He himself conceded that Burbank had made important discoveries despite his crude methods, and ventured the belief that many of America's achievements were due to her backing people who were following unproved "hunches" not verified by logical reasoning.

I told Viscount Goto I was learning many things; Japanese laboratories, in both numbers and equipment, were a source of constant amazement to me, and were superior to ours in their distribution. Good bacteriological examinations could be made in almost every nook and corner of the country. But I also pointed out that Japan, on account of the modern civilization she had adopted, had greatly increased her health hazards, and if she were to keep her place in the sun she must avail herself of health control measures. She had to take cognizance of her diseases caused by faulty nutrition and soil pollution, and also her rising typhoid and high infant mortality rates.

The thoroughness of the Japanese was by no means extended to all branches of medicine. Curiously enough, dentistry was not held in high regard, because their German teachers had not believed in focal infections. The Japanese medical profession itself had the worst teeth I have ever seen.

Leprosy was apparently on the wane, although only the most advanced cases, and these relatively few in number, were segregated. Those at large were under the ever-watchful eye of the police, who saw to it they used only their own utensils and did not come in close contact with well persons.

The increased cost of living had caused more and more crowding and poorer diet in the homes of working people. The most serious disease menace, therefore, was tuberculosis, which had fastened itself upon the country; the incidence was almost twice as high as in the United States or England, and the rates approached the worst slum centers of the world.

Japanese scientists concerned themselves little with the practical application of existing knowledge. It was their constant dream to discover a specific for tuberculosis or some other disease. In their zeal they often made unreliable reports. To prevent these reaching the outside world, a small committee in Tokyo took upon itself the task of suppressing them.

I have never felt more strongly about what is being done in the name of preventive medicine than after visiting a Japanese hospital. It was an arbitrary use of power in a futile endeavor to control things that would never happen. Such force and insistence were placed upon non-essentials that as much effort was wasted in making the machinery run as though a hundred horsepower motor were hitched to a lawnmower.

Japanese hospital rules and regulations made any visitor feel bacteria were going to rise up and bite him. When I once visited a tuberculosis sanitarium, I was put through a most amazing rite. First I was encased in a pair of boots which came to my hips, and then the regulation hospital gown, which was so short on me that a portion of my booted legs was exposed. This caused the attending staff much concern, lest some possible infection might make its way through the area not protected by the gown. Only after a gauze face mask and a hood had been adjusted was I allowed to enter the presence of the patients.

On emerging, I had to wade through a huge tank of bichloride solution, after which an attendant, striving vainly on tiptoe to reach my throat with his atomizer, pulled up a little stepladder beside me, stood on it, and carefully sprayed my respiratory passages to kill any possible tubercles which might be lurking there. Finally, I was requested to gargle, and, feeling thoroughly purified, I was allowed to depart.

In the cholera hospital, the wheels of the ambulance which carried in the patients had to run through troughs of disinfecting solution. The same type of rules had been imposed in Korea during cholera epidemics. At the gateway to public buildings, horses and people were obliged to tramp through similar solutions, and, before any letter could be mailed, the correspondent had to wash his hands in a germicidal basin placed by each mailbox. In the light of modern knowledge their precautions were ridiculous.

In the application of maritime quarantine regulations the Japanese were strict. When an American Assistant Secretary of State was once traveling in the East, he was put in quarantine, because a case of plague had occurred on his ship. In high dudgeon he cabled Washington to get him out, but the Japanese health officers were adamant to all representations. He protested indignantly that this was an unheard of humiliation. His humorless jailers, a careful people, searched the records and found that the King of Sweden had once been in quarantine. Since royalty obviously outranked a mere Assistant Secretary of State, the latter continued to languish until the incubation period was over.

The German-trained men in charge of Japanese medicine adhered to the procedure of the age of bacteriology; they developed knowledge along the lines of Koch, Pasteur, and Lister, but had an entire lack of appreciation of the need to have it used in the lives of the people. Shibasaburo Kitasato was the outstanding medical scientist. The concentration on bacteriology rather than health was largely due to the power of his personality and ability.

A GREAT LITTLE PEOPLE

After Kitasato's memorable achievement in tracking down the plague bacillus, he was loaded with honors. But, unfortunately for the progress of medicine in Japan, he became involved in a dispute with the government, and resigned indignantly from his position as head of the Imperial Institute for Infectious Diseases. Nevertheless, his prestige was so great that by public subscription a laboratory was built especially for him.

Kitasato's action led to a disastrous schism in the medical profession. He not only took the majority of his staff with him but also the leaders in bacteriology, including Shiga, who had discovered a dysentery bacillus and was a most important figure in the Japanese medical world. The government had to build a new organization from the ground up. What one faction wanted, the other fought, although the government, which had no other source of supply, had to buy the various sera and vaccines manufactured by the Kitasato laboratory. The problem was complicated further by the fact that the government owned all the universities, with the major exception of the Keio, which set the pace for the rest. When the Kitasato group threw its weight behind the Keio, the government medical school languished and the rift grew wider.

Because of this cleavage among Japanese scientists, which had lasted for thirty years, all professional dealings with them had to be conducted with delicacy and caution. The jealousy was so intense that when Doctors Flexner and Welch went to Japan, they were received by one group and ignored by the other. They actually had to leave the country and return, so that they might be officially welcomed by the opposite faction.

Through the exercise of care the Rockefeller Foundation had always been able to maintain friendly relations with all parties to the dispute.

I would never compromise with their petty animosities although, since our survey came at a time when anti-American feeling was running so high, I had to allow it to be made more or less under cover; the politicians were afraid if they accepted help openly from America it might interfere with their political future.

Dealing with the Japanese government had one great advantage. Once an arrangement was agreed upon we could be sure it would be

413

faithfully carried out, no matter how the balance of power in politics might shift. German influence in government medical circles was on the wane, and there seemed to be hope that the authorities would subscribe to the concept of applying knowledge to prevent disease and realize that Germany had not progressed so far as America in this respect. As an indication of the change, it was also astounding to see to what extent English was coming into general use, and how rapidly German was declining.

Gradually I came to be accepted as a neutral and could go freely from one group to another. I told them both frankly that, if they could not agree, there was no hope of getting the Rockefeller Foundation to aid them. Eventually I worked them up to a point where they jointly petitioned for us to help them start a Health Institute in which they would both cooperate.

When the Far Eastern Association of Tropical Medicine met in 1926 at Tokyo, Kitasato was still all-powerful. Each time the great man spoke, the awed delegates from all over the Orient were silent. He was chairman, and it was amusing to see that no vote was ever taken; any motion put by him was accepted as unanimously passed. Everything was most amicable. At the first formal meeting the toastmaster made a happy address, quoting from some ancient Japanese writings the impression made upon the Japanese who had first dissected a white man. They had been astounded to find that underneath his skin he was constructed in exactly the same way as themselves.

A great to-do took place over which country's delegate should preside at the banquet to be given by the foreign guests to their Japanese hosts. Finally, unable to reach a conclusion, they compromised on me, who represented no country, and was known to be equally well disposed to all.

Over seven hundred persons assembled in the huge banquet hall of the Imperial Hotel for one of the largest international dinners ever held in Japan. Kitasato, who was sitting on my right, told me much about his early days with Koch, and, to my surprise, admitted that bacteriology now had its back to the wall; further development would probably be along the lines of bio-chemistry. I could not interest him in nutrition as an important factor in disease, although the Japanese themselves, in their own laboratories, had proved the importance of diet by producing stones in the bladders or kidneys of white rats with a diet deficiency, and had dissolved them again with proper diet. But Kitasato, like so many other research scientists, saw no further than the discovery, and, assuming it would immediately be adopted by the people, did not realize that usually more effort is required to bring a discovery into use than has gone into the original research.

After our survey was completed it was obvious that the didactic teaching should be largely supplemented by the inculcation of methods to bring modern scientific knowledge into the lives of the people. To accomplish this a modern school of hygiene and public health for Japan was recommended, and this was finally agreed to by the Japanese government. The development of new knowledge was to be encouraged in every way, but equal importance was to be attached to its practical application.

The chief difficulty in founding a Health Institute in Japan lay with the stubborn elder groups, still headed by Kitasato. He had no faith in it, because he had spent his life in the cloistered seclusion of the laboratory. He did not believe in his heart in what we were recommending, but, because he realized I was above the battle and had no personal objectives in my long persuasive efforts, he finally acquiesced. We inveigled a group of these elder scientists to come to the United States to observe the friendly cooperation in American scientific circles, and see how research workers in bacteriology and the men who applied their discoveries could work in harmony together. The ancients were still dubious after their expedition to America, but they could be counted upon at least not to oppose the venture.

Once the Health Institute had been decided upon, the great problem was how to apportion the control. Admittedly the elders had to be put in charge, but it was very hard for them to change the guiding principles they had acquired in their youth, and the reverence for age was so great that, although the younger men might know better, they were still apt to bow respectfully before the older wisdom. Determined to have a body of younger men with progressive ideas to serve as a check, we stipulated, "You'll have to have an advisory committee."

During the many years required to establish the Health Institute, we brought many of these young men to America on fellowships, selecting the applicants carefully from both government and Kitasato groups, so that by the time the Health Institute should be ready to open its doors, there would be a staff of young men who would have lost to some extent their ancestor worship and would champion their own ideals even against the elders. After this new school has a sufficient number of graduates it is the hope that personal idiosyncrasies, habits of mind, and the old German concept of hygiene, which is still strong, will be overcome, and that the application of preventive medicine will become a reality.

CHAPTER 24. PICKING UP
BROKEN THREADS

THE Harrison bonfire which had blazed so merrily for many years and around which the Filipinos had danced so blithely, finally flickered and went out, leaving only dead ashes. They were still warm when General Wood and former Governor General Forbes came to poke among the ruins to see what of value remained. I was on my 1921 trip and saw a paper with American news only occasionally. I was cognizant that President Harding had appointed these two old friends of mine to report on the condition of the Philippines, but did not know precisely where they were.

In the course of my travels I arrived at Sandakan, Borneo, just in time to see the *S.S. Eastern,* which I had expected to take to Manila, steaming out. I had a choice of waiting in Sandakan several weeks for the regular sailing, or of taking an extra week to retrace my steps to Singapore, and going thence by another line to Manila.

The following morning, still perplexed as to what I ought to do, I was walking along the harbor front. Low down on the horizon I saw faint trails of smoke. "What ships are those?" I asked the Captain of the Port.

"Haven't you heard?" he replied. "Early this morning we received word the Wood-Forbes party was to pay an unexpected visit to the Governor of Borneo."

My gloom lifted as the gossamer wisps grew into black smudges. Just at that moment the Governor's aide came along, and I saw a

417

launch making ready to leave. "Could I go out with you?" I asked him.

"Of course, if you would like to, but I think the Governor is expecting you to accompany him."

"If you don't mind, I'd rather join you."

As we gradually drew near, I recognized the old *General Alava*, an inheritance from the Spanish, and the *Polillo*, the despatch boat of the previous Governor Generals. I could see through my glasses that we also were objects of scrutiny. I was, of course, in civilian clothes, but my face was well concealed by my huge helmet; the arriving party was scurrying about. I could hear the bugle sounding and see sailors lined up stiffly on the deck. At the top of the gangway, the officer saluted smartly.

"Where's the General?" I asked.

"On the quarterdeck, sir."

"Lead the way."

"Aye aye, sir."

General Wood and his staff, former Governor Forbes, Major General Frank McCoy, Colonel Gordon Johnston, Major Edward Bowditch, and other old friends among the members of the Mission were all standing strictly at attention. General Wood was the first to recognize me. I could see him blink. Just then Forbes relaxed his official attitude and ejaculated, "You damned old scoundrel, we're not drawn up at attention to meet you. You're not the Governor."

As we pumped each other's hands enthusiastically, General Wood exclaimed, "This is the most extraordinary coincidence. I've cabled all over the East trying to find you. Imagine running across you in Borneo. You may not know it but you're joining the Mission, and you're going on with us to the Philippines."

Nothing could have pleased me better. Bag and baggage I was transferred to the *General Alava*, and that evening we sailed.

This was a particularly happy occasion. I was back in the midst of many friends whom I had not seen for years, with whom I could reminisce over old battles, old triumphs, and pleasant and amusing experiences we had shared together. Once more we were in harness at the old job of hauling the Filipinos out of the slough. My friends seemed to be equally divided between the two ships, and, since it was impossible for me to be in both places at once, we talked by wireless. I even carried on an animated chess game by wireless with General McCoy.

Seven years dropped away as we inspected island after island which I had so often visited as Director of Health. At each stop we heard the same old charges and countercharges, discovered shocking examples of delayed justice, and heard the same addresses of welcome pitched in the same old florid vein. The independence leaders had agitated well; the keynote of many of these orations was independence, though many Filipinos themselves realized that the time was not yet ripe for independence without a protectorate.

A warm welcome awaited me in Manila. My old associate and prize cholera fighter, Dr. Vicente Jesus, who was now Director of Health, seemed overjoyed at my return to share his responsibilities. He had already had a desk placed beside his, and offered to retire temporarily while I was there. I was never more touched than by this demonstration of trust.

General Wood asked me to stay with him at Malacañan during my visit. My acquaintance with him dated from 1903 when he had been in command at Mindanao. Then and later, when he had been head of the Philippine Division of the Army, we had often consulted together on problems of health. He was a delightful man to be with, urbane, courteous, and full of interesting anecdotes. Like Theodore Roosevelt, his close friend, he surrounded himself with unusual people, and had the gift of setting them at their ease and drawing them out.

One evening when we were alone at Malacañan, coffee and cigars were brought out on the veranda, which overlooked the Pasig River. Between the palm trees the native life could be seen hurrying up and down this artery of trade and traffic in endless procession. The General had been offered the position of head of the University of Pennsylvania, which was clamoring for his return to take up his post there. President Harding had just offered him the Governor Generalship of the Philippines and he was obviously pondering the problem. I obtruded upon his thoughts.

"I don't know your ambitions," I said, "and, of course, it's none of my affair, but I suppose you still would like to be President of the United States. If you stay here I believe you might as well

419

abandon any such idea. If you do a hundred percent job as Governor General, it will be taken for granted. Here you have a political and economic crisis to deal with; some of the things you attempt to do under such conditions will inevitably be failures. These will be seized upon by your opponents, who will make political capital out of them in the United States. You will be too far away to answer any of these slanders. Furthermore, your salary here will barely pay your expenses, whereas at the University of Pennsylvania you will be better off."

"That's quite true," he replied.

"But what's more important," I went on, "in Philadelphia you will be close to affairs. You will be in a strategic position politically, because you can put in an appearance whenever the weather is propitious, and stay in academic retirement when it isn't. After four years here you will be forgotten, especially if things are running well. Obviously, it will be much to your personal advantage to go to Pennsylvania."

General Wood took a long pull on his cigar, and then said slowly but with complete finality, "I believe I can serve my country best in the Philippines. What effect this may have on my career is immaterial."

Though I regretted the benefits he was to lose, I could only admire his decision, particularly in the face of the burden he was assuming.

The Philippines had changed sadly for the worse since I had last seen them. As General Wood remarked to me at Sandakan, "Only here and there could I find a few rusty streaks where the rails had been." Governor Harrison had carried out to the limit his theory of the Philippines for the Filipinos; he had let them ruin themselves. A wise governor general would have tried to prevent this. A small group, surfeited with power, managed to bring about the resignation of Americans against whom they had a grievance, and it so happened that in the normal exercise of duty most of those formerly in control had found it impossible to avoid giving offense in some quarter or other.

The Wood-Forbes Mission found that the government-owned projects had incurred tremendous deficits. Among other things, thousands of railway passes had been issued. Sugar companies had started up on a shoe string and then borrowed government funds without adequate security. One hundred million pesos had been lost in banking schemes. To cap the climax, the silver metal reserve behind the currency had been sold to India, so that the peso had fallen to thirty-eight cents. General Wood had to get an emergency loan authorized by the United States Congress to put the Islands on their feet financially.

The report of the Mission concluded that an immediate grant of independence would be "a betrayal of the Philippine people," and that "under no circumstances should the American government permit to be established in the Philippines a situation which would leave the United States in a position of responsibility without authority."

As soon as General Wood had reestablished financial credit, he turned his attention to the Bureau of Health, which had fallen hopelessly into politics; its ramifications were so extensive that innumerable plums were to be had for the plucking. Since I had built it up originally, he believed I was the one best qualified to resurrect it. The Rockefeller Foundation concurred, and I spent several months making a survey and offering suggestions for its regeneration. The Foundation furnished funds and expert advisers and placed its resources at my disposal.

In order to ensure the fulfilment of my survey I talked to Manuel Quezon, pointing out on a chart how the death rate had risen steadily since I had left, and how the whole future of the Islands depended on getting the Health Service out of politics. He agreed with me completely, and induced the principal leaders of the Legislature to sign a document that they would support me loyally. This they continued to do, even through the thick of their contest with General Wood.

The Health Service was overloaded with old fossil men, educated in past epochs, who had no conception of modern hygiene in its scientific aspects, and who were too old to learn. Improvement was impossible until younger men were trained. Filipino students were sent on fellowships to take post-graduate courses in American schools. As they returned, the standards of the Medical School were gradually raised to their former excellence. Eventually they formed the staff of a new School of Hygiene—with the exception of India the only one East of Suez. The nursing schools were also restored with the aid of imported experts. The slow business of education had to be started all over again to convince the Filipinos of the value of the Health Service. Not until then would the Legislature vote money of its own volition.

The Bureau of Science presented a more difficult problem. Only with adequate guarantees of a certain tenure of office for a number of years could a desirable set of men be induced to accept positions again. The *Philippine Journal of Science* had also lost its standing, but in time its former reputation was to a great extent regained.

The state of the lepers and the steps taken by General Wood to remedy their deplorable situation have already been described. Equally distressing was the condition of the insane. Those under confinement were existing almost like animals and receiving inadequate attention from the authorities. More were roaming the country at will; many insane women were becoming pregnant as fast as nature would allow.

General Wood was horrified to find the extent to which the care of the insane had deteriorated. I was motoring with him one noon on our way to lunch when he happened to spy on the street one of the principal Filipino doctors of Manila. The General, who was always a man of action, stopping his car, hailed the doctor. "I'm going to the insane hospital," he said. "Won't you come along?"

"But I'm just on my way to lunch."

"Skip lunch and come with me."

Such a request from the Governor General could not be disregarded. The doctor perforce joined us. General Wood spent two hours meticulously pointing out every harrowing detail. He had missed lunch but made a convert. The doctor became one of the ardent supporters of appropriations for the large modern asylum which was ultimately erected.

Apparently there was always a genuine desire and willingness on the part of the local people to cooperate with the Rockefeller Foundation cordially and openly. But they were sometimes timid owing to the fear that they might lose prestige and influence among their own people. It was difficult to make much advance, but we did prevent further retrogression and dissolution during this trying period of reconstruction.

On the morning of May 13, 1922, in the midst of our busiest days, the British cruiser *Renown*, bearing the Prince of Wales, now King Edward VIII, dropped anchor in Manila Bay. The Prince landed at noon, but before he could have any lunch he had to review the crack Ninth Cavalry on the Luneta, and the crack Constabulary company at Malacañan. Although he must have already experienced similar demonstrations of local pride hundreds of times, he had to school his countenance to pleasant appreciation. To my mind his charm of manner was much heightened by his apparent embarrassment. Instead of a prince of twenty-eight, he gave the impression of a young boy of eighteen who had never performed such a function in his life.

The Prince had obviously been brought up in the true British traditions of the dangers of the noonday sun. His amazement was manifest when he observed the Governor General essay bareheaded the short journey from the government offices where he had been received to the palace where he was finally to have lunch. He was apparently of two minds over donning his helmet but after a few moments' hesitation concluded to be on the safe side and wear it.

By way of further entertainment, General Wood had arranged a polo match for the afternoon. He and I were watching from the grandstand when by accident our royal guest was struck on the head with a ball. The game was stopped and the Prince was carried off the field.

General Wood exclaimed, "Come on, Heiser! We'd better go over." We jumped into his automobile and dashed across the field to the stable, where we found the Prince lying on a bench with an inch and a half cut in his forehead. A severed artery was spurting a stream of blood with each heart beat.

The Prince, still conscious, blinked up at me with his one good eye and said, "Won't you look after me, Doctor, and have my surgeon help you?"

I clapped a compress on the wound at once, and said, "We'd better do the rest of the dressing at Malacañan. The stable's not a good place."

Tetanus germs may always be lurking about a stable; consequently the recognized practice was to give an anti-tetanus injection for any wound received in the vicinity of one. But I knew that the only serum in town at the moment had been causing the most violent reactions.

I was in a quandary. I retired to meditate. "If the Prince dies of tetanus, I shall be condemned by the entire world for not having given him the injection. On the other hand, if I give him the serum, and he dies of that, the result will be equally bad." I had in my care the most valuable asset possessed by the British Empire; his life might be in my keeping.

I went myself for the serum to the hospital where I received dubious assurance that it was safe. Hoping I was doing the right thing, I ordered the injection made. A cable was immediately despatched to King George V, informing him the injury was slight and that the Prince expected to keep his full program the next day, and a similar message was sent to President Harding.

The Prince was able to attend a luncheon at Malacañan the following noon. I found that he was, as so often described, truly a Prince Charming, but he also had an astounding grasp of the problems of his country. He was quite serious, discussed world events with great judgment, was well-informed on names and places, and seemed to have an extraordinary memory for his experiences in France and for what he had learned on his long journeys in behalf of the Empire.

The Prince and I talked over in detail the Indian situation, with which we both were familiar. I described the hookworm survey in Madras, and suggested that the elimination of hookworm alone would go far toward building up the stamina of the Indians. He asked particularly about the difficulties encountered over caste, race, and religious prejudices.

That night the Prince himself gave a dinner on the *Renown*, at which it was imperative that he appear. Although it was time for the anti-toxin to show a reaction, he succeeded in taking his place at the head of the table. I noticed he was surreptitiously scratching all the time, and suspected what was wrong with him. As soon as the dinner was over, I approached him. "Are you feeling comfortable?" I asked in a professional tone.

He playfully hit me a tremendous punch in the chest. "You know perfectly well I'm feeling miserable. I hardly slept last night at all. Look!" And he displayed the most beautiful case of hives I have ever seen. Fortunately he suffered no other ill effects from the injection.

The Prince's fondness for dancing was common knowledge, and also his idiosyncrasy that his partners should preferably alternate between blonde and brunette, and that none should be as tall as he unless, of course, she happened to be his hostess. His choice of partners, which seemed so spontaneous, was often managed. He would privately have the best dancers pointed out to him and would then ask them to do him the honor; they would sparkle with delight under the exhilarating thought that he had selected them out of all the beautiful bevy.

The publicity attendant on the goings and comings of the Prince caused him much concern. Amusing anecdotes are told about his attempts to attain a measure of privacy. In Japan, where privacy is at a premium, it is said he staged one of his greatest successes. The Japanese were determined that he must be entertained every moment. Once when he came from an officially escorted inspection into the anteroom of the quarters provided for him, he excused himself to the Japanese general detailed to accompany him, walked into his own apartment, and hopped through the French window into his Rolls Royce which his chauffeur, accustomed to these escapes, was driving slowly past, according to instructions. He crouched in the bottom of the car as it passed the sentries and nobody saw him. No sooner was he outside than he quickly changed into the street clothes waiting in the limousine, and immediately abandoned it for a rickshaw.

The general in the anteroom first grew tired of waiting and then alarmed; finally he instituted inquiries. When the news leaked out that the Prince had vanished, the tocsin was sounded. The Japanese pride themselves on being able to locate any foreigner within their gates in a few hours, but they could not find the most conspicuous figure in the world. The Prince frequently changed rickshaws, wandered about, shopped, and when he grew tired returned to the palace and walked coolly into the bedlam of police and detectives.

While the Prince was in Manila we had several sets of tennis together. When, once or twice, he suspected I was not exerting myself, he was much annoyed. He disliked excessively the fanfare and acclaim which greeted his every appearance. When he would walk in from the court everybody would rise. "Look here!" he would say, "I'm just a tennis player."

Although the Prince was able to assume with startling rapidity whatever public attitude fitted the moment, he was fundamentally a sober-minded person. He would often inject a serious note in a frivolous conversation, as when he said self-deprecatingly that he had been able to accomplish very little in the world beyond appearing as the model for "what the well-dressed man will wear." The terrible discomforts of men's dress as decreed by convention in the East seemed to cause him much distress. As soon as he was East of Suez he made it a point never to wear a waistcoat, and to replace the hot black dinner coat with a cool and comfortable white mess jacket. "You travel through the Orient a great deal," he said to me. "Why don't you set the fashion of wearing mess jackets?"

"I'm afraid my influence wouldn't carry very far," I smiled.

"Yes, it would. We'd get the thing started, and think what a boon it would be to men all through the tropics."

Because I was so thoroughly in accord with the Prince's sentiments I agreed to do my bit. When I arrived in Calcutta a few months later I was invited to a formal dinner at the Bengal Club, at which I knew a black dinner coat would be *de rigueur*. But it was so steamy and unpleasant that the mere thought of broadcloth was abhorrent. I decided that I could follow no better sartorial example than that of His Royal Highness, and appeared, therefore, in a mess jacket.

My host was obviously most uncomfortable, but I remained serene. "I see that mess jackets aren't being worn," I remarked affably. "I'll go back and change if you like. It's only a few blocks. But, perhaps I'd better say first that H.R.H. has requested me to wear a mess jacket wherever I go in British territory. If you gentlemen in Calcutta—"

This put a different aspect on the matter. The news that I had been acting as personal physician to the Prince had been cabled all over the British world. A meeting of the House Committee was called at once to discuss this upheaval in all accepted social canons. After weighty deliberation it was agreed that under the circumstances exception should be made in my case. All during the banquet I could see the news going around from mouth to mouth. "H.R.H.—mess jackets." And then they would look intently at me as I sat cool and complacent, a white beacon against the background of oppressive black.

When I attended a second banquet only a few nights later every man in the room was attired in a mess jacket.

Just before the Prince left the Philippines I paid my official farewell call on the *Renown*. He asked me into his quarters and presented me with a silver cigarette case, thanking me for my services, both official and unofficial, and saying, "Doctor, do come and see me in London."

"That would be very pleasant."

"Just let me know in advance. I want you to come down to my farm. I'll show you I sometimes work too."

The visit of His Highness had provided a pleasant interlude in the midst of our labors which, as he had observed, were heavy indeed. Immediately after General Wood's appointment as Governor General, October 5, 1921, the Filipino leaders had been meek as children who had broken their toys through disobedience and wanted them mended. Like a kind father he repaired some of their favorite playthings but others, which had been given them under the mistaken impression they knew how to use them, he removed until such time as they should prove their maturity. If he were to rehabilitate the Islands he must take back the executive powers Governor General Harrison had allowed to lapse. The Legislature's submission was short-lived. After the first year he had to face a terrific political agitation organized against him by Quezon, who consistently opposed every measure General Wood proposed, and accused him of autocratic methods, even going as far as to demand his recall.

In rooting out the graft and corruption which had permeated the government service, General Wood had to make many removals, but even the most justifiable one would cause the most frightful abuse in the Filipino press. The General paid no attention to the clamor, but held to his appointed course. He knew that he had the administration at home behind him.

General Wood was always held up by his opponents as an extreme example of militarism, but in reality he was directly the opposite. I remember one particular occasion when he had a matter he wanted approved by a group of leaders. He invited them to the government office for a discussion. The conference began at nine-thirty in the morning. He set forth his views in great detail. His auditors were not in accord with them, but because of Filipino aversion to joining issue with someone in authority, they remained silent.

General Wood was extremely patient. He expounded everything over again. And a third time. The whole morning went by and the lunch hour arrived. The Governor said, "I suppose you gentlemen are hungry. Won't you take lunch with me?"

The silent opposition became vocal and accepted politely; an agreeable hour was passed in amicable conversation. Afterwards all adjourned once more to the office, and Wood resumed his unruffled round of argument. He talked at the Committee members all the afternoon. They had practically nothing to say—certainly not "yes."

When seven o'clock came, General Wood said, "You gentlemen must be starved. Won't you have dinner with me?"

The session lasted until late in the evening and was begun again the next morning. The second day followed the pattern of the first until finally, worn down by the Governor's unwearying calm, and replete with good food, they capitulated.

Filipino legislators were only silent when it served their purposes. More often, though, they conducted their business with formality, dignity, and decorum, they talked, and talked, always with waving arms and grandiloquent gestures.

General Wood attempted to win his victories by pacific means, but unfortunately he was often forced to use his veto power. As he explained to me, the bills which he vetoed and for which he was being criticized so much in the press had practically all been rejected after consultation with the Filipino leaders. Many of these bills were of a frivolous nature and designed to force any conscientious administrator into exercising his prerogative. Eighty-seven of them were passed the closing night of one Legislature, and it was humanly impossible for any member to know what they all contained. Even Quezon and his co-agitator Osmeña were astounded when they later saw the contents of the bills they had approved.

It was assumed by observers that these bills had been railroaded through with the full understanding of their worthless character and for the express purpose of forcing the General to use his veto power. The charge of tyranny was duly made by the Filipinos.

Even in the United States General Wood was branded as a militarist, and it was said constantly that he was dominated by the sabre and the spur and his methods were anything but pacific. His detractors pointed accusingly at his ex-officio cabinet which was composed of Army officers, sometimes called the cavalry, kitchen, or muchacho cabinet. But the explanation was simple. The Legislature was trying to curtail his activities by their oft-repeated and effective method of cutting down appropriations. These had been so reduced that no money was available to pay for any advisers, and General Wood had been forced to borrow from the Army, which gladly lent its best men.

Fortunately, the character of these officers was such that no accusation could stand the light of investigation. Major General Frank McCoy had had a long and distinguished career as General Wood's aide-de-camp in Cuba and, because of his gift of diplomacy, was to be appointed by President Coolidge to serve as peacemaker in the first presidential election in Nicaragua after the insurrection.

The chief fame of Colonel Gordon Johnston also rests upon his peace time activities. He was doing fine work in connection with the Guardian Society. The quartering of any army upon a people is followed by many illegitimate births. The military occupation had lasted so long in the Islands that the numbers of these children had reached the appalling figure of eighteen thousand. The mestizos of other races—Spanish, Chinese, and English—ranked high socially because their fathers saw to it that they were provided for materially. But the casual American soldier had generally evaded responsibility for his left-handed offspring. Many of the Filipina mothers, poor Cho-cho-sans abandoned by their Pinkertons, were forced to form new connections in which the children of the former alliances played no part. They usually sank to the lowest social strata; many of them were kept by the warmhearted but impoverished Filipina taos. No career was open to the pretty girls as they grew up except that of mistress to prominent Filipinos.

General Wood realized that these Army waifs should quite properly be wards of the country whose soldiers were responsible for their sad plight. We had until this time disgracefully shut our eyes to the situation. The Governor General delegated Colonel Johnston to organize the Guardian Society to take care of them. Many of the fathers who had returned to the United States were traced and made to contribute to their support. The aid of Catholic and Protestant organizations was enlisted, and they were persuaded to provide proper homes and arrange marriages. What had been a tragic situation was ameliorated. Colonel Johnston became foster-father to thousands of *café-au-lait* American orphans.

The loyalty of General Wood's personal following, who were intimately familiar with his daily life, was intense; they bitterly resented all criticism of him, and he, in turn, placed absolute reliance upon their honesty and judgment, and had the gift of eliciting the best in them. He had an original method of keeping associates and subordinates on their toes. On inspection trips in the government despatch boat *Apo*, his traveling office, he would have as his guests representatives of the railroads, the public works, the non-Christian Bureau, or the Health Department, depending on his particular interest of the moment—generally enough to make up a table of twelve to fifteen. At every stop all would go ashore, and, during the first meal afterwards, General Wood would ask each in turn to describe something unusual or particularly interesting he had seen. If anyone were caught napping the first time, he was sure to keep his eyes open the next so that he could contribute.

The real significance of the American work in the Islands had been to protect the masses against the classes. A constant struggle had been waged against the old order of things which tended to give additional privileges to an already privileged class. Because of their illiteracy, the great body of ignorant Filipinos had always been unable to make themselves heard, and for generations had remained in ignorance of their rights.

PICKING UP BROKEN THREADS

Though the politicos' campaign against General Wood was fierce, he retained the admiration and affection of the masses. Certain safeguards had been placed around all the preceding governor generals, but no need of these was ever felt in General Wood's case. Several times I have been riding through the provinces with him in his automobile when an old tao who had heretofore hardly dared lift his eyes to the cacique, now held up his gnarled hand, confident that he would not be rebuffed. General Wood never failed to stop. The tao, with patient eyes and shy smile, would approach in a respectful way, and say he wished to thank the General for all the fine things he was doing for the Filipinos.

As the years went by, one after another, they told more and more upon General Wood's strength. He often admitted to me he felt exhausted after struggling with Filipino officials in the effort to push them to some constructive action. We had all experienced this fatigue, but we did not somehow look for it in a man of General Wood's abundant energy and robust physique.

The Governor had more reason for exhaustion than any of us fully realized at the time. When he had been in Cuba as Governor General years before, he had one day risen suddenly from his desk and his head had come in contact with great force against an old-fashioned oil counter weight lamp, hung low from the ceiling. The triangular iron handle had penetrated his skull, and the injury had been followed by a tumor of the brain and a certain amount of paralysis of the left side. The tumor had twice been removed before he had gone to the Philippines. He should have returned to Dr. Harvey Cushing at the end of his first two years, but had been at that time in the thick of the fight and would not let go.

Because General Wood was an international figure, he was frequently photographed for news reels; often he was shown pre-views. I noted how stoically he looked at them, but it was apparent that it hurt him terribly to watch how painfully he lifted himself in and out of boats or automobiles; he had been so proud of his physical strength.

Only after six years, when he believed his work was nearly finished, would he consent to go home long enough to have the operation performed. But by then the tumor had grown to enormous size.

431

I happened to see moving pictures of the General's landing at Seattle, and was shocked to observe how one of the finest specimens of manhood I had ever known had changed; his entire side had become paralyzed. But even then he insisted on reporting in person and consulting over the best method of winding up his work in the Philippines, which he expected to do as soon as the operation was over. When finally he went to Boston for his long-delayed ordeal the blood vessels in the tumor had become so large that the hemorrhage could not be stopped and he died almost immediately. He had given his life as truly as any soldier on the firing line.

After General Wood's death, even the Filipino leaders who had fought him so bitterly admitted their animosity had been of a political nature only. They realized that, although they had not seen eye to eye with him, he had labored long and well in their behalf.

Henry L. Stimson, formerly Secretary of War in President Taft's cabinet, was appointed General Wood's successor. He had paid a visit to the General in the Philippines some six months earlier, had become conversant with affairs at that time, had approved the Wood policies wholeheartedly, and was prepared to continue them. The fight for the restoration of the powers of the executive had been already won, and Governor Stimson continued to exercise them. No acute question arose during his term; Coolidge prosperity ruled in the Islands as well as at home, and Governor Stimson's main objective was to set about the development of material resources so that the country might rest on a sound economic foundation.

Governor Stimson asked me to be his adviser, and the Rockefeller Foundation made it possible for me to remain longer than usual in the Islands. President Hoover shortly recalled him in 1929 to enter the cabinet as Secretary of State and in his place was selected Dwight F. Davis, D.S.C., donor of the Davis Cup for the international tennis championships, and public-spirited patron of art and culture in St. Louis. As Governor General he continued to be one of the most retiring of men, and consistently avoided publicity. Nothing was attempted which might have caused trouble during those years when the Filipinos were shouting louder than ever for independence. He told me privately he was not satisfied with his accomplishments, but that as long as the United States would not declare a definite policy toward the Philippines it was useless to attempt anything beyond keeping the situation peaceful.

Theodore Roosevelt, Jr., took office upon Governor Davis' resignation. He had inherited to a conspicuous degree his father's charm of manner, and became tremendously popular among the Filipinos. He came from the Governor Generalship of Puerto Rico speaking Spanish, was hail-fellow-well-met with one and all, radiated cheerful enthusiasm, and played upon the heartstrings of the emotional Filipinos who vibrated to his masterly touch. He devoted himself to them and made much of them socially. Not even former Governor Harrison in his heyday had won greater plaudits. I discussed with him, among other things, the anomalies of malaria in the Islands. Like his father he talked so continuously it was difficult to make a point with him, and his conversation was peppered with quotations from Kipling and the Bible in support of his theses.

The last Governor General of the Philippines was Frank Murphy, now representing the authority of the United States in the new Commonwealth. Although many believed his former public services as Mayor of Detroit were not sufficiently broad, by his acts he proved an exceedingly able administrator in a difficult situation, and became well liked by the Filipinos, who admire those who know how to play the political game.

We were morally bound to give the Filipinos their independence. President McKinley made the first commitment, and in the Jones Bill we again assured them they should have independence when they had a stable government. The moot point has always been the definition of a stable government. Does it rest upon the maintenance of law and order? Or upon self-sustaining power economically?

The heart of the question at the moment is indubitably one of economics. The Filipinos have been raised by means of the tariff privileges we have granted them to a standard of living formerly unheard of among Orientals. If we shut them out completely it is hard to see how they can exist.

I have a great deal of confidence in the Filipinos. They in return have a real liking for us, and feel their destiny is with us. Thousands

433

volunteered for service in the World War, although it was too late for them to go to France. They want to retain our goodwill, but we are handicapped because we spend no money to support our views, while opponents are active in propaganda.

Once more the Filipinos are given an opportunity to show their capacity for conducting their affairs in a manner which will be conducive to the general good. Their fate lies, to a great extent, in the hands of Manuel Quezon who of all Filipinos has had most political experience and has made the best use of it. President Quezon of the Philippine Commonwealth is not the same man as Resident Commissioner Quezon who used to play poker with Uncle Joe Cannon backstage in Washington, using an Independence Bill as stakes, and hoping for a lucky break.

Naturally I saw Quezon whenever I went to the Philippines, and visited him at Baguio during his long illnesses. As the years went by I found him increasingly frank.

In the fall of 1935 my telephone rang, and when I answered it a voice said, "I'll bet you don't know who this is."

"You're Manuel Quezon, the coming President of the Philippine Commonwealth," I replied.

"Yes, Doctor, you're right. I'm in the hospital. Will you come down and see me? I want to talk to you."

I went to the hospital. "What a big fool I am," he greeted me. "I let a newspaper friend of mine pick out a doctor. Why didn't I call you up in the first place? Now I want you to tell me whether I should let them operate on me."

"What's wrong with you?"

"Pepino," he called to his man. "Bring me the X-ray plates."

The briefest examination of them showed he had a stone in the kidney.

"The doctors want to take it out. What do you think of these New York surgeons anyhow?"

"They have excellent ones here," I assured him.

"But suppose this were your kidney and your stone. What would you do yourself?"

"I'd go to Dr. Hugh Young at Baltimore. He's been very successful."

"Pepino! Bring me my clothes. Get me a limousine. I'm going to Baltimore."

Then turning again to me, he spoke impulsively, "I want to talk to you on the way to the station. After your long experience in the Islands you know them from a health standpoint better than anybody else. I want you and General MacArthur and General Harbord to come out and advise me. Think it over and let me know whether you'll accept."

I told him honestly that I had little inclination to do so; that I had given many years of my life to establish a Health Service which he had allowed to decay. "See what's been done to the Bureau of Science which is so badly needed by your people," I reminded him.

"Oh, we'll fix that up again all right."

"How are you going to do it?" I inquired. "I've just been talking to Theodore Roosevelt. He says you used to have a revenue of sixty million. Now you have forty; once you are outside the United States tariff wall, you won't have more than twenty. That will barely cover the absolute necessities of government. How's there going to be anything left for the Health Department?"

"I have that all solved," he confidently asserted.

"How?"

"I've just been in Ireland, and have been studying the workings of the lottery there. We can have much better ones in the Philippines, and we'll sell most of the tickets to you Americans. The lottery will be under state control, and directed under the best auspices. It will bring in several million dollars a year anyhow, and perhaps as much as ten million. You can have it all for the Department of Health. I want you to be the only one to say how it is to be spent."

I had no doubt of the sincerity of his intentions. Quezon had admitted once to General Wood that he was swayed by his white blood in one direction and by his Oriental in another, but in spite of himself the predominant sway was toward the white. He has much force, energy, and moral courage. He may have a successful career as well as a tempestuous one. In spite of the many attempts on his life made by his political opponents, he has no physical fear. An automobile salesman once informed him an armored car could be manufactured to protect him against cranks for not much more than the price of the model used by ordinary citizens.

"No, sir, I'll have a landaulet, an open car. A statesman should know how to die in the performance of his duty."

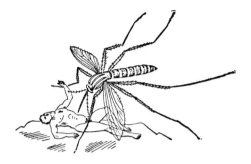

CHAPTER 25.   AN OUNCE OF
                PREVENTION

AMONG all tropical diseases malaria is supreme. In my experience it is the most persistent, the most destructive, the most widespread, and the most difficult of them all to control. Plague is terrible, but the precise method of its transmission is known, and rats can be eliminated. Cholera, smallpox, and beriberi have no excuse for being. Dysentery and typhoid could be wiped out. Though leprosy creates horror it seldom interferes with the march of progress; the poor and lowly are the principal sufferers. But for malaria there is no specific and the problem of prophylaxis is enormous in its complexity and expensiveness. The method of its widespread control is not yet out of its swaddling clothes.

Those races touched by the shaking finger of malaria have undergone a progressive decadence. The "glory that was Greece" faded out before its onslaughts and will not shine again until the minute pools in her broad rocky river beds cease to be a threat. The "grandeur that was Rome" paled centuries ago and only recently has the light flared up. The Campagna, the fertile farmland region around Rome from which the early Republic derived both its food and the men for its conquering peasant armies, has been the scene of recurrent waves of malaria. The drainage operations of the Etruscans had kept it healthy, but under Rome the population steadily declined. When fever and chills swept over the marshlands, the terrified populace sacrificed to the Goddess Mephitis, who, with her bald head, great paunch, swollen veins, and emaciated limbs, typified

437

the essence of horror. The city itself remained free because of the Cloaca Maxima and its communicating system of interlocking porous earthen pipes, which antedated our modern subsoil drainage installations by several centuries.

The barbarians lost army after army of their non-immunes; Alaric himself is said to have died of malaria. Pope after Pope tried to reclaim these Pontine marshes in vain. Not until "Il Duce" led the stagnant waters in huge canals to the sea did the land once more become fertile and the cities once more spring into life. It is magnificent and also startling to see Sabaudia and Littoria, modernistically designed from church to peasant dwelling, rising renascent from the desolation that was.

Whether malaria was endemic in the New World before the arrival of the discoverers and explorers is a matter of dispute. Certainly *calenturas* were mentioned early and often in contemporary accounts. The first Spanish venture of Columbus in Hispaniola had to be abandoned because of the "fevers." Half the inhabitants of Jamestown, encircled by the miasmic Virginia marshes, died within six months of their arrival. Up and down the coast the first settlements were established by the water courses, and even after the pioneers had moved into the primeval forest, in clearing it they left pools and standing water. Moreover, power to saw the lumber and grind the grist to house and feed those who, all unaware, were inviting malaria into their midst, was furnished by innumerable millponds.

From earliest times the connection of marshland and malaria had made itself apparent. Miasmas or mephitic airs arising, particularly at night, from these moist regions, were blamed for the disease, and the neighboring inhabitants believed safety could be assured only by closing every door and window against their entrance. When men began to apply scientific words to their observations of natural phenomena, they claimed malaria was due to the "decomposition of organic matter in low areas which thereby freed poisonous gases." This theory that disease was air borne had been, from time immemorial, accepted as a reason for epidemics. Malaria, especially, was subject to this plausible explanation.

Malaria, "bad air," was first so called by an Italian, Torti, in

1753, and introduced into England in 1827 as a specific name for the malady known variously and vaguely as marsh miasma, paludal poison, ague, jungle fever, hill fever, tropical fever, intermittent and remittent fever, or, simply, fever of the country.

The chills and fever so often described by the ancients were undoubtedly malaria, because the symptoms are so distinctive that there was little chance for confusion. Hippocrates, a native of Aegean Cos, had studied the disease in Asia Minor, where it was prevalent in the Fifth Century B. C., although it had not yet extended to Attica. The Father of Medicine had divided these fevers into quotidian, tertian, and quartan. This same differentiation of types is still retained; in the quotidian form the attack recurs daily, in the tertian every other day, and in the quartan every three days.

The chills, which last perhaps fifteen minutes, are usually accompanied by the most violent paroxysms. I have seen the malaria ward in a hospital actually tremble from the violence of the shivering; a single bed would move on the floor. The initial stage is followed by burning fever which rises to a peak, after which profuse perspiration breaks out and the patient gradually returns to normal temperature, and remains so until the next attack.

The Tenth Century Arabian poet, Al Mutanabbi, described in the following verses the disease which had become his companion.

> "I watch for her time of arrival without desire,
> Yet with the watchfulness of an eager lover,
> And she is ever faithful to her appointed time;
> But faithfulness is an evil
> When it casts thee into grievous suffering."

Malaria is often deadly in its action. In the cerebral form, parasites become so thick in the blood that they clog the capillaries of the brain and cause almost immediate death, and the same may be true if they lodge in the kidneys.

But a far larger number of cases are chronic; the parasites gradually destroy so many red blood corpuscles that extreme anemia results. The patient's liver does not function properly, he has frightful headaches, cannot eat, and takes no interest in anything. The most indicative symptom in the diagnosis of malaria is the enlargement

439

of the spleen "which often makes the belly protrude mightily." I have seen many a child so badly afflicted that his spleen bumped against his side as he walked, rather like a box showing through a bag. This condition is colloquially called ague cake.

Because malaria is age-old, physicians of every period have made attempts at cures. One of the Roman methods was to place under the head of a patient with quartan fever a copy of Homer, opened to the fourth book where the healing of wounded Menelaus is described.

In the Middle Ages treatment was little more efficacious. Patients were bled, were advised to change the air, fed wormwood, lettuce, crocus, linseed, given warm water to make them perspire. At times when an epidemic raged, huge bonfires were lit to purify the bad air.

But long before the disease was given its present name, its remedy was known in South America. In 1600, Spanish missionaries used the bark *quina quina* in Loxa, Peru. Don Francisco Lopez Canazares, Corregidor of Loxa, was himself cured in 1683, and thoughtfully sent a supply of the bark to Lima, six hundred miles away, for the use of Francesca de Rivera, second wife of Don Luis Geronimo Fernandez de Carera, Viceroy of Peru, stricken with tertian fever. She recovered and took a supply back with her to Spain. Her physician, Juan del Vego, followed her with more of the bark, which he disposed of at Seville for one hundred reales a pound.

In 1742 that industrious Swedish naturalist, Linnaeus, who dedicated his life to classifying and naming botanical specimens, made a slight error. He gave this bark the name of cinchona, after the deceased first wife of the Viceroy, Anna, Countess of Chinchon, who had never been to Peru, had never been ill of malaria, and had never taken the medicine. Before that it had been known as Jesuit's Powder or Bark, because the Jesuit order, as the power behind the throne in Peru, had a monopoly of quinine sales. The priests received its weight in gold from those who could afford to pay; to the poor it was free. The supply was never equal to the demand, and in the effort to adjust the balance, the trees of South America were stripped of their bark and largely destroyed.

The failure of the South American governments to protect the source of supply from this destruction brought efforts to cultivate cinchona elsewhere. In 1852 seeds and plants were introduced into the Buitenzorg Botanical Garden in Java, where the Dutch tended them carefully. Four hundred and fifty live plants were transported to India by Sir Clements Markham with great difficulty. Soon the Ceylon planters had the monopoly on production. But then Charles Ledger, in 1865, made it possible for the industry to take a great forward stride by grafting a Brazilian variety on another wild variety which had a strong root system and would flourish in less fertile soil. Until that time cinchona production had not been successful in Java. But the Dutch found they had ideal conditions for the cultivation of this grafted cinchona. The Ceylon planters had to cut down their trees and set tea shrubs in their places.

With perfected technique, the Dutch no longer killed the tree by stripping the bark. They kept the supply perpetual by constant thinning and pruning. Now, only the young twigs, which have the largest percentage of alkaloid, are used for bark. With the monopoly thus secured, the price was kept so high that thousands died because they could not afford to buy. The Dutch always insisted it cost them a great deal to produce quinine, but skeptics suspected that, since the expense of extracting the alkaloid was known to be relatively small, the profits must be unduly large.

The task of breaking the Dutch monopoly seemed for a long time utterly hopeless, but, because the price of quinine was a matter of world-wide importance, I suggested to the Health Section of the League of Nations that this was a type of activity admirably suited to its purposes. The League fell in with this idea and began from Geneva a campaign of "pitiless publicity," subtly planned and beautifully carried out. Its effectiveness lay in its simplicity. The figures of quinine production appeared at stated intervals in League bulletins. "Over nine hundred tons out of a thousand were produced in the Dutch East Indies. The price in 1890 was such and such; now in 1917 it has risen to such and such." The great difference between the early low cost and the later high one told its own story.

Years were spent in bringing down the price. But on each of my European trips I visited Geneva, and each time I talked cheaper quinine. If the officials evidenced a lessening of interest in it, I would spur them on by relating some of the harassing tales I had heard of fellow human beings who were afflicted with malaria and lacked the means for relief. The campaign continued with renewed vigor. Nothing was said directly; no attack was made. But the Dutch found the shoe fitted and began to be sensitive.

The campaign had been progressing for some time when I happened to visit a prominent Dutch gentleman in the Netherlands who owned many shares in a Javanese quinine estate. Unaware of my interest in the subject, he said, "It's terrible! We're gouging the whole world. I'm going to get rid of my stock and wash my hands of the whole business!"

This feeling was shared by so many people and in time the opprobrium became so great that gradually the cost of quinine was voluntarily reduced.

The citizens of the United States can with difficulty comprehend the poverty of the races which are most scourged with malaria, or the blessing which a cheaper drug conveys upon them. We had depended upon quinine exclusively in the Philippines, and had struggled constantly with Chinese druggists who found it profitable to make pills out of lime and sell them at a high price. The credulous Filipinos had been deceived by the similarly bitter taste. We had put the genuine drug on sale at the office of every municipal and township treasurer throughout the Islands at a cost of nine cents for a dozen five-grain tablets. Instead of arresting and fining the Chinese druggist, we had found it far more effective to put him out of the quinine business by offering the drug at a price lower than his bogus lime tablets.

An extract of all the alkaloids in cinchona barks called totaquina, the great advantage of which is its cheapness, is now being recommended by the League of Nations Malaria Commission. The average Filipino, for example, cannot even afford the two and a half pesos for two hundred and fifty grains of quinine, an average treatment, but can usually find the necessary thirty-five centavos for totaquina.

I had naturally suggested to various laboratories throughout the world the possibility of manufacturing quinine synthetically, but had met with little enthusiasm for the idea. I was always assured it would be extremely difficult and costly; the research would be long, and the result problematic. But the indefatigable Germans were undeterred by these considerations. They began experimenting, and have recently produced two synthetic drugs, plasmochin and atebrin. However, they are apparently not yet entirely satisfied with results, because they have made no attempt to capture the world market. In a number of respects, plasmochin and atebrin are more effective than quinine, particularly in treating the malignant types of malaria, but many drugs that seem so good in the first trials prove to have deleterious after effects. Until more is known about these drugs they should only be administered by a physician. Quinine, on the other hand, can be taken by anybody, and seldom more than temporary deafness results from overdosing. Until recently the belief was firmly established that quinine was a specific for malaria, and had a lethal action on the malaria parasite. Later research throws doubt on this sweeping conclusion, but, nevertheless, quinine cannot be dispensed with in malarial treatment.

Nor is quinine a prophylactic for malaria. The drug has not yet been found which will kill all forms and stages of the parasite promptly. Although as long as quinine is taken there will be no attack, the parasites are ever lying in wait, ready to appear, if, as too often happens, the patient wearies at the long and tedious treatment, and stops it too soon.

"The Roman fevers are faithful according to an imprescriptable right. Whom once they have touched they do not abandon as long as he lives."

Thus despairingly wrote Peter Damian in 1060 from his malaria-ridden bishopric of Ostia, the ancient port of Rome.

It is true malaria may recur in one year, or two years, or after many years. The parasites hide away in the deep recesses of the body, such as the spleen and the bone marrow. One of the paradoxes with which the subject of malaria abounds is that often when latent cases are removed to cold climates the disease recurs; it is also true that the colder the climate, the greater the hope for a complete cure.

It had been obvious for a long time that water played an important part, but no one was able to bridge the hiatus between cause and effect until the end of the Nineteenth Century. Then Sir Patrick Manson, who, after his successful demonstrations in filaria, was still eagerly interested in research on the theory of insect transmission of diseases, stimulated Major Ronald Ross, a former pupil, to try various experiments with mosquitoes. Many of these failed but after each disappointment Manson would write Ross letters of encouragement, and would suggest some new method of attacking the problem of malaria transmission.

The hundreds of known varieties of mosquitoes are divided broadly into the culex and anopheles groups. Little was known of their habits except that the male lived on fruit and was quite harmless; only the female bit. Ross had naturally picked upon Culex fatigans, the common tiger mosquito, as the villain. This was readily understandable, because of all the hundreds of varieties it was the most common and annoying in its numbers, its buzz, and its bite.

After laboring for many years Ross finally in 1897 found the same type of cell in a dapple-winged anopheles mosquito that the Frenchman, Laveran, in 1880 had discovered in Algeria in the blood of a human being suffering from malaria.

In this connection it seems only fair to mention that in the beginning Manson believed filariasis was transmitted by water or its emanations, previously contaminated by mosquitoes which had bitten persons with filariasis. It was not until after the American, Dr. Theobald Smith, in 1889 had shown that cattle fever was transmitted by the *bite* of a tick that transmission of filariasis by the *bite* of mosquitoes was proved. In 1894–95 Bruce demonstrated the transmission of trypanosomes by means of the fly, glossina. These discoveries helped clear the path and established the method by which malaria was transmitted.

An anopheline is usually distinguishable because of the little black dots on her wings, which other mosquitoes do not have, and because she looks as though she were standing on her head when biting. A tremendous number of enemies are ready to destroy her; she cannot even stand wind or bright sunshine. Her life history occupies only about one month, but as long as she lives, she has a meal every two to three nights. The swelling from her bite is not large, nor is the itch particularly annoying—sometimes a person does not even know he has been bitten—yet one bite is enough to cause malaria.

Malaria can only be contracted from a mosquito which has previously fed on someone who had malaria parasites in his blood. Years of study were devoted to discovering the complex and almost improbable life cycle of this tiny animal organism called the plasmodium. Many lacunae in our knowledge still remain. But when an infected anopheline bites a human being, with its saliva are introduced a number of rod-like objects, pointed at each end, called sporozoites, which, with graceful undulating movement go swimming off into the blood stream. For eight or nine days they disappear completely from view. Repeated examination of the blood reveals no trace of them, and nobody as yet knows what is taking place. When they next come into view, they have changed their shape completely. Tiny little rings, called schizonts or trophozoites, much smaller than the rods, now are discoverable inside the red corpuscles. These increase rapidly in number and size, some becoming sexual and others non-sexual. Each cell of the latter type at regular intervals divides itself into as many as fourteen smaller ones, and whenever this segmentation takes place, toxins are freed—thus accounting for the periodicity of the disease—and the human host suffers chills and fever.

The sexual forms, the gametocytes, go circulating in the blood stream and do no harm. But if some of that blood happens to be sucked up by an anopheline mosquito of the right variety, then the sexual life of the plasmodium begins. The female cell is fertilized inside the mosquito, and then elongates, penetrates the wall of the mosquito's stomach, and attaches itself to the outside of the gut in the peritoneal cavity. There it begins to grow, and forms a cyst which eventually bursts and frees a vast number of sporozoites. These penetrate all parts of the mosquito's body, some of them lodging inevitably in the salivary glands, ready to be deposited in a human with the mosquito's next meal. During the twelve days required for this process, she cannot infect a human being. At no time, apparently, does she receive any injury from incubating the plasmodia.

Malaria flourishes in a broad zone on both sides of the Equator, where it assumes vast proportions, creating great economic loss and taking a high toll of human lives. It is also endemic for some distance into the temperate zones, diminishing, however, in frequency and severity. Poor old Africa, from which the slave trade broadcast so much disease, is, as usual, assumed to have been the seed bed. But the largest centers are in Asia. In India it is the arch-destroyer; half the three hundred and fifty million population are estimated to suffer from it, and one million die annually. These are stupendous figures. Turkey, Syria, Palestine, Malaya, Siam, Indo-China, Java, Sumatra, the Philippines, and China are all intensely malarial.

In Europe there have been outbreaks in the Netherlands and England until recent times. Huge epidemics occurred during and after the World War in Macedonia, Serbia, Rumania, and Russia. Greece and Italy are badly affected. But in Denmark and Norway malaria is practically unknown. Why some places are exempt or why the seeming immunity of others is suddenly broken down is difficult to explain. Penang was healthy until occupied in 1786 by the British, and became malarious a few years later; clearing off the jungle and exposing the pools did not seem sufficient explanation. Chile and Barbados were free of it until 1927 when cases began to occur.

Though today largely confined to the hot countries, malaria does occur in the United States, at one time extending as far north as Wisconsin. At the first settling it was common in Connecticut, but disappeared, only to return when Italian immigrants, who swarmed in to occupy the abandoned farms, brought the infection in their veins. It was so prevalent in the nineties along the Sound that when the Cambridge crew came over from malaria-free England to compete in the races, during the course of the final training near New London some of the oarsmen caught malaria and subsequently lost to Yale. They claimed it was just another of those damn Yankee tricks.

Year by year the malaria line in this country is receding. The disease was once bad enough in Washington to interfere with the sittings of Congress. But draining and improving the surrounding land has gradually eliminated the anopheles there. In the South, broadly speaking, malaria is largely man-made. Railroad embankments and the more recently built automobile roads were thrown up across the country, and the drainage culverts were often a little higher than the level of the water in the trenches or ditches. These created perfect artificial breeding places for mosquitoes, which added to the ever-present danger from swamps.

Since the aim of the International Health Board was to promote public health so that local health departments could get a legitimate share of appropriations, and as hookworm demonstrations gradually began to achieve this object, the subject of malaria grew more and more important. Accordingly, we embarked on a program which included both a study of the incidence of the disease, and the type and breeding habits of the mosquito responsible, so that control could be attempted at the larvae stage. Our hope was finally to devise means whereby poor communities might effect control at a price they could afford.

In 1916 the International Health Board made a demonstration at Crossett, Arkansas, that a community could be freed of malaria by freeing it of mosquitoes, and within a reasonable cost. When this was successful the work was gradually extended until in 1921 a general attack upon the disease was being made.

The perplexing questions raised from the entomological angle proved malaria to be a paradox of paradoxes. Many ideas and theories were completely upset; even the nomenclature of mosquitoes had to be changed as our knowledge of types was extended. All progress in malaria control is accomplished by a narrowing process. It was a tremendously complex study in itself to determine which mosquitoes caused what disease and where. Yellow fever and dengue, or breakbone fever, as well as filaria and malaria, are transmitted by the bite of a mosquito.

There were over thirty species of anopheles in the Philippines and twenty-two on the Island of Luzon alone, but only one or two were an important factor in carrying malaria. Moreover, a given species might be dangerous in one country and not in another. In Batavia, Java, where the geographical and climatic conditions were practically identical with those of Manila, frightful malaria was transmitted by the same anopheles which was harmless in Manila. To complicate the problem in the South Seas, malaria was extremely severe in the New Hebrides, but was totally lacking in neighboring New Caledonia which was in constant communication with it, and where no quarantine precautions were observed by the French.

Malaria was extremely vicious in Asia, diminishing in intensity with the distance therefrom. The Rockefeller Foundation representative in Siam, Dr. Milford E. Barnes, found thirty-four varieties. There were not quite so many in the Dutch East Indies, only three or four in Dutch New Guinea, in Australian Papua only one, and Fiji, though it swarmed with culex, had no anopheles whatever.

For a long time it was believed in Europe that the maculipennis

447

was the only malaria-carrying anopheles. But several factors seemed confusing. For example, in one section of Italy where the maculipennis was numerous there was no malaria, and in another where it was scarce, malaria was very bad. The larvae of mosquitoes from both regions appeared identical. Finally the simple idea of examining the eggs occurred to a retired sanitary inspector named Faleroni, and, instead of one maculipennis, he was able to distinguish five varieties. Further investigation showed some of these carried malaria and some did not.

Further progress in research in Italy was hampered by the difficulty of finding infected mosquitoes in bedrooms, their common and logical hiding places. Ordinarily not more than four percent of the anopheles in a given region are infected, but if the bedroom is dark the anopheles, after biting, remains and hides there until it is time for another meal. If this bedroom is occupied by a person with malaria the percentage of hazard to others in the home is normally greater than the percentage of mosquito infection in the district. Dr. L. W. Hackett, the Foundation's malariologist in Italy, took one thousand mosquitoes from a bedroom in an Italian home where all the members had malaria, and found in every case the anopheles had fed on cows' blood. It had always been assumed they had been securing nourishment from the humans in the house, but actually they had only been taking shelter after their meal.

The anopheles is not usually found above the 3,000 foot level; 2,000 feet was the height in the Philippines, but under rare conditions it flew higher; 4,500 in Malaya, 6,000 in Mexico, 6,500 in Lebanon, and 8,000 in the Himalayas.

The horizontal flight of the anopheles was discovered to extend far beyond the hundred yards once set as the limit. Although the large sturdy-winged New Jersey culex has been known to travel forty miles, the average distance for the anopheles is about one mile. At Camp Stotsenberg in the Philippines individual mosquitoes would fly over two miles to get a feeding of blood, but the average was too low to do much harm at that distance.

Mosquitoes are most persistent in their search for a blood meal. In Georgia we selected for our experiment a certain swamp caused by one of the numerous limestone outcrops which, wherever they occur in low ground, bring about the accumulation of water, difficult to drain. In this marsh many anopheles were known to breed. The nearest house was a mile away over the crest of a hill, and between the swamp and the house were many pine trees which had been ringed by turpentine gatherers and later died, leaving the branches bare so that mosquitoes could not hide among them. One summer a group of college students was assembled, and each one stationed in a tree with a huge mosquito net. All the insects caught were sprayed with a carmine stain. When released, they invariably flew in the direction of the house, although it was out of their sight and had no lights. If the weather were windy, they might proceed no more than a tree or two, and remain sheltered on the lee side. If the weather were more favorable, they would make greater progress, but always at night. Sooner or later, if they survived, they arrived at the house, ready for the anticipated dinner.

In every survey which was made, the first task was to study the habits of the local mosquitoes. The culprits had to be run down, and then enough facts detected about them so that the proper offense measures might be taken.

In the Philippines malaria was widespread from the Bashi Channel in the North to the Sulu Sea in the South. The approximately two million cases a year resulted in from ten to twenty thousand deaths, although practically none of these occurred in the principal cities of Manila, Cebu, or Iloilo. Malaria interfered with every enterprise. In getting the lumber out of the forests and raising sugar cane in the fields, laborers died by the hundred. Because of malaria, Mindoro, a great and fertile island in sight of the mouth of Manila Bay, was supporting only a sparse population of semi-civilized people. Hundreds had died there under the Spanish régime in the effort to start sugar plantations, and the first American attempts fared little better. Although as a direct cause of death malaria ranked fourth in the Islands, as a humanitarian and economic problem it ranked among the first.

Outside of Manila we had to deal with extensive population shifts during the various harvest seasons. It was the rule that laborers went

449

from their native towns to distant ones or to the mountains to collect forest products. On such occasions they frequently built lean-to shelters along ditches in which anopheles bred abundantly.

It was difficult for the lay mind to associate danger with anything which appeared as harmless as a mosquito. Many of the Filipinos adhered tenaciously to the bad air theory and absolved the mosquito from all blame while she went on with her deadly work. The simple-minded tao could see no direct cause and effect, particularly since the mosquito bite did not annoy him as much as it did a thicker-skinned race. He had sojourned on terms of a "live and let live" relationship all his days.

In Manila, if the innocent day mosquito, the stegomyia persistans, or the equally blameless night mosquito, the fatigans, were allowed to breed, the Bureau of Health was promptly accused of laxness. The fatigans bred in drain pipes, septic tanks, and cesspools, and the persistans chose rain barrels, house gutters, cans and bottles.

During the first year of the mosquito campaign the householder was given instructions by the mosquito squad of the Bureau of Health. Receptacles were emptied, other collections of water were covered with petroleum, and storm gutters were frequently flushed out by the Fire Department. If mosquitoes were thereafter found breeding on private premises, the occupants were listed on the roll of dishonor in the daily newspapers. This procedure had a very good effect. The culprits' names became bywords throughout the town. The few remaining delinquents were taken before the court, where fines for maintaining a nuisance were imposed. The enforcement of these measures resulted in eliminating practically all the mosquitoes which annoy man.

For years we could not account for the absence of malaria in Manila, which had so many anopheles mosquitoes. Furthermore, the great valleys of the Islands were also practically free of the disease. This too was a great puzzle.

Some progress had been made by oiling the surface, draining, and experimenting with larvae eating fish while I was Director of Health. The Bureau of Science had imported Texan gambusia—extraordinary minnows able to live equally well in salt, fresh, running, or stagnant water. But in the Philippines they were unable to fulfill their high purpose because of an even more extraordinary fish. The peripatetic dalag, or mudfish, pursued the tasty gambusia with avidity, and even hopped overland from pool to pool in quest of these delectable morsels. In the fountains and similar places the gambusia were able to keep the water free of larvae; in the ponds and esteros they were quickly eaten by the questing dalag, who himself often furnished food for Filipino appetites.

In spite of all our attempts at control, the problem was by no means near a solution. The campaign was given new impetus when I returned to the Islands in 1921. One evening after dinner Governor General Wood and I were sitting, as was our custom, on the veranda of Malacañan.

"I've a very pleasant surprise for you," the General said, "I've secured a million dollars for you to spend on malaria. According to the health reports, thirty thousand people are dying annually from it, and it's time we wiped it out."

"General," I replied, "I wouldn't know how to spend as much as that productively. From what I've learned about mosquitoes, the mere expenditure of money won't help toward the solution."

"Why not? That's the way they did it in Panama."

"But they never had to sanitate more than a few square miles in the Canal Zone while we have thousands."

"Of course you can get rid of it if you'll drain the swamps. That will cut malaria down right away."

"But, General, we're running into all sorts of contradictions in the study of malaria. Isn't it possible that swamps may not be responsible for malaria here?"

"They have everywhere else. Why not here?"

"Nobody's proved it, and it's not a scientific way of finding out."

"Well, that's the way I want it done!" was General Wood's categorical response.

I considered that the General, himself a medical man, should not have taken such an attitude. "In that case, General, I'd better stop," I said. "I can't proceed that way. It won't be difficult for you to find someone to work on the problem as you may direct, and your method may be right. I hope it is."

The subject was dropped on this uncompromising note. But the next morning, after a good night's sleep, the General, as was his wont, repented his gruffness and was extremely apologetic. "What do I know about malaria? Forget everything I said, and tell me your ideas."

"In the first place, I'd like to know whether all the deaths ascribed to malaria are really due to that cause. And, if they are, I'd like to find out why all the measures we've taken in the malarial districts have so far been practically ineffective. I suggest asking the International Health Board for help in getting a good malariologist here to make a survey."

Wood agreed to this program without a moment's hesitation, and as soon as possible Walter D. Tiedeman was brought to the Islands. He selected four towns, each representing a geographical type—one hill town, one lowland, one bordering a lake, and one lake village influenced by running water from nearby hillsides.

Fortunately the species of anopheles which carried malaria flew only late at night, the exact time depending somewhat on the moon. On dark nights, contrary to mosquito customs in the United States, where the flight begins at sundown, they did not put in an appearance until twelve-thirty or one. We knew that we could sit or move with perfect safety until bedtime—it was impossible to sit on a screened veranda in the Philippines in comfort because the screens shut off the breeze and made the heat intolerable—but must sleep under mosquito bars if we wished to avoid infection.

The Anopheles minimus was already convicted of guilt. But in the Philippines it was never found in the house during the daytime. Before any preventive measures could be taken, its home must be located.

All sorts of experiments were made. Among others, beds were arranged in trees so that biting habits at different elevations might be studied. The beds were baited with men and the sides of the mosquito bars left open. At about eleven the first minimus arrived for her meal, but the bars were not closed until enough had entered for experimental purposes. At two o'clock, after having fed, the insects were becoming distinctly uneasy, at three they were agitatedly seeking an exit, at four they were practically committing mass suicide, jamming their heads between the interstices of the nettings, and even breaking off their wings. They were obviously motivated by some tremendous homing instinct.

After having been sprayed with carmine, the prisoners were released and immediately a hunt was organized. Stones were overturned, blades of grass and leaves scrutinized, tree trunks examined. The search continued for two years and cost thousands of dollars but ultimately the hiding place of the minimus was ferreted out. In the Philippines the streams were always lined with bamboo, and where the current undercut the banks, the bamboo rootlets formed a tangled mass into which the elusive minimus would retreat during the daytime.

It was thus proved that malaria in the Islands was associated with the swift running waters of the foothills. Had Wood's million been spent in draining swamps, it would have been completely wasted.

This fundamental discovery gave us the information required for a fresh start in malaria control. Rice chaff was scattered on the surface of the stream, and as it floated along an observer noted where it stopped in the little eddies. In those places larvae or wrigglers were often found in abundance.

The eggs of the Anopheles minimus were laid among the bamboo rootlets on the surface of the water. Sometimes in the course of one day the larvae would form, and with the chisel-shaped egg breakers on the backs of their heads would cut their way through the shells. They would then lie on the surface to feed, breathing air with tiny tubes pushed up through the surface film, and brushing into their mouths any minute particles which might float their way. These wrigglers would take a week to develop into adult mosquitoes—if the water were cold, even longer.

The problem of eradicating the minimus would have been difficult of solution had we not been able to utilize the wonderful discovery made by Dr. Barber that the acetoarsenite of copper compound known commercially as Paris green, when mixed with ninety-nine parts of fine dry road dust, and released in clouds above the surface of the stream, would kill the larvae. The mixture is so effective that if larvae were living in a dish in a room, and somebody around the

453

corner poured the mixture from one container to another, enough would sift through the air, drift through the open windows, and settle on the dish to kill the larvae.

Paris green had this additional advantage. Water treated with it could be used for bathing, washing clothes, or even be drunk with impunity, whereas pouring oil on water rendered it unfit for use. One of the latest developments is a machine run by a paddle wheel in the stream, which scatters the Paris green automatically over the surface of the water.

The discovery that malaria in the Philippines does not exist in the lowlands but only in the foothill country was turned to immediate use. The Army had established Camp Stotsenberg, with two thousand men, in the supposedly malaria-free foothills, and had employed all the anti-malarial devices effective at Panama. But in spite of every effort, the soldiers still contracted the disease, because the camp had been established in the one place where the Anopheles minimus was to be found in the greatest numbers. The disease was eliminated almost at once by spraying Paris green on the streams that ran down the two valleys leading to the reservation.

In almost every problem of malaria, the basic approach is to survey local conditions and then apply the remedy. It may be as simple as having carabao walk through a stream to disturb the larvae, or compelling natives to turn their discarded cocoanut shells upside down, or it may consist of the most elaborate and expensive engineering operations. In the course of the demonstrations we encountered many baffling problems in engineering. Even drainage operations, when not correctly planned, have sometimes done great damage by creating breeding places where none existed before.

The Rockefeller Foundation now has engineers who travel from country to country with the sole object of advising on malaria control. One of their more important jobs was in Palestine which, governed under mandate by Great Britain, had an efficient health service, but was still unable to cope successfully with malaria.

Palestine has never been self-sustaining; it has been maintained for centuries by the world's charity. Even the Jewish colonies established by the Rothschilds were economically unsuccessful. After the World War the Jews arrived in great numbers at their ancient but long deserted home with the intent of making it self-contained, and of establishing prosperity on a firm agricultural basis. Most of the Zionists were sentimental ancients or young enthusiasts with few children. In spite of all that can be done, no more than a quarter of them are in agriculture. They persist in drifting into shops; Tel-Aviv is a typical East Side New York.

The country as a whole is most desolate. Its series of steep hills and narrow valleys are covered by loose stones about the size of a fist. The few arable sections are found near the seacoast and in the Jordan Valley. In the former, citrus fruit is grown, but the climate is so dry that every orange tree must be surrounded by a dike through which water has to be pumped at frequent intervals, thus creating additional water hazards. The Jordan Valley is fertile, but, owing to the pernicious malaria which abounds there, cultivation has been almost impossible, and those who have made the attempt frequently paid with their health, if not their lives. It was for years impossible to determine the source of the malaria so prevalent in the district around Tiberias, because it was certain anopheles could not breed in the brackish waters of the Sea of Galilee, and no other possible breeding grounds could be located. Finally, some tiny springs were found in the hillside.

American engineers introduced expert methods of dynamiting and blasting to drain the stagnant pools and swamps. Strings of explosive were laid from these to the lowlands and then exploded, making channels instantaneously. Streams that could not be dealt with in this manner were treated with Paris green. The cultivation of the land made available by the irrigation project was in itself a deterrent to mosquito breeding.

Some years ago the All America Cables had a small station on the West Coast of Nicaragua, the staff of which was losing as high as fifty hours a week from sickness among its few employees. One of the Rockefeller engineers was despatched there, and found the station located in a dent in the high hills out of which water trickled and collected in the station. By digging a circular ditch around the back of the town, the weeping water was collected in one place, and

455

there treated with Paris green. One thousand hours of time yearly were saved to that small group of cable employees by this simple device.

In Malaya the economic aspect of malaria was of supreme importance. Along the coast were thousands of miles of alluvial plain, bordered with mangrove swamps, and there was not a village which did not pay toll to malaria. In this vast, sparsely inhabited country, so newly opened to the rubber industry, no domestic animals were kept in the coolie lines, and human beings alone furnished blood for the mosquitoes. Death rates of over two hundred per thousand were not uncommon on some of the estates; nobody knew the answer.

There were three malaria-carrying anopheles in Malaya. The umbrosus dwelt in the jungle, the ludlowii in the brackish water along the coast, and the maculatus bred almost everywhere—in the bottom of a ditch, in a little water from a crack, amid spots of green algae where the water was no more than one-eighth of an inch deep. Because the maculatus is a seepage breeder it is extremely difficult to reach and control.

One of the great problems in Malaya was the constant silting which had occurred in the river beds that took drainage from the tin mine washings. Many of these river bottoms were raised so high that water from them wandered all over the country, forming innumerable pools, big and little.

Paris green had been of inestimable assistance in many places, but it was not all-encompassing. Some question had arisen of its effectiveness against a seepage breeder such as maculatus. On many estates and in many communities it was desired to get rid of culex also, but Paris green had no effect on culex larvae. To kill mosquito larvae Paris green must be eaten. The anopheles feeds at the surface, but the culex feeds with its head hanging below and consequently eats only particles in suspension, missing the Paris green, which floats on the surface.

A thin film of petroleum spread over the surface will kill all mosquito larvae by preventing them from obtaining air. But oil also had its advantages and disadvantages. In many places it was too expensive for use, and it was, of course, ineffective on running streams. From the point of view of supervision oil was favored. The health officer merely had to drive along the road and could see at a glance whether the coolie had done his job, whereas chemical analysis was required to discover whether water had been treated with Paris green.

The principal trouble on Malayan plantations, determined only after long search, was found to have come from cutting down the jungle, because maculatus larvae, which, unlike the adult mosquitoes, loved sunlight, would breed like mad as soon as the pools were exposed, while in the dark they would not multiply. If the planters refrained from felling the jungle, or if after felling they encouraged second growth, the anopheles could be kept under control.

Singapore in the old days was a veritable death trap. Gilbert Brooke, who held the office of Chief Health Officer of Rural Singapore, became so interested that he regarded mosquitoes as his avocation as well as his vocation. He made a hobby of these insects, and was writing a book about them, largely compiled from a huge mass of literature. Brooke read me a long poem from Vergil in the original, and then translated a passage which he interpreted as proving that the gnats therein described must have been culex mosquitoes.

The mosquito danger in Singapore came not only from maculatus but also from ludlowii, although the former was still the chief offender. The cost of dealing with them was high, but fortunately the Straits Settlements in those days of the rubber boom could afford it.

Every time the slightest excavation was made, the maculatus would breed plentifully. The site of the new city reservoir had been an old coffee plantation long abandoned because of its malaria rate. The huge granite boulders in the stream beds which fed it were flattened with dynamite, so that no pools could remain in the dry season. The crevices in rocks with pot holes, which gave rise to such intensive breeding, were filled with cement, making a smooth surface throughout. On the hillsides subsoil pipes were laid, covered with crushed stone and several feet of earth seeded with grass.

The ludlowii breeds in brackish water, Singapore lies right on the sea, and the spring tides always flooded the flats with salt water. Thereafter, when the daily rains diluted these residual pools to

457

the right degree of salinity, the ludlowii flourished. Subsoil drainage was begun for their elimination when the Naval Base, which was to prove British power to the East, was started in 1923. But the short-lived pacifistic Labor government stopped the work, and it was not recommenced until 1925. The onrush of the jungle in tropical lands is so swift that the location of these pipes, laid eighteen months before, was lost and could not even be found. It was necessary to begin the work all over again.

In most of the countries to which I went, the health authorities were exceedingly anxious to secure help in their malaria problems. Pushed more or less by the native members, the Ceylon government was anxious to start an island-wide malaria control campaign, and intimated that large sums, possibly a million rupees, could be made available. But the firm policy of the Foundation was never to embark in any undertaking without a thoroughly competent survey having first been made. This survey revealed that, although there were eighteen types of anopheles on the Island, the only proved carrier was culicifacies. It had a wide range of breeding places—slow moving sandy rivers and pools, but also irrigation channels, quarries, open drains, clear fresh sunlit water, even hoofprints of cattle.

Special attention was paid to Anuradhapura, a section of Ceylon so arid that in the days of its magnificence water had been brought in by canals for storage and irrigation purposes, and thus had created its own malaria problem. We found that reservoirs and canals still leaked abundantly through crawfish holes and seepage along penetrating roots. The hazard of many years ago had been further increased by borrow pits beside the railroad and leaks from rice paddies. It was a question of efficient engineering to make the malaria disappear.

Malaria could be wiped out anywhere if enough money were spent, but the question of economically feasible control, particularly in rural areas, was constantly arising. In Ceylon the survey showed the average per capita cost would be six rupees, and no island-wide campaign would be practicable at this figure.

It is one of the paradoxes of malaria that in India it becomes epidemic with heavy rainfall, while in Ceylon the death rate soars with drought. The reason for this is clear upon analysis. In the

Punjab, the vast plain drained by the Indus, pools are left in the depressions of the land after the rains in July and August, and in these the mosquitoes breed. In Ceylon, the geography is quite different. The south central part of the island is a mass of hills and mountains whose peaks rise to seven thousand feet. From these flow numerous rivers and streams, many of which are only outlet channels for the storm water of the monsoon. Pools remain as drought shrinks the rivers.

In October, 1934, began the worst drought in the history of Ceylon, accompanied by one of the major malaria epidemics of history. In the ensuing seven months, out of a population in the affected district of three million, half had the disease. In some places the infection was one hundred percent. Eighty thousand lives were lost in the period, village life was paralyzed, agricultural operations ceased, trade and business stopped almost completely. The whole medical force was mobilized, the school houses were taken over as clinics, and everybody was supplied with free quinine. At the height of the epidemic, more than sixty thousand a day were treated.

An expert malariologist, supplied by the British government, was at once called into consultation. Hitherto such epidemics had been regarded as inevitable but after an exhaustive study he reported that, although epidemics could not be halted once under way, it should be possible, by combining all known methods and, especially, training the river beds to eradicate breeding places, to prevent their recurrence.

All over the world students, research workers, field and laboratory scientists are working on malaria. Until some method can be devised which is capable of general application, there is little hope of bringing the disease under complete control. The most that can be said today is that if enough money is spent, a malarial district can be made healthy; but it is a long and persistent task, and only unremitting care meets with success.

In the tropics there is no end to malaria control; as soon as anti-malaria measures are stopped, the disease recurs. At one time Bombay was building a new port area, and nearly all crews of ships that anchored in that section of the Bay caught malaria. The situation became so serious that ships were short-handed. It was finally discovered that rain had collected in half-completed basements nearby, and the mosquitoes had bred there, thus infecting the sailors. The work of ridding the port area of mosquitoes was so well done that the city fathers said, "We have no malaria"; and did away with the appropriation.

Malaria at once returned.

Even with the knowledge at our command, malaria control is not always possible. In the East religion sooner or later steps upon the scene. In Bombay the Parsees, who follow a strange cult, were dominant in the business affairs of the city. They are to be encountered everywhere in the city, readily distinguishable by their odd wooden hats, covered with yellowish and black oilcloth. They live in huge tenement-like structures built around a little courtyard in the middle of which is a well, sometimes thirty feet deep. On the roofs are vast cisterns. Both wells and cisterns are uncovered because all Parsees regard the four elements—earth, air, fire, and water—as sacred and uncontaminable.

In Bombay the malaria carrier is Anopheles stephensi, so perfectly urbanized that it will breed in almost any container, and is equally at home in deepest well or high-built cistern. Not until after years of persuasion and the exercise of constant unyielding pressure would the influential Parsees screen their cisterns and wells.

The Parsees ultimately withdrew their objections, but religion must still be dealt with in other parts of India. The recently powerful spokesman, Gandhi, flying in the face of all modern scientific knowledge and ignoring the tremendous number of humans being slain by such small insects, is reported as having stated in the *Times of India*, June, 1935, "We have no right to take the lives of mosquitoes, flies, lice, rats, or fleas. They have as much right to live as we."

CHAPTER 26.

AND MAKE
PERSUASION DO THE
WORK OF FEAR

WHEN I first began traveling for the Rockefeller Foundation, the run from Singapore to Java was a bright spot in
the itinerary. The *Melchoir Treub* and the *Rumphius* were the
crack passenger liners of the K.P.M., the most powerful corporation in the Dutch East Indies. These boats, which resembled luxurious yachts, were built for comfort in the tropics. Passengers could
practically live on deck, taking refuge from the brief but daily showers in little shelters specially provided. The voyage was comfortable
and pleasant. Fat Dutch officials spent most of their time puffing
placidly on cabbagy cigars which glowed like red hot chimneys,
and, in the company of their equally fat Mevvrouws, gulping foaming
schooners of beer at the little deck tables.

With the low Sumatra coast on our right, never out of sight of
islands, we steamed the five hundred miles to broad and shallow
Batavia Bay. At dawn of the second day we approached the breakwater which protects Tandjong Priok. Neither at this modern port
nor at the old capital of Batavia, seven miles away, was there any
hint of the strange beauty hidden within the island. Low-lying Batavia itself looked like any town in Holland. Its stone-walled canals,
with gates to regulate the sluggish flow of the current, sometimes
traversed the centers of the enormously broad avenues, built on the
generous scale of the Dutch themselves.

461

The tidal flats of Batavia, more pestilential than those of Singapore, had offered no terrors to the Seventeenth Century colonists from the Zuyder Zee, who had come from a country in which malaria claimed then an annual tithe. In Batavia, which ironically enough means Fair Meadows, they clung intrepidly to the homes they had erected there. But the mortality was so overpowering—over a million died in twenty-two years of the Eighteenth Century—that the city ultimately was abandoned to natives and commerce; the burghers now come down to it only for working hours, and return as early as possible to Weltevreden (Well Content) where they live in their plastered tinted houses on ground only a little higher but far more healthful.

Even in Weltevreden—Batavia Centrum as it is now called—the heat is intense, and the mosquitoes, although not malaria carriers, made it impossible for me to work in my hotel room. The whole island swarmed with insect life, from butterflies to termites, and at sundown the air was resonant with their throbbing sounds. They were an omnipresent pest.

The Governor General found Weltevreden much too hot. He moved inland to Buitenzorg in the hills which, although not in sight from Batavia, are never much more than an hour from the coast. The world's most beautiful botanical gardens form a private park for his mansion. On the slope of Salak volcano, which through the centuries has fertilized its hillsides, grow specimens of every tree, shrub, plant, and vine known to the tropics. Throughout its spacious acres the Dutch experiment with tea, rubber, cinchona, sugar cane, rice, nutmegs, cloves, and pepper in order to develop them for commerce. Though the fundamental purpose is economic, the faithful botanists who have labored there have never sacrificed beauty to utility. Five thousand out of the six thousand known varieties of orchids open exotic blooms, and tree fuchsias of incomparable beauty are covered with dusky red and purple blossoms. Its primeval forest is watered by a river, and on its numerous ponds float the most marvelous water lilies I have ever seen.

Not many miles from the Botanical Gardens lies a mysterious plantation, encircled by a high stone wall. Within this enclosure, which no visitor ever enters, grow the cinchona trees of Java. The secrets of cultivation and extraction thus jealously guarded have made the Dutch supreme in the production of quinine.

This was by no means the only contribution of the Dutch to medicine. They introduced chenopodium for the cure of hookworm. In their laboratories they had developed the smallpox vaccine, sought vainly for so many years, that would remain effective for long periods under tropical temperature. They were the first to experiment with cholera vaccine on a large scale, testing it on the inhabitants of each alternate block in Batavia. Practically no cases occurred in the blocks protected by the vaccine. In Sumatra, where hundreds of laborers on rubber plantations used to die annually, administering the vaccine had cut the number down to one or two.

In the extremely difficult situations that confronted them, the Dutch seemed to possess to an unusual degree the ability to combine the scientific with the practical. They directed their efforts to finding specific remedies for treating tropical diseases and working out economical methods for dealing with health matters. It was a Netherlander in Java who invented the bored hole latrine, one of the greatest contributions to sanitation in the East. At last in dealing with the terrible problem of soil pollution a method was devised, the chief value of which lay in its simplicity. By boring a hole in the ground fourteen to sixteen inches in diameter and ten or twelve feet deep, preferably to ground water, a cheap, odorless latrine could be made available to all races and to suit all purses. The Americans, who are the well-drillers for the world, soon perfected drilling equipment, as easy to use as a carpenter's augur, which still further simplified installation.

The bored hole latrine has many advantages. Years of research conducted by the Rockefeller Foundation have shown that, under almost all conditions, such latrines constitute no danger to wells or other domestic water supplies.

Even the poorest peasants of Java can afford this safeguard and literally hundreds of thousands are being constructed annually.

Mrs. Marie D. Buck, a prominent teacher in Madras, states: "We expect every student to become a thorough convert to the B. H. L. and to leave us eager to install them in his home, school, and playground, as a disease controller and annihilator of the main reason for making outcastes untouchables. While we feel that control of hookworm and water borne diseases is a worthy ambition, even wider horizons open before us as we realize that if we can spread the B. H. L. all over India, human night soil ceases to become the concern of the outcastes. Then, though we shall not live to see its triumphant conclusion, we shall have struck a death blow at the reason for untouchability."

The Dutch handled ingeniously their peculiar malaria problem along the coast, which was a mass of ponds, artificially made. There fish had been raised for many decades in enormous quantities to help supply proteins for the teeming population. As many as three hundred and eighty varieties were cultivated, including the golden carp which grew to great size and made brilliant spots of color in the market places.

The fish ponds used to be profuse breeders of Anopheles ludlowii which hid in the masses of top algae where minnows could not reach them. To solve the problem thus introduced, deep trenches were dug encircling the bottoms of the ponds, and when the water was drained, as was periodically done, the level would sink so that water remained only in the trenches, where the fish could live temporarily. In this way the surface algae were destroyed and the larvae could be swallowed up by top minnows.

Few people realize what a vast population is under the control of the Netherlands in the Far East. That tiny little country, encompassing few more inhabitants than New York City, has a dependent population of over seventy-five million in Java, Sumatra, Borneo, and New Guinea, all Malayan save the latter. The average revenues from these Eastern subjects are so low that little is left over to meet the cost of modern health safeguards.

In practically all colonies the health departments are starved for funds. Only the crumbs and leavings come their way. But wherever the Rockefeller Foundation could stage a demonstration, with its attendant publicity and startling results, popular interest was directed toward health, and the appropriations for the health departments were almost immediately increased. One of the most valuable services we could render Java would be to bring prestige from the outside to the members of the local medical service, which paradoxically appeared to occupy the lowest status of officialdom. If we could get them to cooperate along our lines of preventive medicine, enormous

464

numbers of people would be affected, but this was not easy of accomplishment because they were convinced of their ability to handle their health problems without outside aid.

I relied on the old familiar hookworm route to gain entrance to Java, and, following my rule to begin with the man at the top, interviewed Alexander W. Frederick Indenburg, the Governor General, a difficult undertaking, since high Dutch officials are not in the habit of seeing casual visitors. With the temperature at ninety, the humidity at saturation point, and not enough breeze to move a piece of tissue paper, I arrayed myself in redingote, heavy trousers, stiff shirt, patent leather shoes, and a silk hat and made my call.

I briefly described to the Governor General the development of the hookworm campaign in the United States; how it had gradually extended to foreign countries, and how it served as an entering wedge to make even the most lowly people acquainted with the good results that followed public health measures; I told him how our Board believed that a system of health could not be imposed upon a people from above, that it must come from below, and that it was only by patience rather than by force that permanent progress in health lines could be gained; I explained how hookworm was so simple that even the most ignorant could understand it, that our experience so far had been that through its treatment a desire was created in the masses for better health conditions, and that as soon as this was accomplished we believed the battle was half won; I laid special stress upon the improvement which might be expected in the economic efficiency of the people, and expressed our desire to make an infection survey in Java; and finally I suggested that, if suitable arrangements could be made, we would send a medical officer to cooperate with the medical officers of his own service.

The Governor General was very polite and affable. He would be happy to look into this, would advise me if anything were to be done, and gave me a letter to his Chief Health Officer, Dr. W. T. de Vogel, who would make the necessary arrangements for the Darling Commission's survey.

Dr. de Vogel intimated that when it came to control measures, his department was probably better able to handle them than our new organization. He agreed readily, however, to let the Darling

Commission make investigations, because pure research would not interfere with his department in any way.

The Dutch like formality and no great results are obtained if a mass of ideas is put to them too quickly. My only hope was to go slowly; caution and more caution was to become for years my motto in Java.

In all the countries I have ever visited, I have found no place where English did not suffice for travel purposes, though it might not always serve in scientific or polite conversation. In communicating with people generally I could usually find a short cut. *Pigi*, which means literally "bring," is a word combining a multitude of purposes in Java and Malaya. By consulting a list of common terms, and saying, "*pigi* this" and "*pigi* that," I could get what I wanted. When Dr. MacCallum was traveling with me, he would step up to a passerby and read a question from the Malay instruction book, but it was comical to watch his face when an unintelligible spatter of sounds piled up against his ear drums. Again and again it happened that after he had completed his contortions in Malay, I would put the question in English and get a perfectly good answer.

The Dutch realized that nobody could be expected to understand their language, and consequently learned English and either French or German as auxiliaries. Because the subtleties of the English language were often too much for them, and because German was more closely allied to their language and also more exact in itself, I frequently found that my German was more intelligible.

I had several amusing experiences with the Dutch inability to grasp the finer points of English. The morning after I had secured permission for the Darling Commission to work in Java, I sent a cable to the home office announcing my success. The girl in the telegraph office looked it over and apparently approved it. Since it was war time, all messages were eyed carefully lest they be in code. But that noon in the midst of a luncheon party I was giving at the Hôtel des Indes, a waiter bent over me and said, "Telephone for you, sir."

The only phone, unprotected by a booth, hung on the dining room wall. I took up the receiver, and above the hum of the many diners I heard a feminine voice, "Are you zee Doctaire Heisaire?"

"Yes."

"Zis morning you have sent one cablegram?"

"Yes, why?"

"Eet ees not zee Eengleesh. It must be zee Eengleesh."

"What's wrong with it?"

"Eet has zee word p-s-y-c-h-o-l-o-g-i-c-a-l. Zat ees not zee Eengleesh."

"Of course it is! It's a perfectly good word."

"No! Eet ees NOT zee Eengleesh."

"I cannot be responsible for your English education. I'll leave it to any English-speaking person."

That seemed to end her doubts, at least momentarily. She began on another tack. "You have anozzaire word. Eet ees also zee code."

"What's that one?"

"D-a-r-l-i-n-g. I have looked in zee dictionary and eet say 'one sweet zing.'"

"Darling is not one sweet thing. It's the name of a man," I assured the girl desperately, aware by this time that the whole dining room had ceased eating and was listening to this absorbing conversation.

"Oh, no-o-o, darling means 'one sweet zing.' It must be zee code. I cannot send eet."

"I insist on your sending it! It has to go through Singapore anyhow. Let them decide."

"Well," hesitatingly, "I don't zink I can send eet."

"You go ahead and send it," I adjured her, slammed down the telephone receiver, and passed through the length of the dining room to the accompaniment of knowing looks from the diners, all of whom were convinced that I had been communicating with "one sweet zing."

The Hôtel des Indes is a remarkable place. Javanese hotels are run on different principles from those of any elsewhere in the world. They are more like small villages, consisting of a series of cottages with two apartments, one above the other. For the time of the guest's occupancy, one of these, composed of veranda, sitting room, bedroom, bath, and cubby hole for the boy assigned to him as his personal servant by the hotel, is his private dwelling. This boy

467

even accompanies him as he makes his way to the dining room in the central building, and waits upon him there.

It is not strange that the Dutch in Java seem to be ponderous with adipose tissue. On one of my subsequent trips I saw two Dutch women who were not fat, which I thought a great sight and scarcely credible. Too much alcohol, little exercise, and, in particular, over-eating, are responsible.

I have never seen anything remotely resembling the Dutch meals. Possibly because of the heat, the men keep curious office hours—from seven to twelve, and from five to eight. Before embarking on the day's arduous duties, they breakfast sparingly on eggs, cold meat, several kinds of sausage, meat pudding, cheese, and coffee, the latter a concentrated syrup from a bottle to which scalding hot water is added. About ten in the morning they reinforce themselves further.

At lunch time comes the famous *rijstafel*. First the guest ladles rice into a soup plate the size of a washbasin. Then a line of waiters —sometimes as many as twenty—advances, every one with a tray containing two to five varieties of food; some of each is supposed to be taken. The many ingredients include chicken, duck, beef, Bombay duck—a form of dried fish tough as leather but with a delightful flavor—eggs, peanuts, shredded cocoanut, all imaginable vegetables from Occident and Orient, beets, beansprouts, water chestnuts, the extraordinary condiments of the East, chutneys and chillies, and curry which turns the mixture yellow and a cochineal red powder which, if taken in any quantity, burns like fire. With a large soup spoon in either hand the diners turn this mountain of food over and over as though they were putting it through a concrete mixer and then consume it to the last grain of rice.

Afterwards, the Dutch, thoroughly groggy, drag themselves groaning to their couches, where they repose until four-thirty. It is then time for tea, and so back to the office. Dinner, the real meal of the day, comes as a welcome finale at nine-thirty or ten, accompanied by a liberal supply of schnapps. Finally they retire exhausted to bed to repair the ravages of the day's toil.

To my astonishment, I several times heard Americans referred to as the heaviest eaters in the world. Since I had never seen anything that remotely resembled the Gargantuan repasts of the Dutch,

468

I was extremely curious. I puzzled until I discovered the answer. When they entered an American hotel or restaurant, believing it the local custom, they would mistakenly start at the top and eat their way through the à la carte bill of fare, a difficult feat, even for those in training.

The appearance of the Dutch, heavy and big-boned, was decidedly unattractive. Nor could the Javanese, with their wizened faces, be judged beautiful by Western standards. Only the mestizos, combining the best features of both races, were handsome. Fortunately there were many of these, because the Dutch and Javanese intermarried freely. Part of many Dutch women's lack of charm was due to the habit of sitting around in sarong and jacket until late in the afternoon. This could be excused on the grounds of the great heat, but not on those of esthetics.

The nights were so sticky and hot in the lowlands, especially since a mosquito net was indispensable, that it was the invariable custom to provide a long bolster called a Dutch wife. By placing one knee over this, the sleeper could expose a larger area of epidermis and receive the benefit of the maximum amount of air.

The Dutch were still far behind other countries in the fundamentals of tropical ventilation, so necessary in a country where the monsoon seldom blew. This seemed odd in the light of their many remarkable conquests of other tropical problems. The homes, scrupulously whitewashed and decorated with blooming plants in the tradition of the old country, had no jutting verandas. Instead, the middle of the front three rooms merely lacked an outer wall. Whatever breeze there might be could enter this open-air sitting room only from one direction.

Cholera was often severe in Batavia before the general application of vaccine. According to a Malay custom, when an epidemic was raging, in order to avoid registering their dead, they used to drag the bodies to the "particular lands" and abandon them there. These were private government grants, exempt from the Dutch health regulations, most of them located in the outlying district of Batavia called Meester Cornelis.

The danger of cholera was also present in rural communities, where villagers bathed their bodies and washed their rice in the same

469

streams which they polluted. These *dessas*, as they were called, were surrounded by rice paddies and cane fields. Most of the houses were built flat on the ground, some made of *suale*, or woven bamboo, others of a substance resembling our adobe. In most cases they had heavily thatched roofs.

Although the Dutch conquered cholera, plague was still an unsolved problem in thickly populated Java. On one of my trips I learned there had been a hundred thousand cases, chiefly in the mountain districts. The authorities asked my opinion, and offered me every facility for visiting the plague area.

In the course of inspecting the districts affected I had a fine opportunity to see a great deal of Javanese village life. We rode in procession with a native official on horseback, and everywhere we stopped we were surrounded by curious multitudes. Even as we inspected the rat-proof houses, large numbers tramped after us. All the countryside came to make a holiday. At many points along the route we were greeted by the native gamelan or anklong bands. At Karangkobar a great show was staged for my benefit which was in many respects similar to the Ifugao fiestas in which I used to participate in the Philippines.

The Dutch method of dealing with plague was to demolish every house in any village in which the disease appeared. In putting the buildings together again, they cleverly split the bamboo poles in half, laying the ends of the semicircle of one section into the concave surface of the other so that no enclosed space for harboring rats was left. Naturally the plague disappeared in that town, but it was more than likely to appear in the one ahead.

After completing the inspection, I informed the Dutch frankly that first of all the primary sources of infection, the grain warehouses in the port cities, should be dealt with, and, since they had only about a million dollars to spend on plague, the method they were pursuing in the villages was not likely to be successful. In attempting to guard against the disease they waited until something happened, and then concentrated heavily on the infection itself. The idea of tearing down and reconstructing fifty thousand houses annually was a program which would have awed any but a determined Dutchman. My advice was to map the roads over which grain was accustomed to travel, because along those routes the plague would surely travel also. Instead of expending so much energy in a town already infected, I suggested taking a lesson from our enemy the fleas, and keeping one jump ahead of them. The wholesale destruction of a town was spectacular, but the otherwise efficient Dutch never caught up with the plague. Their plan was nothing more than a stern chase.

The Dutch, on the other hand, claimed the sectional method I had used so successfully in the Philippines was impossible in Java because rats could not be eliminated from the thickly thatched roofs. Furthermore, it was their duty to keep their population happy, and, since the Javanese never wanted anything done, they believed that in attacking infection after its appearance, they were interfering about as much with native habits and customs as circumstances warranted.

The Malay was not easy to work with. In his native state he was highly superstitious. When asked his name, rather than bring down upon his head the bad luck supposed to follow a direct answer, he would turn to a friend and ask, "What is my name?" Although nominally Mohammedan in Java, he still believed in *hantu*, evil spirits which lived in trees and lurked about the houses at night, and this *hantu* influence was believed to be sinister toward his family, animals, crops, and even his own person.

The Malay inability to stay awake was so serious that the Dutch would not trust the Javanese to operate trains in the darkness; consequently they did not run at night. Because prospective travelers had to be routed out of bed so early in the morning to catch trains, traveling was particularly tiresome. In spite of this inconvenience, however, the two-day trip along the mountain range which ran the length of Java was most scenic and impressive, particularly the section between Batavia and Djokjakarta.

At Djokjakarta the Dutch had compromised with the religion of their subjects, who fervently worshipped the Sultan as divine, by permitting him to keep up a shadow of his former rule. I had an odd feeling that it was, to say the least, unusual to find white Christian soldiers guarding a Mohammedan potentate in a country ruled by a European nation, especially when I recalled that this rule had now extended over a period of several centuries. For my interview with the Sultan I was conducted by a Dutch officer through his *kraton*, loosely called the palace, which, like those of all Eastern potentates, consisted of a series of buildings. Within the stone walls, which sheltered some ten thousand followers, was enclosure after enclosure. The private dwelling of the Sultan was located within the fourth enclosure, as were the harem apartments guarded by the princes, and a public reception room, ornately decorated with gilt carvings and scintillating with mirrors. Pictures of Queen Wilhelmina and the Netherlands royal family certified his loyalty to the source of his income.

The Sultan lived in colorful if not regal surroundings. Within the grounds paraded resplendent birds of paradise and peacocks. Many roosters were also being exercised, each with his special male attendant; cockfighting was one of the Sultan's principal diversions. Glistening shining carp, said to be very highly prized by the Sultan as articles of food, swam lazily in a pond into which drainage from the royal palace emptied.

Enormous pergolas dotted the lawns. In accordance with the tenets of the Mohammedan religion, worship could not be permitted under the clear sky. It was generally assumed that this meant services should be conducted in a mosque, but the Sultan had dodged both the issue and the heat by erecting these open-air structures which were cheap, provided shade, and at the same time might be interpreted as meeting the demands of his religion.

More attractive than the *kraton* were the fairly modern ruins of the nearby Water Palace, built by a Portuguese adventurer. Although when I first saw it, it had been abandoned for only five years, it was already in a state of great disrepair, and the jungle had crept over it. Many underground water-cooled chambers had been built to provide relief from the tropical heat, and from these in all directions led passages, apparently designed to afford ready means of escape.

Less than a hundred years ago was discovered the greatest of all Javanese ruins, which the jungle had swallowed up completely. The Dutch had been loyal to the antiquarian trust left in their hands, and had carefully removed the clinging tendrils from Boroboedoer. This magnificent relic, deserted with the Mohammedan conquest of the island, remained still to bear witness to the physical expression of the Buddhist faith. Tier on tier the huge lava blocks, fitted without mortar, held by no columns and no supporting arches, rose majestically above the plain. Each terrace was decorated with bas reliefs, representing the life of Buddha and symbolizing the spiritual development of man.

From the top of the temple the eye swept the countryside, fecund with rice, sugar, and cocoanuts. The pretty streams, the gentle people, the fertile country, and the harmonious landscape, impressed me with the thought that, after all, man did not defile all he touched, and even did much to make it more beautiful.

Boroboedoer stands as a cherished relic, but the ever-present volcanoes are still regarded with superstitious awe and reverence by the Javanese who live among them. The mild and kindly Tenggerese had a sort of religion, half Brahmin, half animistic, centered around the worship of Bromo, the most famous of Javanese craters, which reared itself from the Zand Zee not far from Soerabaja at the eastern end of the island. The morning I made the ascent the mists in the valleys at sunrise looked like great ocean billows, and the mountain tops stood out like islets here and there. At times I had the illusion that waves were being washed against the shore. Then the mists thinned, and the lowlands appeared dimly, as though seen through clear water.

At Moengal Pass, eleven hundred feet up, we looked down into the "Landscape of the Moon" which was in reality the bottom of the old Tengger Volcano. The narrow and shallow steps cut up to the crater's rim, an hour's ride further, were difficult to climb because they had been deeply covered with ashes from the constant eruptions. Steam explosions were occurring at the bottom with an awe-inspiring noise. At the edge of the crater shelters of huge timbers had been built, and when it was time for an eruption, the guide urged us into one of these. From there I saw the actual eruption, its showers of hot rocks and ashes spurting into the air and thundering down.

On the return journey the atmosphere was transparent and pellucid and the scenery majestic. Java was the most volcanic island for its size in the world, and periodic eruptions from one or more of the craters sent out great clouds of fine ashes which drifted and settled over the landscape. The soil thus fertilized was watered by the daily rains, creating ideal conditions for plant life. Even the tops of the mountains were sown with crops of potatoes, carrots, lettuce, and corn.

All Java was like a garden; not an arable plot went untilled on this island of thirty million inhabitants. Lalang, the universal grass pest of the Eastern tropics, could not grow because of the intensive cultivation. I was always reminded of what would be possible in the Philippines, so impressed was I with the great wealth of Java's products—its sugar, kapok, pineapples, mangoes, cocoanuts, rubber, and spices. Irrigation ditches for the thick-standing rice radiated in all directions like the veins of a leaf. It was strange to see rice being planted and harvested in the same field.

Sugar cane, ten feet high, grew in vast fields. The land was prepared by heaping up, with hoe-like *choncling* tools, large masses of earth between which deep canals were left. Sugar harvesting seemed to be a tremendous operation in which enormous numbers were employed. The roads were literally congested with carts carrying cane to the mills. Throughout the island, traveling by train, motor, or horseback, it was impossible to get out of sight of a human being. Javanese, in their flat, neatly tied turbans, the subdued colors of their raiment producing a terra cotta effect, trooped up and down about their business of gaining a livelihood.

I could not help being impressed by the fact that the white man made beasts of burden out of these people. But it was probably the dense population rather than the Dutch dominance which made them so eager to work. In some places Malays are indifferent and indolent, but in Java, where the struggle for existence is more severe, they are wide awake and ambitious. I have never seen more willing labor anywhere. They seemed to toil from sunrise to sunset with a cheerfulness beyond belief.

When I first went to Java the peasantry were gentle people, cringing and never standing in the presence of Dutch officials, who ruled with a heavy hand, allowing the Javanese only inferior positions in the Civil Service, and maintaining domestic discipline literally by spanking. They had been for years imposing upon these Mohammedan Malays, differing from them in almost every respect, laws and regulations which suited their own ideas of hygiene. But by

474

1926 the Javanese were becoming more and more restive, and more and more aggressive in their resentment. They held parades protesting against Dutch domination, blew up bridges, and killed their masters, who for so many years had punished them as though they were children. The reign of terror was so strong at Weltevreden that every house had to be protected by a night watchman. Thousands of *insurrectos* were sent to exile in New Guinea, where they still remain.

After years of cautious preliminary skirmishing on our part to secure an invitation from Java, the Dutch suddenly capitulated and asked us to cooperate in health work. This surrender was due to an unpremeditated circumstance. I was in Geneva serving on a Commission to draft an International Sanitary Code, of which the retired Chief Health Officer of Java was also a member. Hardly had I finished my address to the Health Section of the League of Nations on the activities of the Rockefeller Foundation when he dashed up, shook my hand, and said, "Now for the first time I understand what the Rockefeller Foundation is trying to do. I'm going to see that you receive an invitation to go to Java at once."

True enough, the invitation shortly arrived.

In the ten years which had elapsed since I had begun my visits to Java, the situation had changed. A new Governor General had been appointed who had become familiar with modern publicity methods while Minister to Washington. He had substituted an official policy of persuasion for that of force in dealing with the Javanese.

The members of the Civil Service, however, trained in the old tradition, found the orders of the Governor General abhorrent, and gave lip service only. We had the feeling we were being allowed to make our demonstration only in order that they might demonstrate to us how wrong we were. We encountered both active and passive resistance on every hand from the rank and file of Dutch officialdom. The Chief Health Officer, Dr. van Lonkhuyzen, said in so many words to our representative, "I'm sorry you've come, and the original invitation was only sent because it was forced upon us by higher Government officials."

We were assigned to Serang, an insurrectionary district about sixty miles from Batavia, which bore the reputation of being particularly cantankerous and difficult. Dr. van Lonkhuyzen freely admitted he did not believe in our campaign of education. It was the old story that it could not be done, at least not in Java, and this he knew because of his long experience.

The Dutch, who heretofore had been administering vermifuges to hookworm cases only when they came into the dispensaries, were now beginning to subject them to an intensive course of treatment. Villagers were brought in by the headman, much the same as cattle would be driven to market. Groups were herded together and then made to pass in single file to a table where the medicine was poured down their throats. The Dutch were greatly interested in their work and proud of it.

Dr. John Lee Hydrick set about proving to the Dutch that in spite of the virtues of their chenopodium, the important thing in Java was to prevent reinfection, and a soil pollution campaign, accompanied by the building of latrines, had to be carried on simultaneously with treatment. He had not been working long when the Dutch, with their old feeling of superiority, stated, "Your methods are too slow; we'll show you how to do it."

The great day came when the comparison of results between the two methods was to be made. The Governor of the district and other officials first examined everything that we had been able to persuade the people to do in the territory in which we were working. They were apparently much impressed until Dr. van Lonkhuyzen said, "The people here have built ten thousand latrines, but we've built one hundred thousand at less expense. I want you to see our installations."

I too was eager. Dr. van Lonkhuyzen, Dr. Hydrick, his secretary, and I set out for Kroja, the village in Central Java where the Dutch had concentrated their work.

At Kroja we dismounted from the automobile and marched in procession to the first latrine, standing new and trim. I lit a piece of paper and threw it down the hole; the latrine had not been used. We marched to the second; it too was as it had been built—and so on down the line, every single one was immaculately clean.

Dr. van Lonkhuyzen, somewhat discomfited, asked the local

Health Officer for an explanation. "It's not customary for the people to begin using the latrines until after they've taken the treatment," was his excuse.

"Your campaign has been going on for some time. Isn't there a town where the people have already been treated?" I inquired interestedly.

"Oh, yes, we have some latrines which have been constructed for several months in another town."

"Let's go there," I suggested.

"Oh, it's much too far, and the heat is too great."

"Well, let's have something to eat first and then go."

After lunch the reluctant officials climbed back into the automobile and we motored forty miles to another village. More hot and more tired, they once again dismounted and once again the procession formed. It was the same story. The latrines which had been built for several months had still not been used.

"I surrender," said Dr. van Lonkhuyzen. "I thought we had something on you. But I'm convinced now. We must have public health education in Java."

Meanwhile Dr. Hydrick was perfecting his technique of instruction. He took advantage of the peculiarly Javanese institution of the *mantri*, a term used to designate a native technician in any field. It was astounding to see to what an extent the *mantri*, who usually possessed a good academic background, was being used in the different government departments. He might be a postal or telegraph helper, or an agriculturist, or a nurse or operating assistant. Since Dutch doctors did not understand what was meant by public health nursing, it too was regarded as a menial duty and delegated to the *mantri*.

Dr. Hydrick learned both Dutch and Malay, and then instructed a selected group of *mantris* in the story of hookworm. Each *mantri* would go into a Javanese home, sit on the floor with all the family collected about him, describe the hookworm, and demonstrate its presence in the soil with the Baermann apparatus. They usually seemed to understand it but, taking no chances, in a few weeks' time he would go back and repeat the story. Upon a third visit he would question them. They welcomed this opportunity to repeat the lessons

477

they had learned. He would ask, "Where does the hookworm live?" or "How do you get anemia?" If they could not answer, the *mantri* knew his instruction had been poor. On the fourth interview the school children were also present. An old grey-headed grandfather might be corrected by a little child. But invariably an animated discussion would begin, all appealing to the *mantri* as judge to decide which was right.

I spent a great deal of time myself going from village to village and from house to house. I saw children singing health songs with gusto, but experience in many countries led me to question whether the words of these songs had any effect or made any impression on the children's minds. This business of bringing the offerings of science to a rural population, and of making them a part of daily lives had many pitfalls and required the patience of Job. Trying to write my impressions amid fiercely biting mosquitoes and thousands of bugs, ants, and flying things that crawled down my neck as well as constantly obscured the page, heightened my admiration for the intrepid souls who stayed there from day to day and struggled with the health problem amid the filth, and, even worse, the skepticism which continued on the part of many of the Dutch officials.

Fortunately we had the full-hearted support of the new Governor General, who said to me, "You know the situation we're up against. We're ready to finance your work up to the hilt. We have one hundred thousand dollars available."

It was not all done at once but when the Dutch Civil Service was finally converted, it entered the field of education with every bit of its abundant energy. Moving pictures, charts, health-mobiles, pamphlets, printed matter—all were used for propaganda purposes. Ultimately a Museum of Health was installed in a large building specially remodeled for the purpose. Open-air movies and speeches were held on the immense Koningsplein in Weltevreden; sometimes as many as thirty thousand Javanese attended.

But these were merely outward manifestations of a complete change in point of view. Helping to bring about this reversal was our great contribution to Java. Every aspirant for the Netherlands Colonial Service had to go to school for several years at the Colonial

Institute in Amsterdam. He learned the Malay language, the folk-lore, religion, and customs. But the whole system of teaching has been changed at its roots. Where once the student was taught to command, now he is instructed in the principles of persuasion.

CHAPTER 27.   HUSTLING

                                    THE EAST

ONE hot June afternoon I set out along the Charun Krung,
the New Road, for the palace of the King of Siam, in 1916
one of the few remaining absolute monarchs in the world. Formerly
Bangkok, the Venice of the East, had had no streets, nothing but
tree-shaded *klongs,* or canals. But King Maha Vajiravudh had tired
of riding on the broad and placid Menam in his Golden Swan, propelled by its sixty paddlers clothed in Tyrian red, whose gold-leaved
blades flashed rhythmically in the sun. He had seen the automobiles
of the Western World and, desiring them for his own use, had in
ten years bordered the *klongs* with over a hundred miles of roads,
so that he could travel from one border of his city to the other in
one of his forty-two cars. Beyond, there were and still are no highways
—nothing but a vast paddy field stretching to the horizon as far as
the eye can reach.

We passed by beautiful public buildings and the brick palaces
of the multitudinous brothers, uncles, cousins, and nephews of the
King. The countless wats were roofed in peacock-hued tiles and
decorated with slim, sharp-pointed, gilt prachidees. These spires,
shooting up suddenly and unexpectedly amid the greenery, were
startling, no matter how often I saw them.

Though the thermometer was at ninety-five I had necessarily attired myself in heavy broadcloth morning coat; the hottest places
in the tropics seem to have a predilection for formal dress on official
occasions. But it was annoying, after all my sartorial preparations,

to have the general effect spoiled. Just opposite the National Museum of Fine Arts a sprinkle of rain peppered my top hat so that it looked as though it had suffered a severe attack of smallpox.

Finally, we reached the bend of the Menam in the heart of the city where the great wall, with its crenelations shaped like the ace of spades, enclosed the King's compound. The sentries at the gate peered suspiciously into the car, ignoring the fact that it was one of the King's own, and that one of the King's own aides was sitting by my side. Once within, we went unchallenged between lines and lines of pickets, who came to attention as the car swept by. I later learned that a cow's crest on the car would admit anyone who had the forty-two ticals to pay for the privilege.

After twisting and turning and passing through three additional sets of gates, all of which had to be opened, we entered the inner enclosure, where Chululongkorn the Great, the King's father, had added the Chakkri Palace to the innumerable other buildings, which displayed all forms of Eastern architecture, simple and ornate. There was located the Dusit Mahaprasit Hall which "held in architectural form not some builder's plan, but an artist's dream of the fantastic." There also was the royal Wat Phra Keo. A myriad small bells under its eaves sweetly tinkled in every little breeze. Thousands of pieces of glass, incrusted in the walls, glinted in the sun; within its sacred interior, high on his altar, sat the Great Emerald Buddha.

After being introduced in one of the reception rooms to a number of military officers, who entertained me most politely in excellent English, I was conducted ceremoniously between rows of military officers of high rank to a one-room bungalow which, in contrast to the splendor of the main palace buildings, was small and unpretentious. I was shown at once into the presence of the King, who was dressed as a colonel of a British regiment. The room was almost filled with admirals, generals, ministers, and other officials, all adorned with gorgeous uniforms.

The short, stout, moon-faced monarch graciously motioned me to a chair and seated himself on a wicker settee. After the usual inanities about the weather had been exchanged, he suddenly asked, "What do you think of our medical school?"

"I'm not prepared to talk about it, Your Majesty."

"I want to know."

"Your Majesty, I hope you'll excuse me."

"But I want to know."

He must have observed that I had been glancing curiously at the semi-circle of faces surrounding us. Apparently believing I was embarrassed at the presence of these dignitaries, he turned to them and said, "You're dismissed."

Nobody moved.

"I say, you're dismissed!" the King reiterated in an unmistakable tone of command.

Expressions of astonishment spread over their faces. Reluctantly, with sabres clanking, they filed out, and the other door closed behind them.

"Now we're alone, tell me about my medical school," the King persisted.

"Your Majesty, really I can't."

"No one ever tells me the truth. I hear only what everybody thinks I'd like to hear. Please give me your frank opinion."

I was conscious of dozens of beady eyes peering between the slats of the Venetian blinds. The obvious assumption was that the King's entourage, who had been barred from the room, were going to make certain their King should not be assassinated.

"Does Your Majesty really want to know?"

"Yes, I do."

"Then, I'll tell Your Majesty. I have visited medical schools all over the world, West as well as East."

"Yes, yes."

"I regret very much to say that Your Majesty's Royal Medical School is the poorest I have ever seen."

As though he were on springs the King leaped up and ejaculated, "This cannot be!" He paced up and down angrily. "This is simply outrageous! This cannot be! Nobody ever told me that."

"Your Majesty asked me for my frank opinion. I've given it."

"But every year I've sent a group of our best young men to Europe and America. Some of them are teaching in the school now."

"I've seen your young men. Many of them have picked up our bad habits, and few of our good ones."

"Don't they use their time properly in America?"

"I'm just making an observation, which is beside the point. The fundamental difficulty is that Your Majesty hasn't a good school."

"My government has no more funds that could be used for that purpose."

"Siam has beautiful colleges of fine arts. What good do they do if the people are sickly and die before their time? It is reasonably assumed that Siam has a death rate of thirty to forty per thousand. Dead people don't enjoy fine arts. The first thing Siam ought to do is get good health."

I went on to explain to him that curing his subjects of hookworm would make them happier and improve their economic efficiency, thereby making little Siam more powerful; further that our sole desire was to cooperate with the medical officers of his own government, but first he would have to produce good ones, and this could only be brought about in a better training school.

"Where do they have a better school?" demanded the King.

"In the Philippines."

"Oh, the United States is disgustingly rich. You Americans pour millions into that country. It's quite understandable, of course, why a school there should have high standards."

"I beg Your Majesty's pardon, but the United States has never contributed anything to the Philippines."

"Then you must grind the Filipinos down with taxes so that they cannot get their heads above water."

"No, Your Majesty, they're the lightest taxed people on earth. Three dollars per capita covers everything. The Siamese tax rate is far higher than that."

"Well, what can I do? I can't afford any more money."

"Your Majesty would not need to. Competent instructors cost little more than incompetent. The Rockefeller Foundation would be glad to supply the nucleus of a foreign staff and provide fellowships so that the Siamese would eventually be able to take over the instruction."

The King thought for a few moments, and then said, "This is my golden opportunity. I'm usually so burdened with foreign advice that I can't take any action that does not trample on the rights of somebody. But now the War has freed me to some extent of advisers. I'd like to pay for my own teachers. Could you recommend suitable ones?"

"I'd be very glad to."

The King then apologized for having lost his temper, and went on to say, "I'm not in a position to suggest these changes myself. But if it could be arranged for one of my family to see the school in the Philippines, and the suggestion came from him, perhaps my foreign advisers would not object. Could you manage to have him received incognito so that he could see the situation as it really is?"

"I'm sure there'll be no question about it. I'm going to the Philippines myself from here."

"He'll be there almost as soon as you are."

This appeared to terminate the interview. The King rose and I also. "Wait a moment," he said, and called a servant to whom he spoke in Siamese. I was conscious that the interview had been prolonged beyond the usual time, but shortly the servant returned with a small plush box in his hand. The King tendered it to me with the words, "I give you this in confirmation of my promise to support the work of the Rockefeller Foundation in Siam."

I bowed myself out. On my return to the hotel, I opened the case and found I had been decorated with the Fourth Class of the Order of the White Elephant, Busanabaran. Its value to me lay in the fact it betokened a pledge from the King to support a movement for bettering health conditions and improving medical education. The receipt of this honor was contrary to custom. It is the usual practice that those upon whom honors are to be conferred are asked in advance to indicate their willingness to receive them. This rule has enabled me to follow out my determination never to accept honors.

Prior to the War, perhaps five hundred Europeans were "employed" by the Siamese government, chiefly on the insistence of Great Britain, France, Belgium, and Germany. Many of these seemed content to draw their salaries and follow any other path than that demanded by the situation.

With advisers of many nationalities often giving conflicting counsel, it was plain how the Siamese had been pulled first in one direction and then in another, all efforts lacking coordination. They had developed into a set of apologists, and were constantly confronted with the necessity of giving the least offense to those whose advice they did not accept. The game of the different legations was to have their nationals appointed to office. The amount of intrigue and countermoves that went on backstage was unbelievable. The community presented the picture of a few whites quarreling among themselves, and a huge native mass that did not know what it wanted.

Because Maha Vajiravudh firmly believed that his numerous white advisers should be replaced with Siamese, he fell in readily with the Rockefeller Foundation policy of extending aid by training and guiding the Siamese and then allowing them to continue the work themselves. The difficulty was to direct the royal attention to health and away from his hobbies of building palaces, repairing wats, and increasing the army and navy.

The King was also said to be busied trying to find surnames for his eight million subjects, none of whom had any. Trying to keep names and titles straight in Siam drove me nearly to distraction. Almost all the officials, and especially the Princes, had more than one, and even these were changed every few months by the King. I sometimes searched for days and even then was unable to find the later names of men I had known well on previous trips. To make matters more difficult for the visitor, the spelling differed in the various provinces.

This son of Chululongkorn, educated at Oxford, had one Occidental idea which conflicted with the Oriental traditions of his country. He had steadfastly refused the request of his subjects that he wed, according to ancient Siamese custom, one of his own half sisters, although he himself was a product of half sister marriages for four generations. The story went that Queen Victoria, whose great pet he had been, had told him polygamy was wicked, and he had promised her not to marry into his own family. He remained in a quandary for years, but finally lifted a commoner to royal rank.

The King's avocation was supposed to be writing plays, but he had also composed a primer on hygiene and education, good in every way except that it recommended a local quack's medicine for stomach trouble. He was supposed to have a deep sentimental interest in insanity, and it was also reported he had paid out of the privy purse the expenses of one year's vaccination campaign.

But the King's medical enthusiasms had been badly directed. The Medical School fully deserved the reputation I had ascribed to it in my interview with him. The entrance requirements were those of the

485

eighth grade. Almost any male was admitted who could read and write and was of average intelligence. The school was deplorably lacking in equipment. No laboratory facilities were provided, and not one microscope was available for student use; in fact, there were only a half dozen serviceable microscopes in all Siam.

In addition to the regular curriculum a course in Siamese therapeutics taught the application of local herbs, barks, flowers, and ground sharks' teeth. The old Chinese materia medica was also included, and drugs were prescribed for dosage without any scientific testing of their medicinal value. The study of physics had to be attempted because the subject had not been taught in pre-medical school. Sometimes the study of anatomy was omitted entirely, because no teacher was available or because the students objected to the odor of the dissecting room. The instructor in bacteriology quite obviously ought to have been working in medicine.

Textbooks in Siamese could not be kept up-to-date because the language lacked means for expressing the recent medical terminology, and consequently neither teacher nor student was able to avail himself of scientific discoveries as they occurred. The only solution appeared to be that classes should be conducted in English, but this, I was assured, was impracticable unless the Siamese could be persuaded of the inadequacy of their own language.

Moreover, the attitude of the students would have to be changed. As one of the professors told me, "Siamese will learn accurately from a book all the steps of an operation, but they have no desire to perform it." They also objected to having examinations held, and the authorities, in the desire to have everything as pleasant as possible, would often omit these annoyances; a favored pupil was sometimes allowed to complete the four-year course in eighteen months. The majority of the students sat in the shade and smoked pink lotus leaf cigars.

Siam's greatest need from a health point of view was undoubtedly the improvement of its medical education. Only thirty students graduated per year, which meant that one new doctor was turned out annually to tend each 266,666 Siamese. The few students educated abroad found when they returned that their profession was so unprofitable and held in such low public regard that they usually went into the army.

486

In the midst of this inefficiency and lack of proper facilities sat Prince Rangsit, who was credited with being one of the genuinely public-spirited men of Siam. Although not himself a doctor of medicine, he had been educated in Germany in pedagogy, and was struggling valiantly to make progress and improve the condition of the school. But he had been able to accomplish little beyond repairing some of the more decrepit old buildings and fitting up additional lecture rooms.

Shortly after I reached the Philippines, Prince Rangsit, using the name of Krom Mom Jainad, arrived. During his stay of almost a month Governor General Harrison arranged for him to see everything that might be of value or interest to him, and I conducted him personally from hospital, to school, to Bureau of Science, and even to the Fire Department, so that he might see how America ran her affairs in the Orient. Whatever lurking suspicions might have remained in his mind as to the altruism of American motives apparently were thoroughly allayed.

In the course of our conversations, Prince Rangsit became more and more confidential, and gave me details of the difficult situation in which Maha Vajiravudh found himself. The King had a good heart and did not desire to believe anything unpleasant about anybody; consequently he was frequently deceived. Prince Rangsit's firm belief was that if the clique which controlled the King's public attitude did not take kindly to the new medical program, its future was hopeless. Too overwhelming a victory for the Allies would also make the situation more precarious for Siam because the balance of power, which made for their sole safety, would be upset.

The beginnings of our long labors in Siam were complicated by the tangled skein of politics. To win the confidence of the Siamese generally was a difficult task. They were suspicious of almost every proposition put before them, although they were somewhat less wary of Americans, than of Europeans or Japanese, who were not demanding their share of appointments. Almost every time they had come in contact with the white race they had lost something. Both French and British, on trumped up excuses, had, in the most approved empire-building fashion, appropriated choice sections of their territory.

More bitter to endure were the extra-territorial rights which had been fastened upon the Siamese by the leading European nations, Japan, and ourselves. The subjects of all countries having consuls in Siam—Great Britain, France, Netherlands, Denmark, Norway, Sweden, Spain, Portugal, Italy, et al.—were exempted from Siamese laws, which were made by royal decree and were not often likely to be in accordance with Western legal procedure. Moreover, every regulation affecting foreigners had to be approved by their home governments, and when no statutes of their own covered the situations, the English common law was used.

The Siamese were allowed to charge only a three percent customs duty, and this did not provide sufficient income. To make up the deficit they were compelled to adopt an onerous and difficult system of taxation such, for example, as taxing each fruit tree. Most important from our point of view, before any sanitary regulation could be put into effect, the consent of the foreign powers had to be secured.

Siam was constantly trying to rid herself of extra-territoriality. Long years ago she had attempted to negotiate a treaty with Great Britain by which this onerous obligation would be abolished in return for the cession of Trengganu, Kedah, and other possessions on the Malay Peninsula. But Great Britain stipulated that the agreement would only be effective when she judged the Siamese courts were functioning to her satisfaction, and that, in any case, a British judge should sit with the court when a British subject was concerned. Siam did not agree, but lost the provinces just the same, and with them some of the richest tin mines in the world.

A health organization in the modern sense was non-existent in Siam. The few health activities carried on were in the hands of foreigners. Our Minister was asked to assist in obtaining two Americans for the so-called Bangkok City Health Service. He submitted two names, but as soon as this news was spread abroad, the British protested and demanded these appointees should hold office only until the end of the War when British successors must be assured. The Siamese government resisted feebly but finally had to agree.

Siam's experience with France, which was nibbling off bits with every treaty, was equally unfortunate. To obtain French approval for the abolition of extra-territoriality, the Siamese had agreed, among other things, to keep a Frenchman, practically in perpetuity, at the head of the Pasteur Institute. It was directed by the French, although built and subsidized at Siamese expense. When I first went to Siam, the War was going badly for the Allies, and France had her back against the wall. The French incumbent had gone to the front, leaving control to Siamese. Mismanagement was evident, the place was dirty, rabbits were dying in their cages. Out of the dozens of biologicals usually manufactured in such an institution, only rabies and small-pox vaccine were being made. I shuddered to think of such tremendous forces being placed in the hands of half-educated and wholly untrained Siamese.

At Prince Rangsit's request I suggested a new head for the Institute. But the French no sooner heard that the Siamese had chosen an American, than the Frenchman was released from service and scurried back to resume his position. Two days later the American, Dr. Ira Ayer, appeared. The bewildered Siamese had to do something about this contretemps and hastily created for him the post of Sanitary Adviser to the Minister of the Interior at a higher salary.

Some years afterwards I was in Siam while a frightful cholera epidemic was raging. I was then on such intimate terms with the leading Siamese that I could talk with the utmost frankness to them in private, because they knew I would not humiliate them in public.

"This epidemic is disgraceful. Why don't you stop it?"

"We would if we could get the cholera vaccine. But M. —— is so busy with his private practice that he has no time to spend at the Institute, and we are forbidden to make the vaccine ourselves."

Eventually the French were shamed out of their attitude, and ceased insisting on the letter of their rights.

Siam had had a long series of American advisers, beginning with Edward H. Strobel from Harvard, who had pleased Chululongkorn so much he had thereafter had a predilection for advisers from that institution. Francis Sayre, a graduate of Harvard Law School, negotiated many of the arrangements for relinquishing extra-territoriality. Upon his successful conclusion of treaties with foreign powers in 1927, Siam was immediately enabled to increase its revenues by advancing the customs duty, thus relieving to a great extent the internal tax burden.

My first impressions of Siam and the Siamese had made me wonder

489

whether we could overcome the mental torpor and lethargy of this race, which appeared to be a hybrid between Chinese and Malay. The more I inquired, however, the more hopeful I became. The barrier to introducing sanitary measures was not insuperable. Although the Siamese had no reverence for the medical profession, or any science, as such, they had no religious objections to killing rats or, from the medical point of view, no taboo as regards human excreta. The population was apparently not increasing, and the million and a half Chinese did most of the productive labor. The Buddhist Siamese, like the Christian Filipinos, controlled only a small part of the commerce of their own country. The earning power of the Siamese laborer was from fifty to one hundred percent greater than that of the majority of other Orientals, so that prospects of the country's being able to support a higher standard of living were excellent.

In Siam there was the greatest divergence between upper and lower classes. The latter were completely illiterate. Culture was confined to a small minority, most of whom had been educated in Europe. They impressed the traveler as being among the world's most pleasant peoples, conversant with art, literature, politics, and the humanities, and were socially gracious.

As I saw our program in Siam, the first step was to start a hookworm campaign; second, to stimulate the government to set up higher medical standards; and, third, to create scholarships for medical students. It was obvious that in Bangkok politics would hamper us to such an extent that I soon discarded the idea of beginning work in the capital. The proper procedure seemed to be to make a rapid survey and to initiate operations in a rural area which was heavily infested, and quickly prove the value of demonstrations.

All sorts of complications had to be smoothed out before hookworm work could be inaugurated. In spite of the King's agreement, his ministers had to be dealt with, one by one, and persuaded to cooperate. Many Siamese officials were frank enough to state they could not understand how such help as the Rockefeller Foundation offered could be entirely disinterested.

The suspicions of the interested foreign powers had also to be quieted. The British Minister and Consul had to be convinced we had no intention of replacing British with American doctors. By diplomatic maneuvering, and our common interest in leprosy, I made friends with Dr. Morden Carthew, the British medical adviser. Though not antipathetic, when I told him of our intention to start in the interior, he denigrated the idea and said we could make no headway with the preponderant lower classes. But if we were determined to continue our foolhardy venture, we should at least confine our activities to the upper classes, who might understand our objectives. And if any progress at all were to be made we must first get on our side the royal princes who, like Rangsit, had been educated abroad. Once the medical profession could be given greater prestige, it might be possible to disregard class distinctions and have men from below in key positions. Social rank was no bar to political advancement in Siam.

But even the upper-class Siamese, in Dr. Carthew's opinion, wanted to be left alone, and resented the disturbance to their tranquillity when it was pointed out to them how much plague or cholera or other disease existed in their midst. "They want to be considered civilized only in order to make favorable impressions on foreigners so that they can negotiate loans. The Siamese are interesting and plausible conversationalists, but when steadfastness is needed, they'll probably fail." On the whole he looked upon what we were trying to do as hopeless.

In spite of Dr. Carthew's warnings, we continued on our chosen path. The preliminary survey indicated as a strategic point of attack the ancient northern city of Chiengmai near the Burmese border, once capital of the Lao kingdom, now a provincial unit of Siam. It had long been an important trade center for Chinese, Burmese, and Siamese, and the teak trade was mainly conducted from there.

On my first visit of inspection to Chiengmai with Dr. Sawyer, my companion on that trip, we traversed a series of plains, dry and warm even in March, and intersected everywhere with klongs, that were the real lines of communication. Each of the three days' journeys ended at a town equipped with comfortable rest houses. "With" provided bed and meals; "without" furnished a cot and allowed the traveler to supply his own bedding and food. The third day we rode on a construction train, sitting in comfortable wicker chairs at the front of a flat car. It was an unexpectedly pleasant method of travel. A canopy protected us from the sun, and, since the car was pushed ahead, the smoke and embers from the wood-burning engine drifted behind us.

As we climbed through cooler mountain passes, dense with bamboo thickets and forests, we could see "elephints a pilin' teak, in the slushy, squdgy creek."

Siam was almost entirely dependent for livelihood and prosperity on rice and teak. The trees were felled, trimmed, and rolled into a stream, where they floated along lazily until the coming of the dry season. On the mud-caked bottom they would lie until the next year's rains once more lifted them forward. Three years of alternate motion and rest sometimes elapsed before the logs finally drifted down the Menam highway to Bangkok.

Almost immediately upon my arrival in Chiengmai I met the British Consul, who invited me to dine with him. "I'd be delighted," I replied. "Where shall I come?"

"I'll send for you."

Twenty minutes before the dinner hour a tiny turbaned mahout, gaily dressed in crimson and white and gold, appeared before me. "The elephant waits," he announced.

"What's that?" I interjected. "I don't want any elephant." But the boy did not know enough English for any extended expostulation, and willy nilly I had to comply with what was apparently the customary method of attending dinner parties in Chiengmai. The little fellow conducted me to the door and with his hook prodded the elephant, which sank ponderously to its knees. I climbed the short ladder into the howdah and seated myself on a cushion. The mahout leaped nimbly to the elephant's head and we were ready. The great beast lumbered to its feet, the howdah lurching precariously. I was not at all prepared for what followed. As we set off I was shot forward and then suddenly back, until I thought my head would be jerked off. It did not seem possible that I could stay aloft.

I was entertained at Chiengmai most cordially. One pleasant afternoon I was received by the Chao Dara, widow of the late Chululongkorn, and daughter of the last Lao King. She lived in royal dignity, and her train of servants were required to enter and leave her presence on their hands and knees. She took me to a spacious open hall where the expert silk weavers of Chiengmai had been gathered together. The fiancée of the King had decided to wear the Lao skirt as court dress instead of the breeches-like penung of the South, and, because the Chao Dara possessed to an unusual degree the gift of artistic expression common to Siamese, the designing of these garments had been entrusted to her. Materials, beautifully patterned in blues, pinks, greens, and reds, shot with gold and silver, were rippling from the busy looms.

Chiengmai was noted for its lacquer craftsmen. One quaint little shop was filled with round lacquer boxes in every stage of manufacture. I gazed in fascination at the dexterity of the workmen as they filled in the interstices of the woven bamboo frames with thick waxy material, then applied a beautiful smooth surface of red, black, or gold lacquer concealing the framework, and, lastly, scratched fine patterns on the surface and filled them in with pigment. The shop was overhung by palms and stately oil trees, and looked at the ruined brick wall of the ancient town across the moat. In this a Lao, armed with a basket-like net hanging from the end of a long bamboo pole, was patiently fishing for the tiny fish that flickered under the lily pads.

Most common of all sights in Siam was the endless procession of priests, bright in their yellow robes, who everywhere, with their begging bowls in their hands, were asking for rice. The greatest charm to the traveler in Chiengmai, as in all Siam, lay in the wats. Almost everywhere I turned rose a temple, glowing in blue and gold and red, or stately in its dim and quiet ruins. The gateways were guarded by grotesque dog-like images that would frighten away a host of evil spirits, unless perchance they were protected by a sense of humor. On the eaves the little bells, designed for the same purpose but in a pleasanter humor, jingled tunefully. At either end a series of overlapping gables, each surmounted by a strange, snake-like projection, suggested to the International Health Board mind a hookworm rampant.

We had sent Dr. M. E. Barnes, an excellent choice, to Chiengmai. His early upbringing had made him at home with the Oriental mind. Born in India, he knew Hindustani, and had a sound linguistic basis on which to build. He learned not only the Lao tongue but also the Siamese, not an easy task because the differentiations between the two are so subtle. The Siamese language is supposed to be among the most difficult in the world—with its seven tones commensurately more

493

difficult than the four-toned Japanese or Chinese. Seldom could a foreigner master all seven, but Dr. Barnes knew enough of them to be able to give public addresses.

The Siamese were always affable and pleasant, ever ready with the making of fine promises, but taking an eternity to carry them out. Dr. Barnes would ask villagers to come to a certain place at a certain time; they would not be there. He would request local officials to make announcements; they would not be made. To cope with this amiable lethargy, Dr. Barnes devised an extraordinarily effective system of using the Buddhist priests. Although most of them were illiterate, they liked to be considered progressive, and Dr. Barnes diplomatically turned this vanity to his own ends. He proved to these bonzes how, when the Rockefeller Foundation cured their people, they would be the ones to reap the rewards of gratitude.

I was fortunate enough to be able to attend the opening meeting of Dr. Barnes' hookworm campaign in the Wat of Amphur Sansai near Chiengmai. It was filled to the walls with men, and even a few women had timidly crept inside the temple door. From the dusky recesses before them a great gilded Buddha, smiling and complacent, gazed out at the sea of dark faces. The dimly-lighted temple, the image, the tall pillars, the chief priest draped in yellow, the reverent audience in their penungs, presented a picture impressively Oriental, and one pervaded with a spirit of satisfaction with things as they are. Seated on their heels on the floor, these men and women waited patiently to receive the message for which they had been summoned. The only foreign intrusive notes were struck by the hookworm chart which hung on the front of the altar, and by the models of latrines displayed on teak tables, carved and inlaid with mother of pearl.

In sing-song Lao Dr. Barnes described the busy little hookworm in their midst; there were signs and sounds of approval. Then Major Boriracksh, Medical Officer of the Siamese Army, added what was obviously enthusiastic corroboration. Although I could understand no word of what was being said, the Siamese seemed like children listening to a story hour.

Dr. Barnes scored a signal success in Chiengmai, and grew to be admired and trusted by the Siamese as few foreigners had ever been.

Because of his achievements there we were able to storm the citadel of Bangkok, and take up the vital questions of a first-class medical school and an efficient health service.

In Bangkok we had more or less the same problems which had confronted us in the Philippines, but nothing like the authority to carry through reforms. The Siamese were so receptive to ideas, and so many people were offering advice gratis, that the result was often a jumble. They had violated all the principles we held dear in the establishment of a medical center by building the main school across the river, and the pathological laboratory on the city side.

Insanity was prevalent, much of it due to overindulgence in the dangerous drug bhang, or hashish, a derivative of Cannabis Indica, the Indian hemp plant. Smoking, chewing, or drinking hashish was an extremely common habit which the government was loth to stop because the foreign advisers made no objection to this source of revenue. The Siamese had abandoned the practice of chaining their insane to posts, and had built an asylum across the Menam from the city proper. But in the year which had elapsed since its building, not a single Siamese official of any rank had paid it a visit. The approach to this series of small buildings, each of which looked unhappily like a cage, was along a beautiful *klong*, shaded with blooming trees, but the pools in the grounds themselves were stagnant and covered with poisonous green slime. A separate enclosure was set aside for mad priests, which made me wonder how many people were driven crazy by religion. Formerly beriberi had kept down the number of patients until the Health Department, under my inspiration, fed them unpolished rice; thereafter so few died that overcrowding became serious and only the city insane could be accommodated.

The public market, which belonged to the privy purse, was highly insanitary. It was completely closed in by a set of crowded and dirty shacks in which lived the people who prepared food and ices for the vendors. In a filthy well were kept fish destined for public consumption. After trying for years to have this market renovated, the Health Department finally took a series of photographs and sent them to the King. He was shocked and at once ordered repairs made. But then the government officials also went to the King, and said, since it was understood the building was to be torn down soon, repairs

495

were useless. This same excuse served to hold up improvements for years.

The serious health problems of Bangkok did not obtrude on the public notice, but the Siamese were extremely sensitive about their mosquitoes, which were criticized by every foreigner. Although not malaria carriers, they were the worst pest I had ever seen anywhere in the world. When I first went to Siam in 1915, at every dinner party my hostess, upon receiving me, would, as a matter of course, hand me a small bottle filled with oil of eucalyptus which I was supposed to pour over myself in liberal quantities in the hope of discouraging insects. But mosquitoes swarmed in such numbers that the preventive was of no avail, and I usually returned to the hotel with my feet, ankles, and hands swollen beyond recognition. Guests used to cover their legs at table with bags. The last time I was there Flit had become popular, and every half hour a servant would pump a liberal supply under the table, while the guests sprinkled neck and arms with Sketalene.

I was often asked by the Siamese what they could do about mosquitoes, and I advised a survey to determine the cost of control. But they never seriously put themselves to the task of eradication.

The man who might have done something about this and other far more important matters was Prince Dhamrong, the leading elder statesman of the royal family. It seemed to me that he represented the highest point Siamese civilization attained under the old régime. He was charming and gracious in his manner, philosophic in his comments, and it was always a pleasure to converse with him. Had there been many others like him our road in Siam would have been far smoother. He had a magnificent estate, a most tastefully furnished house, and a garden beautifully planted with flowers, among which there were many evidences of Buddhist ornamentation. He said he was not only a professed Buddhist, but also one in actual practice. The moral code of Buddhism, in his opinion, was much like that of Christianity.

"I assume you are a Christian as I am a Buddhist," he said. "It has always interested me why religions are so at odds. What they really disagree about is the hereafter. But I as a Buddhist know nothing of it, and you as a Christian know no more. Why should there be all this acrimony about something we neither of us know anything about? The guess of a Buddhist may as well be right as the guess of a Christian."

The official with whom I had most to do was Prince Sakol, pronounced Sakon, one of the King's first cousins who had recently graduated from Oxford and gave promise of becoming very efficient. In 1915 he had been considering going into the Treasury Department, but I had persuaded him to cast his lot in the public health field by showing him the far greater opportunities there. According to a peculiar custom in Siam, each generation of titled persons lost or stepped down one grade of nobility, eventually becoming plain *nais* or misters unless, by the performance of some meritorious deed, new titles were conferred upon them by the King. Prince Sakol was anxious to prove himself, but he labored under the great handicap of having married a German girl when he had been in Europe, and Siam and its rigid social system had seemed very far away. Upon his return he found his wife ostracized and himself looked upon as having lost caste. Nevertheless, by merit and determination, and in spite of the unhappiness of his social lot, he rose steadily and in 1926 succeeded Jainad, the former Rangsit, as Director of Health.

Even Prince Sakol, honest as he was, would exaggerate our alleged shortcomings in fulfilling our part of the contract, and minimize those of the Siamese. His burden of complaint was that our agreement called for two foreign doctors, and he submitted records showing that, owing to vacations, lapses of a few months had occurred during the past two years of the five-year contract. But he ignored the fact that the Siamese had transferred men out of our units or failed to furnish them altogether. Their capacity, like that of trained lawyers, to split into infinite details some inconsequential matter and obscure the important point when it suited their purpose was at times most trying to the patience.

Each year, as their proportionate share of the budget increased, the Siamese seemed to believe that we were taking something out of their pockets. We knew, of course, that this sentiment was a defensive reaction because of their own realized yet unacknowledged shortcomings in complying with their agreement with us.

The Prince who should have been King after the death in 1925 of Maha Vajiravudh (Rama VI) was Songkla, the only available son of the first queen, but practising medicine appealed to him more than a throne. He had received an M.D. from Harvard Medical School, but unfortunately had been recalled for a funeral before he had an opportunity to serve an internship in the United States. The King had frowned upon the idea of any member of the royal family being in a subordinate capacity in the hospital at Bangkok. Prince Songkla, therefore, had gone to the Missionary Hospital at Chiengmai. Because of his talents and influence, he was, above all others, most useful to us in removing friction and adjusting differences. His early death was a great loss to Siam.

On Prince Songkla's refusal to be king, his half brother Prajadhipok was chosen. King Prajadhipok was always quiet, efficient, sincere, and a conscientious worker. But he was not the best of the princes. The power behind the throne was Prince Nagor Svarga, pronounced Lakan Siwan, head of the Supreme Council of Five and an able administrator. He had much initiative, hard common sense, and a desire to have the government administration in Siam reach a high degree of efficiency. He made quick decisions and pushed his projects through to successful conclusions. Although an opponent of Prince Sakol, he was a great friend of Dr. Barnes who, believing he was the man best fitted for the position and anxious to see the Health Department under his direction, persuaded him to become Minister of the Interior.

Hope was expressed on all sides that the new King would inaugurate a more progressive régime. But the putting of princes and other titled persons into high places still continued, regardless of their training for the jobs. The cringing attitude and the deferring, even in scientific matters, to those of higher rank, was common. It was especially amusing to observe the attitude of Prince Sakol's subordinates, who would deliver no opinions until he had given his. Since our views often reached the Prince only through these same subordinates, delays and misunderstandings were inevitable. Many ministers required their heads of departments to sit on the floor in their presence, and during the later years of Prajadhipok the former custom of requiring servitors to approach him on all fours was resumed.

498

HUSTLING THE EAST

Until a few years ago Siam was perhaps the most peaceful country in the world. The people had no democratic rights and did not possess the vote; all orders were issued from the capital at Bangkok. But apparently they were perfectly satisfied and contented to have an absolute monarchy. Almost out of a clear sky came the Revolution, aimed at the princes who, without regard to merit, had so long held all the important offices. Its causes were so ill-defined that nobody could quite put his finger upon them. Among the reasons offered was that America, by its example in granting so many powers to the Filipinos and providing them with an Occidental standard of living, had stirred up the fires of independence smoldering here as elsewhere in the East.

When King Prajadhipok had returned from his cataract operation in New York in 1931, Prince Nagor Svarga had told him a revolution was brewing, but the King would not believe it. "You're the King," said Nagor, "and I can do nothing, but you could stop it if you would do such and such things," and he outlined a course of action. But the King merely intimated he would institute reforms in the near future. Long before he was prepared to move, the revolutionists won over the Army, and then it was too late.

The Revolution of 1932 altered the monarchy from absolute to constitutional, with an elective assembly and an executive council. Most of those who had formerly been assistants now became ministers. On the whole, the best men were chosen, and few reprisals were attempted; the royal family retained most of its property, although all were banished except the King.

I later met Prince Nagor Svarga, now called Parabitra, exiled in Bandoeng, Java. It seemed odd to see this Prince who, at Bangkok had lived in such regal splendor, now occupying a simple bungalow. I called to mind how only a few years before, when the Far Eastern Association of Tropical Medicine had held its 1930 meeting at Bangkok, Prince Nagor Svarga had outdone himself in providing welcome. The atmosphere had been one of hospitality, that in Siam was so peculiarly inspiring with its sincerity. To terminate the festivities, he had given a reception and dinner to one hundred and thirty guests, served luxuriously in his immense grounds. Afterwards he had offered for our entertainment a gorgeous spectacle in which several hundred Siamese portrayed a Buddhist play in dance.

In 1935 King Prajadhipok refused all requests to return from London, whither he had gone for a second operation, because the Revolution had deprived him of so many powers, chiefly that of pardon. He abdicated his throne and remained in England. The present heir apparent is the son of Prince Songkla. His mother is struggling to keep him at school in Switzerland and out of the confusion of Siamese politics.

Many of the trying customs of the old governments are being continued in the new régime. The higher-ups make plans in secret without consulting the bureau chiefs, who never know the objects of the policies they are directed to pursue. The office force finds it difficult to realize the old days are gone, and that they may express opinions without knowing what their superiors think. They still speak in whispers, and wait for all plans to be handed down to them from above.

The great problem in medical education in these later years was whether to have a large number of poor doctors or a small number of very good ones in Siam. The poor ones could undoubtedly give relief to many people, and the few good ones could only reach a limited number. I had been concerned with this question for thirty years and found it exceedingly difficult to decide which was the better course. But I knew that dealing with environmental sanitation such as water and sewage would produce much greater results in the form of a reduced death rate and morbidity than all the junior doctors could ever accomplish. The Siamese ultimately saw the matter from the Rockefeller Foundation point of view.

To Dr. A. G. Ellis belongs the major credit for building up the Medical School in Siam. He had been selected by the Foundation as Director and later employed by the Siamese themselves. It was amazing to me that any human being could have lived through the daily round of disappointment and discouragement. He was able to see the hands of progress move around the clock, although they were turning so slowly no one else could detect their motion. It was due to his sacrificial efforts that the Medical School, with a completely Siamese faculty, became a modern institution.

As far back as 1926 it had seemed advisable for the International

Health Division to withdraw from Siam, for a time at least, until the government, of its own initiative, should present a sound plan for continued cooperation. The attitude was all too prevalent that we were forcing the Siamese to do something they were not convinced they wanted to do, and that we only offered them fellowships, which they keenly desired, in order to bribe them into doing something the value of which they considered debatable. They apparently failed to understand that we were there to help them in their struggle for something better. On the other hand, they were so innocently nice that we had a feeling we ought to help them, and that any failure on their part must be due to their not having understood. My conclusion was that if the Rockefeller Foundation's investment were to yield worth while results, a well-qualified adviser would be needed on the scene for many years.

In 1929 the Foundation finally withdrew completely from Siam except for such an adviser. Dr. Louis Schapiro, who had done brilliant work in Panama, volunteered for this thankless task. He had refused our offer of retirement, although he knew his term of life would be shortened by any strenuous labor, saying he would rather die in harness. He became a tremendous favorite in Siam. It was during his service that a sanitary engineer was brought from the United States to develop the installation of reservoir and pipe line distribution systems in the cities and towns of Siam. By efficient prodding, and helped in every imaginable way by Prince Nagor Svarga, he even succeeded in starting health centers. When Dr. Schapiro died we did not replace him.

In many ways over the years we had saved the Siamese from doing unprofitable and unwise things and often from spending money foolishly. But we had ourselves often forgotten the Siamese were the product of a civilization that did not want to hurry, and that, even when they tried, they were pulled back by the accumulated habits of centuries. The few progressive Siamese were still as scattered corks, bobbing upon a vast ocean, struggling against winds and currents that often carried them far from their goal. Only when I looked back over fifteen years of work could progress be noted. Many men whom I used to see in bygone years had passed on, yet things continued to move, and even made slow advance from an Occidental viewpoint. Graft and corruption, which had been so prevalent, were steadily lessening; efficiency slowly increasing, and finally the Siamese had come to accept, although probably they never completely understood, the Rockefeller Foundation form of altruism.

CHAPTER 28.   PEARL OF
                              GREAT PRICE

O NE by one the fertile regions of the earth have been swallowed
      up by the land-hungry nations. Abyssinia alone remains as the
largest undeveloped area of productive terrain in the world. Even
now most Americans and many Europeans have little idea of its
desirability. This temperate zone paradise in the heart of equatorial
Africa is securely hemmed in by the barren wastes of the Sudan,
the inhospitable shores of West Africa, and the sweltering deserts
bordering the Red Sea. Comparatively few foreigners are familiar
with its clear sparkling days and bright blue skies, or have viewed
its forested mountains and translucent streams. Nevertheless, its European neighbors, Italy, France, and Great Britain, who hold the sterile
Red Sea coast once controlled by Abyssinia, are keenly aware that the
Abyssinian government, in spite of its boasted five thousand years
of continuous existence, has not kept step with the civilized world.
Their urgent craving to unbar the gates to these greener pastures is,
if not excusable, at least quite understandable.

Although my work for the Rockefeller Foundation had, in the
course of twenty years, taken me into practically every portion of
the two hemispheres, it was not until 1933 that I visited Abyssinia,
or Ethiopia, as the inhabitants prefer to have their country called.
The Foundation, which was then engaged in an attempt to eradicate
yellow fever from the world, had cabled me a request to collect for
them some blood samples in that remote mountain land.

One morning in early May, with the thermometer at 115 degrees, the Messageries liner *Leconte de Lisle* anchored off Jibuti, the gateway of Abyssinia. I had expected to make immediate connections for the Abyssinian capital, Addis Ababa. This did not seem unreasonable, since both railway and steamship line were French-owned. But the train, which ran only twice a week, had left ten minutes before our arrival. I had four days to wait for the next one.

Somewhat impatiently I inquired my way to the hotel. It turned out to be much like that one finds in a village in France, even to the little sidewalk café. There French officials and Levantines were trying to shelter their drinks from the dust which rose in clouds as the motor cars chugged laboriously through the hot sandy streets.

The days wore on but the thermometer remained static. Although many years in the tropics had made me pride myself somewhat on my indifference to heat, Jibuti was an oven in which I was slowly being baked. The only way I could get a night's sleep was to throw off blanket, sheet, and pajamas, and turn two large electric fans upon myself. At table an open shirt, no coat, and shorts was the accepted dress.

The United States was at this moment fervently engaged in going off the gold standard. As the dollar tobogganed down, those travelers in foreign parts, including myself, looked on bewildered and helpless. American money, before the War practically unknown, had in succeeding years become standard. American tourists, eager to spend their dollars, had literally made them all mighty throughout the world. The urchin who dived for coins in Jibuti harbor knew their value. Now, almost overnight, this confidence was destroyed.

I trustfully took my American Express checks to the Bank of Indo-China, the only one in town. The cashier shrugged his shoulders; he could quote no rate of exchange. He would, as a special favor to me, cash one check for twenty dollars, but no more. Since the fare to Addis Ababa was almost three times this figure, it appeared that, for lack of a few francs, I might be prevented from carrying out my commission.

In the white hot sunlight I went tramping from place to place, hoping to find some merchant who would take my money. My hopes were not unduly high; I knew the normal reluctance of the French to extend credit would be enhanced considerably by the current financial crisis. It was by the sheerest good luck that I finally encountered a shopkeeper who owed bills in the United States which we could pay with my express checks; from him I obtained seventy dollars.

The first of the long three days required for the railroad journey —the train did not run at night—lay through sand barrens, stippled thickly with black rocks, called, from their obvious resemblance, nigger heads. I could see occasional dust devils whirling in the distance; about noon one of these engulfed the train. I hastily banged the windows shut, but the fine choking dust penetrated everywhere. Without any ventilation, the heat was so intense that sand and sweat caked on my face. My teeth grated on the fine particles and my eyes soon became as bloodshot as those of the desert inhabitants themselves. The one electric light which, with true French economy, was the size of a glass bead, gave little illumination inside the compartment, and had not the slightest effect upon the outer darkness. Water of any sort is rare; the rivers which come rushing from the mountains of Ethiopia are sucked into the desert long before they reach the sea. Moreover, malaria and dysentery, the age-old enemies of man in the tropics which have so often defeated his plans, are ever lying in wait.

After climbing steadily all day long, at nightfall the train pulled into Dire Dawa, at an altitude of nearly a mile, and, in contrast to the coast, delightfully cool and refreshing. This was the border of Ethiopia, the legendary country where Prester John and the Queen of Sheba once had ruled. Pandemonium was raging. At least five hundred of the coffee-colored, hooked-nosed townspeople, gesticulating and shouting wildly, were gathered around the station. I innocently assumed they were celebrating the arrival of the train, but I soon discovered my error. We were to be the victims of their barbaric holiday. In apparent delight at the opportunity of humiliating white people, the black soldiery rudely pushed us into the Customs House with their guns. One after another, the passengers' bags were seized, roughly opened, and each article held up for the edification of the crowd. Whenever a bit of feminine lingerie was flourished triumphantly in the air, the howling mob greeted the display with appreciative shouts of joy. I could sense the resentment of the inspectors, who seemed to regard us with that intuitive aversion which so many Americans feel toward members of the black and yellow races.

When my turn came, I exhibited to the Customs Official a permit from the Ethiopian Minister of Foreign Affairs, which I confidently expected would exempt my personal belongings from being passed in review before the population of Dire Dawa. Without even pretending to examine it, he waved it aside. I asked him, by signs, to take me to his chief. But the latter, glancing at it briefly, merely replied, "We don't know what that is."

Still unwilling to lose faith in the efficiency of this document, I sought the Customs Office up the street. The only comment of the department head was, "We never honor these things"; for the third time I was ordered to open my bag.

Obediently I returned to the station, only to find that the short-lived interest had subsided, and the crowd was melting away. One by one the guards, with the inspection only half over, were also departing, and in a few moments I was left alone with my still unopened bag. It was simplicity itself; I merely summoned a porter to carry it to the hotel.

The second day's ride was somewhat less monotonous than the first. There were occasional scrubby trees and even small patches of cultivated land. The third day we slid through lush valleys, skirted steep river cañons, and chugged up wooded highlands. It was difficult to believe that these Delectable Mountains could be only twenty-four hours away from the arid inferno of the coastal regions. I could well understand why Italian eyes should strain toward them so covetously.

In the last few hours of the third day we mounted abruptly from three to eight thousand feet. From the mountain rim, looking far down over the terraced orchards of apple and pear and peach, and the fields of waving grain, I could see the tiled roofs of Addis Ababa, lying prettily in its grove of eucalyptus trees.

As soon as I had deposited my bag in the hotel, I started out for a brisk walk to stretch my legs and sniff the spring fragrance. I had gone no more than half a mile when I was stopped by sentries, and taken to a guard house. I had not the faintest idea of my offense, but I have always deemed it unwise to display anger under such circumstances. I smiled my pleasantest, and began to pass cigarettes among my captors. They received these overtures amiably, but, whenever I attempted to go on my way, their bayonets promptly barred my passage. I knew not a word of Amharic, the language of the country; but I tried in turn my English, French, German, and Italian—all to no avail. For some thirty minutes we smiled at one another with continued amiability.

Then it occurred to me that perhaps in that direction might lie some military arsenal or government preserve which I was not supposed to see. "Possibly," I thought, "if I am able to show my willingness to return upon my tracks, I may be allowed to leave." I indicated this in pantomime, and, behind the smoke screen of a final round of cigarettes, departed in peace.

The next morning I described my adventure to the American Minister and asked whether he could furnish any explanation.

"Very easily," he assured me. "Nobody is supposed to go unescorted in the streets of Addis Ababa. Any man of social standing must have at least three or four retainers tagging after him. If he's really important, three hundred may follow him to the market place to buy a chicken."

"But I have visits to make and work to do," I protested. "I must be back and forth all the time."

"Don't worry," he replied. "We have a standing arrangement with the government that one uniformed legation guard ranks as high as a retinue of fifty. The two I'm going to lend you will put you well up in the social scale."

Thereafter, where I went, they went. If I walked, they walked. If I rode, they rode; one in front and one behind. If I played tennis, they had to accompany me, as guarantors of my social standing.

My first duty was to pay my respects to Belaten Gheta Herouy Woulde Selassie, Minister of Foreign Affairs. Although Abyssinia had a Parliament of two houses, and a full-fledged cabinet of ten high-sounding ministries, these were generally regarded as the Emperor's window dressing. The exception was Herouy who, for services rendered, had been rewarded with a sort of grand viziership.

I explained to Herouy that I had come to Ethiopia to secure yellow fever blood specimens. There would be no objection, he assured me, provided there were no cost to his government. To my astonishment I learned that the army of Ethiopia was without medi-

507

cal protection—no doctor, no nurses, no splints, not even a box of pills. I discovered later that there was but one native doctor in the whole country, and that even the Emperor's Greek physician was said to have been merely a sergeant in the medical corps of some army. Herouy made it apparent that Ethiopia, beyond controlling the sale of narcotic drugs, had no desire to establish a health service. He regarded leprosy as the country's most important health problem and stated incidentally that he was certain this disease was hereditary in Ethiopia. By presenting him evidence from my own experience, I tried to persuade him to the contrary, but he remained unconvinced.

In contrast to the average Abyssinian, Herouy was coal black and, instead of the usual wavy or even straight hair, he was crowned with kinky white wool. He appeared to have negroid characteristics, but this could hardly have been possible, since the Ethiopians, proud of their Semitic heritage, regard the Negro as fit only for slavery. No one even suspected of Negro blood can attain to any position of importance.

It is unfortunate as well as unintelligent that the people in the United States, without investigation, and with characteristic impulsiveness, have actually encouraged American Negroes to go to Abyssinia to establish friendly relations. Nothing could have caused more irritation. Such typically American attempts at missionary work have ended in complete futility.

In a way it was refreshing to find myself in a country where statistics did not exist. Anybody could prove anything, and opinions assumed the force of facts. Nobody knew whether there were three or fifteen million Abyssinians. They were born and they died without record. But apparently the high birth rate was balanced by the high infant mortality.

The Coptic Church of Abyssinia, an ancient form of Greek Catholicism, was all powerful in the country. Originally it had followed the Nile up from Egypt, and for many centuries had maintained its identity, although cut off from the rest of the Christian world by the Mohammedan encirclement. It was intensely jealous of encroachments on the part of other Christian religions. The priests always considered it a favor when they permitted the missionaries to build hospitals and schools, and made it clear that there must be no proselyting. The latter did their best to fulfill these requirements, but they often forgot, and one of the principal duties of the foreign legations was to straighten out the resultant difficulties.

Four mission hospitals had been built at Addis Ababa, and a few dispensaries were scattered throughout the provinces. These took care of a small portion of the sick; what became of the rest was a mystery. The Swedish Hospital was said to have received substantial grants from the Emperor. The French Menelik Hospital, on the other hand, was treated like a stepchild, and looked it.

Some years ago the Emperor had had a modern hospital constructed and completely equipped. Just before the opening ceremonies, he asked to see the budget. He examined the figures. "We won't open the hospital," was his sole comment.

For several years the building stood idle. Then some American Seventh Day Adventists discovered it. "Here is a beautiful hospital," they said to each other. "Instead of constructing one for ourselves, we shall ask the Emperor for this."

"Oh, yes," Haile Selassie told them. "You may have it as long as it does not cost me anything, and is used for the benefit of my people."

The exultant missionaries went to install themselves, but found to their dismay that much of the equipment had mysteriously disappeared. However, the once-poverty-stricken Menelik Hospital, not far off, had somehow or other come into possession of suspiciously similar instruments. The Adventists wrote a letter, informing the Menelikers that they would appreciate the return of the equipment which now belonged rightfully to them. There was no reply. A second note received the same inattention. The Adventists then returned to the Emperor with their complaint.

"I'll see that you get the instruments," he encouraged them, and promptly took the matter up with the French Legation.

The affair had now become a matter of state. After the usual diplomatic delays, a reply was eventually elicited from the Menelik Hospital authorities. They would not admit that they had these instruments, but, even if they did have them, they could not very well return them. Such an action would be an admission that they had taken them, and consequently a reflection upon their honor.

At last accounts the Adventists were still waiting for their equipment.

As I crossed the veranda of the American Mission Hospital on my first visit there, I observed several advanced cases of confluent small-pox, relapsing fever, and typhus; no isolation ward for such infectious diseases had been provided. But the relatives or friends of stricken ones, hearing of the miracles performed at the Hospital, would leave them in the grounds under cover of darkness, and the doctors made shift to care for them.

Because of these limited facilities, the doctors and nurses themselves suffered terribly from infectious diseases. The quality of their bravery was greater, perhaps, because, in the last analysis, their primary interest lay in religion and not in medicine. Caring for the body was merely a means by which the soul might be saved.

Probably few diseases are more deadly than yellow fever, and nobody as yet has been able to discover an organism. In the course of laboratory research many deaths have occurred among the workers from merely handling the virus. A section of a blood vessel in the leg of a mosquito contains enough poison to kill an adult human being, and one infected mosquito can start an epidemic.

For thirty years the scientists of the world had tried to convey yellow fever to every variety of animal from snake to monkey. Finally Dr. Adrian Stokes, a British specialist, made the important discovery that it could be transmitted to a certain type of Indian monkey, but just at the moment of triumph he contracted the disease and died. His contribution made it possible to proceed with experimental work, and, in time, a practical blood test was developed which could determine whether any people in a given area had ever had yellow fever.

The history of the virtual conquest of yellow fever exemplifies the value and necessity of collaboration in science. Economically a country may be self-sustaining, but in the medical world international cooperation is essential. Any great advance today seldom results from the efforts of one person or one race. British, Americans, French, and Dutch, often working along unrelated lines, all added their little pieces of information which made it possible to put the yellow fever puzzle together.

PEARL OF GREAT PRICE

Dr. Henry R. Carter, inveterate reader and student, supplied one of the missing pieces. He searched through the diaries of the early explorers of America to find some evidence of the existence of yellow fever on this continent before Columbus. He found none. The inevitable conclusion from his work, coupled with other evidence, was that yellow fever had come to America with the slave trade. West Africa was thus established as the seed bed of the disease.

I knew that residents of Addis Ababa would be free from yellow fever, because the stegomyia does not fly above the five thousand foot level. However, the American Mission Hospital contained enough lowland patients for my purposes.

The first time I tried to make tests, the sterilizer refused to work. Then, the doctor upon whom I depended for assistance developed sinus trouble and amoebic dysentery. The ordinary procedure was to collect each specimen in a glass tube and then fuse the end in a Bunsen burner. But there was no gas in Addis Ababa. I tried an alcohol lamp; it was not hot enough. Nor did a blow pipe prove more adequate. Finally, by pumping vigorously on a Primus stove, I managed to seal the glass tubes hermetically. In spite of these difficulties, I had secured thirty blood specimens at the end of three days, although I was somewhat dubious as to their sterility.

The next problem was to contrive some method of keeping the blood specimens on ice during the three days' run to Jibuti. I had to construct an emergency refrigerator, much like those I had formerly used for carrying smallpox vaccine into the Mountain Province of the Philippines. I received sufficient ice from the Addis Ababa brewery to keep the tubes chilled until they could be shifted to the steamer's refrigerator at Jibuti.

I was naturally interested in observing the incidence of diseases other than yellow fever in Addis Ababa. The enormous bazaar was the logical place to seek them. The boisterous, good-natured crowds were milling around the little baskets of native commodities and cheap foreign hardware spread on the ground. Unmistakable cases of leprosy and smallpox were circulating freely among the people.

Nobody apparently minded the jostling and pushing. But the traffic problem had become exceedingly serious with the advent of motor cars, which dashed recklessly over the few asphalt-paved streets, and sent the innumerable curs yelping. Abyssinia, with the aid of Belgian policemen, was trying to install traffic rules. Great difficulty was being encountered with the more primitive forms of transport. The puzzled drivers of donkeys and camels failed utterly to comprehend what was expected. They calmly plodded and padded along, regardless of upraised hand and verbal admonishment. When the vociferous Belgians would come tearing after them, accompanied by interpreters to explain the infractions of the rules, they would merely look puzzled and scratch their pates.

On one of my walks around the town I noted a number of small shelters scattered over the hillside on which stood the rambling congeries of buildings which comprised the royal palace. Squatting under each thatched roof was a forlorn-looking individual, munching his lunch. All were there in accordance with the Emperor's unique method of disciplining government officials with whom he was not pleased. The imperial income was mainly derived from coffee and goatskins, the tribute of the kings or other governments. The only traceable revenue in coin was the customs duty, usually paid in the old Maria Theresa dollar, minted in Austria and imported as a commodity. This money, however, was apparently not sufficient for the Emperor's needs, because it was said the servants' wages at the palace were a year in arrears.

The great depression had affected Abyssinia very little. The landowners had merely required extra duty from their slaves, and the government twice as many goatskins and double the quantity of coffee. Each of the Emperor', unsalaried governors had to collect the additional tribute and also support himself. What was more difficult, he had to keep everybody satisfied. Retaining or losing his province depended upon the number of complaints against him. No questions were asked as to how much of the revenue he diverted to his own uses, but the balance was obviously delicate.

The system worked as follows. A countryman would start to drive a herd of several hundred goats from a distant province to the market place of the capital. Two or three would be appropriated by the first government official he encountered. As he proceeded, his animals would diminish, until he might reach Addis Ababa with only a few stragglers. If this process of depletion could not be accomplished without hard feelings, he would set up a loud outcry.

The unlucky official would be promptly ordered to appear at the palace for an interview at six in the morning. He would take his place under one of the shelters and wait there. The Emperor might not see him for one month, or two months, or even six months. But he had to appear each morning at that same early hour. This chastening process was guaranteed to tame even the most recalcitrant.

Haile Selassie regarded himself as the ranking Emperor of the world. Only the Mikado could approach him in dignity. As for the King of England, he was a mere absentee Emperor, and not to be included among the proper emperors. Haile was now on a tour of his provinces, and was due to stop for the day in Addis Ababa on his way South. He usually saw nobody on such occasions, but through the personal friendship of the American Minister who had known him well in the days when he had been simply Ras Tafari, a Prince of the royal house, I was granted an audience.

I presented myself at the palace and was conducted to an anteroom. The Emperor was always prompt for Europeans and Americans, though his dignity demanded that he keep his own subjects waiting. Almost immediately upon my arrival, the doors were thrown open, and with the prescribed three bows and three steps between, I approached the throne on which was sitting his Imperial Majesty Haile Selassie I, King of Kings of Ethiopia, Conquering Lion of Judah, Elect of God as proclaimed in the seventy languages of Ethiopia, and heir presumptive to Palestine through descent from King Solomon and the Queen of Sheba.

The Emperor was resplendent in a royal scarlet coat, gorgeously decorated with broad bands of gold, and his feet were ornamented with shoes, brocaded in the Chinese manner. He was short of stature, perhaps five and a half feet tall, brown in complexion, with full black beard and a Hebraic cast to his nose.

Haile Selassie was educated in French and speaks it fluently, but he prefers to use his native Amharic, which sounded to me much like Arabic. The interview had to be conducted through an interpreter. I have often found the interpreter system a help rather than a hindrance. If such an intermediary can convey the spirit of what is said as well as the bare words, the pauses, particularly where an ill-chosen word might have a bad effect, permit a more careful phrasing than would otherwise be possible.

I told my royal host how the course of yellow fever was being traced in Africa, and recounted the story of the Panama Canal as an illustration of what sanitation had been able to accomplish. I described the early failure there, and told how the difficulties had been overcome. Although my audience was to have lasted only ten minutes, he became so interested in my social sales talk that he asked me to remain for tea. During the rest of the afternoon I tried to show him how his own country would benefit by the establishment of a sanitary organization.

The Emperor was as thoroughly convinced of the importance of leprosy in Ethiopia as Herouy had been. He showed great interest in the work of the American Mission to Lepers, for which funds were even then being raised. Later he himself opened the Ethiopian Leprosarium with elaborate ceremonies. Nobody knows, of course, the number of lepers at large in Ethiopia, but it is probable that the disease is relatively unimportant there as compared, for example, with the Philippine Islands or India. If similar sums were spent on vaccination, thousands of lives would be saved and innumerable cases of blindness prevented. Or by a cleanliness campaign, at a cost well within his resources, Haile Selassie could free his people from typhus and relapsing fever—both lice-borne diseases.

In my enthusiasm I was led to remark somewhat jocularly on the backward condition of Ethopia. He bore with me in gentlemanly fortitude, then inquired politely, "You are an American, are you not?"

"Yes," I admitted, somewhat puzzled as to the object of his query.

"How many unemployed have you in the United States?"

"About twelve million, I should imagine."

"Well," he continued blandly, "my government has been in continuous existence for over five thousand years. We have no unemployment; we have never had any. We have no starving. All my people have homes to live in. They have clothes to wear. They are happy."

I could think of no answer. I have not yet been able to think of one.

In this interview politics were not mentioned. Elsewhere I inquired assiduously of British, French, and Italians, and, from a composite of their views, tried to ascertain the truth. It appeared that, as late as December, 1925, Great Britain and Italy had made a secret treaty about spheres of influence in Abyssinia. Italy was anxious to run a railway through the highlands to connect her two separated provinces of Somaliland and Eritrea. In return Great Britain was to be allowed to construct a dam at Lake Tsana by which the flood waters of the Nile could be controlled.

Since Americans are generally credited with having no territorial ambitions, the J. G. White Engineering Corporation of New York was employed to make the preliminary surveys for this project. The press of England immediately cried out against it, intimating that this was a clever Yankee trick to regulate the water of the Nile so that Americans would have a stranglehold on the British-owned cotton industry of the Sudan. Not merely was this ironical in view of the secret treaty, but the British editors failed to realize that Americans, even to protect their own markets, seldom have exhibited such foresight.

Finally, with funds furnished by the Sudan, and with the full consent of Great Britain, the survey was made.

Then it developed that the plans, if carried out, would cause the flooding of many Coptic churches in that section of the country. Abyssinia, therefore, rejected the proposals.

However, the English government and the Sudan were so anxious to have the water impounded that still further pressure was exerted on Abyssinia. She finally consented to a second survey, to be paid for by Egypt, an equal sharer in the potential profits of the scheme. Churches subject to flooding were to be protected by coffer dams. The Abyssinians were to take what water they needed for their own crops and to be paid a royalty on all water flowing from the dam.

There remained the question of building a road to the dam site. Great Britain naturally desired to have it constructed from the Sudan. But the Abyssinians vetoed this idea categorically. According to their fundamental policy, all roads in the country should radiate from Addis Ababa. France, Great Britain, and Italy, with amazing celerity, shift sides according to the economic or political interest of the moment. In this case French Somaliland battened parasitically upon traffic to and from Abyssinia, and she trembled for her railroad receipts should a motor road approach Addis Adaba from the South. Consequently France nobly helped the Abyssinians carry their point. It was agreed that the road should be built from the capital to Tsana, a distance of several hundred miles.

In order to finance this undertaking a bond issue was proposed. But the preferred place to float such a loan was the United States, in which foreign bond issues had attained an unenviable notoriety. Consequently, after the medley of promises, threats, and reprisals, nothing has been done.

The Abyssinians had enough political acumen to perceive that their best hope of survival lay in the mutual jealousy of the three big dogs barking outside the Abyssinian manger. Hence they had joined the League of Nations promptly, and whenever any country had encroached, they had clamored so loudly that the aggressor, alarmed at the light of publicity, had withdrawn as gracefully as possible.

When Abyssinia has been arraigned for culpable backwardness, her holding of slaves has usually been made the chief charge against her. It is true that when the Abyssinians wanted more slaves they went out and captured them. A prerequisite to the League was the promulgation of a decree abolishing slave trading. The Emperor, who had been to Europe and had progressive ideas, was full of fine intentions, and wrote stringent regulations punishing it by death— but nobody would enforce them.

I suspect that political agents have used the subject of slavery in Ethiopia for their own propaganda purposes. Earnest people who write articles are legitimately outraged by the situation: no one would wish to condone this state of affairs. I must admit, however, that the slaves, of whom it is estimated there are about three million, seem cheerful and well treated. In almost every way they form part of the household.

PEARL OF GREAT PRICE

After joining the League, the Abyssinians were told they must abandon slavery altogether. When ordered by the Emperor, they obediently released ten thousand. But the slaves owned no land and consequently had no means of earning a living. They did not know where to go or what to do, and promptly ran back to their old masters. A short while ago I was told that the Abyssinians were willing to free all their slaves, but when I was there they were still waiting for the League to explain what to do with them when they were freed.

Raids have been made into British and French territory and the Abyssinians have undoubtedly created disturbances along the border of what the Italians have regarded as theirs. But the Abyssinians may argue with truth that they cannot tell when they have left their own territory, because their hundreds of miles of border are unmarked.

The regular Abyssinian Army, although comparatively small in numbers, is exceptionally brave, and has been well drilled by European officers. The soldiers have always claimed no conscription would be necessary; they liked to fight. Nor had the Emperor, frugal in other things, been niggardly in the matter of military equipment.

I heard several times the story of the American Army Colonel who was one of the three representatives of the United States at the coronation. At his interview with Haile Selassie, this officer had presented a machine gun of the latest pattern. He and his gift were received most graciously and, as a return courtesy, the Colonel was invited to attend a review the next morning. The infantry and the cavalry passed, and then came a number of machine gun companies. Each had a gun the exact counterpart of that which the Colonel had just donated to this backward country.

With his unfailing courtesy the Emperor did not, then or later, mention the matter.

Whatever the outcome of the present movement, it is obvious that Abyssinia cannot remain indefinitely in her present stage of development. If Italy does not find her way in, it is only a question of time before some other country will do so. It may not be with the fanfare of trumpet and beat of drum, but the march of civilization cannot indefinitely be postponed. It is an all-penetrant force, ineluctable and ineludible, before which the Conquering Lion of Judah must ultimately bow.

CHAPTER 29.   PILGRIM'S PROGRESS

CHOLERA has always followed the trail of the pilgrims. Every year the ghats of Benares are dotted with the brown bodies of Hindus who have come from all over India to the Holy Ganges to bathe and drink. Instead of healing all their infirmities and purifying their souls, as they trustfully believe, the filthy water contaminates their bodies.

But in India the danger is centered within the one country. The route of the faithful to Mecca endangers the whole world. From India, Egypt, Persia, Iraq, Turkey, the Malay Peninsula, Borneo, Java, and Mindanao the hordes converge on the Holy City of Mahomet. Seventeen thousand passed through the Quarantine Station at Tor on the Red Sea in one year. With the exception of Egyptians, who are given cholera and smallpox vaccinations on leaving for Mecca, practically none of the pilgrims was protected. Sooner or later cholera appears among them; whole shiploads of these people have tragically perished, although through international action in establishing a quarantine station, and the general use of cholera vaccine, such outbreaks are becoming less frequent.

Each country through which the pilgrims passed wanted to secure a share of this tourist trade, and constantly squabbled as to how the routes should be mapped. In 1927 an International Sanitary Convention at Paris agreed that pilgrims must use certain prescribed sea routes.

We were most anxious to help the nations control disease along these new pilgrim paths, which not only affected the route to Mecca, but also threatened Europe with invasions from the Orient. Through international action, the Conseil Sanitaire Maritime et Quarantenaire d'Egypte was established many years ago, which through its control of quarantine at the Suez Canal has served as a filter to protect Europe against the invasion of dangerous communicable disease. A laboratory at Bagdad, where careful diagnoses could be made, would do much to bring this about. I made several trips there and was well on the way to success when the British decided to give up their mandate.

King Feisal also was in agreement with our ideas, and we discussed it at dinner in his palace, a single-story Moslem building containing many rooms. The gorgeous uniforms of the servants gave the effect of departed glory. King Feisal had been French-educated, but his hatred of the Gaul was so great that he made desperate attempts to speak English, although with poor success. Unfortunately for our plans King Feisal died before anything could be accomplished.

Iraq, because it has proved to be the center of one of the world's great oil districts, has become a rich country. A pipe line runs all the way from Mosul to the Mediterranean at Haifa in Palestine, with a branch to the French in Syria.

As usual the Medical Department lacked funds; the few medical men there had a problem facing them so huge that they resembled pygmies trying to move a mountain with a toothpick. Half the public income went for defense and police; health received but a twentieth.

Of the rural population an indefinite number of thousands were wandering Bedouins who cultivated the soil and drove their cattle to spots favored by weather conditions at particular times of the year. They were an important factor in the spread of disease, and most difficult to control, especially in such matters as smallpox vaccination.

Owing to the rapid increase of power pumping along the Tigris, the area of nearly five hundred miles along its banks between Bagdad and Basra was rapidly coming under cultivation, bringing with it the malaria menace. Another source of danger was the extensive maze of bazaars in Bagdad. The dark cellars, the innumerable underground passages, and the multitude of grain deposits, made rat-proofing almost impossible. Moreover, in some districts fifty percent of the population was estimated to be infected with the bladder variety of bilharzia, although it was not known what variety of snail was responsible. Research work was badly needed.

Scarcely any missionary or other philanthropic aid was rendered to hospitals. The demand for bed space in the Bagdad Hospital far exceeded the supply. Each morning even the desperately sick were carried in litters to the hospital grounds in the hope of being able to pounce upon a bed made vacant through death or discharge. At evening the unsuccessful ones were dolefully returned whence they had come.

In spite of these health handicaps, Bagdad radiated an air of optimism about the bright future of Iraq. None of the thousand British considered it a handicap to live there. In summer the temperature reached as high as 118, but the nights were cool. During the British occupation Government House was a fine building with spacious grounds located beside the Tigris, and with all the swank and military incidental to Government Houses in other British countries. After giving up the mandate, Great Britain still kept the right to have a certain number of judges and to station forces in Iraq west of the Euphrates, to control foreign relations.

Over the border in French-mandated Syria, traveling conditions were far less pleasant than in Iraq. The usual French officiousness cropped up at the border. Although a half-million-dollar bridge over the Euphrates had just been completed to encourage international travel, I had to undergo four customs and two passport examinations at Deir es Zor. The officials refused to return the latter without so-called overtime, rated at a pound and a half per passport, and infinite annoyance was caused by having to tramp from office to office.

Syria was a land of milk and honey compared with the terrible dryness of Palestine. The French were pouring money into it to make it go. After years of disturbances, peace had only been achieved at the point of the sword. The marvelous ancient buildings of Damascus, one of the world's oldest cities, had been half destroyed by French airplanes to give a lesson to the "rebels." The French claimed revolution was in progress, a queer name for non-cooperation. On my last trip I had worked for two days after one of the bombardments helping with the wounded women and children who had been wantonly injured.

Things had quieted down in the Lebanon since the Druses had been given republic status, and Arab schools were made possible under partial self-government. The Health Service was entirely military, and, on the whole, very little had been done for the people of the country. I came away feeling that if we could make a malaria survey it might lead the way to a complete reorganization of health and medical service, and thereby give the Syrians the help in the control of disease they so sorely needed.

When I reached Beirut May 15, 1921, I could find no scheduled sailing for London, where it was imperative that I meet Dr. Vincent on June 1, for discussion of plans for an Institute of Hygiene. No steamship agent could suggest a possible route that would get me there in time. I myself was at my wit's end. In desperation I made the rounds of the harbor, asking everywhere. Finally I located the *Montazah,* an old freighter which carried no cabin passengers; her master said he was bound for Constantinople. On the assumption that I was to be the only passenger I bought a deck passage and purchased a box of oranges, little knowing how invaluable they were to prove, carted them and my bags on board and, feeling terribly sorry for myself, deposited them on the hot, sizzling, iron deck, and sank heavily on to the hatch.

It was rather lonely and I spent an uncomfortable night on the hard planks. The next morning we were in Tripoli, where we were to stay four to five hours. Taking advantage of the stop, I decided to go ashore. In this small town, contrary to my usual luck, I found nobody who could speak any language I knew. Finally I corralled a small boy who watched politely while I made signs to him, intended to convey that I was in a mood to see church architecture. He nodded in apparent comprehension and set off at a brisk pace, I at his heels. Twisting and turning through alleys and byways, we eventually reached a gate in a narrow street on which the boy pounded vigorously. To my astonishment, the doorway framed a lady who greeted me in an American accent. I explained that I also was an American on my way through; my small guide had apparently drawn his own conclusions.

The lady laughed and said the boy had done very well because she and her husband were the only English-speaking persons in town and had been able to use their native tongue only in speaking to each other. She was sure that her husband, Dr. Henry R. Boyes, in charge of the local missionary hospital, would be delighted to talk with me; would I not come in until he returned? She prepared tea, a pleasant change from the poor food of the galley. After tea Dr. and Mrs. Boyes showed me what there was to see in Tripoli, and waved farewell to me from the wharf.

I was appalled to find that I was no longer the only passenger on the *Montazah*. At least one hundred Levantines had now come on board to join me, bringing all their vermin with them. An hour later I had a complete set of my own. Up to that moment I had not known how to kill time; thereafter I had my hands full. A louse bite lasts three to four hours, and I was given no respite. No space on my body larger than a five cent piece was left unbitten. I scratched and scratched and scratched, convinced that my cup of gall was overflowing. But more grief was in store. That night we anchored and clouds of voraciously biting mosquitoes attacked us. At Latakiya we took one hundred cattle on board. Because the hold was full they were stored on the deck, where they bellowed and moaned. With this addition to our company we were decidedly overcrowded, and I had to fight to retain my place on the hatch. I was sure the worst had now happened.

But at Alexandretta several hundred sheep were waiting to be loaded. Though I could not see any possible place for them to be put, it turned out to be simple. They were stowed away under the cattle, and plaintive baas blended with mournful moos. As though bleating and lowing were not enough, the ships' officers—Scotch, Irish, English, Syrian, Greek, and Egyptian—added to the din by arguing and shouting incessantly in all languages.

I could no longer move, but at Mersina, the last Syrian port, more Levantines somehow shoved themselves into the cracks. There was now no space in which to lie down. Food in the galley was running low, but I did not dare make a dash for my share, because I would not only lose my place on the hatch, but also my bags and my oranges. I was reduced exclusively to a citrus fruit diet. I literally had to sit on the crate to keep out the grasping claws of the other passengers.

Adalia was the first Turkish port, but we were not allowed ashore under pain of arrest. Since the Allied occupation was in progress, both Italian and Turkish flags were flying over the public buildings.

The call at Rhodes was ever memorable. Cargo and ever more cargo arrived. Additional cattle were lifted on board by the horns in lots of six. It was a gruesome sight. Without the slightest provocation the crew would hit them with sharp cargo hooks when they were dumped on deck and, with a clatter of hoofs, were regaining their feet. Grass and hay were stuck on a trellis built over their heads. The deck looked and smelled like a barnyard. When the first officer would work his way along on his rounds, with wisps hanging from his clothing and in his hair, he would look exactly as though he had emerged from a haymow.

We anchored almost on the main street of Grecian Khios. Again I could not go ashore, and passed the time totting up our passenger list. I tabulated one hundred and forty cattle, two hundred and eighty-eight sheep, and three hundred and fifty human passengers, for whom one unspeakable toilet had to suffice. The fleas, lice, flies, and bedbugs were uncountable.

Many of my oranges had rotted, and the supply was running low. I had sucked them until my mouth was puckery, and I hoped I might never have to see another again.

After an endless day and night we arrived at Smyrna, from which we were not to sail until evening. Since a number of passengers had disembarked, I decided it would be safe for me to leave my particular niche I had guarded so long. I felt in desperate need of a bath, and it would be something to do to go ashore. I secured a rowboat, but at the pier the Greeks, who were in charge at the time, wanted to retain my passport. I had no intention of giving up anything so valuable. "Oh, no, you don't get that," I said, and returned to my rowboat.

A great wall stretched along the seafront, and I told the boatman to row a mile or so further. When we reached a point where no guards seemed to be in sight, I surreptitiously disembarked and spent a delightful day, chiefly taken up with an elaborate repast and a luxurious hot bath.

My man was waiting for me at the appointed time and place. As we crossed the Bay, I noted with sinking heart that lighters filled with baskets of fresh string beans were converging from all directions upon the *Montazah*. I hoisted myself on board and landed on beans. Not a spare inch was left on deck. Beans were piled over the top hamper, around the smokestack, and in the life boats. The only seat I could find was on a basket of the green legumes high up near the funnel. We were still two days away from Constantinople. I would pull out my watch and look at it. Then I would swear to myself that I would not touch it for a whole hour. I would sit and think over my sins for what seemed many hours and then take a peek. Ten minutes would have passed.

At nine in the morning we went by Chanak and were at last in the Dardanelles. At noon we were abreast of war-torn Gallipoli. The view up the Straits was magnificent; I was able to admire it in spite of the lice. Early the next morning we were in the vicinity of Constantinople. French, British, Italians, and Greeks were all there. The Turks were supposed to be the vanquished, and the Allies were running everything. But all were suspicious of one another; no uniform law, not even a uniform policy, was adopted. Constant bickering went on, and contrary orders were issued.

First Greek quarantine officers boarded us, and all were examined. No disease was found, and after an hour we were cleared. But hardly had the *Montazah* started again when we heard a shrill tooting, "Poo-poo!" and a launch came alongside.

"We've been inspected," the Captain called.

"Who did it?"

"The Greeks."

"Well, we're the Italians."

Down went the anchor and another two hours were wasted.

"Poo-poo-poo!" This time it was the French, who inspected us all over again with much pother. It was now afternoon. Once more we started. "Poo-poo-poo-poo!" This time it was the British.

"We've already been inspected three times," yelled our Captain.

"Who did it last?"

"The French."

"We don't believe in the damned Frogs," and aboard they came.

Not until five were we off the waterfront. I had cabled ahead from Smyrna, and friends were there in a launch to meet me. But in other craft came hungry Turkish boatmen, and I was nearly pulled to pieces before I escaped their clutches. The moment I reached the home of my friends I requested an isolated woodshed. There I disrobed, bathed in an improvised tub, burned my clothes, and ended my intimate association with the vermin.

The eleven nightmare days were at last over.

I arrived in London in plenty of time for my appointment, but I was not to see New York that year. I started back around again under more pleasant circumstances and more civilized surroundings, to attend the meeting of the Far Eastern Association of Tropical Medicine, held that year in Java. By the time I reached Manila I had been away so long that I was eager for home.

Ordinarily, because sailings did not coincide, the trip from Manila to Peiping via Hongkong and Shanghai lasted two weeks. I believed it would be possible to cut the time in half if I could go straight to Shanghai and there make good connections for Tientsin, the port for Peiping. Opportunely I found a Captain of a Norwegian freighter who was going direct. I thought I was making wonderful sacrifices for the sake of the Foundation but, to my amazement, I was taken to beautiful quarters with sitting room, chairs, desk, rugs on the floor, bedroom, and bath. I was never more comfortable in my life. The Captain and I dined together in state. The first day out I remarked, "Is there much news on the air?"

"All you want," replied the Captain. "The wireless operator isn't doing anything. I'll see about it."

Hourly after that I was furnished reels of news about everything from everywhere. I did not know the world was so full of exciting happenings.

In due course early one morning we reached the mouth of the Whangpoo. The pilot boat brought a paper on board, and I read eagerly that four vessels were due to sail from Shanghai that day. The first of these was leaving from some fifteen miles below the city, just about opposite where we were to dock. When the tug which was to transfer me as soon as we had made fast did not appear, I summoned a Chinese sampan, dropped my bags into it, and started for the steamer. But just as we reached the middle of the river, I saw her cast loose and depart.

I had the coolie take me ashore, and carry my bags to the edge of the highway. While I was standing hesitantly, wondering how I could get conveyance up to the city from this forsaken spot, an impressive shiny black touring car came bowling toward me.

I held out both my arms like a semaphore. The Chinese chauffeur pulled to a stop, and a European lady, all alone in the tonneau, began to shriek at the top of her lungs. I had often been told that if a direct order were given to a woman, she would obey. "Shut up!" I commanded.

She stopped with startling suddenness. I explained to her that I had to catch a steamer; I asked if she would be kind enough to take me along with her since no taxi was to be had.

She explained that she was only going a short distance to pick up her husband and was returning home at once.

This would never do. "Put the baggage in the car," I decisively ordered the coolie who had brought me ashore, and who was looking blankly on.

The lady raised her eyebrows in surprise, but made no objection. I climbed into the car and sat down. "Tell your chauffeur to drive to the English Bund!" I said in loud tones.

She hesitated.

"Tell him to drive to the English Bund!" I shouted.

This time she obeyed, and we started off. Then I asked, "Why did you scream like that when I stopped you?"

"There have been terrible hold-ups near here," she explained. "I thought somebody might come to help me." Since she remained quiet, I trusted her fears had been allayed.

We were ambling along at about twenty miles an hour. "This is altogether too slow," I expostulated. "I'll never catch the boat at this rate."

"Oh, they're very strict in enforcing the speed laws around here."

"Tell him to drive faster," I insisted.

Our speed increased to forty miles an hour. We came shortly to the heart of the business section at the Astor House. The traffic light was just changing, and hundreds of rickshaws and other vehicles of all kinds were beginning to move across our path. I knew it would be minutes before we could get under way again. "Tell him to drive through the light."

We dashed across, narrowly missing half a dozen vehicles, and in Shanghai traffic a miss is something to remember. Behind us we heard a policeman's shrill whistle.

"Hurry up or he'll catch us!" I ordered.

Our speed increased to sixty miles an hour, and in a few moments we ground to a stop at the English Bund. My second ship was already in the middle of the Whangpoo.

"Madam, I'm terribly sorry, but I have to catch a boat. The next one leaves from the Chinese Bund."

"What will my husband say?"

"I have no idea, but I have to catch that boat. Tell your driver to hurry to the Chinese Bund."

Somewhat to my surprise she still obeyed. We reached the pier to find the gangplank already pulled in, the ship cast off, and swinging around to let the bow out. I hailed a coolie, and, as the stern almost grazed the pier, I told him to throw the baggage on board. As the stern was already swinging out I leaped after it into the atmosphere, hooked my right arm around the railing, pulled myself on deck, and turned to thank the lady. She had already fled, and I have always since been fearful of Shanghai lest I might meet her husband.

When I had recovered my balance, I looked about me. I was not at all sure of the steamer's destination. I was still standing in the midst of my belongings and wondering, when I heard the dinner gong. This was a welcome sound. I asked one of the sailors who had been eying my unceremonious boarding to direct me to the dining room. I followed his instructions. Only one place was set in the saloon. I sat there. In a few seconds the Captain, a bluff red-faced Britisher, came in. The moment he saw me in his chair, he started to bluster.

"What are you doing here?" he demanded.

"I'm one of your passengers."

"We don't carry passengers."

"Where are you going?" I countered.

"You'll have to get off!"

528

"I can't get off."

"This is a freight boat. We've no room for passengers."

"You haven't answered my question. Where are you going?"

"It's none of your business."

"There's no use getting excited," I said soothingly, and then addressed the steward, "Bring the Captain a plate, knife, and fork." "Captain, do sit down," I urged. "Let's discuss this amicably. I'm going to Peiping, where are you going?"

"We can't take anybody. The pilot's getting off at the bar, and you're getting off with him."

"Let's have a whiskey and soda," I proposed. He made no protest, and we sipped our drinks.

"Where are you going?" I asked again.

"Wei Hai Wei," in surly tones.

"Right on my way, and I've never seen it. Where do you go from there?"

"Chefoo."

"Couldn't be better. Right on my way too. Where do you go from there?"

"Tientsin."

"Fine, that's my port. I'm your passenger."

"Oh, no, you're not." He made as though to rise, but before he could carry out his intent, I suggested, "Let's have another whiskey and soda, Captain."

By the time it too had been partially consumed, the Captain had mellowed, and relations were much more friendly. "You must have a spare cabin somewhere," I insinuated.

A few more sips and the Captain finally melted, "Well, I guess I'll have to take you." He called a steward, ordered a cabin prepared, and I moved in. The Captain and I hobnobbed on the bridge and talked about the weather. A dust storm at sea fortunately provided a topic of conversation. It was red and thick and the ship was covered with it. He added to my meteorological knowledge with the information that it came from the Gobi Desert, and sometimes such storms traveled as far as seven hundred miles over the ocean.

I had a few uneasy moments as we approached Wei Hai Wei, fearing the Captain might carry out his early threat and leave me behind, but he did not. We took on cargo at Chefoo and left. By this time it appeared as though I might be able to get an afternoon train from Tientsin to Peiping. But just then a thick woolly fog enveloped us. The engine stopped; the boat slowed down.

"Captain," I said, "I've gone to extraordinary trouble to get as far as this. I'm still in a great hurry. Can't we get in?"

"Can't be done this afternoon, but I'll tell you what I'll do. I'll have steam up early and still get you to Tientsin in time for the morning train."

"All right," I said, "fine!"

I had a good sleep and awakened at daylight to hear the anchor chain coming through the hawse pipes. The engine started, and then stopped. I knew something was wrong. I pulled on some clothes and dashed to the bridge. "We're never going to get in this way," I said.

"Can't you see the fog?" the Captain retorted irritably. "I'm going to anchor again."

"Did you ever hear of Lindbergh?" I asked.

"That aviator fellow? Certainly!"

"Well, they say he has air sense; he knows where he is when he's flying. Now these Chinese fishermen—I know them. They have fog sense."

"Nonsense! We've every instrument right on the bridge, and we can't tell where to go."

"Let's call a fisherman over and see what he says."

The Captain demurred and made uncomplimentary remarks about land lubbers but in the end he blew his whistle, and soon a tiny Chinese sampan came alongside. Through an interpreter I asked, "How far are we from the mouth of the river?"

"Five miles."

"Could you steer us there?"

"Oh, yes."

I told the fisherman I'd make it worth his while if he could make good his word. The Captain was listening to these arrangements with considerable nervousness, but we were pretty good friends by this time, and he was used to my vagaries.

"Who's going to be responsible if the ship runs aground?" he queried rhetorically.

"We're not going to run aground. You're all deep sea men and don't know how to approach a coast. I'll tell you a trick I learned from a captain who knew his way around in shoal waters. Put out five fathom of chain at the bow anchor, and let it hang. You draw two and a half. Just go slowly and if there's shoal water ahead the anchor will catch."

"Damn it, I'll try," the Captain agreed with an impulsiveness not ordinarily associated with the British, and ordered the anchor chain let out.

Meanwhile, the Chinese made his sampan fast and climbed aboard. Standing at the bow, he gestured this way and that as we slowly plowed forward. Suddenly we emerged into the sunshine. Dead ahead were the two lighthouses which marked the mouth of the Pei-Ho.

I boarded the train and reached Peiping within a week after leaving Manila—a week earlier home for me.

CHAPTER 30.   GRANT BUT
                               MEMORY

AND so I might have gone on mile after mile, year after year,
crossing one ocean after another, from one land to the next,
trudging through rains and snows, sometimes basking in the sunshine
of delightful countrysides, sometimes sweltering in the intolerable heat
of the jungle, encountering everywhere odd, interesting, and con-
genial personalities, many of them engaged in the same endeavor as
myself. But everything must end, and I had seen enough of the
world. On October 31, 1934, I wrote to the President of the Rockefeller Foundation, as follows:

Dear Mr. Mason:

Ever since I had the pleasure of talking with you at New Bedford last
August, I have continued to give serious consideration to the question of
being relieved of the burden of active responsibility in connection with the
International Health Division. I trust it is unnecessary for me to assure you
that I have made every effort to view the matter from all angles. It is
with sincere regret that I cannot escape the reluctant conclusion that I
should respectfully request you to be good enough to have the necessary
steps taken to place my name on the retired list, at your convenience.

As I am sure you realize, I have found it very difficult to reach this
decision, and to adhere to it. Nevertheless, the privilege of having had the
opportunity in the beginning to assist in formulating and inaugurating the
broad policies on which the Foundation's activities in the field of preventive
medicine have been based will always be a source of great satisfaction to
me. The same is true of each of my sixteen trips around the world which

were made in an effort to promote field research and develop methods to bring about the more general use of scientific discoveries and knowledge of such enormous potential benefit to the advancement and well-being of the human race.

The only possible rewards for a life devoted to the public health branch of the medical profession are, of course, such professional standing and respect as one may earn, and the keen satisfaction of unselfish service to others. Perhaps, therefore, I may be pardoned for referring to the really extraordinary comparison of present day conditions, and the backward public health situation of 1914 when Dr. Rose came to the Philippines to interest me in the aims and work of the Foundation. This great progress, for which I rejoice to feel the Foundation is so largely responsible, fairly staggers the imagination. It would be quite impossible even to mention briefly the most outstanding of the accomplishments in each of the forty countries in which I had the privilege of making surveys and proposing programs in the early days of the Foundation. I shall never cease to be grateful to each of those who were charged with the duty of making the decisions which resulted in all of my recommendations being put into effect either directly by, or through the efforts of, the Foundation.

Although (and I believe wisely) the Foundation has not included leprosy among its direct benefactions, I have always been granted liberal facilities to do work myself in this field. Much of the progress that has been made in the control of leprosy throughout the world in recent years has been due to this friendly interest and this example to other organizations on the part of the Foundation. Similar generous treatment has also been accorded me in endeavoring to promote health work in a number of other fields. I deeply appreciate this consideration.

In conclusion, allow me to express to you personally, and through you to all those associated with this splendid organization, my sincere gratitude for the unfailing kindness and cooperation with which I have been surrounded throughout these past twenty years of fascinating service. During the years to come, I shall hope to serve the cause of humanity in ways which will not entail my spending so much time away from home. Regardless of the activities in which I may be engaged, however, I shall always look back upon my connection with the Rockefeller Foundation as my real life work, and shall always consider it both an honor and a privilege to do anything in my power at any time to further its aims.

Sincerely yours,

VICTOR G. HEISER.

AN AMERICAN DOCTOR'S ODYSSEY

Rockefeller Center
New York
January 14, 1935

Dear Dr. Heiser:

Thank you for giving me the opportunity of reading your letter of October 31st to Dr. Mason. What a record it makes! Think of sixteen trips around the world, a life devoted to the public health branch of the medical profession in almost every part of the world and work actually developed in more than forty countries! This is a record of which you may well be proud and which does you the greatest credit.

As Chairman of the Board of the Rockefeller Foundation and your warm friend of many years, I am happy to take this opportunity of expressing profound satisfaction in the work that you have done in your relation with the Foundation. And the best of it is that on the foundations which you have so well laid, there will continue to be built through the years superstructures that will render a continuing and increasing service to the health and the well-being of the peoples throughout the world.

In the hope that you may have in full measure the happy consciousness of work well done and a life well spent, I am,

Very sincerely,
JOHN D. ROCKEFELLER JR.

Dr. Victor G. Heiser
49 West 49th Street,
New York, New York

Perhaps I would never have fully realized how fortunate my lot has been had not the writing of this volume tempted me to peruse many pages of old diaries which might have remained indefinitely unopened in the trunks and boxes to which they had been consigned years ago. But obviously even the more striking experiences of two score years devoted to pursuing my profession in many corners of the world on highways and through trackless lands cannot all be set forth between the covers of one book.

Lack of space has prevented me from making any mention of the months I spent with the armies of Europe during the World War, and the references to China, India, Egypt, Central America and other countries are all too brief. Lack of space also prevents all mention of the years of effort to establish a museum of hygiene on the scale of the

Metropolitan Museum, the fascinating research for speedier relief of accidents occurring among the soldiers of industry, of my work with the Railway Sanitary Commission which happened to have such far-reaching influence, or of the extraordinary spread of child health education throughout the world which I had a part in developing with President Hoover, Dr. Emmett Holt, Dr. Frederick Peterson, and many others.

Such a career as mine has necessarily deprived me of close family ties, and many other experiences which enrich our lives. But the deprivations have been more than compensated by the opportunity to bring the discoveries of the laboratories to disease-bound millions who knew of no possibility of relief and scarcely hoped for any.

Mine has been an extraordinarily happy and satisfactory life. Among other compensations has been the host of friends who have made my path pleasant. In my mind's eye I can picture them in every quarter of the globe, and have a vivid and grateful consciousness that a welcome awaits me in the sixty-odd countries I have visited, should I resume my travel. Laying down active administrative responsibilities and breaking the habits and associations of a lifetime are tinged with unhappiness and a keen sense of personal loss. Yet the realization of an earnest effort to serve and the joy of past accomplishments soften the pangs of regret at this parting.

INDEX

INDEX

INDEX

INDEX

Ilongots, 140, 148
Immigration Law, 33 f.
Indenburg, Alexander W. Frederick, 465
India, plague in, 91; smallpox in, 176, 177, 183; leprosy in, 211, 217; malaria in, 458 ff.
Indian Camp Plantation, 257
Indian Medical Service, 338, 339, 341 f.
Indo-China, 294 f.
Insulin, 283 f.
International Cholera Convention, 18
International Congress on Medicine, Cairo, 34 f.
International Congress on Tuberculosis, 22
International Health Board, 272, 275, 285 ff., 291, 299, 447, 452
International Journal of Leprosy, 263
International Leprosy Ass'n, 263
Iraq, 520 f.
Iwahig, 53

Jacoby, Dr. Abraham, 77
Jacocks, Dr. W. P., 94 ff.
Jaffa, plague in, 94 ff.
Japan, 395 ff.; beriberi in, 205; leprosy in, 217; earthquake, 396 ff.; emigration, 398 ff.; Exclusion Bill, 399 ff.; medicine, 410 ff.; Health Institute, 414 ff.
Java, 461 ff.; beriberi in, 209; leprosy in, 218; public health education in, 475 ff.
Jefferson Medical College, 10
Jefferson, President Thomas, 179
Jenkins, Dr., 17
Jenner, Edward, 178 f.
Jesus, Dr. Vicente, 419
Johns Hopkins University, 276 f.
Johnston, Colonel Gordon, 418, 429, 430
Johnstown Flood, 3 ff.
Jones Act of 1916, 57
Judson, Harry Pratt, 276

Kalingas, 140 f.
Kanakas, 363 f.
Kandy, plague in, 93 f.
Katipunan, 45

Katzoff, Simon Louis, 190
King of Belgium, 286
King Edward VIII, 423 ff.
King Feisal, 323, 520
King Humbert, 22 f.
King Louis VIII, 213
King Maha Vajiravudh of Siam, 480 ff., 487, 490, 495, 498
King Philip IV of Spain, 219
King Prajadhipok of Siam, 498, 499, 500
King Victor Emmanuel III, 23
King, W. L. Mackenzie, 275
Kinyoun, Dr. J. J., 97
Kitasato, Shibasaburo, 81, 412 ff.
Kitasato Institute, 288
Koch, Robert, 103, 199, 298 f., 414
Kuala Lumpur, 206
Kuenen, 209
Kyne, Peter B., 261 f.

Lake Memphremagog, Vt., 32
Lake Mohonk Conference, 195
Lambert, Dr. Alexander, 168
Lambert, Dr. S. M., 363 f., 365 f., 370 f., 374, 376, 377, 378, 393
Landis, Judge K. M., 272
Lankenau Hospital, 10
Laurier, Sir Wilfred, 32
Laveran, 444
Lawshee, Auditor, 51
Lazy worm disease, 273
League of Nations, Commission on Leprosy, 263; Health Section, 441 f., 475
Leake, C. D., 254
Ledger, Charles, 441
de Legaspi, Miguel Lopez, 44
Leiper, Dr. Robert T., 278 f.
Leonard Wood Memorial for the Eradication of Leprosy, 262 ff.
Leprosy, 211; history of, 212 ff.; occurrence in Orient, 217 f., in Europe, 218, in America, 218, in Philippines, 218 ff.; types of, 220 ff.; in Hawaii, 226 f.; examination for, 232 f., *see* Culion; chaulmoogra oil treatment, 248 ff.; other remedies, 254; *see also* Carville

540

INDEX

INDEX

542

INDEX

INDEX

Ultra-violet ray, 75
Uncinariasis, *see* hookworm
Underwear, orange-red, 75 f.
Union Steamship Line, 311 f.
University of Chicago, 267
University of the Philippines, 152
U. S. Public Health Service, 265

Vaccination, smallpox, 178 ff.; in Spain, 179; in Philippines, 179 ff.; opposition to, 188, 189 ff.
Vedder, Captain Edward B., 129, 208
del Vego, Juan, 440
Vincent, Dr. George E., 284 f., 522
Virchow, Rudolf, 22
Visayans, 44
de Vogel, Dr. W. T., 465 f.

Wade, Mrs. Dorothy Paul, 261 f.
Wade, Dr. H. Windsor, 260 f., 263
Walker, Dr. E. L., 164
Walled City, Manila, 40 ff.
Walsh, Governor David I., 266 f.
Walter Reed Commission, 34
Washington, D. C., 10 f., 18 f.
Water, 39 ff., 65, 130 f.; and cholera, 102 f., 106 f., 111, 121 ff.

Waterhouse, Professor Benjamin, 179
Webster, Daniel, 189 f.
Welch, Dr. W. H., 276 ff., 285, 413
Whipple, Dr. George, 277
White ants, 42 f.
White, Major F. Norman, 341
William of Tyre, 222
Wilson, President Woodrow, 53 ff., 175
Wood, Cyrus, 399
Wood-Forbes Mission, 417 ff.
Wood, General Leonard, 34, 138, 148, 188, 189, 237, 239, 248, 260 ff., 387 f., 417 f., 419 ff., 427 ff., 451 f., 453
Worcester, Dean C., 48, 104 f., 124, 131, 140, 141, 144, 151, 152, 164, 227
Wright, Governor, 115
Wright, Frank Lloyd, 397
Wright, Luke E., 48, 49 f.
Wyman, Dr. Walter, 18

Yap, 186
Yaws, 133 ff., 212, 221, 357, 370, 377
Yellow-Dog Dingo, 256
Yellow fever, research, 287 ff.; in Abyssinia, 507, 510 f., 514
Yersin, Alexandre, 81
Young, Dr. Hugh, 434
Young, Owen D., 262

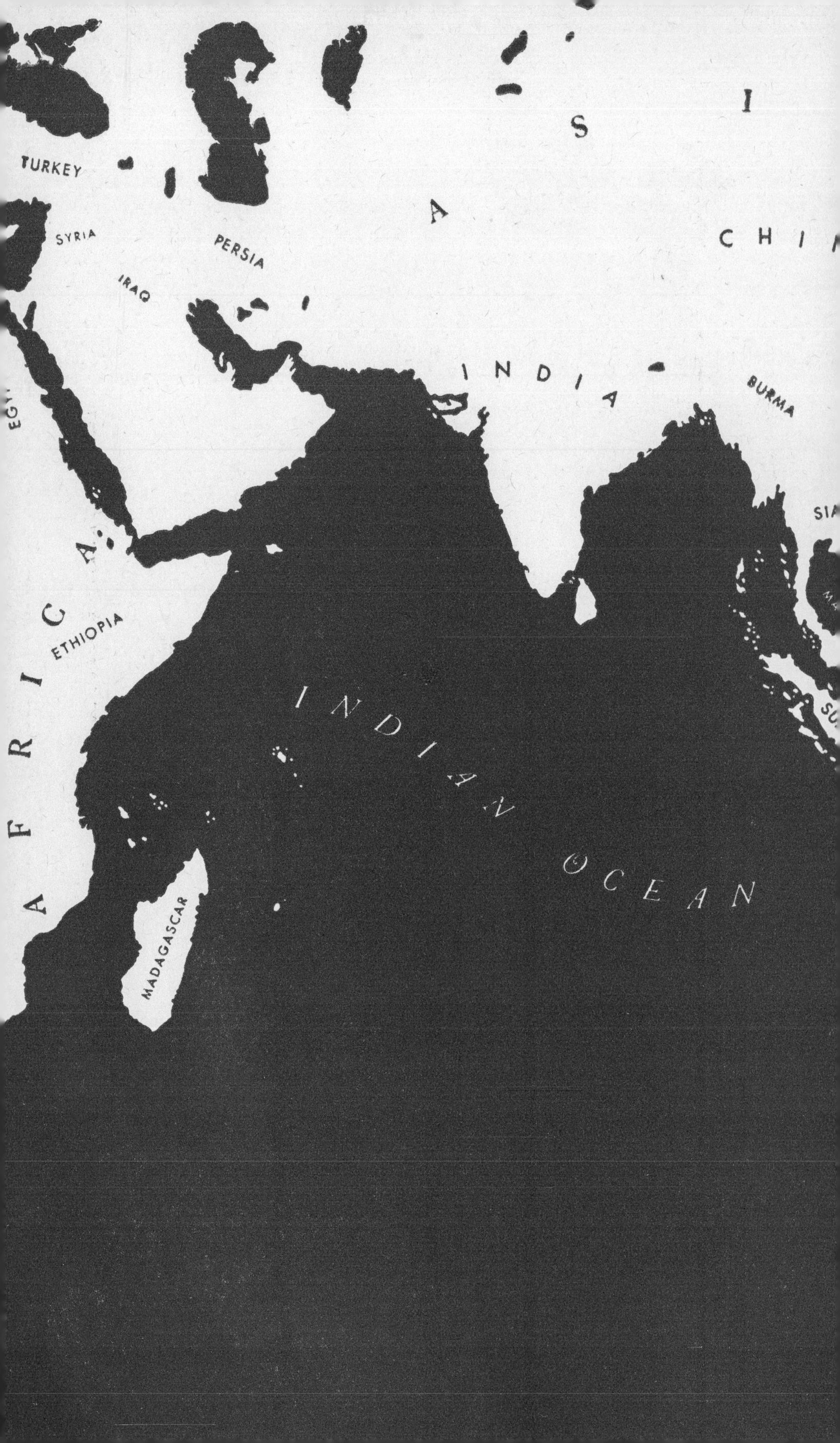
TURKEY
SYRIA
IRAQ
PERSIA
A S I
INDIA
BURMA
A F R I C A
ETHIOPIA
MADAGASCAR
INDIAN OCEAN

The Rights of Children

Edited by Albert E. Wilkerson
With an Introduction by Justine Wise Polier

The Rights of Children

Emergent Concepts in Law and Society

Temple University Press

Philadelphia

Temple University Press, Philadelphia 19122
© 1973 by Temple University. All rights reserved
Published 1973
Printed in the United States of America

International Standard Book Number: 0–87722–052–2
Library of Congress Catalog Card Number: 73–79230

Contents

vi   **Contents**

Preface

The United Nations Declaration of the Rights of the Child states in the Preamble that "mankind owes to the child the best it has to give." The discrepancy between the acknowledgment of debt and the reality of nonpayment in full necessitates the very formulation of a Children's Charter and an articulation of "children's rights."

The concept of the rights of children is at once an ethical judgment about the nature and value of the human being and a statement affirming both the legal assurances and the provision of social resources that a democratic society needs to guarantee its citizens. The thrust of the concept is essentially the same as is found in any other search for "rights," a theme so prominent in the United States at this hour.

Human rights and legal rights cannot be separated except for academic purposes. One cites individual need and expresses social values and aspirations; the other is evidence of the society's depth of conviction through its willingness to translate its ethics into concrete actions.

Human rights and legal rights are relatively sterile unless they are placed in complementary relationship. And both can be relatively useless unless they are supported by a network of human services that reflect a major social policy commitment to health and welfare. Judge Polier underscores this in her introduction, urging that we "exert unremitting efforts to secure services and facilities, without which legal rights can mean little" for the child. A commitment to the rights of every child requires a provision of human services on an institutionalized pattern, replacing residual programs that are aimed only at specific target populations. Such public responsibility for children would make obsolete the present system of plugging in fragmentary programs for the child at the point he is found neglected, dependent, or in trouble with society;

and it would help to avoid the risk of sending a child down a destructive road through sheer insistence upon the technicalities in a legal right.

The capacity of a society to value human rights and the determination to give them substance through legislation and service delivery networks is related to its long process of social maturation. This maturation has to do with an increasing faith in human potentialities and a decreasing fear of wider human freedoms, and to a value orientation that places the individual at the center of the human drama—even above economic systems and political ideologies.

Within this kind of social maturation, the child is discovered, too, as a person. In long historical perspective, this involves moving from a view of the child's worth primarily for his future potential as a carrier of the culture, to perceiving him as an adult in miniature, to seeing him as having a right to the status of childhood with its own needs and peculiarities, to a perception of the child as a person with his own full range of rights with societal mechanisms for their enhancement.

We are just now coming to terms with this latter perception, and this is the content of the present volume. The basic ideal was expressed in the Geneva Declaration on the Rights of the Child (1924) and more recently is enunciated in the ten principles set forth in the United Nations Declaration of the Rights of the Child (1959). That we have advanced as far as we have in refining the specifics summed up in these aspirations, and in translating them into legal assurances, attests to the tenacity of many persons during this century in holding firmly to the belief that a solid legal base is necessary to social processes and social decisions. Not infrequently they stood alone, as "voices in the wilderness." Social work students are discovering in social service delivery and in social policy-planning the legal framework in which human life is lived, as well as the fact that this framework is an important arena for the effecting of social change. Law students are learning that the technicalities of law do not always solve the human dilemma.

The original intent of the juvenile court was to provide a decision-making system for the child, emphasizing his potential development above his immediate accountability for an infraction of the law. The family court has sought to preserve the integrity of the family unit and to enhance parental functioning. To act in the "best interests of the child," as the principle for judicial decision-making, required the concepts of *parens patriae* (the protector of subjects unable to protect themselves) and *loco parentis* (the power to stand in the place of parents). The undiluted juvenile court philosophy has within it assumptions about the competence and the caring nature of the court staff that would lead naturally to best-interest decisions. But the frailties of human beings, wide variations in biases as to what constitutes need and best interests, and the impersonal quality that comes to permeate all organizations have made the ideal somewhat less than the noble venture anticipated. The trend toward a legalistic juvenile court, given impetus by the necessity for guardians *ad litem* (court-appointed advocates, to represent the child's interest in a particular case), and the United States Supreme Court decisions in *Kent v. United States* (concerning legal safeguards for the child transferred to the jurisdiction of an adult court) and *In Re Gault* (concerning a number of basic procedural safeguards) would in undiluted form give the child the kind of rights that no longer set him apart for special care and consideration. The obvious goal for juvenile and family courts is a synthesis of the two extremes. As yet there has not been enough experience with clashes between best interests and legalism to mold a balanced approach to the plights of children.

The purpose in bringing this collection together into a single book is not only to make the material more accessible to professional students, especially in social work and law, and to personnel in child welfare and court services, but in so doing to highlight and encourage professional interest and commitment to an urgent and unfinished social task. In selecting the material, priority was given to those pieces which take the definition or implementation of children's rights a step further, or which identify problems and issues that impede movement in this direction. The collection is not designed as a comprehensive reference book on the rights of children; rather, it is a statement of where we have advanced in critical areas and where we need to go from here, what controversies we are moving through, and what challenges we must meet with an increased vigor. Clearly, "the rights of children" is the central theme in child welfare for the coming decade.

The book is divided into three sections: "The Child as a Person," "Protection of the Child," and "Decisions About the Child." Within these sections are reflected the major issues in child welfare that have to do with children's rights and that are becoming crystallized into specific principles, through court decisions and agency practice. Among these are the rights of children as a generic concept, legal safeguards for the child as a person, the improving status of the illegitimate child, the unborn child and the abortion controversy, implications for the child born by artificial insemination, protection of the neglected or battered child, protection of the child through support obligations of parents or guardians, custody issues, and the question of advocacy and representation.

The collection has certain limitations and omissions. Major case decisions and changes in court and agency practice are being made even as the book is being printed. New areas are emerging rapidly that demand exploration and definition of the rights of children and that offer new challenges for policy-making and resource development. Among these are the right of physically and mentally handicapped children to the full array of medical services and social opportunities; the right of every child to maximum education and assistance in developing his capacity to take advantage of an educational system that is individualized and child-centered; the right of children to a uniform social and legal consensus in the area of emancipation to adulthood; the right of children to search for creative expression and identity within new modes and self-created forms; the extension of protective rights of the child through family planning and through the establishment of a national, state, and community child advocacy system to enhance the quality of life for every child. The 1970 White House Conference on Children began its new decade of interest in children by making some of these areas and these kinds of tasks central to its agenda.

The development of children's rights in all areas requires a new, bold, and sometimes radical set of assumptions that must meet the blunt, challenging question as to whether or not we mean what we say in regard to stated principles in human relations and in the democratic ideal. This calls for a deeper social commitment to the primacy of the child in policy-planning priorities, making viable Principle Eight of the United Nations Declaration: "The child shall in all circumstances be among the first to receive protection and relief."

The community has assumed that the family will ensure the rights of its children and will provide adequately for their needs. Only when this care does not meet a minimal standard—generally as perceived by school or neighbors—does the community intervene through an agency mandated to protect the health and life of children. This kind of community interest at a point of family failure is a last-resort, crisis response. Such agencies have not had the responsibility to set standards, to encourage or demand creative child development, and in essence to carry an advocacy role in child care. Such a principle can seem threatening to the concept of family that gives a total kind of decision-making to natural parents.

The protective service agencies have done a commendable job during the past century, risking the possibility of violating parental rights in the interest of the child. In the past, they have worked, generally quite alone, toward provision of needs for dependent, neglected, and battered children whose environment was critical and frequently life-threatening. Much of the child-welfare legislation received its data and impetus from protective agencies. But the agencies have not been able to promote in a similar way the concept of the rights of children. Alan Keith-Lucas emphasizes the difference between "needs" and "rights," and points to the historical error in social work in equating the two. Social workers have been too easily satisfied with corrective measures that meet immediate needs. Lawyers, hired for a fee to accomplish the client's purpose, have clung with tenacity to an inviolate parental role and have been nearsighted in looking at children's rights. One has to concede that the present system of child protection runs close to violating due process of law for the parent or guardian. And with an orientation toward adult client-rights, lawyers have of course found the social work values in agency procedures and juvenile court hearings a source of professional frustration.

The concept of child advocacy, now being defined across the country in conjunction with the leads from the 1970 White House Conference, and the necessary rethinking of the role of the parent and family, have significant implications for the practice of both social work and law. We must arrive at a frame of reference that does not require trespassing on adult rights in order to protect children, and one that does not leave children at the mercy of their parents. In the long run, this means a community responsibility and accountability for child development and child care, and it will yield a different kind of socio-legal child-parent connection. The forms that this will take are now shadowy, but they will constitute the focus for child welfare for some time to come. And the family will have many new adjustments to make as it perceives itself and its tasks in new lights.

Schools of social work are gearing themselves for practice that concerns itself with risk populations, community responses, and healthy environmental conditions, in addition to the more traditional methods for helping individuals and groups who have already succumbed and have become "cases." Law schools are now giving respectability to family law, child welfare law, and public welfare law. Collaborative educational programs in law and social work are increasing and offer challenging and creative opportunities in broadening the perspectives and competence range of professionals. While social workers and lawyers are historically no strangers to each other, research studies during the past decade have indicated that minimal understanding of the other's purposes and competencies, and antagonisms that result from interaction between the two professional roles, have left the relationship less than desirable. Concern for the rights of children becomes, then, a powerful dynamic for productive interdisciplinary work.

Credit for the book belongs to the authors whose articles appear in the collection. I am indebted in a special way to Professor Thomas A. Coyne, Dean Bernard J. Coughlin, S.J., the Honorable Robert F. Drinan, S.J., the Honorable Robert W. Hansen, Professor Julius A. Jahn, Professor Sanford Katz, and Professor Alan Keith-Lucas for their interest and encouragement in my editing of *The Rights of Children*. The enthusiasm and dedication found in Judge Polier's Introduction reflects the spirit of those concerned with children's rights and services.

As an expression of the concern for the plight of children around the world, the contributors to *The Rights of Children* have agreed that royalties accruing from this publication shall be contributed to the work of UNICEF.

A.E.W.

Introduction

Justine Wise Polier

This volume brings the searchings and critiques of those concerned with the rights and needs of children. The material is valuable for those engaged in the day-to-day tasks of helping individual children and for those seeking more effective ways of doing so through legislation, or by challenging judicial and administrative procedures. Imbedded in the material, however, lies a more profound challenge. One senses the extent to which those concerned with the rights of children are imprisoned within a system which denies access to the very goals they seek. Even writings directed to concrete problems reveal doubts as to whether progress can be made within the present value system of America.

In various ways the presentations raise haunting questions. To what extent has institutionalized justice provided bastilles against the assertion of rights and the liberation of those whose rights have been denied? To what extent has it provided rationalizations for wrongdoing and a shield against self-scrutiny? How far has it been used to provide comfort and haven for the self-righteous? Finally, to what extent has it been exploited as the foe of social change?

"His injured childhood bullied him." These words of the poet Robert Hayden strike to the heart of what, as a society, we have failed to comprehend or overcome. Neither the lifetime tragedy of a Lee Harvey Oswald nor the recoil from his final act of destruction, has achieved recognition that there are no simplistic

The Honorable JUSTINE WISE POLIER, Judge of the Family Court of the State of New York, New York City, is author of *A View from the Bench: The Juvenile Court* (New York: National Council on Crime and Delinquency, 1964), and *The Rule of Law and the Role of Psychiatry* (Baltimore: Johns Hopkins Press, 1968).

xiii

or cheap solutions to the problems that undermine the vitality of our children, destroy their manhood, and sap the health of our society. Institutions, whether judicial or administrative, that largely determine the rights of children, like schools and welfare services, inevitably reflect both the knowledge and the ignorance, both the concern and prejudice, both the generous and the niggardly qualities that have shaped American society.

The recent report of the Joint Commission on the Mental Health of Children once more provides clear evidence that hunger, malnutrition, delinquency, abuse, lack of health care, inadequate education, pittance-welfare, and discrimination remain areas of crisis, if not disaster, for tens of thousands of children throughout the United States in the 1970s. The monumental deficiencies in services are compounded by a lack of determination to tackle the problems of children whose lives are subject to the crippling effects of what we do and fail to do. The 1970 White House Conference on Children announced that prepared reports would offer "a supermarket of proposals." Surely, such a whole-sale display of so many predigested or canned ideas can only obscure what could have been major thrusts. One hopes that it will not diffuse real issues.

Steps taken during the past decade to protect the legal rights of children reflect the hard work of many individuals. Unfortunately, their steps have been paralleled, if not outpaced, by a growing awareness of the low value placed on children. Thus, while we move toward establishing legal rights we are also confronted with the persistent undermining of the basic props that make life meaningful. While our rhetoric reflects the American mythology about children as our most precious resource, our actions conform to a pathology which allows blindness to deprivations that brand children with the stigmata of feeling neither wanted nor needed. It is this pathological blindness that alienates and destroys the capacity in children for caring for others or having hope for themselves.

In speaking of the mythology of concern for children, it should not be seen as a single dragon to be slain. Myths, like dragon's teeth, dominate many interrelated areas of life. Myths of equality, myths of universal justice, myths of human brotherhood, and even myths about parental love and natural rights all require examination. The liberal faith in the achievement of social change and progress through plodding efforts must also be subjected to examination, together with social legislation and resulting institutions, in terms of their reality for another generation rather than in terms of wishful expectations. The protection of legal rights cannot be regarded as a panacea so long as there is a failure to achieve an earthy sense of justice that demands and secures more fundamental social change.

Too many existing institutions, within and outside the administration of justice, have been party to the masking and avoidance of the tragedies and deprivations that shadow the lives of children. Reaction to such obscurantism has understandably led to demands that all heads and hands now be directed to the correction of social wrongs as the cause of individual failures or "wrongdoings." These demands have polarized the position of those dedicated to this goal from that of those committed to meeting the need for services and treatment of children and their families.

As in the comparable polarization in the mental health field of prevention as "against" treatment rather than "with" treatment, an exclusive emphasis on "rights" too often ignores what is needed to save and support a generation now in being. Thus, the insistence by a law guardian that a girl of fifteen be paroled pending a hearing, although the law guardian knew that a pusher of drugs, whom the girl feared, was awaiting her outside the court, illustrates the blind pursuit of legal rights now increasingly embraced by young lawyers who have lost all faith in the value of judicial intervention on behalf of a child.

Small islands of service in which constructive help can be rendered to a few children through the juvenile courts, like good education for a few, are no longer tolerable. Neither are fine generalities about constitutional rights nor blueprints for the future meaningful without builders to dig foundations, to raise structures for human habitation, and to provide skilled persons to service them.

We need the Supreme Court to be on the side of the angels to protect the child as well as the adult from denial of constitutional rights or the hue and cry for vengeance, even when uttered in the name of "law and order." We need administrators of justice who will vigorously pursue and root out judicial abuses in the court, whether of nonfeasance or malfeasance, and who will consistently seek to uncover and correct the defects that develop in all large human institutions. To meet such responsibilities, the administrators will have to do more than rely on efficiency experts or on a response to crisis situations.

The "musty overloaded criminal machinery" which led to the prison riots in New York City during the fall of 1970 exemplify the crisis-reaction syndrome. Judicial administrators and political figures responded to long-existing conditions that violated both legal and human rights only under the whip of fear following public disclosure. The proposals by one district attorney to sentence and deliver convicted defendants to state prison without benefit of pre-sentence probation reports, in order to relieve over-crowding, was characteristic of the approach which all too often combines "efficiency" with dehumanization. Crisis response and efficiency thus fueled cynicism about the possibility of improving and humanizing the administration of justice except in response to violence or threats of violence.

Against such a background, this volume provides the perspective of men and women engaged in seeking to establish the rights of children. I would venture that many thought, when they began their work, that it would be easier to win support for improving the lot of children than adults, and that improvements won for children would provide the key to the doorway for broader social change. Paradoxically, they have discovered that the self-image of a "child-centered society" has failed to open the pathway to protection, to care, to support, and to the recognition that children, too, have rights. The question, still to be answered, is why American society has been least generous toward its children and why the judicial, as well as the legislative and executive branches of government, have been so reluctant and so tardy in protecting the constitutional rights of children.

It has been suggested that anti-child, like anti-poverty, and anti-mental illness attitudes, of which we are often not even conscious, have prevented the implementation of sound objectives. Certainly the continuing use of jails for the detention of children seven decades after the birth of the juvenile court system, and the failure to provide appropriate treatment services have largely negated the purpose and the promise of these courts. The con-clusion is confirmed by the Joint Commission in its description of what happens to mistreated children:

. . . they are bounced around from training school to reformatory to jails, and whipped through all kinds of understaffed agencies, and end up being treated more poorly than caged animals or adult criminals, or incarcerated with chronic adult psychotics in massive warehouses for the mentally ill.

Yet the Juvenile Court movement at the turn of the century was led by men and women concerned with the welfare of children and the development of a new concept of justice for children. They were unwilling to accept the brutish stance of the law as represented by its application of criminal law to children. The harsh, punitive, and bullying role against the child was to be remolded in parental terms. Unburdened or unblessed by scientific complexities, they had faith that concern for each child, understanding of his problems, and assistance to meet his needs could lead to transforming the rebellious or delinquent into a healthy or well-adjusted child. Happily for them, these reformers lived in a period where hopes for a better world seemed limited only by the pace at which it could be achieved. And this, in turn, depended only on the effort put forth. Those halcyon days are gone.

The founders could not foresee that the states would establish juvenile courts throughout the country but fail to provide the staffing or placement facilities needed. They could not have foreseen the isolation of the juvenile or family court from the mainstream of judicial administration, or its treatment as low man on the judicial totem pole, in practice if not in speech. They could not have foreseen the creeping paralysis that would result from inadequate staffing and services. Finally, they could not have foreseen that youth of today would be turned off by judges (part of the establishment) seeking to act as parents, even more than by parents (squares) who spoke or acted in judgmental fashion.

All these unforeseen developments help to explain what may be described as the backlash against both the concept and practice of juvenile courts. This backlash is evident in the stance of law guardians who resort to any legal strategy to "rescue" children or youth from what they regard as the false pretensions of debilitated social courts. They see no justification for the deprivation of freedom that is not compensated for by treatment or significant help. The backlash is also supported by those who see the testing and enforcement of the rights of the poor, defendants in courts, and the mentally ill as an essential step toward the restoration of self-respect. Finally, the backlash receives support from those who perceive social work, welfare, psychiatric treatment as silken cords by which the deprived are ensnared, forced to conform, and bound to the system.

Justification for such backlash cannot be gainsaid. Unfortunately, thus far the drive to protect legal rights has not succeeded in commanding any appreciable increase in skills, services, or institutions essential to constructive help to children in trouble. Nevertheless, the earnest attacks on the judicial establishment, the tearing away at pretensions, the aggressive assertion of the rights of the poor by young lawyers and community groups represent one of the promising forces that have emerged recently. It is needed to awaken political groups to vast problems and to challenge the ignorant, the prejudiced, and the complacent.

Too often, in his single-minded pursuit of legal rights, the young advocate seems unable to differentiate the child's right to every defense against a charge of delinquency from the needs of an addicted or suicidal child for treatment. He sees the Court, probation, and the physicians only as adversaries. To the judge such inability to differentiate is deeply troubling, as he faces an overwhelming calendar, the lack of appropriate services, and his own isolation within the judicial system. A sense of anger and impotence on the part of the young advocate may well be matched by an unspoken sense of uncertainty and impotence on the part of the judge. The advocate sees the judicial establishment as masking or protecting the woeful lack of real services, and, therefore, as not being entitled to be trusted to help the child. The judge sees the advocate as directing his fire at the wrong target.

The juvenile court and the concept of individualized justice it represents are thus caught in a pincer move as a result of the community's withholding of the means with which to function and the disillusionment of those who see only the Court's failures. A dilemma is posed by the realistic alternative. Return to criminal procedures based on a punitive philosophy, the mechanical or whimsical application of penalties, and the availability of even lesser services and facilities hold little promise. The proposed substitution of new administrative bureaucracies raises additional questions as to how legal rights will be protected, in the light of past experience with administrative agencies. Therefore, in this field as in many others, there is urgent need to confront false promises, to protect individual rights, and at the same time, to exert unremitting efforts to secure services and facilities without which legal rights can mean little.

Gains will not be won easily. Yet gains have been made. The establishment of legal rights has protected individual children and classes of children against injuries long ignored. Thus the ending of the disadvantaged status of a child born out of wedlock, the removal of restrictions on the right of a child to freedom to travel to another state, the right to public assistance without requirements of residence, the right to counsel, the right to a fair hearing, and the right against self-incrimination, like the historic decision of *Brown v. Board of Education,* have deepened understanding of where we must go to remove old shackles that have wrongfully deprived children of rights essential to their well-being.

In looking backward, such victories, in establishing what may now seem incontrovertible rights, may appear to have been inevitable. Yet each one was preceded by a newly recognized and articulated concept of a legal right, by strenuous efforts to establish it, resulting finally in one more gain. Each gain, in turn, has led to greater understanding of rights still denied. This process must go on. Hopefully, it will be supported and strengthened, both by those who are rendering direct services to children and by those who are determined that the larger goals of American society must encompass new values that give meaning to the life of every child.

Part I

The Child as a Person

1

United Nations Declaration of the Rights of the Child

A five-point Declaration of the Rights of the Child was stated in 1923 by the International Union for Child Welfare, with 1948 revisions in a seven-point document. The League of Nations adopted the IUCW Declaration in 1924. The following Declaration of the Rights of the Child was adopted by the United Nations General Assembly in 1959.

DECLARATION OF THE RIGHTS OF THE CHILD

PREAMBLE

Whereas the peoples of the United Nations have, in the Charter, reaffirmed their faith in fundamental human rights, and in the dignity and worth of the human person, and have determined to promote social progress and better standards of life in larger freedom,

Whereas the United Nations has, in the Universal Declaration of Human Rights, proclaimed that everyone is entitled to all the rights and freedoms set forth therein, without distinction of any kind, such as race, color, sex, language, religion, political or other opinion, national or social origin, property, birth or other status,

Whereas the child, by reason of his physical and mental immaturity, needs special safeguards and care, including appropriate legal protection, before as well as after birth,

Whereas the need for such special safeguards has been stated in the Geneva Declaration of the Rights of the Child of 1924, and recognized in the Universal Declaration of Human Rights

United Nations, General Assembly Resolution 1386(XIV), November 20, 1959, published in the *Official Records of the General Assembly, Fourteenth Session, Supplement No. 16,* 1960, p. 19.

and in the statutes of specialized agencies and international organizations concerned with the welfare of children,

Whereas mankind owes to the child the best it has to give,

Now therefore,

The General Assembly

Proclaims this Declaration of the Rights of the Child to the end that he may have a happy childhood and enjoy for his own good and for the good of society the rights and freedoms herein set forth, and calls upon parents, upon men and women as individuals and upon voluntary organizations, local authorities and national governments to recognize these rights and strive for their observance by legislative and other measures progressively taken in accordance with the following principles:

PRINCIPLE 1

The child shall enjoy all the rights set forth in this Declaration. All children, without any exception whatsoever, shall be entitled to these rights, without distinction or discrimination on account of race, color, sex, language, religion, political or other opinion, national or social origin, property, birth or other status, whether of himself or of his family.

PRINCIPLE 2

The child shall enjoy special protection, and shall be given opportunities and facilities, by law and by other means, to enable him to develop physically, mentally, morally, spiritually and socially in a healthy and normal manner and in conditions of freedom and dignity. In the enactment of laws for this purpose the best interests of the child shall be the paramount consideration.

PRINCIPLE 3

The child shall be entitled from his birth to a name and a nationality.

PRINCIPLE 4

The child shall enjoy the benefits of social security. He shall be entitled to grow and develop in health; to this end special care and protection shall be provided both to him and to his mother, including adequate pre-natal and post-natal care. The child shall have the right to adequate nutrition, housing, recreation and medical services.

PRINCIPLE 5

The child who is physically, mentally or socially handicapped shall be given the special treatment, education and care required by his particular condition.

PRINCIPLE 6

The child, for the full and harmonious development of his personality, needs love and understanding. He shall, wherever possible, grow up in the care and under the responsibility of his parents, and in any case in an atmosphere of affection and of moral and material security; a child of tender years shall not, save in exceptional circumstances, be separated from his mother. Society and the public authorities shall have the duty to extend particular care to children without a family and to those without adequate means of support. Payment of state and other assistance toward the maintenance of children of large families is desirable.

PRINCIPLE 7

The child is entitled to receive education, which shall be free and compulsory, at least in the elementary stages. He shall be given an education which will promote his general culture, and enable him on a basis of equal opportunity to develop his abilities, his individual judgment, and his sense of moral and social responsibility, and to become a useful member of society.

The best interests of the child shall be the guiding principle of those responsible for his education and guidance; that responsibility lies in the first place with his parents.

The child shall have full opportunity for play and recreation, which should be directed to the same purposes as education; society and the public authorities shall endeavor to promote the enjoyment of this right.

PRINCIPLE 8

The child shall in all circumstances be among the first to receive protection and relief.

PRINCIPLE 9

The child shall be protected against all forms of neglect, cruelty and exploitation. He shall not be the subject of traffic, in any form.

The child shall not be admitted to employment before an appropriate minimum age; he shall in no case be caused or permitted to engage in any occupation or employment which would prejudice his health or education, or interfere with his physical, mental or moral development.

PRINCIPLE 10

The child shall be protected from practices which may foster racial, religious and any other form of discrimination. He shall be brought up in a spirit of understanding, tolerance, friendship among peoples, peace and universal brotherhood and in full consciousness that his energy and talents should be devoted to the service of his fellow men.

Bernard J. Coughlin, S.J.

2
The Rights of Children

The times call our attention to human and to civil rights, and
demand that we recognize and honor, in philosophy and in practice, our conviction about rights in a democratic society. In this
essay I would like to give attention to a neglected aspect of
human rights—the rights of children. The specific theme I would
like to develop is one relating to child welfare: that children have
a special right to the protection of the state by reason of their
dependency.

I propose to develop this theme in four stages. First, we should
review the definition of some terms that are essential to this
subject. Second, as background for examining children's rights,
it will help to reflect on the more encompassing human rights
movement in our society. Third, we shall study the area of the
human rights movement that has impact on the field of child
welfare. Finally, we shall consider the responsibility that the
state has in theory and in fact to guarantee the rights of children.

Some Definitions of Terms

Human Rights

Although people in our society value human rights highly, there is
certainly a lack of unanimity on the definition of human rights.
Because the concept of rights is so central to social welfare and to
the profession of social work, however, it would seem to be of
critical importance for those of us who are totally involved in this

BERNARD J. COUGHLIN, S.J., Ph.D., is Dean of the
School of Social Service, Saint Louis University, Saint Louis,
Missouri. This article is reprinted, with permission, from
Child Welfare 47(1968):133–42.

7

profession to understand and set forth clearly the idea of human rights.

In the construction of our society the Founding Fathers built upon two premises: that all men are created equal, and that they are endowed with certain inalienable rights. I define "right" as a moral power in virtue of which human beings may make just claims to certain things. To use the word "power" in defining "right" may be misleading, because we usually conceive power as belonging only to the physical order. To say that right is a moral power is to distinguish it from physical powers; it is a power that pertains not to the physical but to the intellectual and volitional order. Perhaps the concept of relationship gives added insight into what right is: right implies the existence of a relation between persons and things. And to say that right is a relationship is to say that right does not exist independently, but inheres in persons as a quality that affects not their physical but their moral being.

An everyday example is illustrative. A father comes home from work with a piece of candy that he has bought for his six-year-old boy. He gives the candy to the child. The child kisses his father, thanks him, and goes out into the backyard to play as he enjoys the candy. Minutes later an older boy in the neighborhood—a ten-year-old—sees the six-year-old, comes up to him, grabs the candy from his hand and takes it for himself. Everyone says: "He has no right to do that." The six-year-old's right to the candy obviously is not a natural right, but the example illustrates the just claim that the child has to it. By virtue of a relationship that exists between the six-year-old and the candy, the candy is said to be "his"; this is to say that he exercises a moral power over it, even though he may not exercise physical power over it.

Natural Rights

Now, it is highly important to distinguish between natural and civil rights. Although this is not the occasion to study the matter in depth, it is necessary to compare these concepts briefly in order to achieve greater clarity and insight into the idea of right. Natural right, sometimes called human right, is inalienable. That is, it belongs to man by reason of his very existence as a human person, and therefore is not conferred upon him by parents or church or state or any other individual or community of men. Because it is a moral power and not a physical entity, and because it is inalienable and flows from the very nature of the human person, human right as such can neither be granted nor withheld. People, out of ignorance, malice, or neglect, may deprive a human being of food to the point of starvation and death. This is to deprive him of the benefits that the natural right to food and life are supposed to bestow. But the privation of food does not deprive man of the right to food. Natural right may be ignored or violated, but unlike a purse that can be robbed, natural right is as indestructible as the human person.

Natural or human right, therefore, is not a claim that a person earns as a result of his contribution to the economy or to the social or political order. Neither is it a claim that a person merits by reason of his education, intelligence, or maturity. Human right is based on the idea that the human person is master of himself and his own actions, and that therefore he is not a means to an end, but rather an end unto himself. There are certain things that are due to man simply because he is human. He is created by God with a purpose, and he is a free moral being with respect to that purpose. Integral to his being, therefore, are obligation and responsibility. The human being may justly claim those things that are necessary for the attainment of his purpose and the fulfillment of his responsibility.

It is clear that the correlative of human rights is human responsibility. Natural rights are related directly to this responsibility, since certain things are absolutely necessary for human fulfillment. Man has, for example, the rights to life, food, drink, shelter, and a certain level of physical, emotional, intellectual, and spiritual growth. These are called natural rights because they pertain directly to man's nature, and it is clear that they are unconditional.

Civil Rights

Civil rights, by contrast, are the effect of legal enactment. They are based on natural rights and are the state's explicit enunciation of rights that it guarantees to every citizen. Sometimes the state incorporates certain natural rights in its constitution or code of legislation; by that incorporation they also become civil rights. In other instances the state elaborates and explicates certain natural rights, making application of them to its particular culture and political system. Thus, the civil code incorporates many natural rights. At the same time, in order to facilitate the social process, it guarantees to the citizen certain civil rights that are not natural rights per se. An example of a natural right that the state sanctions as a civil right is the right to life. By reason of this natural right, the state passes a law punishing murder. Another example of a natural right that the state develops into a civil right is the citizen's right to justice, which the state seeks to protect and guarantee, among other ways, by the civil right to trial by jury. Trial by jury is one of a number of possible ways in which a society can guarantee justice in the judicial process. A society such as ours grants this legal right by constitutional guarantee or some other legal form. Citizenship is the entitlement.

Like natural rights, civil rights may be violated. We are all familiar with violations in some of our states of the right to vote as that right is applied to Negroes. Daily our Federal and state supreme courts hear cases and render decisions that concern the denial of civil rights. The significant point is that a citizen's civil rights, like his natural rights, may be denied for reasons of ignorance, malice, or neglect. But this is a denial only of the benefits that the civil rights seek to confer; it is not a denial of the civil right itself. Just as natural rights are inalienable by reason of human nature, civil rights enjoy what, for want of a better expression, we might call "citizenship inalienability."

Dependency

One other concept that is relevant to this subject is that of dependency, and this requires little elaboration. Dependency implies reliance on another for existence or assistance. Because they must rely entirely or partially on others, children are in a particularly vulnerable position. This vulnerability is accentuated in a large, complex, impersonal society. The child cannot initiate steps to rectify injustices against himself. To parents falls the primary responsibility of protecting the rights of children, and parents are accountable to the community at large. In a small society it is relatively simple for the community to supervise this parental task. Relatives, friends, and neighbors are never far away; parental neglect, abandonment, or mistreatment cannot be concealed from certain segments of the community. The modern city is much more anonymous. The very existence of many children is not known beyond the immediate family circle. When the rights of such children are violated, their total dependency is a particularly critical phenomenon.

The Human Rights Movement

In order to provide perspective on recent developments of the human rights movement in child welfare, I should like first to take a broader view of human rights in other areas of social welfare. I am purposely using the term "human rights," and avoiding the term "civil rights," because contemporary historical events tend to make civil rights synonymous with racial justice. Actually, civil rights is much broader than the rights of minority groups. More-over, aside from historical consideration, the term "human rights" is more appropriate for our purpose since, as we have seen, it is a broader concept than "civil rights." A view of recent developments of the human rights movement in related fields of social welfare will convey a broader meaning and a deeper significance to human rights developments in child welfare.

Corrections

In the field of adult corrections, for example, several recent Supreme Court decisions have been handed down that are directed at clarifying the rights of the suspected criminal. The trend of the Court is toward expanding rather than contracting the rights of the accused. One recent case, *Miranda* v. *State of Arizona,*[1] drew wide attention. Miranda had been taken into custody and interrogated in the police station. He was advised neither of his right to remain silent nor of his right to consult an attorney. After two hours of questioning he signed a written confession. At the trial the state, in spite of Miranda's objection, introduced the confession in evidence against him. He was found guilty of kidnapping and rape.

When the case came before the United States Supreme Court, the decision of the lower court was reversed on the grounds that the trial procedure had violated the following constitutional rights of the accused: that "No person . . . shall be compelled in any criminal case to be a witness against himself," and that ". . . the accused [shall] have the assistance of counsel. . . ." As a matter of record, Miranda was convicted on a retrial; the point of the case,

---

1. *Miranda* v. *State of Arizona,* 384 U.S. 491–92 (1965).

however, is the solicitousness of the Court to protect the rights of the citizen even where the evidence conclusively indicates guilt.

Mental Health

In the mental health field, a recent decision by the United States Court of Appeals drew the attention of the country to the constitutional rights of hospitalized mental patients. There are an estimated 500,000 persons in 285 state and county mental hospitals in the United States. All who are acquainted with the level of treatment in many of these hospitals know that large numbers of mental patients receive little more than custodial care. Many of these patients are involuntarily committed by court order. Chief Judge David L. Bazelon gave the court's decision, and in specific reference to the criminally insane man's right to treatment under Federal law, wrote: "The purpose of involuntary hospitalization is treatment, not punishment. . . . Absent treatment, the hospital is 'transform[ed] . . . into a penitentiary where one could be held indefinitely for no convicted offense. . . .' " [2] Where treatment is absent, one may question the constitutionality of mandatory commitment. The Judge added that ". . . a right to treatment in some form is recognized by law in many states." Senator Sam Ervin of North Carolina, who sponsored the 1964 Hospitalization of the Mentally Ill Act, and Chairman of a Senate Judiciary Subcommittee on Constitutional Rights, noted that several experts had advanced the opinion that to deprive a person of liberty on the basis that he is in need of treatment, without supplying the needed treatment, is tantamount to a denial of due process. Court decisions of this kind will have the effect of improving the treatment programs and services in public hospitals for the mentally ill.

Economic Welfare

In the field of public assistance and economic welfare of the family, the human rights movement is goading the conscience of society to devise and accept a minimum economic level to which every citizen has a right. The movement is based on some hard facts about the economy. All families in the society face a common level of need. For all families, as one writer recently put it, "Housing is expected to conform to minimum standards of safety and comfort; foods

2. *Rouse* v. *Cameron,* District of Columbia Circuit, 373 F.2d 451 (1966).

are packaged and priced in standardized quantity and quality, so that Kellogg's Cornflakes will cost about the same in Duluth, Minnesota, and Dothan, Alabama; the same type of shoe is needed to protect from the pavement in Harlem and in Hollywood; the nutritional minimums for healthy childhood are precisely the same in Seattle and in Selma, for a sharecropper's family in South Carolina, for a distressed miner's brood in Appalachia, and for youngsters clustered about a den mother in Scarsdale." [3]

At some point society must face the question: does the family in today's affluent society have a right to a minimum income? However we answer that question, we cannot close our eyes to the economic inequality that exists, an inequality that finds, according to the latest statistics of the Office of Economic Opportunity, 34.3 million citizens below the poverty level. Of that number, 5.8 million are under six years of age, and 13.9 million are under sixteen years of age.[4] When these statistics are considered in the light of our knowledge that as the size of the American family increases the median annual income decreases,[5] then it becomes clear that those who suffer most from the present income distribution are children. Over 40 percent of all families in poverty have children under six years of age.[6] The movement to accept an economic policy that would guarantee to every citizen a minimum income is based on the right to an income minimum; indeed, there are those who assert that this is an actual constitutional right, given the level of economic abundance that characterizes American society.[7]

Legal Services

In the area of legal services and legal protection, especially to the poor, one can see another spearhead of the human rights movement. Illustrations of the inequality of legal protection for the

3. John A. Morsell, "The Civil Rights Struggle and the Welfare of Children," *Child Welfare* 44 (1965):461.
4. *Dimensions of Poverty in 1964* (Washington, D.C.: U.S. Government Printing Office, October 1965), p. 4.
5. Lenore A. Epstein, "Some Effects of Low Income on Children and Their Families," *Social Security Bulletin,* 24, no. 2 (1961):13.
6. *Dimensions of Poverty in 1964,* p. 15.
7. *See* Edward E. Schwartz, "An End to the Means Tests," in Robert Theobald, ed., *The Guaranteed Income* (Garden City, New York: Doubleday and Company, 1965), p. 124.

poor and the wealthy could be chosen from any area of slum life —consumer problems, landlord-tenant relations, housing and education, and so forth. As the Director of the Division of Social Services of the Children's Bureau recently said:

> We hear much these days about legal services for the poor. We know only too well, however, what is happening to many poor people. They have no funds to pay lawyers to defend them when they are victimized by unscrupulous landlords and usurious merchants, nor to free them when they are entangled in a web of policies, regulations, and procedures. For them, freedom from want at this moment may mean only money to buy the next meal for their children or to keep their furniture from being piled on the sidewalk.[8]

We still find it difficult to shake off the attitude that those who are compelled to receive government assistance do not have the same political and social rights as those who can provide for themselves and their families. Because the poor and uneducated usually have little understanding of their legal rights, they are frequently the victims of dilapidated housing, unscrupulous landlords, evictions, discrimination, and punitive legal action. As Attorney General Katzenbach said:

> To us, law and regulations are protections and guides established for our benefit and for use. To the poor, they are a hostile maze, established as an harassment, at all cost to be avoided.[9]

Citizenship entitles every citizen to a minimum of legal protection, which safeguards his just treatment in the marketplace. Therefore, one of our important national goals is equal legal protection under the law for all citizens.

The Rights of Children in Social Welfare

This is sufficient, I think, to give us a perspective of the human rights movement that extends far beyond the rights of children.

8. Mildred Arnold, "Child Welfare Amendments—Where Are We Now?" *Child Welfare* 46 (1967):130.

9. Nicholas deB. Katzenbach, untitled address in *Proceedings of the Conference on the Extension of Legal Services to the Poor* (Washington, D.C.: U.S. Government Printing Office, 1964), p. 6.

Now let us narrow our scope and consider some of the activities that are taking place in the field of child welfare.

Provisions of 1962 Amendments

The 1962 Amendments to the Social Security Act testify to the sweeping concern for the rights of children. Title V, Part 3 of the Act has been amended many times since 1935, but certainly the 1962 amendments stand out for their legislative mandate to serve children. These amendments are based on the child's total dependence and on the recognition of the right that every child has to receive not only economic security but the whole range of social safeguards necessary for his development. The 1962 Amendments are the response of the society to provide for all children all of the services that they need in order to mature.

This legislation seeks to achieve its goal in four ways. First, the amendments require that all political subdivisions of every state must provide child welfare services, so that within the political subdivision there is a solid foundation of opportunity for all children. Second, these services are to be available to all children who have need of them, regardless of legal residence, economic potential, social status, race, religion, or national origin. Third, as this piece of legislation is interpreted by the Children's Bureau, states are encouraged to seek out actively children who need services: the unseen and unknown, those in crowded slums and rural byways, those who are physically abused and those who are uncared for. There is a large number of children in our society who remain unknown and unhelped, who are not given the chance to live full lives because no one searches them out and offers service. We know from political history that civil rights must be fought for. Protective services for children have had an uneven career; this area of social work practice requires aggressiveness to guarantee that the child has what he needs.

A fourth and highly significant element of the 1962 Amendments is the new definition of child welfare, which considerably expands its scope and function. In the initial years of their development, child welfare services were defined largely in terms of foster family care, adoption services, and some institution care for children. The present definition is much broader. Child welfare services now encompass public social services which supplement or substitute for parental care and supervision for the following purposes:

> To prevent and solve problems that result in the neglect, abuse, and delinquency of children.
> To protect and care for homeless, dependent, and neglected children.
> To promote the welfare of the children of working mothers.
> To strengthen the home and to provide adequate care for children away from their homes.[10]

It is clear from this public mandate that the government is assuming responsibility for implementing the rights of all children who need protection, care, and service. It is clear also that in the realization of this much broader function the government will assume a much more aggressive role in protecting the rights of children.

Child-Abuse Laws

Another consideration will make even more emphatic this aggressive role of government in implementing the rights of children. This trend is effectively indicated by the increasing number of child-abuse laws in the states. Although the neglect and abuse of children is nothing new, the degree of violence and the rising incidents of attacks on children by parents and other caretakers are new. The Children's Bureau became aware of these aspects of the problem early in the 1960s. As this trend was documented by case studies and research on the battered child, government began seriously to look into the matter. Under the leadership of the Children's Bureau, technical assistance has been given and a piece of model legislation developed with the hope that individual states would assume responsibility for incorporating the principles of the legislation into state laws that protect children from physical and emotional abuse. One by one, the states have responded by designing and passing child-abuse laws. The strongest and best laws make it mandatory that physicians, interns, and residents report instances of child neglect and abuse to proper state authorities. At the same time, these laws protect anyone against liability who in good faith cooperates with the public authorities in identifying a case of child abuse.

10. *See* Social Security Act, 1935, Title V, Part 3, Section 528.

Health Legislation

Another area of legislation aims to protect the rights of children to health. Some states have enacted legislation to protect children from specific diseases. For example, in California doctors must administer prophylactic medicine to both eyes of every baby within two days of birth, or be guilty of a misdemeanor. This is based on the child's right to be protected from serious eye problems resulting from gonorrhea, and removes from the parents the right to make this decision for the child. Also in California, a 1962 enactment makes it mandatory for parents to supply the school with a statement that their child has been vaccinated against poliomyelitis. In default of such a statement, parents must provide the school authorities with an acceptable explanation for not having vaccinated the child. The purpose of the law is to identify and protect those children whose parents fail through neglect to meet the community's standards of good health care.[11]

Custody

Closely related to this concern of society for a child's right to health care is concern for his right to parental care, affection, and a family environment that fosters full human development. Recent developments in family courts document the human rights movement in this area of child welfare. Not only the increase in the number of divorces, but proceedings in family and domestic relations court lead one to suspect that the husband and wife are so involved in contesting their own rights before the court that the rights of the children involved are forgotten. As Justice Black stated, "Unfortunately, experience has shown that the question of custody, so vital to a child's happiness and well-being, frequently cannot be left to the discretion of the parents. This is particularly true where . . . the estrangement of husband and wife beclouds parental judgment with emotion and prejudice." [12] In a legal system such as ours, where the rights of children and the rights of the family are so intertwined, the status of children in divorce action raises critical questions: Are the rights of children constituted as separate entities apart from parental rights? Are children

11. *See* Helen E. Boardman, "Who Insures the Childs Right to Health?" *Child Welfare,* 42 (1963):122.

12. *Ford v. Ford,* 371 U.S. 187 (1962) at 193.

in divorce proceedings actually parties to the action, with rights that must be considered regardless of the desires of the parents? If so, who is to represent the interests and defend the rights of the child at the trial of a divorce action?

In several recent cases in Wisconsin the State supreme court has taken a decided stand, saying that in divorce proceedings more is involved than the rights of the two contending parties. In such cases the trial court does not function merely as an arbiter between two private parties. Rather, it represents the interests of society in promoting family stability. In a divorce children are always disadvantaged parties, so the law and the court must take positive steps to safeguard their rights and their welfare. With this purpose before it, the court should initiate a social investigation and present information in addition to the evidence produced by either party to the divorce. In 1965 the supreme court of Wisconsin carried this philosophy one step further when it ruled that in every divorce action someone should represent, before the court, the rights and interests of the child.[13]

Juvenile Proceedings

Although we cannot undertake here an exhaustive exploration of every contribution to the human rights movement in child welfare, a paper on this subject must include two recent examples from the juvenile court.

Kent v. United States is important, not only because it was in defense of the rights of children, but because it challenged society to stop paying mere lip service to its juvenile court philosophy of *parens patriae* and to pay the price to make that philosophy effective in practice.

The facts of the case can be quickly recalled. An intruder entered the apartment of a woman in the District of Columbia, took her wallet, and raped her. Fingerprints in the apartment matched the prints of Maurice Kent, a juvenile. Kent was apprehended by the police and taken to police headquarters. The police did not notify the parents of the child; the juvenile court was not informed until a week after Kent was apprehended; he was interrogated by the

13. *See* Robert W. Hansen, "The Role and Rights of Children in Divorce Courts," in George G. Newman, ed., *Children in the Courts—the Question of Representation* (Ann Arbor: The Institute of Continuing Legal Education, 1967), pp. 22–32.

police in the absence of both counsel and parents; he was not advised of his right to counsel nor of his right to remain silent; while thus detained he was fingerprinted. All of this was in violation of the Juvenile Court Act of the District of Columbia.

The juvenile court judge certified Kent to the district court where he was tried as an adult. The fingerprints and the testimony that police had obtained while the suspect was in their custody were presented as evidence. Kent was convicted. When the case reached the United States Supreme Court, however, the decision of the lower court was reversed, on the grounds that the trial was illegal since the procedures used to obtain the evidence that convicted Kent were in direct violation of the Juvenile Code of the District of Columbia.

Mr. Justice Fortas delivered the opinion of the Court and used the occasion to theorize on juvenile court philosophy. The objective of the juvenile court is to provide guidance and rehabilitation for the child as well as protection for society; it is not to fix criminal responsibility, guilt, and punishment. Nevertheless, this philosophy of *parens patriae* is not an invitation to procedural arbitrariness. And in the following words Mr. Fortas questions how serious society is about translating into practice what for seventy years has been termed a juvenile court philosophy:

> While there can be no doubt of the original laudable purpose of juvenile courts, studies and critiques in recent years raise serious questions as to whether actual performance measures well enough against theoretical purpose to make tolerable the immunity of the process from the reach of constitutional guarantees applicable to adults. There is much evidence that some juvenile courts, including that of the District of Columbia, lack the personnel, facilities and techniques to perform adequately as representatives of the State in a *parens patriae* capacity, at least with respect to children charged with law violation. There is evidence, in fact, that there may be grounds for concern that the child receives the worst of both worlds: that he gets neither the protections accorded to adults nor the solicitous care and regenerative treatment postulated for children.[14]

Another Supreme Court decision addressed itself even more pointedly to the rights of children in juvenile court proceedings.

14. *Kent* v. *United States,* 383 U.S. 451 (1966).

In re Gault concerns the right of children to due process in the juvenile court.

The essential facts of this case may be simply stated. Gerald Gault, a fifteen-year-old boy, was arrested while on probation for making lewd and indecent remarks over the telephone to a woman neighbor. Gault was not given counsel, and at the hearing the mother's request that the complaining neighbor be present was denied. The boy was committed to an institution until the age of twenty-one, the period of his minority. Since no appeal was permitted by Arizona law, Gault filed a petition for a writ of habeas corpus with the State court. This petition was denied. The supreme court of Arizona rejected the claim that due process had been violated, basing its argument on the *parens patriae* nature of juvenile court proceedings.

The case was carried to the United States Supreme Court, where the decision of the Arizona court was reversed on the grounds that the child's right to due process had been violated. The Court was vigorous in maintaining that, whatever differences may and should exist between juvenile and adult courts, and however much the state and the court must function in lieu of parents, this is no justification for disregarding rights that the Constitution guarantees to every citizen. "It would be extraordinary," the Court said, "if our Constitution did not require the procedural regularity and the exercise of care implied in the phrase 'due process.' " [15]

Speaking for the Court, Justice Fortas cited a number of juvenile court procedures that disregard the rights of children and should be corrected. Upholding the right of the juvenile to counsel, he said: "The juvenile needs the assistance of counsel to cope with problems of law, to make skilled inquiry into the facts, to insist upon regularity of the proceedings, and to ascertain whether he has a defense and to prepare and submit it. The child 'requires the guiding hand of counsel at every step in the proceedings against him.' " *Powell v. Alabama,* 287 U.S. 45, 69 (1932).[16] The Court refused to accept the argument that the constitutional right not to be compelled in a criminal case to witness against oneself does not obtain in juvenile proceedings because they are civil in nature. Again, in the language of the Court: ". . . the constitutional privilege

15. *In the Matter of Gault, The United States Law Week,* vol. 35, no. 44 (1967):4406.
16. *Ibid.,* p. 4409.

against self-incrimination is applicable in the case of juveniles as it is with respect to adults. We appreciate that special problems may arise with respect to waiver of the privilege by or on behalf of children, and that there may well be some differences in technique—but not in principle—depending upon the age of the child and the presence and competence of parents." [17] Moreover, the Court upheld the right of the child to be confronted by his accusers and the right to cross-examine witnesses with the aid of counsel. "We now hold," wrote Justice Fortas, "that, absent a valid confession, a determination of delinquency and an order of commitment to a state institution cannot be sustained in the absence of sworn testimony subjected to the opportunity for cross-examination in accordance with our law and constitutional requirements." [18]

The Gault case has had a startling impact on the juvenile court. In the judicial system, rights are guaranteed through procedures. In the future juvenile offenders will be protected like adults—by established procedures with respect to arrest, search, seizure, pretrial investigation, notification of charges, advice and representation by counsel, the voluntariness of confession, confrontation by accusers, and cross-examination. Although the Court is aware that "due process" may guarantee justice before the law, happily it also recognizes that procedures alone cannot bring about the treatment and care that the delinquent requires. If it is true, as the Court stated, that the juvenile receives "the worst of both worlds," [19] it is also true that a court can guarantee the best of only one world. The Court is acutely aware of another world that society has left relatively untouched. For the second time within a year the Court called society's attention to its responsibility to care for and treat the child who is delinquent. Given the juvenile court philosophy, without care and treatment there is no justification for intervention. Echoing the *Kent* decision, Justice Fortas wrote:

> The traditional ideas of juvenile court procedure, indeed, contemplated that time would be available and care would be used to establish precisely what the juvenile did and why he did it— was it a prank of adolescence or a brutal act threatening serious consequences to himself or society unless corrected? Under

17. *Ibid.*, p. 4415.
18. *Ibid.*, p. 4416.
19. *Kent* v. *United States*, pp. 23–24.

traditional notions, one would assume that in a case like that of Gerald Gault, where the juvenile appears to have a home, a working mother and father, and an older brother, the Juvenile Judge would have made a careful inquiry and judgment as to the possibility that the boy could be disciplined and dealt with at home, despite his previous transgressions.[20]

Summary and Conclusions

The basis of human rights is the human person. These rights belong to children as well as to the adult citizen. Natural rights are inalienable and inviolable; they are not a reward for accomplishment. No other person, group, or state confers natural rights, but the state and all institutions have the responsibility to acknowledge them and to establish a social order that protects and guarantees under law their free exercise. Because of their dependency, children especially have a claim on this protector and guarantor role of the state.

Since establishing the Bill of Rights and incorporating it into the basic law of the land, our society has valued individual human rights highly. Indeed, this seems almost a truism. But the expansion, complexity, and impersonality of modern society demands that the state take a more active role, especially in assuring the dependent that their rights will not be violated either by other citizens or by the state itself. Accordingly, these times see a movement of human rights that bears directly on the rights of children. Perhaps these rights have always been acknowledged in theory, but there have been many gaps in practice. The present income level of the AFDC Program is a gap; the present quality of institution care represents a gap; supposedly comprehensive child welfare services leave many gaps; the present level of health care represents a gap; the services of juvenile courts have gaps; the child-abuse laws of many states leave gaps; and the educational opportunities for all children have gaps. But we are aware of the gaps, and they are being closed. We have a commitment to close them: It is our commitment to the child because of who a child is. It is our commitment to the society because the child is the future citizen. It is a commitment acknowledged the world over and expressed by the United Nations in its Declaration of the Rights of the Child:

20. *In the Matter of Gault,* 4406–7.

The child shall enjoy special protection, and shall be given opportunities and facilities, by law and by other means, to enable him to develop physically, mentally, morally, spiritually and socially in a healthy and normal manner and in conditions of freedom and dignity.

This is our commitment.

Lois G. Forer

3
Rights of Children:
The Legal Vacuum

"What are the rights of children? What is the law?" These questions are being asked by nonlawyers with increasing frequency. Recently the departments of pediatrics of two Philadelphia hospitals held lectures on this subject. Schools of social work are deeply concerned. Teachers, administrators of institutions for children, jail wardens and even high school and junior high school pupils want to know what the law is with respect to the rights of children.

What Law?

The lawyer who is asked this question may well reply, "What law?" It is an anomalous and incredible fact that there is almost no case or statutory law setting forth the rights of children. Although the United States Supreme Court passes on some 2,500 cases a year and decides on the merits of approximately 400 cases a year, it was not until 177 years after the founding of this nation that the court ruled on a case raising the constitutional rights of a child.[1] The much-discussed *Gault* case (387 U. S. 1), which was decided the following year, 1967, was limited to four procedural points in delin-

The Honorable LOIS G. FORER, LL.B., is Judge of the Common Pleas Court of Philadelphia. As a practicing attorney, she was attorney in charge of the Anti-Poverty Law Office for Juveniles in Philadelphia from 1966 to 1968. She is the author of *"No One Will Lissen": How Our Legal System Brutalizes the Youthful Poor* (New York: John Day, 1970). With slight revisions, this article is reprinted with permission from the *American Bar Association Journal* 55(1969):1151–56.

1. *Kent* v. *United States,* 384 U. S. 541 (1966). Prior cases involving children were not addressed to the question of whether children in contradistinction to adults are entitled to the protections of the Bill of Rights.

quency hearings in juvenile court. Even these rulings are hedged with limitations.[2] The decision did, however, signal a radical change in jurisprudential theory. Contrary to the prior state cases [3] and the views of many authorities on the juvenile court, the *Gault* decision indicates that children do have some constitutional rights. The extent and limits of those rights have not been limned.

Thoughtful persons who deal with the minds and bodies of children are aware of the changing legal climate. They are deeply disturbed by many difficult and sensitive decisions affecting the lives of children that they are required to make, and they seek legal guidance. There are no clear legal answers to their questions. The recent outpouring of legal literature on juvenile delinquency and the juvenile courts is devoted primarily to issues covered by the *Gault* decision or implicit in it.[4] To date the legal profession appears to be oblivious of the vast uncharted area of legal problems involving the lives of children.

It is interesting to speculate on the reasons for this legal vacuum. Almost half of all Americans are under the age of twenty-one. In our highly structured, complex society, many agencies of government take actions affecting children's lives, often with drastic results. Yet there are few cases challenging such actions or alleging that the constitutional rights of the child have been infringed. By contrast, the rights of members of such tiny sects as Jehovah's Witnesses and the Amish have been litigated many times. Issues of limited importance and involving comparatively few people have been before the courts again and again and have been the subjects

2. The Court held that in delinquency proceedings the accused child has the right to notice of the charges, the right to counsel, the right to confront and cross-examine the witnesses and the privilege against self-incrimination. Whether any of these elements of due process must be observed in the preliminary phases of a delinquency case and whether they apply in dependency and neglect hearings were scrupulously left undecided.

3. See, *e.g., In the Matter of Holmes,* 379 Pa. 599, 109 A. 2d 523 (1954).

4. See, *e.g.,* GAULT: WHAT NOW FOR THE JUVENILE COURT, Institute of Continuing Legal Education, Ann Arbor, Michigan (1968); Weinstein & Goodman, *Supreme Court and the Juvenile Court,* 13 CRIME & DELINQUENCY 481 (1967); Welch, *Delinquency Proceedings—Fundamental Fairness,* 50 MINN. L. REV. 653 (1966); *Comment, Criminal Offenders in the Juvenile Court,* 114 U. PA. L. REV. 1171 (1966); Platt & Friedman, *The Limits of Advocacy, Occupational Hazards in the Juvenile Court,* 116 U. PA. L. REV. 1156 (1968); Fort, *Gault: Adversity or Opportunity,* 51 JUDICATURE 53 (1967); Mecham, *Proceed with Caution,* 14 CRIME & DELINQUENCY 142 (1968).

of exhaustive scholarship.[5] There are enormous bodies of law—statutes, regulations and cases—elucidating in minute detail fine distinctions in such esoteric fields as apportionment of income between life tenant and remainderman, the scope of review on appeal, and the possibility of an octogenarian's having issue.[6]

Probably there are many psychological and sociological reasons for the law's neglect of the rights of children. In America's youth-oriented society, adults may have ambivalent feelings toward children. Today a child is an economic liability. He is no longer a source of cheap or unpaid labor on the farm or in the family business. Few parents can look forward to being supported by their children in old age. Campus unrest and the growing juvenile delinquency rate provoke cries of "Get tough!" Such conditions do not give rise to a concern for the rights of young people. Nor have the reformers who devote themselves to problems of crime prevention, rehabilitation of wayward youth and improving the lives and conduct of the underprivileged been notably sensitive to the rights of those whom they have tried to help, particularly when the objects of their solicitude are children. After all, those who are older and wealthier are presumably wiser. They know what is best for the young.

A simpler explanation for the scarcity of law involving the rights of children is the fact that very few children have been represented by counsel. Most of the children in institutions, whether for the delinquent, the neglected or the mentally ill, are indigent. Prior to the *Gault* decision, it was considered inappropriate, if not unauthorized, for counsel to appear in juvenile delinquency proceedings. Even now, two years after the decision, there is still widespread resistance to having defense counsel in juvenile court. In innumerable other situations in which children's welfare and liberty are

5. *Sherbert* v. *Verner,* 374 U. S. 398 (1963); *In re Jenison,* 375 U. S. 14 (1963); Casad, *Compulsory High School Attendance and the Old Order Amish,* 16 KAN. L. REV. 423 (1968); *Kansas* v. *Garber,* 419 P. 2d 896 (Sup. Ct. 1966).

6. Typical of these scholarly discussions are Jaffee, *Administrative Law: Burden of Proof and Scope of Review,* 79 HARV. L. REV. 914 (1966); Leach, *New Hampshire Defertilizes the Octogenarians,* 77 HARV. L. REV. 279 (1963); Berger, *Administrative Arbitrariness—A Reply to Professor Davis,* 114 U. PA. L. REV. 783 (1966); Davis, *Administrative Arbitrariness—A Final Word,* 114 U. PA. L. REV. 814 (1966); Berger, *Administrative Arbitrariness—A Rejoinder to Professor Davis' "Final Word",* 114 U. PA. L. REV. 816 (1966); Davis, *Administrative Arbitrariness—A Postscript,* 114 U. PA. L. REV. 823 (1966).

involved, there is no requirement that the matter be judicially determined or that children have counsel. No provision is made to furnish lawyers for these children. Litigation under the common law system is the crucible in which legal doctrine is forged, refined and solidified. Without counsel, there are seldom appeals or written opinions that would form the basic materials for legal scholarship. Consequently, there is little research or analysis of these problems.

The principal legislation governing children is the juvenile court act. Every state has by statute established a special court to handle cases of neglected, dependent and delinquent children. The primary purpose of such legislation and the principal activity of these courts is the processing of children whose behavior is disruptive to the community, the schools or their families. With minor variations these acts create courts with broad powers and loose procedures. Many juvenile courts do not even have rules of court. Nowhere in the standard juvenile court law or the new Model Juvenile Court Act is there any specification of the rights of a child or the procedures that he may invoke for his protection or to obtain redress for wrongs done to him.[7] The laws governing the treatment of animals are more specific than those with respect to children.

A Blank Slate Is at Least a Clean Slate

Since there is so little precedent, we are in the unusual position of being able to consider a priori what the law ought to be. Social reformers often engage in Utopian speculations about restructur-

---

7. The 1961 California Juvenile Court Law, which was enacted after a careful investigation of the abuses in and mistreatment of children by the juvenile court, provides for a few procedural safeguards. However, it re-enacts the basic structure of the old juvenile court laws and is predicated on the assumption that children have no substantive rights as persons. The act provides in part: "Any person under the age of 21 years who persistently or habitually refuses to obey the reasonable and proper orders or directions of his parents, guardian, custodian or school authorities, or who is beyond the control of such person or any person who is a habitual truant from school within the meaning of any law of this state, or who from any cause is in danger of leading an idle, dissolute, lewd or immoral life is within the jurisdiction of the juvenile court which may adjudge such person to be a ward of the court." CAL. WELF. & INSTITUTIONS CODE § 500 *et seq.* at § 601. There is no provision in this long and carefully drawn statute for the child to invoke the jurisdiction of the court for his own protection against adults or the state or to obtain redress for wrongs committed against him.

ing society, the family or government. Such bold thoughts offer heady excitement but little of practical value to people of good will who want to take at least a first step in the right direction. Lawyers frequently err in the other extreme by presenting a legislative package that deals with specific abuses but fails to consider basic injustices structured in the larger system. This paper tries to avoid both pitfalls. Although urging lawyers to give their attention to the wide range of legal problems involving the rights of minors, it seeks only to ask questions, explore concepts and suggest avenues of inquiry.

Legal rights do not exist separate and apart from daily life. Constitutional and statutory guarantees are meaningful only if they protect the individual from real hazards. If lawyers, courts and legislatures are to devise substantive and procedural laws to guarantee and implement the rights of children today, they will need hard factual information with respect to life as it is actually lived in the teeming inner cities, in the affluent suburbs, in small towns and rural areas. They must put aside preconceived notions of childhood innocence, Biblical ideals of filial devotion, the ethic of hard work and frugality. They must examine reality, unpleasant and shocking though it may be. They must learn how such institutions as schools, reformatories, juvenile courts and hospital clinics actually function, not simply read the reports of statistics and goals. They must study the lives of America's children as they are lived day by day in the family, in school and on the streets. This is not a task for lawyers alone. It requires the *expertise* of many disciplines.

Don't Ask a Lawyer "Who Is a Child?"

Perhaps the first inquiry should be to determine who is a child. At present there is no clear answer. One might say that under the law anyone who is not an adult is a child. But this reply is deceptively simple. A quick glance at the pertinent statutes reveals a patchwork of inconsistent, anomalous and conflicting age levels. At eighteen a boy is responsible for registering for the draft and serving in the Armed Forces. A mother contested that law on the ground that her son was legally a minor and under her control and that she forbade him to register.

This same eighteen-year-old cannot get married without his

parents' consent. If he is married, he is obligated to support his wife. But he cannot give a valid consent to an operation to be performed on her. If he buys an automobile or a motorcycle on the installment plan, he can disavow the contract and not be obligated to pay. If he negligently or maliciously injures persons or destroys property his parents are not responsible for the damage. There are many occupations, such as coal mining and bartending, that he may not engage in. Until 1970, he could not vote.[8] In most states he may not buy liquor. At sixteen, in some states, he may not see certain movies,[9] but he may be tried as an adult for crime and sentenced to a penitentiary with adult criminals. He can also be tried for incorrigibility as a juvenile without a jury and sent to a correctional institution for five years. In many states he will go to the very same jail to which he would have been sent had he been tried as an adult and convicted of a crime. But incorrigibility is not a crime for adults. At sixteen, he can be sent to jail for refusing to attend school.

The adolescent is also denied service on juries, membership in the legislature and on government boards and agencies, control of his property and person, and a multitude of other rights and decision-making powers. The common law was simpler. A child under the age of seven could not be prosecuted for violations of law. From the ages of seven to fourteen, a child was presumed to be lacking criminal capacity. Today, however, thirteen-year-old children are tried and convicted of murder.[10] Even a cursory review of the statutes and cases reveals that minors suffer many legal disabilities with very few compensatory rights or protections.

Primitive Peoples Have No Problem

The perplexing question of how to treat the teen-ager under the law is a peculiarly modern problem. Anthropologists find that in primitive societies there is no anomalous status of being an adolescent or, as we now say pejoratively, a juvenile. At puberty a

8. *Oregon* v. *Mitchell*, 400 U.S. 112 (December 21, 1970).
9. See, *e.g.*, N. Y. Penal Law § 235.21(2); *Mishin* v. *New York*, 383 U. S. 502 (1966); Comment, *Exclusion of Children from Violent Movies*, 67 Colum. L. Rev. 1149 (1967).
10. *Pennsylvania* v. *Moore*, Pa. Sup. Ct., 1968 Term, No. 166, Misc. Docket No. 17.

boy is, after a difficult initiation, inducted into the tribe. He then assumes the obligations of manhood and is given the full rights of an adult. A girl also passes from childhood to adulthood without undergoing an intermediate, indeterminate phase of adolescence.

Contemporary American society has a whole subculture of the teen-ager. There are clothes, magazines and entertainment especially designed for this group. With rare exceptions the teen-ager is both unemployed and unemployable. Without analyzing the economic and societal values served by prolonging childhood and financial dependency until the age of seventeen for the slum dweller and at least twenty-one for the middle-class student, the law must face the serious question of whether such dependency can or should deprive a young person of full legal rights and participation in the life of the community.

Correlative duties are also involved. If the adolescent, at whatever age, is denied full legal rights, then what duties of protection does society owe to him? Concepts of right develop imperceptibly, without scientific proof, technical argument or documentation. When the time is ripe, a declaration is made that certain rights, not heretofore formulated in law, are inalienable, inherent or self-evident. And society grudgingly concedes that such is the fact. Freedom from want, for example, is a peculiarly twentieth-century notion. It is hard to think of another time in history when society would have recognized a right to sustenance on the part of the individual and a correlative obligation on the part of government to support the citizenry. Perhaps we are now ready to recognize that there are certain human rights which all children have and certain corresponding obligations on the part of society to implement those rights.

Four Rights Are Inherent in All Children

I suggest that in formulating a juvenile jurisprudence there are four basic rights which the law should recognize as inherent in all children. These may be described as (1) the right to life, (2) the right to a home, (3) the right to an education, and (4) the right to liberty.

Liberty is the only one of these postulated rights that the courts have considered even indirectly. The decisions are fragmentary

and based upon inexact analogies to the criminal law.[11] They turn
on due process questions of the procedures by which a child is
institutionalized, but skirt the fundamental issue of the right of the
state to deprive a child of his liberty under circumstances in which
an adult could not be removed from society. Children are deprived
of liberty in our complex contemporary world for many reasons.
Alleged delinquency is only one. A child may be removed from
his home, immured and isolated from society and deprived of an
education because he is mentally retarded, emotionally disturbed,
nonconforming, difficult, refuses to attend school or perhaps is just
unloved or unlovable. These are the majority of children whom
the state places in institutions.

The emerging doctrine of right to treatment [12] is an indirect and
perhaps clumsy judicial attempt to mitigate the harshness of depriving the noncriminal person of his liberty. Significantly, the seminal
cases involve adults, not children, although vastly larger numbers
of children are placed in institutions.

The perplexing problem of what to do with these difficult children, who are often sloughed off on the state by their parents,
should be considered, I submit, in the context of the child's right
to freedom. Legality of the commitment would then be the issue—
not the procedures by which he was committed or the quantum of
care that he received or the existence of institutional peonage.
These are inexact and difficult facts to prove and really peripheral
to the question of whether the child (or adult) must be incarcerated
to protect society or to save his own life.

The Right to Life Is Not Self-Evident

The right to life seems self-evident. Once an infant is born, no
one has a legal right to take its life. We would be shocked at the
thought that a parent would be permitted to kill his child. But in
many civilized societies it was a common and accepted practice for
parents to expose an unwanted child, often a girl or a cripple. The
helpless infant was placed on a mountain top and left to die.
Today we call it murder or manslaughter.[13] We would also reject

11. See *In the Matter of Gault,* 387 U.S. 1 (1967).
12. *Rouse* v. *Cameron,* 373 F. 2d 451 (D.C. Cir. 1966).
13. See 60 Nw. U. L. Rev. 399 (1968).

the notion that a parent has the right to maim or deform his child. This, too, is a common practice in some countries to increase the earning capacity of the child who is expected to become a beggar. Binding the feet of infant girls was a sign of caste and privilege in China. Generations of women were thus crippled for life by their parents.

The parent who fails or refuses to provide medical care for his child may be little different from these other parents whose conduct shocks the contemporary American conscience. Natural parents, foster parents and institutions in which children are housed frequently fail to provide necessary medical care and treatment. It is not only infants who are denied care. Older children are equally at the mercy of adults with respect to obtaining medical care. Few children are able to consult a physician on their own. Parental consent is required for hospital treatment and perhaps for psychiatric care even when a teen-ager has money of his own and voluntarily seeks help.

There is little statutory law governing health care for children. Medical treatment is not yet a recognized constitutional right. Although the government does provide some free clinics and the law prescribes certain entitlements under aid to dependent children programs, there are few procedures by which a child may claim these benefits for himself. If medical treatment or surgery is necessary to save the life of a child, most courts will order that such treatment be provided irrespective of the wishes of the parent.[14] These cases usually arise when a child is already in a hospital and the parent refuses to give consent to a blood transfusion or surgery.

There are many other situations, not life or death emergencies but very serious illnesses, in which a child is denied medical care because of the ignorance, poverty or neglect of parents or guardian. Although few statistics are available with respect to the incidence of childhood illness as related to the economic status of the family, it is undoubtedly true that there is more preventable and curable illness among children of poor families than of middle-class and

14. *Applications of President and Directors of Georgetown College*, 331 F. 2d 1000 (D.C. Cir. 1964), *cert. denied*, 377 U.S. 978; *Raleigh Fitkin-Paul Morgan Memorial Hospital* v. *Anderson*, 201 A. 2d 537 (Sup. Ct. N.J. 1964), *cert. denied*, 377 U.S. 985 (1964); see also *Prince* v. *Massachusetts*, 330 U.S. 158 (1944).

well-to-do families. The law fails to provide a structure by which these children can obtain necessary treatment and care. Unless a child is actually committed to a mental hospital or a correctional institution, the juvenile courts do not order medical treatment. Thus a child who is delinquent (criminal) may receive some treatment, whereas a child who is discharged (acquitted) will not receive any medical care unless it is voluntarily provided by his family.

Twenty years ago medicare for the aged sounded improbable and visionary. Today it is a fact. Some system of financing medical care for the poor children in America is a necessity. The poor child may be physically crippled by accident or disease or mentally stunted by malnutrition. The right to life should include a structure by which medical care to cure and prevent such conditions is available.

The right of a child to have a home would appear to be self-evident to most Americans. In many countries today, a sizable proportion of the population is homeless. Adults and children sleep in the streets. Government does not provide shelters or subsistence. In the United States, children are not permitted to sleep in the streets, on vacant lots or park benches. If there is no other place for a child without family or friends, he will be put in a detention center until some place can be found for him. The battered baby is all too familiar to the medical profession. The abused adolescent receives little medical or legal attention. If he (or she) complains of physical mistreatment or sexual abuse, he will often be placed in an institution for an indefinite period, which may be months or years.[15]

Homes for the Friendless

No one believes that a child, if he is incapable of caring for himself or if he does not have a safe dwelling, should be permitted to roam

15. To date legal consideration of the problems of the abused child has been unimaginative and sterile. Reporting statutes are the only remedy seriously considered. Even those who recognize the failure of such statutes to protect the child have continued to rely upon reporting and urge more funds and personnel. See Paulson, *Child Abuse Reporting Laws,* 67 COLUM. L. REV. 1 (1967); Hansen, *Suggested Guidelines for Child Abuse Laws,* 7 J. FAMILY LAW 61 (1967). The obvious remedies of appointment of a guardian and counsel for the child to bring suit against those who have abused him are overlooked.

the streets and forage for himself. Society must provide a home for
him. In the nineteenth century, orphan asylums were a popular
form of charity. They were indeed an improvement over the work-
house and the indenturing or apprenticing of orphans who had to
work for their keep. These asylums were sometimes known by
that dreadful name, "A Home for the Friendless." There are
many friendless children in our large urban centers today, although
few of them are legally orphans. The *de facto* orphan, the child
who has a parent but no home, is a commonplace. Often a parent
refuses to provide for his child. "You take him, Judge. I can't do
nothin' with him," says the mother or father. Very few judges
will compel an unwilling parent to care for his child. If the parent
does not want him, the child will be sent to an institution even
though he has not committed any crime.

The institutions in which such adolescents are placed have all
the characteristics of a jail. A detention center is not a hotel or
boarding school. The children may not leave. They are locked
behind bars or walls. They cannot attend public school. They
have none of the pleasures of life. In the United States today a
child who is deprived of a home is also deprived of his liberty.
Little thought is given to the critical need for nonpenal shelters
for such children. It would cost less to provide boarding schools
than jails. Both the right to a home and the right to liberty are
violated when unfortunate noncriminal adolescents are held in
detention. There have been few legal challenges to this common
and deplorable practice.

The Inverse of an Old Law

The right to an education is simply the inverse of an old law. For
more than half a century, America has had compulsory school
attendance statutes. If a child refuses to go to school, his parents
can be fined and he can be sent to jail. In twentieth-century
America there is no place for illiterates. The community requires
children to attend school so that they will be fit to assume the
responsibilities of citizenship and be gainfully employed. The
concept is valid. But, the results of such laws are often disappointing. Vast numbers of children go through the school system and
despite massive expenditures of public monies remain illiterate and
unemployable. The reasons why Johnny can't read are endless.
One cause, seldom mentioned, may be the statutes themselves.

Compulsory school attendance laws operate like a penal sentence. They prescribe the number of hours, days and years a child must spend in school. When he has served his time, he is released regardless of his skills or lack of them. Often the most ignorant are permitted to leave school early and are encouraged to drop out at or before legal school-leaving age. Possibly a different type of attendance law should be drafted, one that makes legal school leaving dependent upon skills rather than time served. If a child is functionally literate, reasonably well informed and employable at sixteen, why must he remain in school another year if he prefers to get a job? Conversely, just because he is seventeen, should he be permitted to leave if he cannot read or function in the adult world?

Children are often excluded from the public schools because they are disruptive. Many of these children are not "bad" or delinquent. At age eight how bad can a child be? Undoubtedly, these boys and girls are difficult to manage in classes of twenty-five to thirty-five pupils. Consequently, brain-damaged, emotionally disturbed and nonconforming children are pushed out of the school system. Whether these children have a legal or possibly a constitutional [16] right to attend school is unclear. Since most of the children who have been excluded from public school are too poor to afford to retain counsel, this question has not been litigated.

The law has largely ignored the rights of the child vis-à-vis the school system. Again the few reported cases turn on procedural points adopted by analogy from administrative law—the right to a hearing and the right to counsel.[17] While such aspects of due process are important, they are of relative insignificance if the child has no substantive right to attend school. The unresolved and largely unformulated question I would pose as follows: "Does every child have a right to elementary and secondary education suitable to his physical, intellectual and emotional needs at public expense?" It is obvious that some children, because of physical handicaps, severe mental retardation or emotional disturbance

16. Under the equal protection clause, it could be argued that public schooling is an entitlement. If it is available to some children, it must be available to all members of the class. Classification by physical or emotional disability for the purpose of the right to attend school could be deemed arbitrary and unreasonable.

17. *Madera v. Board of Education,* 386 F.2d 778 (2d Cir. 1967); see also Glass, *The Procedural Rights of Public School Children in Suspension-Placement Proceedings,* 41 TEMPLE L. Q. 349 (1968).

cannot function in a regular school program. There are also many normal children who are simply putting in time at school but not learning. They are being deprived of an education as surely as the child who is excluded from the classroom. Neither the educational bureaucracy nor the lawyers have faced the question of the rights and remedies of these pupils.

These are only a few of the many legal and constitutional issues implicit in the lives of American youth today. We neglect them to the prejudice of the young and of the entire community. Children grow up quickly while law cases proceed slowly. We cannot wait for these problems to be resolved piecemeal in fifty-one different jurisdictions by the aleatory processes of litigation. More direct and speedy remedies are required. Lawyers, in cooperation with doctors, educators and sociologists, must devise statutes, rules, regulations and government institutions to formulate and enforce the rights of American children. This is one of the unacknowledged challenges to the legal profession.

Young people today are restless and impatient. They have little faith that the customary legal processes will solve their problems. Neither appeals to belief in law and order and the democratic way nor threats of repressive measures will quiet them. Society will either recognize now the rights of the young and the obligations of government to provide a decent environment, meaningful education and an opportunity to live healthy, free lives or it will have to provide jails and mental institutions later. The price of delay may be far greater than the cost of action.

Robert F. Drinan, S.J.

4
The Rights of Children in Modern American Family Law

Up until about the year 1900 only one person in a family had any legal rights. The husband alone could contract, make debts, and have a legal personality.[1]

With the wave of emancipation statutes, married women have assumed a new and unique position in American law. Married women have all of the rights of single women—except for a few surviving legal disabilities.[2]

Concurrent with this unprecedented emancipation of married women, America has experienced an era when divorce has become startlingly easy and consequently amazingly widespread. We, therefore, witness a totally new moral and legal situation for the married woman; she is legally emancipated with a right to be divorced upon what everyone concedes may well be frivolous grounds.[3]

The law has supplied very few answers to the hard question:

The Honorable ROBERT F. DRINAN, S.J., Member of the House of Representatives, United States Congress, was formerly dean of the Boston College Law School. This article was adapted from an address presented at the annual meeting of the National Council on Family Relations, University of Connecticut, Storrs. The footnotes are those of the editor of the *Journal of Family Law*. The article is reprinted, with permission, from the *Journal of Family Law* 2(1962):101–9. Copyright 1962 by the University of Louisville.

1. 1 Bl. Comm. 442; 2 Bl. Comm. 433; 2 Kent Comm. 143.
2. Madden, *Persons and Dom. Rel.,* §§ 42–48.
3. Washington allows a divorce "for any other cause deemed by the court sufficient, if satisfied that they (the parties) can no longer live together." Ballinger's Ann. Codes & Statutes, § 5716, subd 7. See also Kentucky Revised Statutes 403.020(3)b (for "settled aversion" to wife); Coleman v. Coleman, 269 S.W. 2d 730 (Ky. 1954); Millar v. Millar, 175 Cal. 797, 167 P. 394 (1917) ("ungovernable temper"); Hatchett v. Hatchett, 89 Okl. 176, 214 P. 929 (1923) (Neglect of "duty").

What are the rights of a divorced woman? The law does, however, say at least the three following things about the rights of women permanently separated from their husbands:

1. Such a wife has a right to alimony. Theoretically, she may remain at home and live at ease—even to the point of giving up gainful employment which she held during the life of the marriage.[4]

Such a right to alimony seems inconsistent with the theory behind the drive for emancipation. No erosion of the inherent right to alimony, however, appears to be very firmly operating within American family law.

2. A divorced woman apparently has the right to the name of her husband forever; even if the wife has been outrageously guilty and has violated all of the legal and ethical standards of matrimony she, nonetheless, cannot ordinarily be required to surrender her husband's name.[5] Once again the partnership theory underlying the emancipation statutes seems to be in conflict with a new theory of marriage.

No one has yet raised the question whether a divorced man has a right to have only *one* woman possessing his name.

3. The divorced woman in well over 90 percent of all cases is deemed to have the right to the custody of the children of the marriage.[6] Such right is not an exclusive one, since the father is almost always granted visitation rights. It seems fair to say that American law has not thought out a consistent legal theory by which the once-married but emancipated, and now divorced, woman can fulfill all her duties to her former husband and to the children over whom she has custody.

In view of the fact that the children of divorced parents share in whatever rights the ex-spouses possess, it will be helpful to us to try to analyze the rights of children in three separate areas:

4. Bowzer v. Bowzer, 236 Mo. App. 514, 155 S.W. 2d 530 (1941); Pellegrino v. Pellegrino, 66 N.Y.S. 2d 297 (1946); DeRoin v. DeRoin, 198 Okl. 430, 179 P. 2d 685 (1947); 27A C.J.S. Divorce § 233(6)b. Lump sum settlements would seem to encourage giving up gainful employment. Consult local statutes. See, e.g., Towers v. Towers, 184 Wis. 188, 199 N.W. 75 (1924); Davis v. Davis, 347 S.W. 2d 534 (Ky. 1961).

5. Recovery of maiden name is at *wife's* option. Appeal of Hanson, 330 Pa. 390, 198 A. 113 (1938); Day v. Day, 137 Or. 159, 1 P. 2d 123 (1931); Mitts v. Mitts, 32 Ky. 854, 229 S.W. 2d 958 (1950); Reinken v. Reinken, 351 Ill. 409, 184 N.E. 639 (1933).

6. See for example Klein v. Klein, 47 Mich. 518, 11 N.W. 367 (1882); Wann v. Wann, 85 Ark. 471, 108 S.W. 1052 (1908); Wills v. Wills, 168 Ky. 35, 181 S.W. 619 (1916); Boxa v. Boxa, 92 Neb. 78, 137 N.W. 986 (1912).

I. The rights of children before the modern development of emancipation and divorce.

II. The rights of children within the family prior to any dissolution.

III. The rights of children whose custody is with a divorced woman.

The Rights of Children Before the Modern Development of Emancipation and Divorce

Among the several legal rights which children have always possessed are the following:

(1) A child has a right to be born. According to tradition from time immemorial the willful abortion of an unborn child has always been most reprehensible, if not criminal, at common law.

(2) In view of the fact that a child and a human person were deemed to exist from the moment of conception, the right of a child *en ventre sa mere* to inherit property was beyond dispute.

(3) A modern trend in tort law allows the recovery of an unborn but viable child who has been injured by the tortious conduct of a third party.[7]

(4) Pursuant to one of the strongest presumptions in the law, a child has the right to be legitimate if such a status can be inferred in any way from the conditions surrounding the birth of the child.[8]

(5) Modern legislation and contemporary legal thought seeks to grant to the adopted child all of the rights, so far as is possible, that the natural child would possess.[9]

(6) At common law,[10] and by statute in twenty-nine states, a child born in wedlock has a right to the religion of its father; if born out of wedlock, the child is presumed to have a right to the religion of the mother.

It will be seen, therefore, that legal thought had made some

7. Bonbrest v. Kotz, 65 F. Supp. 138 (D.D.C., 1946).

8. Wallace v. Wallace, 137 Iowa 37, 114 N.W. 527, 14 L.R.A. (N.S.) 544 (1908); Dudley's Adm'r v. Fidelity and Deposit Co. of Md., 240 S.W. 2d 817 (Ky. 1951); Cave v. Cave, 101 S.C. 40, 85 S.E. 244 (1915); State v. Shaw, 89 Vt. 121, 94 A. 434, L.R.A. 1915F, 1087 (1915).

9. Attempts have been made to give adoptive child even greater rights than that of the natural child. Commonwealth v. Finn, 181 A. 2d 887 (Pa. Super. 1962).

10. People v. Bolton, 27 Colo. App. 39, 146 P. 489 (1915); 67 C.J.S. Parent & Child § 129.

development prior to the modern crisis in elaborating on the inherent rights of children.

Rights of Children Within a Family Prior to Dissolution

In all matters where children are involved courts have said with tedious regularity that the welfare of the child is the supreme goal to be attained. No principle is more untiringly recited.

As a result a child can be removed from its parents and placed under a guardian, if such action is deemed to be absolutely necessary.

The law assumes that a child has a right to a happy home. Law and society, therefore, try to provide for such a condition as far as this is humanly possible.

A child within a family has an inherent right to receive not merely the education which the state supplies but, according to the famous Oregon school case, to an education which his parents desire in a nonpublic school. In this famous *Pierce* decision the Supreme Court ruled that the state "cannot standardize" children.[11]

In general, it may be said that the children within a family have inherent moral and legal rights to economic, educational, and emotional security.

The Rights of Children Whose Custody Is Held by a Divorced Mother

In view of the fact that the divorced woman and mother, separated from her husband, is an entirely new phenomenon in western culture, we cannot say too firmly what are the rights of children whose custody she has been granted. The law is, in fact, uncertain as to the rights of the ex-spouse. Consequently, it seems even more uncertain about the privileges which the law should extend to the children with "weekend fathers."

The law generally assumes, however, that the ex-wife has a right to economic security. The law also seeks to give to the ex-wife some emotional security—at least the law will prevent harassment by her former husband.

These rights of the ex-wife exist apparently even though the

---

11. Pierce v. Society of Sisters, 268 U.S. 510, 45 S.Ct. 571 (1925).

wife might have been the sole cause of the divorce. It is, of course, impossible to determine from the legal records of America anything about the ultimate cause of divorce. More than two-thirds of all divorces are granted—usually to the wife—on the grounds of cruelty; but, even if the divorce is granted to a husband for inexcusable conduct on the part of the wife her rights are not necessarily adversely affected. It is interesting to note, however, that Florida has a statute under which a wife who is divorced for adultery loses all right to alimony.[12]

If the rights of an ex-wife are confused in the law, the rights of the children over whom she has custody are no less obscured. In statutes, divorce decrees, and separation agreements, this confusion is increased because very frequently the terms of financial settlement confuse alimony and support for the children. Such confusion is understandable since at common law the rights of the children were not different from those of the head of the family. The overlooking of children's rights in divorce decrees and separation agreements is also the product of the simple fact that children cannot exercise their rights independently of the parent in whose custody they are placed by law.

For several reasons, however, it appears that an emphasis on the rights of children is now needed. The following support this conclusion.

1. There are now some ten to twelve million children in America who do not live with both parents.

2. More and more divorced women remarry, with the result that the status of the children of their first husband in relation to the second husband is very uncertain. Likewise, the rights of the second husband's children by a previous marriage in relation to his present wife are also most uncertain.

3. Stressing the rights of children independently of their father and mother may offer a new and fruitful approach to a tangled and many-faceted problem.

When a divorce decree and custody decision is rendered the court assumes that the children are granted the same rights as if there had been no divorce. At least the court would not concede that the children of this now dissolved marriage have been deprived of any of their pre-existing rights.

---

12. Florida Statutes § 65.08.

Although one cannot say that such an assumption is simply a legal illusion, it is not unjust to state that the law has not confronted the entirely new situation which the law has created.

Today we have millions of half brothers and half sisters, children by a previous marriage, semi-adopted youngsters, stepsons, and foster mothers and fathers. All of this language has been lifted from the law which applied previously to situations where one of the spouses had died. Although the legal names may suffice for identification purposes, the legal names simply do not express the new realities behind the novel situation which America confronts in an age when a second marriage is becoming an almost routine event.

What then are the rights of children whose custody after a divorce has been granted to their mother?

1. The source of all rights of a child is the right to be loved. A family means that the mother and father take vows to love the children whom they bring into this world.

One can argue that a basic compromise of the right of every child to be loved is made whenever the mother and father are allowed to separate. It is difficult to see how a child's right to be loved by both his mother and father can fail to be compromised when the father is excluded from seeing the child except for a few hours every other weekend.

2. After the basic right of the child to the love and companionship of *both* his parents has been compromised by divorce, the child still has a right to the companionship of *one* of his parents. The law still assumes that either the natural mother or the natural father is the best possible person to have custody of the child. Even in states where the comparative rectitude doctrine is employed, virtually no court has ever ruled that both the mother and the father are so guilty of acts involving moral turpitude that neither is entitled to the custody of the child.

Theoretically, if the mother and the father after the divorce fulfill all of their legal duties to their children then all of the legal rights of these youngsters would be fulfilled. Such expectation, however, is a legal fiction, since the children of divorced parents are totally different than any group of persons known previously to the law.

We have noted above that the law assumes that children within a marriage have a right to economic, educational, and emotional security. Clearly no one would want the children of divorced parents to have less than the rights of children whose homes have not been legally dissolved. Let us, therefore, contemplate these three areas of the rights in connection with "half-orphans."

Right to Economic Security

A. A lump sum settlement for the support of children would be the ideal arrangement. Since, however, this is unattainable in most cases, might the law suggest to a father being granted freedom to marry again that he designate a certain percent of his income in advance for the economic security of his child? Such a provision would avoid further legal action, all types of wrangling between the spouses, as well as instill a deep sense of economic security within the minds of the children.

B. Would it be feasible to have a state or federally maintained withholding plan under which a designated amount of a man's income would be periodically withheld and given for the economic security of the children of his previous marriage? It would appear that the federal law has more machinery to implement such a plan than the state law. The machinery, however, is not the important question, but rather, obtaining a widespread consensus for the principle that a man should be required by law to implement the right of his children to economic security.

C. In most support and divorce decrees provisions concerning medical and dental insurance, as well as such things as music lessons and other cultural activities, are generally very unclear. Would it not be wise for lawyers and family court judges to spell out in some detail the inherent obligation of a father to provide for the ordinary and extraordinary costs of those benefits which should not be denied to any child?

D. An intriguing body of speculation and law is growing up around the question of whether or not the giving of adequate support by the father should be required before he is allowed to exercise his visitation rights. From the father's viewpoint, he should not be denied visiting with his children simply because he may be prevented from contributing for a period to their support. From the mother's viewpoint, she cannot understand how a father could help or love a child if he does not support it before spending money on any other venture. From the child's point of view the situation is totally bewildering. We can only imagine what a child might feel when any question or problem arises in connection with the fundamental problem of who supports and maintains the child.

E. Would it be possible that both attorneys in a divorce matter should unite on behalf of the children. If this is not done we may well witness the establishment by counties and states of a "friend of the child" who, as a social worker or lawyer, insists upon the economic rights of the children affected by a divorce.

Is it not most reprehensible for a lawyer to obtain advantages for a father and his prospective second family at the expense of the children of his first marriage?

The Right of Children to Educational Security

Many laws concerning divorce and separate maintenance provide that the father must take care of the education of his children. In view of the fact that all public education is free through high school, it would appear that these laws might well be construed to mean *higher education*. Every third or even every second high school senior now desires to enter college. To finance a college education, however, requires in this modern age years of preparation. Should not a realistic divorce decree therefore specifically require that a father pay a premium periodically on a long-range insurance policy which would cover the college education of his children?

It may be that lawyers for both sides in a divorce case could agree upon an insurance arrangement under which the husband would pay a specified sum so that the medical, dental and educational benefits to which his child has a right would be guaranteed to this youth.

It is difficult for a judge to raise these issues when he is presented with a separation agreement to which both parties have consented. It may well be, however, that family court judges should raise the extremely important question of how the minor children can be expected to obtain a college education on the meager sum provided and agreed to by the husband and wife.

The Right to Emotional Stability

The emotional health of the children of divorced homes is a far more mysterious and complex problem than is the issue of their economic and educational rights. The children of separated homes, where a cold war continues between the ex-spouses, will have serious adjustments to make. Psychologists who are becoming ever more familiar with the problem of the child with two homes tell us that the emotional impact of such a situation upon youngsters is simply enormous.

Perhaps some child as perceptive as Anne Frank will arise to describe the tensions, conflicts, and emotional upheavals that come to a child from having a weekend father and a week-long working mother.

The central issue of the emotional rights of children centers on the question of visitation privileges for the person not having custody. The law has given very little thought to this matter and has simply assumed that a father has an inherent right to see his child. It is not even certain whether the right to visitation exists in the child or in the father or in both.

At least a few students of the matter have questioned the advisability of any visitation rights to the father in particular cases. It would appear that the emotional equipment of some children is simply incapable of handling an inherently complex situation. This is particularly so in the crosscurrents of multi-relationships which arise when both the mother and the father remarry and have children by their second spouses.

The law can hardly be expected to know very much about the unknown sea of the emotional life of children with weekend fathers. Would the appointment of an impartial arbitrator be worthy of consideration? Such an arbitrator would be removed from the adversary proceedings of the parents, would have special training in the psychology of children, and might well be able to secure a result which would not be determined by the accidents of litigation but rather based on the inherent rights to emotional security which all children possess.

Conclusion

The rights of all children to economic, educational, and emotional security should, therefore, be the prime objective of law and society whenever the courts must make a decision affecting the life and future of children. In connection with the second marriage of any man or woman, is it not the obligation of the law to insist that the children who have been born are guaranteed those economic, educational, and emotional privileges which it is the duty of the state to foster and protect insofar as this is humanly possible?

It may be that we need emancipation statutes for children. The legal ideas of a previous day no longer cover the situation in which every fourth American child finds himself. Nothing is more moving than the suffering of a child and, yet, the law, in succumbing to the wishes of adults, has overlooked the predicament which the granting of a divorce will bring to the children involved.

It is time for all lawyers, for judges who have jurisdiction over family matters, for social workers, and all concerned with the sufferings of American children to realize that a new crisis is at hand which is uniquely demanding of a positive solution.

David W. Louisell

5

Abortion, the Practice of Medicine and the Due Process of Law

The current proposals for amendment of the abortion statutes in the United States are generally based on the recommendations of the American Law Institute. Its model statute would permit an abortion by a licensed physician "if he believes there is substantial risk that continuance of the pregnancy would gravely impair the physical or mental health of the mother or that the child would be born with grave physical or mental defect, or that the pregnancy resulted from rape, incest, or other felonious intercourse." [1] All illicit intercourse with a girl below the age of sixteen is included within the definition of "felonious intercourse." [2] Two physicians, one of whom may be the person performing the abortion, must certify in writing the circumstances which they believe to justify it. In the case of an abortion justified on the ground of felonious intercourse, the certificate must be submitted to the prosecuting attorney or the police.[3]

The justification of the abortion would therefore involve no

DAVID W. LOUISELL, J.D., is Elizabeth Josselyn Boalt Professor of Law, University of California, Berkeley. He is the author of *Modern California Discovery: A Text on Discovery in Civil and Criminal Cases* (San Francisco, Berkeley Press, 1963); and co-author of *Principles of Evidence and Proof* (Mineola, N.Y.: Foundation Press, 1968) and *Jurisdiction in a Nutshell: State and Federal* (St. Paul: West Publishing Co., 1968). This article was prepared for a collection of essays, *Morality of Abortion: Legal and Historical Perspectives*, edited by John T. Noonan, Jr., *et al.* (Cambridge: Harvard University Press, 1970). It is reprinted here with permission from the *UCLA Law Review* 16 (1969):233–54.

1. MODEL PENAL CODE § 230.3(2) (Proposed Official Draft, 1962).
2. *Id.*
3. *Id.* § 230.3(3).

48   Abortion, Medicine, and Due Process

judicial process and no representation of the public interest or
that of the father or unborn child. Justification is complete upon
the request of the pregnant woman and certification of two physicians without involvement of any other agency or person. Except
for the certificate to the prosecuting attorney or the police in the
case of felonious intercourse, only the hospital need be informed
of the abortion.[4]

Proponents of liberalizing the abortion laws along the lines of
the American Law Institute proposal insist that the "legitimizing
circumstances" for such abortions are "narrowly defined." [5] Yet
the only factor limiting the discretion of the mother and the two
certifying physicians is that the mother's or the child's physical
or mental "health" must be gravely threatened.[6] There is nothing
in the statute which would aid the physician in making the
determination. It would be fair to assume that, absent any such
guidelines, the area circumscribed by the word "health" will be
broad. The World Health Organization, in 1960, defined health
as "a state of complete physical, mental and social well being,
not simply the absence of illness and disease." [7] One writer has
said that "such a definition of health could be used to establish
legal cause for termination of an unwanted pregnancy for almost

4. It should be noted at the outset that many proponents of liberalized
abortion view the American Law Institute proposals as merely a start in the
direction of completely permissive abortion. See, e.g., L. LADAR, ABORTION
169 (1966): "The complete legalization of abortion is the one just and
inevitable answer to the quest for feminine freedom. All other solutions are
compromises." It has already been argued that a liberal construction of
California's Therapeutic Abortion Act of 1967, CAL. HEALTH & SAFETY
CODE §§ 25950–54 (West Supp. 1968) is called for by considerations of
due process of law. Leavy & Charles, *California's New Therapeutic Abortion Act: An Analysis and Guide to Medical and Legal Procedure,* 15
U.C.L.A. L. REV. 1, 27–28 (1967); *cf.* Note, *The California Therapeutic
Abortion Act: An Analysis,* 19 HAST. L.J. 242, 254 (1967); Comment,
Criminal Law—Abortion—The New North Carolina Abortion Statute, 46
N.C. L. REV. 585, 591 (1968). Nevertheless, these facts should not deter
one from an attempt at honest appraisal of the model statute taken at face
value.
5. Schwartz, Modernizing the Anti-Abortion Laws, 2 (paper delivered to
International Conference on Abortion, Washington, D.C., Sept. 1967).
6. A more objective set of criteria would, of course, be available in the
cases in which abortion is justified on the alternative grounds of rape, incest,
or other felonious intercourse.
7. Quoted in N. MIETUS, THE THERAPEUTIC ABORTION ACT 71 (1967).

any reason whatsoever." [8] At the very least the statutory language provides a fertile ground for the application of individual, subjective notions of what the requisite degree of gravity of risk ought to be in a given case.

The primary question concerning the proposed statutory changes, asked by religious and non-religious persons alike, is whether this easy path to destruction of the fetus potentially conflicts with our ethic of reverence for human life, and the legal norms crystallized in the constitutional mandates of equal protection and due process of law. The question should be considered in the context of the law's historic attitude respecting the fetus as a human person.

The progress of the law in recognition of the fetus as a human person for all purposes has been strong and steady and roughly proportional to the growth of knowledge of biology and embryology. In earlier times the uncertain knowledge of embryology inevitably caused some doubt as to whether or not the unborn child was a human person. Yet even the early English cases resolved scientific, as well as moral and philosophical, doubts in favor of the unborn.

Legal Recognition of the Fetus as a Human Person

The Unborn Child in the Law of Property

The English courts held that an unborn child is within the description in a devise to "children living at the time of his [life tenant's] decease" [9] and is also within the description of a testamentary disposition to children "born in her [testatrix] lifetime." [10] The case of *Wallis v. Hodson* [11] allowed a posthumous child to have an accounting of her father's intestate estate years after her birth

---

8. Byrne, *A Critical Look at Legalized Abortion,* 41 L.A. BAR BULL. 320, 349 (1966).

9. Doe *dem.* Clarke v. Clarke, 2 H.Bl. 399, 126 Eng. Rep. 617 (C.P. 1795). Language in the case indicates that it was the court's unequivocal opinion that the unborn child was a human being: "[A]n infant *en ventre sa mere,* who by the course and order of nature is then living, comes clearly within the description of 'children living at the time of his decease.'" *Id.* at 401, 126 Eng. Rep. at 618.

10. Trower v. Butts, 1 Sim. & Stu. 181, 57 Eng. Rep. 72, 73 (Ch. 1823).

11. 2 Atk. 114, 26 Eng. Rep. 472 (Ch. 1740).

where her mother and second husband held the property.[12] The unborn child was also considered to be a life in being for purposes of the perpetuities rule even where it was not to the benefit of the unborn child to be so considered.[13]

The American cases, based upon English common law rules, reached much the same results. Faced with the necessity of making decisions involving considerations of the existence of pre-natal life and given the uncertain knowledge of embryology, American courts chose, uniformly, to treat the unborn child as a human being. A posthumous child is able to take under a will description bequeathing property to those "living at my (testator's) decease."[14] The unborn child can also take, under a will, as a tenant in common with its own mother.[15] It can have a sale of land set aside where the sale involves descendant land, a portion of which is held to vest in the unborn child prior to its birth.[16]

12. *Id.* at 117, 26 Eng. Rep. at 473. The Lord Chancellor states, "both by the rules of the common and civil law, she [the unborn child] was, to all intents and purposes, a child, as much as if born in the father's life-time."

13. Thellusson v. Woodford, 4 Ves. 227, 31 Eng. Rep. 117 (Ch. 1798). Buller, J., in replying to the contention that the unborn child is a nonentity, said: "Let us see, what this non-entity can do. He may be vouched in a recovery, though it is for the purpose of making him answer over in value. He may be an executor. He may take under the Statute of Distributions. [citation] He may take by devise. He may be entitled under a charge for raising portions. He may have an injunction; and he may have a guardian." *Id.* at 322, 31 Eng. Rep. at 163. In answer to the contention that an unborn child is to be considered as being alive only in those cases when it is to its own benefit, he replied: "Why should not children *en ventre sa mere* be considered generally as in existence? They are entitled to all the privileges of other persons." *Id.* at 323, 31 Eng. Rep. at 164.

14. Hall v. Hancock, 32 Mass. (15 Pick.) 255 (1834). Chief Justice Shaw quoted with approval the language of the Lord Chancellor in *Wallis v. Hodson,* quoted in part in note 12 *supra. Accord,* Barnett v. Pinkston, 238 Ala. 327, 191 So. 371 (1939); Cowles v. Cowles, 56 Conn. 240, 13 A. 414 (1887); McLain v. Howald, 120 Mich. 274, 79 N.W. 82 (1899). In *Hall* the court also explicitly negates the applicability of the "quickness' requirement found in the criminal law cases, to cases involving issues of descent and distribution. *See* discussion of criminal law cases in notes 27–42 *infra,* and accompanying text. CAL. PROB. CODE § 250 (West 1956) provides: "A posthumous child is considered as living at the death of the parent." Section 255, amended as recently as 1961, provides that an illegitimate child is the heir of his mother, whether the child is "born or conceived."

15. Biggs v. McCarty, 86 Ind. 352 (1882).

16. Deal v. Sexton, 144 N.C. 110, 56 S.E. 691 (1907). The court recognized that constitutional rights of the unborn child are at stake when it stated: "If we hold, as we must, that the inheritance vested immediately in the plaintiff, while *en ventre sa mere,* upon the death of the father, the con-

The suggestion that the unborn child is a legal non-entity was clearly rejected in *Industrial Trust Co. v. Wilson.*[17] Here the court held that a posthumous child was to begin sharing in the proceeds of a trust at the date of her father's death rather than upon the date of her subsequent birth. Thus, the child was an actual income recipient prior to the event of her birth.

The state of the law in American courts is fairly well summed up in *In re Holthausen's Will,*[18] where a New York court states that: "It has been the uniform and unvarying decision of all common law courts in respect of estate matters for at least the past two hundred years that a child en ventre sa mere is 'born' and 'alive' for all purposes for his benefit." [19]

The requirement, stated in certain cases,[20] that the courts recognize pre-natal existence only for the benefit of a child subsequently born alive, has been suggested by some to indicate that the courts have merely developed a rule of construction and that these cases are no authority on the question of whether or not the unborn child does, in fact, have any legal rights.[21] But when a lawsuit is commenced on behalf of an unborn child on the theory that property rights accrued to him while he is still in gestation, almost inevitably that child will have proceeded to term and been successfully born or will have miscarried or been stillborn before the case which decides his rights is adjudicated and the opinion written. Thus at the time the court speaks, the child, by his representative, is actually before the court requesting some kind of relief. Similarly, where a lawsuit is based on accrual of property rights to a child prior to his birth, but is commenced after his birth, he is likewise before the court when the opinion is written. Under such circumstances it is understandable, but really gratuitous and

clusion must follow that such inheritance ought not to be divested. . . . [A] person must have an opportunity of being heard before a court can deprive him of his rights, and . . . an unborn child, not having been made a party, can recover from those claiming his title." *Id.* at 110–11, 56 S.E. at 692.

17. 61 R.I. 169, 200 A. 467 (1938).

18. 175 Misc. 1022, 26 N.Y.S.2d 140 (Sur. Ct. 1941).

19. *Id.* at 1024, 26 N.Y.S.2d at 143.

20. *In re* Well's Will, 129 Misc. 447, 221 N.Y.S. 714 (Sur. Ct. 1927). The court states: "It is well settled that a child en ventre sa mere, *which is subsequently born alive* and capable of living, is considered a child living, so as to take a beneficial interest in a bequest or devise when the description is 'child living.'" *Id.* at 451, 221 N.Y.S. at 719 (emphasis added).

21. *See In re* Scanelli, 208 Misc. 804, 142 N.Y.S.2d 411 (Sur. Ct. 1955).

superfluous, for the court to observe that the child must have been born alive. The observation is only dictum; it does not necessarily require a different result in those cases where the observation is inappropriate.[22]

One may speculate that the psychological motivation for these decisions in the property realm is the instinctive desire to avoid excluding the unborn child because of the accidental factor that his birth was delayed beyond the ancestor's or testator's death; that such decisions proceed more from a pragmatic sense of fairness and realism than from a philosophic conclusion of the existence *in utero* of autonomous human life. But this is only speculation. And whatever the motivation for the decisions, they are clear-cut holdings that a child in gestation is a human person, hence an autonomous legal entity capable of possessing property. Of course in deciding these cases the courts have not been primarily interested in essaying philosophical propositions, and their opinions naturally have been couched in phraseology appropriate to the resolution of controversies. The most significant fact is that the courts have given the unborn child the same rights, in respect to property, that have been traditionally considered constitutionally protectable when held by others.

Moreover, the property rule which recognizes human life in the unborn child prevails whether or not it inures to his personal benefit, and even where it works a detriment to him. Thus, in *Barnett v. Pinkston*[23] a child born two months after the death of his father was held to be a "living child" at the death of his father. The child lived only several hours, leaving its mother as its sole heir. She died a few days later. The remainder that had vested in the child was held to have passed to her and through her to her heirs. The court's recognition that a child en ventre sa mere is a child in esse, thus produced no personal benefit to the child.[24] In

---

22. See note 24 *infra*.

23. 238 Ala. 327, 191 So. 371 (1939).

24. This issue would be further refined by a case where an heir of an unborn child to whom property rights accrued, but who miscarried or was stillborn, claimed those rights through the child. No case upholding or denying such a claim has been found. If there be none, the explanation is likely in practicalities: the relative rarity of the situation, the lack of motivation to make the claim on the part of the heirs who presumably often would be the child's parents, and the like factors. *Quaere,* as to the effect on such a claim of a statutory provision such as that of Cal. Civil Code

In re Sankey's Estate [25] a child conceived but not born was held bound by a decree entered against the living heirs.

The common law's recognition of the unborn child as a human person for property law purposes appears to reflect a basic psychological evaluation that in law, as in ordinary thought, "child" includes the conceived but as yet unborn. Apparently the civil law and its terminology reflect the same normative use of language. In the Digest of Justinian appears:

> Qui in utero sunt, in toto paene iure civili intelleguntur in rerum natura esse. (Unborn children are in almost every branch of the civil law regarded as already existing.) [26]

The Unborn Child in the Criminal Law

The criminal law historically has afforded the unborn child a substantial amount of protection. Not always, however, has this protection been extended throughout the entire period of gestation. Nor, at common law, was it possible for the unborn child to be the object of the crime of murder. [27] The hesitancy of the criminal law to convict someone for a capital offense where the victim could not be perceived in the normal, visual manner is understandable. A charge of homicide could be sustained, however, where the child was born alive and then died due to injuries inflicted upon it while still in its mother's womb. [28] At least in those instances when the aborted fetus lives for a short time outside the womb, the proposed statute will have succeeded in legalizing what the common law clearly and historically regarded as murder. [29]

---

§ 29 (West 1954): "A child conceived, but not yet born, is to be deemed an existing person, so far as may be necessary for its interests in the event of its subsequent birth. . . ."

25. 199 Cal. 391, 249 P. 517 (1926).

26. I. AUGUSTI, CORPUS JURIS CIVILIS—DIGESTA, Lib. 1, tit. 5, s. 26. *See also id.* s. 7.

27. Clarke v. State, 117 Ala. 1, 23 So. 671 (1898); Jackson v. Commonwealth, 265 Ky. 295, 96 S.W.2d 1014 (1936); Morgan v. State, 148 Tenn. 417, 256 S.W. 433 (1923).

28. Clarke v. State, 117 Ala. 1, 23 So. 671 (1898).

29. Recent reports from Sweden indicate that the killing of the fetus after removal from the womb is often the case due to procedural complexities and a general lack of manpower. Women qualifying for legalized abortions are often forced to wait as long as the sixth month of pregnancy before the operation is accomplished. Very often the fetus is able to put up quite a struggle for life after it has been removed from the womb at this late stage.

The common law's protection of the unborn child by criminal sanctions was principally by punishing abortion as a distinct misdemeanor. By the majority rule the offense was committed only if the child had reached the stage of gestation known as "quickening." It was held that a conviction of abortion could not be sustained unless the prosecution established that the required degree of development had been reached.[30] In *Foster v. State*,[31] the court was very explicit in stating the reason for the requirement as a practical necessity, but was somewhat less successful in justifying it on a logical basis:

> In a strictly scientific and physiological sense there is life in an embryo from the time of conception, and in such sense there is also life in the male and female elements that unite to form the embryo. But law, for obvious reasons, cannot in its classifications follow the latest or ultimate declarations of science. It must for purposes of practical efficiency proceed upon more everyday and popular conceptions, especially as to definitions of crimes that are *malum in se.* . . . That it should be less of an offense to destroy an embryo in a stage where human life in its common acceptance was not yet begun than to destroy a *quick* child, is a conclusion that commends itself to most men.[32]

Even at common law, however, some courts refused to deny protection to the unborn child during the stage of development prior to quickening and held that abortion was just as illegal at that time as at a later period.[33] Other courts expressed dissatisfac-

---

Essay, TIME, Oct. 13, 1967, pp. 32–33. *See also* address by Professor Ian Donald, Free Trade Hall, Manchester, England, Dec. 5, 1966: "Make no mistake about it. An unborn baby, even a very small one, can put up a determined fight for life. An abortion can be born alive and can kick and go on kicking for quite a long time. It is not difficult to see this as a sort of slow murder. On the other hand, the baby can be killed while still inside. Is there so much difference?" Quoted in N. MIETUS, *supra* note 7, at 16.

The recent California legislation includes the provision: "In no event shall the termination [of pregnancy] be approved after the 20th week of pregnancy." CAL. HEALTH & SAFETY CODE § 25953 (West Supp. 1968). Already serious dispute has arisen as to whether "approved" means authorization of the abortion by the hospital committee, or performance of the abortion.

30. Smith v. State, 33 Me. 48 (1851); Commonwealth v. Bangs, 9 Mass. 386 (1812); State v. Cooper, 22 N.J.L. 52 (1849); Foster v. State, 182 Wis. 298, 196 N.W. 233 (1923).

31. 182 Wis. 298, 196 N.W. 233 (1923).

32. *Id.* at 301–02, 196 N.W. at 235.

33. Mills v. Commonwealth, 13 Pa. 630, *aff'g* 13 Pa. 633 (1850).

tion with the common law requirements but stated that it was up to the legislature to abolish the "quickening" element.[34]

As the legislatures of the various states began to codify existing law during the 19th century, the anticipated change in the abortion laws occurred. The quickening requirement often was abolished [35] so that the fetus was protected from the moment of conception throughout the entire period of gestation. Some jurisdictions extended protection by the means of a foeticide statute [36] which made destruction of the fetus at any stage of development a criminal act and in some cases, where the fetus was "quick," made such destruction a capital offense.[37] States which prohibited abortion by specific statutes aimed at foeticide abolished "quickening" as an element of the crime while those states which utilized regular homicide (manslaughter) statutes generally retained that element.[38] But there was a minority view under which a conviction of manslaughter could be sustained for destruction of the fetus at any stage of gestation.[39] The trend, however, was to protect the fetus by specific anti-abortion laws rather than by application of homicide statutes and, with the former, distinctions based on the various stages of fetal development were not generally made.

Historically, the common law had recognized the inviolability of the unborn child by providing for suspension of execution of pregnant women under death sentence, at least when "quick." [40]

34. Mitchell v. Commonwealth, 78 Ky. 204 (1879). The court stated: "That the child shall be considered in existence from the moment of conception for the protection of its rights of property, and yet not in existence, until four or five months after the inception of its being, to the extent that it is a crime to destroy it, presents an anomaly in the law that ought to be provided against by the law-making department of the government." *Id.* at 209–10.

35. *See, e.g.,* CAL. PENAL CODE § 274 (West 1954).

36. Hans v. State, 147 Neb. 67, 22 N.W.2d 385 (1946).

37. *See* Passley v. State, 194 Ga. 327, 21 S.E.2d 230 (1942).

38. Thus Wisconsin held that where the death of the mother resulted from an illegal abortion it was immaterial whether the fetus had quickened, but where the prosecution was for the death of the child he must have quickened. State v. Walters, 199 Wis. 68, 225 N.W. 167 (1929); State v. Dickinson, 41 Wis. 299 (1878).

39. *See* State v. Atwood, 54 Ore. 526, 102 P. 295 (1909).

40. 1 W. BLACKSTONE, COMMENTARIES *456 (W. Jones ed. at 651, 1916); 2 M. HALE, PLEAS OF THE CROWN *413–14 (1st Am. ed. at 412–13, 1847). *See generally* Hazard & Louisell, *Death, the State, and the Insane: Stay of Execution,* 9 U.C.L.A. L. REV. 381 (1962).

This solicitude continues in modern statutes without regard to the stage of pregnancy.[41] Statutes imposing criminal sanctions protective of children's right of support from their parents also apply to the unborn child.[42]

The Unborn Child in the Law of Torts

Perhaps no other area of the law has undergone such a dramatic reversal as that of the law of torts in recognizing the legal existence of an unborn child.[43] Until World War II most American courts denied recovery in tort to the child who had been harmed by negligent injury to his mother while she carried him. This denial was predicated upon several factors, including the difficulty of proving causation in view of the then deficient state of medical knowledge. The primary reason for denying recovery, however, was reliance upon the statement of Justice Holmes in *Dietrich v. Northampton,*[44] that "the unborn child was a part of the mother at the time of the injury. . . ."[45] Since the rejection of this view in 1946, in the case of *Bonbrest v. Kotz,*[46] the law has proceeded apace to recognize the unborn child as a human being in this area as it had in others.

Many of the early cases required that the unborn child have reached the stage of viability at the time the injuries were inflicted in order to maintain an action.[47] The modern trend, however,

41. *E.g.,* CAL. PENAL CODE §§ 3705–06 (West 1954).

42. *E.g., id.* § 270 (West Supp. 1968): "A child conceived but not yet born is to be deemed an existing person insofar as this section [child neglect] is concerned."

43. *See* W. PROSSER, HANDBOOK OF THE LAW OF TORTS § 56 (3rd ed. 1964).

44. 138 Mass. 14, 17 (1884).

45. *Compare* with the statement made by Holmes, J., the holding which appears to have been the settled rule, in Prescott v. Robinson, 74 N.H. 460, 69 A. 522 (1908), that the mother could not recover on her own behalf for injuries sustained by her unborn child. The mother had, unsuccessfully, claimed that the unborn child was a part of her.

46. 65 F. Supp. 138 (D.D.C. 1946).

47. *Id.;* Scott v. McPheeters, 33 Cal. App. 2d 629, 92 P.2d 678 (1939) (CAL. CIV. CODE § 29 [West 1954] expressly provides that the fetus is to be deemed an existing person); Tursi v. New England Windsor Co., 19 Conn. Supp. 242, 111 A.2d 14 (1955); Damasiewicz v. Gorsuch, 197 Md. 417, 79 A.2d 550 (1951); Keyes v. Constr. Serv., Inc., 340 Mass. 633, 165 N.E.2d 912 (1960); Williams v. Marion Rapid Transit, Inc., 152 Ohio 114, 87 N.E.2d 334 (1949); Mallison v. Pomeroy, 205 Ore. 690, 291 P.2d 225 (1955); Seattle-First Nat'l Bank v. Rankin, 59 Wash. 2d 288, 367 P.2d 835 (1962).

has been to reject the viability distinction and to allow recovery whenever the injury was received, provided that the elements of causation are properly established.[48] Where the child has died due to injuries received while in the womb, the cases have allowed recovery based on wrongful death actions where the fetus has reached the stage of viability. At first, recovery was limited to those cases in which the child was born alive and then died due to injuries received prior to birth.[49] But perhaps the most significant

48. Hornbuckle v. Plantation Pipe Line Co., 212 Ga. 504, 93 S.E.2d 727 (1956); Daley v. Meier, 33 Ill. App. 2d 218, 178 N.E.2d 691 (1961); Bennett v. Hymers, 101 N.H. 483, 147 A.2d 108 (1958); Smith v. Brennan, 31 N.J. 353, 157 A.2d 497 (1960); Kelly v. Gregory, 282 App. Div. 542, 125 N.Y.S.2d 696 (1953); Sinkler v. Kneale, 401 Pa. 267, 164 A.2d 93 (1960); Sylvia v. Gobeille, 220 A.2d 222, 223–24 (R.I. 1966), where the court said: "While we could, as has sometimes been done elsewhere, justify our rejection of the viability concept on the medical fact that a fetus becomes a living human being from the moment of conception, we do so not on the authority of the biologist but because we are unable logically to conclude that a claim for an injury inflicted prior to viability is any less meritorious than one sustained after." W. PROSSER, *supra* note 43, § 56. "Viability" of a fetus is not a constant but depends on the anatomical and functional development of the particular baby. J. MORISON, FOETAL AND NEONATAL PATHOLOGY 99–100 (1963). The weight and length of the fetus are better guides than age to the state of fetal development, and weight and length vary with the individual. Gruenwald, *Growth of the Human Fetus*, 94 AM. J. OBSTETRICS & GYNECOLOGY 1112 (1966).

49. Worgan v. Greggo & Ferrara, Inc., 50 Del. 258, 128 A.2d 557 (1956) (not certain whether child was born alive or was stillborn); Steggall v. Morris, 363 Mo. 1224, 258 S.W. 2d 577 (1953); Cooper v. Blanck, 39 So.2d 352, (La. Ct. App. 1923); Hall v. Murphy, 236 S.C. 257, 113 S.E.2d 790 (1960); Shousha v. Matthews Drivurself Serv., Inc., 210 Tenn. 384, 358 S.W.2d 471 (1962); Leal v. C. C. Pitts Sand & Gravel, Inc., 419 S.W.2d 820 (Tex. 1967) (child lived two days; question of liability when stillborn left open).

The jurisdictions which persist in the notion that recovery in tort for injury to the fetus is conditioned on the child being born alive, do so for policy reasons: difficulty of proof, danger of double recovery if the mother also sues for miscarriage, or the peculiarity of language of the wrongful death statute involved. *See generally* W. PROSSER, *supra* note 43, § 56. The requirement of survivorship as a condition to redress tortious injury does not detract from jural recognition that a right came into existence at the time of the injury. Survivorship may be a condition precedent to an enforcement of a right, but hardly confers retroactively rights not in existence at the time of the injury. The common law was replete with instances of torts not remediable because the victim died before enforcement of his rights. "If it were conceded that killing the plaintiff was a tort toward him, he was none the less dead, and the tort died with him." *Id.* § 121, at 923. Who would have contended that the law did not recognize a tort in trespass, for assault and battery, or for medical malpractice simply because none of the actions survived if the victim died?

cases for proving the legal existence of a child prior to birth have
been those very modern decisions which allow the parents, or
survivors, to maintain such an action where the child is stillborn.[50]
Thus, the unborn child, to whom live birth never comes, is held
to be a "person" who can be the subject of an action for damages
for his death.

In *Porter v. Lassiter*,[51] such an action was allowed even where
the child had not reached the stage of viability at the time the
fatal injuries were received. In 1967 the Supreme Court of
Massachusetts [52] allowed recovery where the child had not reached
that stage and died a few hours after birth. The court, after
noting that it had allowed recovery for wrongful death following
prenatal injury to a viable child, said:

> In the case at bar, where the fetus was not viable, we must
> decide whether there is a sound distinction from the situation
> where the fetus is viable. . . .
>
> In the vast majority of cases where the present issue has
> arisen, recovery has been allowed. . . . To the extent that the
> views of textwriters and legal commentators have come to our
> attention, they are unanimously of the view that nonviability
> of a fetus should not bar recovery. . . .
>
> We are not impressed with the soundness of the arguments
> against recovery [alleged lack of precedents, the avoidance of
> speculation or conjecture as to causation, and the encouragement
> of fictitious claims]. They should not prevail against logic and
> justice. We hold that the plaintiff's intestate was a "person"
> within the meaning of [the wrongful death statute of Massachu-
> setts].[53]

50. Gorke v. Le Clerc, 23 Conn. Supp. 256, 181 A.2d 448 (1962); Hale
v. Manion, 189 Kan. 143, 368 P.2d 1 (1962); Mitchell v. Couch, 285 S.W.2d
901 (Ky. 1955); State v. Sherman, 234 Md. 179, 198 A.2d 71 (1964);
Verkennes v. Corniea, 229 Minn. 365, 38 N.W.2d 838 (1949); Stidam v.
Ashmore, 109 Ohio App. 431, 167 N.E.2d 106 (1959); Poliquin v. Mac-
Donald, 101 N.H. 104, 135 A.2d 249 (1957). *See also* Wendt v. Lillo, 182
F. Supp. 56 (N.D. Iowa, 1960); Valence v. Louisiana Power & Light Co.,
50 So. 2d 847 (La. Ct. App. 1951); *contra,* Estate of Powers v. City of Troy,
380 Mich. 160, 156 N.W.2d 530 (1968) (strictly limited meaning of "person" under wrongful death statute); Padillow v. Elrod, 424 P.2d 16 (Okla.
1967), *criticized in* Note, *Torts: Prenatal Injuries—Viability and Live Birth,*
21 OKLA. L. REV. 114 (1968).
51. 91 Ga. App. 712, 87 S.E.2d 100 (1955).
52. Torigian v. Watertown News Co., 352 Mass. 446, 225 N.E.2d 926
(1967).
53. *Id.* at 448, 225 N.E.2d at 927.

59   David W. Louisell

One could predict, confidently so before the current pressures for abortion liberalization,[54] that actions for the wrongful death of unborn children generally will be allowed without regard to the stage of fetal development at the time of death.

Other areas of tort law have also recognized the civil rights of the unborn child. Thus, an unborn child has been held to be a "child" or "other person" allowing him to bring an action for the death of his father where the death occurred prior to the child's birth.[55] The fetus has also been held to be an "existing person"[56] and a "surviving child"[57] under various wrongful death statutes.

The tort law developments discussed in this section manifest another instance where the law has overcome cultural lag to get abreast of scientific realities. As put in *Scott v. McPheeters:*[58]

> The respondent asserts that the provisions of section 29 of the [California] Civil Code are based on a fiction of law to the effect that an unborn child is a human being separate and distinct from its mother. We think that assumption of our statute is not a fiction, but upon the contrary that it is an established and recognized fact by science and by everyone of understanding.

Equity's Protection of the Unborn Child

Provision for the appointment of a general curator to the person or property of a child conceived but not yet born, to act for him until his birth and thereafter to render an accounting, seems to bespeak the same regard for the unborn as for the born infant.[59] An unborn child can have an action brought by a guardian appointed for the purpose to have the father compelled to support the child prior to its birth.[60] A court may also order the appoint-

---

54. *Cf.* Estate of Powers v. City of Troy, 380 Mich. 160, 156 N.W.2d 530 (1968).

55. La Blue v. Specker, 358 Mich. 558, 100 N.W.2d 445 (1960).

56. Herndon v. St. Louis & S.F.R.R., 37 Okla. 256, 128 P. 727 (1912).

57. Texas & P. Ry. v. Robertson, 82 Tex. 657, 17 S.W. 1041 (1891).

58. 33 Cal. App. 2d 629, 634, 92 P.2d 678, 681 (1939).

59. QUEBEC CIVIL CODE, arts. 337–38, 345 (1967); *see* Montreal Tramways v. Leveille, [1933] 4 D.L.R. 337, 341 (Sup. Ct. Can. 1933).

60. Kyne v. Kyne, 38 Cal. App. 2d 122, 100 P.2d 806 (1940); Metzger v. People, 98 Colo. 133, 53 P.2d 1189 (1936). CAL. CIV. CODE § 29 (West 1954) provides that a child conceived but not born is to be deemed an existing person for the protection of its interests. The *Kyne* court read this section together with § 196a of the same code and held that one of these "interests" was the right to have the father compelled to support it.

ment of a special guardian as a procedural device to effectuate its
decree for the administration, over religious objection, of medically
necessary blood transfusions to save a pregnant woman's life or
that of her unborn child.[61] The court, admitting that it is a
difficult question as to whether an adult may be compelled to submit to blood transfusions,[62] had no difficulty in ordering the
transfusion here because it was "satisfied that the unborn child
is entitled to the law's protection" when a transfusion is necessary
to save its life.[63] The significance of this recognition of the right
of the unborn child is perceived when it is realized that it prevailed
over the cogent countervailing claim to the free exercise of
religion.[64]

Professor Prosser's summary of the status of the unborn child
well puts the legal, judicial and social consensus:

> [M]edical authority has recognized long since that the child is
> in existence from the moment of conception, and for many
> purposes its existence is recognized by the law. The criminal law
> regards it as a separate entity, and the law of property considers
> it in being for all purposes which are to its benefit, such as
> taking by will or descent. . . . All writers who have discussed
> the problem have joined . . . in maintaining that the unborn
> child in the path of an automobile is as much a person in the
> street as the mother.[65]

Abortion, the Practice of Medicine and Historic Legal Norms

Even where it is apparent, however, that a legally protectable
life is present it must be recognized that the legal right to life is

61. Raleigh Fitkin-Paul Morgan Memorial Hosp. v. Anderson, 42 N.J.
421, 201 A.2d 537, *cert. denied,* 377 U.S. 985 (1964); Hoener v. Bertinato,
67 N.J. Supp. 517, 171 A.2d 140 (1961).

62. *See* Application of Georgetown College, Inc., 331 F.2d 1000 (D.C.
Cir.), *cert. denied,* 377 U.S. 978 (1964); *In re* Estate of Brooks, 32 Ill. 2d
361, 205 N.E.2d 435 (1965); Louisell, *Transplantation: Existing Legal
Constraints,* in ETHICS IN MEDICAL PROGRESS 78, 82 (1966); *cf.* State v.
Perricone, 37 N.J. 463, 181 A.2d 751 (1962) (blood transfusion to child
notwithstanding parental objection).

63. Raleigh Fitkin—Paul Morgan Memorial Hosp. v. Anderson, 42 N.J.
421, 423, 201 A.2d 537, 538, *cert. denied,* 377 U.S. 985 (1964).

64. *Compare* Sherbert v. Verner, 374 U.S. 398 (1963); West Virginia
State Bd. of Educ. v. Barnette, 319 U.S. 624 (1943). *See generally* Gian-
nella, *The Difficult Quest for a Truly Humane Abortion Law,* 13 VILL. L.
REV. 257, 278–79 (1968); Louisell, *The Man and the Mountain: Douglas
on Religious Freedom,* 73 YALE L. J. 975 (1964).

65. W. PROSSER, *supra* note 43, at 355.

not absolute. Capital punishment, the concept of a justifiable war, and the principles of self-defense of a mortally threatened victim of assault all involve the legal taking or forfeiture of life. In the case of capital punishment, the legal right to life is forfeited only for grave reason after the convicted person has been afforded his full rights to the due process of law. With respect to self-defense and justifiable war there exists a notion of illegal aggression or at least derivative wrongfulness on the part of the one whose life is taken, and a motivation of survival, in an emergency situation, on the part of the legally innocent party who commits the homicide.

It must be asked how the proposal of the American Law Institute accords with these stated principles of the law. The model statute allows the termination of a pregnancy solely on the basis of a medical judgment. It is obvious that such matters as concern the physiological feasibility of abortion and surgical techniques and risks to the mother are matters for medical expertise and judgment. But the problem of the legitimacy of a given operation is more than merely a medical one; it also involves legal, moral, ethical, theological, philosophical, sociological and psychological considerations. These realities cannot be undone merely by calling the problem "medical." "How simple would be the tasks of constitutional adjudication and of law generally if specific problems could be solved by inspection of the labels pasted on them." [66] The historical function of physicians has been to diagnose and heal, not to adjudicate. Rabbi Immanuel Jakobovits has put it well:

Physicians, by demanding that as the practitioners in this field they should have the right to determine or adjudicate the laws governing their practice, are making an altogether unprecedented claim not advanced by any other profession. . . .
. . . A physician, in performing an abortion or any other procedure involving moral considerations, such as artificial insemination or euthanasia, is merely a technical expert; but he is no more qualified than any other layman to pronounce on the rights or legality of such acts, let alone to determine what these rights should be, relying merely on the whims or dictates of his conscience. The decision on whether a human life, once conceived, is to be or not to be, therefore, properly

66. Trop v. Dulles, 356 U.S. 86, 94 (1958).

belongs to moral experts, or to legislatures guided by such experts.[67]

Contrariwise, under the model statute the physician is to decide who shall have life and who shall have death.

Often in human affairs medical expertise may determine aspects of a problem without purporting to be dispositive of the whole problem. In the case of the defense of insanity in a criminal prosecution, medical testimony is highly relevant to the issue of responsibility; but we do not submit the issue to the decision of a jury of psychiatrists. To the contrary, even where the problem appears predominately a medical one, increasingly a societal judgment is sought. If war is too important for the generals, the ultimate issues of life and death are too important for the surgeons. Medical defense committees and screening committees used in malpractice litigation utilize the services of clergy, lawyers and other thoughtful persons in addition to physicians.[68] When kidney disease threatens to be fatal, and the possibilities for dialysis are limited, with apparently increasing frequency the choice of the beneficiaries is left to a "jury" of lay people.[69]

In order to make the question of the legitimacy of an abortion solely a medical judgment it must be assumed that no human life, other than that of the mother, is involved in the termination of the pregnancy. The American Law Institute accomplishes this by drawing a distinction between abortions which occur late in pregnancy and those which

> occur prior to the fourth month of pregnancy, before the fetus becomes firmly implanted in the womb, before it develops many of the characteristic and recognizable features of humanity, and well before it is capable of those movements which when felt by the mother are called "quickening." There seems to be an obvious difference between terminating the development of such an inchoate being, whose chance of maturing is still somewhat *problematical,* and, on the other hand, destroying a fully formed

67. *Compare* Jakobovits, *Jewish Views on Abortion,* in ABORTION AND THE LAW 124, 125–26 (1967), *with* Hellegers, *Law and the Common Good,* COMMONWEAL, June 30, 1967, at 418.

68. D. LOUISELL & H. WILLIAMS, TRIAL OF MEDICAL MALPRACTICE CASES ¶ 7.02 (1960).

69. Alexander, *They Decide Who Lives, Who Dies,* LIFE, Nov. 9, 1962, at 102; Sanders & Dukeminier, *Medical Advance and Legal Lag: Hemodialysis and Kidney Transplantation,* 15 U.C.L.A. L. REV. 357, 371 (1968).

viable fetus of eight months, where the offense might well become ordinary murder if the child should happen to survive
for a moment after it has been expelled from the body of the
mother.[70]

It is submitted that this approach involves arbitrary distinctions
which, in fact, are not medically supportable. How is the chance
of maturing of the specified inchoate being "problematical" other
than as all life is "problematical"? "[O]nce spermatozoon and
ovum meet and the conceptus is formed, . . . roughly in only
20 percent of the cases will spontaneous abortion occur. In
other words, the chances are about four out of five that this new
being will develop." [71] Implantation in the womb "normally
occurs within eight (8) days of fruitful intercourse," [72] a skilled
embryologist can positively identify the humanity of the embryo
shortly after conception, and even a layman can "easily recognize
human features by the sixth week." [73] Medical evidence would
indicate that the various stages of development are merely labels
which have been placed upon what is in fact the steady, constant
growth of the human being and are no more significant as tests
of life itself than are the more commonly used labels of infancy,
adolescence, maturity, middle-age, and old-age. The only real
difference between the "inchoate being" and the eight-month-old
fetus is that the latter is somewhat older than the former. This
would hardly seem to justify the conclusion that one of the
fetuses represents human life, in its generally accepted form, while
the other does not.

70. MODEL PENAL CODE § 207.11, Comment (Tentative Draft No. 9,
1959) (emphasis added).
71. Noonan, *Abortion and the Catholic Church: A Summary History,* 12
NATURAL L. F. 85, 129 (1967). Noonan also points out that the conceptus
is qualitatively distinct from the elements, spermatozoon and ovum, which
meet to form it. The newly conceived being possesses what is not possessed
by these individual components: the genetic code, the transmitter of all
those potentialities which make men human. F. GOTTLEIB, DEVELOPMENT
GENETICS 17 (1966). At the same time this new being represents a dramatic
jump in potentiality for survival. Of the 200,000,000 to 300,000,000 spermatozoa in a normal ejaculate, only one has a chance of developing into a
zygote. J. BAXTER, FRAZER'S MANUAL OF EMBRYOLOGY 5 (1953). Of the
1,000,000 oocytes in a female infant, 390 at most have a chance of being
ovulated. G. PINCUS, THE CONTROL OF FERTILITY 197 (1965). Note from
the text the chances of survival of the conceptus, absent deliberate abortion.
72. N. MIETUS, *supra* note 7, at 16.
73. *Id.* at 17.

Many proponents of liberalized abortion choose to ignore the basic question of whether human life is involved. The effect of this, given the historic legal and prevailing medical judgment that life is present from the moment of conception, is to turn our traditional hierarchy of values upside down. The mother's interest in her own welfare and happiness is to be placed above the life of the unborn child, contrary to the historic rule recently repeated by the New Jersey Supreme Court that "the right of their (parents') child to live is greater than and precludes their right not to endure emotional and financial injury."[74] The new morality would undermine the classical justification for taking life. A man may take the life of an assailant who threatens him with fatal or grave bodily harm but he may not do so when the assailant merely threatens his automobile or other valuable possession.[75] Historically the right to human life has been subordinate to no lesser claim than a superior right to life; now physicians may prescribe it as subordinate to considerations of physical or mental health, fear of defective offspring, or revulsion of carrying an illegally conceived child. Thus is the Judaeo-Christian ethic of reverence for life replaced by an ethic of reverence for welfare, convenience, or happiness. It is ironic that the proposals for liberalizing abortion laws are made by a generation that is reconsidering and often abandoning capital punishment.

It seems fair to conclude that the abortion proposal of the American Law Institute comes not as a further evolutionary step in the law's perception of the value, intrinsic dignity and essential equality of human life. To the contrary, it confronts the law's evolution with a countermovement. It would justify the weighing of the right to life on scales open only to utilitarian weights. The unborn child, concededly morally blameless, may be sacrificed in the interests of the mother's mental health or the social interests in avoiding a defective person who might become a welfare charge, because those interests by the ethos of the day are regarded as more socially significant than the claim to life. The right to life becomes relative not only to others' right to life, but to others' health, happiness, convenience and desires for freedom from avoidable burdens. And the scales-master is to be not a neutral

74. Gleitman v. Cosgrove, 49 N.J. 22, 227 A.2d 689 (1967).
75. R. PERKINS, CRIMINAL LAW 889–909 (1957); Daube, *Sanctity of Life*, 60 PROC. ROYAL SOC'Y MED. 1235, 1237 (1967).

agent such as a court, but the person who desires to avoid the burden.

It may be conceded that many of the hardships of the human situation can be avoided or mitigated by a refusal to put up with burdensome or unpleasant life embodied in a child in the womb. (Parenthetically one may ask, who can appraise whether the moral trauma consequent upon a decision to avoid the burden may not produce a still weightier one?) Life in a sense is cheap; there are multiple ova and sperm; where one union produces an idiot, the next may result in a genius. Some lawyers, like many of their fellow citizens, seem convinced that the abortion proposal is justified for pragmatic reasons, or at least represents the lesser of evils in relation to illegal abortion. Some at least purport to believe that the fetus is only tissue of the mother and hence is disposable at her will. But no utilitarian appeal, however plausible or attractive in its promise of social betterment, can hide from the percipient lawyer the hard fact that the proposal is not legal evolution but revolution. It reverses the trend of the law, a trend heretofore taken as one of the badges of progress in man's hard climb to civilization.[76]

Pearl S. Buck has put with the incisiveness of artistic insight the ethos that underlay our historic legal norm, in pointing out why it was worthwhile to rear a child retarded from phenylketonuria:

[C]ould it have been possible for me to have had foreknowledge of her thwarted life would I have wanted abortion? Now with full knowledge of anguish and despair, the answer is no, I would not. Even in full knowledge I would have chosen life, and this for two reasons: First, I fear the power of choice over life or death at human hands. I see no human body whom

---

76. Perhaps lawyers are most inclined to feel that what *has* been *should* be. It can be argued that the author, in appraising the abortion proposals derives too much significance from past decisions protective of human life (although the recent decisions in the tort area are something else again). Do modern longevity and population explosion render obsolete the old learning on the inviolability of innocent human life? Abortion proponents who refuse to take refuge in the pretense that their proposals do not involve human life, and who frankly argue that in this genetically-manipulable, organ-transplantable era, society must have power to authorize life-death decisions, deserve credit at least for their intellectual candor. Better forthrightly to face the "Brave New World," than to hide one's head in the sands of pretense!

I could ever trust with such power—not myself, nor any other. Human wisdom, human integrity, are not great enough. Since the fetus is a creature already alive and in the process of development, to kill it is to choose death over life. At what point shall we allow this choice? For me the answer is—at no point, once life is begun.

. . . .

It can be summed up, perhaps, by saying that [to] this world, where cruelty prevails in so many aspects of our life, I would not add the weight of choice to kill rather than to let live.[77]

Abortion and the Law as Teacher

Little wonder that the lawyer's mind, faced with so abrupt a reversal of the law's trend, seeks to extricate the law from its predicament. For he sees that the law will be at war with itself, something of a schizophrenic, if on the one hand it protects the unborn from the tort feasor who is only negligent, yet subjects him to deliberate destruction at the will of his mother. Thus it has been suggested that it would be better for the law to abandon the abortion field to the domain of private conscience only, rather than to begin the process of deciding who will live and who will die.[78] For where will the process end? How long will it be before the senile, the retarded, the psychopathic are also regarded as too inconvenient, or too socially burdensome? The *carte blanche* permissiveness will be intolerable at least to the religious conscience of numerous citizens. If this is to be the wave of the future, let the law withdraw from the swim. Further, withdrawal may be facilitated, even effected, by the abortifacient pill of tomorrow's chemistry.[79]

It is easy to understand and hard to criticize the motive for such a proposal. Any port in a storm. But the port may prove to be an illusion; the escape hatch from the predicament too broad. Law and morality are not coterminous. But can society afford a

77. *Foreword* to THE TERRIBLE CHOICE: THE ABORTION DILEMMA (R. Cooke, A. Hellegers, R. Hoyt, & H. Richardson eds. 1968).

78. *See, e.g.,* Remarks of Robert F. Drinan, International Conference on Abortion, Washington, D.C., Sept. 1967.

79. Survey, *Church-State: A Legal Survey—1966–68,* 43 NOTRE DAME LAW. 684, 712–13 (1968).

proclamation of the law's lack of concern in matters of life and death?

If it be objected that in any event the prohibition of abortion is not effectively enforced, the argument proves too much. Who would advocate abandonment of the laws against perjury because of lack of enforcement? [80] The frequent invocation of the experience under the late unlamented eighteenth amendment seems beside the point. An unwanted dietary principle cannot be coerced; but does the right to life involve no more than that? Likely the abortifacient pill will make enforcement of anti-abortion laws even more difficult, although it must be remembered that free availability of the pill presupposes the law's toleration of its manufacture and distribution. In any case, if the de facto withdrawal of the law from the field will be a function of the pill, would it not be wiser to await the event rather than anticipate it by public pronouncement of the legitimacy of foeticide? The law is a teacher, sometimes a great teacher. Do we want it to *teach* the legitimacy of easy abortion, even assuming it must tolerate it?

Abortion and the Due Process of Law

Some lawyers will feel that, if easy abortion must be the wave of the future, they should at least construct dikes of due process against the most flagrant abuses in the threatening floods of the new permissiveness. They will contend that at a minimum they must prevent the orderly execution of the unborn from deteriorating into uninhibited lynching. Such due process instincts are laudable and attempts to construct machinery to effectuate them not wholly hopeless. The dilemma of course is that the crucial decision—that it is permissible for man to decide who shall live —will already have been made by the legislature. If the courts acquiesce in the constitutionality of that decision, what is left to achieve under the rubric of due process?

Something may be left. Judicial inquiry might reveal that a mother's claim of grave injury to her mental health is under the facts of a particular case so trivial as to be sham in relation to

80. *See, e.g.,* McClintock, *What Happens to Perjurers,* 24 MINN. L. REV. 727 (1940).

the child's presumed desire to live. Fraudulent claims of rape or incest might be exposed. Fear of a gravely defective fetus might be shown by cross-examination of the proposing physician, and by other evidence, to be insubstantial.

To these suggestions objection may be made that the inexorable and rapid flight of the period in which abortion is medically feasible precludes such judicial inquiry; that due process is a luxury of leisure. If nature has itself ordained the impossibility of applying standards of fundamental fairness in appraising a claim to abortion, perhaps that is something of judgment on the intrinsic quality of the act. Perhaps what cannot be done fairly should not be done at all. The law, however, is steeped in experience of dealing with time emergencies and has in other areas been able to devise techniques of accommodating to emergency circumstances, *e.g.,* the temporary restraining order.

Appointment of a guardian to represent the fetus would seem feasible and would be the minimum starting point for any attempt at due process that is more than a sham. The guardian obviously would have to be one not under the domination of the mother or the recommending physician. The guardian would appear for the fetus at the judicial hearing on the petition for the abortion. A possible alternative to a judicial hearing would be an administrative one before an interdisciplinary board with at least a limited right of judicial review. The board might consist of independent physicians, lawyers, sociologists, theologians and lay persons. A model for the judicial review might be that recommended to review administrative determinations respecting alleged intervening insanity of those under death sentence.[81] Provision for expedition would have to be made.

If experience proved that the foregoing ideas, rooted in common law experience and development, were not feasible in the new area of legalized abortion, perhaps we could borrow from the extra-litigious procedures of continental jurisprudence.[82] Under that approach a judge would be charged to make on his own initiative judicial inquiry into the substantiality of the claim for abortion under the statutory standard.

There would seem to be no inherent psychological or moral

---

81. *See* Hazard & Louisell, *supra* note 40.
82. *See* Ehrenzweig, *The Interstate Child and Uniform Legislation: A Plea for Extralitigious Proceedings,* 64 MICH. L. REV. 1 (1965).

reasons for medicine to oppose attempts to construct for abortion applications a machinery of due process. The medical profession should be wary of preempting the abortion decisional prerogative by a statute that would formally ordain the legal right of two physicians to justify an abortion under the nebulous standards proposed.[83] Even the strongest proponents of liberalized abortion admit that, at least, the potential for human life is present in the early stages of gestation. In principle, the medical profession should be reluctant to exchange its historic role of champion in the struggle for life, for the role of even a well-intentioned judge-executioner. Moreover, physicians as much as any men stand in need of the due process of law, and should realize that the rights of any of us are secure only while those of all are secure.[84]

But the best possible attempts at due process would be largely thwarted by the necessarily limited scope of inquiry permissible under a statute authorizing easy legal abortion. Hard questions would naggingly lurk in the background, pressing for their own resolution under historic notions of due process and equal protection,[85] and frustratingly would be denied consideration. What

83. "Mental health of the mother" is particularly nebulous and susceptible to subjective value judgments. Yet the first Report to the Legislature on Implementation of California's Therapeutic Abortion Act shows that out of 282 abortions approved, 238 were on the ground of the mother's mental health. CALIF. DEP'T OF PUBLIC HEALTH, REPORT TO THE LEGISLATURE ON CALIFORNIA'S THERAPEUTIC ABORTION ACT, Tab. 1 (Jan. 1968).

84. D. LOUISELL & H. WILLIAMS, THE PARENCHYMA OF LAW 157, 165 (1960).

85. A constitutional argument, that the law's conclusive preference for the wishes of the mother, even when grounded in considerations far less than those of life itself, over the claim of the unborn child to life, would deny the latter as a human being the equal protection of the law, is not here pursued. The essentials of this argument have already been well put by Noonan who, after showing the insubstantial or at least inconclusive nature of the arguments advanced by supporters of easy abortion to distinguish fetal from other human life, states:
"[H]uman beings with equal rights often come in conflict with each other, and some decision must be made as [to] whose claims are to prevail. Cases of conflict involving the fetus are different only in two respects: the total inability of the fetus to speak for itself and the fact that the right of the fetus regularly at stake is the right to life itself.
. . . .
The perception of the humanity of the fetus and the weighing of fetal rights against other human rights constituted the work of the moral analysts. . . .
. . . .

type of evidence should be admissible, where the very reason for the proceeding is a legislative judgment that innocent life is to be forfeited for reasons not necessarily having to do with the preservation of the mother's life, but only with her rights to health and happiness, or with the prospect of having a possibly defective child? What criteria are to be relied upon in passing on the child's right to be born? Does a potentially defective child have a lesser claim on this right than a normal one who is the product of rape? And what of the interests of the father who under the proposed statute is not to be consulted or even informed of the abortion? [86]

Conclusion

Easy legal abortion presents a genuine and disturbing reversal of the law's steady progress toward recognition of the dignity, value, and essential equality of human life. It is a negation of the constitutional guarantee of equal protection of the law.[87] It is a loveless act offensive to both the religiously and humanistically predicated conscience of our common-law tradition.[88] Attempts to justify it on the ground that the fetus is not fully human want for logic, because to pick any moment other than that of conception as the starting point of human life is artificial and arbitrary. All human life, whether fetal, infant, adolescent, mature, or aged, is in the process of becoming.[89] Abortion can be justified only

---

The commandment [love your neighbor as yourself] could be put in humanistic as well as theological terms: Do not injure your fellow man without reason. In these terms, once the humanity of the fetus is perceived, abortion is never right except in self defense. When life must be taken to save life, reason alone cannot say that a mother must prefer a child's life to her own. With this exception, now of great rarity, abortion violates the rational humanist tenet of the equality of human lives." Noonan, *supra* note 71, at 130–31.

86. *See* Carroll & Louisell, *The Father as Non-Parent,* 210 CATHOLIC WORLD 108–10 (December, 1969).

87. A legislative decision for liberal abortion is of course ultimately subject in American society to constitutional appeal to the courts by one with standing to complain.

88. Noonan, *supra* note 71.

89. "Humanity is an attribute which anyone conceived by a man and a woman has. . . . Any attempt to limit humanity to exclude some group runs the risk of furnishing authority and precedent for excluding other groups in the name of the consciousness or perception of the controlling group in the society. . . .

. . . A being with the human genetic code is *homo sapiens* in potency; and

if society has the right to prescribe the conditions of continuing life, and to authorize the weighing of the right to life against other values. To concede such a societal right is to depart from the Judaeo-Christian ethic of reverence for human life.[90]

Confronted with the threat of such a reversal of the law's posture, some lawyers would prefer that the law abandon the field rather than explicitly succumb to the threat. To take this escape, however, is to denigrate the function of law as teacher.

If society insists on legal abortion, the law's last line of defense is to attempt to erect machinery calculated to bring as much due process as possible into the methodology of abortion. But the law must not pretend to do the impossible. The machinery of the most skilled proceduralists will hardly substitute for Albert Schweitzer's principle of Reverence for Life, or equivalently manifest that principle's ethical affirmation of life. As he put it:

> Let a man once begin to think about the mystery of his life and the links which connect him with the life that fills the world, and he cannot but bring to bear upon his own life and all other life that comes within his reach the principle of Reverence for Life, and manifest this principle by ethical affirmation of life. Existence will thereby become harder for him in every respect than it would be if he lived for himself, but at the same time it will be richer, more beautiful, and happier. It will become, instead of mere living, a real experience of life.[91]

---

his potential capacity to reason makes him share in the universal characteristic of man. Man is always in the process of learning. No one is full human. If the fetus is potentially human, so is the adult. Capacity to be human alone is common." *Id.* at 128–29.

As to the aged, one is reminded of the story about Justice Holmes who, queried as to why he was pursuing Greek in his twilight years, replied: "Why, to improve my mind, of course."

90. The senile grandparent, the retarded child, the defective fetus and infant may be dire afflictions. But to abide them has been a hallmark of Christian civilization. Is the burden too heavy for the richest country in its most affluent hour?

91. A. SCHWEITZER, OUT OF MY LIFE AND THOUGHT 179 (1963).

Elliott L. Biskind

6
Legitimacy of Children Born by Artificial Insemination

To the "Doctor's Dilemma" now has been added the "Court's Dilemma." Is a child illegitimate when born by artificial insemination to a married woman through the use of the semen of a third party donor [1] with the consent of her husband?

The basic problem is the necessity to overcome, by clear and convincing evidence,[2] the presumption of legitimacy, one of the strongest presumptions known to the law. This problem is complicated by the irrelevant issue of adultery.

What will overcome this presumption, then, is irrefutable proof of the husband's sterility, or impotence to a degree that he cannot emit semen. Evidence of either or both of these infirmities must relate to the time when conception did or could have taken place.[3] If the proof is not clear and convincing, and during the

ELLIOTT L. BISKIND, LL.B., is editor in chief, Clark Boardman Company, Ltd., New York. He is editor of *Harvey Law of Real Property and Title Closing* (New York: C. Boardman, 1966) and co-author of *The Revised Penal Law Handbook* (New York: C. Boardman, 1967). This article first appeared in *Boardman's New York Family Law* and subsequently in the *Journal of Family Law*. Revised by the author, it is reprinted with permission from the *Journal of Family Law* 5 (1965): 39–50.

1. Artificial insemination through the use of a third party's semen will be referred to as heterological insemination or A.I.D., while artificial insemination through the use of the husband's semen will be referred to as homologous insemination or A.I.H.

2. In *In re* Newin's Will, 29 Misc. 2d 614, 213 N.Y.S. 2d 255 (1961), the phrases used to denote the necessity for clear and convincing evidence are "a very heavy burden of proof on the one challenging legitimacy, even to the extent of proof of negative facts," "most convincing evidence," and "the party asserting illegitimacy must disprove every reasonable possibility of legitimacy by credible evidence, not by presumptions, even if this requires proof of a negative."

3. Houston v. Houston, 199 Misc. 469, 99 N.Y.S.2d 199 (1950); Schatkin, *Disputed Paternity Proceedings*, 2d ed., pp. 366–367.

time of conception the husband and wife engaged in intercourse, no matter how unsatisfactory the attempts may have been, the presumption of legitimacy will stand like the Rock of Gibraltar.

In *L. v. L.*,[4] the husband suffered from a psychological impotence. His wife artificially inseminated herself with his semen and produced a child.

Whether impotency or sterility warrants a holding that a husband is not the father of the wife's child depends upon the degree and cause of either, and upon the weight to be given the medical testimony. In *Doornbos v. Doornbos*,[5] the husband had been tested for sterility before resort was had to A.I.D. However, the record showed (1) that natural intercourse took place within the time of conception, and (2) the wife's gynecologist testified that sterility *and* impotence must be present to negate the possibility of conception through natural intercourse. Under the circumstances of that case he testified that he could not state definitely whether or not the child had been conceived by artificial insemination or by natural intercourse. Another unusual feature of that case was pregnancy after the first injection, which, the gynecologist stated, was unusual.[6]

According to Stedman's Medical Dictionary,[7] there are three types of sterility. Aspermatogenic sterility is due to a failure to produce living spermatozoa. Dysspermatogenic sterility is due to some abnormality in production of spermatozoa, e.g., lacking in adequate motility. Normo-spermatogen in the male is due to some cause other than failure to produce live, normal spermatozoa, e.g., blockage of the seminiferous passages.

Impotence is lack of power in the male to copulate. This lack of power may be due to a physical or emotional cause. Physical inability has one of three causes: atonic, caused by a paralysis of the motor nerves; paretic, caused by a lesion of the central nervous system; and sensory. Emotional inability generally results from one or more of the following: traumatic experiences of infancy and childhood; fear; repressed hostility and unconscious conflicts triggered by ambivalence, homosexuality, and narcissism. The great

4. [1949] Probate Div. 211 [1949] 1 All. Eng. L.R. 141.

5. 23 US L Week 2308, No. 54-S-14981, Superior Court of Cook County, app dism on procedural grds. 12 Ill App. 2d 473, 139 NE. 2d 844 (1956).

6. *See:* Levisohn, *Dilemma in Parenthood; Socio-Legal Aspects of Human Artificial Insemination,* 36 Chicago- Kent L. Rev. 1, n56 (1959).

7. 20th rev. ed.

majority of cases of impotence fall into the second category, as physical inability is said to be quite rare.

If any type of sterility is claimed, it must be proven to have existed at the approximate time when the artificial insemination occurred. If the medical or laboratory evidence on this point concerns a test made some time prior or subsequent to that time, such evidence, while competent, is accorded little weight, for in many cases of sterility the condition is not permanent.

Assuming that the evidence is satisfactory as to the time of the test, the quality of the test is important. In *People* v. *Guiseppe*,[8] there was received in evidence a physician's report of his laboratory examination of the defendant's semen, which read:

> Above semen ejaculate findings represent a very poor specimen for successful insemination and satisfactory insemination and satisfactory fertility purposes. Consensus of medical opinion would be that this specimen would not be adequate to impregnate.

Characterizing the report as cautious and as leaving an inference that there might be a difference of medical opinion as to the defendant's fertility, the court issued a paternity order against the defendant on the basis of complainant's evidence.

Birth of a child through A.I.D. appears to be more difficult to prove when impotence is claimed rather than sterility. Except, perhaps, for paretic impotence, an impotent male may emit normal spermatozoa. If there is a history of attempted intercourse at or about the time of the artificial insemination, there is no justification for holding a child born within the normal gestation period, calculated from the time of the intercourse and the A.I.D., to be illegitimate. To so hold violates the requirement that only clear and convincing evidence can eliminate the presumption of legitimacy.

If husband and wife are living together, and assuming the absence of clear and convincing evidence of the husband's inability to procreate, legitimacy will be presumed "though the wife has harbored an adulterer."[9]

Potent, indeed, the presumption is, one of the strongest and

8. 97 N.Y.S. 2d 486, aff'd 276 App. Div. 1102, 96 N.Y.S. 2d 848 (2d Dept 1949), lv to app den 277 App. Div. 879, 98 N.Y.S. 2d 220.
9. Matter of Findlay, 253 N.Y. 1, 10, 170 N.E. 471 (1930).

most persuasive known to the law . . . , and yet subject to the sway of reason. . . . At times the cases seemed to say that any possibility of access, no matter how violently improbable, would leave the presumption active as against neutralizing proof. . . . By and large, none the less, the courts are generally agreed that countervailing evidence may shatter the presumption though the possibility of access is not susceptible of exclusion to the point of utter demonstration. Issue will not be bastardized as the outcome of a choice between nicely balanced probabilities . . . in a futile quest for certainty. Some of the books tell us that to overcome the presumption, the evidence of non-access must be "clear and convincing" . . . ; others that it must lead to a conclusion that is "strong and irresistible" . . . ; others that it must be proof "beyond all reasonable doubt." . . . What is meant by these pronouncements, however differently phrased, is this and nothing more, that the presumption will not fail unless common sense and reason are outraged by a holding that it abides.[10]

In *Gursky* v. *Gursky*,[11] the court refers to "the believable testimony," the "medical proof," and to the "evidence in the case," including the formal admissions made on the part of the plaintiff husband, as sustaining the defendant wife's position that there had been a failure of the consummation of the marriage. The court then observed that, as a result of medical advice and "plaintiff's condition," the parties investigated the possibility of artificially inseminating the wife. This was done, with the signed consent of both parties. The court then found that "as a result of said artificial insemination" a child was born to the wife, but the birth certificate listed the plaintiff husband as the father.

Much of the balance of the opinion is devoted to a discussion of legitimacy, concluding with the observation that a child born to a married woman whose father is not the woman's husband, is illegitimate, and that the birth is a result of the mother's adultery, citing the Illinois case of *Doornbos* v. *Doornbos*.[12]

It is to be regretted that the court did not detail the evidence of the plaintiff husband's "infirmities." At the same time, it must

10. *Id*. at 6, 7, 8, 170 N.E. at 472–473.
11. 242 N.Y.S. 2d 406 (1963). *See* Strnad v. Strnad, 190 Misc 786, 78 N.Y.S. 2d 390 (1948).
12. Note 5, *supra*.

be assumed in the absence of availability of the record,[13] that the court was satisfied the evidence was clear and convincing and overcame the presumption of legitimacy.

This much is known about *Gursky*. There were constant, but apparently "unsatisfying" attempts at normal intercourse prior to the artificial insemination. The husband did emit semen, even though he was incapable of attaining complete erection. But, the parties claimed, the semen was left "on the sheets." In this situation it is impossible to present clear and convincing evidence that no semen reached the wife's uterus.

An analogous situation was present in *Russell* v. *Russell,*[14] where the court found that the wife had had no sexual intercourse with her husband nor with "any other man," but had become pregnant through physical contact (without penetration) between hers and an unknown man's sexual organs. The court called it "fecundation, *ab extra.*"

The trend today is to narrow rather than enlarge the area in which children are labeled illegitimate. The entire concept of illegitimacy has been built up essentially because of property rights, with little or no regard to the human rights involved. When a husband consents to the artificial insemination of his wife because of his own physical or psychological sexual inadequacies but permits his name to be listed on the birth certificate as the father, it would seem that a presumption of legitimacy born of the recognition that it is necessary to remove from children the stigma of illegitimacy, should operate as an estoppel against both a wife and husband contravening or contradicting his parenthood.[15]

Such a situation occurred in *People* v. *Dennett,*[16] where the parties, with two children, had separated. The separation agreement referred to "issue of the marriage" and included provision

13. Records in filiation proceedings in New York are sealed by the court.
14. [1924] A.C. 687. *See also:* [1943] 2 All. E. R. J40 (P.D.A.)
15. *See:* Anonymous v. Anonymous, 208 Misc. 633, 143 N.Y.S. 2d 221, 225 (1955): "A wife will not be permitted to bring an action to declare that her husband is not the father of a child born during lawful wedlock without proof of non-access or impotency and *will be denied relief even then in the absence of proof that it is for the best interests of the child."* (Emphasis supplied.) *See also:* Vohmann v. Michel, 185 N.Y. 420, 78 N.E. 156 (1906).
16. Misc. 2d 260, 184 N.Y.S. 2d 178, (1958).

for the support of the wife "and children." It also provided for the father's visitation rights with respect to "the children." With respect to custody, the agreement recited that the wife shall have the care and custody of the two children "of the marriage." Shortly after the execution of the agreement, the wife established residence in Nevada, where she obtained a divorce. The separation agreement was incorporated into the decree, which provided that "said agreement and all of the terms and provisions of same and all matters pertaining to the care, custody and control, support and maintenance of the minor issue of this marriage to whit . . . are hereby incorporated herein . . . and the custody of said minor children is hereby awarded to the parties as provided in said agreement. . . ."

Some time later, the former husband instituted a habeas corpus proceeding to enforce his visitation rights. The mother resisted on the ground that both children were born as a result of heterological artificial insemination.

The court held that both the acknowledgment of paternity in the separation agreement and in the Nevada decree estopped the mother from claiming that the children were not the issue of the former husband.

With respect to homologous insemination, there can be little, if any, quarrel with the assertion that children born as a result are legitimate. This device is resorted to when the husband has no physical disabilities but purely psychological ones, which make it difficult, if not impossible, for him to engage in the normal sexual act.

Children born of heterologous insemination should not be stigmatized with illegitimacy when the husbands of their mothers had freely consented to the practice which resulted in their births, and had permitted their names to be registered as the fathers. It is not suggested that a child born of secret insemination without either the knowledge or consent of the wife's husband also should be legitimatized. The solution to the problem of the former group is simple, and requires only legislative recognition that such children are legitimate.

Under Louisiana law, legitimacy does not depend necessarily upon birth during marriage. A formal method of acknowledging the legitimacy of children born out of wedlock is present in Articles 200 and 203 of the Louisiana Revised Code. They provide that a parent may acknowledge legitimacy of a child by making a declaration to that effect before a notary. Courts of Louisiana have also held that a child born illegitimately may prove its subsequent legitimization by other competent evidence that its parents recognized its legitimate status.

In *In re Slater's Estate*,[17] decedent died intestate, a resident of New York State, and his alleged daughter was granted letters of administration. In a proceeding to revoke the letters, it was claimed that the daughter was the decedent's illegitimate child. The decedent had been born in Louisiana. While domiciled there, he became the father of the administratrix by a woman concededly not his wife. The administratrix claimed she was legitimatized under Louisiana law which must be recognized in this state.

In this case the evidence regarding recognition of the child's legitimate status included testimony of an aunt that she was present at the child's christening, that the father was there, and that the father's brother acted as godfather in sponsoring the child. There was testimony of a former schoolmate of the mother, who also was present at the baptismal ceremony, that the decedent spoke of and referred to the administratrix as his child and daughter. In addition, the baptismal certificate naming the child and the parents was received in evidence. While this certificate was not itself sufficient to show acknowledgment of legitimacy, taken with the other evidence it did establish the fact in issue, and the court held that the administratrix was the legitimate child of the decedent under the Louisiana law and was therefore entitled to letters of administration.

With respect to "adultery," it is defined as, "The sexual intercourse of two persons, either of whom is married to a third person; unchastity; unfaithfulness."[18]

"Chastity" is defined as, "Free from sexual impurity; modest; virtuous."[19]

In the same context, "unfaithfulness" is defined as, "not true to marriage vows."[20]

In *Doornbos* v. *Doornbos*,[21] notwithstanding the absence of clear

17. 195 Misc. 713, 90 N.Y.S. 2d 546 (1949).
18. Funk & Wagnalls New College Standard Dictionary.
19. *Ibid.*
20. *Ibid.*
21. Note 5, *supra.*

and convincing testimony that the child was born by artificially impregnating the mother with a donor's semen, the court held the child illegitimate, and then, in what is essentially dicta, concluded that heterological insemination is adultery. In an earlier Illinois case it was held that the definition of adultery does *not* include artificial insemination,[22] and, as late as 1958, a Scottish court also so held.[23]

In a Canadian case,[24] the court found that the child born to the wife was the result of her actual adultery (employing the term in its accepted meaning) and not of heterological insemination as she had claimed. Nevertheless, the court expressed its opinion (*dicta*) that A.I.D. is adultery. It reasoned:

> It is admitted that there is no direct authority upon the exact point. . . . The sin or offense of adultery, as affecting the marriage, . . . may be traced from the Mosaic Law down through the canon or ecclesiastical law to the present date. . . . In its essence, adultery was an invasion of the marital rights of the husband and wife. The marriage tie had for its primary object the perpetuation of the human race. The Church of England's marriage service—the voice of the Ecclesiastical Courts of England—gives the first of the causes for which matrimony was ordained, that of the procreation of the human race. Can anyone read the Mosaic Law . . . without being convinced that had such a thing as artificial insemination entered the mind of the law-giver, it would have been regarded with the utmost horror as an invasion of the most sacred rights of husband and wife, and have been the subject of the severest penalties? . . . The essence of the offense of adultery consists . . . in the voluntary surrender to another person of the reproductive powers or faculties of the guilty person. Sexual intercourse is adulterous because in the case of the woman it involves the possibility of introducing into the family of the husband a false strain of blood. Any act of the wife which does that would, therefore, be adulterous.[25]

22. Hoch v. Hoch, 44-C-9307, Circuit Court of Cook County.
23. Maclennan v. Maclennan [1958], Sess. Cas. 105 [1958], Scots L.T.R. 12. *See:* Payne, *Artificial Insemination Heterologous and the Matrimonial Offense of Adultery in the United Kingdom,* 40 N.C.L. Rev. 111.
24. Orford v. Orford, 49 Ont. L.R. 15, 58 D.L.R. 251 (1921).
25. 49 Ont. L.R. at 21, 22, 58 D.L.R. at 257–258. "The history of artificial insemination is said to have begun with the first successful breeding of mares by the Arabs in 1322. Don Ponchom followed with successful experiences with fish in 1420. Leewenhoek and Ham's discovery that sperm were motile was followed by Ludwig Jacobi's successful revival of the work

This reasoning is to be questioned. While in committing adultery a married woman may surrender to another person "her reproductive powers or faculties," as a rule she does not do so, for contraceptive measures usually are employed. Pregnancy is not, normally, her purpose in committing adultery. It is the last thing she or her partner wants. Adultery is committed for sexual gratification which is acquired by the physical contact between male and female and by the consummation of the act itself. Not only is this physical gratification absent in A.I.D., but the donor and recipient never consciously lay eyes upon one another.

If it is adultery, is the physician, if a man, also guilty? [26] And what if the physician is a female? Or is the donor guilty? [27] Furthermore, who is the father of a child so born, the physician who impregnated the woman, but with semen not his own, or the donor who had neither knowledge of the identity of the recipient

---

with fish in 1742. Then followed epochal experiences on many sides from which the names of Malpighi and Rossi, Spallanzani, Heape, Marshall, Allbrecht, Plonnis and Sir Everett Millais stand out in bold relief. Iwanow and the Russian school brought about the grand scale use of artificial insemination in animal breeding and since that time many other countries have scored similar successes. About the middle of the sixteenth century Eustachius is said to have had the first successful human case. In the last decade of the eighteenth century John Hunter had his celebrated experience using the vaginal route of insemination. Lesueur and others, including Nicholas of Nancy, succeeded in the same manner. In America, Marion Sims successfully employed intrauterine insemination in 1866. A long list of French investigators including Gigon, Girault and Gerard reported multiple successes. 'The modern work in this field began with Rohleder who reported in 1904 the first pregnancy from material recovered by testicular puncture, although Dickinson had reported two cases of heterologous artificial insemination at an International Congress in London the year before. Several series of successes were subsequently reported including the one of Abbett in which there were eleven pregnancies out of thirty-seven cases, Schorohowa with twenty-two successes out of fifty, Warner with six pregnancies out of nine and Seguy's second series of nine cases reported in 1935. The first application of eugenics to the practice of artificial insemination must be credited to Seymour in 1936. It was not until 1943 that the first report of a successful use of sperm transported by airplane is to be found in the literature.' Koerner, *Medicolegal Considerations in Artificial Insemination*, 8 La. L.R. pp. 484, 487 (1947–1948)."

26. N.Y. Penal Code Law, § 255.17, defines adultery: "Any person is guilty of adultery when he engages in sexual intercourse with another person at a time when he has a living spouse, or the other person has a living spouse." Thus, both participants are guilty even though one is unmarried. This may not have been the Legislature's intent.

27. *Ibid.*

of his semen, nor whether his semen actually was used? If the child is illegitimate, who of the two, the physician or the donor, is to be held liable for its support?

It is rare to find adultery committed with the consent of a spouse, while heterological insemination occurs almost invariably with the active and written consent of the husband. There is, therefore, no "invasion of the most sacred rights" of a husband, and if there be such "invasion," it is with his consent. Similarly, labeling A.I.D. adultery because it will introduce a "false strain of blood" into the family, something the husband is supposed to regard with horror, is untenable, for he has agreed that this be done, just as he agrees that this be done when he consents with his wife to adopt an illegitimate child whose parents are unknown to him. In neither instance is he a deceived husband.

In his *Collected Legal Papers,* Mr. Justice Holmes wrote:

An ideal system of law should draw its postulates and its legislative justification from science. As it is now, we rely upon tradition, or vague sentiment, or the fact that we never thought of any other way of doing things, as our only warrant for rules which we enforce with as much confidence as if they embodied wisdom.

If society persists in branding as illegitimate a child born by artificial insemination (A.I.D.) employed with the consent of the mother's husband (assuming clear and convincing evidence of paternity), there would seem to be no justification to stigmatize the mother as an adulteress when both intent and the elements of adultery are absent. Sexual intercourse with the donor does not occur. Unfaithfulness is not involved, since that term is synonymous with extra-marital and secret sexual intercourse. Furthermore, illegitimacy is birth of a child out of wedlock and does not necessarily import adultery. Science has developed a method of impregnating women whose husbands, unable to do so, consent to the procedure. Weighted down with centuries of tradition and accumulation of "vague sentiment," courts label this method as adultery, with as much confidence as if this superficial definition "embodied revealed wisdom."

The New York City Health Code contains regulations for the practice of artificial insemination. If forbids anyone other than a licensed physician to engage in the practice and then only in accordance with the regulations of the Department of Health.

Section 112 of the New York City Health Code reads:

Artificial Human Insemination—No person other than a physician duly licensed to practice medicine in the State of New York shall collect, offer for sale, sell or give away human seminal fluid for the purpose of causing artificial insemination in a human being or except in accordance with the regulations of the Board of Health of the Department of Health of the City of New York.

The Board of Health Regulations read:

Regulations Governing the Providing of Seminal Fluid for Artificial Human Insemination.

Regul. 1. A person from whom seminal fluid is to be collected for the purpose of artificial human insemination shall have a complete physical examination with particular attention to the genitalia at the time of the taking of such seminal fluid.

Regul. 2. Such person shall have a standard serological test for syphilis and a smear and culture for gonorrhea not less than one week before such seminal fluid is obtained.

Regul. 3. No person suffering from any venereal diseases, tuberculosis or infection with brucella organisms, shall be used as a donor of seminal fluid for the purpose of artificial human insemination.

Regul. 4. No person having any disease or defect known to be transmissible by the genes shall be used as a donor of seminal fluid for the purpose of artificial human insemination.

Regul. 5. Before artificial human insemination is undertaken, both the proposed donor and proposed recipient shall have their bloods tested with respect to the RH factor at a laboratory approved for serology by the Board of Commissioner of Health. If the proposed recipient is negative for the RH factor, no semen shall be used for artificial insemination other than from a donor of seminal fluid whose blood is also negative for this factor.

Regul. 6. Where artificial human insemination is performed, the physician performing the same shall keep a record which shall show:

(1) The name of the physician.

(2) The name and address of the donor.

(3) The name and address of the recipient.

(4) The results of the physical examination and the results of the serological examinations, including the tests for the RH factor.

(5) The date of the artificial insemination.

Such records shall be regarded as confidential and shall not be open to inspection by the public or by any person other than the Commissioner of Health, an authorized representative of the Department of Health or such other persons as may be authorized by law to inspect such records. The custodian of any such records, the said Commissioner or any other person authorized by law to inspect such records shall not divulge any part of any such records so as to disclose the identity of the persons to whom they relate except as provided by law.

While these regulations have the force of law, they are not, of course, conclusive of the question whether or not A.I.D. is adultery. Nevertheless, it bespeaks a recognition by the medical profession, in that city at least, of the prevalence of the practice, its clear acceptance that it does no violence to morality or medical ethics, and its recognition of the need for supervision and control. This should be accorded great weight by the courts. Or is it suggested that the New York City Health Department has promulgated rules to regulate the practice of adultery?

In this discussion the question of non-access has not been discussed, for in those states where such evidence is inadmissible, a child born to a married couple is a child born within wedlock and therefore legitimate. In those states where such evidence is admissible, the question of the child's legitimacy does exist.

While we still retain the distinction between legitimate and illegitimate children, the trend in most of our states is to hide illegitimacy behind an innocuous birth certificate which merely lists the birth of a child and the name of the mother, omitting any identification of the father. As society becomes more enlightened, it is expected that the courts will become more vigilant in enforcing the rule of evidence that before a child born to a married woman is held to be illegitimate, there must be clear and convincing evidence of that fact. Also it is expected that the courts will make greater use of the estoppel rule, where a husband and wife to whom a child has been born, allegedly by A.I.D., acknowledged legitimacy of the child by registering their names as the parents.

While it may be too early to expect state legislatures to establish the legitimacy of an A.I.D. child when the husband executes his written consent to the process, it is not utopian to suggest that a variation of the Louisiana rule be adopted pending more enlightened legislation. As stated above, this rule provides that a child born out of wedlock may be legitimatized by positive action on the part of the father acknowledging the child to be his by listing his name as the father in the birth records. The variation suggested for an A.I.D. child would be for the mother's husband to make a similar declaration of paternity. This differs little from the estoppel rule when the husband lists his name as the father, but the advantage of such legislation would be to make the rule a positive one rather than a negative one, and to eliminate litigation with respect to the child's legitimacy.

The status of illegitimacy has its origins in property rights. Originally, no moral stigma attached to an illegitimate child. This stigma has been superimposed upon the original concept. The stigma is gradually disappearing, but what remains is the problem of an illegitimate child's right to inheritance. It may inherit from its mother, but not from its father, unless, after a hearing, an order of paternity has been entered.[28] If an A.I.D. child is to be held the child of the mother's husband, either through the use of the estoppel rule or through legislation along the lines of the Louisiana rule holding an A.I.D. child the legitimate child of the mother's husband if the A.I.D. process was performed with the husband's written consent, then the rules regarding the child's inheritance rights must conform to this new standard.

With respect to support of an A.I.D. child, in an unusual California case,[29] the wife had a child through artificial insemination with the husband's consent. He was named as the father in the birth certificate, although he denied knowledge of the contents of the certificate. However, he treated the boy as his son for about four years, until the couple separated. At the separation, the wife told the husband that she wanted no support for the boy and consented to a divorce, which the husband obtained. In the divorce decree, jurisdiction was retained "regarding the possible support obligation of plaintiff in regard to a minor child born to defendant." The decree did not refer to the child as being born "of the parties." Some time later, the mother required public assistance, which was supplied until she was able to resume work. The former husband had never paid for support of the child, although the district

---

28. N.Y. Estates, Powers and Trusts Law, § 4–1.2; Matter of Consolazio, 54 Misc. 2d 398, 282 N.Y.S. 2d 905 (1967).

29. People v. Sorensen, 63 Cal. Reptr. 462 (1967).

attorney had demanded it. The Municipal Court found the father guilty of violating § 270 of the California Penal Code, which places responsibility for support only upon the father, whether the child is legitimate or illegitimate. The burden of proof to establish the father's parenthood is upon the prosecution. Since it was not disputed that the mother's former husband was not the actual father, the prosecution sought to uphold the conviction on the theory of estoppel, namely, that he had treated the child as his own for four years. Apparently this theory was sought to be bolstered by § 230 of the California Civil Code, which provides for the adoption of an illegitimate child by the actual father's publicly acknowledging it as his own, with the consent of his wife, if he is married, and otherwise treating it as if it were a legitimate child.

In reversing the Municipal Court, the California Court of Appeal observed that § 230 was not applicable, since it was not the natural father who was involved, but the former husband of the mother, and held that a conviction could not be sustained upon an estoppel in order to prove an essential element of a crime.

The Supreme Court, however, reversed, and for the purpose of legitimatizing the child, held the husband to be the father. To stigmatize an artifically conceived child as illegitimate "serves no useful purpose." [30]

As for a recent and significant case of first impression, *In Matter of Anonymous,* Kings County, N.Y., 74 Misc. 2d (____), a husband was listed as the father of a child born of consensual AID. Subsequently, the wife was divorced and remarried, and her second husband sought to adopt the child. But the first husband refused his consent (see N.Y. Domestic Relations Law, Sec. 111), claiming he was "not the father." Permission was then sought to dispense with his consent. Surrogate Sobel dismissed the petition, holding that New York's strong policy in favor of legitimacy, absent persuasive evidence of the husband's sterility, required application of the presumption of legitimacy, with the first husband's consent required for adoption.

---

30. 437 P 2d 495, 498; see Smith, *Artificial Insemination: No Longer a Quagmire,* 3 A.B.A., Fam. L. Q. 1 (1969).

Part II

Guarantees for the Child

Irving Weissman

7

Guardianship:
Every Child's Right

We are a nation committed to governance by law, not men, but we tolerate uncontrolled authority over children. We are committed to respect the rights of the individual, but we tolerate constant violation of the rights of children. We are committed to making citizen participation effective in common affairs, but we tolerate ineffectiveness in the making of citizens.

These paradoxes root in an old problem in the relation between the child and his elders, on the one hand, and his state, on the other. They point up the fact that we have not yet achieved any satisfactory resolution of the basic questions involved:

Is the child a person with legal rights or merely a body subject to the whims and wishes of whoever may have possession?

If he is a person with legal rights, how is the child's body to be protected against unauthorized possession and control by others and how are his rights to be made effective for his everyday functioning?

The Legal Quandary

There is cruel irony in the contrast between the commitments to children in law and the practices followed by courts and community agencies dealing with children.

The law books of every state in the nation affirm the child's rights as a person and also acknowledge the responsibility of the

IRVING WEISSMAN, M.S.W., retired as professor of social work in the Graduate School of Social Work, Rutgers–The State University, New Brunswick, New Jersey. This article is reprinted with permission from *The Annals of the American Academy of Political and Social Science* 355 (1964): 134–39.

state for protecting the person and rights of the child. Two broad legal doctrines have evolved in law to serve this purpose.

The first of these doctrines imposes the legal status of minor on all children below an age varying from eighteen to twenty-one in the different states. This expresses an official presumption that persons so young are too immature physically, emotionally, intellectually, and socially to be expected to deal with their life situations themselves. Accordingly, the thinking is that "as a general rule, a minor child cannot select where he should live or how, or enter into litigation, or consent to medical or other professional care and services." [1]

The second protective doctrine complements the first by taking cognizance of the legal disabilities imposed upon the minor child. It supplies a legal remedy in the form of a guardian of the person of the child.[2] The guardian is vested with powers and duties to furnish the child responsible representation so that his personal rights can become functionally effective in his everyday life situations. Two major types of guardians are supplied by law: the natural guardian, who is the child's own parent(s) or adoptive parent(s), and the legal guardian.[3]

In the view of guardianship law, the legal guardian ranks second only to parental guardians in order of essentiality for the effective functioning and well-being of the child. This is the meaning to the requirement of presence or consent of a "parent or guardian" in transactions with a child. The law predicates two principles to be governing in the child's interpersonal relationships: (1) A legal guardian will be supplied the minor child whenever he is without proper guardianship from his parents so that the child's person and legal rights will be continuously in competent hands identified with his interests and welfare. (2) A judicial process will be used in establishing a child with a legal guardian so that

1. *Legislative Guides for the Termination of Parental Rights and Responsibilities and the Adoption of Children* (U.S. Children's Bureau Pub. No. 391; Washington, D.C., 1961), pp. 5–6.
2. Hereafter in this article the words "guardian" and "guardianship" will be used to refer only to the child's person. It should be noted that guardianship law extends the protection of the state to the incompetent adult as well as the minor child and does so in matters of property rights as well as personal rights.
3. A so-called *guardian ad litem* can be appointed by a court to represent the child in a specific court action.

the exercise of authority and control by the legal guardian over the person and rights of the child will always be accountable at law.[4]

There seems to be wide recognition of the beneficence of this body of law in assuring every child a responsible, competent, personal agent to protect and act for him during his minority. Yet, in the actual practice of the courts and social agencies working with children, this law is almost completely neglected.

Neglect by Courts

Some facts and reasons for this neglect have been brought to light by recent studies and reports.

Major findings of a study [5] which focused on the courts with jurisdiction to handle guardianship cases, commonly called probate courts, support these generalizations:

The need for guardianship is not being met. In communities which included nearly 1,350,000 minor children of whom 142,000 were estimated to be living apart from their parents, legal guardians were supplied for only 1,450 in the year of study.

The appointment of the legal guardian is perfunctory in manner. The courts generally accept the petition of the first person who files one, often do not see the child or proposed guardian personally, give no notice to persons who may have a legitimate

4. Little legal, judicial, or social research has been undertaken on this subject. A literature has emerged only in recent years. See the following in addition to specific citations elsewhere in this article: Sophonisba P. Breckenridge and Mary Stanton, "The Law of Guardian and Ward with Special Reference to the Children of Veterans," *Social Service Review,* Vol. 17 (September 1943); *Standards for Specialized Courts Dealing with Children* (Washington, D.C.: U.S. Children's Bureau, 1954); A. Delafield Smith, *The Right to Life* (Chapel Hill, N.C., 1955), pp. 112–52; Robert Emmett Clark, "Legal Aspects of Guardianship," Irving Weissman, "Social Aspects of Guardianship," Irene Liggett, "Community Aspects—What Guardianship Means to the Child," *The Child at Law,* 28th Ross Pediatric Research Conference, 1958, pp. 33–47; *Standard Family Court Act* (New York: National Probation and Parole Association, 1959); and "Symposium on Guardianship," *Iowa Law Review,* Vol. 45 (1960).

5. Irving Weissman and others, *Guardianship: A Way of Fulfilling Public Responsibility for Children* (U.S. Children's Bureau Publication No. 330; Washington D.C., 1949).

interest in the appointment, and, for the most part, leave actual arrangements to the attorney of the petitioner desiring to be named legal guardian.

The courts are poorly equipped for the job. These courts have diverse functions. Their attention centers primarily on constituting and administering guardianships over property, from which they derive fees. The judges have no special background for work with children. Their staffs do not include social workers nor is use made of community social agencies in investing and evaluating petitions for guardianship.

The guardianship is exercised without accountability at law. The courts generally maintain no contact with the legal guardian. No follow-up is made unless a petition for removal of the legal guardian is presented. No formal termination of the guardianship takes place. Often the guardianship lapses before the child has achieved majority age without the court knowing it.

The guardianship doctrine has not been adequately developed in the statutes. In contrast to extensive modernizing of provisions for administering property rights in estates, the statutory provisions for protecting the personal rights of children have undergone little modification over the years.[6]

An administrative type of guardianship has emerged. The enormously increasing numbers of children who become beneficiaries of veterans' and social security programs are often found to be, in the judgment of agency representatives, without competent parents who may receive and administer the payments to which the children

---

6. What seems to have happened is a fragmentation of the protective role of the state. New laws have been enacted creating new courts to deal with legal problems of children, conspicuously juvenile courts and family courts. New proceedings have been proliferated which demand court action on what has happened to children often as a consequence of improper guardianship—neglect, abuse, exploitation, nonsupport, getting in trouble with the law, running away, and so on. Of special interest in this connection are, first, that these new laws and new proceedings have not been reconciled with the law of guardianship and, indeed, are often contradictory and overlapping and, secondly, the retention in the law of many states of the doctrine of *in loco parentis,* which confers a sort of guardianship in fact upon persons who take children into their homes ostensibly to care for them.

are entitled. For these children, the agencies are increasingly designating so-called "representative payees" under authority of federal statutes. These payees are empowered to make such decisions as whether to invest the money for the child's future or use it for his current needs, and exactly how. There is no recourse to the courts to remove from parents and—or—legal guardians the power to make such decisions, where the funds involved are small, which inheres in their legal responsibilities.[7]

Social agencies feel an unsettling impact. Troublesome guardianship questions have arisen for community social agencies in connection with adoptions, placements in foster care, protective service, and handling of special funds which become available for children in care. Concern has arisen over the congruence of the professional and authority roles carried by agencies in serving children whose guardianship is unclear or indefinite.

Neglect by Social Agencies

A recent study based on state samples representing nearly 500,000 children served by public and voluntary agencies in the United States,[8] provides sad but striking evidence of confusion between the professional and authority roles assumed by agencies serving children whose guardianship is unclear or indefinite.

In this study, the "child in need of guardianship" was a principal diagnosis for 8 percent of children served by public agencies and 5 percent of children served by voluntary agencies. It ranked among the first three problems in 16 percent of children served by public agencies and 11 percent of children served by voluntary agencies.

Moreover, in the words of the report, the diagnosis presenting "the single, most important problem was neglect, abuse, or exploi-

---

7. A similar type of procedure has been adopted as a temporary measure by the Federal Bureau of Family Services as a means of improving the management and use of payments made under Aid to Families with Dependent Children (AFDC). The program limits the use of "protective payees" to a maximum of 5 percent of a state's AFDC cases for a period of one year. See Bureau of Family Services State Letter No. 634 (March 19, 1963).

8. Helen R. Jeter, *Children Problems and Services in Child Welfare Programs* (U.S. Children's Bureau Pub. No. 403; Washington, D.C., 1963).

tation by parents or others responsible for the child's care." [9]
For 36 percent of the children, this was the principal problem.
For 46 percent, it was among the first three problems.

The diagnosis "neglect, abuse, or exploitation of the child" is
explained as follows: [10]

> Whatever the exact situation, these are children for whom a
> parent, relative, or other older person responsible for the child's
> care had failed to provide a suitable home, not because of finan-
> cial need, but because of psychological incapacity or unwilling-
> ness to meet the situation. Many of the parents were surely
> mentally ill, some were alcoholic, others, as many schedules
> noted, were themselves too "immature" to make suitable homes
> for their children.

Despite the magnitude of children diagnosed to be in need of
guardianship and suffering from such consequences as neglect,
abuse, and exploitation, the report carries no classifications or statistics indicating the initiation of legal action with reference to the
guardianship of children served.

The report includes, however, three classifications of legal service provided children served.[11] The statistics show 3 percent or
fewer children receiving these services from public or voluntary
agencies. The categories included the investigation of independent
placements in adoption at the request of the court, investigations in
connection with other court services, such as divorce, and agency
petitions for award of legal custody of children from the court.
However, in relation to the last category, the report notes that, for
42 percent of children served by public agencies and 35 percent
of those served by voluntary agencies, a court had given legal
custody of the child to the reporting agency before the study was
undertaken.

Who were these children for whom the agencies asked legal
custody? The report describes them as follows: [12]

9. *Ibid.*, p. 17.

10. *Ibid.*, pp. 19–20.

11. In some states, such as New Jersey, the State Bureau of Children's
Services has statutory authority to petition for and assume the powers of
legal guardianship over children served. The Bureau is empowered to give
up the guardianship without returning the child to the court. On February
29, 1964 a total of 2,849 children were reported to be in agency guardianship. See *Report,* New Jersey Department of Institutions and Agencies,
Bureau of Research, March 18, 1964.

12. *Ibid.*, p. 148.

The highest percentages of children in the legal custody of public agencies were those whose parents had died. Of all the children in the study who had lost one or both parents by death, 48 percent of those served by public agencies and 25 percent by voluntary agencies were in the legal custody of the reporting agency. In the voluntary agencies, however, 60 percent of those whose parents were not married to each other were in legal custody.

What powers and duties does legal custody confer? A spelling out is furnished by the United States Children's Bureau,[13] which recommends that the term "legal custody" should be used uniformly in state laws to mean: [14]

a legal status created by court order embodying the following rights and responsibilities: the right to have physical possession of the child or youth; the right and the duty to protect, train and discipline him; the responsibility to provide the child with food, clothing, shelter, education and ordinary medical care; and the right to determine whether and with whom he shall live. . . .

Does an award of legal custody make legal guardianship unnecessary where a child has no parents living or where parental rights have been terminated? The rest of the above quotation provides the considered answer of experts: [15]

. . . *provided,* that these rights and responsibilities shall be exercised subject to the powers, rights, duties and responsibilities of the guardian of the person of the child or youth, and subject to any residual parental rights and responsibilities.

And what are these "powers, rights, duties and responsibilities of the guardian of the person" to which the exercise of legal custody must be subject? Another Children's Bureau legislative guide spells these out as follows: [16]

"Guardianship of the person" with respect to a minor means the

13. Frequently, state laws are vague or fail to provide any definition of the terms used in statutes. For some years, the U.S. Children's Bureau has been working with representatives from the legal, judicial, and social welfare fields on the drafting of suggested language and principles to be incorporated in state legislation relating to children. A number of states have made this basic start in clarifying, co-ordinating, and unifying their laws on children.

14. *Proposals for Drafting Principles and Suggested Language for Legislation on Public Child Welfare and Youth Services* (Washington, D.C.: U.S. Children's Bureau, 1957), p. 23.

15. *Ibid.,* pp. 23–24.

16. *Legislative Guides for the Termination of Parental Rights and Responsibilities and the Adoption of Children, op. cit.,* pp. 2–3.

duty and authority to make important decisions in matters having a permanent effect on his life and development and to be concerned about his general welfare. It includes but is not necessarily limited either in number or kind to: the authority to consent to marriage, to enlistment in the armed forces of the United States, and to major medical, psychiatric and surgical treatment; to represent the minor in legal actions; and to make other decisions concerning the child of substantial legal significance; the authority and duty of reasonable visitation, except to the extent that such right of visitation has been limited by court order; the right and responsibility of legal custody except where legal custody has been vested in another individual or in an authorized social agency; where the parent-child relationship has been terminated by judicial decree with respect to the parents, or only living parent, or when there is no living parent, the authority to consent to the adoption of the child and to make any other decision concerning the child which the child's parents could make.

In short, an award of guardianship carries with it greater rights and responsibilities than an award of legal custody. The child needs a legal guardian to safeguard his rights while he is in an authority relationship with an agency vested with legal custody and in a professional relationship with those serving him. The Bureau takes the logical position [17] that agencies serving children should be given the duty to petition for the appointment of a legal guardian of the child when there are grounds for belief that the natural or adoptive parents are not in a position to exercise their guardianship functions effectively. It recommends, however, that officers or employees of the agency vested with legal custody should not themselves become legal guardians, lest there be conflict between the official duties they carry and the personal loyalty they must give the child they are serving as guardian.

Implications

I believe the implications of this defining language and these precisely drawn distinctions between terms of child law are obvious for the improvement of the law, the judicial process, the welfare services for children: No child should be without guardianship at any

17. *Proposals for Drafting Principles and Suggested Language for Legislation on Child Welfare and Youth Services, op. cit.,* pp. 42–43.

time. The law must be modified, correlated, and unified to reflect this basic commitment to children already advanced by the doctrines of minority and guardianship. Court and agency objectives, policies, and procedures must be brought into harmony with this concept so that practices might reflect active concern with the child's legal rights as a member of a democratic society.

Eric Gordon Andell

8
A Minor Has an Absolute Right to Sue His Parent for a Negligent Tort

Plaintiff, a two-year-old child, was burned by hot ashes which were left adjacent to a barbecue pit in a city park. The plaintiff sued the City and County of Honolulu for negligence. The city counterclaimed against the parents of the child for contribution pursuant to the Uniform Contribution Among Joint Tortfeasors Act,[1] alleging that the parents' negligence was either the sole or contributing cause of the plaintiff's injuries. The lower court dismissed the counterclaim, but granted leave to the City and County of Honolulu to appeal to the Supreme Court of Hawaii for a decision on whether a parent could be joined as a joint tortfeasor in an action brought by the child. On appeal to the Supreme Court of Hawaii, *held,* reversed as to dismissal of the counterclaim. Contribution under the Uniform Contribution Among Joint Tortfeasors Act depends upon whether the plaintiff child can enforce liability against his parents. In Hawaii, a child can enforce liability against his parents. *Peterson v. City and County of Honolulu,* 462 P.2d 1007 (Hawaii 1970).

In the United States, three State supreme court cases established the parent-child immunity rule as American common law.[2] In 1891

ERIC GORDON ANDELL, J.D., a practicing attorney, is a partner in the firm of Andell & Wayne, Houston, Texas. This article is reprinted with permission from the *Houston Law Review* 8 (1970): 183–89.

1. HAWAII REV. STAT. § 663–11 (1968) states:
For the purpose of this part the term "joint tortfeasors" means two or more persons jointly or severally liable in tort for the same injury to person or property, whether or not judgment has been recovered against all or some of them.
2. The parent-child immunity rule does not appear to be rooted in the English common law. The common law recognized an action between parent and child for breach of contract, and also a suit in tort for injuries to property. McCurdy, *Torts Between Persons in Domestic Relation,* 43 HARV. L. REV. 1030, 1057 (1930).

the Supreme Court of Mississippi in *Hewellette v. George*[3] ruled that a minor child cannot sue his parent for an action sounding in tort. The *Hewellette* court, citing no prior authority for such a rule, denied a daughter recovery against her mother for wrongfully detaining her in an asylum.[4] The court felt a public policy respecting the peace of the families composing society and, in general, the best interests of society barred a minor child from suing for personal injuries sustained at the hands of the parent.[5] After the *Hewellette* decision, the Tennessee Supreme Court in *McKelvey v. McKelvey*[6] denied a child recovery against her father for criminally assaulting her. Similarly, the Washington Supreme Court in *Roller v. Roller*[7] denied a suit by a daughter against her father for raping her.

State courts pursuing the immunity rule have advanced several reasons to justify their position. Those most often cited include the assurance of domestic tranquility;[8] the right of the parent to discipline and control his child;[9] the danger of fraud and collusion between parent and child;[10] and, the danger of draining family funds in favor of one child.[11]

The immunity rule generally has not been adopted without strong criticism. Vigorous dissenting opinions appeared in some cases,[12] and in others exceptions to the rule were made.[13] The California Supreme Court, which originally applied the immunity doctrine in

---

3. 68 Miss. 703, 9 So. 885 (1891).

4. *Id.* Most States today allow a minor to enforce both his contractual and property rights against his parents. For a collection of authorities on this point see Comment, *Child v. Parent: Erosion Of The Immunity Rule,* 19 HASTINGS L. J. 201, 203 nn.14, 15 (1967).

5. 9 So. at 887.

6. 111 Tenn. 338, 77 S.W. 664 (1903).

7. 37 Wash. 242, 79 P. 788 (1905).

8. *E.g.,* Hewellette v. George, 68 Miss. 703, 9 So. 885, 887 (1891); Reingold v. Reingold, 115 N.J.L. 532, 181 A. 153, 155 (Ct. Err. & App. 1935).

9. *E.g.,* Barlow v. Iblings, 156 N.W.2d 105, 107–08 (Iowa 1968); Chaffin v. Chaffin, 239 Ore. 374, 397 P.2d 771, 774 (1964).

10. *E.g.,* Luster v. Luster, 299 Mass. 480, 13 N.E.2d 438, 440 (1938).

11. *E.g.,* Roller v. Roller, 37 Wash. 242, 79 P. 788, 789 (1905).

12. *E.g.,* Hastings v. Hastings, 33 N.J. 247, 163 A.2d 147, 151 (1960) (Jacobs, J., dissenting); Wick v. Wick, 192 Wis. 260, 212 N.W. 787, 788 (1927) (Crownhart, J., dissenting).

13. *E.g.,* Emery v. Emery, 45 Cal.2d 421, 289 P.2d 218, 223 (1955); Dunlap v. Dunlap, 84 N.H. 352, 150 A. 905, 910 (1930); Borst v. Borst, 41 Wash.2d 642, 251 P.2d 149, 156 (1952).

its entirety, began to allow recovery to the child when the parent's act was willful or malicious.[14] The rationale for this exception was succinctly stated by Justice Traynor:

> While it may seem repugnant to allow a minor to sue his parent, we think it more repugnant to leave a minor child without redress for the damage he has suffered by reason of his parent's willful or malicious misconduct.[15]

Similarly, the Supreme Court of Washington refused to apply the immunity doctrine when the court felt that willful or wanton behavior on the part of the parent constituted an abandonment of the normal parent-child relationship.[16]

Numerous State courts have decided that parent-child immunity expired when, at the time of the suit, the parent or child was dead.[17] These courts reasoned that the child or his representative could then maintain a suit in tort against the estate of the deceased parent since none of the social or legal justifications for the rule still were applicable.[18]

Another trend developed which allowed recovery to a child when the injury occurred within the scope of the parent's business or vocation.[19] In 1930 the Supreme Court of New Hampshire in *Dunlap v. Dunlap*[20] for the first time gave redress to a child for a tort committed by a parent for negligence in his business. The child, employed by his father for the summer months, was injured when the staging on which he was working collapsed. The court

14. Emery v. Emery, 45 Cal.2d 421, 289 P.2d 218, 224 (1955).
15. *Id.*
16. "[A] parent who takes a child in an automobile with him and drives it while he is intoxicated is temporarily abdicating his parental responsibilities and is not entitled to the immunity. . . ." Hoffman v. Tracy, 67 Wash.2d 31, 406 P.2d 323, 327 (1965); *accord,* Cowgill v. Boock, 189 Ore. 282, 218 P.2d 445, 453 (1950).
17. For a collection of authorities on this point see Comment, *Child v. Parent: Erosion Of The Immunity Rule,* 19 HASTINGS L. J. 201, 214 n.102 (1967).
18. *E.g.,* Palesey v. Tepper, 71 N.J. Super. 294, 176 A.2d 818, 819 (1962). *Contra,* Gunn v. Rollings, 250 S.C. 302, 157 S.E.2d 590 (1967). The court in *Gunn* said that if the child has no right to sue his living parent for the parent's negligence, he has no right to maintain an action against the parent's estate. *Id.* at 592–93.
19. *E.g.,* Signs v. Signs, 156 Ohio St. 566, 103 N.E.2d 743, 748–49 (1952); Dunlap v. Dunlap, 84 N.H. 352, 150 A. 905, 911 (1930). *Contra,* Barlow v. Iblings, 156 N.W.2d 105, 112–13 (Iowa 1968).
20. 84 N.H. 352, 150 A. 905 (1930).

reasoned that by employing his son, the father had surrendered his parental control.[21] The court also emphasized that the father had liability insurance and that such insurance removed any danger of family discord,[22] for in reality the child was suing the insurance company.[23]

Following *Dunlap,* the Virginia Supreme Court of Appeals, in *Worrell v. Worrell,*[24] denied immunity to the parent when the daughter, a passenger on the bus her father owned, was injured due to the negligence of the driver. The *Worrell* court cited *Dunlap* with favor and concluded that the presence of liability insurance covering a parent in his business or vocational capacity removed all reasons for immunity.[25]

In *Signs v. Signs*[26] a child was injured when a gasoline pump caught fire on the business premise of the father's partnership. The court determined that the child could sue since the parent was engaged in business, a non-parental function, at the time of the injury.[27]

Widespread liability insurance and the increasing frequency of negligent automobile collisions induced some State courts to hold parents liable to their children for ordinary negligence.[28] In 1963 the Supreme Court of Wisconsin in *Goller v. White*[29] allowed a

21. *Id.* at 911.
22. *Id.* at 913.
23. *Id.* at 915.
24. 174 Va. 11, 4 S.E.2d 343 (1939); *accord,* Lusk v. Lusk, 113 W. Va. 17, 166 S.E. 538 (1932) (Daughter was injured while riding on a school bus owned by her father).
25. 4 S.E.2d at 350.
26. 156 Ohio St. 566, 103 N.E.2d 743 (1952).
27. *Id.* at 749–49; *accord,* Trevarton v. Trevarton, 151 Colo. 418, 378 P.2d 640 (1963) (Recovery allowed when injury to child is not connected with any parental duty). *Contra,* Borst v. Borst, 41 Wash.2d 642, 251 P.2d 149 (1952) (Immunity disappears while dealing with child in a nonparental transaction).
28. Hebel v. Hebel, 435 P.2d 8, 15 (Alas. 1967); Briere v. Briere, 107 N.H. 432, 224 A.2d 588, 590 (1966); Goller v. White, 20 Wis.2d 402, 122 N.W.2d 193, 197 (1963). *Contra,* Bulloch v. Bulloch, 45 Ga. App. 1, 163 S.E. 708, 712 (Ct. App. 1932) (The insurer cannot be liable when the insured parent is not); Downs v. Poulin, 216 A.2d 29, 33 (Me. Sup. Jud. Ct. 1966) (The existence of liability insurance should not create a cause of action where none existed before); Hastings v. Hastings, 33 N.J. 247, 163 A.2d 147, 150 (1960) (The presence of insurance makes the opportunity of fraud greater between the parent and child, and the insurer cannot adequately protect himself).
29. 20 Wis.2d 402, 122 N.W.2d 193 (1963).

child to sue for injuries suffered due to the negligent driving of his parent. The court felt that the prevalence of liability insurance was a factor to consider when deciding whether to abrogate parental immunity in negligence actions.[30] In 1966 the Supreme Court of New Hampshire reached the same conclusion, reiterating that the availability of insurance cannot be ignored when considering the child's right to sue.[31] In 1967 the Alaska Supreme Court, though clearly limiting its decision to the facts before the court, allowed a minor child to sue for injuries sustained due to the negligent driving of the insured parent.[32]

The current trend is for States to abolish the immunity rule. Both Minnesota and Wisconsin abrogated the immunity doctrine with two exceptions: (1) Where the alleged negligent act involves an exercise of parental authority over the child, and (2) where the alleged negligent act involves an exercise of ordinary parental discretion with respect to the provision of necessities.[33]

In 1966 the New Hampshire Supreme Court in *Briere v. Briere* [34] abolished parental immunity for torts. Although the court did not state that insurance was a necessity, the court stressed that the prevalence of insurance should not be ignored in determining whether an individual has the right to sue.[35]

In *Gelbman v. Gelbman*,[36] the New York Court of Appeals held that a parent could sue his child for negligent operation of a motor vehicle. The court in *Gelbman* first acknowledged that the immunity doctrine was the law of the State.[37] Then it noted the exceptions that New York had made previously and concluded that such exceptions did not support the immunity rule but attested to its primitive nature.[38] The court overruled its earlier decisions and eliminated the immunity role. While in this case a parent was suing a child, the court expressly overruled all previous New York decisions which had prohibited a child from suing a parent.[39]

30. *Id.* at 197.
31. Briere v. Briere, 107 N.H. 432, 224 A.2d 588, 590 (1966).
32. Hebel v. Hebel, 435 P.2d 8, 15 (Alas. 1967).
33. Silesky v. Kelman, 281 Minn. 431, 161 N.W.2d 631, 636 (1968); Goller v. White, 20 Wis.2d 402, 122 N.W.2d 193, 198 (1963).
34. 107 N.H. 432, 224 A.2d 588 (1966) (automobile accident).
35. *Id.* at 590.
36. 23 N.Y.2d 434, 245 N.E.2d 192, 297 N.Y.S.2d 529 (1969).
37. 245 N.E.2d at 192–93.
38. *Id.* at 193.
39. *Id.*

Subsequently, two New York Supreme Court cases allowed children to sue their parents.[40] Both courts relied on *Gelbman,* nothing that *Gelbman* had completely abolished the parent-child immunity rule in New York.[41] The courts concluded that the right of the child to sue his parent in tort was an absolute right. One court specifically recognized that this right is *not dependent on the presence of insurance.*[42]

The first instance in which a Hawaii Court considered intra-family immunity was in *Tamashiro v. DeGama.*[43] The *Tamashiro* court allowed parents to sue their unemancipated child, joined as a third party defendant, for the negligent operation of a motor vehicle. The court stated that when a parent is injured by the acts of his child, family harmony is already disrupted and there is no reason not to allow recovery.[44] The court also stressed that where there is insurance coverage, intra-family discord is reduced since the true defendant in such cases is the insurer.[45] Furthermore, the court asserted that while collusion is a possible consequence of allowing suits between parent and child, the judicial system is ade-quate to discover collusion when it occurs.[46]

Later that year, the Hawaii Court extended *Tamashiro* in *Peter-sen v. City and County of Honolulu.*[47] *Petersen* held that a child can enforce liability against his parents, regardless of the presence or absence of insurance.[48] The *Petersen* court, noting its decision in *Tamashiro,* reasoned that if a parent can sue his child, the child should be allowed to sue his parents.[49] The court further concluded

40. D'Ambrosio v. D'Ambrosio, 60 Misc.2d 886, 304 N.Y.S.2d 154, 156 (Sup. Ct. 1969) (Child injured in automobile collision); Howell v. Howell, 60 Misc.2d 871, 304 N.Y.S.2d 156, 158 (Sup. Ct. 1969) (Child riding in automobile injured by father's negligence).

41. Cases cited note 40 *supra.*

42. Howell v. Howell, 60 Misc.2d 871, 304 N.Y.2d 156, 158 (Sup. Ct. 1969).

43. 51 Hawaii 74, 450 P.2d 998 (1969). *But see* Scruggs v. Meridith, 135 F. Supp. 376 (D.C. Hawaii 1955). The court in *Scruggs* stated that the territorial courts had not decided the question whether a child could sue a parent in tort, but that in their opinion the better rule was not to allow an unemancipated minor to sue his parents for a tort sounding in mere negli-gence. *Id.* at 377.

44. 450 P.2d at 1001.

45. *Id.*

46. *Id.* at 1001–02.

47. 462 P.2d 1007 (Hawaii 1970).

48. *Id.* at 1008.

49. *Id.*

that "minor children are entitled to the same redress for wrongs done them as are any other persons." [50]

States following the immunity doctrine view domestic tranquility as the main policy factor in not permitting a child to sue his parent.[51] The *Petersen* court dismisses this policy consideration, contending that once harm has come to the child, harm to the family relationship has already occurred and the prohibition of suits will not aid in restoring family harmony.[52]

This contention presupposes that the harm caused to the child by the negligence of his parent automatically results in family discord. This assumption is questionable, especially in light of the facts in this case. In *Petersen* it was the parents' negligence in the supervision of their two-year-old child that allegedly contributed to the child's harm. Arguably, no family discord resulted under these circumstances. Consequently, if there is no family discord, the question remaining is whether the lawsuit itself will create discord. In *Petersen* the court was not faced with this question because the child was not suing his parent. The Court fails to consider the situation in which little or no family discord is caused by the acts of the parent, but where the presence of a lawsuit might cause substantial family friction. Other courts, while allowing recovery in an increasing number of cases, still recognize that the immunity doctrine is desirable when its application prevents family discord.[53]

The *Petersen* court also stated that "parent-child negligence suits will be allowed in Hawaii regardless of the presence or absence of insurance coverage." [54] This position is clearly a breakaway from *Tamashiro,* where insurance, though not expressly the basis for the holding, was emphasized.[55] New York is the only other jurisdiction stating that the right to sue the parent in tort is not dependent on the presence of insurance. However, the New York cases which eliminate the immunity doctrine all involve automobile accidents and in New York automobile insurance is *compulsory,* thereby eliminating the necessity for the immunity rule.

50. *Id.* at 1009.
51. Cases cited note 8 *supra.*
52. 462 P.2d at 1009.
53. *E.g.,* Silesky v. Kelman, 281 Minn. 431, 161 N.W.2d 631, 636 (1968); Dunlap v. Dunlap, 84 N.H. 352, 150 A. 905, 909–10 (1930); Goller v. White, 20 Wis.2d 402, 122 N.W.2d 193, 197 (1963).
54. 462 P.2d at 1008.
55. Tamashiro v. DeGama, 51 Hawaii 74, 450 P.2d 998, 1001 (1969).

The presence of insurance is the major contributing factor in other jurisdictions which have either abrogated [56] or modified [57] the immunity rule. With the presence of insurance, the suit in reality is against the insurer, which minimizes family discord arising from the suit. Therefore, the presence of insurance isolates the parent from financial burden and protects the family funds from being drained in favor of one child. As a result of the *Petersen* holding, financial hardship might befall an uninsured parent involved in negligent torts other than or including automobile accidents.[58]

The Hawaii Supreme Court has adopted the rule that a child who is injured by the negligence of his parent has the absolute right to bring suit.[59] It is submitted that the court did not adequately recognize that there may be times when the allowance of a suit against the parent might cause substantial family friction and financial burden. In the instant case the court was safe in allowing contribution because not only was there minimal friction resulting from the acts of the parent but there was little potential friction from the counterclaim. Rather than completely rejecting the immunity doctrine, the court might have allowed the counterclaim on grounds that no inter-family friction was likely in a suit by a third party against the parent. Such a decision still would have allowed recovery in *Petersen,* while retaining the flexibility to deny an intra-family suit resulting in substantial disruption to the home.

56. *E.g.,* Briere v. Briere, 107 N.H. 432, 224 A.2d 588 (1966).
57. *E.g.,* Worrell v. Worrell, 174 Va. 11, 4 S.E.2d 343 (1939).
58. In all other jurisdictions that have abolished the immunity doctrine, the cases have involved moving vehicle accidents. *E.g.,* Gelbman v. Gelbman, 23 N.Y.2d 434, 245 N.E.2d 192, 297 N.Y.S.2d 529 (1969).
59. 450 P.2d at 1008. In *Petersen,* the court reasoned that "whether contribution may be had from a person depends upon whether the original plaintiff could have enforced liability against him, had he chosen to do so." *Id.,* citing Tamashiro v. DeGama, 51 Hawaii 74, 450 P.2d 998 (1969). Consequently, the court seemed to feel that it was impossible to allow the defendant contribution as against the child's parents unless they established an absolute rule allowing the child to sue the parent.

E. Thomas Cox

9
Indigent Children and Fiscal Clearing

It is the policy of the law to protect the interests of minor children incapable of looking after their own affairs.[1] Where any indigent child,[2] who is cared for at state expense, has legally responsible relatives or friends in another state willing to provide a home for the child even though they are financially unable to support him, it will be in the child's best interests that he be placed with them.[3] However, the administrative procedures and policies of state welfare departments often retard or prohibit such transfers through the use of fiscal clearing [4] when the financial burden of supporting the indigent child threatens to shift to the receiving state.[5] Realiz-

E. THOMAS COX, J.D., a practicing attorney, is an associate in the firm of Booth, Pritchard & Dudley, Fairfax, Virginia. This article is reprinted with permission from the *Washington and Lee Law Review* 28(1971):423–33.

1. *See, e.g., In re* Guardianship of Carlon's Estate, 43 Cal. App. 2d 204, 110 P.2d 488 (1951); *In re* Anderson's Estate, 20 Ill. App. 2d 305, 155 N.E.2d 839 (1959); Zoski v. Gaines, 271 Mich. 1, 260 N.W. 99 (1935); Fiorella v. Fiorella, 241 Mo. App. 180, 240 S.W.2d 147 (1951); Pieri v. Nebbia, 178 Misc. 388, 34 N.Y.S.2d 317 (1942); Tart v. Register, 257 N.C. 161, 125 S.E.2d 754 (1962). This policy is based on the theory that the state, as *parens patriae* should protect the child against those who might take advantage of him.

2. The term "indigent" is commonly used to refer to one's financial ability, and ordinarily indicates one who is without means of comfortable subsistence. Weeks v. Mansfield, 84 Conn. 544, 80 A. 784 (1911). *See also* note 49 *infra.*

3. If the child's interest will be better promoted by awarding the custody to a non-resident the court will not hesitate to do so because of the residence of the applicant. *See* note 1 *supra.*

4. "Fiscal clearing" is the term specifically applied by Judge Justine Polier of the New York Family Court to the financial processing involved in the transfer of indigent children. *See In re* Paul and Mark, 64 Misc. 2d 382, 315 N.Y.S.2d 12 (1970).

5. The term "receiving state" refers to that state to which the indigent child is being sent and the term "custodial state" denotes the state in whose custody the child remains pending fiscal clearing.

ing that the financial burden of supporting the child would now fall upon them, some receiving states, before admitting the indigent child, require the custodial state to agree to retain financial responsibility.[6]

Fiscal clearing has its historical source in the English law of public assistance which was known as the Elizabethan Act of 1601 For the Relief of the Poor.[7] This Act established the principle of local responsibility for indigents as taxation was imposed upon the parishes for the public support of local indigent adults and children.[8] Under this public assistance policy special attention was given to the vocational training of indigent children. The imposition of local responsibility resulted, however, in attempts to reduce this relief burden.[9]

In 1662 a statute was passed placing "strangers" in a class unentitled to relief.[10] In their efforts to combat vagrancy and mendicancy the English localities developed rules regarding the settlement and removal of potential paupers. Local jurisdictions passed laws which called for the forced removal of paupers from the locality if they had not lived in the parish for the time required

6. Many states require not only that the consent of the state welfare board be obtained before any dependent child be brought into the state, but a bond must be furnished to insure that the child will not become a public charge. *See, e.g.,* IND. ANN. STAT. §§ 52-509 to -510 (1964); MASS. ANN. LAWS ch. 119, § 36 (1965). Other states avoid the indemnity bond arrangement by merely requiring the custodial state to sign a guarantee to retain welfare responsibility. *See* MICH. STAT. ANN. § 16.414(d) (Repl. Vol. 1968). Fiscal clearing will be the term used throughout to refer to such guaranty and indemnity procedures.

7. 43 *Elizabeth* ch. 2 (1601).

8. *See* Reisenfeld, *The Formative Era of American Public Assistance Law,* 43 CAL. L. REV. 175, 178 (1955) (hereinafter cited as *Reisenfeld*).

9. *Id.* at 181.

10. Such an effort came with a 1662 statute: "That it shall and may be lawful, upon complaint made by the churchwardens or overseers of the poor of any parish, to any justice of peace, within forty days after any such person or persons coming so to settle as aforesaid, in any tenement under the yearly value of ten pounds, for any two justices of the peace, whereof one to be . . . of the division where any person or persons that are likely to be chargeable to the parish shall come to inhabit, by their warrant to remove and convey such person or persons to such parish where he or they were last legally settled. . . ." Act of 1662, 13 & 14, Car. II c. 12, as quoted in *Reisenfeld* at 181–82. This statute provided for the forced removal of "strangers" who were really unwanted indigents. *See also* Mandelker, *Exclusion and Removal Legislation,* 1956 WIS. L. REV. 57, 58; Note, *Depression Migrants and the States,* 53 HARV. L. REV. 1031, 1032 (1940).

by statute.[11] Colonists transplanted similar laws to America during the seventeenth century.[12]

Due to the increase in population and economic development of the colonies during the American eighteenth century, new methods were devised to accommodate welfare recipients.[13] The erection of local almshouses for children, the tightening of settlement laws, and the further development of provisions for the removal of unsettled paupers are examples.[14] States enacted exclusion and removal statutes based on the English statutory and judicial practice and these did receive some court support.[15] In *New York v. Miln*,[16] the Supreme Court dealt with a New York statute which imposed upon the master of a vessel the obligation to report to the authorities the last legal settlement, age and occupation of every passenger brought into the port of New York from another state or country. The Court upheld the statute as

> competent and as necessary for a State to provide precautionary measures against the moral pestilence of paupers, vagabonds, and possibly convicts, as it is to guard against the physical

11. *Reisenfeld* at 192–200.

12. The colonies authorized the public support of indigent children; provided for their education; farmed out to foster homes the children of indigent parents; held that the home residence of the child was liable for all support expenses given the child by another residence; sent poor children to work in the public workhouses; and provided for the apprenticeship of poor children. *Id.*

13. *Id.* at 223.

14. *Id.* at 223–24.

15. The statute 1662 also provided for the compulsory removal to his place of residence of any person "likely to become chargeable." Thus evolved the practice of removal. This statute allows relief administrators to transport to their place of settlement persons who were ineligible for relief as well as prohibited persons thought to be potential relief recipients from acquiring a settlement. Mandelker, *Exclusion and Removal Legislation,* 1956 Wis. L. Rev. 57, 58. In regards to exclusion laws, the state imposed civil and criminal liability upon anyone who brought a poor person into a locality with knowledge or intent that the individual will become a public charge. *Id.* For a discussion of the constitutionality of exclusion legislation, see text accompanying notes 33–38 *infra*.

16. New York v. Miln, 36 U.S. (11 Pet.) 357 (1837). A few convictions under laws against bringing indigents into a state have been upheld by state courts. *See* State v. Cornish, 66 N.H. 329, 21 A. 180 (1890); Winfield v. Mapes, 4 Denio 571 (N.Y. 1847). There were Supreme Court dicta that the state could defend against indigents which were brought in and likely to become public charges. *See* Passenger Cases, 48 U.S. (7 How.) 140, 155 (Wayne, J., concurring), 190–91 (Grier, J. concurring), 193–94 (Taney, J. dissenting) (1848); Prigg v. Pennsylvania, 41 U.S. (16 Pet.) 417, 440 (1842).

pestilence which may arise from unsound and infectious articles imported. . . .[17]

By 1940, local responsibility for the poor, indigent exclusion procedures and settlement were being determined by statute.[18]

To these restrictions upon freedom of movement some states added more legislation which concerned the interstate travel of children, especially the indigent.[19] The Uniform Transfer of Dependents Act was approved in 1935 by the National Conference of Commissioners on Uniform State Laws and the American Bar Association.[20] The Act has been adopted by eleven states [21] and authorizes the state welfare agency to enter into reciprocal agreements with the custodial state relating to the acceptance, transfer, and support of the indigent child. It is also provided that no state shall be committed to the support of persons who were ineligible in the opinion of the receiving state.[22]

The idea of reciprocal agreements [23] has not been ignored by

17. 36 U.S. at 369.

18. *See* Note, *Depression Migrants and the States,* 53 HARV. L. REV. 1031, 1033 (1940). As of 1940, thirty-eight states required a resident to live in the jurisdiction one year before he was eligible for public assistance; twenty-eight states provided that settlement could be lost by non-residence during a period equal to or shorter than that required to gain one. Regarding the development of exclusion statutes, by 1940 twenty-seven states made it a misdemeanor to bring an indigent into the state or imposed a fine for so doing. Some states even provided that non-settled indigents could be forcibly removed. *Id.* at 1033-34.

19. *In re* Higgins, 46 Misc. 233, 259 N.Y.S.2d 874, 878 (Family Ct. 1965).

20. UNIFORM LAWS ANN. 9C at 216 (1935).

21. The 11 states are California, Colorado, Connecticut, Delaware, Louisiana, Maine, Minnesota, North Dakota, Pennsylvania, South Dakota and Virginia. CAL. WELF. & INST'NS CODE §§ 18400–18401 (West Ann. 1966); COLO. REV. STAT. ANN. §§ 119-5-1 to -5-4 (1963); CONN. GEN. STAT. ANN. § 17-293 (1958); DEL. CODE ANN. tit. 31, § 119 (1953); LA. REV. STAT. ANN. §§ 46:01–02 (1950); ME. REV. STAT. ANN. tit. 22 § 4191 (1964); MINN. STAT. ANN. §§ 261.25, 261.251 (1959); N.D. CENT. CODE § 50-06-11 to -06-12 (1960); PA. STAT. tit. 62 § 209 (1968); S.D. CODE § 28-16-7 (1967); VA. CODE ANN. § 63.1–99 (Repl. Vol. 1968).

22. *Id.*

23. The prefatory note to this Act gives a reading of the purpose or idea behind the Act: "In recent years there has been a great change of sentiment . . . upon which the transfer of public dependents by the states should be effected, and experience has demonstrated the wisdom of having legislation passed which will enable each state to confer upon its public welfare officials the right to enter into reciprocal agreements for the interchange of dependents, rather than in attempting to have uniform settlement laws." UNIFORM LAWS ANN. 9C at 218–19.

other states. New York is one of six states that has enacted a statute providing for interstate compacts on the placement of children.[24] The statute provides that the custodial agency retains financial responsibility for the child unless the receiving state agrees to provide welfare assistance for the indigent child. Based on the statutory provisions, New York can avoid having to support the child.[25] In addition to these compacts some states have enacted separate statutes which affect the mobility of children in need of placement. For example, Michigan states that it is a misdemeanor for a county agent to bring about the transportation of an indigent child into Michigan without the welfare district's official approval.[26] Arkansas has provided that the Arkansas State Department shall administer all child welfare activities including the regulation and importation of indigent children.[27] If these statutes, compacts, and uniform acts are considered along with the state statutes requiring indemnification as to the child's public liability,[28] a wide network of restrictions upon the child's placement in a receiving state is apparent.

In 1941, the United States Supreme Court in *Edwards v. California* [29] held unconstitutional a California exclusion statute [30] which made it a crime to knowingly bring a poor person into the state. This decision, which forced the first breach in the statutes based on the English Poor Laws,[31] employed the commerce clause as a vehicle to consider the state's interference with interstate commerce.[32] The Court determined that the exclusion statute burdened

24. N.Y. SOCIAL SERVICES LAW 374a (McKinney 1966).

25. The other five states that have complementary legislation are Kentucky, Maine, New Hampshire, North Dakota, and Wyoming. *See* KY. REV. STAT. ANN. § 199.341 (1969); ME. REV. STAT. ANN. tit. 22, §§ 4191–4200 (1964); N.H. REV. STAT. ANN. §§ 170-A:1 to -A:6 (Supp. 1970); N.D. CENT. CODE § 14-13-01 to -13-08 (Supp. 1969); WYO. STAT. §§ 14-52.1 to -52.9 (1957).

26. MICH. STAT. ANN. § 16.450(1) (Rev. Vol. 1968).

27. ARK. STAT. ANN. § 83-109 (Repl. Vol. 1960).

28. *See* note 6 *supra*.

29. 314 U.S. 160 (1941).

30. *See* notes 15 and 18 *supra*.

31. Mandelker, *Exclusion and Removal Legislation*, 1956 WIS. L. REV. 57.

32. 314 U.S. 174, 176. The Court referred to *Milk Control Board v. Eisenberg Farm Products,* which explained the commerce clause: "This court has repeatedly declared that the grant [commerce clause] established the immunity of interstate commerce from the control of the States respecting all those subjects embraced within the grant which are of such a nature as to demand that, if regulated at all, their regulation must be prescribed by a single authority." 306 U.S. 346, 351 (1939).

the indigent citizen's constitutional right of interstate travel which was found not to admit of diverse treatment merely because paupers were involved.[33]

In 1969, the Court in *Shapiro v. Thompson*[34] extended its holding in *Edwards* and held that residency requirements for state welfare recipients were unconstitutional. *Shapiro* involved statutory provisions[35] which denied welfare assistance to residents of the state who had not been present within the jurisdiction for at least one year immediately preceding their application for such assistance. The Court held that, absent a compelling state interest, the statutory provisions violated the equal protection clause of the fourteenth amendment since the classification of residency touched upon the fundamental constitutional right of interstate travel.[36] The Court concluded that the statutory purpose of inhibiting the migration by needy people into the state is constitutionally impermissible.

Though the Court has yet to rule on whether the receiving state can require the sending state to retain financial responsibility, *Edwards* and *Shapiro* have served as a basis upon which the Family Court of New York, in two cases, extended the law by ruling fiscal clearing practices to be unconstitutional.[37] In the first of these cases, *In re Higgins,*[38] a family court judge was presented with a demand by Michigan authorities that New York sign a guarantee[39] promising the three-year-old child would not become a public charge in Michigan. Michigan deemed this necessary in order to validate a private arrangement that had been made for the child

33. 314 U.S. at 175–77. Paupers were held to be entitled to the same rights as any other United States citizen.

34. 394 U.S. 618 (1969).

35. Connecticut and Pennsylvania and the District of Columbia statutes were involved.

36. 394 U.S. at 638. According to the Court if a migrant had to operate under such a statute he would be greatly inhibited in his interstate freedom of travel. "An indigent who desires to migrate, resettle, find a new job, and start a new life will doubtless hesitate if he knows that he must risk making the move without the possibility of falling back on state welfare assistance during his first year of residence, when his need may be most acute." *Id.* at 629.

37. *In re* Paul and Mark, 64 Misc. 2d 466, 315 N.Y.S.2d 12 (Family Ct. 1970); *In re* Higgins, 46 Misc. 2d 233, 259 N.Y.S.2d 874 (Family Ct. 1965).

38. 46 Misc. 2d 233, 259 N.Y.S.2d 874 (Family Ct. 1965).

39. *See* MICH. STATS. ANN. § 16.414(d) (Repl. Vol. 1968).

to live with his maternal aunt in Michigan.[40] The mother, who was living in New York, died while the father was in prison. The New York court decided it did not have the power to comply with this requirement and that the demand for such an agreement deprived the child of her constitutional right to freedom of travel. The court analogized the Michigan fiscal clearing demand to the exclusion statute in *Edwards v. California*. The analogy appears correct in that both statutes were discriminatory by creating two classes of citizens. In *Edwards*, California recognized that local indigents were entitled to welfare and freedom of travel and determined that non-resident indigents were entitled to neither. In *Higgins*, Michigan could deny relief to non-resident children and consequently their freedom of travel, but a local child did not encounter these restraints. Just as *Edwards* struck down the exclusion statute, *Higgins* ignored Michigan's attempt at discriminatory fiscal clearing.

In *In re Paul and Mark*,[41] Judge Polier made use of the *Higgins* analogy to the *Edwards* case as a foundation for considering the constitutionality of California's attempt at fiscal clearing. The decision involved a mother who, realizing she could not support her three children, placed them in a New York welfare agency. Subsequently, she moved to California, rehabilitated herself, established a home and requested that her children be reunited with her. Despite the recommendations of a California welfare agency and the New York agency, New York was advised by California that the children could not be reunited with their mother pending fiscal clearing with California. California wanted New York to retain legal liability for the children since the mother could not earn enough to support the children without state assistance.[42] The New

---

40. The pertinent section of the statute gives the state welfare department the power to ". . . approve the placing of a child of this state in a family home of persons unrelated to the child by a person not a resident of this state . . . by an agency or organization with no place of business in this state. Within approval of the proposed placement shall be obtained from the State department. Such person, agency or organization shall furnish the state department with such information as it may deem necessary regarding the child and the prospective foster parents and such guaranty as is required by the state department to protect the interests of the county in which the child is to be placed." *Id.*

41. 64 Misc. 2d 466, 315 N.Y.S.2d 12 (Family Ct. 1970).

42. It is not obvious from the facts as given in the case whether California was basing her demand for guaranty on a statute or on informal welfare

York court found no justification for keeping the children from their mother in light of the *Edwards* analogy [43] and *Shapiro's* rejection of both direct (exclusion statutes) and indirect (residency laws) attempts by state agencies to discourage the right of freedom to travel.

The residency requirements invalidated in *Shapiro* are similar to the California and Michigan fiscal clearing demands[44] in that they imposed a condition upon indigents in need of welfare who wished to enter the state. *Shapiro,* in striking down the residency requirement as a threat to the constitutional right to equal protection of the laws, cited *Sherbert v. Verner,*[45] which stated that this constitutional challenge cannot be answered by the argument that public assistance benefits are a "privilege" and not a "right." [46] Fiscal clearing appears to be unconstitutional in that public assistance is a child's right and if he is eligible in one state, it would seem that he should be eligible in any state in which he resides.[47] Such a result is implied by the reasoning of Judge Polier in *In re Paul and Mark.*

A child's well-being is, however, within the state's constitutional power to regulate.[48] This power is limited to regulations that promote the welfare of the child and his physical, mental, and moral development.[49] All other considerations should be deferred or subordinated to the child's interests.[50] In light of this limitation it seems that where the indigent child's welfare would be promoted

---

policy. However, California has enacted the Uniform Transfer of Dependents Act. CAL. WELF. & INST'NS CODE § 18400 (West 1966). This Act allows a state to avoid financial responsibility through reciprocal agreements.

43. *See* text accompanying notes 37–39 *supra.*

44. *See* text accompanying notes 37–40 *supra.*

45. Sherbert v. Verner, 374 U.S. 398, 404 (1963).

46. *Id.*

47. *See* Slaughter House Cases, 83 U.S. (16 Wall.) 36, 77 (1872). This is not to suggest that a child should be able to reap the benefits of double welfare payments. *See* text accompanying notes 50–51 *infra.*

48. *See, e.g.,* Ginsberg v. New York, 390 U.S. 629, 639 (1968). The case involved a statute prohibiting the sale of obscene literature to minors and this was held to be a constitutional exercise of state police power, notwithstanding the fact that the Court indicated that had minors not been involved in the sale, the literature may have been subjected to a different test.

49. *See, e.g.,* Abdul-Rahman Omar Adra v. Clift, 195 F. Supp. 857 (D. Md. 1961); Weatherton v. Taylor, 124 Ark. 579, 187 S.W. 450 (1916); Williams v. Williams, 110 Colo. 473, 135 P.2d 1016 (1943); Workman v. Workman, 191 Ky. 124, 229 S.W. 379 (1921).

50. *Id.*

by transporting him to another state, the receiving state should not require fiscal clearing that would disregard the child's well-being. *Shapiro* has affirmed another restriction upon the state's right to regulate child welfare where the state has enacted legislation that classifies the children. Where a classification serves to penalize the exercise of a constitutional right, unless shown to be necessary to promote a compelling governmental interest, the legislation is unconstitutional.[51] Just as residency laws could not qualify under a compelling governmental interest in *Shapiro,* fiscal clearing would appear to fail in like manner.

States attempt to justify fiscal clearing procedures, contending that they are based on permissible state objectives despite the fact that they penalize the exercise of the constitutional freedom to travel. The state objectives have yet to be specifically delineated but fiscal clearing would be sanctioned as allowing for budget predictability, preventing double payment to children, and saving welfare costs.[52] These objectives failed to justify residency laws and by analogy they also seem to fall short of validating fiscal clearing. Double payment (the possibility of two states paying the same recipient child) might be prevented by requiring that the migrant child give legal proof of his prior residency before assistance is given by the receiving state. Notice to the last state of custody would eliminate the possibility of double benefits.[53] The suggestion that the receiving state's budget would remain predictable through the use of fiscal clearing is cancelled by *Shapiro* which held that new residents are not required to give advance notice of their need for welfare assistance.[54] The contention that fiscal clearing will save state welfare costs by forcing the sending state to

---

51. 394 U.S. at 634. To qualify as a compelling state interest the action must bear a reasonable relationship to the achievement of the governmental purpose asserted as its justification. The state must have so cogent an interest in the action as to justify the infringements upon personal liberty. *See* Skinner v. Oklahoma, 316 U.S. 535, 541 (1942); Korematsu v. United States, 323 U.S. 214, 216 (1944); Bates v. Little Rock, 361 U.S. 516, 524–25 (1960). Restrictions of liberties must be justified by clear public interest, "threatened not doubtfully or remotely, but by a clear and present danger." Thomas v. Collins, 323 U.S. 516, 530 (1944).

52. These arguments were used to sanction residency requirements in *Shapiro* and would appear to be the likely arguments of those states employing fiscal clearing practices.

53. 394 U.S. at 637.

54. *Id.* at 635.

retain the support obligation is defeated by the equal protection clause. According to *Rinaldi v. Yeager*,[55] the equal protection clause imposes requirements of rationality and non-discriminatory application upon state law. In other words, a state cannot impose special burdens, in this instance restricted freedom of travel, upon defined classes without the distinctions that are drawn having some relevance to the purpose for which the classification is made.[56] Fiscal clearing seems to be discriminatory in its application as incoming indigent children are met with clearing requirements that can deny the child state welfare where resident indigent children do not encounter such treatment. In light of the Supreme Court's holding in *Rinaldi,* it would seem that such a classification would not be justified by an attempt to save money by limiting welfare payments.

Moreover, the social philosophy recognized in this country for thirty-five years since the adoption of the Social Security Act in 1935 [57]—that every person in the country should have access to basic income to meet the essential needs of life—is in conflict with restrictions on indigent aid.[58] It is not wrong for a person to move to another state because there are superior educational, medical, or other social welfare provisions there.[59] According to the Social Security Act a state shall

> provide . . . that all individuals wishing to make application for aid to families with dependent children shall have the opportunity to do so, and that aid to families with dependent children

55. 384 U.S. 305, 309–10 (1966). *Rinaldi* involved an attempt to reduce expenses by requiring prisoners to reimburse the state out of their institutional earnings for the cost of furnishing a trial transcript. This was held unconstitutional because it did not require similar repayments from unsuccessful appellants given a suspended sentence, placed on probation, or fined.

56. *Id. Cf.* Baxstrom v. Herold, 383 U.S. 107, 111 (1966). *Baxstrom* involved a statute which invidiously discriminated against the mentally ill. The classification was invalidated by the same test mentioned in text.

57. Social Security Act, 42 U.S.C. § 301 (1964).

58. *See* Note, *Residence Requirement for Public Relief: An Arbitrary Prerequisite,* 2 COLUM. J. OF L. AND SOC. PROB. 133, 143 (1966), citing Simons, "Our Obsolescent Residence Laws," Speech presented at Fifty-ninth California State Conference on Health and Welfare, in Berkeley, California, May 3, 1960. The Social Security Act is an enactment of progressive social legislation intended to alleviate a citizen's economic insecurity. Rivard v. Bijou Furniture Co., 67 R.I. 251, 25 A.2d 563 (1941).

59. *Id. See also* 394 U.S. at 630.

shall be furnished with reasonable promptness to all eligible individuals.[60]

Those states which wish to take advantage of federal funds [61] must conform to these requirements of the Social Security Act.[62] Fiscal clearing, by avoiding financial responsibilities for incoming indigent children, appears to permit states to ignore the mandate of section 402 which provides for payments of federal money by the state to all eligible individuals.[63] States have the power to determine in a non-arbitrary manner who is entitled to public assistance, but fiscal clearing as applied by states such as California and Michigan in the aforementioned New York cases is inconsistent with the philosophy that all should have access to a basic income to meet the essential needs of life.

The concurring opinion of Justice Douglas in *Edwards v. California* presents another possible approach by which fiscal clearing might be challenged. Douglas concluded:

> The right to move freely from State to State is an incident of national citizenship protected by the Privileges and Immunities Clause of the Fourteenth Amendment against state interference.[64]

Although Douglas admitted there was no specific constitutional guarantee of freedom to travel, he concluded that even before the fourteenth amendment it was a fundamental right.[65] Fiscal clearing results in this same type of restraint upon a child exercising his

60. 42 U.S.C. § 602(a)(9) (1964). The term "dependent child" means a needy child who has lost his parents by reason of death, continued absence, or physical or mental incapacity. 42 U.S.C. § 606(a)(1) (Supp. 1964). The term is modified to permit a child to be treated as a dependent when placed in a foster home or child care agency. 42 U.S.C. § 608 (1964).

61. The funds come from the Federal plan for aid to families with dependent children which provides funds to the states for distribution to parents of needy children. The state plan for assistance is submitted to the Federal government and upon approval the state becomes eligible for federal funding. For a full discussion of this plan see *King v. Smith,* 392 U.S. 309 (1968).

62. Williams v. Dandridge, 297 F. Supp. 450, 454 (1968). 42 U.S.C. 602(b) (1964) authorizes the Secretary of Health, Education and Welfare to approve state plans which impose a year's residence requirement on any child residing within the state. In light of *Shapiro,* this is unconstitutional.

63. Though paid to an adult guardian, the financial assistance is treated as a benefit to the child. *See* Williams v. Dandridge, 297 F. Supp. 450 at note 9.

64. 314 U.S. at 178.

65. *Id.*

rights of national citizenship. When an indigent child, desiring to enter another state, is subjected to fiscal clearing practices by the receiving state which seeks to protect itself from any new financial burden, such a child is relegated to an inferior class of citizenship. In light of the reasoning of Justice Douglas, such a relegation is unconstitutional under the privileges and immunities clause and infringes upon the child's fundamental rights.

Although fiscal clearing may restrict a child's right to travel, some form of administrative procedure may be necessary to prevent payment by more than one state.[66] As implied by the language in *Shapiro,*[67] such a procedure might consist of exchanging data which would notify the custodial state that the child had been entered on another state's welfare rolls. Requiring proof of previous residence from the indigent child would make him eligible for local assistance and would allow the receiving state to notify the prior custodial state. In view of *Shapiro,* the imposition of any further burden upon the incoming indigent child would seem to discourage the child's constitutional right of freedom to travel. Since fiscal clearing would impose additional burdens, it follows that these may restrict an indigent child's right to travel and hence be unconstitutional.

66. *See* text accompanying notes 48–51 *supra.*
67. *See* Shapiro v. Thompson, 394 U.S. 618, 639 (1969).

Lindsay G. Arthur

10
Should Children Be as Equal as People?

In the beginning it was written that "all men are created equal."
The words carried a magic in their simplicity; even though those
who declared them really meant only that all white, adult, proper-
tied, Christian males are created equal. But the words as they were
written have been a lodestone: the restrictive adjectives are being
removed, each with its own struggle. The courts say that non-
whites are equal, legislatures write laws commanding it. Property
is only distantly remembered as a qualification for equality, lack of
it is now an assurance that all the essentials of life will come free.
The church is so well protected by its separation from the state that
it has substantially lost its influence on public affairs. Females are
struggling for equality. Now the last adjective is being assaulted.
From Berkeley to Columbia, from Kent to Gault, from Haight
to hair-do's, from vodka to voting to Viet, the non-adults are
demanding equality. But should children be as equal as people?

> . . . nor shall any state . . . deny to any person . . .
> the equal protection of its laws.

Should children go before children's courts, or, if they are equal
should they go before "real" courts—with real prisons? Should
children have extra laws, such as for drinking, smoking, curfew,
disobeying teachers, or, if they are equal, should they only be
charged for "grown-up" offenses?—and drink what they please.
Should children who commit criminal offenses with dangerous
weapons be treated as dangerous criminals?—even if they're only

The Honorable LINDSAY G. ARTHUR, J.D., is District
Judge, Juvenile Division, State of Minnesota. This article
is reprinted with permission from the *North Dakota Law
Review* 45(1969):204–21. Copyright 1969 by the University of North Dakota School of Law.

seven years old. If a woman is married to a drunkard, she can get a divorce; but can a child, if his mother is a drunkard?—and where does he go next? If a man's home provides him no satisfactions, he moves on; should a child?—can a child?

Should people be as equal as children? All children are provided a free education; are adults denied equal protection of the laws if they must pay? All children receive food, shelter, and clothing with no strings attached; is it unconstitutional not to do the same for adults? All children are virtually guaranteed a woman's loving care; are all men entitled to the same guarantee? Should people be as equal as children?

Equal Protection

Counsel?

> . . . no single action holds more potential for achieving procedural justice for the child in the juvenile court than the provision of counsel.[1]
>
> The juvenile needs the assistance of counsel to cope with problems of law, to make skilled inquiry into the facts, to insist upon regularity of the proceedings, and to ascertain whether he has a defense and to prepare and submit it.[2]

The question is no longer whether counsel should be provided, but when, and in what depth. Consider: at the arraignment, the court offers to appoint a lawyer and to continue the case for a few days to allow consultation. Because it would mean an additional hearing, an additional half-day's pay lost, the family rejects the offer. Is the child denied counsel?

Consider: the child desires an attorney and the parents have adequate money but refuse to spend it for a lawyer's fee. Is counsel a necessity for which the parents must pay? Can the court order them to pay on pain of contempt or can the court charge the fees to the long-suffering taxpayers?

Consider: the Bar Association provides a list of lawyers who have volunteered to represent juveniles, but none of the lawyers have read *Gault,* the Juvenile Code, or "Standards for Juvenile and

1. REPORT OF THE PRESIDENT'S COMMISSION ON LAW ENFORCEMENT AND ADMINISTRATION OF JUSTICE, THE CHALLENGE OF CRIME IN A FREE SOCIETY 86 (1967).
2. In re Gault, 387 U.S. 1, 36 (1967).

Family Courts." [3] Is the child proffered knowledgeable counsel? Can such counsel comprehend the various and delicate interrelationships of court, child, parent, probation officer, police, public, press, school, peers, or institutions? Can any nonmetropolitan court afford to have specialized counsel always available?

Consider: should counsel advocate what the child, his client, wants—what the parents think best for the child—or what counsel thinks best for the child?

Consider: should counsel see only the clerk's file? Or should he also see the police file, the social history and the social worker's notes and sources? Further, should counsel be given access to school and psychological data? If all of these should be provided, how much time and how many lawyers will be needed? [4]

Counsel is a constitutional necessity, which should be chargeable to the parents. He should insist upon time to acquaint himself with the facts and the law, hear all that the court sees and hears, cross-examine those who purvey information or opinion to the court and advocate that which his client would seek if his client were mature of thought.

Care?

> . . . the evidence discloses that . . . [the parents] are caught in a vicious circle of physical incapacity, emotional strain, and financial distress beyond their capabilities to master. The net result has been a destruction of any reasonable hope for a home environment compatible with the welfare of the three young children. [5]

Children are entitled to parental care. Obviously, if parents can

---

3. CHILDREN'S BUREAU, DEP'T OF HEALTH, EDUCATION, AND WELFARE, PUB. NO. 437, STANDARDS FOR JUVENILE AND FAMILY COURTS (1966).

4. "In [disposition] hearings . . . all evidence helpful in determining the questions presented, including oral and written reports, may be received by the court. . . . [T]he parties or their counsel shall be afforded an opportunity to examine and controvert written reports so received and to cross-examine individuals making the reports. Sources of confidential information need not be released." UNIFORM JUVENILE COURT ACT § 29-d (promulgated July 30, 1968, by the National Conference of Commissioners on Uniform State Laws). This position was endorsed by the National Council of Juvenile Court Judges at their annual convention in Chicago, June 25, 1968, but with a vigorous and almost unanimous dissent to the last phrase.

5. Kennedy v. State, 277 Ala. 5, 166 So.2d 736, 737 (1964).

not, or will not, provide adequate care, society intervenes with expert social counseling. If this is not sufficient, the children are removed temporarily while the parents and the home are brought up to minimal standards. If, despite the best available efforts, there is no hope of achieving such standards, the children are removed permanently and placed for adoption or made wards of the state. It is neat and efficient—and frightening in its aspect of the social camel's nose prodding under the parental tent. Four words determine whether parents keep or lose their children: "adequate care" and "minimal standards." The parents are charged with child neglect. They are told they may lose their children, which, among other reactions, they feel as a personal insult. They fight back, hard.[6] As in delinquency, the court becomes more involved in yesterday's muck than in tomorrow's help—and the help is made that much harder to accept.

What is "care" becomes important. Physical care: food, shelter, housing, these are easy to measure. Supervisory care: awareness and control of the child's conduct and teaching self-discipline, these can also be measured, though far too often they are measured in a delinquency proceeding rather than a neglect proceeding. "Parental neglect, excessive weakness, categorical leniency destroy respect for the law and for those charged with its enforcement."[7] Emotional care: giving the child love, an identity and a sense of security are difficult to measure and yet they are possibly the most important elements for a stable society. "When I did something good, I should have gotten some gratitude or something; and when I did something wrong, I wasn't punished enough. (My parents) just didn't care very much about me."[8]

Society, and its courts, should be concerned with what children need, not with muckraking and labeling what they and their parents have done. The focus should be forward: to provide for future needs, not backward: to correct for past misdeeds.

6. "When existing parent-child relationships fail to meet—or allegedly fail to meet—commonly accepted community standards, an intense human drama almost inevitably develops." Todd v. Superior Court, 68 Wash.2d 587, 414 Pac.2d 605, 606 (1966).

7. J. Edgar Hoover, Remarks to Masons, Oct. 1965.

8. Comment by an anonymous parolee from Minnesota State Training School for Girls on "Open Mike for Teens," WCCO Radio, Minneapolis, March 5, 1967.

Equal Privacy

Silence?

The privilege can be claimed in any proceeding, be it criminal or civil, administrative or judicial, investigatory or adjudicatory.[9]

If the police are questioning a boy about rape, as in *Kent;* or threatening phone calls, as in *Gault,* it is obvious and easy to say that the accused is entitled to silence, and to be told of his right to it. "He needs someone on whom to lean lest the overpowering presence of the law, as he knows it, . . . crush him." [10] "[T]he statements of adolescents under 18 years of age who are arrested and charged with violations of law are frequently untrustworthy and often distort the truth." [11]

[I]t seems probable that where children are induced to confess by "paternal" urgings on the part of officials and the confession is then followed by disciplinary action, the child's reaction is likely to be hostile and adverse—the child may well feel that he has been led or tricked into confession and that despite his confession, he is being punished.[12]

Silence is golden and the right to it can be precious. But there are problems. Confessing to a policeman is rather obviously a prelude to unpleasant consequences; but what of confession to a school principal or a coach who passes it on to the police? Should school principals or coaches be required to give the *Miranda* warning? Testifying at a court trial is at the very vortex of unpleasant consequences; but what of testifying at a parent inquiry which results in loss of driving privileges, an early curfew, or a spanking? May children take the Fifth Amendment with all authority? And if not all, then should the child have the protection of privileged communication as to those with whom he has no right of silence?

A child should have the right of silence in all matters with the police, and in investigations by the schools and other public agencies of conduct criminal for adults; and his communications on child offenses to the schools and on all matters with his parents should be privileged.

9. In re Gault, *supra* note 2, at 47, *quoting from* Murphy v. Waterfront Commission, 378 U.S. 52, 94 (1964) (concurring opinion).

10. Haley v. Ohio, 332 U.S. 596, 600 (1948).

11. In the Matter of Four Youths, 89 Wash. L. Reporter 639 (1961), *as quoted in* In re Gault, *supra* note 2, at 55.

12. In re Gault, *supra* note 2, at 51–52.

Hearsay?

> . . . the court conferred privately with the daughter. . . .[13]

When should children testify? Tests for determining their competency are well settled: respect for the oath and capacity to relate observed facts.[14] But when should they *have* to testify? It is common in custody fights for one party to demand that the child be brought forth and ordered to state her preferences publicly with both parents watching, and then the other side demands to cross-examine. How cruel must courts be? Some courts clear the courtroom of all except counsel and the reporter and all questions are put by the judge. But the child knows, and is afraid and confused —and the child's susceptibility has been propagandized by the person who brought her to court. Hence, this procedure is almost as cruel and almost as meaningless. Some judges interview the child alone, without record or counsel. But this is a denial of confrontation, and any appeal taken is at least partially without transcript. Moreover, this procedure only slightly lessens the fear, propaganda —and the trauma. Children talk best in their native habitat. What they say when pressures of emotion and strangeness are absent is more apt to be true, somewhat analogous to *res gestae.* Obviating the need for children to come into court will prevent trauma to the children, trauma which accomplishes little since court testimony of children is not very reliable.

Under reliable circumstances, out of court statements made by children pertaining to their relationship with their immediate family should be admissible as an exception to the hearsay rule.

Search?

> We can agree that the father's "house" may also be that of the child, but if a man's house is still his castle, in which his rights are superior to the state, those rights should also be superior to the rights of the children who live in his house. We cannot agree that a child . . . has the same constitutional rights of privacy in the family home which he might have in a rented hotel room.[15]

The watchword in recent appellate decisions is that children are entitled to "fairness." Unreasonable search and seizure is as cer-

13. Aske v. Aske, 233 Minn. 540, 543, 47 N.W.2d 417, 419 (1951).
14. State v. Triblett, —— Minn. ——, 162 N.W.2d 121 (1968).
15. State v. Kinderman, 271 Minn. 405, 409, 136 N.W.2d 577, 580 (1965).

tainly barred by "fairness" for juveniles as it is by "civil rights" for adults. So far the answer is simple, but with children there are the problems that come from dependence. Can school officials search a child's locker for marijuana—or .38's? Can a probation officer search a child for switchblades—or zips? Can a YMCA director search a child's tote basket for LSD—or yellow jackets? Can a parent search a child's dresser for stolen records—or hub caps? Somewhere there is a line. Parents cannot be reduced to search warrants nor school principals to Miranda warnings—or can they? If equality is the principle, if children are as equal as people, then children have the same rights to privacy and mothers should not read mail, or diaries, or insist on meeting dates. But, repeat *but,* if parents have a right to invade the privacy of their children, where does inequality stop: at home, church, school, psychologist's office, or the police station? Should inequality stop at age fourteen, seventeen, nineteen, or at emancipation? A cruel rule may be necessary but one which lets parents be parents and schools be schools and doctors be doctors, and lets them inquire into the needs and problems of children and act according to their best judgment.

Those legally responsible for providing children with necessities should be entitled to make, or authorize, reasonable—or unreasonable—searches and seizures.

Arrest?

> . . . the law of arrest does not apply to the taking into custody of minors.[16]
> Such action shall not be deemed an arrest but shall be deemed a measure to protect the health, morals, and well-being of the juvenile.[17]

A child may be taken into custody without the safeguards of observation or reasonable suspicion that protect an adult. But what does the child receive in return: a separate place of detention—in some metropolitan areas; friendly and interested counsellors—sometimes; no bars on the windows, no echoing corridors, no clanking locks—just psychiatric screen, shiny tiled walls, and electronic listening. It doesn't seem an even shake! Liberty is at least

---

16. In re James L. —— Jr., 25 Ohio Op.2d 369, 194 N.E.2d 797, 798 (1963).
17. State v. Smith, 32 N.J. 501, 161 A.2d 520, 534 (1960).

as precious to children, maybe more so, since time curiously means so much more to children who have so much more of it. Everyone arrested is allowed one phone call. Everyone knows this axiom to be true, even though finding it in any lawbook makes an interesting search. How effective is one phone call to an absent or drunken parent, or to a friend whose mother says he's in bed, or doing his homework, or to a lawyer—and how many children know a lawyer?

Arrest for children is at least as serious as arrest for adults. It should have the same rules whatever name is given it and a call should be completed to a supportive, competent adult advising him of the arrest within a reasonable time.

Equal Innocence

Bail?

> The right to release without excessive bail, guaranteed by constitutions and statutes in criminal cases, is neither historically nor logically a part of civil or equitable proceedings such as occur in juvenile court. . . .[18]

Bail is money deposited to guarantee return of an arrested person at his next hearing. Does a twelve-year-old child appreciate the difference between five hundred dollars and five thousand? Can he comprehend how many hours of sweat go into five hundred dollars, or how many shoes, hamburgers, aspirins or blankets it will buy? Does he care that his father has mortgaged his home, or his mother her engagement ring? Can children understand money— someone else's money—well enough to be bound by it? A child should not be detained in the first place unless he is dangerous or a runner.[19] If he is dangerous, money or bail will not make him less so, especially the money of someone intimate enough to ante it up for the child and thus probably so intimate as to be, to the child, responsible for the confinement in the first place. And if the child is a runner, isn't he most apt to be running from precisely the people who will be offering the bail?

Bail should not be available for children unless it is clearly

18. REPORT OF THE COMMITTEE ON JUVENILE DELINQUENCY (CRIMINAL LAW SECTION) OF THE AMERICAN BAR ASSOCIATION, CONSTITUTIONAL RIGHTS IN JUVENILE COURT PROCEEDINGS (1966).

19. *Supra* note 3, at 60.

*demonstrated that the money or the bond or the property will in
fact be compelling upon the child to return for the subsequent
hearing.*

Grand Jury?

. . . [T]he constitutional right to a grand jury indictment as a
preliminary to prosecution is inapplicable to juvenile court proceedings involving children charged with misdeeds.[20]

A grand jury protects a citizen from the expense and stigma of
a criminal charge. In juvenile court, counsel is guaranteed and the
lack of a public trial guarantees that no stigma or inference will
be attached to the mere fact of a charge.

*The reasoning for the Grand Jury does not exist for children.
Cessante ratione legis, cessat ipsa lex.*

Notice?

Notice, to comply with due process requirements, must be given
sufficiently in advance of scheduled court proceedings so that
reasonable opportunity to prepare will be afforded, and it must
"set forth the alleged misconduct with particularity." [21]

The immediate tendency of many juvenile courts was to shift to
the jargon of indictments, making the notice satisfactory to appellate courts—and considerably less intelligible to the family. The
essential is *plain* language,[22] with sufficient detail as to time, place,
names, and actions to advise of the claims which will be presented
to the court. Amassing of synonyms and adjectives actually works
toward a denial of due process by obfuscation. But the right to
notice raises other problems: is the *child* entitled to notice and are
both parents, if separated? What of the offense which comes to
light in the pre-disposition investigation? Can the court consider it
without further notice and arraignment? Must the notice specify
the particular subdivision of the particular statute allegedly violated and be held to this and no other? What facts must be pleaded
and proven to demonstrate "incorrigibility," "waywardness," or
"habitual misconduct"? If a child steals a car to escape a drunken

20. Antieau, *Constitutional Rights in Juvenile Courts,* 46 CORNELL L. Q.
387, 393 (1961).
21. In re Gault, *supra* note 2, at 33.
22. In re Hitzemann, —— Minn. ——, 161 N.W.2d 542 (1968).

father, must the pleader be forced to choose either delinquency or neglect, or is "fact pleading" permissible? The public is concerned that courts intervene into the lives of individuals when necessary, but only when necessary. The family is concerned with knowing what it is that has called down authority upon them. And the court is concerned with what, if anything, the child needs which the court can provide.

The notice must allege sufficient facts to show the child's need and the court's authority, in language a layman can understand.

Proof?

We live in a sea of semantic disorder. . . .[23]

"Beyond a reasonable doubt," "fair preponderance of the evidence," "clear and convincing" and "persuasive to reasonable men" are standards that have been advanced. At the risk of being sacrilegious, it is suggested that however much the standard mouthings are defined, the test that will in fact be applied is simply whether the trier of the fact is "pretty sure," or not. It matters little when what formula is ordered, only that he who applies it realizes that American liberty is a precious thing.

After all, what we are striving for is not merely "equal" justice for juveniles. They deserve much more than being afforded only the privileges and protections that are applied to their elders. A niggardly and indiscriminate granting of concepts of justice applied to adults will stunt the growth of the juvenile court and handicap the progress of future generations.[24]

Equal Trial

Speedy Trial?

All the powerful reasons that have long justified the draftsmen of our constitutions in enshrining the right to a speedy trial apply in cases where juveniles are accused of misconduct.[25]

The argument is made that speedy trial is a criminal right and therefore not available in juvenile proceedings which are by nature

23. Pres. Dwight D. Eisenhower, State of the Union Message, Jan. 1960.
24. Chief Justice Earl Warren, Address to the National Council of Juvenile Court Judges, Vol. 15, No. 3 Juv. Ct. Judges J. 14 (1964).
25. Antieau, *supra* note 20, at 398.

noncriminal.[26] That the consequences of juvenile court dispositions may be at least as unwanted by the child as criminal sentenc-
ing is unwanted by adults was pointed out in *Gault,* with the
comment that:

> it would be extraordinary if our Constitution did not require
> the procedural regularity and the exercise of care implied in the
> phrase "due process." [27]

Local Trial?

> In all criminal prosecutions, the accused shall enjoy the right
> to a . . . trial [in] the State and district wherein the crime
> shall have been committed. . . .[28]

Most juvenile codes provide for trial, at least optionally, not
at the county where the offense was allegedly committed but at
the child's county of residence upon the theory that the child is
better protected in his home county by his parents, better known
in his home county to those who must devise a treatment for him,
and better supervised in his treatment in his home county by the
court where he will be living. The theory is sound in all respects,
but it seems to run counter to the Constitution unless:

> Where it is to the child's own interest, the criminal analogy
> can be disregarded and the jurisprudence can revert to the
> child's welfare, and to the pre-Gault concept of the juvenile
> court as a derivation of equity, interested in best using society's
> power to help children.[29]

Subpoena?

What can be in doubt? What can be said in opposition?

Public Trial?

> Anyone who enjoys seeing his name in print as a lawbreaker
> is a potential criminal, and the sooner he's put away the
> better.

*   *   *

Publicity is painful but necessary. Most people have good

26. Harling v. United States, 295 F.2d 161 (D.C. Cir. 1961).
27. In re Gault, *supra* note 2, at 27–28.
28. U.S. CONST. Amend. VI.
29. *See* State ex rel Knutson v. Jackson, 249 Minn. 246, 82 N.W.2d 234
(1957).

youngsters they want to keep away from the hoodlums. How can they do it if they don't know who the hoodlums are?

*   *   *

Giving publicity to a delinquent doesn't destroy him. In all cases I have seen it has improved his behavior.

Judge Lester Loble [30]

In one short year . . . in the court presided over by (Judge Lester Loble) there has been a 58 percent increase . . . in juvenile felony cases. . . .[31]

Publicizing a juvenile delinquent brands him—and his brothers and sisters—and isolates him into the company of other delinquents, with little preventative effect. But, not publicizing delinquency proceedings threatens both the child and the public, in that their proper interests will be arbitrarily handled—or ignored. Traditionally the adult courts have accepted the public's "right to know" as a needed protection both to the accused and the victim, and upon an unproven belief that punishment is a deterrent to others. In their brief history of only some seven decades, the juvenile courts have accepted the child's "right to privacy" as a more needed protection from public retribution. There are five principal influences attributed to public trial. First, it protects the accused from an arbitrary court. But a lawyer, a court reporter, and an appellate court can provide better protection. Second, it assures the victim that an eye has been given for his eye. But the *lex talionis* has been repealed.[32] Third, it deters others from criminal conduct by fear of known punishment. But there is better authority to the effect that the real deterrent is the fear of getting caught.[33] Fourth, it drives the guilty into further crime by isolating them into a criminal environment, publicity's real fault.[34] Fifth, it protects the public from judicial disregard of dangerous conduct, publicity's real value. A simple rule which protects the public

---

30. *Montana's Experiment with Juvenile Crime,* Vol. 75, No. 6 AMERICAN LEGION MAGAZINE 50 (1963).

31. *Open Hearings in Juvenile Courts in Montana,* Statement by the National Council on Crime and Delinquency (Nov. 1964).

32. The gospel according to St. Matthew (circa 110) Ch. 5, v. 38–44.

33. "It is accepted in the police world that it is not fear of punishment that deters the criminal, but fear of being found out." Kurt Lindroth, Deputy Director of State Police for Sweden, *quoted from* THE ROTARIAN 32 (Aug. 1968).

34. *See* "Comment" to UNIFORM JUVENILE COURT ACT, § 24, *supra* note 4.

without needless harm to the accused, and without duly restricting freedom of the press requires that: *news media should be accorded full access to juvenile court proceedings, but should be forbidden to identify any participating juvenile.*

Jury Trial?

A jury trial would inevitably bring a good deal more formality to the juvenile court without giving a youngster a demonstrably better fact-finding process than trial before a judge.[35]

A jury of peers is a protection to both the public and the individual from authority and judicial whim. Peers have a degree of sympathy, they can relate to the accused and understand in some measure his idiom and his world. But children are children's peers, and children can't be tried by a jury of children. Yet adults can't understand long hair, and teeny-bop talk, and the driving fear of being left out, and the perplexing problem of identity for a changing body with a changing mind in a changing world. Adults can be taken in by giving a hoodlum a suit, a tie, and a crew cut, and adults can be put out by the normal rebellion of children striving for independence. Possibly judges who are in constant touch with juveniles come closest to being their peers—if empathy is peerage. And in a court of equity, from which the juvenile courts have evolved, it was thought that: *where remedies were needed beyond law's rigidities, justice can better come from judges than from juries.*

Confrontation?

. . . the right to confront witnesses . . . essentially includes the right of effective cross-examination by defendant's counsel of witnesses against the defendant.[36]

If the right belongs to the child to see and hear everything the judge sees and hears, it's a little thing; if it belongs to the parents it's a little more; if to counsel, certainly quite a deal more. Children may not be mature enough to absorb adverse testimony and react with intelligent counterattack. Parents become emotional about criticism of their children—and far more emotional at sug-

---

35. Paulsen, *Fairness to the Juvenile Offender,* 41 MINN. L. REV. 547, 559 (1957).
36. 32 J. OF AM. TRIAL LAWYERS 570 (1968).

gestions it may be parental fault. Counsel can protect the rights involved, and can better comprehend and be unemotional about the domestic can-of-worms that appears in so many delinquency and neglect cases.

Confrontation without a lawyer is nearly meaningless. Counsel is the essence of the right, he knows the questions to ask—and not to ask.

Equal Guilt

Double Jeopardy?

> The doctrine of double jeopardy is one of ancient origin and is designed to prevent the prosecution of a person a second time when he has already been subjected to the risk of "life and limb" in a prior trial. The concept clearly contemplates that the action which bars a second prosecution must be instituted in a court which has the power to . . . punish . . . [but] . . . the juvenile act does not contemplate the punishment of the children. . . .[37]

Children are not punished by the courts; but then neither are adults. They are both reformed and rehabilitated, they are made penitent. "The fact of the matter is that, however euphemistic the title, a 'receiving home' or an 'industrial school' for juveniles is an institution of confinement. . . ."[38] If a child is threatened denial of his liberty, however high the motive of him who denies it, is the liberty any less important than that of an adult?

If a child's freedom of movement has been put at stake, for whatever noble purpose, he has been in jeopardy.

Punishment?

> In making dispositions some judges will use some device that will "shock" the child . . . fines can be used constructively, if they are not too heavy. . . .[39]

Are "shock" dispositions "cruel and unusual"? Watch a seventeen year old suburban boy when his license is suspended for drinking beer! Are fines or restitution, which to a child amounts

37. Moquin v. State, 216 Md. 524, 140 A.2d 914, 916 (1958).
38. In re Gault, *supra* note 2, at 27.
39. ADVISORY COUNCIL OF JUDGES OF THE NATIONAL PROBATION AND PAROLE ASSOCIATION, GUIDES FOR JUVENILE COURT JUDGES, 79–80 (1957).

to the same thing, "excessive"? If a child wraps a stolen car around a telephone pole, is $2,000.00 restitution, ordered as part of delinquency rehabilitation, an excessive fine? Is it "cruel" to require delinquents to clean soft drink cans from the side of a highway—or is it involuntary servitude? Curiously, the Constitution does not prohibit cruel punishments nor does it prevent unusual punishments; it only prohibits cruel *and* unusual punishments. Flogging is cruel, but apparently may be used if it always has been. Taking care of senile patients is unusual, but may apparently be used if it is not traumatic. What is prohibited is "considerations of expediency, the satisfaction of public indignation, or example . . . [as] . . . contrary to the whole spirit of the juvenile act." [40]   Fines and restitution may be used, if not excessive for the *particular* child.

The great advancement of the juvenile courts is that they can be imaginative and flexible: that they can design a package of dispositions to fit the needs of a particular child.

Transcript?

> . . . an indigent parent who is . . . aggrieved is entitled to a free transcript, the cost of which shall be assumed by the county out of appropriate welfare funds. [41]

Appeal without a transcript is like reviewing a book without reading it. Yet how much should the transcript contain—just formal testimony and exhibits, or the social report with its hearsay and conclusions? When it is free, what controls should be used to prevent overordering? Should it contain everything the judge hears and sees, including a probation officer's casual corridor comment, or a newspaper story? And how does one include the personal knowledge that a judge in a smaller community has of the people in his district? The need for a transcript of the arraignment and the adjudicatory hearing are obvious. The dispositional hearing is more difficult: it is far less formal—or should be; it includes more discussion than evidentiary presentation; it may be based on opinions, phone calls with counsel, hearsay and much consideration of facial expression, chosen attire, tone of voice, gait, gum, glare, slouch— all the ingredients important in the decision, but impossible for

---

40. State v. Myers, 74 N.D. 297, 22 N.W.2d 199, 201 (1946).
41. In re Munklewitz, —— Minn. ——, —— N.W.2d —— (1968).

inclusion in a transcript. But the disposition is almost entirely for the trial judge.[42]

A transcript of that which is transcriptive and necessary to the appealed issue is sufficient—if appellate courts continue to recognize the impact of un-transcriptive matter.

Appeal?

> This court has not held that a State is required by the Federal Constitution "to provide appellate courts or a right to appellate review at all." [43]

Appeal, next to the right of counsel, is the great protection against an arbitrary, ignorant or uncaring trial court. "The powers of the Star Chamber were a trifle in comparison with those of our juvenile courts. . . ." [44] Appeal *should* be as of right. It *should* be readily available and financially feasible. It *should* be expeditious, particularly for children for whom treatment should be temporally close to misconduct. Morris Kent was in his twenties when his case was remanded to the court for children. Appeal *should* be anonymous, consistent with the juvenile doctrine of confidentiality: the Gault boy, the Kent boy, the Whittington boy have either too much stigma or too much status. Other children, who should appeal, are often loath to follow them—or their parents shun the publicity.

Appeal is the only real protection against an improper trial court. It should be easily and readily available.

Equal Expression

Religion?

> . . . the educated Chinese conscience . . . does not insult God by believing that he is a merciless Legalist, a stick-and-carrot deity who rules through a system of unimaginable rewards and awful punishments. . . .[45]

May children choose their religion—or lack of it? If they are old

42. In re Lewis, 11 N.J. 217, 94 A.2d 328 (1953).
43. In re Gault, *supra* note 2, at 58.
44. Doscoe Pound, Foreword to YOUNG, SOCIAL TREATMENT IN PROBATION AND DELINQUENCY xxvii (1937), *quoted from* In re Gault, *supra* note 2, at 18.
45. BLOODWORTH, THE CHINESE LOOKING GLASS (1967).

enough to drive, to die, to procreate, to marry, to drop out of school—are they old enough to drop out of church, to move to an "activist" church, or to follow Malcolm X? When can children decide that they are fed up with Sunday School, except the dancing, hay-riding, boy-meets-girl part? If they enjoy the right to counsel, regardless of their parents, do they also enjoy the right to freedom of religion regardless of their parents—or does religion matter that much any more or is religion too important to trust to the young?

> A child old enough to die is old enough to affirm, "O unbelievers! I will not worship that which ye worship; nor will ye worship that which I worship. . . . Ye have your religion, and I my religion." [46]

Statement?

> When a nation silences criticism and dissent, it deprives itself of the power to correct its errors. [47]

Do children have the right of free speech—in four-letter words? Do they have the right of free press—in scurrilous, underground rags? Can children criticize their teachers or their parents? May parents censor? May parents listen in on their children's phone calls? May they read their children's mail, both incoming and outgoing? If children have the right of silence, do they also have the right of expression? If children are entitled to cross-examine witnesses who accuse them, do they also have the right to cross-examine parents who accuse them? How far do we go with equality? If children are to be as adults, must they not then lose their childhood? If children are too immature to speak, to print, to assemble, to petition, to worship, are they not also too immature to resist search, to waive counsel, to confront witnesses, to read notice? If children are incapable of exercising some rights, how can they be capable of exercising others?

Children should be allowed to speak their dreams and their accusations privately or in public when they are mature enough to listen to the accusations of others and accord them their dreams and their frustrations.

46. The Koran (circa 652), Ch. 109.
47. Henry Steele Commager, Historian.

Conduct?

> . . . a nation bent on turning out robots might insist that every male have a crew cut and every female wear pigtails. But the ideas of "life, liberty, and the pursuit of happiness," expressed in the Declaration of Independence, later found specific definition in the Constitution itself, including of course, freedom of expression and a wide zone of privacy. I had supposed those guarantees permitted idiosyncracies to flourish, especially when they concern the image of one's personality and his philosophy toward government and his fellow men.[48]

Can children do as they please? Obviously not. They can't hurt others; but can they hurt themselves? They can't hurt the sensibilities of others but can they wear their skirts short, or their hair long? Must they wash, and shave, and use curlers, and brassieres? Must they come home when ordered by law or custodian? But if society, or churches, or schools, or policemen, or parents can limit attire, or appearance, can they also limit speech, and press, and assembly? Are children to be deprived of all right of decision the day before their twenty-first birthday—and have full right of decision the next day? Shouldn't maturity and judgement be the test, rather than the calendar? But then, of course, many adults might lose *their* rights.

Let children have their fads and their foibles; so long as the sensibilities of too many others are not invaded too much, it is the safety value of youthful effervescence, and the re-germination of our culture.

Equal Waiver

> We appreciate that special problems may arise with respect to waiver of the privilege by or on behalf of children, and that there may well be some differences in technique—but not in principle—depending on the age of the child and the presence and competence of parents.[49]

If children are equal, or even a little bit equal, they have rights. Rights can be the bane of existence for Authority. Rights can't

48. 37 U.S.L.W. 3023 (1968).
49. In re Gault, *supra* note 2, at 55.

be just presumed to be known, they must be made known. Rights
have to be observed, or Authority will be humiliated by the courts'
suppression of evidence. Rights get in the way of Authority's
proper investigation. But they *can* be waived, and for adults this is
Authority's out, because Authority can easily persuade adults to
waive—sometimes Authority can hardly finish intoning the *Miranda* Formula before admissions come bubbling out. An adult
can waive for himself his own right to silence, to counsel, to
notice, to confrontation, or to jury—but can a child? He's too
young to drink, to marry, to contract, or to soldier. Is he too
young to waive? Can anyone waive for him? If there is no waiver
possible without a lawyer, how can the police investigate a car
theft or a "gang shag"? How can a department store investigate a
shoplifting or obscene shouting? How can a school investigate
truancy or nickel-and-dime extortion? How can a physician investigate battering or incest? How can a welfare worker investigate
incorrigibility due to immorality by night or abandonment by day?
Pragmatism demands waiver; fairness refines the demand. A
method for juvenile waiver is a fundamental necessity, a method
which will protect the child and not hamstring the public. It
cannot be founded upon age because some hoodlums are constitutionally sophisticated at thirteen and some Boy Scouts ignorant
at eighteen of their protections from Authority, and some people
are not endowed with the brains ever to learn. So waiver cannot
be a factor of age. Neither can it be founded upon the presence
of an adult because some parents are uncaring or afraid, and
some school people uninterested except in peace and order, and
some probation officers are almost Authority themselves. There
will never be enough lawyers to be available whenever a child
has a right to exercise. It must be a method usable by the police
in the turmoil of tempers and by the judiciary in the calmness
of courtrooms.

*Waiver should be permitted by a child of whatever age, or in his
behalf by a concerned adult of whatever relationship, if the child
or the friend understands the right to be waived, the consequences
of waiving it, and believes waiver not to be harmful to the child.*

Conclusion

A child at birth has no ability to choose between optional
courses of conduct. Gradually he learns to recognize increasingly

complicated facts. Gradually he learns to forecast the consequences of increasingly complicated acts. Gradually he learns to compare the advantages and disadvantages of increasingly complicated available alternatives. He should be given the freedom to choose between alternatives only when he can recognize each alternative, forecast its consequences, and compare the advantages and disadvantages. Without such maturity, his choice between available alternatives may be needlessly harmful to himself, or to others. But for every choice which he is too immature to make, as for every need he is unable to provide, he is entitled to the protection of a mature person who will make the choice and provide the need in his best interest.

Some day a person's identification card will show his Maturity Quotient which will change from time to time, but not much more often than his height and weight and face. It will be very useful for determining when a person may drink or drive or vote or read pornography or choose his church or authorize search or understand notice or, most important, waive counsel. Until then we must devise more complicated and more rigid restrictions and grants of juvenile freedom and juvenile equality.

Should children be as equal as people? Certainly not. They should not have equal liberty: they should have less. Neither should they have equal protection—they should have more. How much less and how much more will depend on the maturity of the particular child at the particular time.[50]

---

50. For a careful and exhaustive casebook treatment of juvenile court law by two leading experts in the field, *see* M. PAULSEN AND O. KETCHAM, JUVENILE COURTS (1967).

Harry D. Krause

11
The Bastard Finds His Father

Levy v. Louisiana [1] and *Glona v. American Guarantee & Liab. Ins. Co.* [2] may turn out to be two of the most significant cases of the U.S. Supreme Court's 1967 term. On the basis of the equal protection clause, these cases held that illegitimate children could recover for the wrongful death of their mother and that a mother could recover for the wrongful death of her illegitimate child. These holdings went against a long-standing interpretation of Louisiana's wrongful death act which had restricted such recoveries to legitimate children. On the surface, these cases seem innocuous enough, and so far they have generated little excitement. Indeed, if the relationship between the illegitimate child and mother had been their only meaning, the cases *would* be unimportant because in nearly all states and particulars, this relationship today is the same as that between legitimate child and mother. However, the truly important question raised by *Levy* is whether and to what extent the manifold discriminations still imposed by state and federal law in the relationship between *father* and illegitimate child are subject to constitutional attack. The first judicial returns on this question now are coming in from several state supreme courts.

(1) On the appealing and basic issue of the illegitimate child's

HARRY D. KRAUSE, J.D., is Professor of Law, University of Illinois at Urbana-Champaign. He is reporter-draftsman, Committee of Commissioners on Uniform State Laws, and Chairman of the Committee on Paternity, American Bar Association. He is author of *Illegitimacy: Law and Social Policy* (New York: Bobbs-Merrill, 1971). This article is reprinted with permission from *Family Law Quarterly* 3 (1969):100–11.

1. 391 U.S. 68 (1968).
2. 391 U.S. 73 (1968).

right of support from his father, the Supreme Court of Missouri [3] held that "the decisions of the United States Supreme Court compel the conclusion that the proper construction of our statutory provisions relating to the obligations and rights of parents . . . affords illegitimate children a right equal with that of legitimate children to require support by their fathers."

(2) The Supreme Court of Colorado [4] held unconstitutional a (now repealed) Colorado statute which allowed the jury to assess damages in illegitimate paternity cases, because it imposed a substantially different support obligation from that owed a legitimate child, especially insofar as subsequent modifiability was concerned. The holding is of particular interest because it applied *Levy* not only to the rights of the child against the father, but also extended to the father's right not to be "more liable" to an illegitimate child than to a legitimate child.

(3) Earlier in Ohio,[5] on the other hand, the Supreme Court decided the question of the illegitimate child's right of support *against* the illegitimate. A four-to-three decision failed to consider *Levy* fully and held not only that *Levy* applied solely to the intimate relationship between mother and child but also that questions of such importance should be left to the legislature. The minority considered *Levy* controlling.

(4) The Louisiana Supreme Court,[6] when deciding *Levy* on remand, seemed to believe that *Levy* applies to the father-child relationship as well as to that between mother and child: "The United States Supreme Court has held that, as alleged in the petition in this case, when a *parent* openly and publicly recognizes and accepts an illegitimate to be *his* or *her* child and the child is dependent upon the *parent,* such an illegitimate is a 'child' as expressed in Civil Code Article 2315."

(5) A lower New York court [7] postulates: "In the light of the decisions of the United States Supreme Court on May 20, 1968, state statutes which discriminate against children on the basis of a classification as to whether they were born in or out-of-wedlock

3. R—— v. R——, 431 S.W.2d 152, 154 (Mo. 1968).
4. Munn v. Munn, 450 P.2d 68 (Colo. Sup Ct. 1969).
5. Baston v. Sears, 15 Ohio St.2d 166, 239 N.E.2d 62 (1968).
6. Levy v. Louisiana, 253 La. 73, 216 So.2d 818 (1968).
7. Storm v. None, 57 Misc. 2d 342, 291 N.Y.S.2d 515, 519 (Family Ct., N.Y. City 1968); *cf.* Trent v. Loru, 57 Misc. 382, 292 N.Y.S.2d 524, 530 (1968).

must be held to violate the Equal Protection Clause of the Constitution. Certainly there is no area in which such statutes should be more carefully scrutinized than where the support, the care, and the education of a child depend on their interpretation."

(6) In North Dakota,[8] the Supreme Court considered still another question raised by *Levy,* namely whether *Levy* opened intestate succession *through* the mother to the illegitimate. The Court flatly held that a North Dakota statute denying such succession is unconstitutional. One may assume that the court would have done the same had an inheritance from or through the father been in question.

(7) A recent decision of the Wisconsin Supreme Court [9] failed to consider (or even mention) *Levy* when it decided that an illegitimate child has no right to recover for his father's wrongful death under Wisconsin's wrongful death act. The latter defined eligibility in terms of the rather progressive intestacy statute which allows the illegitimate to inherit if paternity has been formally established. While the court seemed to have no doubt regarding the fact of paternity (father and mother had been engaged), the case failed on the issue of formal ascertainment which had been prevented by the father's death prior to the child's birth. The constitutional issue that should have been discussed (but was not recognized) is whether and to what extent the equality requirement limits the state in setting up formal standards of proof of paternity.

(8) A New Jersey appellate court [10] case did worse than the Wisconsin court when, on facts very similar to those of the Wisconsin case, it considered but rejected *Levy.* The chief argument mustered by the New Jersey court was that distinctions on the basis of illegitimacy are reasonable in the father-child relationship (even though *Levy* may forbid them in the mother-child context) because paternal descent is more difficult to ascertain than maternal descent. This case is now on appeal.

None of the cases that has been decided so far has attempted a careful analysis of the meaning and limits of the equal protection clause. The decisions favorable to the illegitimate have applied *Levy* point blank and have concluded without further ado that

8. Michaelson v. Undhjem, 162 N.W.2d 861 (N.D. 1968).
9. Krantz v. Harris, 40 Wis.2d 709, 162 N.W.2d 628 (1968).
10. Schmoll v. Creecy, 104 N.J. Super. 126, 249 A.2d 3 (1969).

discrimination against the illegitimate is unconstitutional. The negative decisions have employed three basic arguments against the extension of *Levy:* 1. *Levy* applies to the more intimate mother-child relationship only and thus cannot be extended to the father-child relationship. 2. The uncertainty of proof in the father-child relationship distinguishes it from the more easily ascertainable mother-child relationship. 3. Questions of such importance should be left to the legislature. These "reasons" will be dealt with in order.

1. While it is true that the *Levy* case involved the mother-child relationship, the illegitimate's claim against his father does not rest on an analogy to his claim against his mother. Rather, it rests on comparison with the *legitimate* child's rights against his father and, more specifically, on the answer to the question whether "legislation denying to the illegitimate rights against his father that are granted to those of legitimate birth is . . . related to a proper public concern with respect to which legitimate and illegitimate children are not situated similarly." [11] This question is the real issue in these cases. It was answered in the *Levy* case with regard to the child's relationship to his *mother* to the effect that no proper legislative purpose justifies discrimination between legitimate and illegitimate children. Therefore, it should be inquired (a) whether there are legislative purposes which support legislation discriminating between legitimate and illegitimate children in the *father*-child context that are not present in the *mother*-child context and (b) whether such other or additional purposes pass the test of the Fourteenth Amendment. This question was not dealt with by any of the courts since *Levy,* although one earlier (father-child) case [12] pointed in the right direction: "Significantly, a very persuasive argument can be made that a decision contrary to ours would deny appellant's daughter her Fourteenth Amendment right to equal protection of the laws, since there is no valid social reason, for purposes of welfare legislation, for distinguishing between members of the class 'illegitimate children' and other members of the broader class 'children' to which the members of the more narrow class belong."

2. The argument relating to uncertainty of paternity is sound in

11. Krause, *Equal Protection for the Illegitimate,* 65 MICH L. REV. 477, 486 (1967).
12. Armijo v. Wesselius, 440 P.2d 471, 474 (Wash. 1968).

all cases in which paternity is uncertain. However, it is absurd to argue that because there is no proof in some cases, no obligation should be imposed in cases where there is proof. In the cases in question paternity was known.

3. The referral to the legislature begs the question which is whether the equal protection clause requires equality. If it does, then it is the duty of the courts to ensure equality with or without implementing legislation and, if necessary, in contravention of opposing enactments.

Justice Douglas may be criticized for having produced an un-scholarly opinion on so important a subject. His opinion furnished a deserving target for Justice Harlan's biting dissent.[13] However, although at first hearing the dissenters sound almost more plausible than does Justice Douglas they, too, did not take time to think things through. What follows is an attempt to clarify some of the issues that future cases should discuss.

This much is clear: Whatever the analytical inelegance of *Levy,* the case prohibits law discriminating against the person of il-legitimate birth in his relationship with his mother *because no rational legislative purpose supports such discrimination.* Is there another legislative purpose applicable to discrimination in regard to the relationship between father and child? Just what did Louisiana have in mind with its statutory scheme discriminating against the illegitimate?

Seeking to justify the statute, the Louisiana Court below had held that "denying illegitimate children the right to recover in such a case is actually based on morals and general welfare because it discourages bringing children into the world out of wedlock."[14] In its brief, the State of Louisiana had argued that its purpose was not punitive but positive—"the *encouragement* of marriage as one of the most important institutions known to law, the preservation of the legitimate family as the preferred environment for so-cializing the child, and the preservation of the security and certainty of property rights linked with family status."[15]

---

13. This is discussed in detail in Krause, *Legitimate and Illegitimate Offspring of Levy v. Louisiana—First Decisions on Equal Protection and Paternity,* 36 U. Chi. L. Rev. 338 (1969).

14. Levy v. Louisiana, 192 So.2d 193, 195 (La. Ct. App. 1967).

15. Brief for the Attorney General, State of Louisiana as Amicus Curiae at 4–5, Levy v. Louisiana, 391 U.S. 68 (1968).

Encouraging marriage is indeed a valid legislative purpose. The fault in Louisiana's argument lies in the constitutional requirement that a fair connection exist between a statute and a valid purpose, in this instance between the status of the illegitimate child under the law and his mother's (or father's) conduct. If there is any connection, it lies in the expectation that a potential mother will be so concerned about the treatment that awaits her illegitimate child at the hands of the law that she will adjust her conduct accordingly. The rising illegitimate birth rate illustrates that vast numbers of illegitimate mothers are not guided by this. But even if there were an effective relationship, it would not be permissible to punish an innocent non-party for someone else's undesirable conduct. Justice Douglas held the discrimination "invidious" because "no action, conduct, or demeanor of (the illegitimate children) is possibly relevant to the harm that was done the mother."[16] In his concurring opinion in *Smith* v. *King,* Justice Douglas expressed this point even more cogently when he compared the stigma of illegitimacy to the "archaic corruption of the blood, a form of bill of attainder."[17] There is no reason to think the proper legislative purpose of encouraging marriage any more valid when it is related to legal discrimination in the illegitimate child's relation with his father than when related to the mother. Actually, the law's failure to impose a substantial economic burden on the illegitimate father may be more likely to encourage illegitimacy than marriage.

A wide variety of other arguments that might be viewed as supporting legal discrimination between legitimate and illegitimate children in their relations with their fathers have been discussed and refuted elsewhere.[18] These arguments include a supposed legislative intent to discourage promiscuity, to protect the family, to emphasize the actual child-father relationship that exists in a family unit, to allow the father a choice in recognizing or not recognizing his child. Little purpose would be served here by repeating this discussion which demonstrated that the true basis for the legislatively imposed discrimination is found in history, not reason.

16. 391 U.S. at 72.
17. 392 U.S. 309, 336 n.5 (1968).
18. Krause, *Equal Protection for the Illegitimate,* 65 Mich L. Rev. 477, 489–500 (1967).

Ascertainment of Paternity

There would seem to be only one factor that seriously differs as to the father. This is the problem of ascertaining paternity which always will remain the irreducible minimum relevance of birth out of wedlock. As discussed above, this point belongs in the realm of proof. If there is no proof, no relation should be imposed. If there is proof, there is no problem. But there is one further question here—can the law remain inactive? Equality vis-à-vis the father means nothing if the father remains unknown. The rationale of the equal protection approach (which runs in terms of the rights of the illegitimate child) therefore implies that the interest primarily at stake in the paternity action is that of the child. This contrasts sharply with existing paternity statutes which usually run in favor of the mother and do not concern themselves with "rights" of the child. The primacy of the child's interest will now require recognition. At the least, it will be necessary that the child, by his representative, be a party to an action involving his paternity, regardless of other parties (such as the mother) who may assert their own interests in the same action. It also must be recognized that it will not be enough merely to provide rights to the child on whose behalf an action is actually brought. Since the child cannot act for himself in the short time after his birth when there is hope of finding the father, a mechanism should be provided to ascertain the illegitimate's paternity whenever possible and desirable in his best interests. Even if no support is sought or if the putative father is unable to pay support and likely to remain so, a proceeding to declare the child's paternity may be a necessary safeguard of an illegitimate child's potential inheritance from his father or paternal relatives. In this connection, Justice Harlan's concern with the possibility that the administration of estates will be excessively burdened with paternity litigation is of considerable merit.[19] Definite and reasonable standards of proof of paternity will have to be provided *legislatively* to avoid just that. It seems clear, however, that the legislatures will not be free to set any standard of proof of paternity they deem fit. While there is no doubt that it is "rationally permissible," indeed necessary, that an illegitimate child prove paternity by other means than a legitimate child (who

19. Levy v. Louisiana, 391 U.S. 68, 80–81 (1968).

merely shows the marriage certificate of his parents), the fulfillment of the constitutional equality standard cannot be allowed to
depend on (and perhaps be thwarted by) unduly burdensome and
unreasonable requirements of proof of paternity that a state may
wish to set up. The standards that are set must meet the test
of reasonableness.

Other problems that beset the paternity action are not related
directly to the constitutional argument. It may be hoped, however, that the forthcoming new look at our illegitimacy laws
under *Levy* will carry further than minimally required or implied
by the equality standard. Questions such as civil or criminal
proceeding, trial by jury or judge and the weight and admissibility
of scientific evidence have gone too long without intelligent
answers. It is certain that the current paternity prosecution
practice in many metropolitan areas is abhorrent. Blackmail and
perjury flourish, accusation often is tantamount to conviction,
decades of support obligation are decided upon in minutes of
court time and indigent defendants often go without counsel or a
clear understanding of what is involved. But there *is* an alternative.

Assuming now that paternity has been ascertained in a given
case—is there any further justification for denying the illegitimate
a legal relationship with his father similar to that enjoyed by a
legitimate child? And if, as seems fairly obvious at this point, no
permissible legislative purpose supports the wholesale discrimination imposed by our present order on illegitimates as a class, may
narrower distinctions fairly be drawn in specific cases?

Perhaps so. However, our present law is not cast in terms of
rational distinctions that make actual sense. It is governed instead
by the broad criterion of illegitimacy which is either grossly over-
or underinclusive in terms of any rational categories that may be
defined. Thus it falls short of the equal protection test. Among
others, these laws include support laws which do not concern
themselves with need or actual dependency but with legitimacy;
intestacy laws which on the basis of legitimacy alone pass an
inheritance to a legitimate fifth cousin rather than give it to an
illegitimate son; cases or statutes interpreting wills or trusts which
prescribe that "child" or "issue" means *legitimate* child or issue,
without reference to the testator's or settlor's actual intent; tax
laws which provide favorable inheritance tax rates to legitimate
children but treat illegitimates as unrelated; custody laws which

often deny the support-paying father as little as a right of visitation, not on the basis of fitness but on the basis of illegitimacy;
federal welfare laws that are interpreted to provide benefits for
legitimate children only and state workmen's compensation and
wrongful death acts that do the same. These laws are not only
bad—they are invalid.[20]

If equality is the standard, some question arises as to what this
means. Should equality be sought through legal neutrality or must
the law act affirmatively to help the illegitimate approximate the
situation of the legitimate child? As mentioned above, affirmative
action to ascertain paternity would seem indicated whenever this
is possible and in the child's best interests. A more difficult
question is whether the illegitimate's right of support should be
extended beyond the father's death by providing a liquidated
support claim against the father's estate. This would make the
illegitimate somewhat more than equal since the father may
disinherit his legitimate child without making provision for support (but of course he is far more likely to do that to an illegitimate
than to a legitimate child.) While this is one arguable preference,
it may be said with respect to most other problem areas that even
"if legal *neutrality* is inadequate to compensate for inequality in
fact, to have the law take *affirmative* steps toward factual equality
opens . . . a Pandora's box of difficult problems of value judgment, prejudice and preference."[21] Although somewhat similar
problems are now being discussed at the fringes of the racial
equality requirement, the illegitimate's claim probably should be
limited to the degree of equality that neutral laws can furnish.

To be sure, much of the national problem of illegitimacy—one
in fifteen children is now born illegitimate and in some urban
areas the rate exceeds fifty percent—lies in the public sector and
requires public help in social and economic terms. But there it
lies as an integral aspect of the poverty problem and the criterion
for public help is poverty, not illegitimacy. If, by reducing social
and economic poverty, public relief also reduces illegitimacy and
some of its burdens, this does not overlap with the ground covered

20. This is discussed in detail in Krause, *Legitimate and Illegitimate
Offspring of Levy v. Louisiana—First Decisions on Equal Protection and
Paternity*, 36 U. Chi. L. Rev. 338 (1969).
21. Krause, *Bastards Abroad—Foreign Approaches to Illegitimacy*, 15
Am. J. Comp. L. 726, 751 (1967).

here. Here the focus is on the *private* resources that the law should make available to the illegitimate to provide him an even start in life. These resources are his parents, especially his father. If public relief must alleviate some of the worst aspects of illegitimacy, in a society that thinks in terms of the primacy of individual—not collective—responsibility, the relief that is the subject of this paper must ultimately take over the task. *Consider that our present laws deny one in four Negro children a legal relationship with his father.*[22]

22. In his brief *amicus curiae* filed with the U.S. Supreme Court in the *Levy* case, this author noted that, although the Louisiana Wrongful Death Act employed no racial criterion on its face, it operated far more severely upon Negroes as a class than upon whites. This covert discrimination came about in two ways. First, disproportionately more Negro children than white children are born out of wedlock. In Louisiana in 1965, the U.S. Department of Health, Education and Welfare reported, 8,276 illegitimate children were born to Negroes and 1,158 were born to whites. *U.S. News and World Report,* Oct. 2, 1967 at 85. The national picture is similar. In 1963, the Vital Statistics Division of the Public Health Service, U.S. Department of Health, Education and Welfare, estimated that the white illegitimacy rate was 30.7 per 1,000 live births; the non-white rate was 235.9. (While the non-white classification includes Orientals, Indians and Negroes, Negroes so predominate numerically (more than 90%) that the non-white classification reflects the Negro figure with reasonable accuracy. U.S. Bureau of the Census, *Statistical Abstracts of the United States* 28 (1967).) See United States Department of Labor, Office of Policy Planning and Research, *The Negro Family: The Case for National Action* (hereafter referred to as *The Moynihan Report*) 8–9, 59. By 1965, the white rate was 39.6 and the Negro rate was 263.2 per thousand live births. *U.S. News and World Report,* Oct. 2, 1967 at 84. These figures drastically understate the problem, for among the impoverished urban Negroes the illegitimacy rate has been rising much faster than it has risen nationally. In the District of Columbia, the illegitimacy rate for non-whites grew from 21.8 percent in 1950, to 29.5 percent in 1964. *The Moynihan Report* at 9. In impoverished areas of the District the 1963 rate was 38 percent. *Id.* at 70. In Harlem, the non-white illegitimacy rate in 1963 was more than 43 percent. *Id.* at 19. In some areas of Chicago, the illegitimacy rate stands at 38 percent. Champaign-Urbana [Illinois] News Gazette, Feb. 14, 1966, p. 13. In Central Harlem, illegitimacy stood at 54.2 percent in 1967. N.Y. Times, July 1, 1967.

The second and even more important reason that made the statute disproportionately more burdensome for Negroes than for whites is that a high percentage (70%) of white illegitimate children are adopted and thereby achieve status under the Wrongful Death Act, at least with regard to their adoptive parents, whereas very few (3–5%) Negro illegitimates find adoptive parents. U.S. Department of Health, Education and Welfare, *Illegitimacy and its Impact on the Aid to Dependent Children Program* 35–36 (1960).

Conclusion

Whatever the outcome as to any specific instance of discrimination, no rational reason supports the wholesale discrimination imposed by our present legal order. It seems clear that a great advancement in the legal position of the illegitimate will be realized under the *Levy* case without harm to existing institutions.

Griffin v. County School Board, 377 U.S. 218 (1964), involved a comparable point because, on its face, the closing of the public schools of Prince Edward County to white and Negro children was not discriminatory. However, the Supreme Court unanimously held the school closing "to deny colored students equal protection of the laws" because "[c]losing Prince Edward's schools bears more heavily on Negro children in Prince Edward County since white children there have accredited private schools which they can attend while colored children until very recently have had no available private schools, and even the school they now attend is a temporary expedient." If the uneven numerical incidence of illegitimacy among Negroes and whites in itself provides an analogy, the fact that adoption facilities are open and widely utilized by white illegitimates improves the analogy. The analogy was perfected by a Louisiana statute which forbids interracial adoption and thereby closes to Negroes, solely on the ground of race, one method of escape from the discrimination under the Wrongful Death Act. LA. REV. STAT. §9:422 (1950). (Loving v. Virginia, 388 U.S. 1 (1967), of course, presumably voids this statute.)

Applying the national percentages on white adoptions (70%) and non-white adoptions (4%) to the 1965 Louisiana illegitimacy figures (1,158 white, 8,276 Negro) it may be estimated that only 347 white children remained unadopted, whereas 7,945 Negro children remained unadopted. *This means that 95.8 percent of all persons potentially affected by the operation of the Louisiana Wrongful Death Act were Negroes.* For all practical purposes this means that the criterion of *illegitimacy* as used under the Louisiana Wrongful Death Act was synonymous with a *racial* classification.

It was not contended, of course, that the construction of the Louisiana statute against illegitimates, at least in its inception, had a racially discriminatory intent. Nor was it contended that a statute which happens to fall most heavily upon one particular group is for that reason alone unconstitutional. However, it was suggested to the Court that Louisiana is a Southern state with a long history of racial discrimination and that the operation of the Wrongful Death Act, if accidentally, fits perfectly into a pattern of legislation which often is only a thinly disguised cover for racial discrimination. For example, in 1960 Louisiana amended its constitution to deny the right to vote in federal and state elections for a period of five years after the birth of an illegitimate child, to both parents of an illegitimate child. *La. Const,* art. 8, §§ 1(5), (6). *See* brief for NAACP Legal Defense and Educational Fund, Inc. and National Office for the Rights of the Indigent as *amici curiae* at 18–20, Levy v. Louisiana, 391 U.S. 68 (1968). The Supreme Court, perhaps wisely, stayed clear of this aspect of the controversy.

The family will not cease to exist. This is a tired concern. For example, in the eighth century, St. Boniface described the English "both Christians and pagans, as refusing to have legitimate wives, and continuing to live in lechery and adultery after the manner of neighing horses and braying asses," and wrote to King Ethelbald: "Your contempt for lawful matrimony, were it for chastity's sake, would be laudable; but since you wallow in luxury, and even in adultery with nuns, it is disgraceful and damnable. . . . Give heed to this; if the nation of the Angles, . . . despising lawful matrimony, gives free indulgence to adultery, a race ignoble and scorning God must necessarily issue from such unions, and will destroy the country by their abandoned manners." [23]

We still have adultery and we still have families. Indeed, if we did not still have families—there could be no adultery. Similarly, if there were no families, there would be no legitimacy, and consequently no illegitimacy.[24] If equal rights are sought for the child without a family, it is only on the assumption that the family will remain.

The Equal Protection Clause has set the standard that must be met. We may rely on the courts to chart a haphazard route through the difficult questions touched on above and see the answers vary from case to case and court to court. On the other hand, we may answer the complicated question of whether legitimates and illegitimates are situated similarly for the fair purposes of a particular law through detailed, preferably uniform, legislation that centers on the interests of the child and embodies the equality principle of the Fourteenth Amendment.[25] The latter course seems clearly the better. It is indeed fortunate that a committee of the National Conference of Commissioners on Uniform State Laws was recently appointed to study the need for uniform legislation in this area.

23. DURANT, THE AGE OF FAITH 487 (1950).
24. Have the Ethopians achieved the perfect solution (? ? ? !): "Le mariage est prohibé entre parents." Art. 582, Parente, Code: livre II, titre IV, Ch. III in David, Le Droit de la Famille dans le Code Civil Ethopien (1967).
25. Cf. Krause, *Bringing the Bastard into the Great Society—A Proposed Uniform Act on Legitimacy*, 44 TEX. L. REV. 829, 832–41.

Elizabeth J. du Fresne

12

The Rights of Foster Children to Financial Benefits of Foster Parents Under Federal Statutes

"If not by birth . . ." *

From the conception of the American Republic, the traditional Continental emphasis on bloodline has been noticeably absent. It has been replaced by a doctrine of individual worth, ostensibly based on merit rather than on geneology. The French commentor, de Tocqueville, remarked in 1840 in his study *Democracy in America:*

> Thus not only does democracy make every man forget his ancestors, but it hides his descendants and separates his contemporaries from him, it throws him back forever upon himself alone and threatens in the end to confine him entirely within the solitude of his own heart.[1]

This quote beautifully describes the abstract individual's role in a theoretical, wholly democratic America; but the actual individual in his own little part of America would be quite lonely in the

ELIZABETH J. DU FRESNE, J. D., is a practicing attorney in Miami, presently Civil Rights and Law Reform trial and appeal lawyer with the Economic Opportunity Legal Services Program, Inc. of Dade County, Florida. This article, revised by the author, is reprinted with permission from the *Journal of Family Law* 7(1967):613–35.

* Edmund, illegitimate son of Gloucester, in *King Lear,* says in Act I, Scene ii:

> Wherefore should I
> Stand in the plague of custom, and permit
> The curiosity of nations to deprive me
> . . . Let me, if not by birth, have lands by wit.

1. Part II, 2d Book, ch. 2 (Modern Library ed., 1960).

"solitude of his own heart." From the practical perspective, it can be easily observed that a democracy, like most other political forms, is composed, not of individuals, but of family units. Perhaps, in a democracy, this family unit has less influence as to the final success or failure of each family member in society than does the corresponding Old World unit, but the unit still remains all-important in many aspects of democratic existence.

The problem with which this article will deal is that of the foster child [2] and his federal rights to benefits flowing from his foster family. There is no better example of an individual who has truly "forgotten his ancestors." Yet, in the forgetting of past ties, there is no matching adoption of new ones, beyond those of custom and affection. The foster child is so completely separated from his contemporaries that he is left, not only in "solitude," but in a legal no-man's-land. Few cases or legislative enactments acknowledge the existence of such individuals. Only in recent years have the respected institutions of society begun to hesitatingly accept such persons as "members of the family." Of these institutions, the law has been among the most ponderously slow in enlarging its concept of the family. Whether in a democracy or not, there is a near sacred worth attached to family membership. The law in its mystic role of guardian of societal values has been determined to protect the accepted norm.

The concept of the family is not a static condition that needs only be viewed dispassionately to be correctly evaluated and assessed. Rather than constant, it is a perpetually changing way of viewing a group of humans.

At one time family feelings merged with tribal allegiances. Later this very kind of "community of man" sentiment led to divergent results: (1) both the extreme attachment to the Fatherland which in Nazi existence obliterated ties to one's closest relations, and the passive acceptance of the Orwellian Big Brother State which

2. For the purposes of the present study, the term "foster child" shall include all those persons who live in a parent/child relationship with its usual duties and obligations without benefit of any legal recognition of such parent/child relationship. Persons falling within this class range from stepchildren to dependent relatives, from unrelated children put in the home by the Court as part of a juvenile delinquency charge to babies who are in the process of being adopted. It also includes those persons usually designated by the limited meaning of the term "foster child," i.e. children taken to care for on a somewhat temporary basis for payment from state welfare branches.

marks much of the non-productive aspects of modern socialism; and (2) the partial submergence of personal family divisions in the communal farms of New Israel. In each of these situations the term "family" is a term of art, more or less significant, more or less defined, blending with a vague but superior entity.

This process is not clearly present in American society, and thus the individual family unit must be precisely defined. The search for precision has been costly. It has cast countless individuals who have not observed legal niceties in their relationships into a position where they cannot inherit from the only parents they ever knew.[3] The discrimination is not limited to the probate court; it reaches out to restrict a foster child's participation in practically every facet of possible financial benefit.

Place of the Foster Child in American Society

The incongruity of the modern circumscription of the foster child's rights is highlighted by the history of the custom of

3. Some background information on the foster child under inheritance law is pertinent since many of the federal statutes under consideration herein either specify or have been interpreted to imply that the state law on devolution of personal property shall govern the eligibility for benefits of foster children.

At common law there was no duty to support a foster child, Ladd v. Welfare Commissioner, 217 A.2d 490 (Conn. 1965); and unless they were specifically designated and named in the will, they could not inherit through the general class categories of "children" or "issue" or "heirs," *In re* Rick's Will, 258 N.Y.S.2d 171. (Sur. Ct. 1965).

This harsh reasoning has been somewhat mitigated by statutory changes in the individual states, but there is no true "consensus" on the issue today.

The earliest cases of the United States Supreme Court have supported a liberal construction of words of devise and descent. *E.g.* Den v. Baskerville, 52 U.S. (11 How.) 329, (1850): " 'Children' has a legal significancy, extending as the case may be to grandchildren, and even to illegitimate children. . . ."

Recent state cases reflecting a similar policy are exemplified by *In re* Grace's Will, 261 N.Y.S.2d 236 (Sur. Ct. 1965) in which adopted grandchildren were included in the term "issue" and other generic terms expressing parent/child relationship, absent on explicit purpose to exclude the child. However, there are many cases like Bryant v. Thrower, 239 Ark. 783, 394 S.W.2d 488 (1965) in which birth or adoption were interpreted as creating permanent relationships while the foster parent condition, specifically called *in loco parentis* here, was considered a mere temporary setup.

In Rodrigues v. Vivoni, 201 U.S. 371 (1905), Mr. Justice Holmes read "issue" to cover an unrelated foster child, but the case has not had far-reaching effects because it was muddied by the presence of much Spanish law.

"fostering." [4] It sprang up in ancient Ireland. There children were placed with their fosterers at a young age and the relationship thus created was thought to be much stronger than blood ties. The custom is said to have grown up in order to give poor families a chance to let their children better themselves and to give wealthy families persons to whom their fortunes might pass. [5] To understand how far away that original purpose is, one has only to realize that a foster child today has no assurance that he will be allowed to receive any share in his "parents' " estate, and, in some states, is barred from receiving anything at all if natural children exist.

Until 1926, there was no legally recognized process of adoption in America, so all the thousands of children living with persons other than their natural parents were part of the "foster child" category. [6] The establishment of adoption did not eliminate or substantially decrease the number of foster children to be contended with. [7] States have become more aware of the necessity for providing means of support other than "relief" and public institutions. A great number of statutes have tended to create more foster home situations. [8]

The Negro community alone gives rise to thousands of foster homes each year, as manifested by the fact that only a minority of Negro children, attaining the age of eighteen years, have lived

4. The verb "foster" means, according to *In re* Norman's Estate, 295 N.W. 63, 66 (Minn. 1940), to nourish or provide with food; hence, to rear, air or encourage. As an adjective, the opinion continues, "foster" means "affording, receiving or sharing nourishment, nurture, or sustenance, although not related by blood, or by ties of nature, or the like."
The opinion also discusses the welfare-department-appointed "foster parent" and says the remuneration fixed for the rearing of a foster child is "fosterlean."

5. BLACK'S LAW DICTIONARY 784 (4th ed. 1951).

6. AMERICAN BAR ASSOCIATION. SESSION ON FAMILY LAW, SUMMARY OF PROCEEDINGS (Washington, D.C. 1960), quoted in Dix, *A Legal Dissertation For Parents and Those in Loco Parentis,* 2 J. FAM. L. 6 (1962).

7. The suggestion is made in Simsarian, *Foster Care Possibilities in a Suburban Community,* 11 CHILDREN 97–102 (1964), that although the past tendency has been to recruit foster parents from the lower income areas of the city or from rural farms, in the future more and more homes in higher income sections of suburbia will also be open to foster children. The survey conducted in the highest income county, of the highest income area of the country (Bethesda-Kensington, Md.) showed that of the 60 families interviewed, 12 had provided fulltime foster care for children for 4 months or more.

8. W. BROCKELBANK, INTERSTATE ENFORCEMENT OF FAMILY SUPPORT 30–31 (1960).

all their lives with both of their natural parents.[9] Deterioration of the Negro family structure has been cited repeatedly as the fundamental source of the weakness of the Negro community today.[10] The result of this breakdown of the family is the creation of more foster relationships. Since the Negro family has the largest number of children and the lowest income of any ethnic group, it is likely that neither the natural nor the foster home is adequately equipped to support these children.[11] At the present rate of "overproduction," it has been estimated by the Department of Health, Education, and Welfare that in 1972, one out of eight Americans will be non-white.[12] Thus the problem will become increasingly more significant in the next few years.[13]

Foster care is, of course, not limited to lower class Negroes [14]— but in that instance the need for participation in financial benefits can be dramatically illustrated because without such benefits, small though they may be, the child is almost certain to become completely dependent upon the state for its sustenance. Since, under some state plans, foster children who are neither related to their foster parents nor placed with them by a state agency are not eligible for Aid for Dependent Children, these children may well end up in state institutions.[15] This seems to be a result which defeats the very purpose of welfare legislation.

9. THE NEGRO FAMILY: THE CASE FOR NATIONAL ACTION, Office of Policy, Planning, and Research, U.S. Dept. of Labor, 9 (1966).
10. *Id.* at 5. "Family structure of lower class Negroes is highly unstable and in many urban centers is approaching complete breakdown."
11. *Id.* at 25. The majority (56%) of Negro children receive public assistance under Aid For Dependent Children at one point or another during their childhood. At the present time 14% of America's Negro children are on AFDC as compared to 2% of the white children, p. 12.
12. *Id.* at 25.
13. *Id.* at 30. "By destroying the Negro family under slavery, whites broke the will of the Negro. Although the will has reasserted itself in our time, it is a resurgence doomed to frustration unless the viability of the Negro family is fully restored."
14. CHILDREN'S AGENCY, SOCIAL SECURITY ADMINISTRATION, ESSENTIALS OF ADOPTION LAW AND PROCEDURE, CB PUB. NO. 331, (1949). There the example is given of all the countless young men, white and non-white alike, who were at loss as to how to explain to the Army during World War II that the neatly printed form calling for next-of-kin needed to be answered by a name of one who was, in fact, no legally recognized kin.
15. The policy and purpose of legislation for dependent children is to provide a means of support for dependent children in a home atmosphere rather than the impersonal process of institutionalization, Ladd v. Welfare Commissioner, 217 A.2d 490 (Conn. 1965).

No single law concerned with the well-being of children can be truly evaluated by itself. A federal agency has issued a statement of policy that reads as follows: "The principles and the standards essential for full protection of children must be the foundation of the whole network of statutory and administrative provisions benefiting children." [16] What are these "principles and standards"? Can they be found embodied in the statutes? This appears unlikely since a goodly portion of the federal statutes leave the standard of eligibility up to the devolution laws of the individual states—a highly diversified standard at best; a highly arbitrary and irrelevant standard frequently.

Federal Statutory Provisions

The statutes themselves might be divided into three categories: [17]

1) Those in which Congress has defined "child" explicitly in the context of the statute; [18]

2) Those in which Congress has provided that "child" be defined by state law; [19] and

3) Those in which the term "child" stands alone and the courts must provide the standards and interpretation.[20] In examining individual federal statutes, an attempt shall be made to discover whether there exists any common purpose behind the statutes granting financial benefits to "children," and whether there is any consistent criteria for judging whether foster children are eligible for these benefits.

The statutes under consideration are quite varied in the situations from whence their benefits arise and, although representative, do not pretend to cover the subject definitively. The question of foster children's rights to benefits is new to the courts, in the sense that it has not often been before the bench for ruling; but the question is also as old as the human family [21] in that the aban-

16. *Supra* note 14, at 3.

17. Categories suggested by a note on *The Rights of Illegitimates under Federal Statutes*, 76 HARV. L. REV. 337 (1960).

18. *E.g.*, Longshoremen and Harbor Workers Act, 85 U.S.C. § 902(14) (1958).

19. *E.g.*, Social Security Act, 42 U.S.C. 416(e) (1958).

20. *E.g.*, Federal Death on the High Seas Act, 46 U.S.C. § 761 (1958).

21. One of Western Civilization's early legends is the story of Romulus and Remus, who had a wolf for a "foster mother."

doned or orphaned child has always been cared for and, presumably, dealt with in some manner after his foster parents' demise.

Although the ancient manner of "caring for" may well have amounted to sharing a corner at which to beg alms, the awakened social consciousness of America lends a more literal meaning to "care for." As an example of this mass conscience in action in the law, consider the Longshoremen and Harbor Workers Act,[22] prototype for Workmen's Compensation legislation throughout the country.[23] The act falls within the first classification of statutes: those in which Congress has defined the term "child." Insofar as the definition in the federal statute is complete in itself, that definition is binding upon any interpreting agency.[24] The LHWA's statutory construction of the limits of "children," included as beneficiaries under its provisions for compensation to families in the event of death or disability, is one of the most liberal:

> "Child" shall include a posthumous child, a child legally adopted prior to the injury of the employee, a child in relation to whom the deceased employee stood in loco parentis for at least one year prior to the time of injury, and a stepchild or acknowleged illegitimate child dependent upon the deceased, but does not include married children unless wholly dependent on him.[25]

Certainly such a definition goes far in substantially supporting the purpose of the legislation of which it is part. By looking to the actual day-to-day relationship of the persons involved, rather than by mechanically applying an antiquated conception of a narrowly defined family unit, persons who were actually dependent[26] upon the wage earner will be eligible to be compensated for their very real loss. Such policy is expressed by the Alaskan District Court in a decision concerned with the Alaskan Workmen's Compensation Act, an act modeled after the federal LHWA:

> . . . Not only is there no reason why those who stand in loco parentis to dependent children should be denied such benefits, but it would seem to be sound public policy to provide such

22. 88 U.S.C. §§ 901–950 (1958). Hereinafter LHWA.
23. *Supra* note 17, at 339.
24. Ellis v. Henderson, 204 F.2d 173, 175 (5th Cir. 1953).
25. 33 U.S.C. § 902(14) (1958).
26. The federal statute has been found not to require dependency if the child is under 18 in the cases Turnbull v. Cyr, 188 F.2d 455 (9th Cir. 1951), and Maryland Drydock Co. v. Parker, 37 F. Supp. 717 (D.C. Md. 1941).

benefits in view of the fact that one of the objectives of the
Workmen's Compensation system is to provide support for those
made destitute by the death of their provider.[27]

The opinion continues in a generalized discussion of Workmen's
Compensation laws, concluding that there has been a "trend . . .
toward enlargement and liberalization . . . rather than contraction
and restriction." [28]

The broad lines of LHWA belie the old adage that a statesman cannot afford to be a moralist. He cannot afford not to be,
or at least give the impression of being, a moralist. Obviously
there is a moral—or, better, a utilitarianly ethical—principle
behind the drafting of laws so that they include the widest possible
range of persons in their beneficiary categories. The persons who
disagree would probably believe that politicians cannot bother
themselves with the foster children's trivial percentage of the population when the conditions of all children must be improved. If one
thing can be learned from the strength of the appeal of the Negro's
cause in modern society, it is that in America, there still exists a
predominant belief that a government must protect and nurture
the minorities. Hopefully, in the light of the civil rights movement,
the "objective rather than moral" argument will become increasingly weaker. Those who are strong and prosperous can wait for
services which bring extra comfort while those who are poor and
weak are given the minimum to endure. The foster child is already
weaker than other children through the lack of solidarity of his
world. The child who has one foster home often has many.[29]

Restrictive Effect of Reference to State Laws

Statutes with flexible definitions of family membership, like the
Longshoremen and Harbor Workers Act, will undoubtedly become more numerous if the trend towards less rigid family lines

27. Juneau Lumber Co., Inc. v. Alaska Industrial Board, 122 F. Supp.
663, 664 (D.C. Alaska 1964).
28. *Id.* at 664. *Contra,* Stellmah v. Hunterdon Corp., 211 A.2d 201
(N.J. Super. 1965) in which 99 C.J.S. *Workman's Compensation* § 141
(2)(b) is quoted approvingly. The child in question resided with the wage
earner pending a formal adoption. Since the adoption was not a legally
accomplished fact prior to the wage earner's death, the child was not entitled
to recover under the state act as a dependent of the wage earner.
29. *Supra* note 9, at 25.

becomes a societal actuality. However, until such time, the situation will continue to be one marked by confusion. The federal purpose becomes more and more markedly to apply compensation to all those children who because of a dependence upon the deceased individual suffered loss. The state laws on descent and distribution are distinctly tighter in their view of the family—and, perhaps, understandably so, since they are not concerned with compensating individuals who have suffered loss, but with making proper allocation among his relations of whatever assets the deceased possessed at death. Since one is compensatory in nature and the other is only an ordering of rights to assets already ascertained, it is strange that again and again the latter provides the test for eligibility to the former. The two types of statutes are not analogous as to purpose or function, but still the parochial perspective of state intestate succession law can determine a child's qualification for the supposedly compensatory federal welfare benefits.[30]

An example of the contradictory effect of the strict state standard's utilization in welfare activity is found in a comparison of the legislative history of the Federal Employer's Liability Act [31] with the act's subsequent operation. The Congressional records reveal that the act's beneficiary provision [32] was intended by its drafters to: "Certainly . . . be as broad, as comprehensive, and as inclusive in its terms as any of the similar remedial statutes existing in any of the states which are suspended in their operation by the federal legislation upon the subject." [33] One of the class of statutes so suspended in its application to the designated class of employees

30. *Contra,* 3 SUTHERLAND ON STATUTORY CONSTRUCTION § 7205 (13 Ed., 1943), in which liberal interpretation of statutes in order to accomplish the statute's general purpose is advocated.

31. 35 Stat. 65; 45 U.S.C. § 51, *et seq.* Hereinafter referred to as FELA.

32. Although there are several alternative parts of the statute, depending upon whether death was instantaneous or a disabling injury occurred, the beneficiary list is the same as in § 51 herein quoted: "In case of the death of such employee, [the employer shall be liable] to his or her personal representative for the benefit of the surviving widow or husband and children of such employee; and, if none, then of such employee's parents; and, if none, then of the next of kin dependent upon such employee, for such injury or death resulting. . . ." There is no indication in the entire text of the statute that Congress intended the use of state statutory standards, Comment, *Beneficiaries Under the Federal Employer's Liability Act,* 19 WASH. & LEE L. REV. 105 (1962).

33. S. REP. NO. 433, 61st Cong., 2d Sess. 12–15 (1910); H.R. REP. NO. 513, 61st Cong., 2d Sess. 6 (1910).

is the workmen's compensation acts of the several states.[34]   An example of the terms of one of these acts is offered in the Tennessee Workmen's Compensation Act.[35]   Upon showing of actual support, a stepchild, an illegitimate minor sister, a nephew, and unrelated children have been held qualified as proper beneficiaries.[36] The federal court decisions on FELA matters arising in Tennessee have been correspondingly generous, despite rigid intestate provisions in the Tennessee Code.[37]   Most other state statutes in the Workmen's Compensation field are equally broad in the base standard for beneficiaries.   And yet—until quite recently, there was almost universal adherence to the severely constricted definition of state succession statutes.   Largely responsible for this widespread judicial attitude is the well known Supreme Court decision of *Seaboard Air Lines Railroad v. Kenney:* [38]

---

34. Pizzitola, *FELA: Jensen v. Elgin,* 40 TEXAS L. REV. 40 (1962).

35. TENN. CODE ANN. §§ 28–107 (1956). For a good general discussion of the act, *See* Shelley v. Central Woodwork, Inc., 207 Tenn. 411, 340 S.W.2d 896 (1960).

36. *Supra* note 34, at 41, for detailed description of Tennessee's beneficiary categories. For the matter of unrelated children as beneficiaries, *See* Kinnard v. Tennessee Chemical Co., 157 Tenn. 206, 2 S.W.2d 807 (1928); Memphis Fertilizer Co. v. Small, 160 Tenn. 235, 22 S.W.2d 1037 (1930); and Wilmoth v. Phoenix Utility Co., 168 Tenn. 95, 75 S.W.2d 48 (1934). In all these cases, the test used is dependency, not relationship.

37. *E.g.,* Tune v. Louisville and Nashville Railroad Co., 223 F. Supp. 928 (M.D. Tenn., 1963). Therein one finds expressed beliefs concerning the FELA's purpose which reflect the sentiments of the drafters, examined above. The court states that "under the Federal Employer's Liability Act the crucial test is one of dependency." The court views the act as creating "two rights: one for the benefit of an injured employee during his lifetime but which does not survive his death; the other, an entirely new right in the beneficiaries to compensate them for *their* loss upon death." [Emphasis by the court]. Since the FELA is not a survival act, "the rights of action which accrues to the beneficiaries is based on injury to them, not the deceased, and is measured by the amount of loss suffered by them." The beneficiaries, therefore, have a right completely apart from that of the deceased had he lived.

The court concludes that since the test utilized is one of dependency "therefore even unrelated children are entitled to compensation if actually dependent. . . . To deny these children the right to seek recovery primarily serves to punish them for a condition not of their own making, and conceivably will place on the state and on the public the burden of their support."

38. 240 U.S. 489 (1916), considered the definitive case dealing with Federal Employer's Liability Act. Accord, Murphy v. Houma Well Service, 409 F.2d 804 (5th Cir. 1969).

Under our dual system of government, who are next of kin is determined by the legislation of the various states to whose authority that subject is normally committed. It would seem to be clear that the absence of a definition in the Act of Congress plainly indicates the purpose of Congress to leave the determination of that question to state law.[39]

The key words "next of kin" have often been read since *Kenney* [40] as a signal that intestate succession laws of the states will govern.[41] Yet, in the light of Congressional intent already considered above,[42] it is apparent that the phrase is not an accurate guideline for determining what standard the drafters thought they were incorporating in the federal statute; in fact, the reliance upon state inheritance statutory standards directly contradicts the desires of Congress. Justice Cardozo warned of this danger in the majority opinion of *Van Beech v. Sanbine Towing Co.*:

> Death statutes have their roots in dissatisfaction with the archaism of the Law. . . . It would be a misfortune if a narrow or grudging process of construction were to exemplify and perpetuate the very evils to be remedied.[43]

Such construction seems to be the weight of authority for dealing with the FELA. Is this true of all instances in which the government is aligned with or is actually the employer? A full answer to that question can only come from Title 5 of the United States Code which is concerned with the "Executive Department and Government Officers and Employees." The exclusive remedy of an employee of either the government or an agent of the government,

39. *Id.* at 490. Contra, Huber v. Baltimore & Ohio R I Co. 1041 F. Supp. 646, 650 (D. Md. 1965), in which the court said: "I therefore conclude that the better view is that dependent illegitimate children should be compensated unless such compensation inflects with the clearly enunciated state policy." The court further held in Huber that no such strong policy existed in Maryland even though the Maryland statutes do not include illegitimate in the term "children" for the purposes of inheritance, descent or distribution of real and personal property. Huber dealt, as did Kenney, with the FELA.

40. Prior to Kenney the Supreme Court had offered two tests for "children" as beneficiaries: "minor dependent" in Michigan Cen. R.R. v. Vreeland, 227 U.S. 59 (1912) and "dependency and pecuniary loss" in Gulf Col. & Sante Fe Ry. v. McGinnis, 228 U.S. 173 (1912).

41. Middleton v. Luckenbach, 70 F.2d 326 (2d Cir.), *cert. denied,* 293 U.S. 577 (1934).

42. *Supra* note 33.

43. 300 U.S. 342 (1937).

injured in the course of the performance of his duty, is by means of this statute;[44] in other words, such employee and his heirs are barred from suit under the Federal Tort Claims Act.[45] The employee and his heirs may, however, recover under the provisions of the Federal Employees' Compensation Act.[46] This act is supplemented with another arrangement for the benefit of heirs, the Federal Employees' Group Life Insurance plan.[47] There is no definition offered of the word "child" in either of these statutes although the term "heir" is found frequently in the text of the statutes.[48] The use of the word "heirs" indicates that these statutes are patterned after survival acts and thus reference to the inheritance laws of the states is more appropriate than with the compensatory acts.[49] Disregarding the individual nature of the state standards for a moment, there is still some doubt whether or not a foster child generally has a legally enforceable insurable interest in the life of his foster parent. Although such an interest was not acknowledged by the common law, it may accrue under "particular circumstances such as dependency, expectation of aid or benefit when needed,"[50] and, in such circumstances, the foster child who is eligible under his state's inheritance statutes[51] is acceptable as a beneficiary under the federal program.[52]

44. DeSousa v. Panama Canal Co., 202 F. Supp. 22 (D.C.N.Y. 1962); United States v. Martinez, 334 F.2d 728 (10th Cir. 1964).

45. Precluded by 28 U.S.C. § 1346(b) & § 2671. See also: McNicholas v. United States, 226 F. Supp. 965 (D.C.Ill. 1964).

46. 5 U.S.C. 757(b). Accord, Rhodes v. United States, 216 F. Supp. 732 (D.C. Cal. 1962), aff'd & modified, 335 F.2d 379; cert. denied, 379 U.S. 951 (1962): Case points out that heirs of airplane crash victims who were government employees were limited in their right to recover under § 757(b). Those who may recover are specified as "legal representatives, spouses, dependents and next of kin" in § 751.

47. 5 U.S.C. §§ 2091–2103.

48. LaBove v. Metropolitan Life Ins. Co., 164 F. Supp. 808 (D.C.N.J. 1958). The case states that since Congress has offered no definition of "child," the court must look to the states.

49. Supra note 17, at 443.

50. Young v. Hipple, 273 Pa. 439, 117 A. 185 (1922).

51. In discussing the mixed-up doctrines connected with the Federal Employees' Group Life Insurance Act, the court in Tatum v. Tatum, 241 F.2d 401 (9th Cir. 1957) said at 405: The "one point of unanimity is that state law will govern."

52. Metropolitan Life Ins. Co. v. Thompson, 250 F. Supp. 476 (D.C.Pa. 1966), rev'd 368 F.2d 791 (3d Cir. 1966). Ed note. This case and the problems involved in referring to state devolution laws for a definition of "child" are discussed in Note, 7 J. Fam. L. 512 (1967).

Unlike the previous statutes concerned with government employees, Chapter 30, the Civil Service Retirement Program,[53] specifically defines each eligible beneficiary:

> § 2260: "Child" means an unmarried child, including (1) an adopted child and (2) a stepchild or recognized natural child who received more than ½ of his support from and lived with the member or employee in regular parent-child relation. . . .

> The term "child" for purposes of § 2261 [54] of this title shall include an adopted and a natural child but not a stepchild.[55]

This definition on its face excludes all foster children except some few specially designated stepchildren.

Although the Federal Employees' Health Benefits Program [56] also offers a positive definition, it specifically includes foster children:

> § 3001 (d): "Member of family" means an employee's or annuitant's spouse and any unmarried child (1) under the age of 21 year (including (A) an adopted child, and (B) a stepchild, foster child or recognized natural child who lives with the employee or annuitant in a regular parent-child relationship), or (2) regardless of age, who is incapable of self support because of mental or physical incapability that existed prior to his reaching the age of 21 years.[57]

It was amended to include foster children because of the inequity of their exclusion.[58] The Civil Service Commissioner gave the example at the hearings on the bill of the disproportionate burden that had in the past been placed on three employees who were

53. 5 U.S.C. §§ 2251–2261 (1958).

54. For lump-sum awards.

55. Although the act seems to be following the traditional limited family concept, a trading of the amendments to the act through Public Law 89–407 § 1, 80 Stat. 131, April 25, 1966, shows a very slight liberalizing trend. *E.g.,* the last amendment changed the time a stepchild must live with his stepparent from 5 to 3 years.

H. Rep. No. 33, Sen. Rep. 1070, 89th Cong., 2d Sess. (1966) reflect opinions showing a move toward wider scope to those included in the concept of family for the statute.

56. 5 U.S.C. § 3000, *et seq.*

57. § 3001(D) was amended to its present form in 1964 when "21" was substituted for "19" in clauses (1) and (2) and "foster child" was inserted following "step child" in clause (1)(8). Pub. L. 88–284 § 1(3).

58. 1964 U.S. Code, Cong. & Ad. News, at 2088.

raising a grandchild, a niece, and a minor brother. He went on to say that foster children are customarily included in family membership by other large employers and insurers and the amendment brought the federal program in line with the general practice. Since this is the largest health benefit program in the world,[59] the effect of Congress's decision to extend coverage to foster children could well be far-reaching.

As the largest single employer in the country, the federal government is, of course, highly influential in its policy decisions concerning such things as a foster child's ability to participate in the benefits of a health program for employees. Often merely an expression of policy in an official, though unenforceable, manner will have the effect of law. This is especially apparent in the armed services.[60] Although the policy statements in each service's book of regulations may be technically a mere suggestion, in practice the suggestion often becomes a command. An example, in which foster children benefit [61] along with all other dependents of men serving in the military, is the encouragement of proper support payments to one's family.[62] The Armed Forces are lacking in general legal authority to require support payments, even though

59. *Id.* at 2089. There are over 2 million federal employees and 4 million family members. The plan ranks among the most complete of all coverage available.

60. *See* Toms, *Support of Military Dependents,* 6 J. FAM. L. 15, (1966); 37 U.S.C. § 231(g), § 252; and United States v. Robson, 164 F. Supp. 80 (N.D. Ohio 1958).

61. But foster children's benefits will vary with the jurisdiction in which they make their domicile. Since there is no federal law of domestic relations, family support is primarily a matter of state concern. Note, 7 J. FAM. L. 309 (1967). Generally courts have held that once a foster parent has assumed the *in loco parentis* relationship with the child, he is liable for the child's support. Marquess v. La Bois, 82 Ind. 550 (1882).

Once a separation or divorce occurs, however, the husband has usually been upheld in his refusal to continue contributing to the support of a foster child, since, in the act of leaving the home, he has terminated any legal obligation due the child. Chestnut v. Chestnut, 247 S.C. 332, 147 S.E.2d 269 (1966).

62. Army Regulations No. 600-20; Change No. 7, ¶ 37a (19 Oct. 1963): "Support of dependents by men of the Army involves a serious responsibility which is of direct concern to the Army. Failure on the part of a member to carry out this responsibility not only reflects adversely on the Army as a whole, but is entirely inconsistent with Army standards of honor."

Bupersinst, "The Navy will not be a haven or refuge for personnel who disregard or evade their obligations to their families . . ." No. 1620.1 C ¶ 4a (31 Oct. 1962).

such duty has been reduced to a judgment,[63] but they can, and do, incorporate into the military establishment many unofficial sanctions for those who fail to meet their obligations.[64]

Military Foster Parents

Once the military foster parent becomes a veteran, the legal rights [65] which accrue to the foster child multiply. When the child is named a beneficiary of the National Service Life Insurance policy,[66] he is eligible for the benefits regardless of his specifically defined legal status in the family of the insured.[67] If, however, he is not designated as a beneficiary, most of the rewards under the Veterans' Administration's authorization are governed by the definition appearing in 38 U.S.C. § 101 (4):

> The term "child" means . . . a person who is unmarried and
> (A) who is under the age of 18 years;
> (B) who, before attaining the age of 18 years, became permanently incapable of self support; or
> (C) who after attaining the age of 18 years and until completion of education or training (but not after attaining the age of 21 years) is pursuing a course of instruction at an approved educational institution;
> and who is a legitimate child, a legally adopted child, a step child who is a member of veteran's household or was a member at time of veteran's death, or an illegitimate child but, as to the alleged father, only if acknowledged. . . .[68]

Although nothing in the definition explicitly deals with the foster child's eligibility,[69] there are a number of published administrative decisions concerned with the *in loco parentis* relationship.[70] The

63. 6 J. FAM. L., *supra* note 60, at 22.
64. *Id*. at 34.
65. Veterans' Benefits, title 38, U.S.C.
66. *Id*. at §§ 701–24.
67. *Supra* note 17, at 339.
68. His definition applies to all benefits under the Veterans' legislation except those in § 5020 and a few other specified sections of title 38.
69. In determining a foster child's right to benefits from the Veterans' Administration, one must first establish whether the foster parent is in fact included in the meaning of "eligible veteran," that is, one who "a) died of a service-connected disability, or b) had a total disability, permanent in nature, resulting from a service-connected disability or who died while a disability so evaluated was in existence." 38 U.S.C. § 1701 (1958).
70. *E.g.,* 1948 A.D.V.A. 793; 1945 A.D.V.A. 675.

crux of these decisions seems to be that a foster relationship that has existed for more than one year prior to the veteran's injury or death does engender certain rights in the foster child. The decisions speak of applying the common law rule, but reach results contradictory to the old policy and seem, instead, to apply a flexible "dependency" test.

Since the majority of hearings concerning veterans' benefits are handled within the Veterans' Administration Agency,[71] case law on the subject is uncommon. In other areas, such as claims arising under the Federal Tort Claims Act,[72] reported cases and other legal authority [73] are far more plentiful, and unfortunately proportionately more often conflicting.[74] The act itself is one of those in which Congress chose to provide that the state law will govern.[75] When Congress spells out its desires in the text of a statute, the case law hopefully will reflect a similar clarity of interpretation. The Supreme Court in the recent instance of *Richards v. United States* stated the judicial view of the statute in almost the same words as did the legislative drafters: "The Government shall be treated in accordance with the law of the place where the act or omission occurred." [76] Foster children, like all others bringing suit under the act, find their right to a cause of action established by their corresponding right under state law to bring suit against

71. One source of case law on the Veterans' Administration is the litigation arising under the Federal Torts Claim Act, hereinafter discussed in detail. Examples of such cases can be found in: United States v. Rifolfi, 318 F.2d 467 (2d Cir. 1963) and Christopher v. United States, 237 F. Supp. 787 (D.C. Pa. 1965).

72. 28 U.S.C. § 1346 *et seq.* (1958).

73. For a good examination of one aspect of this field, as well as a fairly representative sampling of cases, see: Johansen, *Wrongful Death Recovery Under Federal Torts Claims Act,* 38 N.D. L. Rev. 603 (1962).

74. *Compare,* Granade v. United States, 237 F. Supp. 211 (D.C.N.Y. 1965), in which it is stated that the "entire statutory scheme of remedies against the United States is based on the principle that where there is a remedy available in the form of compensation systems, there is no concurrent right to sue under § 1346 or 2671, *et seq.* of title 28 . . . ," *and* United States v. Muiz, 374 U.S. 1150 (1963) in which the presence of a compensation system is said to not preclude a suit against the United States for negligence under subsection (b) of § 1246 or § 2671 *et seq.*

75. 28 U.S.C. §§ 1346(b) & 2671 (specifically dealing with air crashes): "The government's liability should be determined in accordance with the law of the place where the negligence occurred." This directive is read as also encompassing the determination of the status of beneficiaries that fall outside the defined classes.

76. 369 U.S. 1 (1962).

a private individual in the same situation as the Government.[77] The state law referred to is not the limited view of intestacy provisions, but, rather, the far more liberal perspective of state personal injury, survival, and wrongful death statutes.[78] Under the authority of such statutes, it is quite possible that foster children will be treated more equitably than they would be under the intestacy law standard.

The Middleton Case

Although the Federal Death on the High Seas Act [79] has a lesser significance in any general survey of law than does the Federal Torts Claims Act, it has produced one of the single most influential studies of the policy behind federal compensatory-beneficiary statutes. In *Middleton v. Luckenbach S.S.*[80] the right to recover for wrongful death on the high seas was held to be governed exclusively by federal statute, as distinguished from the law of the forum or the law of the deceased individual's domicile, and, that "parent, child, or dependent relative," [81] as beneficiaries in whose name suit might be brought under the statute, included illegitimate children and the mother of illegitimates. The opinion reasons that:

> In the federal statute we are considering there are no words requiring a mandate of state legislature to inform us as to their meaning; no local law is necessary. The words are to be construed by judicial determination, since there is no legislative definition of a parent or child such as is to be found and which is necessary in a "next of kin" statute. Unlike the statutes wherein the words "next of kin" are used and which therefore might require legislative interpretation, the statutes using the words

77. Weaver v. United States, 334 F.2d 319 (10th Cir. 1964): Subsection (b) of §§ 1346 & 2671 *et seq.* of title 28 "is designed to render the United States liable for its torts in essentially the same manner and to the same extent as private individuals would be in like circumstances under the law of the place where the wrong occurred."

78. 38 N.D. L. Rev., *supra* note 73, at 704–705.

79. 46 U.S.C. § 761 *et seq.* (1958).

80. 70 F.2d 326 (2nd Cir. 1934); *cert. denied,* 293 U.S. 577 (1934). Accord, In Re: Risdal & Anderson, Inc., 266 F. Supp. 157 (D. Mass. 1967); Doyle v. Albatross Tanker Corp., 260 F. Supp. 303 (S.D.N.Y. 1965).

81. 46 U.S.C. § 761: Compensation will be granted for actual pecuniary loss suffered by decedent's wife, husband, parent, child, or dependent relative.

"parent and child" have, in the cases, received interpretation by the judiciary alone.[82]

There is no right of inheritance involved in the Federal Death on the High Seas Act since it confers a right of recovery to dependents, not for the benefit of an estate, but "who by our [the court's] standards are legally or morally entitled to support."[83] Since the act is seeking to compensate those dependents who have actually undergone a loss of support, there is no apparent reason for differentiating foster children from other dependents. The words of the court, although directed to the illegitimate plaintiffs in the case at hand, apply with equal force to the plight of foster children:

> Humane considerations and the realization that children are such no matter what their origin . . . [shall govern]. The purpose and object of the statute is to continue the support of dependents after a casualty. To hold that these children or the parents do not come within the terms of the act would be to defeat the purpose of the act. The benefit conferred beyond being for such beneficiaries is for society's welfare in making provisions for the support of those who might otherwise become dependent.[84]

The "similarity of the statutory language" of the Federal Death on the High Seas Act and the Jones Act [85] has been mentioned in a leading case on the latter statute, *Civil v. Waterman SS.*[86] In that case the majority of the circuit court cited *Middleton* [87] with agreement. Judge Learned Hand, in his dissenting opinion, offered the more tangible test of *Michigan Central Railroad v. Vreeland:*

> The pecuniary loss is not dependent upon any legal liability of the injured person to the beneficiary. That is not the sole test. There must, however, appear some reasonable expectation of

---

82. 70 F.2d 326 (2d Cir. 1934); *cert. denied,* 293 U.S. 577 (1934).

83. Foster children whose foster parents stand *in loco parentis* are certainly due support legally, Marquess v. La Bois, 82 Ind. 550 (1882).
See note *supra* 17, 344–46. The article finds the most closely analogous state law to be, not inheritance, but support. Yet state support laws specify those who may force another to support them, while this act's beneficiaries include not only those with a right to support but also all relatives who are in fact supported.

84. 70 F.2d 326 (2d Cir. 1934); *cert. denied,* 293 U.S. 577 (1934).

85. 46 U.S.C. § 688 *et seq.*

86. 217 F.2d 94 (2d Cir. 1954).

87. 70 F.2d 326 (2d Cir. 1934); *cert. denied,* 293 U.S. 577 (1934).

pecuniary assistance or support of which they have been deprived.[88]

The difficulty in evaluating the efficacy of "dependency," "support," or "pecuniary loss" as tests is that there really is no federal guide for precedent. The Supreme Court has said that "Congress followed the general principles of conflicts of laws: namely that since the statute of the sovereign creates the right of action for a statutory tort, the sovereign therefore determines to whom the cause of acion should be given." [89] But the manner in which the sovereign shall determine such matters is left hanging.

Both the Jones Act and the Railroad Retirement Act [90] are concerned with circumstances surrounding the common carrier; at that point the parallel ends. The Railroad Retirement Act is among the most stringent of the intestacy-like statutes. Besides incorporating the restricting qualifications set forth in § 416(c)(e) and (g) and § 402(H)(3) of Title 42 of the Social Security Act, this statute goes on to add further conditions of receiving benefits:

> (ii) A "child" shall have been dependent upon its parent employee at the time of his death; shall not be adopted after such death by other than a stepparent, grandparent, aunt or uncle; shall be unmarried; and less than 18 years of age. . . .[91]

If a "child" meets these qualifications, he still must be competent under the laws of descent and distribution of the state in which the employee is domiciled at death.[92] The hierarchy of obstacles is somewhat less oppressive when one remembers the chief purpose of this statute is to secure annuities for railroad personnel in their old age.[93] The emphasis is on the prevention of poverty in one's last years, rather than on the welfare of youth. Still, it is unnecessary to rule against one small class of youths as beneficiaries on the grounds of lack of legal relationship, when dependency exists.

---

88. 227 U.S. 59 (1912).
89. Spokane and Island Empire Railroad Co. v. Whitley, 237 U.S. 487 (1915).
90. 45 U.S.C. § 220 *et seq.* (1958).
91. 45 U.S.C. § 228(e)(1) (1958).
92. Freeman v. Railroad Retirement Board, 192 F.2d 51 (5th Cir. 1961); *cert. denied,* 343 U.S. 909 (1952).
93. Flanagan v. Railroad Retirement Bd., 332 F.2d 301 (3d Cir. 1964).

The Copyright Act [94] also is not primarily a compensatory act for young people, but a statute designed to protect a federally created property right.[95] In its concern for the continuation or transmission of this right, it acts much like a will; that is, an author has a statutory right during his lifetime which upon his death is devolved to named beneficiaries whose rights are dependent upon and derivative from the author's.[96] *DeSylva v. Ballentine*,[97] a case whose dubious claim to fame rests in the naming of a famous song writer's illegitimate child as beneficiary, held that the determination of "next of kin" required reference to the law of the state which created those legal relationships. Justice Harlan, writing for the court, said that it was "really a question of descent of property and we think the controlling question under state law should be whether the child would be the heir of the author." [98] The same question would seem to control the rights of foster children but there is no pertinent case law to establish precedent.

Although not every one can write a song and thus leave a beneficiary to continuing royalties, almost every American citizen is affected at some time by the Social Security Act.[99] The Act was designed originally as a general societal protection measure of the New Deal and was amended in 1939 to cover dependents of those who are unable to accumulate an estate sufficient to care for dependent children after the death of the workers, rather than allow them to become, of necessity, wards of the state.[100] With such a broad purpose to the legislation, one might imagine an equally generous, all-encompassing definition of beneficiaries in the statute. Although there are different qualifications for benefits in the various portions of Title 42, the following is representative:

§ 416(e)—Definition of "child":
    1) the child or legally adopted child of an individual, and
    2) a step child [101] who has been such a step child for not

94. 17 U.S.C. § 1 *et seq.* (1958).
95. Tune v. Louisville and Nashville Ry. Co., 223 F. Supp. 928 (M.D. Tenn. 1963).
96. *Id.*
97. 351 U.S. 570 (1956).
98. *Id.* at 572.
99. 42 U.S.C. § 301 *et seq.* (1958).
100. Ray v. Social Security Board, 73 F. Supp. 58 (D.C. Ala. 1947).
101. Harris v. Ewing, 87 F. Supp. 151 (D.C. Ala. 1949) held that wage earner's stepchild who had not been legally adopted by him was not entitled

less than one year immediately preceding the day on which application for child's insurance benefits is filed or (if the insured individual is deceased) the day on which such individual died.[102]

A more comprehensive set of definitions is printed in the Regulations of the Social Security Agency:

Family Relationship
§ 404.1101 Determination of Relationship
   Whether a claimant bears the necessary relationship for entitlement under Title III of the Act [42 U.S.C.A. § 401 *et seq.*] as wife, husband, widow, widower, child, or parent of the insured individual upon whose wages and self-employment income an application is based is determined as follows: . . .
404.1109 The term "child" means a claimant who:
(a) Is the legally adopted child of the individual . . .
(b) Is the stepchild of the individual . . .
(c) Is neither the stepchild nor legally adopted child of the individual upon whose wages and self employment income his application is based but has the status of a child of such individual under applicable state law.[103]

The last provision, "applicable state law," causes a foster child to be a recipient of benefits in California and barred from recovery in Pennsylvania. The courts have taken the phrase as an "unqualified directive" to apply the personal property devolution law of the state.[104] Survivor benefits seem to be determined strictly on intestate provisions rather than on dependency.[105]

---

under state law to inherit from the stepfather's estate, but that this was not controlling in determining whether the stepchild was entitled to death benefits where Congress explicitly declared in the act that a stepchild was entitled to benefits conferred upon a child regardless of state laws pertaining to devolution of estate.

102. Chapter 7: Old Age Benefits. A tracing of the amendments to this definition shows a gradual liberalization of coverage. *See:* Pub. L. 85–840 § 302(a) and Pub. L. 86–778 § 207(b), 208(c).

103. 20 C.F.R. § 404, Subpart L: Family Relationships.

104. Bloch v. Ewing, 105 F. Supp. 25 (S.D. Cal. 1952); Hobby v. Burke, 227 F.2d 932 (5th Cir. 1955): "Determination of eligibility under the Act for child's benefits requires the Administrator to apply such law as would be applied in determining devolution of intestate personal property by the courts of the state in which such insured individual . . . was domiciled."

105. Federal Register, Aug. 27, 1964. Under employee's benefits under the S.S. Act it was found that under the Old Age, Disability, and Survivors' Insurance benefits, a stepchild's dependency upon his stepfather is determina-

Strangely discriminative examples could be given of children who were fed, clothed, sheltered, educated, doctored and cared for in every way for their entire lives by the insured only to be barred from survivor's benefits due to the law of their domicile, but these examples would do no more than briefly highlight the contradictory effect of intestacy standards applied to welfare legislation. Such examples are becoming less frequent as modern courts attempt to achieve just results without exactly sticking to the letter of the statute. In *Gonzales v. Hobby*,[106] for example, a dependent illegitimate child, who could not inherit personal property in the state in question, was declared to "have a right to inherit his estate in identical terms and proportions as legitimate children in other jurisdictions" and thus "the child cannot be excluded from benefits even if the child were not legitimate or adopted . . . or . . . had been adopted by some other individual."

Another source of liberalization of survival beneficiary clauses of the act may be surprising; that is, rights accruing under the Civil Rights Act [107] in conjunction with the Social Security provisions. In Civil Rights cases, federal courts must use "that combination of federal law, common law and state law as will best be adopted to the object of civil rights law and must use their powers to facilitate, not hinder, procedures in the vindication of one's civil rights." [108] Federal courts have traditionally not been allowed to hear wrongful death or personal injury suits in the absence of specific federal or state statute granting them such right. But, § 1988 of the 1958 Civil Rights Act said that deficiencies in suitable remedies under federal law shall be supplemented by state laws utilized in federal courts, thus giving a federal forum for protection of person and property.[109] Since Congress intended on extending one's protection of rights into death itself, § 1988 allowed adoption of the state survival and wrongful death statutes to accomplish this.[110] Now the question arises: if a person deprived of his civil rights dies while insured under the Social Security Act, will the more liberal

tive, i.e. if he was living with or receiving half his support from stepfather he is eligible by federal standard and state law is inapplicable.

106. 110 F. Supp. 893 (D.P.R. 1953).

107. 42 U.S.C. § 1988 (1958).

108. Brown v. City of Meridian, 356 F.2d 602 (5th Cir. 1966).

109. 14 STAN. L. REV. 386 (1962).

110. Comment, "Civil Rights: Survival of Actions," 47 VA. L. REV. 1241 (1961).

survivor and wrongful death statutes govern his children's eligibility, rather than the intestate provisions?[111] The answer at this point is a weak "maybe."[112] If the answer becomes a strong "yes," it will have a tremendous effect on litigation in this area. The United States Supreme Court decision in *Levy v. Louisiana* should have the effect of increasing the chances of reform in the standards applied to plaintiffs wrongful death actions.

> The rights asserted here (of illegitimates to sue under the state wrongful death statute for the loss of their mother) involve the intimate, familial relationship between a child and his own mother. When the child's claim of damage for loss of his mother is an issue, why, in terms of "equal protection," should the tortfeasors go free merely because the child is illegitimate? Why should the illegitimate child be denied rights merely because of his birth out of wedlock? He certainly is subject to all the responsibilities of a citizen, including the payment of taxes and conscription under the Selective Service Act. How under our constitutional regime can he be denied correlative rights which other citizens enjoy?
>
> Legitimacy or illegitimacy of birth has no relation to the nature of the wrong allegedly inflicted on the mother. These children, though illegitimate, were dependent on her; she cared for them and nurtured them; they were indeed hers in the biological and in the spiritual sense; and in her death they suffered wrong in the sense that any dependent would.
>
> We conclude that it is invidious to discriminate against them when no action, conduct, or demeanor of theirs is possibly relevant to the harm done to the mother.[113]

Although the *Levy* decision was solely concerned with the rights of illegitimates, its stress on "biological" rather than "legal" relationships is important in that it shows a desire at the highest level of the court system to look beyond the limitations of the descent and distribution inheritance statutes. This apparent relaxation of reliance on inheritance statutes has not, as yet, brought about any significant changes in the legal attitudes concerning foster children and wrongful death actions.

One liberalization move that was taken of late has nothing to do

---

111. Question of a similar nature posed in Brazier v. Cherry, 293 F.2d 401 (5th Cir. 1964), *cert. denied,* 368 U.S. 921 (1964).

112. *See* Monroe v. Pape, 365 U.S. 167 (1961) for a criminal case which might lead to a positive answer.

113. Levy v. Louisiana, 391 U.S. 68, 71–72 (1968); companion case, Glona v. American Guarantee & Liability Co., 391 U.S. 73 (1968).

with civil liberties. However, some liberalization has occurred in the realms of federal compensation for death of a parent. In the Social Security provisions relating to "Compensation for Disability or Death to a Person Employed at a Military, Air, or Naval Base Outside the United States," the agency suggested, and Congress adopted, an extension of the standards of the Longshoremen and Harbor Workers Act,[114] to cover persons working on defense bases outside the geographical boundaries of the United States.[115] Special provisions applying the same standard to contractors and their employees in foreign United States defense bases were also added to Title 42.[116] The effect of the workmen's compensation standard is to bring foster children of such employees within the qualifications for benefits.

Conclusion

Whether a foster child is included in beneficiary clauses if his father is a sailor building a Vietnamese airstrip, and not included if his father enlists, may not appear unbearably important in the daily game of "What Is the Law?" but the effect of any arbitrary discrimination is the weakening of the entire structure of a democratic schema. If the drafters of these statutes truly seek the goals implicit in the term "welfare," they must signify their intent by providing federal standards which will complement such an end. In the present state of things, the foster child has equal rights in one state, no rights in another, and is a second-rate citizen in a third. The establishment of a single, clearly defined federal purpose and standard would remove the foster child from the legal vagaries of the several states. This article has suggested that the purpose remain as it is: the compensation for loss of the foster parent and reward of a sum which would keep the child, whenever possible, from becoming dependent upon the public; and that the standard of actual dependency be accepted as the test for eligibility to benefits of all compensatory statutes. Let the foster child not have to turn "to wit" as did the Shakespearean character Edmund when he was deprived of lands because of base birth, but let him achieve, "if not by birth," by a legal system designed to protect those who cannot protect themselves.

114. 88 U.S.C. § 901 (1958).
115. 42 U.S.C. § 1651 (1958).
116. 42 U.S.C. §§ 1701–1706 (1958).

Robert E. Shepherd, Jr.

13
The Abused Child and the Law

He was found dead in his crib by a family friend who had
stopped in at the home. A bottle of sour milk was in his crib
and maggots were crawling around in his soiled diaper. The
mother had gone to visit an aunt, leaving the child alone, and
did not learn of the child's death until she was called two hours
later. When she was interrogated by police she stated that she
had noticed "nothing unusual wrong" with the baby and that she
fed him regularly and bathed him daily. Although she had been
advised to bring the child to the well-baby clinic, she had never
done so because she "just didn't get around to it." [1]

This brief case history exemplifies the neglect, or omission, aspect
of a growing medico-legal problem, involving both acts of commission and omission, which has just begun to capture the public's
attention and concern. The other, or commission, aspect is represented by the following example:

A six-week-old infant was admitted to the hospital because of
swelling of the right thigh of four days' duration. The mother
stated to the examining physician that the child had fallen from
its crib and struck its right leg on the floor. X-ray examination
revealed complete fracture through the mid-shaft of the right
femur with posterior displacement of the distal fragment. The
patient was in Bryant's traction for two weeks and was discharged in good condition after application of a hip spica.

ROBERT E. SHEPHERD, JR., LL.B., is a former partner
in the firm of Steingold, Shepherd & Steingold, Richmond,
Virginia. He is currently Assistant Attorney General for the
state of Virginia. This article, revised by the author, is
reprinted with permission from the *Washington and Lee
Law Review* 22(1965):182–95.

1. Adelson, Homicide by Starvation, 186 J.A.M.A. 458, 459 (1963). The
child was seven months and two days old at its death and weighed 7.7
pounds as compared with a normal weight of 17 pounds and its birth weight
of 6.1 pounds.

175   Robert E. Shepherd, Jr.

A few weeks later the child was admitted to another hospital with multiple contusions and abrasions. Investigation by the social service department indicated that the father had thrown the child on the floor, shattering the cast and inflicting serious head trauma resulting in bilateral subdural hematomas. The child was recently seen in the pediatric clinic, where multiple signs of intracranial damage were noted. The child is now blind and mentally retarded.[2]

Hardly a day goes by now when we can pick up the newspaper without reading of some child having been admitted to a hospital with either severe malnutrition or multiple injuries.[3] This is not a new problem; it is as old as mankind. However, it is just in the past few years that society has concentrated on the problem and actively sought to discover some practicable solutions.

The first suggestion of the problem of overt child abuse was made by Dr. John Caffey in 1946 when he noted the coincidence of long bone fractures and subdural hematomas; he felt that in the absence of a reasonable history of trauma, many of these cases raised the possibility of intentional ill treatment.[4] Four years later, Lis, Frauenberger and Smith once again brought these injuries to the attention of the medical community.[5] Upon the foundation laid by these medical pioneers, further studies expanded upon, and confirmed, Caffey's initial reaction.[6] The medical profession responded

2. Fontana, The Maltreated Child: The Maltreatment Syndrome in Children 45–46 (1964) (hereinafter cited as Fontana).
3. While writing this article the Richmond, Virginia, newspapers reported two aggravated cases of suspected child abuse. In the first case, a five-month-old girl was admitted to a Richmond hospital with "broken bones in both legs, both knees, her right ankle, her right arm and several broken ribs. The child also had second degree burns over part of her body and bruises around her eyes. . . ." Richmond News-Leader, Mar. 15, 1965, p. 6, col. 2. A couple of weeks later it was reported that a policeman in Fairfax County, Virginia, had been charged with the murder of his seven-month-old daughter by beating her in the stomach. Richmond Times-Dispatch, Mar. 28, 1965, p. 8-B, col. 5.
4. Caffey, Multiple Fractures in the Long Bones of Infants Suffering from Chronic Subdural Hematoma, 56 Am. J. Roentgen. 163 (1946).
5. Lis & Frauenberger, Multiple Fractures Associated with Subdural Hematoma in Infancy, 6 Pediatrics 890 (1950); Smith, Subdural Hematoma with Multiple Fractures, 63 Am. J. Roentgen. 342 (1950).
6. Altman & Smith, Unrecognized Trauma in Infants and Children, 42A J. Bone Joint Surg. [Amer.] 407 (1960); Bakwin, Multiple Skeletal Lesions in Young Children due to Trauma, 49 J. Pediat. 7 (1956); Caffey, Some Traumatic Lesions in Growing Bones other than Fractures and Dislocations: Clinical and Radiological Features, 30 Brit. J. Radiol. 225 (1957); Fisher,

rapidly and late in 1961 the American Academy of Pediatrics scheduled a symposium on the problem at its annual meeting. Dr. Charles H. Kempe and his colleagues in Denver published a definitive study of the problem and established several valuable guideposts for the diagnosis of this syndrome which they christened, "The Battered Child Syndrome." [7]

Other professions, particularly social workers, met the challenge posed by these perceptive physicians. Leontine Young, Helen Boardman, Elizabeth Elmer and others presented different perspectives and posed challenging questions about what could or should be done once the syndrome has been identified.[8] The Children's Bureau of the U.S. Department of Health, Education and Welfare called a conference of experts to formulate recommendations for meeting these challenges, and this group recommended to the states the adoption of mandatory reporting legislation.[9] However, before considering proposed statutory schemes, it is desirable to examine the law relating to abuse, and the hallmarks of abuse.

It has been observed, with perhaps a tinge of the dramatic, that the laws dealing with child abuse have been far less numerous and less stringent than the laws pertaining to animal abuse. It is fact that one of the earliest and most publicized cases of child abuse pointed up the element of truth in the previous statement. Late in

---

Skeletal Manifestations of Parent-Induced Trauma in Infants and Children, 51 Southern Med. J. 956 (1958); Jones & Davis, Multiple Traumatic Lesions of the Infant Skeleton, 15 Stanford Med. Bull., No. 3, p. 259 (1957); Miller, Fractures Among Children: Parental Assault as Causative Agent, 42 Minnesota Med. 1209, 1414 (1959); Silverman, The Roentgen Manifestations of Unrecognized Skeletal Trauma in Infants, 69 Am. J. Roentgen. 413 (1953); Woolley & Evans, Significance of Skeletal Lesions in Infants Resembling Those of Traumatic Origin, 158 J.A.M.A. 539 (1955).

7. Kempe, Silverman, Steele, Droegemueller & Silver, The Battered-Child Syndrome, 181 J.A.M.A. 17 (1962) (hereinafter cited as Kempe). See especially Ray E. Helfer and C. Henry Kempe, The Battered Child; and Helfer and Pollock, The Battered Child Syndrome, 15 Advances in Pediatrics 9–26 (1968).

8. Boardman, A Project to Rescue Children from Inflicted Injuries, 7 Soc. Work, No. 1, p. 43 (1962) (hereinafter cited as Boardman); Elmer, Abused Young Children Seen in Hospitals, 5 Soc. Work, No. 4, p. 98 (1960); Elmer, Identification of Abused Children, 10 Children 180 (1963); Morris, Gould & Matthews, Toward Prevention of Child Abuse, 11 Children 55 (1964); Young, Wednesday's Children (1964) (hereinafter cited as Young).

9. Children's Bureau, U.S. Dep't of Health, Education & Welfare, The Abused Child (1963).

the last century a church worker, while visiting in a tenement, was informed that a young child, named Mary Ellen, in the same building was beaten daily and appeared to be seriously malnourished. Investigation proved these reports to be true and the church worker sought to have Mary Ellen removed from this environment. Her efforts with the police and the district attorney's office met stone walls and in desperation she turned to the Society for the Prevention of Cruelty to Animals. She argued that Mary Ellen was being treated like an animal and was, after all, a member of the animal kingdom. With its assistance, an action was brought based on this theory and the unfortunate child was removed from her parents.[10]

Blackstone pointed out that under Roman law a father had the absolute power of life and death over his children, but that under English law the father "may lawfully correct his child, being under age, in a reasonable manner; (d) for this is for the benefit of his education."[11] In this country the courts have taken two different approaches with respect to the limits of parental discipline. One is that the parent, or one *in loco parentis,* is the sole arbiter as to the degree of punishment and all punishment is *per se* reasonable which does not result in disfigurement or permanent injury, or is not inflicted maliciously.[12] The other approach, and the one preferred by the majority, is that the parent has a "right to punish a child within the bounds of moderation and reason, so long as he does it for the welfare of the child; but that if he exceeds due moderation, he becomes criminally liable."[13] If the punishment is excessive,

---

10. Fontana at 8–9.

11. 1 Blackstone, Commentaries *452.

12. Nicholas v. State, 32 Ala. App. 574, 28 So. 2d 422 (1946); Dean v. State, 89 Ala. 46, 8 So. 38 (1889); Boyd v. State, 88 Ala. 169, 7 So. 268 (1889); State v. Jones, 95 N.C. 588, 59 Am. Rep. 282 (1886).

13. Carpenter v. Commonwealth, 186 Va. 851, 44 S.E.2d 419, 423 (1947). See also Emery v. Emery, 45 Cal. 2d 421, 289 P.2d 218 (1955); Hinkle v. State, 127 Ind. 490, 26 N.E. 777 (1890); State v. Fischer, 245 Iowa 170, 60 N.W.2d 105 (1953); State v. Washington, 104 La. 443, 29 So. 55 (1901); People v. Green, 155 Mich. 524, 119 N.W. 1087 (1909); State v. Koonse, 123 Mo. App. 655, 101 S.W. 139 (1907); Clasen v. Pruhs, 69 Neb. 278, 95 N.W. 640 (1903); Richardson v. State Board, 98 N.J.L. 690, 121 Atl. 457 (1923); State v. Liggett, 84 Ohio App. 225, 83 N.E.2d 663 (1948); Stanfield v. State, 43 Tex. 167 (1875); State v. McDonie, 89 W. Va. 185, 109 S.E. 710 (1921); Steber v. Norris, 188 Wis. 366, 206 N.W. 173 (1925); State v. Spiegel, 39 Wyo. 309, 270 Pac. 1064 (1928); Annot., 89 A.L.R.2d 396 (1963); Perkins, Criminal Law 878–880 (1957); 1 Wharton, Criminal Law and Procedure § 344 (1957).

the perpetrator may be guilty of either assault and battery, or murder, depending upon the results of the beating.[14] However, when an unintentional killing results from an unlawful assault, the usual rule is that the person inflicting the injuries and causing the death is guilty of involuntary manslaughter.[15] Some states provide by statute that a homicide is excusable if caused by a parent while lawfully correcting a child, if the bounds of moderation are not exceeded.[16] Many states now provide penalties for a distinct offense of child abuse.[17]

The problem of neglect is somewhat different from a legal standpoint as it is largely based on statute. However, even without a statute, it is held to be the rule that if a child dies as a result of the parents' failure to provide food, shelter or clothing, and the parents are able to provide these necessities, then the parents may be guilty of manslaughter or, if the deprivation is willful, murder.[18] The law of neglect has developed into a broad enough field to command the attention of a separate article, encompassing in its civil and criminal aspects such things as medical treatment, education, emotional neglect and many other varied problems.[19]

Affording the foundation for these statutory and common-law rules is the principle that the interests of the state as *parens patriae* are superior to the rights of the parents, or those *in loco parentis*.[20]

14. Wharton, supra note 13, at § 259.
15. 40 C.J.S., Homicide § 58 (1944); Karl v. State, 144 So. 2d 869 (Fla. Dist. Ct. App. 1962); State v. Tornquist, 254 Iowa 1135, 120 N.W.2d 483 (1963).
16. 4 Vernier American Family Law § 232, pp. 19–20 (1936); State v. England, 220 Ore. 395, 349 P.2d 668 (1960).
17. See, e.g., Va. Code Ann. § 40-112 (Repl. Vol. 1953); Cal. Pen. Code § 273a (1964 Cum. Pock. Part). However, the offense is normally just a misdemeanor. The California offense was raised to a felony as recently as 1963.
18. Wharton, supra note 13, at § 297; Biddle v. Commonwealth, 206 Va. 14, 141 S.E.2d 710 (1965).
19. 39 Am. Jur., Parent and Child §§ 103–121 (1942); 67 C.J.S., Parent and Child §§ 91–99 (1950); 4 Vernier, American Family Law § 234 (1936); 1 Wharton, supra note 13, § 298; Levy, Neglected Children in Mississippi, 29 Miss. L.J. 165 (1958); Mulford, Emotional Neglect of Children (1958); Note, Compulsory Medical Treatment—Another Step in the State's Expanding Power over Children?, 41 Geo. L.J. 226 (1953); Note, The Law of Parent and Child in New England, 36 B.U.L. Rev. 622 (1956); Note, The Neglected or Delinquent Child: On Appraisal of New York's Juvenile Court System, 36 Cornell L.Q. 156 (1950).
20. 30 Am. Jur., Parent and Child § 15 (1942); 67 C.J.S., Parens Patriae (1950); 67 C.J.S., Parent and Child § 10 (1950); 43 C.J.S., Infants § 4

This is a somewhat unpalatable doctrine in a democracy because it connotes totalitarianism, and it has consequently been balanced in the courts by the constitutional rights of the parents.[21] In modern American society, it is not used as a device for the aggrandizement of the state, but rather as a shield for the protection of the child.

We have seen how the problem first received general attention and have briefly explored the law pertaining to abuse, but how serious is the problem? There have been few surveys which sought to determine the extent of child abuse on a nationwide level. In 1962, the Children's Division of The American Humane Association initiated a project to obtain data on child abuse cases reported in the newspapers.[22] From January through December of 1962, a total of 662 cases were reported in newspapers in 48 of the states and the District of Columbia.[23] Over 55 percent of the children were under 4 years of age, and of the 178 children who died from their injuries almost 54 percent were children under two years of age.[24] Parents were responsible for some 72 percent of the injuries and 75 percent of the fatalities.[25] Another survey resulted in the reporting from 71 hospitals of 302 cases of abuse, with 33 deaths and 85 instances of permanent brain injury, in one year.[26] The same survey elicited from 77 District Attorneys the information that they had knowledge of 447 cases with 45 deaths and 29 cases of brain injury in a similar period.[27] And yet none of these surveys even purport to be complete.

One hospital in the District of Columbia reported 40 cases of "battered" children in a four-year period.[28] Figures kept by the Massachusetts Society for the Prevention of Cruelty to Children in

---

(1945); Note, Compulsory Medical Treatment—Another Step in the State's Expanding Power over Children?, 41 Geo. L.J. 226, 226–27 (1953).

21. 30 Am. Jur., Parent and Child § 16 (1942). "We have not yet adopted as a public policy the Spartan rule that children belong, not to their parents, but to the state." In re Tuttendario, 21 Pa. Dist. 561, 563 (1911).

22. Children's Div., The American Humane Assoc., Child Abuse—Preview of a Nationwide Survey 3 (1963).

23. Id. at 4.

24. Ibid.

25. Id. at 5.

26. Kempe at 17.

27. Ibid. Official statistics for 1963 reflected 389 homicides of children under five years of age. U.S. Dep't of Health, Education and Welfare, 2 Vital Statistics of the United States—1963, Part II, table 1–25 (1965).

28. Symposium: Battered Child Syndrome, 20 Clin. Proc. Child. Hosp. (Wash.) 229, 231 (1964).

1960 showed well over 100 cases in that state alone.[29] The Coroner of Cuyahoga County, Ohio, revealed that in a seventeen-year period there were 46 homicides of young children there.[30] In a six-month period, 71 cases were reported to child welfare workers and public health nurses in Iowa.[31] In 1960, the Children's Hospital of Los Angeles reported 14 young patients to the authorities with careful documentation of abuse, and in only the first six months of 1961, 11 cases were identified.[32] An Arkansas poll resulted in replies from 71 physicians, of whom 65 percent reported having treated battered children, with most having done so two or three times.[33] An intensive study was conducted by the 25 members of the pediatric staff of one hospital over a two-week period when they saw 5,039 children in offices, hospitals, clinics, or homes, and 90 suspected cases of battering were seen as out-patients and 31 more among the hospitalized children.[34] The Children's Hospital of Pittsburgh reported 50 cases in a ten-year period from 1951– 1960.[35] The Cook County Family Court reports receiving about 100 abuse cases each month, and the admission rate of abused children at Cook County Hospital is up to about 10 a day.[36] The Tidewater Division of the Office of the Chief Medical Examiner of Virginia reports 14 deaths from abuse or neglect between July of 1963 and January of 1965.[37] These local statistics readily demonstrate that what national statistics we have are only the visible part of the proverbial iceberg. And yet the bulk of these local statistics relate only to battering and not to neglect. In 1962 the National Society for the Prevention of Cruelty to Children in England dealt with 24,716 cases of neglect and 4,118 cases of abuse.[38] In New

29. Fontana, Donovan & Wong, The "Maltreatment Syndrome" in Children, 269 New Eng. J. Med. 1389 (1963).

30. Adelson, Slaughter of the Innocents, 264 New Eng. J. Med. 1345 (1961).

31. The Child-Abuse Problem in Iowa, 53 J. Iowa Med. Soc. 692 (1963).

32. Boardman at 44.

33. Potts & Forbis, Willful Injury in Childhood, 59 J. Arkansas Med. Soc. 266, 267 (1962).

34. Platou, Lennox & Beasley, Battering, 23 Bull. Tulane Med. Fac. 157, 161 (1964) (hereinafter cited as Platou).

35. McHenry, Girdany & Elmer, Unsuspected Trauma with Multiple Skeletal Injuries during Infancy and Childhood, 31 Pediatrics 908 (1963).

36. Fontana at 7.

37. Letter from H. H. Karnitschnig, M.D., Deputy Chief Medical Examiner of Virginia, with autopsies attached, March 23, 1965.

38. Editorial, Brit. Med. J. 1544 (Dec. 21, 1963). These statistics show that this is not just an American problem. See also Selander, Kroppslig

York City alone, in 1962, over 5,000 dependency and neglect cases came to the attention of the children's courts.[39]

The magnitude of the problem in numbers alone can scarcely be doubted. In fact, it has been stated that if complete statistics were available, the maltreatment of children could be a more frequent cause of death than leukemia, cystic fibrosis and muscular dystrophy, and it may rank with automobile accidents and encephalitis as causes of disturbances of the central nervous system.[40] A more recent epidemiological study by Gil raises some questions as to the extent of abuse in that only 5,993 physically abused children were brought to the attention of authorities during 1967 across the nation.[41]

The emotional and psychological trauma of "battering" and neglect may be more serious than the physical aspects of the syndrome, and certainly much more costly to society. For example, in Sheldon and Eleanor Glueck's classic analysis of juvenile delinquency it was discovered that 13.5 per cent more of the mothers and 23.7 per cent more of the fathers of delinquents were erratic in their disciplinary techniques than the parents of nondelinquents.[42] Similarly, 17.1 per cent more of the fathers of the delinquent group were overstrict, 21 per cent more of the mothers, and 33.1 per cent more of the delinquent's fathers resorted to physical punishment than in the nondelinquent group.[43] As Professor Glueck pointed out, "[T]he delinquents were much more the victims of the indifference or actual hostility of their fathers and mothers, and were in turn, less attached to their parents." [44] One study of seven boys who had made murderous assaults and one boy who had committed murder revealed definite evidence that three of the boys had been severely beaten periodically by their parents and there was some evidence that the others had likewise suffered beatings.[45]

Misshandel av Smabarn (Willful Injuries to Infants), 70 Nord. Med. 1192 (1963).

39. Fontana at 7.

40. Id. at 6.

41. Gil, Physical Abuse of Children: Findings and Implications of a Nationwide Survey, 44 Pediatrics 857 (1969). However, reported cases may represent less than 10 percent of the actual cases of physical abuse, and physical abuse is only part of the problem. See Letters to the Editor in 45 Pediatrics 509 (1970).

42. Glueck & Glueck, Unraveling Juvenile Delinquency 131 (1951).

43. Id. at 131–132.

44. Id. at 133.

45. Easson & Steinhilber, Murderous Aggression by Children and Adolescents, 4 Arch. Gen. Psychiat. (Chicago) 27, 29–32 (1961).

Another study of six prisoners of middle-class backgrounds convicted of first degree murder revealed that four of the six men
had been badly abused by their parents.[46] Several sources, including those cited above, have theorized that there is a casual connection between child abuse and subsequent antisocial conduct by the
youthful victims.[47] A high proportion of the parents inflicting abuse
were themselves maltreated as children.[48]

The tolls of neglect and abuse are indeed terrible—in twisted
minds and lives as well as twisted bodies. It is an awesome challenge to society. Thus far the challenge has been met part way
through the advocacy of mandatory reporting legislation for cases
of child abuse. As previously pointed out, the Children's Bureau
of the Department of Health, Education and Welfare was a moving
force behind the drive for this legislation. Basically, the Children's
Bureau statute consists of six sections, as follows: 1) A statement
of purpose; 2) A requirement that physicians, interns or residents
must report any injuries to a minor child they have reasonable
cause to suspect were inflicted by other than accidental means;
3) An oral report to an appropriate police authority is required
immediately and a report in writing shall follow; 4) Civil and
criminal immunity from liability and freedom from participating in
any judicial proceeding is granted to anyone making such a report
in good faith; 5) A provision that neither the physician-patient
privilege nor the husband-wife privilege shall be a ground for
excluding evidence; and 6) A penalty provision making a knowing and willful violation of the act a misdemeanor.[49] This model
act, with variations, has been the basis for most of the statutes
passed. California was the first state to provide for mandatory

46. Duncan, Frazier, Litin, Johnson & Barron, Etiological Factors in First-
Degree Murder, 168 J.A.M.A. 1755, 1758 (1958).
47. Curtis, Violence Breeds Violence—Perhaps?, 120 Amer. J. Psychiat.
386 (1963); DeFrancis, Interpreting Child Protective Services to Your Community 23–24 (1957); DeFrancis, Protective Services and Community Expectations 9–10 (1961); Miller, supra note 6, at 1212; Rheinstein, The Child
at Law, Report of the Twenty-eighth Ross Pediatric Research Conference 70
(1958). Fontana at 9 quotes Dr. Menninger as believing that every criminal
was an unloved and maltreated child. See also Silver, Dublin & Lourie, Does
Violence Breed Violence?: Contributions from a Study of the Child Abuse
Syndrome, 126 Amer. J. Psychiat. 404 (1969).
48. American Humane Assoc., Guidelines for Legislation to Protect the
Battered Child 4–5 (1963); The Battered-Child Syndrome, 4 The Sciences,
No. 7, 12 (Dec., 1964); Fontana at 18–19; Kempe at 18.
49. Children's Bureau, supra note 9, at 11–13.

reporting of injuries intentionally inflicted by any means,[50] but it was not until recently that a statute was passed specifically pertaining to injuries to children.[51] Since California's pioneering effort, all of the other 49 states, the District of Columbia and the Virgin Islands have passed similar legislation.[52] All this has occurred in the space of a very few years.

A number of different approaches have been taken in the drafting of these statutes. Some states have amended pre-existing statutes, while others have passed wholly new laws. A number of the states have incorporated their acts into the penal or criminal laws, and other states have placed them in the general or welfare laws. However, the bulk of the states have more or less followed the pattern established by the Children's Bureau Act.[53]

It is very definitely felt that the purpose clause of any such Act should state that the legislature intends for the provision of protective services by the appropriate agencies, under rules established by the agency. One criticism of many of the enactments is that they are too penal in nature, reflecting an emphasis on punishing the parent or abuser, rather than protecting the child.[54] Also, many physicians felt that the mere reporting of abuse is futile unless some system is established to insure that positive and effective action is taken to follow through on the reports.[55] Second, despite the criticism by some groups,[56] it is felt that the statute should be limited to hospitals, clinics, and members of the healing

---

50. Cal. Pen. Code Annot. §§ 11160–11162. This statute was originally enacted in 1929.

51. Cal. Pen. Code Annot. § 11161.5 (Supp. 1970).

52. For analysis of the variety and history of these statutes, see McCoid, The Battered Child and Other Assaults Upon the Family, 50 Minn. L. Rev. 1 (1965); Paulsen, Parker & Adelman, Child Abuse Reporting Laws: Some Legislative History, 34 Geo. Wash. L. Rev. 482 (1966); Paulsen, The Legal Framework for Child Protection, 66 Col. L. Rev. 679 (1966).

53. See Children's Div. American Humane Assoc., Review of Legislation to Protect the Battered Child 2 (1964).

54. Conference, Richmond, Virginia Community Council, March 29, 1965; Editorial, 1 Lancet 543 (1964); Editorial, 266 New Eng. J. Med. 1063 (1962); Harper, The Physician, The Battered Child and the Law, 31 Pediatrics 899 (1963) (hereinafter cited as Harper); Hoel, The Battered Child, 46 Minnesota Med. 1001 (1963); Letter to Editor, 267 New Eng. J. Med. 572 (1962); McCort & Vaudagna, Visceral Injuries in Battered Children, 82 Radiology 424 (1964); Young at 136.

55. Editorial, 188 J.A.M.A. 386 (1964); Report of Committee on Maternal and Child Care, AMA, 190 J.A.M.A. 358 (1964).

56. Ibid.

professions, principally for the reason that these cases are often admittedly difficult to identify and these groups are best equipped to exercise the necessary discretion.[57] Next, the report should be made as soon as practicable in writing, possibly preceded by an oral report if it is felt that time is of the essence, to an official agency charged with the responsibility for protective services in the community. This has been the most controversial aspect of these statutes since most of the acts provide for the report being made to the police, thus emphasizing the punitive aspect of the legislation.[58] A clause should provide for immunity from civil and criminal liability resulting from such a report, although there is probably little practical need for such immunity since malice would have to be proved to render the reporting physician or other person liable for defamation under existing law.[59] The value of such a clause is largely psychological in encouraging reports, although it would also preclude the rather remote possibility of having to defend a claim.[60] It does seem unfortunate that it is necessary to provide for legal immunity in order to secure the performance of a humane act.[61] In states with the physician-patient privilege, a clause should probably be included to place reports of child abuse outside the ambit of such privilege. Once again, this provision is

57. Young at 136.
58. Id. at 138; Braun, Braun & Simonds, The Mistreated Child, 99 Calif. Med. 98, 102 (1963); Delsordo, Protective Casework for Abused Children, 10 Children 213 (1963); Editorial, 269 New Eng. J. Med. 1437 (1963); Ten Bensel & Raile, The Battered Child Syndrome, 46 Minnesota Med. 977 (1963). One solution would be a special unit of police such as that used in Los Angeles. Boardman at 48–51; Erwin, The Battered Child Syndrome, 130 Medico-Legal Bulletin 5–6 (1964); Swanson, Role of the Police in the Protection of Children from Neglect and Abuse, 25 Fed. Prob. 43 (1961); Young at 138.
59. Harper at 902; Erwin, supra note 58, at 6–7; Ferguson, Battered Child Syndrome, 65 J. Kansas Med. Soc. 67 (1964). The general rule is that there is a qualified or absolute privilege in favor of reports of suspected criminal violations. 33 Am. Jur., Libel and Slander § 137 (1941); Prosser, Torts § 95, esp. p. 620 (2d ed. 1955); Schoepfer, Legal Implications in Connection with Physical Abuse of Children, in Protecting the Battered Child 29–30 (1962); Shartel & Plant, The Law of Medical Practice §§ 4–04 –05 (1959). See also Louisell & Williams, Trial of Medical Malpractice Cases para. 8.13 n.57 (1965 ed.).
60. Harper at 902.
61. Louisell and Williams have discussed this unfortunate trend with respect to the so-called "Good Samaritan" statutes. The rationale expressed therein is equally applicable here. Louisell & Williams, supra note 59, at para. 21.42.

185   Robert E. Shepherd, Jr.

probably not necessary since this privilege is almost always personal to the patient, and the patient would be the child and not the parent or person inflicting the injuries.[62] However, as before, such a clause would have a beneficial effect in dissipating to a certain degree the physician's natural reticence to make such a report.[63]

Finally, it is felt that such a statute should *not* have a penalty clause. The identification of an abused child is obviously not as simple as the recognition of a gunshot wound.[64] To provide a penalty for the failure to report a case of child abuse when its identification requires the exercise of a considerable amount of judgment and discretion is unduly harsh. Also, realistically, such a provision is unenforceable and therefore useless. The efforts of a number of brilliant pediatricians and radiologists have made the identification of the "battered child" an easier task through the application of the following indices of suspicion: 1) age characteristically under three years; 2) general health of child indicative of neglect; 3) characteristic distribution of fractures; 4) dispropor-

62. Harper at 900–902; Annot., 2 A.L.R.2d 645, 647 (1948); McCormick, Evidence § 105 (1954); Payne, The Physician-Patient Privilege in Virginia, 1 U. Rich. Law Notes 26, 29 (1958); Shartel & Plant, supra note 59 at § 7–16; Stetler & Moritz, Doctor and Patient and the Law 252–274 (4th ed. 1962); 8 Wigmore, Evidence § 2386 (McNaughton rev. 1961). See State v. Tornquist, 254 Iowa 1135, 120 N.W.2d 483, 494–495 (1963). See also Note, Exception to Use of Physician-Patient Privilege in Child Abuse Cases, 42 U. Det. L.J. 88 (1964). See State v. Tornquist, 254 Iowa 1135, 120 N.W.2d 483, 494–95 (1963).

63. This reticence on the part of physicians is, of course, the major reason that reporting legislation has been, and is, deemed necessary. This slowness to recognize the problem is largely due to a natural reluctance to believe a parent capable of abusing his own child. See Dodge, Medical Implications of Physical Abuse of Children, in Protecting the Battered Child 23 (1962); Kempe at 19. Also, many physicians feel that this is a problem involving only the lower socio-economic classes. Boardman at 44. That this is not necessarily true may be seen in the reports of numerous cases involving children from higher groups. Barta & Smith, Willful Trauma to Young Children, 2 Clin. Pediat. (Phila.) 545, 553 (1963); Kempe at 18. One suspected case has been mentioned in the literature involving the child of a physician and his nurse wife. Crawford, The Battered Child Syndrome, 14 Juv. Ct. Judges J., No. 3, 18, 18–19 (1963). See also a more recent survey in Silver, Barton & Dublin, Child Abuse Laws: Are They Enough? 199 J.A.M.A. 101 (1967).

64. Hoel, supra note 54. However, there are statutes requiring reports of gunshot and knife wounds, communicable diseases and suspicious injuries. 41 Am. Jur., Physicians and Surgeons § 10 (1942); Shartel & Plant, supra note 61, at § 7–08; Stetler & Moritz, supra note 64, at 81.

tionate amount of soft tissue injury; 5) evidence that injuries occurred at varying times and are in different stages of resolution; 6) cause of recent trauma; 7) suspicious family history; 8) history of previous similar episodes; and 9) no new lesions during the child's hospitalization.[65] However, even with the application of these indices, and others, identification still requires a considerable amount of judgment. For example, the Tulane study [66] revealed that of two physicians who each saw about 250 patients under similar circumstances, one reported 17 suspected cases of battering and the other reported none.[67]

Mandatory reporting legislation is not the unanimous choice of all persons concerned about child abuse and it is not a panacea.[68] The great need is for programs for protective services because society cannot stop with the mere reporting of a case.[69] However,

---

65. Fontana at 22; Fontana, Donovan & Wong, supra note 29, at 1393; Connell, The Devil's Battered Children, 64 J. Kansas Med. Soc. 385, 391 (1963); Teng, Singleton & Daeschner, Skeletal Injuries of the Battered Child, 6 Amer. J. Orthoped. 202 (1964).

66. Supra note 34.

67. Id. at 161.

68. In fact, there is a very good argument that such legislation is theoretically unnecessary. For example, the Attorney-General of Kansas has rendered an opinion which would make the enactment of reporting legislation in that state redundant. He advised that—1) a physician was already under an obligation to report cases of child abuse, as they constituted violations of the law, and particularly in view of Sections nine and ten of the Code of Ethics; 2) the physician's testimony would not be subject to a claim of privilege by anyone other than the child; and 3) there would be no personal liability on the part of the physician if he rendered and reported only his medical opinion. Ferguson, supra note 59. A reporting statute could create some problems as it would tend to concentrate attention on the abused child to the exclusion of his siblings. Also, the legislation could increase the danger to the child if its emphasis were penal because it could cause the child's parents to neglect bringing him for medical treatment from fear of prosecution. Reinhart & Elmer, The Abused Child, 188 J.A.M.A. 358, 360 (1964).

69. Child Welfare League of America, Standards for Child Protective Service (1960); DeFrancis, Children Who Were Helped Through Protective Services (1960); DeFrancis, Community Cooperation for Better Child Protection (1959); DeFrancis, The Court and Protective Services (1960); DeFrancis, The Fundamentals of Child Protection (1955); DeFrancis, Interpreting Child Protective Services to Your Community (1957); DeFrancis, Protective Services and Community Expectations (1961); Delsordo, supra note 58; Philbrick, Treating Parental Pathology Through Child Protective Services (1960); Wald, Protective Services and Emotional Neglect (1961). The state of Idaho has established an excellent statutory scheme for the provision of protective services. Idaho Code Ann. § 56–204A(a) (Supp. 1969).

it is a first step, and an essential first step. Over 50 percent of these children will be subjected to additional injuries if returned to their previous environment without some action being taken.[70] Many medical societies have advocated the passage of such legislation, perhaps with some reservations, but with a surprising amount of agreement.[71] My recommendations for a statute which would meet the qualifications set forth above are as follows: [72]

Section 1—*Purpose*. In order to protect children whose health and welfare may be adversely affected through the infliction, by other than accidental means, of physical injury, or through physical neglect, requiring the attention of a physician, the legislature hereby provides for the mandatory reporting of such cases by physicians or institutions to the appropriate public authority. It is the intent of the legislature that, as a result of such reporting, protective social services shall be made available in an effort to prevent further abuse or neglect, safeguard and enhance the welfare of such children, and preserve family life wherever possible.

Section 2—*Reports by Physicians and Institutions*. Any physician, including any licensed doctor of medicine, licensed osteopathic physician, intern or resident, having reasonable cause to suspect that a child under the age of ———[73] brought to him or coming to him for examination, care or treatment has had serious physical injury or injuries inflicted upon him other than

70. Fontana at 21; Erwin, supra note 58, at 4.
71. Dodge, supra note 63, at 25; Editorial, 115 J. Louisiana Med. Soc. 322 (1963); Editorial, 269 New Eng. J. Med. 1437 (1963); Editorial, 47 Rhode Island Med. J. 89 (1964); Montana, The Neglect and Abuse of Children, 64 New York J. Med. 215, 219–220, 223–224 (1964); Hoel, supra note 54; Mintz, Battered Child Syndrome, 60 Texas J. Med. 107 (1964); Pascoe & Peterson, Protective Law Needed for Battered Child Reports, 60 Texas J. Med. 887 (1964); Schrotel, Responsibilities of Physicians in Suspected Cases of Child Brutality, 42 Cincinnati J. Med. 408 (1961); Report of Committee on Maternal and Child Care, AMA, 190 J.A.M.A. 358 (1964). This latter report was adopted by the House of Delegates of the American Medical Association in June, 1964. Several other statements have reported the legislation and pleaded for the attention of the medical profession and others. The Child Abuse Problem in Iowa, supra note 31; Editorial, The Battered Child Problem, 181 J.A.M.A. 42 (1962); Physical Abuse of Children, Virginia Welfare Bull., p. 4 (Oct. 1963); Platou at 157; Sheriff, The Abused Child, 60 J. S. Carolina Med. Ass'n 191 (1964); Toland, Abuse of Children—Whose Responsibility, 28 Conn. Med. 438 (1964).
72. See Children's Div., American Humane Assoc., Guidelines for Legislation to Protect the Battered Child (1963).
73. The maximum age utilized in the state for Juvenile Court jurisdiction should be inserted here.

by accidental means, or is suffering from serious physical neglect, shall report or cause reports to be made in accordance with the provisions of this Act; provided that when the attendance of a physician with respect to a child is pursuant to the performance of services as a member of the staff of a hospital, clinic or similar institution he shall notify the person in charge of the institution or his designated delegate who shall report or cause reports to be made in accordance with the provisions of this Act.

Section 3—*Nature and Content of Report; to Whom Made.* A report in writing shall be made, and an oral report if, in the judgment of the attending physician, time is a material factor in preventing further abuse or neglect, to an appropriate protective services agency. Such reports shall contain the following information if known: (a) The address and age of the child; (b) The address of the child's parents, step-parents, guardians, or other persons having custody of the child; (c) The nature and extent of the child's injury or injuries, or evidence of neglect; (d) Any evidence of previous injuries or neglect, including their nature and extent; and (e) Any other information which in the opinion of the physician may be helpful in establishing the cause of the child's injury, injuries or neglect.

Section 4—*Immunity from Liability:* Anyone participating in the making of a report pursuant to this Act shall have immunity from any liability, civil or criminal, that might otherwise be incurred or imposed.

Section 5—*Evidence Not Privileged.* The physician-patient privilege shall not be a ground for excluding evidence regarding a child's injuries or neglect, or the cause thereof, in any judicial proceeding resulting from a report pursuant to this Act.[74]

It has previously been pointed out that this article cannot hope to encompass the complete scope of child abuse, active or passive. It is a broad field and one which has largely been neglected by the legal profession in general, and legal writers in specific. The whole field of child law cries out for intensive and careful study. As the ɔurnal of the American Medical Association expressed it:

For centuries the young child has been regarded as a chattel of his parents. By making abortions illegal except under limited

74. A separate section should provide for the establishment of protective services through the existing or proposed public welfare agencies or duly licensed private agencies, and under rules prescribed by the State Board of Welfare or other comparable agency. See, e.g., Iowa Code Ann. § 56–204A(a) (Supp. 1969). See also Daly, Willful Child Abuse and State Reporting Statutes, 23 U. Miami L. Rev. 283 (1969).

circumstances, civilized society now protects the child in utero. It should continue giving adequate protection through the early years of life when the child is still too young to defend himself.[75]

The law must seek greater interdisciplinary communication in attempting to solve the problems of a mobile and rapidly changing society. The subject of this article represents one area in which the law has lagged somewhat behind medicine and social work in seeking solutions to a growing problem of acute concern. The channels of communication between the professions must be kept open and cooperation must be deliberate and continuing, rather than coincidental and sporadic.

75. Editorial, The Battered-Child Syndrome, 181 J.A.M.A. 42 (1962).

Part III

Decisions About the Child

Thomas A. Coyne

14
Who Will Speak for the Child?

The problems facing us with regard to the family are often quiet, formidable ones. Yet, the manner by which we decide custody raises difficult questions. Family law is a vital field. Though it may not command the drama of the newsprint devoted to student unrest, racism, or the generation gap, those matters are not unrelated to the way in which the state treats the problems of the family.

When Custody Arises

When the marital tie is severed by divorce or separation, the courts must decide what to do with children born to the parties of the marriage. Yet, marriages ended by court action are not the only situations in which questions of custody arise. When a child is born out of wedlock, the law must determine who is to be charged with the child's care and supervision.[1] Furthermore, even if a child is born of a marriage, the question of his welfare can come before a court, though neither parent attempts to sever the marital relationship. A child's parents may die or disappear, thereby making judicial supervision necessary. Even when a child has parental supervision, it is not unknown for a court to interfere in the family unit to protect the child's welfare. It is now commonplace for a juvenile court to exercise jurisdiction over children when the family is dysfunctional. For example, when a child is living with parents who

THOMAS A. COYNE, J.D., is Professor of Law and Assistant Dean, California Western Law School, San Diego. This article is reprinted with permission from *The Annals of the American Academy of Political and Social Science* 383 (May 1969):35–47.

1. California provides that "the mother of an illegitimate unmarried minor is entitled to its custody."—CAL. CIV. CODE § 200 (West 1954).

are not willing to exercise proper care and control over him, a juvenile court may remove the child from his environment.[2]

Indeed, though the parents may be loving and in agreement about the care of their child, a juvenile court may still deprive them of custody so that the child can receive necessary medical treatment contrary to the principles of the parents. Moreover, the juvenile court may be brought into family matters when a father and mother are of different religious backgrounds and each wants the child reared according to his or her own standards.

What has been said indicates that there are limits to parental prerogatives and that the state decides just what those limitations will be. The state assumes the power to protect children regardless of whether the family is a going healthy unit, or is malfunctioning, or is broken. And parents still have much to say about how they want to raise their children. A child's position with the law, however, is not so clear.

A child is, of course, considered to be a human, and this sets him apart from the family furniture, pets, and other possessions. But a child does not possess full legal capacity. He is a minor until he attains the age of twenty-one.[3] The child can be subject to military service before he becomes an adult for many legal purposes. He is held responsible for his torts.[4] If a minor is a party to litigation, he must be represented by a guardian. He has no legal capacity to make a contract, but if he does, he may recover as if he were an adult.[5] He cannot give binding consent to a medical operation before his majority.[6] An action, however, may be maintained in his behalf for injuries sustained by him before birth, and his parents may maintain an action for his death before birth.[7] The point is that before the age of twenty-one, a human being is a minor with certain legal disabilities.[8]

---

2. Not unlike other states, California grants a juvenile-court jurisdiction over "any person under the age of 21 years . . . who is in need of proper and effective care or control."—CAL. WELF. & INST'NS CODE § 600 (West 1966).

3. "Minors are all persons under 21 years of age."—CAL. CIV. CODE § 25 (West 1954).

4. PROSSER, HANDBOOK OF THE LAW OF TORTS 1024 (3d ed. 1964).

5. CORBIN, CONTRACTS § 6 (1963).

6. Lacey v. Laird, 166 Ohio St. 12, 139 N.E. 2d 25 (1956).

7. PROSSER, *supra* note 4, at 354.

8. California provides, however, that a person who is eighteen and married has the legal capacity of an adult.—CAL. CIV. CODE § 25 (West 1954).

From birth to age twenty-one, a child is constantly changing, and during this period, he is a ward of his parents. But he may also be a ward of the juvenile court when the state decides to intervene. The state considers itself to be the parent of the country and, therefore, responsible for all persons who lack full legal capacity. This idea is expressed by the Latin phrase *parens patriae*.

It has been suggested that the concept of the state acting as *parens patriae* of all children originated in the medieval practice which recognized the sovereign's right to a profitable guardianship of the property of incompetents. Because of a printer's error, the word "enfant" was substituted for the word "ideot" in a text written by Lord Coke. By the time this error was corrected in a subsequent edition, it had become accepted that courts of chancery had jurisdiction to decide whose ward a child would be.[9] Regardless of how the court's jurisdiction came into being, the doctrine of *parens patriae* dates back to an England of two centuries ago, and it has found its way into American court opinions.[10]

What Standards Apply

Because a child does not have the physical properties of an adult or the same legal capacities, the juvenile courts have developed some rules in custody cases to help them in their efforts to decide what is in the "best interests of the child." Judge Benjamin N. Cardozo, one of our most capable judges, had this to say about that guiding principle:

> The chancellor in exercising his jurisdiction . . . upon petition does not proceed upon the theory that the petitioner, whether father or mother, has a cause of action against the other or indeed against any one. He acts as *parens patriae* to do what is best for the interest of the child. He is to put himself in the position of a "wise, affectionate, and careful parent," and make provision for the child accordingly. . . . Equity does not concern itself with such disputes in their relation to the disputants. Its concern is for the child.[11]

What the court is actually called upon to do is to play God with

---

9. Foote, Levy & Sander, Cases and Materials on Family Law 394 (1966).

10. 16 Vand. L. Rev. 961 n. 7 (1963).

11. Findlay v. Findlay, 240 N.Y. 429, 433–34, 148 N.E. 624, 626 (1925).

respect to a child. This responsibility becomes all the more awe-some when we consider that there is a general rule to the effect that the mother and father, unless declared unfit, have the right to the custody and care of their children.[12] This presumption of parental right to custody does not, of course, operate when a choice between parents has to be made. In that event, one parent gets custody even though the other is not unfit. However, the idea of parental right is a very strong factor when the choice is between a parent and a third person, and this may at times lead to unfortunate results.

While we may recall with some nostalgia the old maxim that "blood is thicker than water," it may be to a child's best interests not to be a ward of his natural parents. The ties that cement the members of a family into a unit of solidarity are not necessarily the result of a blood relationship; they arise and are formed by role-playing and by an intimate sharing.[13]

Suppose we have a child who, at the age of two, has a guardian appointed because the father, who is absent, assents to the appointment and the mother is unfit. Three years later, the parents of the child petition the court for custody of the child on the basis that the father has always been a fit person and that the mother has now become such. The guardian, the child's paternal aunt, is a single woman of thirty-eight. She is a registered nurse, very attached to the child, and the child considers the aunt to be her mother. The guardian plans to send the child to college. The parents have visited the child infrequently and have contributed nothing towards her support. They love the child, but she apparently has no emotional attachment to the parents. The father believes that he will be able to see that the child goes to college. Who should have the child?

A court decided that the guardian should keep the child because both parents were unfit. The factors which the court thought made the parents unfit were the infrequent visits, no contributions for the child's support, and the actions and attitude of the mother in court.[14]

If the court had been concerned only with the principle of the "best interests of the child," there would have been no necessity for

12. 27 C.J.S. Divorce § 308 (1959).
13. Clifford v. Woodford, 83 Ariz. 257, 265, 320 P. 2d 452, 457 (1957).
14. Wilkins v. Wilkins, 324 Mass. 261, 85 N.E. 2d 768 (1949).

it to find that the parents were unfit. However, the presumption of parental right made the question of parental fitness essential.

On the other hand, if the presumption of parental right does not enter into the court's decision, the best interests of the child will probably be measured by the reference of a judge to his own ideas of what kind of environment is best for a child. This would not require a judicial determination that what the parent is or has to offer is unacceptable.

Consider this statement by a court where it was presented with a choice between a father and maternal grandparents:

> The Bannister home [maternal grandparents] provides Mark [seven years of age] with a stable, dependable, conventional, middleclass, middlewest background and an opportunity for a college education and profession, if he desires it. It provides a valid foundation and secure atmosphere. In the Painter home [father], Mark would have more freedom of conduct and thought with an opportunity to develop his individual talents. It would be more exciting and challenging in many respects, but romantic, impractical and unstable.[15]

The court awarded the grandparents custody of the child without finding that the father was unfit for some more customary reason, such as being habitually drunk, immoral, or mentally ill. Without the discipline of the presumption of parental right, a court may be tempted to consider itself omniscient.

In making a decision about the best interests of a child, perhaps the court should give preference to the natural parents, but *only* when all other alternatives have equal merit. Maybe then the blood relationship should sway the decision in favor of the parent. A presumption of parental right should not be paramount to the best interests of the child. Happily, there is some evidence of a tendency to subordinate parental interests to the child's welfare.[16]

The Relevancy of Parental Rights

A juvenile-court judge is in a difficult position in a custody case where the best interests of the child mean one thing to him, another

15. Painter v. Bannister, 258 Ia. 1390, 140 N.W. 2d 152 (1966). A California court awarded the father custody of the child in August 1968, when he refused to send his son back after a visit and the grandparents filed a court action for custody.

16. Foster, Jr., & Freed, *Child Custody,* 39 N.Y.U. L. Rev. 423, 435 (1964).

to the father, and still another to the mother. In a fairly recent custody case in California, the court was confronted in a divorce case with these facts. The mother's religious beliefs included the idea that she could not associate with any person who did not belong to her sect. Her husband had disassociated himself from this group. The mother testified that she felt it was her duty to instruct her five-year-old son in her spiritual standards and that since the father did not subscribe to these beliefs she felt compelled to prevent her son from seeing his father.

The court which first considered this matter found that the temporal environment available to the child in the custody of either parent would be substantially equal and that each parent was fit. But that court concluded that the best interests of the child would be best served by granting custody to the father. On appeal, the decision was reversed,[17] and the mother was granted custody.

It was established that the mother's religion would prevent the child from eating in a public or private place unless alone or in the exclusive company of other members of the sect. This religion would also prohibit the child from engaging in extracurricular activities at school, from watching or participating in public or private entertainment such as card-playing or television, from having toys or pets, from celebrating Christmas, and from reading any form of literature except the Bible. Though the higher court stated that the best interest of the child is the guide in custody cases, it said that Section 138 of the California Civil Code required custody to be awarded to the mother when a child is of tender years and other things are equal. Moreover, the court believed that the Constitutions of the United States and of the State of California gave protection to the mother's religious freedom. It felt that she could not be deprived of the custody of a child of tender years, other things being equal, where, as here, her religious beliefs were not immoral, illegal, or against public policy. The result of this decision is quite disturbing, for its effect was to take the child from custody granted the father in an interlocutory judgment of divorce two years earlier.

The record of this case is replete with what the mother and the father thought were the best interests of the child and with what the court thought when it decided that the best interests of the child should rest on the mother's constitutional right to religious

17. Quiner v. Quiner, 59 Cal. Rptr. 503 (1967), *rehearing granted; dismissed by stipulation.*

freedom. The relevancy of the mother's constitutional rights to the child's best interests remains unclear. The child was as much a person as his mother, and, perhaps, he should have been seen as having some rights, too.

Another case may help to illustrate the complexity of custody proceedings when a child's best interests are affected by the opposing religious views of his parents. The Supreme Court of Wisconsin was called on to review a lower court's decision awarding custody to the father.[18] The lower court had been influenced by the mother's testimony by which she had professed to be an agnostic, and it concluded that "a home in which a firm faith in deity is professed, is considered one of its foundations, is preferable to one in which doubt, skepticism or agnoticism [sic] is professed." [19]

A fundamental principle in Wisconsin custody-determinations is the rule of preference in favor of a mother, though the welfare of the child is the polestar. Consequently, the appellate court reversed the decision on the grounds that a court would be warranted in denying a mother preference because of her religion only when it involved beliefs dangerous to the child's health or morals. This higher court concluded that no danger to the child's health or morals had been shown and that it was improper for the trial court to give any weight to the matter of religion. The higher court noted in passing that the right to religious freedom under the Constitution of the United States included the right to non-belief. Again, we see that a child's future is made to depend to some degree on the rights of his parent.

Perhaps an avenue should be open for someone to speak for the child. He is not represented by the attorneys for the parents. Their allegiance is to their clients. The child might at least be accorded the power to prevent his disposition from depending on the rights of others. Maybe we are still treating the child as property that results from a marriage, and not as a human being.

Conformity Versus Parental Values

Of course, the parents may be united in their view of what is in the best interests of a child, but their opinion may be contrary to the orthodox view held by the community. Much of the custody

18. Welker v. Welker, 24 Wis. 2d 570, 129 N.W. 2d 134 (1964).
19. *Id*. at 136.

litigation in this area concerns the refusal by parents to give their consent to medical care for the child because the parents have religious beliefs opposed to such care.

As judge of a juvenile court, what decision would you make with these facts? The mother and father are Jehovah's Witnesses, and one of the tenets of their religion forbids blood transfusions. Their infant child has a circulatory problem which is not curable; however, it will not be fatal if blood transfusions are administered. The parents refuse, and the child's condition is critical. A petition is filed before you asking that the custody of the child be removed from the parents so that their consent to the transfusions will be unnecessary. The parents appear before you, and both evidence sincere parental concern and affection for their child. They urgently argue that you would violate their freedom of religion as guaranteed by the Constitution of the United States if you deprive them of custody for the purpose of giving their child the transfusions. If your decision is to deprive the parents of custody, then you would make the same disposition of the case that a court actually made.[20]

The court reached its decision by finding that the refusal by the parents, on religious grounds, to submit their infant to the transfusions needed to save its life amounted to statutory neglect. Because of this finding, the court was able to appoint a guardian and to award him custody for the purpose of authorizing transfusions.

But suppose you were a child in such a case and that you had the knowledge, skill, and experience to enable you to make a decision. The choice might very well be to receive the transfusion and live, without any regard to the religious beliefs of parents.

Religion is not the only parental prerogative which may have to yield to convention. During this century, the universal education of children has gained acceptance. Yet it is still possible for a child to receive an education without the assistance of a public or private school. A father and mother may be literate though they do not meet the requirements specified by a state for teaching in public or private schools. Although evidencing sincere belief that it is to the best interests of their child that he receive his instruction from them, parents may be punished for refusing to

20. State v. Perricone, 37 N.J. 462, 181 A. 2d 751, *cert. denied,* 371 U.S. 890 (1962).

send their child through the mass education system. Even if their child's achievement level and the quality of his education compares favorably with conventionally educated children, the parents may be deprived of custody so that the child can receive an education which conforms to public dictates.[21]

The Family as a Unit

An inquiry into the best interests of a child may produce differences of opinion when it is directed to the parents and to the court. And if the child himself is capable of assessing his own position, he may have an alternative of his own to suggest. Such an alternative would merit the skill of an advocate who would represent the child.

The possibility that a child may have his own proposal to suggest to the court is an important facet of this difficult problem. A father and mother have identical twins, fourteen years of age. These are their only children. During the last year, one of the twins developed a kidney ailment which has resulted in the permanent malfunction of one of his kidneys. The doctors have advised the parents that the disease is seriously weakening the child's remaining kidney and that no cure is presently known. If the disease continues, the child's life expectancy is likely to be no more than one year. It is believed that a kidney transplant will cure the ailing twin, and doctors recommend that the donor be the healthy twin. Only one kidney is necessary to perform kidney functions. But the removal of the kidney from the donor does gives that child less protection in case he should contract a kidney ailment. Furthermore, any major surgery entails risk and can be fatal. Yet, the chance of survival in kidney transplants is 75 percent when the donor is an identical twin, and it is less than 1 percent if another blood relative donates.

Both of the children know these facts and want to go through the transplant process which the doctors recommend. However, the parents are skeptical and refuse to give consent. They feel that the chances are slim that the operation will be successful; that the surgery creates future risk for the donating twin; that the disease may be arrested without surgery; and that it would be

21. *Cf.* People v. Turner, 121 Cal. App. 2d 861, 263 P. 2d 685 (1953), *appeal dismissed,* 347 U.S. 972 (1954).

immoral to give consent to an operation which could be fatal to one or both of their children.[22]

If a petition were filed before you asking that you take custody from the parents so that the transplant could take place, you might think that not only is a "Solomon-like" solution impossible but also that a court may not be the proper place for this particular question. If the state is on one side of a case and the parents on the other, the determination of what is best for a child is difficult enough. But if we introduce the child himself as a party in interest and the family unit as another party, we will complicate further what is already sufficiently complex.

Not only does the child have no advocate in a custody proceeding before a court, unless delinquency is involved, but his preference as to whose ward he will be is usually treated as simply one other factor in the total sum of best interests, if it is considered at all.

The Age of the Child

Some states have, by statute, given the court authority to consider what the child wants. In California, for example, a court may consider preference if the child is of a sufficient age to form an intelligent choice.[23] But this statute is not aimed at securing any right to the child. Its purpose is to grant the court the discretion to consider preference if the court desires to do so. Indeed, the way in which this preference is made known is, by the common practice of the judge, to question a child as to his preference of custodians.[24] The child has no advocate to assist him in his stage of the proceedings, or in any other stage for that matter. While the California statute does not specify the age which a child must have attained before his preference will be considered, some jurisdictions have set the age at fourteen.[25] But, regardless of the child's age, if he is old enough to talk, his preference and the reasons for his choice ought to be formally before the court.

Custody is, however, often determined without any considera-

---

22. FOOTE, LEVY & SANDER, *supra* note 9, at 387–88.
23. CAL. CIV. CODE § 138 (1) (West 1954).
24. I THE CALIFORNIA FAMILY LAWYER, § 15.20 (1962).
25. OHIO REV. CODE ANN. § 3109.04 (1953).

tion of the child's preference. This point may be demonstrated by reference to an actual case. At the divorce of the parents, the custody of the children, one seven years old and the other nine, was awarded to the mother. Shortly thereafter, the mother became ill, both physically and mentally, and allowed the paternal grandmother to have physical custody of her children. The mother's recovery was slow, and the father petitioned the court to change custody to him. The court granted his petition with the stipulation that a rehearing would be held ten months later, after the children had lived with the father and visited with the mother. The judge further stated that he made the order for the purpose of giving the children an opportunity to be able to express an intelligent opinion concerning their custodial future.

By the time of the rehearing, the children were ten and twelve years of age. Despite the original statement of the judge that the children should voice their preference at the rehearing, another judge returned custody to the mother without giving the children a voice. This decision was affirmed on appeal.[26] Since the children were under fourteen years of age, the court found that the trial judge did not abuse the discretion accorded him in deciding best interests without the opinion of the children. But a child has no control over his age, and the reason for his preference may be just as valid at age twelve as at age fourteen. And in a situation like this, where the parents are divorced, there is no family unit to make a decision which might conflict with the court's concept of best interests. Both parents, however, were represented by counsel in the case just discussed. And, no doubt, each attorney tried to convince the court that the child's welfare would be benefited by the grant of custody to his client.

Surely if a guardian *ad litem* must be appointed to appear for a child if he is a party to a civil suit, that same child should have a spokesman when the matter being decided is his environment while he is developing into an adult.

Not only may the child's age determine whether or not a court must hear his preference; it may shape the court's decision in another way. Many states give preference to a mother as a custodian if a child is young or "of tender years," provided that

26. Robelet v. Robelet, 130 C.A. 2d 244, 278 P. 2d 753 (1955).

other things are equal. At the same time, if both parents are suitable, preference is given to the father if the child is older.[27] These preferences recognize that a child is continually developing. If it is impossible for him to have both a father and a mother, at certain stages of his development it would be better for him to have a mother. At other stages, a father would be more beneficial.

Children Without Parents

The discussion up to this point has involved custody proceedings where the sincere efforts of the parents to do what they think best for their children is unquestioned. But parents are human, and they can err. They can also intentionally violate the best interests of their minor offspring. They may die, or become incompetent, or even abandon their children. In this latter circumstance, the juvenile court is asked to choose a guardian. This means that neither father nor mother is available and that the court must interfere in an attempt to create parents. Here the child is probably the only party who may disagree with the disposition made by the court.

The judge in a guardianship proceeding is guided by the "best interests of the child." In the absence of parents to choose from, the court is often guided by statute as to preference. Preference may be in this order: "[1] to one who was indicated by the wishes of a deceased parent; [2] to one who already stands in the position of a trustee of a fund to be applied to the child's support; [and] [3] to a relative." [28] The child's preference may also be considered if, as in a choice between parents, he is of sufficient age to form an intelligent preference. But do not assume that a guardianship proceeding is an advocacy proceeding because there are no parents to seek custody. The court has discretion to decide who the guardian will be, and there is no counsel to represent the child and urge a particular alternative before the court.

When Parents Fail

But, passing from those instances where the family unit fails to

27. "As between parents adversely claiming custody, neither parent is entitled to it as of right; but other things being equal, if the child is of tender years, custody should be given to the mother; if the child is of an age to require education and preparation for labor or business, then custody should be given to the father." CAL. CIV. CODE § 138 (2) (West 1954).

28. CAL. PROB. CODE, § 1407 (West 1956).

function because its parent figures are unavailable, there are, unfortunately, many instances where the parents are available but
their conduct violates the child's welfare. Concern here is not
centered on juvenile delinquency (though that problem is great
and alarming), but on "parental neglect." The victims of this
conduct we might refer to as "neglected" or "dependent" children. Prior reference has been made to sincere parental action
which violates community standards and gives the juvenile court
authority to take custody away from the parents. But our interest
here is in the following type of situation.

A husband and wife have marital difficulties, and this causes
constant quarreling between them. Their children, a girl seven
years old and a boy nine, are often awakened by the shouting of
the parents. At times, they are taken by one of the parents from
their house in the middle of the night, and they sleep in the car
with that parent, or lodge elsewhere, until the matter which caused
the strained relationship is forgiven. On one such occasion, the
mother calls the police and complains that the father has taken
the children away with him. A policeman and a juvenile-proba-
tion officer are sent to locate them. The children are found,
ill-clad and poorly housed, at the home of the father's parents,
and the probation officer takes them to the city guardian's home.
The following morning a complaint is filed in the juvenile court by
the state, alleging that the children are neglected.

The judge enters an order placing temporary custody in the
court until a hearing can be held. At the time set for the hearing,
both parents appear and are represented by counsel. The hearing
discloses that both parents love their children. They agree that
what has occurred in the past is detrimental to the welfare of the
girl and boy and that their marital difficulties may be beyond
solution. But both testify that it would be to the children's best
interest to remain in the home. They contend that it is better to
have the love and affection of the natural parents than any other
alternative open to the court. The state thinks that the children
are neglected, and it urges the court to place them in the custody
of the county welfare department pending changed circumstances
in the home. If marital difficulties continue in their past severity,
then the state recommends that the children be placed in a foster
home or be subject to adoption as the consent of the natural
parents is not necessary for an adoption when the parents have
been deprived of custody because of neglect. The judge talks to

the children in his chambers and finds that they are quite attached to each parent. Though the quarreling of the parents makes the children sad, neither fears that the mother or father will intentionally abuse him or her, and they are anxious to return home.[29]

Though these parents are not providing a satisfactory home life for their children, they are the authority figures in a family unit. Should the state interfere in this scheme? Suppose you were an attorney and that you were asked by the court to represent the children and to advocate what their best interests would be; what factors would you consider?

The judge has heard counsel for the parents and counsel for the state. Both inform him what each feels is necessary for the children's welfare. Traditionally, the role of the judge in an adversary system is to hear the opponents present the facts as they see them. The judge then makes a decision as a trier of fact and not as a finder of fact or as an inquisitor. If you were the judge, would you not welcome an advocate for the children? Though counsel for the parents and the counsel for the children might agree on certain points, perhaps their conclusions would, or ought to be, based on different factors. The judge would hear different points of view presented by independent voices, and this might help him arrive at a wiser decision.

Most statutes concerned with parental neglect are limited in their scope to situations in which the child's care does not meet community standards as to what constitutes an adequate supply of food, clothing, shelter, education, or medical care. In the situation just presented, vary the circumstances so that the children are clean, well-dressed, and at the mansion of the father's parents. In addition, alter the situation to read that though the parents say they love their children, the evidence shows that they are cared for by an employee. The parents see their children, but seldom do they spend much time with them because of social engagements. The children think they love their parents, but they really do not know them.

If you were asked to speak for the best interests of the children, perhaps you would assess the situation as one of "emotional neglect" and consider it as serious as the matters previously described as the usual meaning of neglect. You might wonder

29. *Cf. In re* Douglas, 164 N.E. 2d 475 (Ohio Juv. Ct. 1959).

whether the state ought to interfere with the family when the neglect refers to conduct which denies the children the love and affection which they need for emotional stability.

Where a parent has acted cruelly or violently or battered a child, it may be apparent to the child, court, and state that the best interests of the child dictate that custody be removed from the offending party. But this does not mean that the child still does not need a spokesman. Given that the child needs to be removed, the court's discretion as to the child's future is broad. If the other parent is fit, chances are that he or she will be granted sole custody. If that is not possible, then foster care, adoption, or the orphanage are the principal alternatives. The merits or demerits of each of these possibilities are not the subject of this discussion. But certainly a spokesman for the child would want to look into all available alternatives and assess them in light of the interest of the child whom he represents.

Changes in Society and the Law

Whether a custody question is raised because the marital bond is intentionally severed, or the parental conduct does not conform to community standards, or the parents do not function by reason of death or incapacity, "it is the settled rule that . . . a very broad discretion is vested in the trial courts" [30] to decide the matter.

The judge makes the ultimate decision of custody by standards that have been discussed. Though the best interest of the child is the framework by which he reaches his decision, that seemingly magic phrase is filled in by other factors: *inter alia,* presumption of parental right; the age of the child; the preference of the child; religion; and community values or standards. The judge is the one who considers these factors. And one might say that when they relate to the child, their reference is to his status, that is, to his age, and not to any right he may have. Though the preference of a child over fourteen years of age might be brought before the court, it does not compare to the right which a parent has to follow his religion and still retain custody as long as his beliefs do not endanger the health or morals of the child.

30. Prouty v. Prouty, 16 Cal. 2d 190, 191, 105 P. 2d 295, 296 (1940).

Codifications of the standards and considerations in determining custody have been offered.[31] These proposals do not differ much from those now found in most jurisdictions. Perhaps there may be some merit to our having uniform guidelines throughout the country, as an award of custody is never final, and a subsequent custody proceeding may be outside the state which made the previous award. But greater precision in the standards may be impossible if we are to preserve the necessary flexibility required in an infinite variety of factual situations. In any event, efforts to correct the imprecision of the standards will not lead us to the area most in need of improvement.

And then there are those, some of them lawyers, who make serious proposals to set up a nonlegal bureau, instead of a court, to handle custody matters. The effect of this would be to take away substantially from the field of law the responsibility for the solution of family problems.

The beginning of this century saw the development of disciplines whose contributions have not always been appreciated or incorporated in the legal process. Social changes have caused a decline in the economic dependence of family members upon the family group. The increasing mobility of our population has meant that the child finds that many of his educational and recreational needs are supplied by community institutions rather than by the home. The roles of the individual members of the family group may be changing, but this does not signal the disintegration of the family. What signals there are might profitably be read by the judicial institutions now serving the family.[32]

A Return to Advocacy

The juvenile court is largely a twentieth-century innovation. The attitude which fostered its development was one of benevolence. It was not an adversary proceeding in its inception, as the common law has known that term. A child before that court was not represented by counsel who would defend him in a delinquency action, as would be the case with an adult in court on a criminal charge. Moreover, the child had no counsel to urge that the

---

31. Foster, Jr., & Freed, *Child Custody,* 39 N.Y.U. L. Rev. 615, 628–29 & n. 143 (1964).
32. Foote, Levy & Sander, *supra* note 9, at 5.

judge award custody in some manner because it would further the child's welfare. In both delinquency and custody cases, the judge acted as the finder of fact in deciding what disposition would be in the best interests of the child. But the judge was authorized, and in some jurisdictions compelled, to ask the assistance of other disciplines. Psychology, psychiatry, and medicine assisted the judge in his fact-finding process.

"[Though] the highest motives and most enlightened impulses led to a peculiar system for juveniles . . . unknown to our law," [33] the cloak of the Constitution has recently been thrown over the juvenile court when its jurisdiction is invoked to dispose of a child alleged to be delinquent and subject to commitment to a state institution.

The "delinquent" classification may be just as much the result of parental neglect as the "neglected" or "dependent" child situations which result from lack of parental care. The child is a victim in both instances. But delinquency means more. It means that the child is alleged to have done an act which, if done by an adult, would constitute a crime. Or a child may be accused of delinquency because he is habitually truant, incorrigible, ungovernable, or beyond the control of his parents or other guardian. In this kind of proceeding before the juvenile court, the outcome may be punishment, whereas in a custody matter arising from neglect, dependence, or otherwise, the concentration is not on any offense the child is alleged to have committed. Nor is the attention focused on the child as an offender.

When a determination is to be made as to whether a juvenile is a "delinquent" as a result of alleged misconduct on his part, with the consequence that he may be committed to a state institution, the Supreme Court of the United States has made the juvenile proceeding an adversary matter. The Court said that in this type of proceeding, the child has a right to notice of the charges against him; to counsel; to confrontation and cross-examination of the witnesses against him; and to freedom from self-incrimination.[34] The Court observed that "unbridled discretion, however benevolently motivated, is frequently a poor substitute for principle and procedure." [35]

33. *In re* Gault, 387 U.S. 1, 17 (1967).
34. *Id.* at 10.
35. *In re* Gault, 387 U.S. 1, 18 (1967).

It is true that the child in the Supreme Court case was fifteen years of age, and had been committed by the juvenile-court judge to a state industrial school until twenty-one, whereas in a nondelinquency matter where custody is at issue, there is no incarceration. But a young child whose custody-determination is ill-considered may have to spend a longer period of time in an environment much more detrimental than a school designed to rehabilitate.

If counsel is required in the delinquency proceeding, then maybe we should require the child to have an advocate in the custody proceeding. The role of counsel would, no doubt, be different in those two kinds of proceedings. The attorney representing an accused delinquent gathers all of the facts available which would show that the child has, indeed, not done the act alleged. If the child has, then counsel attempts to secure the consequence which he thinks best suited for his client. At any rate, his investigation may very well make use of the psychologist, psychiatrist, doctor, and social worker. Not only is he concerned about the mental and physical health and educational needs of the child, but he is also concerned about the parents. This may be relevant because one possible disposition of a delinquent child is the return of custody to his mother and father. Their mental and physical health, employment, living conditions, and financial state are all pertinent to the best interests of the child.

Who Can Speak for the Child?

Let the child be a person and have rights in a custody proceeding. Make it a truly adversary proceeding. Give him a spokesman, for his parents and the state will have their own advocates. Take the fact-finding task from the judge and avoid the possibility that the unrepresented child will suffer from the abuse of discretion which so concerned the Supreme Court in the delinquency proceeding. Counsel for the youth would need to come to a decision as to the best interests of the child by acquainting himself with his client's characteristics. He must assess the health, personal, and educational needs of the child. The advocate should have free rein to introduce into evidence any medical, psychological, psychiatric, or juvenile-probation-department reports about the child or his parents, provided, of course, that copies are available to adverse parties in advance of the proceeding and that the authors of the reports are made available for purposes of examination and cross-examination.[36]

The child's advocate would want to know the same things about the parents that interest the lawyer in the delinquency proceeding. If the child is capable of voicing a preference and telling why he so chooses, the attorney may want to know this. Should it materialize that there is no adverse party, we might obligate the state to appear. This would prevent a situation in which counsel for the child would, in effect, be able to exercise the same broad, but undesirable, discretion that the judge has traditionally had in custody cases. Counsel for the state and child might agree on most points, but that does not mean that the child needs no representation. If the advocates inform the judge of the facts, then he may try them, and what is presented to him in the record must support the verdict.

No changes in the law as to standards for best interests may need to be made. The presumption of parental right will probably not be paramount to the child's best interest if the child has a spokesman. And while the religion of the parents may be relevant, their spiritual convictions ought not to defeat consideration of the child's welfare just because those beliefs are not dangerous to his health or morals. If the child has an advocate, then this person would have an opportunity to urge that the best interests of the child are harmed even though his client's health and morals are not threatened.

Legal change typically lags far behind social change. Our legal machinery in custody proceedings is not functioning as it should. The innovation of the juvenile court was doubtless an improvement. It allowed the law to treat children differently from adults. Recognition was given to the vulnerability of youth. But the broad grant of discretion to judges prevented the proceedings from being truly adversary.

Although the law is aware that a child needs his own special forum, the law has not as yet been able to see that a child really is a person in custody matters, that he has rights of his own, and that he needs his own advocate.

36. FOSTER, JR., & FREED, *supra* note 31, at 620.

15
Provisions for the Care of Children of Divorced Parents:
A New Legal Instrument

There is clear evidence that longevity is one of the major causes of the increasing incidence of divorce.[1] Concurrently there has been a sharp drop in the mortality rate in childhood and adolescence. As a consequence of these simultaneous changes, increasing numbers of minor children have divorced parents and for more years. The law must deal with these increasing numbers flexibly. It may be necessary, therefore, to develop new legal instruments for the protection of the interests of the children of divorced parents.

In *Ford v. Ford*,[2] decided by the U.S. Supreme Court in 1962, Mr. Justice Black wrote: "Unfortunately, experience has shown that the question of custody, so vital to a child's happiness and well-being, frequently cannot be left to the discretion of the parents. This is particularly true where, as here, the estrangement of husband and wife beclouds parental judgment with emotion and prejudice." [3]

When a marriage fails, the usual procedure for providing for the welfare of children, whether created by private agreement or by a battle in court, is either to award exclusive custody to one parent, or to divide custody between parents at some specified

LAWRENCE S. KUBIE, M.D., D.Sc., is Clinical Professor of Psychiatry, School of Medicine, University of Maryland, and Senior Consultant in Training and Research, Sheppard and Enoch Pratt Hospital, Towson, Maryland. This article is reprinted with permission of The Yale Law Journal Company and Fred B. Rothman & Company, from *The Yale Law Journal* 73(1964):1197–1200.

1. JACOBSON, AMERICAN MARRIAGE AND DIVORCE (1959); Kubie, *The Disintegrating Impact of "Modern" Life on the Family in America and Its Explosive Repercussions,* in LIEBMAN (ED.), EMOTIONAL FORCES IN THE FAMILY 157 (1959).
2. 371 U.S. 187 (1962).
3. 371 U.S. at 193.

intervals in time, such as vacations, holidays, etc., or to entrust custody to a court-appointed guardian. Usually, however, a court-appointed guardian is viewed as a last resort, because it does not meet the child's need for parents; the other usual dispositions are rigid, and can be altered only by the complicated process of adjudication.

Since the needs of children change during the years before they reach maturity, whatever provisions the law makes for them should be flexible. Yet the many combinations of provisions which are ordinarily incorporated in separation agreements and divorce papers have three inflexible attributes in common: (a) an effort to achieve a compromise between the demands and feelings of contending parents; (b) an absence of any machinery first for discovering and then for serving the changing needs of the child; and (c) a built-in tendency to be less flexible than a child's welfare requires.

No one can foresee the future. Therefore the usual provisions can have at best an accidental relationship to the emotional needs of children as these change over the years. There may be times when a child needs the constant attention and affection of his mother, others when his father's masculine image is of primary importance. Furthermore not only the child but the parents and their relationships may change. One or the other may marry or become ill. Such changes create new emotional needs in the child. Although courts can and do change custody provisions in efforts to meet changing needs, parents are reluctant to invoke the machinery of the law for this purpose unless there are overwhelming reasons for doing so, because the judicial machinery is slow and expensive and may involve a degree of publicity which in itself is damaging to the children and undesirable for the parents.

In order to provide a satisfactory compromise between the parents and to gain that flexibility which is necessary for the child, it is necessary to develop new legal instruments for the protection of the interests of the children of divorced parents. Such a new approach is surely conceivable; but since I am not a lawyer, my only right to claim that the following suggestion is feasible derives from the fact that it has already been incorporated into a large number of separation and divorce agreements, which have been drawn up by eminent law firms in several states. The essence of the proposal consists of joint custody of the child, the appointment of a confidential adult-ally for the child and a committee chosen by the parents to decide questions on which the parents are unable to agree.

The specific steps are as follows. Upon separation or divorce the parents agree that the child's interests are paramount, and that neither of them shall have an exclusive right to custody. They accept the responsibility to attempt to decide together by mutual agreement every question that has a bearing on the welfare of their child or children, *e.g.*, where the child shall live and with whom and for how long, where the child shall go to school and the kind of school, what kind of medical or psychological help the child may have if needed, what kind of vacations to spend and where and with whom, etc.

If and whenever the parents cannot reach an agreement on any matter of concern to the child, they agree to submit the issue to a committee which they themselves choose at the time they make the agreement, and to accept unconditionally the committee's decisions, and to be guided by it. The committee will act at the instance of either parent, and the failure of the other to present his side when given the opportunity does not make the committee's decision ineffective.

(There are arguments for the relative simplicity of choosing a single individual for this task rather than a committee; but in practice it has proved almost impossible to persuade any one individual to carry so heavy a responsibility alone, and relatively easy to persuade even the same individual to serve on a committee. Furthermore, the committee offers a degree of continuity, stability and weight of authority which no one individual can supply.)

The parents select the members of this committee by mutual agreement, and directly or through their respective counsel secure the necessary consents to serve. It is usual to ask a pediatrician, a child psychiatrist or child analyst, an educator and/or an impartial lawyer or clergyman. The parents grant to the members of the committee the right to replace any member who withdraws or becomes ill or dies; but in choosing such a replacement the committee must have its choice approved by the two principals, or where necessary by their respective legal advisors.

The parents further agree that each child shall have one trusted adult-ally outside the family circle with whom the child can talk in confidence. They choose this person from a list of available certified specialists in child psychology, child psychiatry or child analysis. The purpose of this is to make sure that someone who has experience with the highly specialized skills of interviewing and drawing out children will always be available to explore in confidence the child's reactions to parents, homes, schools, camps, doctors, and all similar factors for the guidance of both the parents and the committee. It is rarely easy for a child to talk to adults, and least of all to his own warring parents. Under these circumstances, to talk to either will make a child feel disloyal to the other. He will be able to talk to an adult-ally who is outside of the family without this inhibiting restriction. As already indicated, such an adult-ally should have had technical training and experience in the highly specialized art of listening to children. Given such training, he can then inform the committee of what the child thinks and feels, thus providing a sound basis for the committee's decisions.

Finally, the agreement stipulates that the committee will have no role in the financial guardianship of the children, but will deal only with their spiritual, educational and psychological welfare and general health. It is obvious that it will have to confer at times with the financial guardians of the child concerning the economic feasibility of its recommendations.

The advantage of this proposal is that primary emphasis is placed on discovering and serving the child's changing needs. As those needs change, at least one of the parents will presumably perceive the change, and either persuade the other or bring the problem before the committee which, aided by the child's ally, will be able to evaluate the situation free from the parents' biases. Adjustments can thus be made without publicity, controversy, or great expense. The child will also have the psychological advantage of retaining active contact with both parents. Unless one or the other parent has been flagrantly brutal and destructively amoral in relation to the child (in which case the other parent presumably would not enter into such an agreement in the first place), it is always disturbing to children to be substantially removed from contact with either parent; because this gives rise to a secret feeling that there are first-class and second-class parents. The difficulties which this feeling produces can be traced through later years and even into the ultimate marriages of these children. Therefore, a framework within which both parents maintain contact and can work in harmony is psychologically of value to the child. Continuing relationship with both parents has been available in limited measure through the customary provisions for joint custody, but the lack of adequate machinery for resolving disagreements has often rendered joint custody impractical and has led to the disruption of the relationship of the child to one parent or the other. It is this mechanism which the committee provides.

No individual and no committee can hope for the wisdom of Solomon. One need not expect that no mistakes of judgment will occur. Yet it is likely that the committee will arrive at wise conclusions more consistently than the parent. No parent can evaluate his own children's needs apart from his own feelings. No matter how sophisticated, mature, and generous the parents may be, each must in some measure have an axe to grind. A committee of friendly outsiders provides not only special competence, but also an essential degree of objectivity. The likelihood of sound decisions is still further increased by the fact that they can benefit by the information and the counsel offered by the special adult-ally of the child, for which the agreement provides.

In practice, such committees have done more than solve disputes. Their mere existence often protects the parents from reaching an impasse. As a result, such committees have had to be called into action only rarely. I have seen parents who had squabbled for years behave with restraint and generosity under the civilizing influence of the externalized conscience which the committee comes to represent. Furthermore the parents will have chosen the committee from among people they both know and respect; and they will be ashamed to appear before it to admit that they have failed to reach agreement. Nor will a parent lightly reject the decision of a committee after the committee has been called into action, both because of the high moral force which the committee represents, and because of the new problems which such a rejection would initiate. I have only once seen a parent even attempt to reject a committee's decision.

At this point, lawyers usually ask whether a court, which has of course the right to scrutinize committee decisions, would accept the committee device and enforce its decisions. I cannot answer this question, because to the best of my knowledge it has never been tested. However, since such a plan as this is intrinsically fair to both parents, since it places consideration of the welfare of the child above the pride of parents, since it has been entered into freely by the parents, and since the committee will have considerable competence, any parent who rejects the decision of a committee would come into court with a case which was strongly weighted against him. Certainly no better machinery is available to any court for determining a child's best interests than is available to the committee with the aid of the child's specially qualified ally.

Alan Keith-Lucas

16
"Speaking for the Child":
A Role-Analysis and Some Cautions

When one takes it upon oneself to represent a child's right or his interest, as lawyer or as child welfare worker, in court or in any other place where the rights or interest of a child are being considered, one needs to be clear in what sense one is actually "representing" the child. Unfortunately the terminology of many lawyers and social workers is misleading and has given rise both to muddled thinking and to a form of advocacy that sometimes does more harm than good. Perhaps new terms or phrases are needed to clarify roles in a number of essentially different situations:

Five different types of situations would suggest differential roles.

1. *The attorney or social worker may actually be representing what the child desires.* Thus the attorney who spoke for the teenager who sued a stepfather for alienation of the mother's affection [1] spoke directly for the child, as he would for an adult client. So does the lawyer or social worker who reports a child's preference for one or the other parent, or neither, in a custody case. Here, representation is direct and the adult can properly be said to represent the child. Thomas A. Coyne gives a number of good examples in his article, "Who Will Speak for the Child?" [2] Clearly there should be an expansion of this kind of representation, including perhaps representing the right of a child to an order permitting certain actions, if arbitrarily forbidden by parents or guardians, or enjoining them from certain demands if the child

ALAN KEITH-LUCAS, Ph.D., is Alumni Distinguished Professor in Social Work, University of North Carolina, Chapel Hill.
1. *Taylor v. Keefe,* 134 Conn. 156, 56 A 2nd, 768 (1947).
2. See chapter 14.

feels deeply enough about it to be willing to refer the matter to arbitration or court decision.

2. *The child may have rights of an objective nature or established by law.* To obtain this he needs a representative, since he is legally an "infant," unable to speak with his own voice. Such rights might be to an inheritance, or to damages from a third person, or to some legal status such as legitimacy. Here again there seems to be little question of the nature of the representation, even though the child may be incapable of asking for such help. But when the "right" involved is more nebulous and is something which the parents or guardians of the child would normally be expected to provide, or even to permit, and the child is not demanding this right in his own person, a very different situation exists.

3. The third category can be expressed as *a case in which someone believes a child to have rights which the parent or guardian is failing to implement.* This is the area which gives the most trouble. Three major points must be stressed.

First, except in situations where the "right" involved is one very generally recognized, such as the right to an education, to medical care, to reasonable freedom (for example, not being chained to a bed), to adequate food and clothing, and to freedom from serious physical harm (and sometimes not even then, for there can be various interpretations of most of these things) what is being sought by the juvenile court worker or a protective agency, either through its attorney or directly, is not a right so much as it is someone's concept of what a child needs. But needs and rights are not synonymous, except in the view of the kind of social worker or lawyer who is convinced that his theory of child-rearing is so infallible that it should be enshrined in law, or in irresistible pressure on the child's natural guardians to change their ways. To elevate believed needs into rights, as Emma Lundberg does in her book *Unto the Least of These* [3] can easily lead to particular and ephemeral theories of child-rearing being imposed on family life. Anyone aware of how rapidly such theories change and indeed reverse themselves, as well as those who are aware of different cultural practices in child-rearing, cannot but be wary

3. Emma O. Lundberg, *Unto the Least of These: Social Services for Children* (New York: D. Appleton-Century-Crofts, 1947), p. 4.

of such intervention, quite apart from any theory of the right of a family or of a culture to follow its own customs.

The corollary to this is that the child's "rights" as distinguished from his "needs"—that is, those factors on which there is general and almost universal agreement as due any child—should be enshrined in law specifically as personal rights, and, additionally, there must be some mechanism for requiring their provision in all communities. Much so-called parental neglect is not an act, or a failure to act, on the part of parents, but an occurrence traceable to community conditions or to lack of resources. It is no good establishing the right of medical care for a child if medical care is lacking, or is available only to those with moderate incomes.

Declarations of "Children's Rights" such as those of the United Nations [4] or the Mid-Century White House Conference on Children and Youth [5] speak in general to this kind of right, as well as to some less tangible ones, but do not specify them in law. General statements of a child's "rights" to happiness, or love, or recreation, cannot be so translated or enforced, and are subject to so many different interpretations that they must be considered needs, not rights. In general, their inclusion in such documents tends to prevent the establishment of more concrete rights in law. What would be needed to create more general rights for children is an amendment to the Constitution, and this indeed might be considered.

The necessity to distinguish needs, however desirable, from rights is the essential problem in questions of "emotional neglect." Unless the neglect is so obvious that it offends all canons of decency, or is expressed in clearly unacceptable actions, such as cruel and unusual mental punishment,[6] emotional neglect is largely a matter of opinion. Many British parents send children of eight to boarding school. Is this emotional neglect? Some parents demand instant obedience from children. One can argue, and indeed

4. Published by the United Nations Office of Public Information, New York; adopted in 1959.

5. *Proceedings of the Mid-Century White House Conference on Children and Youth,* Raleigh, N. C., 1951.

6. Examples might be isolation of the child for lengthy periods, or holding him up to community ridicule or shame, as, for instance, sending a twelve-year-old enuretic to school in conspicuous diapers, or a boy to school dressed as a girl.

many children have expressed this thought, that overpermissiveness is a quite serious form of emotional neglect. So, obviously, is its opposite. Some cultures permit very little expression of affection. Some consider close personal contact the primary need of the child. Who has the right to decide? The Painter-Bannister case [7] in which the Court denied custody to a father on the grounds of his supposedly "romantic, impractical and unstable" although "more exciting and challenging" way of life highlights the problem.

Second, the so-called advocate for the child is not actually speaking for the child. He is putting forth his own theory of the child's welfare in opposition to that held by the child's natural representatives, that is, his parents. Let us suppose that a father spanks his child. If the spanking is unnaturally severe, resulting in serious injury, and administered perhaps in hysteria, a child protective worker or an attorney might reasonably be said to be representing the child when he brings the situation to court. But if the spanking, although severe, is a disciplinary measure, perhaps unwise but nevertheless administered in good faith, what is opposed is not the right of the child and the right of the parent, but the opinions of the parent and the opinions of the state, or society, or the social work profession, or an individual social worker, or lawyer, as to what the child's best interests are. This is so even if the child strongly resents the punishment. Necessary discipline is one way of meeting a child's needs, as we admit when we say casually that a child "needs a good spanking." The issue at point is not the parent's right to discipline, but the method, severity, and effectiveness of the means employed.

To present this difference of opinion as a conflict between the rights of parent and child, as is so often done, is not only to try to compare two utterly different things—the needs of a child and the parents' rights and responsibilities as natural guardians to the child are entirely different categories of right—but confers on the state, or the social worker, or the lawyer an entirely specious moral authority as spokesman for the underdog. This false emotionality is all too frequently exploited by that type of social worker, lawyer, or judge—and there are too many of them— whose choice of a field of practice is dictated more by an unre-

---

7. *Painter v. Bannister,* 258 Ia. 1390, 140 N.W. 2nd, 152 (1966).

solved conflict with his own parents than by any real concern with rights or justice. This is one of the real but often unrecognized problems in all child welfare activity.

Such thinking also tends to put the parent in the position of one whose rights naturally conflict with those of the child. Parents are classed almost by definition as oppressors, seeking to exercise their own selfish rights, to the child's detriment. Children's rights or needs can only be enlarged, therefore, at the expense of the parents' rights and needs. But as anyone who has ever worked with dependent children knows, one of the primary rights or needs of most of these children is to belong to and to be under the guidance of their natural parents despite inadequacies, even mistreatment in the home. It is not a sentimental belief that blood is thicker than water, or a conventional acceptance of the family as a convenient sociological institution that establishes the parent as the primary spokesman for the child, not to be relieved of this responsibility and right except for serious dereliction or incapacity.[8] It is the need of the child himself for family identity, and the trauma incident on its disruption.

Children recognize this. They do not, in general, see the intervener on their behalf as "speaking for them." They see him as intervening between their parents and themselves and as competitors with their parents. A few come to see in time the justice of the intervention, and if their parents either deliberately or casually cease contact with them or continue to reject them, may accept the interveners as substitute parents; but the great majority do not. Many children, after years of institutional or foster-family care, seek out or return to parents. Ask any group of judicially separated, neglected children whom they would turn to first if they were in serious trouble, and seven out of ten will name their parents.

This does not mean that judicial separation of parents and children is not quite often necessary, either for a time, or, in some cases, throughout childhood. But if those claiming in such cases to be "advocates for children" were confronted with the reality that what they are doing is not "representing a child" but differing with the parent or guardian about what is good for the child, much more good planning could be done in the child's interest

8. See, for instance, *Mill v. Brown,* 31 Utah 473, 88 Pac 609 (1906).

and many more familites either could be kept together or helped to reunite. I would suggest that such people be frankly recognized not as advocates for the child but as *parental interveners.* To recognize them as such is no disparagement of their interest in the child, their desire to do him good, or their objectivity.

The term "intervener" also stresses another important point. Although parent and "intervener" both present their concept of the child's interest, they do not do so on even terms. The intervener must show not only that what he has to offer is more in the child's interest than what the natural parent can offer; he must also show that what the parent can offer is inadequate or harmful. Otherwise the door is open for an unlimited redistribution of children to those homes where they might be believed, according to the psychological theories of cultural preferences of the time, to be best advantaged. It would make of the state *parens patriae* with a vengeance. Before the "best interests" of a child become the concern of the state, child-enthusiasts notwithstanding, the state must establish the right to intervene.[9] There must in fact be a finding of neglect, delinquency, or dependency. The state cannot be assumed to have a continuous, overriding, and supervisory interest in each child, with the power to order changes of custody at will, unless the state is indeed totalitarian. Particularly is this true in view of the inequalities of opportunity in our society. Until these are righted, such a doctrine would justify, in the minds of some child-advocates, the removal of most poor children and their placement with the reasonably well-to-do. Or it would justify unwise removal if they did not actually recognize the right of the child wherever possible to his own family and culture, even if his needs may not be fully met by other criteria.

The third point is that the child may actually have rights not so much against the parent but against his so-called "representative." This has been recognized in delinquency cases—*Kent* and *Gault* are instances—but not in neglect or dependency ones. To assume that the foster-care agency which will remove him from the home in his "representative"—although it often presents itself in this light—is to conceal this possibility and may leave the child defenseless at times when he has a real need for protection. It is hardly consistent to believe that a child may have rights adversary

9. See Thomas D. Gill, "The Legal Nature of Neglect," *NPPA Journal,* 6 (no. 1, January 1960):1–16.

to that of his parents but not to those of foster parents or child welfare agencies.

Coyne's suggestion that a third person, an "advocate for the child," should be a party to neglect proceedings—a suggestion made by this writer in an article in 1949—recognizes this fact but seems to need further clarification of role.[10] Coyne's argument is that parent and state (or agency) are in adversary positions and that the child therefore needs an advocate of his own. To the extent that the parent is concerned solely with possession of the child and regards him wholly as valuable property, emotionally or materially, and to the extent that the agency is acting out of indignation with regard to the parent's actions, and is seeking freedom to exercise its own parental powers, this may be true. But it is to traduce many parents and many capable and dedicated child welfare agencies to assume that this is always so. Each party is asking in fact that its version of the child's needs and rights be accepted by the court. An attorney "representing the child" may be more objective in estimating the child's needs, although there is no guarantee that he will be so. Many children —and neglected children to perhaps a greater degree than others, since they have often needed to develop this skill in order to survive—are expert manipulators and can persuade someone not trained or experienced in planning for dependent children that their interest demands a plan which is not always objectively good for them. In actual practice a good professional child-welfare agency's plan in most cases will be, for purely experiential reasons, more realistic. Such agencies may in fact act as both parental interveners and, together with psychologists and psychiatrists, as expert witnesses on children's needs (not rights). In my 1949 article I suggested a form of court procedure in which the social agency presented to the judge its considered belief about what a good and practical plan for a child would be, and the judge was charged with the responsibility of determining whether the state had established its right to substitute this plan for that of the parents. Some such distinction between social and legal determination seems to be necessary.

What a third person could do in such a situation is in effect: (1) to insist that the child's interest be considered by the court,

10. Alan Keith-Lucas, "Social Work and the Court in the Protection of Children," *Child Welfare League Bulletin* 28(1960):3–6.

rather than having the action become a purely adversary struggle for possession; he acts therefore as a representative of the child's stake in the proceedings; (2) to represent any established *rights* of the child, as distinct from his needs, that other versions of his needs may have overlooked; this would include any rights he might have against the agency planning to care for him; (3) to represent, if this has not been done, the child's wishes in the conflict; or (4) to offer the court a third point of view, not necessarily more child-centered than that of the parents or the professional expert, but perhaps representing the judgment of the man in the street.

Unless attorneys are to be trained in child welfare practice, and become thoroughly familiar with, say, the effects on a child of foster-family care, residential treatment, and group care, both in general and in the specific resources available in the community, it is hard to see how they can have superior wisdom about a childs' needs. Dr. Coyne's suggestion that they get to know the child and study psychological reports merely creates an amateur child development "specialist." The presentation and interpretation of psychological reports, and the prediction of the likely effects of various treatment or placement plans should be left to professionals in this field. If it is considered that an agency or department is likely to be self-seeking, a socio-legal bureau to act as an expert witness should be established. In this respect it might be wise to recognize the differential contribution of lawyer, social worker, and psychiatrist or psychologist to the determination of the child's interest.

The lawyer can speak of established rights, stake in any proceedings, status, or contractual relationships of parent and child, and how these intermesh with widely held general propositions and precedents in our society. With regard to a child's emotional or social needs he is, however, generally no more expert than any reasonably well-informed citizen and is prone, for instance, to accept much too wholly propositions or even myths about the effects of environment, discipline (or the lack of it), and other influences on the child. The "lay" or "common sense" point of view has its place in such determinations, since more expert points of view need eventually to be expressed in understandable and practical terms. But as an exercise in the state's responsibility to determine the child's best interest, it is frequently a very clumsy and possibly harmful criterion, particularly where the child has suffered from deprivation and has needs that cannot be identified solely from observation of the "average" child reared in a stable family.

The psychiatrist or psychologist is skilled in individualizing the needs of a particular child. He can help estimate such things as the damage done by present conditions, the child's inherent potential to act or behave differently or to withstand shock and separation, his essential normality or abnormality; and he can to some extent clarify the nature of those influences that would assure optimal functioning. However, he is not normally an expert either in rights or in the practical provision of these influences in existing social conditions or services.

Many social workers claim to have some expertise in psychological and sociological evaluation. Despite Schultz's almost total denial of the profession's knowledge in these areas,[11] most social workers have rather more knowledge in this field than the average layman and somewhat more concept of normal and abnormal child growth. But this is not the principal contribution they can make. A competent child welfare worker is, or should be, an expert in the structure, likely outcome, availability, and practicality of alternative parent plans in general, in the specific community, and to some extent in relation to a child's particular situation. He knows, for instance, how agency foster care, institutionalization in specific settings, termination of parental visiting, placement with a relative, day care, or radical environment and cultural change are likely to affect a child in general. And, with the help of knowledge gained from the psychiatrist or psychologist, and from his preliminary exploration of the parents' and the child's attitudes towards such plans, he can estimate the impact in particular. He can assess better than anyone else whether and under what conditions this can be realized productively in the present situation. He knows something about the timing, the explanation of the court's decision both to parent and child, and the administrative freedom necessary to make removal of the child from his own

11. Leroy G. Schultz, "The Adversary Process, the Juvenile Court and the Social Worker," *UMKCL Law Review* 36. (no. 2, Summer 1968) 288–302. In contrast, Edgar Silverman, in his "Lawyers and Social Workers," *Crime and Delinquency* 6 (no. 3, July 1960):264, claims for social workers the ability to "interpret the meaning of behavior."

home a constructive rather than a destructive process. Because, too, he deals largely with children who are separated from their parents, he usually has specialized knowledge of the effects of separation and divided loyalties in a child's life. Although to some extent this knowledge is experiential, enough operational research and detailed observation and testing of process is available to him to constitute a body of special knowledge.

All three elements are clearly necessary in order to assure the child's best interests. It should be recognized too that however undesirable a situation may appear to be, short of being clearly destructive of life or health, there may be factors both in the relationships of child and parent and in the nature of available alternatives to suggest that the best interests of a child are served by not disturbing the status quo. There are some children who, because of strong negative as well as positive ties to parents, find it almost impossible to prosper away from home.

The four functions suggested for the "attorney for the child" are in fact functions which, if the action is recognized as being for the child's benefit, are by present juvenile court philosophy supposedly exercised by the judge. The judge should decide on the basis of evidence between the versions of need presented to him by the parent and the agency; he should take into consideration the child's point of view, and determine what rights are involved. The attorney is therefore present to ensure that the judge does in fact consider these aspects of the case.

Such an attorney cannot then claim to represent the child's interest except in a limited way. He can represent the child's stake in the proceedings and his established rights but not, with any accuracy, his needs.

4. Fourth in the types of situation that suggest differential roles in "speaking for" the child *involves instances where there may be conflict between the child's natural guardians,* as in the case of divorce, or where a foster parent or relative with whom a child is living claims to be the child's guardian by virtue of having exercised parental powers, as if he were in fact the parent. This differs from the situation described in (3) in that no professional child welfare group is concerned, and, in the case of divorce, in that the child is the innocent victim of a conflict in which his welfare is not the cause of the action. Here the child needs someone to speak not only to his rights but also to his needs, and here

again can be envisaged a socio-legal bureau to speak both as a representative of the child's stake in the proceedings, and as an expert witness concerning the child's believed needs.

The situation is, however, somewhat different if there be admitted the possibility that as a result of a custody dispute the child's custody may be given to a third person, or to an agency. If this is possible, it means that by suing for divorce a parent subjects his fitness to exercise parental powers and responsibilities to judgment that would not normally be taken unless neglect or delinquency charges had been filed. Perhaps courts should be empowered to take this action on the specific intervention of a "parental intervener," only by maintaining either that (1) the quality of care that either parent could provide singly would constitute neglect,[12] or (2) the very nature of the conflict between the parents is such that the child would be seriously harmed in either parent's home. This, it seems to me, would have to be established somewhat objectively and perhaps in a separate proceeding. The only other alternative is to make it clear in law that a child in a divorce action becomes by definition a child in need of protection by the state, and that to sue for divorce makes one's child automatically an allegedly dependent or neglected child, and thus subject to state determination of his "best interest." If this is established as a principle, the same should be true of children who are the subject of adoption procedures that fail (as, for example, if the adoption is denied), and for those who have lived a year or more in privately arranged or casual foster care. These are also situations which in the present state of the law require a showing that the child is being harmed by the arrangement before the state can intervene, and this leads naturally to consideration of the fifth situation.

5. *When the natural guardians voluntarily or through incapacity fail to exercise the responsibilities of guardianship,* the child needs a representative of a different kind. One of the incredible things about most family law, at least as it is practiced, is that a child has the right to be cared for, fed and clothed, but not to have a

---

12. A case decided by the Illinois Supreme Court, *Giacopelli v. Florence Crittendon Home,* 16 Ill. 2nd, 556, 158 N.E. 2nd, 613 (1959). The barring of a father from recovery of his child given away in adoption without his knowledge, on the basis of "best interests" without showing of his unfitness, seems to me on the face of it a very dangerous precedent.

permanent representative make major parental decisions in his life, to take note of the care he may be receiving, say, from a temporary foster home or institution, and to assent to such things as early marriage, adoption, enlistment in the armed forces, or surgical care, if his own parents are out of the picture. Only if the child has an estate is a guardian normally appointed.

In many jurisdictions these powers are somewhat vaguely assumed to follow custody, which is itself a rather vague status, being held sometimes to mean mere physical possession of the child and sometimes a legal status assigned by a court. Yet custody is by nature temporary and does not necessarily create the type of interest and mutual confidence, nor the long-range view of the child's welfare, that guardianship requires. Nor, particularly in view of community and institutional neglect, is it psychologically sound to equate the inability to provide daily care for the child with the ability to watch over the child's ultimate interests. Many a parent who has neglected a child through the strains engendered by poverty, the need to work to support him, the fact of inadequate housing, or even the physical and emotional strains of child-rearing still remains capable of exercising discerning guardianship and is indeed the person to whom the child looks for this kind of decision.

The United States Children's Bureau, in its *Standards of Specialized Courts Dealing with Children*,[13] wisely insists that the parent should retain guardianship rights and responsibilities, even where custody has been reassigned, until he is proved incapable or unwilling to exercise this power. Child welfare agencies in those states where judges are inclined to "terminate parental rights"—that is, to dissolve guardianship responsibilities as well as to reassign temporary custody—know how often in cases of neglect they have had in practice to ignore such orders; the parents remain in the child's mind (as well as their own) the child's ultimate representatives and decision-makers.

When, however, parents, either because they are not aware of this responsibility (many courts give the impression, even though they do not say so, that parental rights and responsibilities have been dissolved at the granting of custody), or because they are

13. *Standards of Specialized Courts Dealing with Children* (Washington, D.C.: U.S. Government Printing Office, 1954), p. 74. See also p. 17 for definition of "Guardian of the Person."

discouraged, or because they genuinely wish to divest themselves of this responsibility, disappear or maintain a very tenuous contact, the child is often left without a representative. His custodian may be the last person the child is willing to put in this place. All too often the custodian is seen as the one who has supplanted or discouraged the parent. The child may have rights he needs to assert against the custodian. Yet the law does not in general recognize his right to any such lodestar in his life. A *guardian ad litem* may be appointed in a particular case, but this is not the same thing. Some states permit the natural guardian's powers to be dissolved if the parents fail to exercise their responsibility for a year after placement, in order to free the child for adoption,[14] but this is little help to the older or unadoptable child.

This is a situation in which a child badly needs a representative, not so much of his rights or interests, although these may be involved, but of parental force. Some child welfare agencies and communities provide a social worker with some of these characteristics who remains interested in the child wherever he may be placed; but this is a right that should be established in law, should involve, with older children at least, some expression of choice, should generally not be invested in an agency or a child-care professional but in a relative, a minister, a godparent, a family friend, or someone with a personal rather than a professional interest in the child.

We have now identified five different relationships to a child's rights or needs which are normally spoken of as "speaking for," "representing," or being an "advocate" for a child. These are:

1. Direct representation of a child or of his established rights;
2. Parental intervention in cases of alleged neglect or dependency;
3. Representation of the child's stake in the proceedings;
4. Expert witness to a child's believed needs;
5. Permanent representative, or guardian.

These are very different roles, requiring different skills and different identifications. If they are all subsumed under a single heading, inspired by a genuine but indiscriminate enthusiasm for a child's "rights," and if needs and rights are not distinguished,

14. Shad Polier, "Amendments to New York's Adoption Laws," *Child Welfare* 38 (no. 7, July 1970): 1–4.

not only will many children be denied their rights but there is real danger of a kind of socio-legal enlargement of the *parens patriae* concept that is directly contrary to the spirit of *Kent* and *Gault*.

There remains, however, one form of advocacy for the child that is badly needed, and on which lawyers and social workers need to cooperate. This is the effort to establish in law the rights of children, in which should be included the right to his own parent whenever possible, as well as his right to various benefits and protections, both individually and in requiring that society make these rights available. This will be done best if social workers and lawyers together recognize their respective skills and roles and concretize their contributions on behalf of all children.

David N. Levine

17
Child Custody:
Iowa Corn and the Avant Garde

The custody of eight-year-old Mark Painter has occasioned a great deal of discussion and comment concerning the legal rules applicable to custody cases. Since the Iowa Supreme Court purports to follow, and cites with approval, the custody guidelines formulated by the Family Law Section of the American Bar Association, it may be of special interest to examine the recent custody decisions of that jurisdiction and evaluate the manner in which the Family Law Section's model act has been applied.

When the parties to a custody action are the natural mother and father, it is universally agreed that the best interests of the child will govern placement. But when the parties are a parent (or parents) and "strangers," the unanimity of opinion disappears.

Some states, abandoning their reliance on the best interests of the child, adhere to the "natural right" of parenthood.[1] This notion rigidly compels a court, in discharging its role of *parens patriae,* to award the parents custody, unless the parents are proved unfit. An unfortunate vestige of the feudal era, the "natural right" theory blindly presumes that the interest of the child will most adequately be fulfilled under the aegis of and in residence with the biological parents.

Other states, however, eschew the automatic determination in

DAVID N. LEVINE, J.D., is a practicing attorney in New York City. This article, reprinted with permission from the *Family Law Quarterly* 1(1967):3–9, was prepared with the assistance of Professor Henry H. Foster, Jr., New York University Law School.

1. People ex rel. Kropp v. Shepsky, 305 N.Y. 465, 113 N.E.2d 801 (1953). Raymond v. Cotner, 175 Neb. 158, 120 N.W.2d 892 (1963); *In re* Mathers, 371 Mich. 516, 124 N.W.2d 878, 126 N.W.2d 722 (1963). Commonwealth ex rel Ruczynski v. Powers, 206 Pa. Super. 415, 212 A.2d 922 (1965). Root v. Allen, 151 Colo. 311, 377 P.2d 117 (1962).

favor of the parent-party.[2] Regardless of whether a non-parent is involved, they maintain their dedication to the goal so often articulated and sought in custody cases—the promotion of the satisfactory development of the child, i.e., the best interests of the child. Thus, the operative dominance of the minor's welfare punctures the inviolability of the "natural right" theory and relegates it to the role of an aid in the court's ultimate disposition.[3] Especially in cases where the non-parent has stood *in loco parentis*,[4] the courts applying the "best interest" test do not purport to summarily dismiss the right of the parent. Instead, they seek to unemotionally analyze the alternatives by considering a wide variety of pertinent factors, including the reports of sociological investigators and the testimony of psychologists and psychiatrists.

Three recent decisions of the Iowa Supreme Court, *Painter v. Bannister*,[5] *Alingh v. Alingh*,[6] and *Halstead v. Halstead*,[7] reflect that state's concern with the vital matter of custody and are significant because they apply the "best interest" test to disputes between natural parents and so-called "strangers."

Painter v. Bannister. Following the untimely death of his mother and sister, five-year-old Mark was temporarily entrusted to his maternal grandparents by his father in July, 1963. Having remarried in November 1964, the father requested the return of Mark, but his request was denied by the grandparents. On appeal, the Supreme Court of Iowa reversed the lower court's decision which held for the father. Acknowledging the presumption of parental preference, the court relied heavily on the testimony of a child psychologist and focused its attention on the psychological ramifications of a custodial switch at this time in young Mark's life. The testimony also revealed Mark's strong identification with the Bannisters and his acceptance of Mr. Bannister as his "father figure." In deciding against a change, the court noted the probability, on the basis of analogous psychological studies and Mark's former history of instability, that he might "go bad" if removed from the security of the Bannister home.

2. Root v. Allen, 151 Colo. 311, 377 P.2d 117 (1962).
3. Thein v. Squires, 250 Iowa 1157, 1158, 97 N.W.2d 156 (1959).
4. Chapsky v. Wood, 26 Kan. 650 (1881).
5. 140 N.W.2d 151 (Iowa, 1966).
6. 144 N.W.2d 134 (Iowa, 1966).
7. 144 N.W.2d 861 (Iowa, 1966).

Alingh v. Alingh. After each was injured at the hands of the mentally-ill mother, first Stephan, age four months, and then his infant sister Robin were surrendered to their paternal grandparents by their father. A 1958 habeas corpus proceeding, instituted by the father, was denied and this 1965 action by the grandparents was brought to compel the return of the children unlawfully taken by the father. Affirming a decision for the grandparents, the Iowa Supreme Court ruled that the presumption of parental preference does not arise when, as here, a prior custody decree is *contra.* Utilizing the "best interest" test unadulterated by the presumed right of the parent, the court found the cogent reasons needed to remove the children from their grandparents' home after nine and ten years, respectively, were lacking. There was also tacit reliance on the emotional unfitness of the mother, who, it was found, became unstable only when confronted with her maternal responsibilities.

Halstead v. Halstead. At age two, Phillip was brought to his paternal grandparents' home by his mother. Three years later, following her divorce from Phillip's father, her second husband, she married a third time and moved to Texas, leaving Phillip with his grandparents, with whom he has remained. The Iowa Supreme Court reversed the decision of the lower court, which had granted the mother custody after the natural father's death in 1965. The court found the overwhelming evidence favoring the retention of the custodial arrangement in order to continue serving Phillip's best interest, outweighed the presumptive right of the mother. Based on what is called "the humanities of the case," the court found no cogent reasons—other than the understandable desire of the mother to have custody—to transfer Phillip from the wholesome surroundings to which he had become accustomed and in which he had become well-adjusted during his ten-year stay.

The Iowa courts had long labored under the statutory recognition of parental preference,[8] although recent years had seen a gradual erosion of its strength.[9] More clearly defined was the state's dedication to the paramount importance of the welfare of

8. Iowa Code 1939, Sec. 12573, 12574.
9. Iowa Code Ann. Sec. 633.559 (1964), Finken v. Porter, 246 Iowa 1345, 72 N.W.2d 445 (1955), Kouris v. Lunn, 136 N.W.2d 502 (Iowa, 1965).

the child. The *Painter* case illustrates the efforts of the Iowa Supreme Court, in grappling with a difficult fact pattern, to give meaning to the latter doctrine at the expense of the former. Although the *Painter* court could not have known that *Alingh* and *Halstead,* whose fact patterns seem more suitable to the court's approach and result, were soon to follow, those cases elaborate the *Painter* doctrine and give a clearer indication of the manner in which the best-interest test may be satisfactorily applied.

Justice Stuart, speaking for the court in *Painter,* attached little significance to the fact that, despite the grave misfortunes he faced following the tragic death of his wife and daughter, Harold Painter relinquished custody of Mark only on a *temporary* basis. It is suggested that the strong justification for the initial separation might have been given greater weight, lest even parents who temporarily relinquish custody for the best interest of the child, e.g., as when natural parents are seriously injured and unable to properly care for the child, may be deterred from so doing fearing their inability to regain the child.[10]

Even the Family Law Section's 1963 model act speaks only to a *prima facie* right of the *de facto* custodian, not an automatic one.[11] The concern of the Family Law Section was with absolute rules (like the "natural right" theory) which lacked the sufficient flexibility to account for varying circumstances. Obviously, a contrary rule that the *de facto* custodian *must* be awarded custody, would be equally rigid and undesirable. Fortunately, *Alingh* and *Halstead* indicate that no such automatic intransigent application will follow.

The justification for Harold Painter's placement of Mark with the Bannisters did not prevail against the likelihood of an adverse psychological impact on Mark, if he were returned to his father. This was the court's conclusion drawn from the testimony of Dr. Glenn R. Hawks, a child psychologist and the only expert witness to be heard. His comments, virtually ignored by the lower court, spoke only to Mark's successful readjustment to life with the Bannisters, his prior history of instability and the psychological ramifications of the alternatives facing the court. Dr. Hawks, in analyzing the custody problem, also made a dichotomy between

10. 79 Harv. L. Rev. 1710, 1714 (1966).
11. Foster and Freed, *Child Custody*, 39 N.Y.U.L. Rev. 615, 628.

"long term" and "short term" placement, and stated that the immediate and current interests of Mark demanded that he remain with the Bannisters. Although we leave the sufficiency of his testimony to others,[12] his emphasis on the importance of the "father figure" to Mark, his strong identification with the Bannisters as "parents," and the need for continuation of stable relationships with those to whom he has grown accustomed, is shared by other experts.[13]

In addition to the emotional needs and interests of Mark, the Iowa Court unfortunately involved itself in a comparison of the parties' relative milieus. Its parochial social observations come through as an example of Grant Wood Gothic. The smug and self-righteous attitude implicit in the decision is regrettable and has produced a flood of unfavorable comment.[14] The result reached in the actual case may or may not be in the ultimate best interests of Mark. There are reasonable arguments in favor of a retention of custody with the grandparents as well as for a return of Mark to the natural father and new stepmother. Alternatively, it may be that Mark's immediate and current interests required only a *temporary* retention by the grandparents.

Concern for the psychological welfare of the child is often implied in the criteria used in implementing the best interest test, i.e., the bonds of affection between the parties and the child, the personality and character of the parties,[15] but is only rarely expressed under current practice.[16] The wisdom of such an approach to child custody is evidence of a court's willingness to give something more than lip service to the best interest standard. Thus Twentieth Century thinking in the area of child psychology and psychiatry might well join forces with the progressive case law in the area to create a *prima facie* right in the "parent by association," where the "natural right" of the parent was found in conflict with and subordinate to the best interest of the child.[17]

12. 79 HARV. L. REV. 1710, 1715 (1966).
13. Burlingham and Freud, *Annual Report of a Residential War Nursery,* pp. 1054–57; Young, *Placement from the Child's Viewpoint,* p. 1057–58; Freud, *Safeguarding the Emotional Health of Children,* p. 1059; From GOLDSTEIN AND KATZ, THE FAMILY AND THE LAW, The Free Press, 1965.
14. SATURDAY REVIEW, March 26, 1966, pp. 26, 44; NEW YORKER, April 2, 1966, p. 36. LIFE, March 4, 1966, pp. 101–2.
15. Ross v. Pick, 199 Md. 341, 86 A.2d 463 (1952).
16. Foster and Freed, *supra,* p. 436.
17. See, generally, 73 YALE L. REV. 151 (1963).

The question of the length of time needed to establish the adult as a "parent by association" and his relationship to the child as a viable, meaningful one, is a factual matter for the court to evaluate. But, if twenty-four months was deemed a sufficient time period in *Painter,* it should have come as no surprise that the court found as it did in *Alingh,* where Stephan and Robin had been in the home of their grandparents for ten and nine years, respectively, and in *Halstead,* where young Phillip had spent the last ten of his twelve years in his grandparents' home. In each case, the court gave serious consideration to the time spent in the custodial home, and, in *Halstead,* to the strong preference of the child.

Despite their common result, however, each of the cases is factually distinguishable. While *Alingh* was contested by both the natural parents against the maternal grandparents, *Painter* was brought by a recently remarried natural father, and *Halstead* by a recently remarried mother. Further, while Mark Painter's father was a wholly fit person, Philip Halstead's mother had absented herself from the boy for nearly ten years (save for six brief visits), and Stephan and Robin Alingh's mother had battered them in their infancy and was still under psychiatric care. In neither *Halstead* nor *Painter* was there a prior custody decree as there had been in *Alingh.*

These factual nuances raise sundry and ancillary questions for the court to ponder: What effect will a stepmother or stepfather have on the child's development? What effect will the presence of new stepbrothers or stepsisters have on his development? How strong are the child's present ties of affection with his *de facto* guardian? These nuances of fact patterns also portend the inequitable results which arise if their relative significance to the welfare of the child were ignored, or, worse, superceded by an exercise of dubious Mendelism, labeled "natural right."

Both the *Alingh* and *Halstead* results seems not only plausible, but, in light of their facts, necessary. Hazel Alingh, the mentally ill mother who had beaten both her children during their infancy, was a parent whose fitness was certainly open to question, although the court did not speak directly to this matter. In implementing the best-interest standard, the court properly ignored the testimony of the woman's analyst, who recommended the return of the children without ever interviewing them and admitted that the mother was "aghast" at the thought of their return. Citing Stephan's satisfactory development, the court was justifiably "reluctant to interfere in something that has been all right for ten years." [18]

The matter of Phillip Halstead's custody seemed to be even less troublesome. After a ten year stay in his grandparents' home, Phillip was a happy, well-adjusted twelve-year-old who preferred to stay with his grandparents. Simply stated, the court could find no cogent reasons to compel the transfer of the boy from where he "belongs" and has a "right" to stay.

The vexatious and difficult problem of child custody poses a formidable challenge to the law. In keeping pace with the advances made by the behavioral sciences, as well as our enlightened notions about the benefits to children of a wholesome, secure home life, the courts must not be straitjacketed by the outdated notion of an automatic determination in favor of the parent party. It is indeed ironic that *Painter v. Bannister,* the *cause celebre* of recent custody case decisions, should be one that adopts "the best interests" rule. The tragic cases in the past almost invariably have been ones where the court applied a "blood is thicker than water" approach and transferred the child from persons he regarded as parents to a "stranger" who was not identified by the child as a parent. The dogma of "natural right," which inhibits thoughtful inquiry into the latent problems of child development, should not govern, especially when the non-parent has stood *in loco parentis* for a substantial period of time and become a "parent by association." To the desired end—the successful development of the child and the furtherance of his best interest—the courts should encourage and give serious consideration to psychological and psychiatric testimony. The reports of social investigators should likewise be solicited.[19]

It should be noted, however, that none of this implies an abdication of judicial responsibility. In the final analysis, the court alone must discharge the duty of administering to the needs of its wards. But that judgment must be intelligently appraised, not rigidly predetermined.

18. *Supra,* at 137.
19. Foster and Freed, *supra,* 615–22.

Robert W. Hansen

18
Guardians Ad Litem in Divorce and Custody Cases:
Protection of the Child's Interests

The ex-wife took the child out of the state to live in Michigan, which she probably had no right to do.

The ex-husband went to Michigan, got the child and brought it back with him to Milwaukee, which he certainly had no right to do.

The ex-wife brought a motion asking the court to hold the husband in contempt of court.

The ex-husband brought a motion for change of custody of the child to him.

When the combined motions came on to be heard, I appointed a guardian *ad litem* to represent the minor child, set a hearing on custody thirty days later, directed the Family Court Conciliation Department to evaluate the custody placement alternatives and report to the Court at the hearing. The child was ordered returned to the mother who had legal custody, pending the outcome of the hearing.

Why a Guardian?

When two terriers fight over a bone, the bone does not join the fighting. But a child is not a thing or an object to go as a prize to the winner of a contest. It is a precious, unique, individual human being. The whole future life of the child will be affected by the court's decision in the matter of custody. Where it is to live, under what conditions it is to be reared, where it is to go to school, what training or guidance it is to receive, are involved in

The Honorable ROBERT W. HANSEN, LL.B., widely known for his juvenile and family court work, is a Supreme Court Justice in the State of Wisconsin. This article is reprinted with permission from the *Journal of Family Law* 4(1964):181–84.

the decision. Will such basic interests of the child be adequately represented or even presented to the court by the attorneys for the warring litigants? If a child's rights to damages for injuries sustained in an accident are to come before a court, a guardian *ad litem* must be appointed before a trial can be had or a settlement approved by the court. If it appears that children, known or unknown, may have an interest in the estate of a deceased person, the probate court appoints a guardian *ad litem* to represent the interests of such possible heirs. Is not a minor and dependent child whose parents are involved in a divorce case entitled to similar representation, at least in those cases in which custody becomes a matter of dispute between the parties or concern to the court?

When a Guardian?

The practice in Milwaukee's Family Court is to appoint a guardian *ad litem* to represent the children involved when custody becomes a matter of dispute between the parties. This conflict may be revealed at the pre-trial hearing before the Family Court commissioner on *pendente lite* support orders, or at the time of trial before the court. In our family court, issues as to custody matters, if they are in dispute, are not decided at the time of trial—a separate hearing on custody only is ordered, usually ninety days after the trial date, preceded by an investigation or evaluation of the alternatives by the Family Court Conciliation Department. In addition, even if there is no actual contest, where there is reason for grave concern as to the welfare of the children, a custody investigation and hearing is scheduled. These are likely to be cases in which the mental or emotional health of the custodian appears to be less than robust, where there are indications of neglect of the children, where the children appear to be having difficulties in school adjustment or other areas. Actually, I believe that the day will come when legal representation of the children's interests will be required in all divorce cases. We limit the program to cases where there is a dispute as to custody or reason for concern as to the welfare of the children concerned.

What's the Guardian's Role?

When the hearing on child custody is held, the guardian *ad litem* representing the child or children participates in the hearing with the same rights and opportunities as counsel for the parties. He may subpoena and present testimony of witnesses. He may cross-examine the parties or witnesses testifying on behalf of either party. He is asked to make a statement or recommendation on behalf of the children at the conclusion of the taking of testimony. He does have an additional resource in our county in that we have a family court conciliation department with a staff of qualified social service workers, trained in child welfare as well as marriage counselling work. An investigation or evaluation of the custody alternatives is court-ordered in all cases in which a guardian *ad litem* is appointed. This provides background information to the guardian that otherwise he would have to seek out for himself.

Where's the Authority?

When the children are named in the pleadings or by order of the court as actual parties to the action, the law in Wisconsin requires that a guardian *ad litem* be appointed by the court to represent their interests. This procedure is followed in all cases where the husband denies the paternity of a child born to the wife during the time of the marriage. If objection was made by either party to the appointment of a guardian *ad litem* to represent the children, the family court judge could order them impleaded as parties to the action on the issue of custody. However, up to now, and this is a rather new proposition in our court, we have relied upon the inherent power of the court to implement that "concern for the welfare of the child" to which appellate courts in all states have so often referred. "The polestar remains the welfare of the child," Supreme Court Justice Myron Gordon said in the recent Wisconsin case of Welker v. Welker.[1] It would be hard for me to believe that any appellate court anywhere, since the sole and only purpose of appointing a guardian *ad litem* is to make certain that the welfare of the minor children is properly represented and protected, would deny to a trial court the right to take this affirmative step to protect the children's rights.

1. 24 Wis.2d 570, 129 N.W.2d 134 (1964).

Who Pays the Guardian?

When this court policy of appointing guardians *ad litem* for the children in divorce cases where custody is an issue was adopted by Milwaukee's two Family Court judges, it was agreed that the fee for the services of the guardian, as set by the Court, would be ordered paid by either or both of the litigants. Where the value of property is in dispute, the parties must expect to pay for the services of the court-appointed real estate appraiser. Where the sanity of a party litigant becomes an issue, the parties must expect that somehow either or both will pay for the services of the court-appointed psychiatrist. So we reason that, where custody is in dispute or at issue, the parties, either or both, should be expected to pay for the services of the court-appointed guardian *ad litem*. In some cases, of course, the ability to make such payment may be completely absent; and, in such cases, the guardian may well end up having performed an uncompensated service to the court and the children. Those who know the bar of our community know that this will be no stumbling block to the operation of this program. For a good many years, the local bar has staffed a voluntary defender plan in our misdemeanor court. A panel of cooperating attorneys donate at least one day each year to the completely uncompensated chore of representing indigent defendants in misdemeanor cases. A lawyer's time may be his stock in trade, but his willingness to perform a civic duty is the hallmark of his profession.

This idea of having someone to speak up for the rights of the children in disputed custody matters in divorce cases is a beginning in adding a new dimension to domestic relations actions. It insures legal representation as well as court concern for the rights of children involved in the dissolution of marriages. It is an insurance policy against the children becoming mere pawns in a power contest or prizes to be awarded to the winner in a court dispute. As our Supreme Court, speaking through Justice Horace Wilkie, said in the case of Kritzik v. Kritzik:[2] "In making his determinations as to what conditions of a divorce judgment would serve the interests of the children involved, the trial court does not function solely as an arbiter between two private parties . . . It is his task to determine what provisions and terms would best guarantee an

2. 21 Wis.2d 442, 124 N.W.2d 581.

opportunity for the children involved to grow to mature and responsible citizens, regardless of the desires of the respective parties. This power, vested in the family court, reflects a recognition that the children involved in a divorce are always disadvantaged parties and that the law must take affirmative steps to protect their welfare." The appointment of a lawyer as guardian *ad litem* to represent a child where custody is in dispute is, we contend, such an "affirmative step" to insure that the child is treated as a person with rights, not as an object to be fought over.

Sanford N. Katz

19

Foster Parents Versus Agencies:
A Case Study in the Judicial Application of
"The Best Interests of the Child" Doctrine

It is generally conceded that, in the area of child welfare, social service agencies have the expert knowledge and methods for making enlightened custodial dispositions. Consequently, courts rely on agency decisions and have come to utilize agencies as the intermediate placement for a child whose custody must be resolved. Child welfare agencies are given the authority to choose the custodian for a child on a temporary, permanent, or indefinite basis, and may, at times, be authorized to supervise the placement of the child.

In a certain sense, the court is surrendering its jurisdiction by its reliance on the welfare agencies, and this delegation of decision-making power may have far-reaching consequences. Whether welfare agencies use their power as wisely as courts assume depends largely on what we mean by "wisely" and on what agency is involved. In general, courts unfortunately have neither the time nor the facilities to supervise agency placements, and it is only when an individual has been rejected as a qualified custodian that courts have an opportunity to review agency practices.

A recurring problem which courts face is the need to resolve the conflict which arises when foster parents challenge the decision of agencies that have disqualified these persons from continuing their relationship with or adopting their foster child. This article will explore the role of courts in resolving these disputes and will suggest some criteria by which the courts may be guided in deciding such questions.

SANFORD N. KATZ, J.D., is Professor of Law, Boston College Law School, Brighton, Mass. He has written widely on the relationship between social work and law. This article is reprinted with permission from the *Michigan Law Review* 65(1966):145–70.

The Case of Laura

Agency Participation

The history of Laura, the five-and-a-half-year-old child whose cus-tody was at issue in the New York case of *In the matter of Jewish Child Care Association,*[1] is similar to that of many other children who are similarly involved in the struggle of foster parents to adopt children over the objections of placement agencies. When Laura was thirteen months old, she was placed by the Jewish Child Care Association, a foster care agency, with Mr. and Mrs. Sanders, a childless couple in their thirties. Laura's mother, eighteen years old and unwed, had been unable to care for the baby at birth and had placed her with the New York City Department of Welfare, which transferred the child's custody to the Jewish Child Care Associa-tion (hereinafter referred to as the Agency).

At placement, the Sanders were required to sign a document in which mutual promises were exchanged.[2] Among other things, the

1. 5 N.Y.2d 222, 183 N.Y.S.2d 65, N.E.2d 700 (1959).
2. The following is an example of the kind of agreement entered into by the Agency and the Sanders:
In consideration of being accepted as foster parents by the Jewish Child Care Association [hereinafter referred to as the Agency], we agree as follows:
1. The child placed with us will be accepted by us as a member of our family, and will receive our affection and care as foster parents. The Agency will furnish a monthly board payment, payable at the end of each month. At the time of placement, we will be notified of the specific rate for the child placed with us.
The Agency will provide for the child's clothing, medical and dental ex-penses.
We will be reimbursed for certain other expenditures made, as described in the Foster Parents' Manual, provided they have been previously autho-rized by the Agency.
2. We will notify the Agency of any change or plans for change in our own life, which may affect the child placed with us. This will include, but is not limited to, vacation plans, illnesses, job changes, moving, and any change in the composition of our family.
3. We will notify the Agency immediately if the child placed with us be-comes ill, and we will comply with the Agency's arrangements for medical and dental care.
4. We are aware that the Agency has the responsibility for making plans with regard to the child's relationship with his or her own relatives. We will cooperate with the arrangements made by the Agency worker for visits be-tween the child and his or her own relatives.
5. We acknowledge that we are accepting the child placed with us for an

couple promised to accept Laura as a member of their family and, as foster parents, to give her affection and care. They promised to follow the Agency's regulations regarding the boarding arrangement, notification of and care during the child's illnesses, and changes in living conditions that would affect the child, such as modifications caused by vacations, job changes, and other events. They also agreed to cooperate with the Agency's plans for continuing a relationship with the child's natural mother. Should the couple be unable to continue as foster parents, they promised to work with the Agency in making an orderly transition to another placement. The Sanders acknowledged that they were accepting Laura for an indeterminate period and were aware that the "legal responsibility for the child" remained with the Agency.

During the first year after placement, the Sanders spoke with the Agency about adopting Laura. They were told that adoption was not possible and were asked to help the child understand who her natural mother was. The child had seen her natural mother once during the first year of placement. During the second year of foster care, the Sanders again mentioned their desire to adopt Laura. The Agency refused to consider the proposal and required the couple, as a condition for keeping the child, to sign a statement acknowledging that they had the child only on a foster home basis.[3] Despite the signed statement, the Sanders persisted in their

indeterminate period, depending on the needs of the child and his family situation. We are aware that the legal responsibility for the foster child remains with the Agency, and we will accept and comply with any plans the Agency makes for the child. This includes the right to determine when and how the child leaves us, and we agree to cooperate with arrangements made toward that end.

6. Should we find ourselves unable to continue giving foster care to the child placed with us, we will notify the Agency promptly, and will cooperate with the Agency in making the change of placement as easy as possible. For this reason, we will give the Agency as much time to make such change as is needed, unless our situation is emergent.

Date _____

Signature of Foster Mother _____
Signature of Foster Father _____

Countersigned:
Agency Social Worker _____

GOLDSTEIN & J. KATZ, THE FAMILY AND THE LAW 1021–22 (1965).

3. The legal enforceability of a statement of this kind or of the child placement agreement is open to question. In Adoption of McDonald, 43 Cal. 2d 477, 274 P.2d 860 (1954), foster parents signed an agreement with

efforts to adopt Laura, unsuccessfully seeking approval from the child's natural mother, grandmother, and other relatives. When the Sanders requested permission to take Laura with them on an out-of-state vacation, the Agency refused, asserting that the child should be returned to her natural mother during that time. Laura, then four, had lived with the Sanders for three years and had seen her natural mother only twice. She was not to see her mother again until the litigation over her custody began.

The Sanders' constant efforts to adopt Laura in contradiction of their statements, along with the Agency's belief that the couple had become too emotionally attached to the child, prompted the Agency to demand Laura's return. The couple refused and the Agency brought a writ of habeas corpus to demand the child's release from the Sanders' home. As seen from the perspective of the foster parents, the Agency's action was potentially beneficial for various

---

an adoption agency which included, among other provisions, a requirement that any request for the adoption of the child placed with them had to be approved by the agency, and a stipulation that if after one year the agency was satisfied with the training of the child and the character of the foster parents' home, it would allow the adoption. The agreement further provided that the agency had the right to remove the child previous to legal adoption if at any time the circumstances warranted it. About eight months after the placement of the child, the foster father committed suicide. Later the agency demanded the return of the child. The foster mother refused to give up the child and petitioned a court for adoption without securing the agency's consent. The trial court granted the adoption, having concluded that the agency's consent was unnecessary.

One of the arguments which the agency made in its appeal to the California Supreme Court was that the foster mother was estopped from pursuing the adoption by virtue of the agreement she and her husband signed at the time of placement. Addressing himself to this argument, Justice Traynor wrote: "The [State] department [of Social Welfare] . . . has no power by regulation or otherwise to add to or detract from the rules for adoption prescribed in the Civil Code. . . . Thus, neither appellant, the department, the county agency, nor any private agency had the right by regulation or by agreement to deprive petitioner of the rights granted her by section 226 of the Civil Code to petition the court and have the court determine whether the petition should or should not be granted. If the department could give a licensed agency the right to control the adoption of a relinquished child, it could give such an agency the right to control the adoption of any child not subject to parental control. The statutory provisions governing adoptions cannot be so circumvented.

In a proceeding such as this the child is the real party in interest and is not a party to any agreement. It is the welfare of the child that controls, and any agreement others may have made for its custody is made subject to the court's independent judgment as to what is for the best interests of the child." *Id.* at 461, 274 P.2d at 868; See also CAL. CIV. CODE § 224(n) (Supp. 1964).

reasons. It allowed the Sanders to bypass administrative remedies and to obtain an immediate judicial review of the Agency's decision denying their adoptive suitability. Considering their strained relations with the Agency, the Sanders' chances for administrative relief would probably have been slim. Furthermore, since a habeas corpus proceeding is a method by which a court may explore the child's welfare [4] beyond the narrow issue of the legal right to custody,[5] the fact that the Agency was the legal guardian of Laura did not place it in a significantly advantageous position vis-à-vis the Sanders.

The Trial

In the trial court proceedings to determine whether Laura's "best interests" would be served by a custodial change, much of the testimony was focused on the effect that the proposed change would have on the child's natural mother as well as on the child's own physical and emotional well-being. The line of questioning in which the trial judge and the attorneys engaged seemed to be based on the underlying assumption that the goal of the proceedings was to determine how Laura's needs could best be secured in light of the inability of the natural mother to raise the child.

The trial judge heard testimony from the foster parents, representatives of the Agency, the Department of Welfare, and a psychiatrist. The Agency acknowledged that the Sanders had taken good care of the child and were providing her with a comfortable home environment. However, it claimed that, because of the great love of the foster parents for the child, Laura should be removed from their custody and placed in a "neutral environment" where foster parents would be called "aunt" and "uncle" instead of "mother" and "father" and where "there would not be this terrible

---

4. See, *e.g.,* New York *ex rel.* Halvey v. Halvey, 330 U.S. 610 (1947); Berry v. Berry, 219 Ala. 403, 122 So. 615 (1929); Porter v. Chester, 208 Ga. 309, 66 S.E.2d 729 (1951); Heuvel v. Heuvel, 254 Iowa 1391, 121 N.W.2d 216 (1963). Even the matter of child support may be explored. See Howarth v. Northcott, 152 Conn. 460, 208 A.2d 540 (1965). *Contra,* Buchanan v. Buchanan, 170 Va. 458, 197 S.E. 426 (1938); Pugh v. Pugh, 133 W. Va. 501, 56 S.E.2d 901 (1949). But some jurisdictions limit the court's inquiry on habeas corpus to the narrow issue of the legal right to custody. See, *e.g.,* May v. Anderson, 345 U.S. 528 (1953) (Ohio).

5. See New York Foundling Hosp. v. Gatti, 203 U.S. 429 (1906); Pukas v. Pukas, 129 W. Va. 765, 42 S.E.2d 11 (1947).

pull on the child between her loyalty to her foster parents and her mother." [6] In other words, the Agency did not claim that the foster parents were depriving the child of love, but rather argued that they were indulging her with too much love. The effect of their indulgence on the child, the Agency urged, was a strain on her relationship with her natural mother.

A large part of the trial consisted of the interrogation of a psychiatrist called by the foster parents. In his testimony, he analyzed the effect of a custodial change on Laura's emotional development. In his opinion, the Sanders' love for the child had positive rather than damaging emotional effects; indeed, Laura's removal from her foster parents would be detrimental to her emotional growth. He stated that latency was a critical period in a child's development and that, at Laura's age, she needed the security of a sustained relationship with her foster parents.

The trial judge apparently either was not sufficiently convinced by the psychiatric testimony or was persuaded by the Agency's argument that the child was becoming too attached to her foster parents, thus threatening her "relationship" with her natural mother. He decided to remove Laura from her foster parents and to allow the Agency to regain custody and place her in a "neutral environment." [7] After the intermediate appellate court affirmed the decision of the trial court, [8] the Sanders appealed to the New York Court of Appeals, which held in favor of the Agency in a split (4–3) opinion. [9]

6. 5 N.Y.2d 222, 227, 183 N.Y.S.2d 65, 68, 156 N.E.2d 700, 702 (1959).

7. Jewish Child Care Ass'n v. Sanders, 9 Misc. 2d 402, 172 N.Y.S.2d 630 (Sup. Ct. 1957), aff'd, 174 N.Y.S.2d 335 (App. Div. 1958), aff'd, 183 N.Y.S.2d 65, 156 N.E.2d 700, 704 (Ct. App. 1959).

8. Ibid. The basis of the New York Supreme Court's opinion was as follows: "Respondents have, the court feels, become fond of the child to an extent which has resulted in an attempt by them to induce the mother to permit an adoption by them; she has resisted these efforts and the conflict has resulted in this proceeding. The petitioner believes (quite correctly in the court's opinion) that it cannot suffer its established practice to be set at naught solely because respondents believe they can contribute more to the child's welfare than petitioner and the mother can.

The court does not believe that the best interest of this child will be served by the condonation of a disregard of their own obligations and agreements by the respondents, however well-intentioned they may be." Id. at 403, 172 N.Y.S.2d at 631.

9. 5 N.Y.S.2d 222, 183 N.Y.S.2d 65, 156 N.E.2d 700 (1959).

The Appeal

In the New York Court of Appeals' report, there is a discernible and major shift in emphasis from that found in the lower court's opinion. The trial court viewed "the best interests of the child" doctrine in terms of securing Laura's health needs in light of her natural mother's condition. The New York Court of Appeals first concentrated on the legal status of the claimants and then interpreted "the best interests of the child" in terms of the continuity of family loyalty and the law.

To the majority of the Court of Appeals, the fact that the Sanders were Laura's *foster,* rather than natural or future adoptive, parents was crucial. The court perceived foster parenthood as something less than full parenthood. By showing "extreme love," "affection" and "possessiveness" and by acting more like natural than like foster parents, the Sanders, in the court's estimation, had gone beyond the limits of their role as set out in the placement agreement. In essence, what the majority took as conclusive in the case, namely the "vital fact . . . that Mr. and Mrs. Sanders are not, and presumably will never be, Laura's parents by adoption," [10] was the very issue the court was to decide.

The court stressed its concern for preserving the natural ties between Laura and her mother. "In considering what is in Laura's best interests," the court wrote, "it was not only proper, but necessary . . . to consider the facts in terms of their significance to Laura's eventual return to her own mother." [11] And later the court stated:

> What is essentially at stake here is the parental custodial right. Although Child Care has the present legal right to custody . . . it stands, as against the Sanders, in a representative capacity as the protector of Laura's mother's inchoate custodial right and the parent-child relationship which is to become complete in the future.[12]

Finally, in its concluding remarks, the court crystallized its main preferences as follows:

> [T]he more important considerations of the child's best interests, the recognition and preservation of her mother's primary love

10. *Id.* at 229, 183 N.Y.S.2d at 70, 156 N.E.2d at 703.
11. *Id.* at 228, 183 N.Y.S.2d at 69, 156 N.E.2d at 703.
12. *Id.* at 229, 183 N.Y.S.2d at 70, 156 N.E.2d at 703.

and custodial interest, and the future life of the mother and child together are paramount.[13]

Family loyalty. The parental right to custody, the doctrine referred to by the court as both "paramount" and "fundamental," holds that any biological parent is entitled to the custody of his child unless the parent is affirmatively shown to be unfit.[14] Many courts have claimed that the right is based on principles of morality and natural affection.[15] However, the common-law history of the doctrine reveals that it may have been created for considerations of wealth rather than the dictates of a moral code. During the feudal period, custodial rights, which had commercial value, were subject to transfer and sale; a child was a financial asset to his father. During this early period, therefore, a custodial right was a property right.[16] In time, as concern developed for the child's welfare and as the mother was legally considered a joint custodian together with the father, the emphasis shifted from the property theory of custody toward the personal status theory.[17] That is, the natural parents, because of their relationship to the child, were presumed to be the custodians best fitted to serve the child's needs.

At first glance, the parental right to custody may seem to be a doctrine competing with "the best interests of the child" approach. Indeed, the parental right theory has been described as a secondary doctrine in child custody matters.[18] Perhaps, however, it is more

13. *Id.* at 230, 183 N.Y.S.2d at 71, 156 N.E.2d at 704.

14. See, *e.g.,* Roche v. Roche, 25 Cal. 2d 141, 152 P.2d 999 (1944); McGuire v. McGuire, 190 Kan. 524, 376 P.2d 908 (1962); Stout v. Stout, 166 Kan. 459, 201 P.2d 637 (1949); *Ex parte* Barnes, 54 Ore. 548, 104 Pac. 296 (1909). See also Iowa CODE § 633.559 (1963).

15. See, *e.g.,* Wilkinson v. Wilkinson, 105 Cal. App. 2d 392, 233 P.2d 639 (Dist. Ct. App. 1951); Acomb v. Billeiter, 175 So. 2d 25 (La. Ct. App. 1965); In the matter of Lewis, 35 Misc. 2d 117, 230 N.Y.S.2d 481 (Surr. Ct. 1962); Anonymous v. Anonymous, 15 Misc. 2d 389, 181 N.Y.S.2d 311 (Sup. Ct. 1959); People *ex rel.* Kropp v. Shepsky, 305 N.Y. 465, 113 N.E.2d 801 (1953).

16. See Sayre, *Awarding Custody of Children,* 9 U. CHI. L. REV. 672, 676–77 (1942); tenBroek, *California's Dual System of Family Law: Its Origin, Development, and Present Status, Part II,* 16 STAN. L. REV. 900, 925 (1964).

17. For many purposes, however, the child is still treated as property; there has been a shift, but not a substitution.

18. Simpson, *The Unfit Parent: Conditions Under Which a Child May Be Adopted Without the Consent of His Parent,* 39 U. DET. L.J. 347, 354–60 (1972); *Alternatives to "Parental Right" in Child Custody Disputes Involving Third Parties,* 73 YALE L.J. 151, 152–53 (1963).

appropriate to say that the parental right doctrine is often treated
as if it were an expression of "the best interests of the child." Most
frequently courts, invoking the parental right doctrine when they
prefer to award custody to the child's natural parents rather than
other claimants, assume that the disposition best serves the child's
welfare.[19] When custody is awarded to others, it is likely that courts
will simply state that "the best interests of the child" demand such
a disposition,[20] or that "the superior rights" of parents, or the presumption in their favor, must yield to "the best interests of the
child." [21] It seems safe to say that when courts invoke the parental
right doctrine to award custody to the natural parents, they are
merely articulating an archaic notion, based upon a preference for
the continuity of blood ties or the preservation of kinship loyalty,
in order to justify a decision. It is a significant aspect of *Child Care*
that the majority was more concerned with the *symbol* of natural
family loyalty than its *fact*. As indicated previously, Laura's natural
mother had seen the child twice in four years, and Laura's loyalty
to her would seem, at best, to be more imaginary than real.

Integrity of the law. In his final remark in his opinion for the
Court of Appeals, Chief Judge Conway came to grips with what
appeared to be his primary concern. While the interests of Laura
and her natural mother (but apparently not those of the foster
parents) were of significant importance, another factor was involved. The integrity of the law, as manifested in the child-placement contract and in the administrative decisions of a private
agency, had been challenged. In order to maintain authority, these
administrative policies had to be affirmed and the child-placement
agreement enforced: "[T]he program of agencies such as Child
Care . . . may not be subverted by foster parents who breach
their trust." [22]

The majority in *Child Care* was again concerned with symbols.
Judge Conway seemed compelled to preserve the sanctity of legal

19. See, *e.g.,* Roche v. Roche, 25 Cal. 2d 141, 152 P.2d 999 (1944); Stout
v. Stout, 166 Kan. 459, 201 P.2d 637 (1949); Bond v. Bond, 167 So. 2d 388
(La. Ct. App. 1964); *Ex parte* Barnes, 54 Ore. 548, 104 Pac. 296 (1909).
20. See, *e.g.,* Kennedy v. State Dept. of Pensions & Security, 277 Ala. 5,
166 So. 2d 736 (1964); Forbes v. Haney, 204 Va. 712, 133 S.E.2d 533
(1963).
21. See, *e.g.,* Bond v. Bond, 167 So. 2d 388 (La. Ct. App. 1964); Mouton
v. St. Romain, 245 La. 839, 161 So. 2d 737 (1964).
22. 5 N.Y.2d 222, 230, 183 N.Y.S.2d 65, 71, 156 N.E.2d 700, 704 (1959).

doctrines and, indirectly, the reputation of a community institution. The Sanders had been a threat both to the integrity and the stability of the placement contract [23] and to the prestige of the Agency. To give Laura to her foster parents would have been to reward persons who had failed to fulfill their promises and who had undermined the Agency's decision. It seems that by protecting community institutions, the court shifted its focus from Laura's welfare to other matters: the continuity of legal doctrine and the prestige of a social service agency.

Child custody proceedings, more than other litigation, may be merely a cover for the real conflicts: a power struggle between individuals, institutions, or individuals and institutions, which culminates in a decision that indicates a preference for certain social values over others. It is sometimes said that, in child custody disputes between divorced parents, the child may act as a tool of the parents and the court as an arena in which the parents can display their mutual hostilities. In *Child Care,* one was not witnessing an intra-family conflict, but rather a struggle between community institutions: welfare agency and foster family. The important question before the court was not necessarily who should be awarded custody of Laura, although this inevitably was resolved, but whose decision-making power was to be recognized, the welfare agency's or the foster parents'. In *Child Care,* the Agency prevailed, and the decision therefore may be described as one which furthered the best interests of the *Agency.* Whether it was in the best interests of the child is hard to say. The psychiatrist and a dissenting judge thought it was not.[24]

Toward Clarifying "The Best Interests of the Child"

Assuming that the preservation of biological ties, the maintenance of the sanctity of contract law, and the protection of the prestige of a social service agency were the basis for the court's decision in

23. *But see* note 3 *supra.*
24. In his dissenting opinion, Judge Froessel anticipated the ultimate result of the case, multiple placements for Laura. He wrote: "If Laura is to be bandied about meanwhile from family to family until she is transferred to her mother, each such change will be extremely difficult for the child, as testified to without contradiction by the psychiatrist at the hearing. Why multiply the shocks? And if the mother never chooses to take Laura, and that does not appear to be unlikely from the record before us, the child could not find a better home than she now enjoys." 5 N.Y.2d at 235, 183 N.Y.S.2d at 75, 156 N.E.2d at 707.

Child Care, the question remains: were these considerations relevant to determining the custodial disposition that would further Laura's best interests? This question is difficult to answer unless one first defines for oneself "the best interests of the child," for the doctrine has no absolute definition. Nor is there uniformity in the results of the cases in which the doctrine has been applied. In general, all that can be said is that, as the doctrines of "bona fide purchaser" in the law of real property and "good faith" in negotiable instruments, so "the best interests of the child doctrine" is a mandate from the legislature, directing the judge to use his discretion in making a disposition.[25] Obviously, such an interpretation of the doctrine permits what has, in fact, taken place in *Child Care:* the use of value preferences dominant in the community and reflected in important community institutions.

Perhaps a reason for the constantly shifting bases of child custody opinions relating to establishing and reorganizing the parent-child relationship [26] is that courts feel there are few legal tests to which these decisions can be subjected. This conclusion may be unsound. Legal precriptions existing in other areas, such as the standards relating to supervising the parent-child relationship, might be useful as guides. In this section, an effort will be made to formulate criteria for deciding custodial disputes and to provide a framework that might be helpful in narrowing and disciplining a court's scope of inquiry during both the information-gathering and the evaluating stages of the decision. Furthermore, the proposed analytical scheme might provide judges a means by which they can express their preferences.

Purpose of the Parent-Child Relationship

Our cultural preferences may cause one to assume that a child is

25. See, *e.g.,* Conn. Gen. Stat. Rev. § 46–24 (1958) (the court can "make any order which it deems reasonable"); Ill. Rev. Stat. ch. 40, § 19 (1956) (the court shall make a custodial disposition "as shall appear reasonable and proper"); Minn. Stat. § 518.17 (1947) (the court shall make a custodial disposition "as it deems just and proper"); Neb. Rev. Stat. § 42.311 (1960 Rev.) (the court shall make a custodial disposition "as it shall deem just and proper"). See also Foster & Freed, *Child Custody, Part I,* 39 N.Y.U.L. Rev. 423, 438 (1964).

26. The terms establishment and reorganization of the parent-child relationship refer to the substantive and procedural requisites for becoming a natural, adoptive, foster, neglected, and emancipated parent or child. The term "supervision" refers to governmental administration of established and reorganized parent-child relationships. This terminology is developed in Goldstein & J. Katz, *op. cit. supra* note 2, at 1–5 (1965).

best reared in a family setting. The task in child placement is to find a family that will fulfill a child's needs. One way of determining these needs is to try to identify what the community expects the family, particularly parents, whether natural, adoptive, or foster, to provide for a child. Or, we may try to identify the goals of the parent-child relationship, regardless of what kind of parent is involved.[27] Answers are provided in reported cases, statutes, and prevailing middle class mores about parental responsibilites, but the

27. In much of the legal literature, a distinction, perhaps artificial and distracting, is made between foster care (giving rise to the foster parent-child relationship) and adoption. Foster care is regarded as temporary and adoption is considered permanent. See, *e.g.,* Clevenger v. Clevenger, 189 Cal. App. 2d 658, 11 Cal. Rep. 707 (Dist. Ct. App. 1961); Estate of McCardle, 95 Colo. 250, 35 P.2d 850 (1934); Schneider v. Schneider, 25 N.J. Misc. 180, 52 A.2d 564 (Ch. 1947); Griego v. Hogan, 71 N.M. 280, 377 P.2d 953 (1963); Taylor v. Taylor, 58 Wash. 510, 364 P.2d 444 (1961). This distinction can be interpreted in a number of ways. For example, it may relate to the duration of the status. Or, it might be suggestive of the legal implications that flow from either status: foster case gives rise to ambiguous relationships while adoption creates fixed legal relationships similar to and sometimes identical with those between parents and their natural children. The following discussion may raise doubts about these assumptions. Also, it may lead one to question whether Mr. and Mrs. Sanders' status as foster parents should have been "the vital fact" for decision.

Foster parent refers to the status that arises when one not related, by either direct parental blood or through formal legal proceedings officially establishing an adoptive parent-child relationship, assumes the role generally regarded in the community as the one held by a parent. In traditional legal terminology, he would be one who stands in loco parentis. This doctrine, an illustration of a legal fiction, holds that people who act *as if* they were natural parents are legally held to the same standards as parents. To determine the status, courts tend to apply agency law notions, namely whether the parent "held himself out to the world" as a parent. For a full discussion and history of the doctrine, see Schneider v. Schneider, *supra.*

Foster status may arise in numerous ways, for instance, through direct or indirect formal judicial authority, by a formal or informal arrangement, or by voluntarily caring for a foundling. It also includes parents of a child placed in their custody prior to a final adoption decree and parents who hold themselves out as adoptive parents believing in the validity of an adoptive decree which is legally defective. Further illustrations include the situation that arises when a court awards guardianship and custody to persons other than the natural parents, or when a court awards a social welfare agency guardianship and custody of a child with the power to delegate (usually through an agreement that has the appearance of a legal contract) the parental role to persons chosen by the agency. This is what occurred in Laura's case. A not infrequent situation that may give rise to the foster parent-child relationship is that in which one accepts into his home and treats as his own a child surrendered by his parents. This may occur by a formal or informal agreement or through abandonment. On the other hand, one is an adoptive parent only at the culmination of valid legal adoption proceedings.

discussion below will be restricted primarily to cases involving the state's supervision of the parent-child relationship. The pattern that emerges from these cases suggests a concern for promoting (1) order, integrity and family loyalty; (2) financial security; (3) health and education; and (4) morality and respect.

Order, integrity and family loyalty. At birth a child is considered to be in the custody of his natural parents. Some have looked upon the family relationship that is established at this time as a trust which parents hold for the benefit of their child and the state.[28] In reality, however, due to the sheer necessities of the circumstances, parents assume control over and have immediate supervision of their infant to the exclusion of others. Except for certain compulsory governmental health measures during the first few weeks of their child's life, such as the silver nitrate treatment at birth and perhaps the PKU (phenylketonuria) test later, natural parents have the power to make decisions affecting their child's life.[29]

In legal terminology, a parent's control over and supervision of his child is called the "parental right to custody," and, if it can be included in the bundle of rights associated with marriage, establishing a home and rearing children, it can be claimed as a right that is "so rooted in the traditions and conscience of our people as to be ranked as fundamental," [30] and, therefore, constitutionally protected. The United States Supreme Court has employed substantive due process to protect the family, especially the husband-wife and parent-child relationships, from unwarranted governmental intrusion. This principle of protecting the freedom of the family is supported by cases beginning with *Meyer v. Nebraska,*[31] in which the Court held invalid a state statute prohibiting the teaching of the

28. See, *e.g.,* Gardner v. Hall, 132 N.J. Eq. 64, 26 A.2d 799 (Ch. 1942); Lippincott v. Lippincott, 97 N.J. Eq. 517, 128 Atl. 254 (Ct. Err. & App. 1925); Elliot v. Elliot, 235 N.C. 153, 69 S.E.2d 224 (1952).

29. Many states have statutory provisions regulating the silver nitrate test. See, *e.g.,* CONN. GEN. STAT. REV. § 19.92 (1958); FLA. STAT. § 383.05 (1965); ILL. REV. STAT. ch. 91, § 108 (1963). Minnesota specifically waives the test if parents object to it. MINN. STAT. § 144.12(8) (1965 Supp.). New York has enacted a statutory provision requiring the administering of the PKU test. See N.Y. PUB. HEALTH LAW § 200-a.

30. Griswold v. Connecticut, 381 U.S. 479, 487 (1965) (Goldberg, J., concurring).

31. 262 U.S. 390 (1923).

German language to children who· had not passed the eighth grade, and *Pierce v. Society of Sisters,*[32] in which the Court ruled unconstitutional a law preventing the operation of private schools. *Meyer* and *Pierce* were considered to involve fundamental rights protected by the due process clause of the fourteenth amendment.

The principle that there is a realm of family life which the state cannot invade, save for some compelling reason such as protecting children from imminent danger, was reinforced by *Prince v. Commonwealth of Massachusetts.*[33] In that case, the United States Supreme Court held that Massachusetts child-labor laws were not unreasonable restrictions on either a parent's right to rear children, especially with regard to teaching and practicing a particular faith, or a child's right to observe that faith. For the purpose of illustrating the extent to which the Court believes the parent-child relationship should be secure and free from unreasonable interference from the state, Mr. Justice Rutledge's words are relevant:

> It is cardinal with us that the custody, care and nurture of the child reside first in the parents, whose primary function and freedom include preparation for obligations the state can neither supply nor hinder. . . . And it is in recognition of this that these decisions [*Pierce v. Society of Sisters* and *Meyer v. Nebraska*] have respected the private realm of family life which the state cannot enter.
>
> But the family itself is not beyond regulation in the public interest, as against a claim of religious liberty. . . . Acting to guard the general interest in youth's well-being, the state as *parens patriae* may restrict the parent's control by requiring school attendance, regulating or prohibiting the child's labor and in many other ways. . . . The catalogue need not be lengthened. It is sufficient to show . . . that the state has a wide range of power for limiting parental freedom and authority in things affecting the child's welfare; and that this includes, to some extent, matters of conscience and religious conviction.[34]

Although it was the privacy of the husband-wife relationship that had been invaded by the State of Connecticut's restriction on the use of birth control devices in *Griswold v. Connecticut,*[35] that case

32. 268 U.S. 510 (1925).
33. 321 U.S. 158 (1944).
34. *Id.* at 166–67.
35. 381 U.S. 479 (1965).

has ramifications for the parent-child relationship. In *Griswold,* Mr. Justice Douglas extracted from the Bill of Rights a penumbral right of marital and familial privacy. Mr. Justice Goldberg's interpretation of the ninth amendment gave additional support to precedent affirming the goal of integrity and security in the family. The significance of his remarks about the husband-wife relationship for that of the parent-child should be apparent.

> The entire fabric of the Constitution and the purposes that clearly underlie its specific guarantees demonstrate that the rights to marital privacy and to marry and raise a family are of similar order and magnitude as the fundamental rights specifically protected.
>
> Although the Constitution does not speak in so many words of the right of privacy in marriage, I cannot believe that it offers these fundamental rights no protection. The fact that no particular provisions of the Constitution explicitly forbids the State from disrupting the traditional relation of the family—a relation as old and as fundamental as our entire civilization—surely does not show that the Government was meant to have the power to do so. Rather, as the Ninth Amendment expressly recognizes, there are fundamental personal rights such as this one, which are protected from abridgment by the Government though not specifically mentioned in the Constitution.[36]

That the parent-child relationship should be secure, stable, orderly and free from unreasonable interference by the state or others is further emphasized in cases which establish the right of a parent to procedural due process and other procedural advantages when the custody of his child is being litigated. The due process clause of the fourteenth amendment requires a court to notify a natural parent and to give him an opportunity to participate in a proceeding designed to determine his child's custody. Some courts have analogized parents' rights in their children to "property rights" within the protection of the due process clause;[37] others have maintained that these rights are protected by the guarantee of liberty.[38]

In addition to procedural due process, there is a procedural pref-

---

36. *Id.* at 495–96 (concurring opinion). See also Poe v. Ullman, 367 U.S. 497, 551–52 (1961) (Harlan, J., dissenting).
37. See, *e.g.,* Brooks v. De Witt, 178 S.W.2d 718 (Tex. Civ. App. 1944).
38. See, *e.g.,* Stubbs v. Hammon, 135 N.W.2d 540 (Iowa 1965).

erence given to natural parents in that the burden of proving a natural parent's unfitness is placed on the individual who desires to gain custody of a child over the natural parent's objection.[39] The decision of the United States Supreme Court in *Armstrong v. Manzo* [40] illustrates the extent to which the Court will go to protect a natural parent's right to his child. In that case, the issue was whether an adoption decree was valid when secured by the child's natural mother and her second husband without notification to the first husband, the child's natural father. Although the natural father had subsequently obtained a hearing on his motion to vacate the decree because of the lack of notice and had presented evidence at that hearing in an attempt to establish the necessity of his consent to the adoption, the Court held that the decree was invalid. The failure of the adoption court to provide the natural father an opportunity to contest the adoption was more than a routine denial of procedural due process, because the court's action permanently deprived "a legitimate parent of all that parenthood implies." [41] The natural father's absence in the adoption proceedings gave the adoptive applicant (second husband) an undue advantage since he did not have to carry the burden of proving his own qualifications and the natural father's unfitness. In the subsequent hearing on the motion to vacate the decree, this crucial allocation of the burden of proof was reversed, for the natural father, since he was the moving party in that hearing, was required to demonstrate affirmatively his fitness to have custody of the child. The Court, realizing the decisiveness of the location of the burden of proof, was unwilling to deprive the natural father of his procedural preference in the adoption proceeding.

Another, perhaps indirect, indication of a community policy favoring the integrity of the parent-child relationship is that the law discourages and may even prohibit the unconditional voluntary termination of the parent-child relationship, regardless of the type of parental status. Criminal sanctions attach to parents who fail

39. Professor tenBroek convincingly demonstrates that the burden of proof in favor of parental fitness applies mainly to members of the middle classes, but is substantially relaxed as to the poor. In cases involving the poor, "parental fitness" is *examined* rather than presumed. tenBroek, *California's Dual System of Family Law: Its Origin, Development, and Present Status, Part III,* 17 STAN. L. REV. 614, 676 (1965).

40. 380 U.S. 545 (1965).

41. *Id.* at 550.

to fulfill the incidents of the right to custody: companionship, financial support and health care.[42] It is doubtful whether any state permits the voluntary legal termination of the parent-child relationship unless there is a satisfactory placement available for the child or unless there is reason to believe that denying the termination petition will be detrimental to the child's welfare.[43] Thus, natural parents probably would not be allowed to terminate the full range of their duties, whether the child be healthy or handicapped, in the absence of a showing that the action would serve the child's welfare.[44]

In the adoptive parent-child relationship, the goal of order and integrity is also maintained. Once the adoptive status is legally established, the adoptive parent's duty and right to control and supervise his adopted child, even to the exclusion of the child's natural family, is preserved in the same way as the custodial right of the natural parent.[45] Courts are reluctant to set aside an adoption decree, or to terminate or annul an adoption. Some courts have taken the position that, absent express statutory authority clearly establishing grounds sufficient for terminating the adoption, adoptive parents cannot be relieved of their parental obligations.[46] Jurisdictions having statutory provisions allowing termination or annulment in certain circumstances, such as a child's misconduct, his physical or mental illness unknown at the time of adoption, or when the best interests of the child demand termination, tend to

42. These are usually found in child neglect statutes. See, e.g., ALASKA STAT. § 11.35.010 (1962); ARIZ. REV. STAT. ANN. § 13–801 (1956); COLO. REV. STAT. § 22–2–1 (1963); IND. ANN. STAT. § 10–815 (1956); MD. ANN. CODE art. 27, § 88(b) (1957); MASS. GEN. LAWS ANN. ch. 273, § 1 (1957 Supp. 1965); OHIO REV. CODE ANN. § 2151.99(B) (1963); WIS. STAT. § 947.15 (1961).

43. The Model Adoption Act drafted by the U.S. Department of Health, Education, & Welfare provides for the voluntary termination of parental rights regardless of the availability of satisfactory placement. See CHILDREN'S BUREAU, U.S. DEP'T OF HEALTH, EDUCATION & WELFARE, LEGISLATIVE GUIDES FOR THE TERMINATION OF PARENTAL RIGHTS AND RESPONSIBILITIES AND THE ADOPTION OF CHILDREN 12–13 (1961).

44. This parallels the law of assignment: one may assign one's *right's* but not one's duties (delegation of duties leaves one responsible unless there is a novation).

45. See Odell v. Lutz, 78 Cal. App. 2d 104, 177 P.2d 628 (Dist. Ct. App. 1947).

46. See, e.g., Allen v. Allen, 214 Ore. 664, 330 P.2d 151 (1958).

apply these provisions narrowly.[47] Thus, adoptive parents may not divest themselves of their custodial duties merely because they are dissatisfied with their child, regret their decision about adoption, or think they made a bad deal.[48] This is true even if the adoptive child's natural parents wish to resume a legal relationship with him.[49] Adoption is said to create "a for better, for worse situation," [50] and is therefore seemingly more protected than the marriage of the adoptive parents, which may be dissolved by divorce.

It is said that the parental right to custody not attach to foster parents unless specifically decreed by a court; in other words, foster parents seem to have more duties than rights. This statement, however, may be misleading, for foster parents may in fact enjoy the right to custody without benefit of the label. A *de facto* custodial interest develops in a foster parent when the foster relationship continues over a length of time. Courts are reluctant to interfere with this interest and, if they do interfere, the foster parent is generally entitled to notification and an opportunity to appear and defend his interest.[51] A continuing foster relationship, if secure and orderly, is typically protected even against a natural parent's unreasonable intrusion.[52] If a natural parent wishes to interfere with the foster parent relationship, he must, as any other individual, carry the burden of proving the foster parent's unfitness, as well as the burden of showing that the child's needs will be served best by another custodial arrangement.[53]

Under certain conditions, a foster parent may terminate his relationship with his foster child. The most important of these conditions is that the foster parent must intentionally perform a positive act—which ordinarily implies obtaining the consent of all parties in

47. See, *e.g.,* Buttrey v. West, 212 Ala. 321, 102 So. 456 (1924); Pelt v. Tunks, 153 Colo. 215, 385 P.2d 261 (1963); Mulligaw v. Wingard, 72 Ga. App. 539, 34 S.E.2d 305 (Ct. App. 1945) *trans. from* 198 Ga. 816, 33 S.E.2d 269; Succession of Williams, 224 La. 871, 71 So. 2d 229 (1954); *In re* Pierro, 173 Misc. 123, 17 N.Y.S.2d 233 (Surr. Ct. 1940).

48. See, *e.g.,* Parsons v. Parsons, 101 Wis. 76, 77 N.W. 147 (1898); *In re* Adoption of L (Essex County Ct., P. Div.) 56 N.J. Super. 46, 151 A.2d 435 (1959).

49. See *In re* Adoption of L., *supra* note 48.

50. *In re* Adoption of a Minor, 214 N.E.2d 281 (Mass. 1966).

51. See *In re* Adoption of Cheney, 244 Iowa 1180, 59 N.W.2d 685 (1953).

52. See Cummins v. Bird, 230 Ky. 296, 19 S.W.2d 959 (1929).

53. See State v. Knight, 135 So. 2d 126 (La. App. 1961).

interest—severing *all* aspects of the relationship.[54] Announcing a decision to terminate the relationship while continuing to live with the child is insufficient.[55] A foster parent may not choose to honor his right to enjoy companionship and fail in his duty to support.[56] Presumably, therefore, the policy discussed above of protecting and sanctioning an established and subsisting relationship is not applicable when a foster parent decides to terminate that relationship. The context in which questions are raised about the foster parent's power to terminate the foster parent-child relationship is usually a stepfather's refusal to continue to support his non-adopted stepchild after he has divorced the child's natural mother. Courts normally reason that the order which was present in the relationship has been disrupted by the divorce and that no purpose would be served by requiring the continuance of the duty to support, correlative to the right to custody, in the absence of a sustained relationship. New York, however, goes further than most juris-

54. See, *e.g.*, Lewis v. United States, 105 F. Supp. 73 (N.D. W. Va. 1952); Leyerly v. United States, 162 F.2d 79 (10th Cir. 1947); Young v. Hipple, 273 Pa. 439, 117 Atl. 185 (1922).

55. See Capek v. Kropik, 129 Ill. 509, 21 N.E. 836 (1889); Schneider v. Schneider, 25 N.J. Misc. 180, 52 A.2d 564 (Ch. 1947).

56. That there is a duty to support under these circumstances is evident from public welfare law. The "man-in-the-house" rule, or, as it is sometimes called, the "substitute parent" policy, was stated in People v. Shirley, 55 Cal. 2d 521, 524, 360 P.2d 33, 34 (1961): "[U]nder regulations of the State Board of Social Welfare a stepfather living in the home is responsible for the support of the mother of a needy child unless incapacitated and unable to support. . . . A man living in the home assuming the role of spouse has the same responsibility as that of a stepfather for the mother and the needy children. . . ."

An illustration of state welfare regulations pertaining to the "substitute parent" policy is found in Part III, Section V of the *Georgia Manual of Public Welfare Administration,* dealing with the eligibility conditions for the Aid to Families with Dependent Children Program (AFDC). Subdivision (5) of Section V(3) disqualifies needy dependent children from the program if they are found to have a "substitute father." The subdivision states: "(5) *Substitute Father:* A man living in common-law relationship with a woman is considered a substitute father of any child had by that woman, or any child that woman has had by another man. Further, a man living in common-law relationship with a woman is responsible for the support and care of his and her children, regardless of whether or not he is married to another woman. Regulations place the same responsiblity on this man as if he were the legal husband. The rules for establishing deprivation are the same as those used in establishing it in a legal-father situation." GEORGIA STATE DEP'T OF FAMILY AND CHILDREN'S SERVICES, DIV. OF SOCIAL ADMINISTRATION, MANUAL OF PUBLIC WELFARE ADMINISTRATION 7 (1964). See also Pacht, *Support of Dependents in the District of Columbia: Part I,* 9 HOW. L.J. 20, 36–38 (1963); tenBroek, *supra* note 39.

dictions in requiring a step-parent, after divorce or death of the
spouse, to support the spouse's child if his failure to provide such
support would place an economic burden on the state.[57]

Financial security. The statutory obligation which both natural and
adoptive parents have to support their children probably rests more
on the policy of preventing children from becoming economic
burdens on the state than on any other notion.[58] The level of financial security demanded of parents is one that would enable a child
to be housed, fed, clothed, educated, and given medical care in a
manner which satisfies minimum but acceptable community standards. Providing a child with bare subsistence is insufficient. Also,
since support duties are a public responsibility to which both
criminal and civil sanctions attach, these duties cannot be avoided
except in extraordinary circumstances, such as destitution;[59] merely
renouncing or improperly delegating the duty is without force.[60]
When natural or adoptive parents make no provisions for support,
those who do provide for the child may seek restitution from the
parents.[61]

57. Department of Welfare v. Siebel, 6 N.Y.2d 536, 190 N.Y.S.2d 683
(1959), *appeal dismissed,* 361 U.S. 535 (1960), *construing* N.Y. CITY DOM.
REL. CT. ACT § 101(5). In 1962 the New York Domestic Relations Act was
repealed. Section 101(5) was reenacted in N.Y. FAMILY CT. ACT § 415
(1963). See also tenBroek, *supra* note 39. This is just one illustration of
the "Dual System of Family Law." The New York rule establishes a different law for step-parents of poor children than applies to those step-parents
in more comfortable positions. The reason may well be the fiscal consideration of saving tax money.
58. See Porter v. Powell, 79 Iowa 151, 44 N.W. 295 (1890); Crain v.
Mallone, 130 Ky. 125, 113 S.W.2d 67 (1908); Holland v. Beard, 59 Miss.
161, 42 Am. Rep. 360 (1881); State v. Thornton, 232 Mo. 298, 134 S.W. 519
(1911); Geary v. Geary, 102 Neb. 511, 167 N.W. 778 (1918); Garlock v.
Garlock, 279 N.Y. 337, 18 N.E.2d 521 (1939). See also Jones, *The Problem
of Family Support: Criminal Sanctions for the Enforcement of Support,* 38
N.C.L. REV. 1. 13 (1959); Pacht, *supra* note 56, at 21.
59. See, *e.g.,* Watts v. Steele, 19 Ala. 656, 54 Am. Dec. 207 (1851); *In re*
Estate of Weisskopfs, 39 Ill. App. 2d 380, 188 N.E.2d 726 (1963); Fruen v.
Fruen, 228 Minn. 391, 37 N.W.2d 417 (1949); Libby v. Arnold, 161 N.Y.S.
2d 798 (N.Y. City Dom. Rel. Ct. 1957).
60. See, *e.g.,* Rogers v. Rogers, 93 Kan. 114, 143 Pac. 410 (1914); Huff-
man v. Hatcher, 178 Ky. 8, 198 S.W. 236 (1917); State v. Bell, 184 N.C.
701, 115 S.E. 190 (1922).
61. See, *e.g.,* Commonwealth v. Kirk, 212 Ky. 646, 279 S.W. 1091
(1926); Greenman v. Gillerman's Estate, 188 Mich. 74, 154 N.W. 82
(1915); Worthington v. Worthington, 212 Mo. App. 216, 253 S.W. 443
(1923). See also Jones, *supra* note 58, at 12, 13.

The fact that a person has only a foster relationship with his child will ordinarily not relieve him of his support duty. Courts and statutes, enforcing a foster parent's support duty, speak of the doctrine of in loco parentis and in effect state that persons acting like natural parents assume support duties as if they were natural parents.[62] Foster parents, therefore, may also be required to reimburse those who undertake to support their children.[63] The support responsibilities of foster parents may be imposed by contract. In a formal child placement, in which the agency contracts with foster parents to provide a child with care and daily necessities, it can be said that the agency transfers its duty of support to the foster parents, although the agency probably continues to have subsidiary liability. Foster parents would be subject to civil liability if they failed to fulfill their obligations.

Health and education. Natural and adoptive parents have a duty to establish an affectionate relationship with their children and to nurture and protect their physical and emotional well-being. Also, they are expected to provide their children with guidance and to offer them the opportunity for educational development. Courts use the in loco parentis doctrine to impose these same responsibilities on foster parents.

One context in which courts are asked to enforce health responsibilities is where a parent has failed to provide his child with the necessities of health care. For instance, the parent, natural, adoptive or foster, may be required to compensate a physician who has provided professional services for a child without the knowledge of the parent.[64] A more immediate expression of a community policy protecting children's health is found in instances of child neglect.

62. *In re* Harris, 16 Ariz. 1, 140 Pac. 825 (1914); Howard v. Randolph, 134 Ga. 691, 68 S.E. 586 (1910); Faber v. Industrial Comm., 352 Ill. 115, 185 N.E. 255 (1933); Foreman v. Henry, 87 Okla. 272, 210 Pac. 1026 (1922); Rosky v. Schmitz, 110 Wash. 547, 188 Pac. 493 (1920); Ellis v. Cary, 74 Wis. 176, 42 N.W. 252 (1889). See also *In re* Adoption of Cheney, 244 Iowa 1180, 59 N.W.2d 685 (1953); Brummitt v. Com, 357 S.W.2d 37 (Ky. Ct. App. 1962); Britt v. Allred, 199 Miss. 786, 25 So. 2d 711 (1946); Austin v. Austin, 147 Neb. 109, 22 N.W.2d 560 (1946); Hollis v. Thomas, 42 Tenn. App. 407, 303 S.W.2d 751 (1957); State *ex rel.* Gilroy v. Superior Court, 37 Wash. 2d 926, 226 P.2d 882 (1951).

63. See Rudd v. Fineberg's Trustee, 277 Ky. 505, 126 S.W.2d 1102 (1939).

64. See, *e.g.,* Greenspan v. Slate, 12 N.J. 426, 97 A.2d 390 (1953).

The state may spell out the scope of parental responsibilities by establishing health standards [65] when a child is in immediate danger of death because of parental failure to consent to a surgical operation or blood transfusion, or when a child has been starved or mistreated, to mention only a few extreme examples. This prescription of health standards is indicative of what the state will *not* tolerate: parents who severely deprive their children of physical safety, emotional security, or comfort. Discovery of violations of these standards may lead to criminal prosecution, temporary or permanent loss of custody, or state supervision of custody.

Just as there is no clear statement of what constitutes the maximum or ideal of good health, neither is there any judicial or statutory expression of the extent to which parents must enlighten their children.[66] The educational duty which rests on the parents begins with the birth of the child, and the duty is essentially, although not entirely, uncontrolled. There is almost no state supervision of the duty to educate until a child reaches five or six, although governmental control could be assumed prior to those ages if the child were "neglected" by not having received rudimentary education. When their children reach the age of five or six, parents are expected to enroll them in educational institutions under state regulation, to refrain from interfering with school attendance, and, in fact, to encourage their children's attendance until they reach a specific age (usually sixteen). State compulsory education acts contain criminal sanctions which apply to parents who fail to fulfill their responsibilities. Whether parents must provide their children with educational opportunities beyond statutory compulsory education is an open question, depending perhaps on the economic and social situation of the parents. Recent trends in appellate case law

65. See, *e.g.,* Mitchell v. State, 39 Ga. App. 100, 146 S.E. 333 (1929); People *ex rel.* Wallace v. Labrenz, 411 Ill. 618, 104 N.E.2d 769 (1952), *cert. denied,* 344 U.S. 824 (1952); Morrison v. State, 252 S.W.2d 97 (Mo. Ct. App. 1952); Stehr v. State, 92 Neb. 755, 139 N.W. 676 (1913); *In re Carstairs,* 115 N.Y.S.2d 314 (N.Y. City Dom. Rel. Ct. 1952); People v. Pierson, 176 N.Y. 201, 68 N.E. 243 (1903).

66. A recent Ohio case held that parents have a duty to educate their children in areas grossly neglected in the schools, such as sex education. The court reversed the conviction of a mother for contributing to the delinquency of her minor daughter by instructing her in the use of birth preventive measures, ruling that the conviction violated the mother's constitutionally guaranteed right of free speech. See State v. McLaughlin, 4 Ohio App. 2d 327, 212 N.E.2d 635 (1965).

suggest that parents may in fact be required to support their children in college.[67]

Morality and respect. Closely associated with the parental duty to nurture health and education is the parent's responsibility to teach his child respect and to provide him with a moral environment in which he may develop sound character. This responsibility imposes on a parent, whether natural, adoptive or foster, an obligation to train his child in differentiating "right" from "wrong," and to develop his child's conscience. It also requires a parent to teach by example, that is, to conduct himself in a manner that his child may emulate. Furthermore, although this duty is rarely articulated, the parent is expected to instill in his child respect for the parent as an individual and an authority figure, and, as the child matures, to implant in him respect for other persons and authorities in society. To assist in the development of respect for authority, courts give parents wide latitude in the exercise of their disciplinary powers. An underlying reason for this latitude is the thought that one way in which children learn to adjust to the mandates of society is through the proper use of discipline.

The moral conduct expected of parents is rarely defined in terms of specific religious dogma since, as individuals, parents are not required to follow the dictates of a particular religion, although the tenets of the dominant Judeo-Christian culture may influence the standards of parental conduct. The moral conduct necessary to fulfill parental responsibilities usually encompasses notions of "common decency, cleanliness of mind and body, honesty, truth-

67. Courts are presently split as to whether a college education is a necessity for which the father must provide. One Ohio court has held that a college education is not included among the "necessaries" which a parent is "legally required" to furnish a child. Ford v. Ford, 109 Ohio App. 495, 167 N.E.2d 787 (1959). But another Ohio court, in the same year, held that whether a college education is a necessary is a relative matter and "considering the progress of society and our nation's need for citizens educated in the humanities and sciences, a college education is necessary where the minor's ability and prospects justify it." Calogeras v. Calogeras, 163 N.E.2d 713, 720 (Ohio Juv. Ct. 1960). It has been stated that the most important factors in determining a father's liability for the expenses of a child's education are the father's ability to pay and the child's capacity for further education. Pincus v. Pincus, 197 A.2d 854 (D.C. Ct. App. 1964); Hoffman v. Hoffman, 210 A.2d 549 (D.C. Ct. App. 1965). See also Commonwealth v. Rice, 206 Pa. Super. 393, 213 A.2d 179 (1965); O'Brien v. Springer, 202 Misc. 210, 107 N.Y.S.2d 631 (Sup. Ct. 1951); Commonwealth v. Decker, 204 Pa. Super. 156, 203 A.2d 343 (1964).

fulness, and proper respect for established ideals and institutions." [68] A parent is free to choose the method by which his child will be inculcated with a sense of morality, and he need not utilize religious training for this purpose. In fact, courts have consistently stated that parents have no duty to give their children any religious training. Parents are, therefore, as free to ignore religion in their home as they are to rear their children in a particular faith.[69]

Relevance of the Goals of the Parent-Child Relationship to Child Custody Disputes

It is interesting to observe the reluctance of courts to set anything but minimum and often only vague standards when enforcing parental duties. Yet when courts are faced with the problem of establishing a new parent-child relationship, they seem to feel that the factors which are decisive in that context are radically different from those relevant in the administration of an existing relationship. Thus, in invoking "the best interests of the child" doctrine when choosing a custodian, courts might ignore the community expectations of parenthood which have been discussed above and make a disposition entirely inconsistent with our notions of parental responsibilities.

Examples of the courts' lack of specificity in enforcing parental duties are found in cases involving a child's financial security, where courts rarely say anything more than that the child must be provided with a decent standard of living, whatever that may be. It is also unclear whether the standard of the child's education should be set at a minimum level or at the highest potentialities of the child.[70] Questions about the extent of parental responsibilities are unanswered in other areas. For instance, what are the standards for furthering a child's physical and emotional well-being beyond requiring a parent to protect his child from immediate dangers? Must the parent take positive steps to ensure optimum good health?

68. See L v. N, 326 S.W.2d 751, 755 (Mo. 1959).
69. Courts have generally stated that it is outside the province of the law to regulate religious activities in the home. See, e.g., Abington School Dist. v. Schempp, 374 U.S. 203 (1963); Lynch v. Uhlenhopp, 248 Iowa 68, 78 N.W.2d 491 (1956); Wojnarowicz v. Wojnarowicz, 48 N.J. Super. 349, 137 A.2d 618 (Ch. 1958); Paolella v. Phillips, 27 N.Y. Misc. 763, 209 N.Y.S.2d 165 (Sup. Ct. 1960); People ex rel. Sisson v. Sisson, 271 N.Y. 285, 2 N.E.2d 660 (1936); Hackett v. Hackett, 78 Ohio L. Abs. 485, 150 N.E.2d 431 (Ct. App. 1958).
70. See note 67 supra.

Should the standard for physical health be set at seeking high athletic attainment? As to the emotional health of the child, should the standard be the ability to be stimulated, to form positive relationships with others, to participate effectively in group activities? Does a parent's responsibility to further a child's respect for others include promoting equal respect for persons of all races and religions and in all levels of the social strata? The lack of answers to these questions may be attributable to the courts' failure to consider them seriously.

Courts tend to be more specific when faced with questions of morality and religion, but their decisions are most frequently phrased in negative terms. In order to teach a child social responsibility, special ethical training is not necessary, nor need the spiritual aspects of life be encouraged by attending religious services.[71] Organized religions are not necessarily preferred over other ethical systems, including atheistic systems,[72] and one religious faith is not preferred over others,[73] although there seems to be a certain reluctance to favor individuals with unusual or unpopular views over those who follow Judeo-Christian beliefs. These decisions best illustrate the dichotomy which may exist between the goals of parenthood and the application of "the best interests of the child" doctrine to the initial selection of custodians. Parents in an existing relationship are permitted considerable discretion in the regulating of their child's moral development. However, in custodial dispositions, the courts may look to the religious, philosophical and political qualifications of the applicants and construe "the best interests of the child" so as to discriminate against persons adhering to certain, perhaps unorthodox, ideologies.

In a recent and now celebrated Iowa case, *Painter v. Bannister*,[74] Mr. Painter, the natural father of a seven-year-old boy, brought a writ of habeas corpus against Mr. and Mrs. Bannister, the child's maternal grandparents, to regain custody of the child. After the child's natural mother had died in 1963, his father had arranged for the grandparents to care for him in their home. A year later,

71. See, *e.g.*, Welker v. Welker, 24 Wis. 2d 570, 129 N.W.2d 134 (1964).
72. See, *e.g.*, Cory v. Cory, 70 Cal. App. 2d 563, 161 P.2d 385 (Dist. Ct. App. 1945).
73. See, *e.g.*, Angel v. Angel, 74 Ohio L. Abs. 531, 2 Ohio Op. 2d 136, 140 N.E.2d 86 (C.P. 1956).
74. 140 N.W.2d 152 (Iowa 1966), *petition for cert. filed,* 35 U.S.L. Week 3082 (U.S. Sept. 3, 1966) (No. 518).

the father remarried and asked the grandparents to return the child. They refused, and the father brought the present action. In 1965, the trial court granted the writ and awarded Mr. Painter custody of his son, but stayed execution of the judgment until the matter could be determined on appeal. In February 1966, the Iowa Supreme Court reversed the decision of the lower court, stating that the best interests of the child would be promoted by allowing the grandparents to retain custody.

The factors which the Iowa Supreme Court viewed as material in choosing the grandparents' home and way of life over the natural father's make it apparent that in child custody cases courts clearly move beyond the goals of parenthood discussed earlier. Because of their discretionary powers, the courts may in fact frustrate these goals. Note the Iowa court's language in describing and comparing the characteristics of the Painters and the Bannisters:

> We are not confronted with a situation where one of the contesting parties is not a fit or proper person. . . . As stated by the psychiatrist who examined Mr. Painter at the request of Bannisters' attorneys: "It is evident that there exists a large difference in ways of life and value systems between the Bannisters and Mr. Painter, but in this case, there is no evidence that psychiatric instability is involved. Rather, these divergent life patterns seem to represent alternative normal adaptations."
>
> It is not our prerogative to determine custody upon our choice of one of two ways of life within normal and proper limits and we will not do so. However, the philosophies are important as they relate to Mark and his particular needs.
>
> The Bannister home provides Mark with a stable, dependable, conventional, middle-class, middlewest background and an opportunity for a college education and profession, if he desires it. It provides a solid foundation and secure atmosphere. In the Painter home, Mark would have more freedom of conduct and thought with an opportunity to develop his individual talents. It would be more exciting and challenging in many respects, but romantic, impractical and unstable.

> The house in which Mr. Painter and his present wife live . . . "is a very old and beat up and lovely home. . . ." The large yard on a hill in the business district . . . is of uncut weeds and wild oats. The house "is not painted on the outside because I do not want it painted."

Mr. Painter is either an agnostic or atheist and has no concern for formal religious training. He has read a lot of Zen Buddhism and "has been very much influenced by it." Mrs. Painter is Roman Catholic. They plan to send Mark to a Congregational Church . . . on an irregular schedule. [The court also noted that Mr. Painter is a political liberal.]

These matters are not related as a criticism of Mr. Painter's conduct, way of life or sense of values. An individual is free to choose his own values, within bounds, which are not exceeded here. They do serve however to support our conclusion as to the kind of life Mark would be exposed to in the Painter household. We believe it would be unstable, unconventional, arty, Bohemian, and probably intellectually stimulating.

Were the question simply which household would be the most suitable in which to raise a child, we would have unhesitatingly chosen the Bannister home. We believe security and stability in the home are more important than intellectual stimulation in the proper development of a child.[75]

These excerpts indicate that "the best interests of the child" doctrine permits a court to camouflage its own values, provincial community values, or the interests of dominant local institutions. Absent guidelines, there is no method for evaluating the application of the doctrine. Review, then, becomes as unpredictable as the decision of the trial court because an abuse of discretion cannot be subjected to any discernible standards. Presently, appellate review of child custody cases serves either to reaffirm the values previously expressed by the lower court or, more rarely, to substitute the preferences of the appellate court for those of the lower court.

Summary

The main purpose of this discussion was to illustrate what one might call the minimum goals of parenthood. These goals, found in cases involving the supervision of the parent-child relationship, may be helpful in determining factors relevant for the purpose of choosing custodians. To summarize, the following appear to be the basic goals of the parent-child relationship: to maintain an orderly, stable and loyal relationship so that the government will not be required to intervene in that relationship; to provide a financial base

75. *Id*. at 154, 155, 156.

which will enable a child to mature into a healthy adult and to acquire the skills necessary to participate in and contribute to the economic processes of society; to nurture the child's physical and emotional safety, health and comfort; to provide a child with guidance and the opportunity for educational development; to teach a child respect for his parents, other authorities and human beings; and to train a child in social responsibilities.

Conclusions and Recommendations

The judicial role in child custody matters should be creative. The court should conduct an inquiry, independent of the agency's, to find the specific family unit best fitted for the child. This inquiry necessitates studying closely the familial patterns actually established. But this examination should not be exclusive. The court should widen the scope of inquiry beyond the immediate claimants. It should investigate alternative placements if it is not fully satisfied either with the qualifications of the persons claiming custody or with the immediate plans for the child. Further, courts should require concrete plans for a child rather than be forced into deciding a custody case on the basis of agency assumptions which may be unrealistic or influenced by factors that have no connection with the welfare of the child. According to this concept of the information-gathering stage of the judicial process, the trial court's approach in *Child Care* was not adequate. The court's failure to question the Agency's assumptions and plans for the child was serious. If it had directed a re-examination of the Agency's plans to place Laura with "neutral parents," it might have discovered that "neutrality" or a non-human environment is foreign to child placement policies.[76] In fact, a "neutral environment" could not have been found.[77]

76. In commenting on the *Child Care case,* Miss Lydia Rapoport has written: "We do know nothing can flourish in a neutral environment, least of all a human being. Whatever arguments and current re-evaluations there may be of the work of Spitz and Bowlby, they have convincingly demonstrated that "neutrality" or a non-human environment produces non-human beings and even physical atrophy. We do know, with a fair degree of certainty, that the greatest damage to healthy psychological development is instability—and the kinds of impediments that interfere with the process of identity formation. We also know that long-term separation (after the capacity for the development of object relationships—at whatever age various experts may decide this is) causes damage. Perhaps one cannot talk

There should be some limitations, however, on the judicial role. Abuse of judicial discretion, such as the arbitrary determination found in *Child Care,* should be checked. It is suggested that the use of judicial discretion be restricted by clarifying "the best interests of the child" doctrine in terms of the specific community goals of the parent-child relationship discussed above. That is, when choosing a custodian for a child, the following questions should form the basis for the court's investigation and decision:

1 What disposition will provide the child with a stable, orderly, and loyal parent-child relationship, thus lessening the likelihood that the state will have to interfere with the relationship in the future?
2 What disposition will furnish the child with the economic base necessary for him to become a useful and productive member of society?
3 What disposition will provide the child with an environment that will foster physical and emotional health?
4 What disposition will furnish the child with an environment that will encourage educational goals?
5 What disposition will provide the child with an environment that will promote equal respect for all human beings and will give him an opportunity to mature into a morally stable and responsible adult?

The purpose of framing "the best interests of the child" doctrine in terms of these general questions is to direct the scope of inquiry

of permanent damage because of the maleability of the human organism. However, I am convinced that the scarring process is permanent. All this, the child care agencies know very well. It would be impossible for foster parents to create a climate of neutrality and still carry out their parental obligations and role. It struck me that the child care agency, for whatever reasons, was confused regarding its central obligation: that of the well being of the child." Rapoport, "Safeguarding the Child's Best Interests: A Discussion" (unpublished paper presented at the American Orthopsychiatric Association Meeting in San Francisco on April 13, 1966).

77. The ironic sequel to *Child Care* was that the "neutral environment" suggested by the Agency was not the ultimate placement for Laura; she experienced multiple placements (almost predicted by Judge Froessel in his dissenting opinion, see note 24 *supra*). Within two years after the New York Court of Appeals' decision was rendered, Laura had been in two settings. The child was first placed with her natural mother and then in her maternal grandmother's home. See GOLDSTEIN & J. KATZ, THE FAMILY AND THE LAW 1033–34 (1965).

to particular operative factors serving community goals. Furthermore, the questions may furnish a checklist for organizing the amorphous data that is produced in child custody disputes.

Once the scope of judicial inquiry is narrowed, the next task is an evidentiary one. Courts should draw on the knowledge of various disciplines. Information gathered from fields such as psychiatry, psychology, sociology, social work, theology, and education may demonstrate the extent to which certain characteristics of the child and the claimants are important in achieving the objectives of the parent-child relationship. The behavioral sciences also can aid in answering perhaps more fundamental questions, namely, the effect of parental personalities and behavior on a child, the extent to which environment outside the family affects the child, and the impact on the child of both his maturation and his socialization. The result of such an approach will hopefully be that the child is the true beneficiary of a custodial dispute, not the parents and not the agencies.

20

The Role of the Social Worker in Family Court Decision-Making

The social worker in the Family Court is delegated two functions: the task of helping the troubled individual work his way out of his current dilemma and the task of contributing to the judicial decision-making through a process of assessment. While models of helping are being questioned and reexamined by the profession itself, the assessment task presents its own problem and requires clarification as to the nature of the social worker's professional role and expertise. The lack of clarity, or at minimum an inadequate statement of it, is no doubt among the critical constraints operative within the frequently alienated relationship between the social worker and lawyer.[1] The cases of *Kent v. United States* and *In re Gault* require a reexamination of roles and challenge the boundaries of expertise for the individuals who participate in social and legal decisions about children.

Juvenile and domestic relations courts are based upon the assumption that judicial decisions concerning children are to be made individually in the "child's best interests." The social worker's

ALBERT E. WILKERSON, D.S.W., is associate professor, Graduate School of Social Administration, Temple University, Philadelphia. O. DUANE KROEKER, M.S.W., is associate professor, School of Social Work, University of Missouri.

1. Sanford N. Katz, "The Lawyer and the Caseworker: Some Observations," *Social Casework* 42 (January 1961):10–15; Edward E. Mueller and Philip J. Murphy, "Communication Problems: Social Workers and Lawyers," *Social Work* 10 (April 1965):97–103; Homer W. Sloane, "The Juvenile Court: An Uneasy Partnership of Law and Social Work," *Smith College Studies in Social Work* 35 (June 1965):213–31; Homer W. Sloane, "Relationship of Law and Social Work," *Social Work* 12 (January 1967): 86–93.

tangible part in the decision-making process is his social study and the report of his findings. The social study has been perceived as an "investigative" effort, and the social report as an objective background "assessment" of the data in terms of community values and child welfare needs. The social report, frequently with a recommendation as to disposition, is available at the hearing to help the judge choose from the several possible alternatives available in any given case.

Shielded from standard procedures in direct and cross-examination, and given an edge by being in the employ of the court, conflict between the social worker and lawyer is an expected outcome. The lawyer neither fully grasps nor fully trusts the social worker's role, and he is unable to deal with the assumptions and content in the social report within the framework of his own professional mode of behavior—the adversary process. Further, since social work relies substantially upon other fields for its knowledge content, the matter of the sources and extent of the social worker's knowledge in the social and behavioral sciences raises questions in the mind of the lawyer and should, if it does not, raise questions for the social worker assigned to the case.

The literature on the role of the court social worker, for the most part, has not grasped the dynamic interplay inherent in functional roles and in which differing and even abrasive professional postures are natural. The purpose here is to define the role of the court social worker in terms that are more accurate in the reality of practice, functionally appropriate as to professional purpose and competence, and comprehensible to other disciplines operating within the Family Court setting. The proposed definition restores to the task of assessment a social representation and social accountability, so basic to the practice of "social" work. It centers social work expertise in role and role behaviors rather than in "knowledge." And it rejects the assumptions that a social report can or should be an objective account of a social situation, that the social worker remain nonpartisan, and that the social worker be treated in a hearing differently from other expert witnesses. For the sake of continuity, illustrations are drawn from the area of child custody. Role is a generic concept, and the definition is applicable to social work practice within the court setting in the "best interests" of any child, whatever his plight.

Representing Community Interest in Child Welfare

The social worker represents in a tangible, visible way the community's interest in child welfare. The wide agreement on inclusion of the social worker as a vital component of a court staff attests to the necessity for a social representative who stands for certain values and norms in decisions about children.

The social worker, in this stance, does not represent the particular child, but rather he represents professionally the community's concern, investment, expectations, and desire for well-being as to the child welfare problem reflected in the case at hand. He stands for the human need of every child to be related to a permanent unit of "significant others." And he stands for the social necessity for sound child welfare services as a means to enhance the possibilities for developing a more viable society.

The question is raised when one speaks so sweepingly of "society" and "community" as to just who they are that the social worker represents and from which segment of the population he draws his child-welfare standards. The question, while real, is largely academic. It is unfortunate, but apparently true, that in many instances child welfare "standards" simply mean the minimum that the child's immediate community will tolerate at a given moment. Yet, despite this reality, the standards become the maximized level that can be reached at that point in time through a representation of the societal consensus that every child has the right to the fullest possible input for his individual needs. As society's representative, the social worker must prod the community itself to give shape and content to the very thing it says it wants, but under competing priorities has not sufficiently provided. It is society's best intent, actualized or not, that is given life and vitality through professional social work practice. Thus, the social worker holds up a standard, and, in holding it, moves the intent toward a higher level of fulfillment.

The Family Court exists, together with other child welfare resources, because the family as a social institution is unable to meet all the demands in child-rearing and problem-solving. The organizational arrangement of the court is designed to accommodate for this lack, and it is not by accident that certain institutional roles are represented. The specialized function represented by each professional, and expressed in defined procedures and protocol, prompts differing behaviors within any organizational arrangement, as specializations combine to carry out the basic organizational purpose.[2] The social worker and the lawyer each bring to the case situation a perception and a value priority peculiar to their professions. This does not mean that one is more concerned than the other about the needs of the child. It means only that they operate out of assumptions and orientations that are not identical and which at points are likely to be at variance as opinions as to "need" differ and role tension is heightened. Specialized functions introduce dynamic differences, and these differences should be valued as the matrix from which solid judicial decisions can evolve. The suggestion, abundant in the literature, that the social worker and lawyer need to learn how to collaborate better and come to a consensus more readily around mutual cases—as though working within the model of the clinical "team approach" to problem-solving—is neither realistic nor desirable. Instead, it is out of the understanding of the differences in role, and clarity in understanding the boundaries of the other's expertise, that ground rules can be drawn and working relationships be most productive.

As for the lawyer's role, only in recent decades has the concept of the rights of the child as a person moved toward replacing the concept of the child as parental property. A perception of children as parental possessions denies their rights as individuals. And a perception of them as subjects of litigation, however humane the concern, is an underestimation of the significance of the proceedings for the future of any given child. Judge Hansen of the Milwaukee Court has stressed the necessity for a definition of the legal status of children in separation and divorce cases as "interested and affected parties to the action, with rights that are to be determined and defended. . . ."[3] That the child himself needs legal representation is a conclusion that emerges naturally out of a status of party to the action. In disputed custody cases, court appointment of a lawyer to represent the child as *guardian ad litem* appears to have been a positive experiment in several states. Judge Hansen

2. Amitai Etzioni (ed.), *Modern Organizations* (Englewood Cliffs, New Jersey: Prentice-Hall, Inc., 1964), pp. 105–7.

3. Robert W. Hansen, "The Role and Rights of Children in Divorce Actions," *Journal of Family Law* 6 (1966):1–14.

takes it a step further in anticipating that "the day will come when legal representation of children's interests will be required in all divorce cases." [4]

The working relationship between the social worker and lawyer, clarified through sharpening of functional difference, can be made even more meaningful through disagreements that call for collaboration with other disciplines such as medicine, psychology, and psychiatry.

This kind of approach to child custody necessitates a clearer social-policy statement of children as individuals. Rights must be translated into law and better child welfare resources. The cumulation of uniform and more specific statutes for children, guaranteed through legal and social services, will be their only real "bill of rights."

Integrating Knowledge in Regard to a Particular Child

The social worker's role of representing professionally the community's interest and investment in sound policy and practice in child welfare becomes specific as he moves to fulfill an assessment task in a given case. Here his role is defined through his *integrating knowledge in regard to a particular child,* and not as competence in making clinical judgments.

The practice of a profession is generally taken to represent the application of a body of knowledge to a particular human condition. This, of course, has not been the line of development in social work, a profession in which theory has emerged from practice. With the social work role not fully comprehended as the essence of his expertise, it is not strange that the social worker has been imputed a high level of expertise in the social and behavioral sciences. The profession itself created a further distortion, attempting to incorporate psychoanalytic knowledge, but knowing it only cursorily and without possessing appropriate methodology to make it appropriate and consistently meaningful.

Assessment of a case on clinical judgments and social science theory is substantially an intellectual exercise. For example, in assessing the child's needs and best interests in custody petitions

4. Robert W. Hansen, "Guardians Ad Litem in Divorce and Custody Cases," *Journal of Family Law* 4 (1964):181–84. See reprint in this collection.

involving fit parents, the critical issue generally arises around either the child's mothering needs or concern about development of psychosexual identity. Unfortunate biases are built into judicial decision through psychoanalytic and "scientific" influences which have given some assumptions a sacred quality.

During the first quarter of this century, the father's property right to his children was replaced with the presumption that a father and mother have equal claim to custody in cases of separation or divorce. The premise that joint and equal guardianship is natural to both parents seems to have been a result of the recognition of the rights of women. The emergence of women's rights coincided with the introduction of psychoanalytic thought in the United States and its influence upon conceptions of child development. In the succeeding decades, the psychological significance of the mother in the child-rearing process has given her a first priority in custody decisions. The declared prima facie rights of separated or divorced parents to equal custody potential is negated by common practice. Thus, "equality," as recognized in the right of petition, and "equality" in the probability of judicial response to the claims, are in no way synonymous.

The bias in awarding babies and young children to the mother is based on the belief that their "best interests" require natural mothering. This belief not only gives recognition to the psychological implications, but implies also support for a perception of the mother as the stable factor in the continuity of a family unit. While the child's need for warm and consistent mothering is well-substantiated, one cannot leap to the conclusion that it is best provided by the natural mother. Further, the enthusiasm for the mother's role as the prime psychological stability element in family living has not been validated in research on the fatherless family. The father's custody plan for a young child should provide for a suitable mother substitute. His provision might have within it the possibility of creating more of a semblance of a viable family unit than could be effected by the mother who anticipates heading her own household.

The age and sex of the child also become determining factors through focus upon psychological theories as to the parental function in shaping the child's sex identity and social role. Here again, the decision for maternal custody is weighted, except perhaps in cases involving the older teen-age child who expresses strong preference for residence with the father. Unfortunately, the significance of the father to healthy child development in the nondysfunctional family has not been sufficiently emphasized and researched. Studies on the one-parent family point to the distortions created by the father's absence but do not shed light on his contribution as a carrier of the essentials for parenthood. But whatever the comparative merits for parenthood existing in the mother and father roles, serious consideration should be given to moving away from linking the age and sex of the child to psychological and social theories of role model. As in the instance of preferential awards of children of "tender age" to the mother, this practice involves generalization around a single variable. It does not take fully into account the possibilities in hereditary and cultural determinants, as well as the impact of socialization models outside the family. The best interests of both the child and society can well be transmitted through a focus upon the actualization of the humanity and the uniqueness of the child, rather than upon his acquiring predetermined psychological and social behavior patterns. Herzog and Sudia capture this in their suggestion: "A more important consideration may be the child's conception of what it means to be a human being and what to expect from and offer to other human beings." [5]

The equal rights of parents to unbiased outcome is a prerequisite for all other guarantees that an adjudication will be made solely for the welfare of the child. Custody decisions that are biased for or against the mother or father are based upon a priori assumptions that need experimentation and testing. In the meantime, decisions must continue to be made. Present knowledge and rational thought would suggest that the "maternal" versus "paternal" not be viewed as a central issue in decision-making but only as a single variable among many variables in any given case.

Although the expertise of the social work practitioner lies in his role and role behavior, and not in a specific body of knowledge, it is obvious that certain "knowledge" must apply if he is to act intelligently. Two areas of knowledge are necessary for the court social worker in his task of assessment. First is an "understanding of the phenomenon served," as Smalley [6] phrases it, and second is

5. Elizabeth Herzog and Cecelia E. Sudia, "Fatherless Homes: A Review of Research," *Children* 5 (September-October 1968):180.

6. Ruth Elizabeth Smalley, *Theory for Social Work Practice* (New York: Columbia University Press, 1967), p. 134.

the knowledge of the community resource network. Understanding the phenomenon does imply a basic grounding in research findings about the problem and how these findings are useful in the decision-making process in a particular case.

In addition to this kind of basic "understanding," there is available to the social worker knowledge of what happens to children when certain welfare alternatives are chosen. The validity of this knowledge rests in decades of cumulative social work experience gradually being subjected to empirical verification. In the absence of full verification, the social worker can defend his assessment on a case basis, not unlike the lawyer's method of documentation through precedents.

Also appropriate to the social work purpose in child welfare is a body of knowledge that concerns growth and development needs and patterns of the individual at every age. Not only are there specific developmental tasks of a child at a given age, culturally defined, but there is within every child a growth potential of vital social import. The social worker is responsible for knowing human growth and development patterns, for assessing the child's needs as against current institutional arrangements for meeting child welfare needs, and for standing for the belief in the particular child's untapped potential.

The social worker should be expected to have knowledge and skill in assessing specialized needs of children, such as those of the socially disadvantaged, the emotionally disturbed and the mentally retarded, and the child who is neglected or battered. This is especially valuable when the immediate dilemma has developed out of a basic problem which the parent has not recognized or cannot admit. The parent of the retarded child may say in all honesty, for example, that the child is "not retarded, he's just a little bit slow." The parent of the emotionally disturbed child may perceive him as "head-strong," "undisciplined," or just plain "bad." The neglectful parent may be so engulfed in a struggle with personal inadequacies and limited resources that the condition and consequences of neglect are not apparent to him. And the denial and parental collusion in cases of the battered child were known to social workers in protective agencies long before the medical observations and roentgen studies brought the child's circumstance to national attention.

As the social worker brings to bear on the assessment his understanding of child welfare needs and the impact of community resources, the cumulated data on the results of certain kinds of decisions made "in behalf of" children, and the clinical judgments of other professional disciplines, he evolves a social-service statement of the needs of the child as they relate to the contestants.

Enhancing the Potential for Positive Outcome

There is probably no other client situation with which social workers and lawyers come into contact that is more filled with raw self-interest, potential for open conflict among parties concerned, and a will of clients to subdue each other, as is child custody and the associated problems of visitation and support. Entering a custody petition or drawing up a custody agreement in separation or divorce cases opens a scene of action for intensifying old disharmonies, justifying one's claim of innocence in the marriage breakdown, rewarding the less guilty party and punishing the more guilty, and proving to one's self, to the other person, and to the immediate community the worth of the one parent in contrast to the other. The child, whose life is to be shaped in no small way by the outcome, can easily be the object of the conflict rather than party to the action, or even the subject for whom society, the parents, and the court avow that his "best interests" are the sole consideration.

The charge to the social worker in the decision-making around custody, as noted, lies in his study of the social data, or child-care plans, of each parent, and an assessment of each plan. The most important piece of data within the parental plan is the parent himself, and crucial to the social report is an evaluation of his capacity for parenting.

Immediately evident is that in determining and assessing parental "plans," the task of the social worker goes beyond gathering and ordering data that will provide the judge with background material upon which to make a sound decision. The social report is by nature a value judgment, a statement of professional preference. And it carries the biases natural to the situation, those stemming from assumptions both in the field of child welfare and social work practice and from the social worker's own values and perspectives as a person.

Thus, the thrust of the study and report is clearly partisan, and recently it is being recognized as such.[7] The social worker's

7. LeRoy G. Schultz, "The Adversary Process, the Juvenile Court and the Social Worker," *UMKC Law Review* 36 (1968):288–302.

task in assessment is to present a point of view. There is no way to report "objective social data" in these cases, and even so, hard facts are not the stuff out of which decisions about children are made. The role of the social worker as the institutional child welfare spokesman, and his presentation of a partisan statement, need to be conceptualized more clearly and recognized as such by the parents, lawyers, and judge. There is no priority in arriving at agreement with the points of view of the lawyers or with the judge's biases, since each is also expressing a point of view as to how the child's needs can best be met and his interests served.

No matter how rational and sound the custody decision, it can be only in the child's best interest if both parents choose to make it so. And if the decision solves no more than the right to day-to-day care of the child, the results of a child with divided loyalties and a victorious parent versus a defeated parent lead to destructive consequences. The task of assessing carries with it the responsibility to help the parents and the child with the impact of the assessment, to take in the issues and varying points of view, and to anticipate the aftermath of the alternative finally selected.

A helping process, then, is built into the assessment task and through it the social worker *enhances the potential for positive outcome.* Discussion with each parent as to the child's needs, his capacity to meet those needs, and his projections emerging out of hurt and retaliation help him to make his purpose and focus at one with the court—arriving at a child-centered decision. This is not easy for parents to do, and it requires all the skill in human relationship that the social worker can muster. Throughout the helping-assessing task, the possibility of the parents' putting the child's interest above their own is increased if they understand that the social worker is not for or against either of them as individuals, and that he is not the only advocate for the child's interests. But rather, he is charged with helping to make a decision which is child-centered and socially based, and for which he is socially accountable.

Conclusion

The social worker's professional identity in the Family Court is formulated by the institutional interest which he represents—namely, the community's investment in the family and child welfare, and by its concern for each child as an individual in his own right. Operating within the differing norms and institutional context of the judiciary as a host-setting, the social worker's role is oriented from a framework of value priorities which requires his professional behavior at times to be in sharp variance with the more pervasive legal roles dominant in the judicial process. While it is characteristic of organizational behavior to minimize role tension in order to enhance organizational interests and goals, the very requirement of the social worker's presence with a professional task different from that of the lawyer should form the basis for perceiving potential role conflict in essentially positive rather than negative terms. Role conflict should be viewed in its potentially constructive and creative aspects. The implicit dynamics represent at least an approximation of the adversary process which, in undiluted form, is not likely to be the most useful procedure in arriving at the child's best interests. The critical dimensions of the social worker's functional role in the assessment task in a Family Court derive from his representation of society's interest in the developmental needs of children, as a bearer of the community's humanistic norms within a problem-solving context, and as a broker of community resources in child welfare.

21

In Re Gault:
Children Are People

On June 15, 1964, fifteen-year-old Gerald Gault was committed to an Arizona state industrial training school for the remainder of his minority [1] because he and a friend, Ronnie Lewis, had telephoned a Mrs. Cook a few weeks earlier and made mildly lewd remarks to her.[2] Shocked by the boys' remarks, Mrs. Cook called the Gila County, Arizona, sheriff who promptly traced the telephone call, apprehended Gerald and Ronnie and took them to the Gila County juvenile detention center.[3] When a probation officer, Mr. Flagg, questioned the boys, they admitted making the telephone call; each blamed the other.[4] Probation officer Flagg detained the boys at the center pending a juvenile court hearing.

Later that afternoon, Gerald's mother returned home from work to discover that the authorities had taken her son to the juvenile center.[5] She went to Juvenile Hall where Flagg explained that he was holding Gerald for making a lewd telephone call and that the juvenile court judge would consider Gerald's case at a hearing the next day.[6]

Juvenile Court Judge McGhee decided to commit Gerald to the state industrial school after two hearings—the jurisdictional and adjudicatory hearing on June 9th and the dispository hearing on

JANET FRIEDMAN STANSBY, LL.B., is a member of the firm of Morrison, Foerster, Holloway, Clinton & Clark, San Francisco. This article is reprinted with permission of the *California Law Review* and Fred B. Rothman & Company, from the *California Law Review* 55(1967):1204–18.

1. *In re* Gault, 387 U.S. 1 (1967).
2. Record at 79, *In re* Gault, 387 U.S. 1 (1967) [hereinafter cited as Record].
3. 387 U.S. at 4–5.
4. Record at 45, 50–51.
5. *Id*. at 29.
6. *Id*.

June 15th.[7] Gerald, his mother, and probation officers Flagg and Henderson attended both hearings. In addition, Gerald's older brother was present at the first hearing; Ronnie Lewis and both boys' fathers were present at the second.[8] Mrs. Cook did not attend either hearing.[9] Neither Gerald nor his parents were represented by counsel at either hearing, and no one told them that they had a right to counsel. Judge McGhee questioned Gerald at both hearings but did not tell him that he could refuse to answer questions.[10] Because the court kept no record of either hearing, it is impossible to determine exactly what any of the participants said. Gerald and his parents claimed that although Gerald admitted dialing Mrs. Cook's number and asking if the person who answered was Mrs. Cook, he denied making any of the lewd remarks.[11] Judge McGhee testified that Gerald admitted making some of the less serious remarks.[12] No one disputed that at the end of the first hearing Mrs. Gault had asked the judge whether he would commit Gerald to the industrial school, and the judge had replied, "No, . . . I will think it over." [13]

Gerald returned home on June 11th or 12th, and on the same day probation officer Flagg sent Mrs. Gault a note informing her that the court would hold "further hearings on Gerald's delinquency" on June 15th.[14] At that hearing, Judge McGhee decided to commit Gerald to the industrial school. Because Arizona does not provide for appellate review of juvenile court decisions,[15] Gerald and his parents attacked Judge McGhee's action by applying for a writ of habeas corpus. An Arizona Superior Court found Gerald's commitment proper, and the Arizona Supreme Court affirmed that judgment. The United States Supreme Court noted probable jurisdiction of the Gaults' appeal [16] and then reversed the Arizona court.[17]

Gerald and his parents argued before the Arizona courts and the United States Supreme Court that they did not receive due

7. Brief for Appellee at 9, *In re* Gault, 387 U.S. 1 (1967).
8. 387 U.S. at 5, 7.
9. *Id.*
10. *Id.* at 43–44.
11. *In re* Gault, 99 Ariz. 181, 184–85, 407 P.2d 760, 763 (1965).
12. Record at 57–59.
13. *Id.* at 31; Brief for Appellant at 5–6, *In re* Gault, 387 U.S. 1 (1967).
14. 387 U.S. at 6.
15. *Id.* at 8.
16. 384 U.S. 997 (1966).
17. *In re* Gault, 387 U.S. 1 (1967).

process in the juvenile court hearings because they were not accorded certain specific rights guaranteed to adults charged with crime: (1) the right to counsel; (2) the privilege against self-incrimination; (3) the right to confront and cross-examine witnesses; (4) the right to formal, timely notice of the hearings, charges and possible consequences; (5) the right to an appeal; and (6) the right to a record.[18]

Although the Arizona Supreme Court held that juveniles charged with delinquency are entitled to due process, it defined juvenile due process as encompassing fewer procedural safeguards than those afforded adults charged with criminal conduct. The Arizona court held that juveniles do not have a right to be represented by counsel; that the juvenile's parents do have a right to retain counsel but not to have counsel appointed; that the juvenile court judge need not inform a child appearing before him that he may remain silent; and that although both parents and child have a right to notice of the charges and of hearings, the informal notice probation officer Flagg gave Mrs. Gault was sufficient to satisfy that requirement.[19] The court declined to decide whether a juvenile has a right to confront and cross-examine witnesses because Gerald did not deny the charges and "the relevancy of confrontation arises only where the charges are denied." [20] The Arizona court affirmed its prior holding that there is no right to an appeal from a juvenile court adjudication and consequently held that the juvenile court need not record its proceedings.[21]

The United States Supreme Court agreed only with the Arizona court's holding that a juvenile is entitled to due process; it disagreed completely with the Arizona court's definition of juvenile due process. In a lengthy, wide-ranging opinion by Justice Fortas, the court held that: (1) a juvenile is entitled to timely and complete notice of the charges against him, and notice at the time of the first hearing is not timely; (2) a juvenile whom the state may commit to an institution is entitled to the assistance of counsel, and the state must provide counsel for indigent juveniles; (3) a juvenile is entitled to a warning that he need not answer questions; and (4) a juvenile is entitled to confront and cross-examine witnesses against him.[22] The majority opinion did not

18. *Id*. at 10.
19. *In re* Gault, 99 Ariz. 181, 189–91, 407 P.2d 760, 766–68 (1965).
20. *Id*. at 191, 407 P.2d at 768.
21. *Id*. at 192, 407 P.2d at 768.
22. 387 U.S. at 33, 41, 55–57.

decide whether the juvenile is entitled to an appeal or to a record of the court proceedings.[23]

The *Gault* case raises problems concerning the procedure a juvenile court should employ during the adjudicatory stage of a juvenile hearing. Generally, juvenile courts have jurisdiction over children who have acquired the status of delinquency by violating a state or municipal statute. The purpose of the first stage of the juvenile court hearing, the jurisdictional or adjudicatory stage, is to find facts. The judge must determine that the child committed the act alleged in order to find him a delinquent subject to the juvenile court's jurisdiction. At the second, dispositional stage, the judge decides what the state should do with the child. The Gaults challenged neither the juvenile court judge's dispositional decision nor the procedures used in reaching that decision. Because they challenged only the procedures he followed at the adjudicatory stage of the hearing, the United States Supreme Court limited its opinion to a consideration of those procedures.[24] This Comment will do likewise.

Pre-Gault Juvenile Court Systems

Individualized Justice

The Arizona court's narrow interpretation of juvenile due process was dictated by its concept of juvenile court philosophy:

> [J]uvenile courts do not exist to punish children for their transgressions against society. The juvenile court stands in the position of a protecting parent rather than a prosecutor. . . . The aim of the court is to provide individualized justice for children.[25]

Individualized justice is a recurring theme in literature dealing with the juvenile court system and in appellate cases reviewing juvenile court decisions.[26] Juvenile courts stress individuation

23. *Id.* at 58.
24. *Id.* at 13.
25. *In re* Gault, 99 Ariz. 181, 188, 407 P.2d 760, 765 (1965).
26. *See, e.g., In re* Holmes, 379 Pa. 599, 109 A.2d 523 (1954), *cert. denied,* 348 U.S. 973 (1955); Commonwealth v. Fisher, 213 Pa. 48, 62 A. 198 (1905); Alexander, *Constitutional Rights in Juvenile Court,* in JUSTICE FOR THE CHILD 82 (M. Rosenheim ed. 1962); Mack, *The Juvenile Court,* 23 HARV. L. REV. 104 (1909); Skolar & Tenney, Jr., *Attorney Representation in Juvenile Court,* 4 J. FAMILY LAW 77 (1964).

almost to the exclusion of justice. Individuation means that treatment depends on what a person is, not on what he has done. Juvenile statutes typically define as delinquent a child who has done no more than violate a municipal ordinance; hence, almost any child may be subject to juvenile court jurisdiction.[27] Society fines an adult who disobeys a littering ordinance but may treat a juvenile who violates the same ordinance in exactly the same way it treats a juvenile who commits murder.[28]

The legal justification for individual justice is found in the doctrine of parens patriae: Towards its wayward children the state acts not as governor but as parent.[29] Because a child who engages in delinquent conduct needs care, the state, as a loving parent, intervenes to care for him. It is obviously in the child's best interest that the state care for him and cure him of the problems which resulted in his delinquency. Therefore, procedural formality should not block a finding of delinquency. The judge should admit any evidence which will aid him because he is acting as a parent attempting to determine whether the child needs treatment. The child should have to answer questions, because his answers will help the judge to make that determination. A lawyer is not necessary to protect the child because there is nothing from which he needs protection. A finding of delinquency brings the child beneficial, rather than harmful, results.

In a similar vein, the parens patriae argument justifies denying juveniles most of the rights guaranteed adults accused of crime.[30] But remove the keystone and the arch collapses. If juveniles in fact receive no more than custodial care and treatment,[31] if the state incarcerates them and deprives them of their liberty but does not treat them, then they deserve the procedural protections afforded adults. Most juvenile statutes, however, seem to accept the parens patriae doctrine and mold the procedural safeguards of determining delinquency around the presumption that adequate

27. Paulsen, *Fairness to the Juvenile Offender,* 41 MINN. L. REV. 547, 555 (1957); *see, e.g.,* CAL. WELF. & INST'NS CODE § 602 (West 1966).

28. *See,* CAL. WELF. & INST'NS CODE §§ 725, 731 (West 1966).

29. *See, e.g.,* Paulsen, *supra* note 27, at 549.

30. *See, e.g.,* the Arizona court's discussion of juvenile court philosophy in its *Gault* opinion. *In re* Gault, 99 Ariz. 181, 407 P.2d 760 (1965).

31. *See* Sheridan, *Gaps in State Programs for Juvenile Offenders,* 9 CHILDREN 211–12 (1962): "With few exceptions, the 'treatment' programs . . . go little beyond meeting needs for the care of children away from their own homes, some not even this far."

facilities for treatment are available. Courts accept the lack of procedural regularity, assuming that the state will act in the child's best interests but not asking what rehabilitative facilities are available.[32]

In the name of individualized justice and its keystone, the rehabilitative ideal, one appellate court upheld a juvenile court's finding of delinquency based on a policeman's claim that an adult's confession implicated the juvenile in a robbery. Although the adult later retracted the part of his confession incriminating the boy, the appellate court held that because the juvenile judge could believe the confession rather than the retraction, he had sufficient evidence to find the boy delinquent.[33] Another court upheld a fourteen-year-old's commitment for the duration of his minority because he made a "bomb scare" telephone call to the police.[34] A third court affirmed a juvenile court's waiver of jurisdiction over a boy who was not represented by counsel in the juvenile proceedings.[35] The boy did not attempt to persuade the juvenile court to retain jurisdiction because he mistakenly thought he had a perfect defense to the murder charge which he would face in adult court. The court held that the failure to appoint a lawyer did not constitute a denial of due process because denial of counsel in the juvenile court did not deny the boy his day in court; however, it might have meant that the day was in criminal rather than juvenile court, and that a guilty verdict could have severe consequences. A lawyer would have understood the inadequacy of the boy's defense and might have been able to persuade the juvenile court not to waive jurisdiction. In all of these cases, the state, claiming to protect a child, did not afford the procedural protections which it would have had to grant an adult in like circumstances.

Due Process and Equal Protection for Juveniles

Two practical flaws have marred the ideal of individualized justice for juvenile offenders; both concern rehabilitation, the announced

32. *See, e.g., In re* Gault, 99 Ariz. 181, 188–89, 407 P.2d 760, 765–66 (1965).
33. *In re* Holmes, 379 Pa. 599, 606, 109 A.2d 523, 526 (1954), *cert. denied,* 348 U.S. 973 (1955).
34. State *ex rel* Toney v. Mills, 144 W. Va. 257, 107 S.E.2d 772 (1959).
35. People v. Dotson, 46 Cal. 2d 891, 299 P.2d 875 (1956).

goal of individualized justice. First, juvenile facilities do not adequately perform the training, counseling, and guidance functions which the rehabilitative goal requires.[36] Second, because rehabilitation has also become the goal of adult penology, it no longer distinguishes the juvenile system from the adult system.[37]

The first flaw raises a due process issue. The Constitution prohibits a state from depriving a person of liberty without due process of law.[38] Due process means different things in different contexts. In proceedings to determine whether a person has committed a criminal act and so may be deprived of his liberty for punitive purposes, due process demands strict procedural safeguards. On the other hand, in proceedings to determine whether a person is in need of care and treatment and should be deprived of liberty so the state will be better able to treat him, due process may require fewer procedural safeguards.[39] If the juvenile delinquent actually receives custodial care rather than treatment, the state may have difficulty justifying lax procedural safeguards in the name of treatment.

The second flaw raises an equal protection problem. The state accords an adult offender extensive procedural protection but denies similar protection to a juvenile who the state claims committed the same offense. However, the Constitution demands some rational basis to support differences in treatment not reflecting differences in the nature of conduct.[40] Originally, advocates of the juvenile court system distinguished the adult who, if guilty, was punished from the juvenile offender who, if guilty, was rehabilitated.[41] However, because one of the major goals of current adult penology is rehabilitation through treatment,[42] a rehabilitative disposition no longer differentiates an adjudication of delinquency from a finding of criminal guilt. The equal protection clause,

36. *See* Sheridan, *supra* note 31.
37. "The cold, hard truth, however, is that the theory of punishment and retribution has long since played but a minor role in enlightened criminal courts, and they, too, have adopted as their major purpose treatment and rehabilitation." Quick, *Constitutional Rights in the Juvenile Court,* 12 How. L.J. 76, 78–79 (1966).
38. U.S. CONST. amend. XIV, § 1.
39. Rouse v. Cameron, 373 F.2d 451, 453 & n.9 (D.C. Cir. 1966), dealing with the right to treatment of persons incarcerated after having been found not guilty by reason of insanity in a criminal trial.
40. *See* Yick Wo v. Hopkins, 118 U.S. 356, 373–74 (1886).
41. *See* Mack, *The Juvenile Court, supra* note 26, at 106–09.
42. Quick, *supra* note 37, at 78–79.

therefore, seems to require that the state either grant a juvenile charged with delinquency the same procedural safeguards granted an adult accused of criminal conduct or find some distinction sufficient to justify different procedures. That the child is younger and less knowledgeable suggests that he should receive more procedural safeguards; there seems to be no difference which justifies a lower standard of procedural protections for juveniles than for adults.

The Juvenile's Admissions

Most juveniles admit the delinquency petition's factual allegations [43] and many appellate courts treat the admission as a waiver of rights which they might otherwise grant the juvenile. For example, courts have held that having admitted the facts the juvenile need not confront the witnesses against him; [44] that because he does not dispute the facts, the juvenile does not need a lawyer; [45] that because he does not contest the allegations, neither he nor his parents need time to consider the allegations against him and decide what response to make.[46] Moreover, because by admitting the facts the juvenile has already incriminated himself, he has no occasion to invoke a privilege against self-incrimination. Unfortunately, the courts have not recognized that the admission which results in denying so many procedural rights may itself result from denying other rights and from a system which gives so much discretion [47] to the juvenile court judge. The Supreme Court's decision in the *Gault* case will obviate some of the problems arising from admissions, because the judge now must tell the child that he need not answer questions. In addition, the Court implied that state officials must give juveniles the warnings which *Miranda v. Arizona* [48] requires officials to give adults.[49]

It has been suggested that individualized justice requires an in-

43. Judge Paul W. Alexander, Judge of the Court of Common Pleas, Lucas County, Ohio, estimated that 99% admit involvement. Alexander, *Constitutional Rights in Juvenile Court,* 46 A.B.A.J. 1206, 1208 (1960).

44. *In re* Gault, 99 Ariz. 181, 191, 407 P.2d 760, 768 (1965).

45. People v. Dotson, 46 Cal. 2d 891, 895, 299 P.2d 875, 877 (1956).

46. *In re* Gault, 99 Ariz. 181, 190, 407 P.2d 760, 767 (1965).

47. The judge has substantive as well as procedural discretion. See discussion following note 58 *infra.*

48. 384 U.S. 436 (1966).

49. 387 U.S. at 55. *Cf. In re* Buros, 249 A.C.A. 61, 57 Cal. Rptr. 124 (1967).

formal hearing in which the judge and juvenile work together for the child's best interests free from the psychological pressures of a public trial.[50] However, because the judge and the juvenile may disagree about whether commitment is in the child's best interest, the two are necessarily adverse. It is central to Anglo-American legal theory that the state should not force a person to prove his adversary's case, and for this reason alone the state should not be permitted to pressure the juvenile into making admissions.

Even if the child knows that he need not answer questions, he may sense that the judge will react adversely if he does not cooperate, and the judge will be likely to commit an uncooperative child to a state training school. If the child cooperates, on the other hand, the judge may place him on probation. The atmosphere in which the judge questions the child is highly coercive: The juvenile rarely has a lawyer to advise him;[51] his parents are usually poor and often foreign-born,[52] knowing as little as their child about judicial procedure and as impressed as he by the juvenile judge's power. A person subjected to interrogation in such an atmosphere must clearly understand his rights if they are to retain substance.[53]

The child's admission has the same effect as a plea of guilty to a criminal charge. The adult who pleads guilty also waives many procedural rights [54] also in hope of receiving a more favorable disposition. But the adult is guaranteed a lawyer to advise him [55] and therefore knows that he need not plead guilty. Furthermore, there is a limit on the sentence which the court can impose upon the adult if it finds him guilty. That limit turns on the nature of the act of which the court finds him guilty, and the prosecution has to prove he committed a specific and clearly defined act. The juvenile, on the other hand, has no lawyer to guide him. In addition, he knows that no matter how minor his wrongful act,

50. See Paulsen, *supra* note 29, at 559-62.
51. Skoler & Tenney, Jr., *supra* note 26, at 80–81, report that 59% of the responses to a survey made by the National Council of Juvenile Court Judges stated that attorneys appeared in 0%–5% of juvenile court delinquency cases; 22% reported representation in 6%–10% of juvenile court delinquency cases.
52. See Paulsen, *Juvenile Courts, Family Courts, and the Poor Man*, 54 CALIF. L. REV. 694, 695–98 (1966).
53. *Cf.* Miranda v. Arizona, 384 U.S. 436 (1966).
54. *See* 22 C.J.S. *Criminal Law* § 424(1) (1961).
55. Escobedo v. Illinois, 378 U.S. 478 (1964).

the judge can commit him until he reaches the age of twenty-one. In fact, he knows that the judge need not find he committed any specific acts but only that he is "in danger of leading an . . . immoral life," [56] or becoming "habitually delinquent." [57] It is certainly not surprising that few juveniles dispute the factual allegations against them. It seems unfair to coerce the child to admit the facts and then to claim that his admission waives many procedural rights.

The Specific Rights Claimed in the Gault Case

The juvenile court philosophy, the system's failure to rehabilitate delinquents, and the coercive nature of juvenile court questioning are inherent in the juvenile court system as it exists today. Because each procedural right which the Supreme Court considered in *Gault* is different, each requires separate consideration. The right to counsel, without which all other rights are meaningless, will receive first consideration.

Right to Counsel

The last few years have seen the criminal defendant's right to counsel vastly extended from the literal language of the sixth amendment that an accused may retain counsel in his defense. Because counsel's advice is so important to a fair trial, the right to counsel for indigents now includes the right to have the court appoint counsel.[58] To make the right meaningful, the police must warn a criminal suspect of his right to have attorney's advice during pretrial custodial interrogation.[59] On the other hand, before *Gault,* few states required that juveniles charged with delinquency be advised of their right to counsel or provided for appointment of counsel.[60] The Arizona court went so far as to imply that the juvenile did not have the right to retain counsel, although his parents did.[61]

A lawyer assigned to represent a juvenile will help the court

56. *E.g.,* CAL. WELF. & INST'NS CODE § 601 (West 1966).
57. *E.g., Id.*
58. Gideon v. Wainwright, 372 U.S. 335 (1963).
59. Miranda v. Arizona, 384 U.S. 436 (1966).
60. *In re* Gault, 387 U.S. 1, 37 n.63 (1967).
61. *See In re* Gault, 99 Ariz. 181, 407 P.2d 760 (1965).

ascertain the truth just as does a lawyer assigned to represent an adult. A juvenile needs a lawyer's advice to understand the law and its processes at least as much as does an adult. Commentators and courts have argued that counsel is unnecessary in juvenile court because the hearing is not adversary in nature and because the judge and probation officer protect the child.[62] There are two answers to this argument: First, whether or not it is adversary, the juvenile hearing is a proceeding which may result in incarceration. The child's liberty is precious to him, and he should have a lawyer to help him protect that liberty. In addition, although statutes, commentators, and judges have contended that a finding of delinquency is not the same as a criminal conviction,[63] it actually carries with it many results just as serious as those accompanying criminal conviction.[64] Second, a lawyer's presence need not create a hostile atmosphere in the juvenile courtroom. The reverse may even be true. The lawyer can explain to the child what is happening, discuss with the child the philosophy behind juvenile courts, and help the child to understand the judge's dispositional decision.[65] The child is more likely to accept as an ally the lawyer who supports him and presents his side of the story to the judge than the probation officer who acts as a prosecutor and presents the allegations which support a finding of delinquency to the judge, or the judge who may send him to reform school. Because he has an ally in his lawyer the child may be more willing to accept the juvenile court as an institution set up to help rather than punish him.

In addition to helping the child understand what the court is doing to and for him, a lawyer may be able to help the court in several ways. He can gather facts about the child's actions which may throw a different light on the probation officer's allega-

62. See In re Holmes, 379 Pa. 599, 603, 109 A.2d 523, 525 (1954), cert. denied, 348 U.S. 973 (1955); Mack, supra note 26.

63. See, e.g., CAL. WELF. & INST'NS CODE § 503 (West 1961); In re Gault, 99 Ariz. 181, 187, 407 P.2d 760, 764 (1965); Mack, supra note 26, at 109.

64. See, e.g., In re Gault, 387 U.S. 1, 24–25 (1967); In re Holmes, 379 Pa. 599, 612, 109 A.2d 523, 528–29 (1954) (dissenting opinion), cert. denied, 348 U.S. 973 (1955), In re Contreras, 109 Cal. App. 2d 787, 789–90, 241 P.2d 631, 633 (1952).

65. See generally Allison, The Lawyer and His Juvenile Court Client, 12 CRIME & DEL. 165 (1966); McKesson, Right to Counsel in Juvenile Proceedings, 45 MINN. L. REV. 843 (1961).

tions. He may be able to present objective arguments to the judge, which the child cannot clearly present. More abstractly, a lawyer's presence in the juvenile courtroom may be beneficial to the system itself. Because the juvenile's lawyer is an advocate and protector of his client's interests, he will constitute a built-in check against abuse by the judge of his vast discretion.[66]

Finally, the reasons which led the Supreme Court to expand the right to counsel afforded adult criminal defendants apply to the juvenile system. A criminal defendant needs a lawyer at his trial because alone he will be unable to present his defense adequately.[67] The legal system is a complex machine; those trained in the law are best able to run that machine. A layman accused of crime cannot defend himself adequately because he lacks knowledge of procedural and substantive law. The layman's lack of legal knowledge may be relatively unimportant in juvenile courts—his lack of procedural knowledge because of the juvenile system's flexibility and his lack of substantive knowledge because in juvenile courts the punishment does not fit the crime. However, the layman is also inadequate as an advocate because he is not trained to uncover relevant facts, to assess them, and to present them in a meaningful and well-organized fashion. This aspect of the layman's inadequacy is as important in juvenile hearings as in criminal trials because facts are equally important in each. A lawyer representing the child will better present the facts than will a probation officer who is biased in favor of a finding he recommended.

The criminal defense attorney advises his client so that he will be better able to make decisions about such questions as whether to plead guilty, whether to take the stand, and whether to answer questions. The juvenile needs advice no less than the adult. He is younger, less likely to understand exactly what he is deciding, and possibly more likely to be influenced by what he thinks others—the judge and probation officer and perhaps his parents—want him to decide. Counsel's presence at juvenile hearings will therefore aid both the juvenile offender and the juvenile court. The Supreme Court's holding that juveniles have the same right to counsel as adults perhaps more than any other aspect of the *Gault* decision

66. *See* Paulsen, *Fairness to the Juvenile Offender,* 41 MINN. L. REV. 547, 571 (1957).
67. Gideon v. Wainwright, 372 U.S. 335 (1965).

will result in better juvenile court procedures and greater fairness to juveniles.[68]

The Privilege Against Self-Incrimination

Before the *Gault* case made the privilege against self-incrimination —including the right to be informed of the privilege [69]—obligatory in juvenile proceedings, courts sometimes denied juveniles the privilege; when they did grant it, they often did not require a warning to the juvenile that he had the right to remain silent.[70] In *Gault* the state court did not decide whether a juvenile judge could compel a juvenile to incriminate himself. It did decide that juveniles did not have a right to be told that they need not answer questions.[71] In effect, as the majority of the Supreme Court held, this holding made the privilege meaningless. If the child has a lawyer who can explain the privilege to him and help him decide whether to answer questions, a warning by the judge may not be a necessary part of the privilege. But the child is more likely to believe that he does not have to answer questions if the judge gives him a warning. Because the child probably wants above all to win the judge's approval, the privilege has less meaning if the juvenile believes that the judge will disapprove of his refusal to answer.

The main argument against granting juveniles the privilege against self-incrimination is that rehabilitation will be easier if the child admits his wrongs and tries to cooperate with the judge and probation officer who want to help him.[72] This argument

68. *See generally* Allison, *supra* note 65; Antieau, *Constitutional Rights in Juvenile Courts,* 46 Cornell L.Q. 387 (1961); McKesson, *supra* note 65; Paulsen, *Fairness to the Juvenile Offender,* 41 Minn. L. Rev. 547 (1957); Quick, *supra* note 37, at 91; Schinitsky, *The Role of the Lawyer in Children's Court,* 17 The Record of the Association of the Bar of the City of New York 10 (1962); Skoler & Tenney, Jr., *supra* note 26.

69. 387 U.S. at 55. Justice White dissented from the part of the Court's opinion which included the right to be told of the privilege. He stated that the case did not present the question of whether a juvenile should have the privilege. *Id.* at 64–65.

70. *See In re* Gault, 99 Ariz. 181, 191, 407 P.2d 760, 767–68 (1965); *In re* Dargo, 81 Cal. App. 2d 205, 209, 183 P.2d 282, 284 (1947); People v. Lewis, 260 N.Y. 171, 174, 177, 183 N.E. 353, 354–55 (1932), *cert. denied,* 289 U.S. 709 (1933).

71. *In re* Gault, 99 Ariz. 181, 191, 407 P.2d 760, 767–68 (1965).

72. Paulsen, *Fairness to the Juvenile Offender,* 41 Minn. L. Rev. 547, 561 (1957); *see* Van Waters, *The Socialization of Juvenile Court Procedure,* 13 J. Am. Inst. of Crim. L. & C. 61, 65 (1922).

considers the juvenile hearing as part of the treatment which the child receives. It fails to consider that a hearing in which the child is coerced into answering questions may not be rehabilitative. Perhaps it is better to show the child that justice is fair than to have him admit his wrongs and repent.[73] It is almost impossible to obtain empirical, objective data to support either position. Therefore, even if the hearing is considered solely a rehabilitative experience, it is not clear that the privilege should be denied.

In addition to being part of the juvenile's rehabilitation, the juvenile hearing is the means for deciding whether the child needs treatment.[74] If denying the privilege promotes the truth, such denial will aid the judge to make the proper determination as to whether the state should treat the child. But it is not clear that forcing the child to answer produces truth. He may say what he thinks the judge wants to hear. Because he is likely to believe that the judge will prefer an admission and repentance to a denial,[75] he may confess in order to receive favorable disposition. Therefore, refusal of the privilege will not necessarily aid the judge to ascertain the truth. Finally, because the disposition juveniles receive is in fact punitive as well as, or instead of, rehabilitative, it seems far more just to require the probation officer to prove that the child did something which justifies depriving him of his liberty than to compel the child to incriminate himself. Being a child should not deprive the juvenile of strict standards for determining the need for his incarceration.

Confrontation and Cross-Examination

The right of an accused to confront and cross-examine witnesses against him is closely related to the privilege against self-incrimination. If the courts do not grant juveniles the privilege, or need not inform them of it, juveniles will usually admit the delinquency petition's factual allegations, and the state will have no need for witnesses to prove those allegations. Because the Arizona Supreme Court found that the juvenile court judge did not have to warn Gerald that he need not answer questions, it did not have to decide

73. *In re* Gault, 387 U.S. 1, 51–52 (1967).
74. *See In re* Holmes, 379 Pa. 599, 611, 109 A.2d 523, 528 (1954), *cert. denied,* 348 U.S. 973 (1955) (dissenting opinion).
75. *See* Van Waters, *supra* note 72.

whether Gerald had a right to confront and cross-examine witnesses. Because the United States Supreme Court held that Arizona should have afforded Gerald the privilege, and that his admissions were therefore inadmissible, that Court had to decide whether a juvenile had the right to confront and cross-examine witnesses against him. The Court held that states have to permit confrontation and cross-examination. The holding seems obviously correct; if the child does not admit the allegations, the state will have to produce witnesses to convince the judge of the child's delinquency. It seems unfair to admit testimony by witnesses whom neither the child nor his attorney may cross-examine.[76] Indeed, cross-examination is almost invaluable in exposing falsehood and bringing out the truth.[77]

Notice of the Hearing and of the Charges

The Gaults argued, and the Supreme Court agreed, that the juvenile authority did not give them adequate, timely notice of the charges against Gerald, although Mrs. Gault did know when both hearings were scheduled and on what facts Officer Flagg based his allegation of delinquency.[78] The notice which Mrs. Gault received was not formal, and she obtained notice of the first hearing only by going to the detention home. In addition, the state court held that neither the juvenile nor his parents had a right to receive notice of the specific facts on which the state based its delinquency allegation before the first hearing.[79] Therefore, the Supreme Court found the Arizona juvenile statute unconstitutional in not requiring adequate notice; furthermore, the Court required that adequate notice be timely and found that notice received at the first hearing was not timely.

76. More difficult problems arise in the dispositional stage of the juvenile hearing, at which the court admits less definite evidence. Many judges use social workers' reports, distilled from numerous conversations, to aid them in their dispositional decisions, and it would probably be harmful to require that every witness appear in court. Perhaps the best compromise would be to permit the juvenile's attorney to study the disposition report, and if he challenges parts of it, to require witnesses, sworn testimony and cross examination to prove those parts.

77. Pointer v. Texas, 380 U.S. 400, 404 (1965).

78. Record at 40.

79. *In re* Gault, 99 Ariz. 181, 189–90, 407 P.2d 760, 766–67 (1965).

Right to a Record and to an Appeal

The last two rights which Gerald and his parents demanded were the rights to an appeal and to a record. The Court did not confront the issue whether a juvenile should receive those rights. Because Gerald's case was reviewed by means of habeas corpus proceedings, it is clear that juvenile court decisions will not be immune from appellate scrutiny merely because they are not directly appealable. Therefore, in the *Gault* case, as in earlier criminal cases,[80] the Supreme Court found it unnecessary to hold that a person incarcerated by a state court has a constitutional right of appeal.[81]

The equal protection argument requiring the State to grant juveniles and adults the same procedural protections because there are no meaningful differences between the juvenile court hearing and the criminal trial applies as well to the right to an appeal as to the right to counsel. But the majority of the Court based its decision on due process, not equal protection,[82] and so was not compelled to hold that the state must grant an appeal. Further, it is possible to argue that juveniles, like adults, are granted the right to review, although that review is by means of habeas corpus, not appeal.

Conclusion

The *Gault* decision will have numerous and immediate effects on juvenile court systems around the country. Perhaps only the California and New York juvenile systems will be unaffected. In the other states, legislatures will have to rewrite juvenile statutes which permit the lax procedures condemned in *Gault;* juvenile judges who have become accustomed to running their courts without interference will have to listen to lawyers argue for juvenile offenders [83] and will have to inform juveniles that they need not answer questions which the judge and the probation officer ask;

80. Douglas v. California, 372 U.S. 353 (1963); Griffin v. Illinois, 351 U.S. 12 (1956).

81. The Court held that there is no constitutional right of appeal in McKane v. Durston, 153 U.S. 684 (1894) (criminal case).

82. See text accompanying notes 44–46 *supra.*

83. However, most juvenile court judges are not opposed to attorney representation of juveniles. Skoler & Tenney, Jr., *supra* note 26, at 96.

probably most important, juveniles who have received individualized, sometimes incomprehensible, treatment in juvenile hearings hopefully will now receive justice and fairness. The changes will undoubtedly be difficult; they will also almost certainly be beneficial. No longer will children be second-class citizens when they come before the juvenile court; no longer will the juvenile court be a kangaroo court.[84]

Gault will not serve as a panacea for all the problems of juvenile courts and the juvenile court system. Indeed, it would be surprising if one opinion in one case could solve all the problems which have arisen in over half a century.[85] The almost absolute discretion vested in the juvenile court judge at the dispositional stage of the juvenile hearing is the root of the most serious problems remaining. Because of that discretion, a juvenile may do what he thinks will please the judge even though he has the right to do otherwise. Because of that discretion, the lawyer in juvenile court will have to attempt to protect his juvenile client without antagonizing the judge. Because of that discretion, the exercise of constitutional rights may not place the juvenile in any better position than he would be if he failed to exercise those rights—the judge can commit him to an industrial training school whether he has broken a law or is "in danger of leading an immoral life."

Discretion, in someone, is a necessary corollary of individual treatment, which is still an aim of juvenile justice. Therefore, the problems stemming from discretion cannot be solved by eliminating discretion. A possible solution might be to separate the discretionary functions from nondiscretionary ones. The juvenile hearing is often divided into two parts, adjudicative and dispositional.[86] It would seem possible to have a different person preside over each part of the hearing, so that the impression made by the juvenile at the adjudicative hearing would not influence the dispositional decision. Indeed, the dispositional decision might be better made by a committee of psychiatrists and social workers, trained to treat people, than by a judge, trained to preside over an impartial hearing and to make nondiscretionary determinations

---

84. *In re* Gault, 387 U.S. 1, 28 (1967).
85. The first juvenile court act was adopted in Illinois in 1899. *In re* Gault, 387 U.S. 1, 14 (1967).
86. See text accompanying note 7 *supra*. *See also* CAL. WELF. & INST'NS CODE §§ 701–02 (West 1961).

of fact. Legislatures, not courts, will have to act if different persons are to preside over the different parts of the juvenile hearing. One may hope that the legislatures which must rewrite juvenile statutes so that they conform to the *Gault* standards will consider also making basic changes not required by *Gault*. The Supreme Court has taken the first step towards more just treatment for juvenile offenders, and hopefully state legislatures will take the next one.

Part IV

Epilogue

Albert E. Wilkerson

22
Children's Rights

The rights of children is a developing concept, diverse in scope and content, and ranging from reference to deeply psychological states to basic environmental necessities and legal status. It is a concept for international concern. The immediate requirements for its implementation as a social guarantee are different in various parts of the world. The rights to emotional security, to education, to sound custody decisions, and to meaningful visitation with a separated or divorced parent reflect a certain level of cultural development of a country. A statement of these rights for the Western child is appropriate because both knowledge and resources make them clearly a present possibility. Emphasis upon some of these rights would seem utopian in underdeveloped countries where the rights to childhood survival, minimal parental care, and elementary public health services are of critical import.

The rights of children must become a concept widely accepted as a primary social value that influences social policy and social planning at every level. The family is the unit most immediately affected by attitudes, policies, and guarantees as to children's rights, and to speak of the concept is to wrestle with the deep psychological feelings aroused by the terms "parents," and "family." While making available to parents the range of resources necessary for effective parenting, we need to be more explicit about the social expectations of parents and parental accountability to the community for the form and quality of child-rearing.

An acceptance of the child as a person, not a parental property or a cherished creature in process of becoming an adult, admits fully to his human and legal rights. At certain ages and under certain circumstances, the child cannot care for himself, protect himself, speak for himself, or make prudent choices in his own best interests. The task of meeting these needs has been given to the parents as a responsibility basic to the notion of family. Perhaps the term "parental responsibility" should be substituted for "parental rights," emphasizing the social obligation and account-ability rather than suggesting a kind of finality that cannot rationally be granted. It cannot be granted because we must perceive every child as everybody's child, for whatever happens to him happens to each of us, too. This does not mean that parental rights as they are now understood should be taken lightly. It does mean, however, that the child has superseding rights to expect fulfillment of the parents' responsibilities toward him.

Thus, ensuring the rights of the child begins with strengthening parental capacities and provision of social resources to maximize the possibility of the child's development within his own home. Here he can achieve a healthy balance between dependence and independence, develop a personal identity, learn the meaning of relating positively to "significant others," and in time become an emancipated adult who can effectively negotiate the rewards of the social system. When parents fail, legal and social welfare provisions can be activated, and the community begins to act in the place of parents in determining the child's best interests. These provisions remain inadequate. We are too timid.

Some guarantees have to do with the fact that the child is a person in his own right. Others have to do with measures to be taken when family functioning breaks down or when the family cannot cope alone with special needs or problems of the child. A minimal amount of work has been done in the areas in the first category. Among the problems greatly needing exploration, policy decisions, and frameworks for policy implementation are the rights to protection through prenatal care, to economic sup-ports such as a national children's allowance program, to appro-priate and maximum educational opportunities, to medical treat-ment in mental illness, mental retardation, and other severe handicaps, and to truly rehabilitative services for the delinquent child. The question of the age of emancipation of the child requires comprehensive study, leading to uniformity in state stat-utes. The child is now emancipated in uneven stages. At a varying age, and varying by state, he is considered an adult as concerns for example the right to work, to enter marriage, to vote, to make legal contracts, to manage his estate, and to be viewed as a delinquent child rather than a "criminal." On a more strictly psychological level, the family and other basic social institutions that serve as the immediate environment for shaping the life of the child should respect his right to individuality and difference, acting on the assumption that creativity derives from difference rather than conformity.

The White House Conferences on Children have served since 1909 as pacesetters in child welfare, defining and highlighting critical problems. To a significant extent, the Conferences determine areas for concentration in child welfare for the following decade. Rather than choosing a single theme for the 1970s, the Conference opted for a comprehensive range of concerns, rights, and proposed structures and programs. Among the more promising priorities stated are family-oriented child development programs (health services, day care, and childhood education), guaranteed children's allowances, a national child health-care program, a plan for early identification of special needs and a responsive service delivery system, new options in forms of public education, a reformed juvenile justice system, the establishment of a high-level child advocacy agency, and a commitment to the concept of the rights of children. These issues, perceived from a national perspective, reflect the necessity for a macro-approach to child welfare that will enhance the quality of life for all children.

Despite decades of dedicated work on the part of social workers, attorneys, judges, medical personnel, community leaders, and agencies like the societies for the prevention of cruelty to children, the Children's Division of the American Humane Association, the United States Children's Bureau, and the Child Welfare League of America, the nation with the greatest resources for child development has done a relatively poor job. The general plight of children in the United States, particularly but not exclusively the children of the poor, is a major source of shame.

The concept of the rights of children has emerged from the more concrete, immediately critical, socially visible, and psychologically threatening problems associated with child custody, child support in separation and divorce, delinquency, illegitimacy, child neglect and child battering, and the right-to-life controversy. These have been emphasized in this volume because it is here that trails have been slowly blazed and guideposts established. The assessment of what has been achieved in these areas of family malfunction or breakdown is both encouraging and disappointing. As pioneer efforts and as incremental gains, they are exciting and filled with forward thrusts. As measured against a reasonable ideal fully within our capability, they represent only a beginning.

Perhaps we can determine best how far we have advanced in establishing children's rights, and how far we have yet to go, by restating some of the crucial issues remaining in areas that have long been central concerns in child welfare.

Three areas can be dealt with quickly. As for the area of adoptions, the current struggle between courts and social agencies points to the ambivalence about whose interests come first, parent or child, and what constitutes the best interests of the child. If respecting the rights of the natural parent were a guarantee to the child's rights and needs, the problem would be relatively simple. But this assumption has not been borne out in social agency and court experience, and judges are handicapped by the lack of the kind of research in child development that would give them a more solid basis upon which to make or reverse adoption decisions. As for economic maintenance of the child of the poor family, the state of public assistance speaks for itself. Clearly, we are not committed to the guarantee of economic support of the child in risk populations, although there seems to be rapid movement in that direction. The question of willingness to provide for the child is probably not the problem; the issue, rather, is that historically the unemployed, able-bodied adult is automatically suspect. Like the problem of aid to dependent children, the area of foster care constitutes a national crisis. Foster care was designed to preserve the connection between the child and his natural parents through the provision of temporary care for the child and through developing the parental capacity of the parents. For the most part, it has not worked that way. Instead, it tends to provide a childhood of temporary and changing relationships with substitute parents, denying the child a prolonged and stable experience with any one family that he can call his own. The price of waiting indeterminably for parents who cannot or will not develop acceptable parenting requirements is paid by the child. The question that neither social agencies nor courts can answer is this: by what criteria does one rationally determine that, given resources and services, enough time and effort have been supplied, and that the child now has the right to a permanent, created family.

Custody, visitation, and child support form a triad of complex problems involving the needs and rights of children of separated or divorced parents. The critical issues in custody decisions in the case of "fit parents" are that the prima facie rights of both parents to an equal custody claim be in practice equal (instead of biased toward the mother), that visitation be planned in such a way and in sufficient length of time so as to ensure the possibility for the child to continue a meaningful relationship with both parents, and that child support be an integral part of a custody decision and that it include long-term plans for higher education. Perhaps more difficult is the problem of determining the child's best interest in cases involving a third party, such as a relative, a social agency, or a nonrelative holding de facto custody. In uncontested custody cases in divorce proceedings, parental preference—or more likely, parental bargaining and compromise—does not ensure that the agreed-upon arrangement best meets the child's needs. And in none of these cases is there any guarantee of the child's rights as a party to the action. The determination as to the child's needs and the assurance of his rights are easily mistaken as synonymous. The "rights" of the child can be protected only by a new consensus as to his legal stake in the action, and by legal representation. Assessment of the child's "needs" is a value preference resting heavily in the assessor's concept of child-rearing—a preference essentially for a content and an environment that one deems necessary for a particular kind of growth and development. In assessing needs, the social worker, the lawyer, and other professional persons in a given case often come into conflict centering around differing preferences. This conflict, if the aim is agreement, is misunderstood. Instead, the encounter should involve the essence of professional roles, in which the differences in task, assumptions, and expertise become the dynamics—rather than the negatives—in shaping decisions that so much involve the destiny of the child. The thrust for the rights of the child in *Kent v. United States* and *In re Gault* has implications too for decision-making in custody matters, tempering the socialized court with due process and the adversary approach.

The support obligation of a parent tends to result in a piecemeal plan, as part of the aftermath of a broken family relationship, and is generally conceptualized on a short-sighted week-to-week basis. The child too frequently is the one who bears the burden of a fact which most parents soon discover—that they cannot afford the financial costs of separation or divorce. The plight becomes further complicated through remarriage of the father and his subsequent request to reduce the support payment for the first set of children in order to meet his obligations to the second. Child support should be an integral part of the custody decision or arrangement. The plan should be conceived on a long-term basis, including provision for meeting health-care contingencies. It should extend not merely to the child's age of emancipation but should include the opportunity for higher education. The support obligation should extend after the death of the parent, with a priority claim upon continuance through his estate. To ensure as far as possible that the child's needs will be met and his rights protected, parents in unbroken families should anticipate the possibility of orphanhood by making arrangements for guardians of the person and estate of the child. Long-overdue attention is being given to establishing the rights of the illegitimate child and the foster child as to inheritance.

The philosophy of the socialized court was a recognition of the delinquent child's need for protection and rehabilitation. The rights accorded adult criminals did not seem either necessary or appropriate, since the focus is upon interest in the child rather than concern with the offense. Placement of the juvenile in a correctional setting is done on the assumption that a rehabilitative treatment program best serves his needs, and thus serves the needs of society. But the therapeutic potential in these settings is primarily in the area of wishful thinking, and the court's acting on the basis of clinical judgments has often served only to isolate the juvenile from those community processes in which the possibility for resocialization is found. Thus the theory underlying the procedures leading to dispositions has led essentially to violation of basic rights in due process of law, the foundation of personal guarantees in a democracy. Aside from the discounting of rights in procedural matters, the role of the judge as the wise and benevolent parent, without the constraints that obtain in other kinds of judicial proceedings, is no doubt too much responsibility to place upon an individual, no matter what his qualities and qualifications. During the past several decades, voices were heard occasionally with the resounding question: "To what extent can a court be socialized without violating individual rights?" The cases of *Kent* and *Gault* in a sense culminated the efforts to bring about a "renaissance" in the juvenile court, centering primarily upon protection of the child's rights through procedural safeguards. The two decisions have set into motion increased activity to ensure the juvenile's legal rights and to recast professional role behaviors in a way that can achieve more effectively the original intent of the socialized court. The 1971 decision of the Supreme Court to deny the juvenile the right to trial by jury illustrates the way in which the concepts of "rights" and "best interests" must be balanced.

The societal value reflected in the principle that every child is everybody's child—a romantic phrase but nonetheless accurate in terms of the social accountability of parents—has not applied to the illegitimate child, who essentially has been nobody's child, a nonperson. The illegitimate child, together with the foster child, the battered child, and the neglected child, is being rediscovered. The rediscovery of the illegitimate child seems to be taking place primarily through a concern that pursues his plight through test cases to establish his legal rights. Thus it may be that his humanity will have to be verified by first testifying to his rights as a person under the law. If this is a roundabout way of claiming him as an authentic human being, so it was in a roundabout way that his present status historically became tainted through coercive efforts to maintain a prescribed concept of the family. Heaped upon him too has no doubt been the projection inherent in the common human fear of being a nonentity. The child born of unmarried parents is losing his stigma as we slowly learn that the very fact of his existence accords him legitimacy, that the child of unmarried parents does not shake the validity of the marital family, and that the deeper meaning of "family" lies in the quality of affectional bonds.

Society's role in ensuring the child's right to "protection," in its narrower meaning, has been carried by Societies for the Prevention of Cruelty to Children, and increasingly in recent years by public agencies, with a consistent commitment without parallel in any other area of children's rights. Well-known is the story of the first thrust in the United States toward protective legislation and services in 1874, and the early necessity to use for the child the statutes pertaining to the prevention of cruelty to animals. The critical predicament of the child neglected and battered within his own home has come to national attention only during the past decade. Improved legislation fortunately is the result, including mandatory child-abuse reporting laws and immunity clauses. The need is urgent for increased social services and resources to help prevent and ameliorate conditions leading to neglect and battering. While protective services might at points infringe upon parental and civil rights, the priority is determined in Principle Eight of the United Nations Declaration of the Rights of the Child, which states: "The Child shall in all circumstances be among the first to receive protection and relief." The means must be discovered wherein the civil liberties of adults are ensured in instances of protective intervention for the child, but not at the child's expense.

The rights of the unborn child rest essentially upon the premise that conception—not birth—marks the beginning of an individual's life. With this assumption, the unborn child is the possessor of human life, a separate being from his mother. Thus, the right of the child to life and protection of life is abridged by legalizing adult preference in abortion. Until very recently, abortion was seen basically within the context of religious beliefs, particularly related to the Roman Catholic Church. Concern has now broadened into the realm of general human ethics and human rights. The real controversy, of course, lies not so much with the single question as to the right of the unborn child to birth, but rather his right in a priority relationship to his mother's right not to be a parent if she so chooses. The point of view expressed by groups such as Women's Liberation gives an unqualified priority to the rights of the mother. As in so may other areas of human behavior and conflict, it is difficult to arrive at a fully rational view, since the values of each group are diametrically opposed. Each side has some rather convincing points. It is doubtful that in the right-to-life controversy the rights of the unborn child will be inviolate. Probably one can hope only for a sound compromise.

Social work and law are in this decade focused upon the task of helping to change or create systems which provide more effectively for the development of human potential, afford opportunity, prevent individual and social breakdowns, and maximize availability of resources for individual problem-solving. Central to these tasks in social service delivery, social policy and planning, and the practice of law is the concept of children's rights. A cornerstone for the field of child welfare for today, it is essential that the concept gain full recognition as a principle in human relationships.